T0073798

CCNP Collaboration Cloud and Edge Solutions

CLCEI 300-820

Official Cert Guide

JASON BALL, CCSI No. 33717
TJ ARNESON, CCSI No. 35208

Cisco Press

CCNP Collaboration Cloud and Edge Solutions CLCEI 300-820 Official Cert Guide

Jason Ball and TJ Arneson

Published by:
Cisco Press

1 2021

Library of Congress Control Number: 2021944062

ISBN-13: 978-0-13-673372-0
ISBN-10: 0-13-673372-7

Warning and Disclaimer

Trademark Acknowledgments

Special Sales

For information about buying this title in bulk quantities, or for special sales opportunities (which may include electronic versions; custom cover designs; and content particular to your business, training goals, marketing focus, or branding interests), please contact our corporate sales department at corpsales@pearsoned.com or (800) 382-3419.

For government sales inquiries, please contact governmentsales@pearsoned.com.

For questions about sales outside the U.S., please contact intlcs@pearson.com.

Feedback Information

At Cisco Press, our goal is to create in-depth technical books of the highest quality and value. Each book is crafted with care and precision, undergoing rigorous development that involves the unique expertise of members from the professional technical community.

Readers' feedback is a natural continuation of this process. If you have any comments regarding how we could improve the quality of this book, or otherwise alter it to better suit your needs, you can contact us through email at feedback@ciscopress.com. Please make sure to include the book title and ISBN in your message.

We greatly appreciate your assistance.

Editor-in-Chief: Mark Taub	**Copy Editor:** Bill McManus
Alliances Manager, Cisco Press: Arezou Gol	**Technical Editor(s):** Daniel Ball Jeffrey Hubbard
Director, ITP Product Management: Brett Bartow	**Editorial Assistant:** Cindy Teeters
Executive Editor: Nancy Davis	**Cover Designer:** Chuti Prasertsith
Managing Editor: Sandra Schroeder	**Composition:** codeMantra
Development Editor: Ellie Bru	**Indexer:** Erika Millen
Senior Project Editor: Tonya Simpson	**Proofreader:** Donna Mulder

Americas Headquarters
Cisco Systems, Inc.
San Jose, CA

Asia Pacific Headquarters
Cisco Systems (USA) Pte. Ltd.
Singapore

Europe Headquarters
Cisco Systems International BV Amsterdam,
The Netherlands

Cisco has more than 200 offices worldwide. Addresses, phone numbers, and fax numbers are listed on the Cisco Website at **www.cisco.com/go/offices**.

About the Authors

Anyone who has worked with **Jason Ball** or has sat in one of his classes knows that his enthusiasm for collaboration is matched only by his engaging zeal for teaching. Jason's current position as a solution readiness engineer in Collaboration for Cisco awards him with the opportunity to create and provide training to Cisco partners on new, innovative collaboration solutions as Cisco releases them. He has been operating as a collaboration engineer for more than 11 years and holds 19 different certifications, including a CCNP Collaboration certification and a Cisco Certified Systems Instructor (CCSI) certification. He has been teaching Cisco Voice, Video, and Collaboration certification courses for as many years as he has been involved with Cisco.

Some of the accomplishments that Jason has achieved include serving as a subject matter expert (SME) for two certification courses Cisco has developed: the TVS Advanced Services Course and the CIVND2 certification course for the former CCNA Collaboration certification. He also wrote the Video Infrastructure Implementation (VII) Advanced Services course for Cisco, coauthored *CCNA Collaboration CIVND 210-065 Official Cert Guide* (Cisco Press, 2015), and was the sole author of *CCNP and CCIE Collaboration Core CLCOR 350-801 Official Cert Guide* (Cisco Press). Jason currently resides in Raleigh, North Carolina, with his wife and two children.

TJ Arneson is a Cisco Certified Systems Instructor (CCSI) who has had a history with Cisco products since his enlistment days in the U.S. Army. He has obtained both the CCNP Routing & Switching and Collaboration certifications. TJ's current position is a Customer Success Specialist for Cisco Systems, where he is enabling and empowering customers through the Customer Experience (CX) team under the Service Provider theater. TJ currently resides in sunny Tampa, Florida. When he is not working, he is either fishing in Tampa Bay or grinding levels in video games with his wife.

About the Technical Reviewers

Jeff Hubbard, CCNP Collaboration, CCSI No. 34456, is an engineering project manager with Cisco focusing on training products in the Cloud Collaboration segment. He has been in the technology industry for more than 30 years in a wide variety of roles, and devoted himself solely to Cisco products beginning in 2008, when he started working as a Cisco Certified Systems Instructor with an emphasis on video and voice solutions. In his free time Jeff is an avid motorcyclist and spends most of his time exploring the less-traveled dirt roads of Colorado's Rocky Mountains.

Daniel Ball is a leader in Cisco Collaboration technologies, with a strong background in higher education. He is currently a senior training specialist for PCH Collaboration, focusing on programmability and API integrations. Daniel also maintains a growing YouTube channel called Collab Crush, which is dedicated to promoting quality training for the Cisco Collaboration solution. Daniel received a Bachelor of Arts degree from the University of Texas at Austin and a Master of Science degree in Education from Shenandoah University. His Cisco certifications include CCNA Route/Switch, CCNA Collaboration, and CCNP Collaboration. Currently, Daniel lives in Kobe, Japan, with his wife, Miki, and two daughters, Midori and Hana.

Dedications

I would like to dedicate my contribution in this book to my wife of 24 years. The love, encouragement, and support she has offered have been the strength that has sustained me throughout this endeavor. Every accomplishment I have achieved has been encouraged by her cheering for me from the sidelines. She is the best partner and friend anyone could ask for.

—*Jason*

I would like to dedicate my half of this book to my wife of 8 years as she has been through deployments, heavy travel for work, and the strain of working on her own career on top of that. Jessica has always been a best friend and has grown into a partner in the journey of life.

—*TJ*

Acknowledgments

TJ and I want to acknowledge and thank the technical editors who have also contributed greatly to this book. Jeff Hubbard, it is unfathomable to think about how much both of us have been through, and how much we have learned in the nine and a half years we have worked together and formed our friendship. You have helped challenge and shape me as much as I have done the same for you. Daniel Ball, you are more than a brother to me. Obviously, we have gone through a lifetime of experiences together, but the last 15 years of our lives have proven to be the most formative to our bond. You helped me take that leap into the world of technology, and I would not be where I am without your inspiration.

We would also like to express our gratitude to Eleanor Bru, development editor of this book. We were so incredibly lucky to work with her on this text. She has always been a strong professional who takes the time to ensure the job gets done correctly the first time. Without her, this book would not have been possible, as she worked patiently with us to make this book a reality.

The perceptiveness and expertise of project editor, Tonya Simpson, were integral and vital to this book. Her keenness of insight, understanding, and intuition enabled us to produce quality material. We are thankful for her expertise as we could not accomplish this without her.

Finally, we would like to acknowledge Nancy Davis. You, too, have been a huge part of the success of this book. You constantly had to stay on top of TJ and me to ensure we met our deadlines, and you offered great feedback in the chapters that helped shape the final version of this book. You were always professional, yet gentle and easy to work with. We have enjoyed working with you and would love the opportunity to work with you again.

Contents at a Glance

Online Elements

Reader Services

Other Features

In addition to the features in each of the core chapters, this book has additional study resources on the companion website, including the following:

Practice exams: The companion website contains an exam engine that enables you to review practice exam questions. Use these to prepare with a sample exam and to pinpoint topics where you need more study.

Interactive exercises and quizzes: The companion website contains interactive hands-on exercises and quizzes so that you can test your knowledge on the spot.

Key Term flash cards: The companion website contains interactive quizzes that enable you to test yourself on every glossary term in the book.

To access this additional content, simply register your product. To start the registration process, go to www.ciscopress.com/register and log in or create an account.* Enter the product ISBN 9780136733720 and click Submit. After the process is complete, you will find any available bonus content under Registered Products.

*Be sure to check the box that you would like to hear from us to receive exclusive discounts on future editions of this product.

Contents

xiv   CCNP Collaboration Cloud and Edge Solutions CLCEI 300-820 Official Cert Guide

Online Elements

Introduction

The Implementing Cisco Collaboration Cloud and Edge Solutions v1.0 (CLCEI 300-820) exam is a 90-minute exam associated with the CCNP Collaboration and Cisco Certified Specialist – Collaboration Cloud & Edge Implementation certifications. This exam tests a candidate's knowledge of collaboration cloud and edge solutions, Expressway configurations, and Cisco Webex Teams hybrid and emerging technologies. The course, Implementing Cisco Collaboration Cloud and Edge Solutions, helps candidates to prepare for this exam.

TIP You can review the exam blueprint from the Cisco website at https://learningnetwork.cisco.com/s/clcei-exam-topics.

This book gives you the foundation and covers the topics necessary to start your CCNP Collaboration or CCIE Collaboration journey.

The CCNP Collaboration Certification

The CCNP Collaboration certification is one of the industry's most-respected certifications. To earn the CCNP Collaboration certification, you must pass two exams: the CLCOR exam covered in *CCNP and CCIE Collaboration Core CLCOR 350-801 Official Cert Guide*, and one Collaboration concentration exam of your choice, so you can customize your certification to your technical area of focus.

TIP The CLCOR core exam is also the qualifying exam for the CCIE Collaboration certification. Passing this exam is the first step toward earning both of these certifications.

The following are the CCNP Collaboration concentration exams:

- Implementing Cisco Collaboration Applications (CLICA 300-810)
- Implementing Cisco Advanced Call Control and Mobility Services (CLACCM 300-815)
- Implementing Cisco Collaboration Cloud and Edge Solutions (CLCEI 300-820)
- Implementing Cisco Collaboration Conferencing (CLCNF 300-825)
- Automating and Programming Cisco Collaboration Solutions (CLAUTO 300-835)

TIP CCNP Collaboration now includes automation and programmability to help you scale and customize your Collaboration infrastructure. If you pass the Automating and Programming for Cisco Collaboration Solutions (CLAUTO 300-835) exam, the Implementing and Operating Cisco Collaboration Core Technologies (CLCOR 350-801) exam, and the Developing Applications Using Cisco Core Platforms and APIs (DEVCOR 350-901) exam, you will achieve the CCNP Collaboration and DevNet Professional certifications with only three exams. Every exam earns an individual Specialist certification, allowing you to get recognized for each of your accomplishments, instead of waiting until you pass all the exams.

There are no formal prerequisites for CCNP Collaboration. In other words, you do not have to pass the CCNA Collaboration or any other certifications in order to take CCNP-level exams. The same goes for the CCIE exams. On the other hand, CCNP candidates often have three to five years of experience in IT and Collaboration.

Cisco considers ideal candidates to be those who possess the following:

- Working knowledge of fundamental terms of computer networking, including LANs, WANs, switching, and routing

- Basics of digital interfaces, public switched telephone networks (PSTNs), and Voice over IP (VoIP)

- Fundamental knowledge of converged voice and data networks and Cisco Unified Communications Manager deployment

The CCIE Collaboration Certification

The CCIE Collaboration certification is one of the most admired and elite certifications in the industry. The CCIE Collaboration program prepares you to be a recognized technical leader. To earn the CCIE Collaboration certification, you must pass the Implementing and Operating Cisco Collaboration Core Technologies (CLCOR 350-801) exam and an eight-hour, hands-on lab exam. The lab exam covers very complex Collaboration network scenarios. These scenarios range from designing through deploying, operating, and optimizing Collaboration solutions.

Cisco considers ideal candidates to be those who have five to seven years of experience with designing, deploying, operating, and optimizing Collaboration technologies and solutions prior to taking the exam. Additionally, candidates will need to possess the following:

- Understand capabilities of different technologies, solutions, and services

- Translate customer requirements into solutions

- Assess readiness to support proposed solutions

- Deploy a Cisco Collaboration solution

- Operate and optimize a Cisco Collaboration solution

The Exam Objectives (Domains)

The Implementing Cisco Collaboration Cloud and Edge Solutions v1.0 (CLCEI 300-820) exam is broken down into four major domains. The contents of this book cover each of the domains and the subtopics included in them as illustrated in the following descriptions.

The following table breaks down each of the domains represented in the exam:

Domain	Percentage of Representation in Exam
1: Key Concepts	25%
2: Initial Expressway Configurations	25%
3: Mobile and Remote Access	25%
4: Cisco Webex Technologies	25%

The following topics are general guidelines for the content likely to be included on the exam; however, other related topics may also appear on any specific delivery of the exam. To better reflect the contents of the exam and for clarity purposes, the following guidelines might change at any time without notice. Here are the details of each domain and where the exam objectives are covered in the book:

Domain 1: Key Concepts		Chapter Where This Is Covered
1.1	Describe the complications of NAT in a Collaboration environment	Chapter 10
1.2	Describe the purpose of ICE, TURN, and STUN	Chapter 10
1.3	Describe Expressway media traversal	Chapter 10
1.4	Describe protocol interworking on the Expressway	Chapter 3
1.4.a	SIP < > H.323	Chapter 3
1.4.b	IPv4 and IPv6	Chapter 3
1.5	Describe Expressway Licensing	Chapter 1
1.5.a	Option keys	Chapter 1
1.5.b	Release key	Chapter 1
1.5.c	License consumption	Chapter 1
1.6	Describe SIP media encryption mode	Chapter 5
1.6.a	Auto	Chapter 5
1.6.b	Force encrypted	Chapter 5
1.6.c	Force unencrypted	Chapter 5
1.6.d	Best effort	Chapter 5
1.7	Describe Expressway Core dial plan elements	Chapter 7
1.7.a	Transforms	Chapter 7
1.7.b	Search rules	Chapter 9
1.7.c	Zones	Chapter 9
1.7.d	Regular expressions	Chapter 4
1.7.e	Pipes and links	Chapter 8
1.8	Describe key Expressway settings	Chapter 2
1.8.a	DNS	Chapter 2
1.8.b	Network interfaces	Chapter 2

Domain 1: Key Concepts		Chapter Where This Is Covered
1.8.c	Certificates	Chapter 5
1.8.d	QoS	**Chapter 2**
1.8.e	Clustering	Chapter 11
1.8.f	Network firewall rules	Chapter 2
1.9	Describe Expressway backup and restore procedure (standalone and cluster)	Chapter 2
Domain 2: Initial Expressway Configurations		
2.1	Configure key Expressway settings	Chapter 2
2.1.a	DNS	Chapter 2
2.1.b	Network interfaces	Chapter 2
2.1.c	Certificates	Chapter 5
2.1.d	QoS	Chapter 2
2.1.e	Clustering	Chapter 11
2.1.f	Network firewall rules	Chapter 2
2.2	Configure Expressway Core dial plan elements	Chapter 7
2.2.a	Transforms	Chapter 7
2.2.b	Search rules	Chapter 4
2.2.c	Zones	Chapter 9
2.2.d	Regular expressions	Chapter 4
2.2.e	Pipes and links	Chapter 8
2.3	Configure toll fraud prevention on Expressway series (no custom CPL scripts)	Chapter 7
2.4	Configure a Business to Business (B2B) collaboration solution	Chapter 12
2.4.a	DNS records (focus on Microsoft DNS)	Chapter 10
2.4.b	Certificates (focus on Microsoft CA)	Chapter 5
2.4.c	Traversal Zones	Chapter 10
2.4.d	Neighbor Zones	Chapter 9
2.4.e	Transforms	Chapter 7
2.4.f	Search rules	Chapter 9
2.4.g	SIP trunk integration with Cisco Unified Communications Manager	Chapter 9
2.5	Troubleshoot a Business to Business (B2B) collaboration solution	Chapter 12
2.5.a	DNS records (focus on Microsoft DNS)	Chapter 12
2.5.b	Certificates (focus on Microsoft CA)	Chapter 12
2.5.c	Traversal Zones	Chapter 12
2.5.d	Neighbor Zones	Chapter 12

Domain 1: Key Concepts		Chapter Where This Is Covered
2.5.e	Transforms	Chapter 12
2.5.f	Search rules	Chapter 12
2.5.g	SIP trunk integration with Cisco Unified Communications Manager	Chapter 12
Domain 3: Mobile and Remote Access		
3.1	Configure a Mobile and Remote Access (MRA) solution	Chapter 14
3.1.a	DNS records types (not platform-specific)	Chapter 14
3.1.b	Certificates (not platform specific, covers Unified Communications Manager, IM&P, Expressways, Unity Connection)	Chapter 14
3.1.c	Unified Communications traversal zones	Chapter 14
3.1.d	Unified Communications configuration on Expressway	Chapter 14
3.1.e	HTTP allow list	Chapter 14
3.1.f	SIP trunk security profile on Cisco Unified Communications Manager	Chapter 14
3.2	Troubleshoot a Mobile and Remote Access (MRA) solution	Chapter 15
3.2.a	DNS records (focus on Microsoft DNS)	Chapter 15
3.2.b	Certificates (focus on Microsoft CA, covers Unified Communications Manager, IM&P, Expressways, Unity Connection)	Chapter 15
3.2.c	Unified Communications traversal zones	Chapter 15
3.2.d	Unified Communications configuration on Expressway	Chapter 15
3.2.e	HTTP allow list	Chapter 15
3.2.f	SIP trunk security profile on Cisco Unified Communications Manager	Chapter 15
Domain 4: Cisco Webex Technologies		
4.1	Describe the signaling and media flows used in a Cisco Webex Video Mesh deployment	Chapter 20
4.2	Configure Webex Hybrid Services/Connector	Chapter 16
4.2.a	Calendar Service (Office 365, Microsoft Exchange, One Button to Push)	Chapters 16 and 18
4.2.b	Message Service (Deployment requirements; Expressway requirements, certificates, CallManager prerequisites, IM&P prerequisites, deployment models)	Chapters 16 and 19

Domain 1: Key Concepts		Chapter Where This Is Covered
4.2c	Directory Services (Deployment requirements; deployment models, infrastructure requirements, active directory configuration, synchronization, Webex user service assignment)	Chapters 16 and 17
4.2.d	Video Mesh (Deployment requirements including: bandwidth, clustering, endpoint support, video call capacity, ports and protocols, deployment models)	Chapters 16 and 20
4.3	Describe Cisco Jabber for Cloud and Hybrid deployments with Cisco Webex Messenger	Chapter 21

Steps to Becoming a CCNP Collaboration Certified Engineer

To become a CCNP Collaboration Certified Engineer, you must first take and pass the CLCOR 350-801 exam. Passing this exam alone will automatically earn the Cisco Certified Specialist – Collaboration certification. You will then need to pass one of the collaboration specialization exams of your choosing, such as the CLCEI 300-820 exam. Passing these two exams will earn you the CCNP Collaboration certification. All Cisco certification exams are managed by the Pearson Vue testing organization. Use the following steps to sign up for your Cisco exam.

Signing Up for the Exam

The steps required to sign up for the CCNP Collaboration CLCEI 300-820 exam are as follows:

1. Navigate to **https://home.pearsonvue.com/cisco**.

2. To schedule a Cisco exam, you must first have a CCO ID you created on the Cisco website. Then you must create a Pearson VUE login and link it to the CCO ID. After all this is created, you must sign in to the Pearson VUE site to schedule the exam. Click **Sign In** from the column on the right side of the screen and enter your login credentials.

3. Once signed in click on the View exams button.

4. In the Find an Exam box, enter **300-820** and then click the **300-820: Implementing Cisco Collaboration Cloud and Edge Solutions** name when it appears. Click **Go** to proceed to the next screen.

5. Select either the **At a test center** or the **Online at my home or office** option for where you want to take the exam, read through the information on the screen related to your choice, then click on the next button at the bottom of the screen.

6. Continue to follow the steps on the screen. The options will vary based on your selection from the previous step. You will also need to provide payment for the exam you're scheduling. The CLCEI 300-820 exam costs $300 USD.

Facts About the Exam

The exam is a computer-based test. It consists of multiple-choice questions only. To take the test, you must bring two forms of ID; one must be a government-issued identification card with a photo. The second can be any official ID with your name on it, such as a Social Security card, employee ID card, or credit card, as long as it has your signature on it.

About the CCNP CLCEI 300-820 Official Cert Guide

Although this book does not map sequentially to the topic areas of the exam, all topic areas on the exam are covered in this book. This book cannot contain the personal experience and hands-on exposure to the equipment needed to answer some of the questions that may be asked in the exam. However, it was our intent to write this book in a manner that provides a slow buildup to the technologies that are being tested so that you will not only be better prepared to pass the test but also develop a solid understanding of the underlying technologies examined in this book. This book also uses a number of features to help you understand the topics and prepare for the exam.

Objectives and Methods

This book uses several key methodologies to help you discover the exam topics on which you need more review, help you fully understand and remember those details, and help you prove to yourself that you have retained your knowledge of those topics. This book does not try to help you pass the exam only by memorization; it seeks to help you to truly learn and understand the topics. This book is designed to help you pass the CCNP CLCEI 300-820 exam by using the following methods:

- Helping you discover which exam topics you have not mastered

- Providing explanations and information to fill in your knowledge gaps

- Supplying exercises that enhance your ability to recall and deduce the answers to test questions

- Providing practice exercises on the topics and the testing process via test questions on the companion website

Book Features

To help you customize your study time using this book, the core chapters have several features that help you make the best use of your time:

- **Foundation Topics:** These are the core sections of each chapter. They explain the concepts for the topics in that chapter.

- **Exam Preparation Tasks:** After the "Foundation Topics" section of each chapter, the "Exam Preparation Tasks" section lists a series of study activities that you should do at the end of the chapter:

  - **Review All Key Topics:** The Key Topic icon appears next to the most important items in the "Foundation Topics" section of the chapter. The Review All Key

Topics activity lists the key topics from the chapter, along with their page numbers. Although the contents of the entire chapter could be on the exam, you should definitely know the information listed in each key topic, so you should review these areas.

■ **Define Key Terms:** Although the CCLEI exam may be unlikely to ask a question such as "Define this term," the exam does require that you learn and know a lot of terminology. This section lists the most important terms from the chapter, asking you to write a short definition and compare your answer to the glossary at the end of the book.

■ **Complete Memory Tables:** Open Appendix C from the book's website and print the entire thing or print the tables by major part. Then complete the tables.

■ **Review Questions:** Confirm that you understand the content that you just covered by answering these questions and reading the answer explanations.

■ **Web-Based Practice Exam:** The companion website includes the Pearson Test Prep practice test engine that enables you to take practice exam questions. Use it to prepare with a sample exam and to pinpoint topics where you need more study.

How This Book Is Organized

This book contains 21 core chapters. Chapter 22 includes preparation tips and suggestions for how to approach the exam. Each core chapter covers a subset of the topics on the CLCEI 300-820 exam. The core chapters map to the CLCEI 300-820 exam topic areas and cover the concepts and technologies that you will encounter on the exam. Refer to the exam objective/chapter mapping table as a reference to see which objectives are covered in which chapters. Also, each chapter includes a list of objectives covered in that chapter for easy reference.

The Companion Website for Online Content Review

All the electronic review elements, as well as other electronic components of the book, exist on this book's companion website.

To access the companion website, which gives you access to the electronic content with this book, start by establishing a login at the Cisco Press website and registering your book. To do so, simply go to https://www.ciscopress.com/register and enter the ISBN of the print book: **9780136733720**. After you have registered your book, go to your account page and click the **Registered Products** tab. From there, click the **Access Bonus Content** link to get access to the book's companion website.

Note that if you buy the Premium Edition eBook and Practice Test version of this book from Cisco Press, your book will automatically be registered on your account page. Simply go to your account page, click the **Registered Products** tab, and select **Access Bonus Content** to access the book's companion website.

Please note that many of our companion content files can be very large, especially image and video files.

If you are unable to locate the files for this title by following the preceding steps, please visit https://www.pearsonITcertification.com/contact and select the **Site Problems/ Comments** option. Our customer service representatives will assist you.

How to Access the Pearson Test Prep Practice Test Software

You have two options for installing and using the Pearson Test Prep software: a web app and a desktop app. To use the Pearson Test Prep software, start by finding the registration code that comes with the book. You can find the code in these ways:

- **Print book:** Look in the cardboard sleeve in the back of the book for a piece of paper with your book's unique PTP code.

- **Premium Edition:** If you purchase the Premium Edition eBook and Practice Test directly from the Cisco Press website, the code will be populated on your account page after purchase. Just log in at https://www.ciscopress.com, click **Account** to see details of your account, and click the **Digital Purchases** tab.

- **Amazon Kindle:** For those who purchase a Kindle edition from Amazon, the access code will be supplied directly from Amazon.

- **Other Bookseller eBooks:** Note that if you purchase an eBook version from any other source, the practice test is not included because other vendors to date have not chosen to vend the required unique access code.

NOTE   Do not lose the activation code, because it is the only means with which you can access the QA content with the book.

Once you have the access code, to find instructions about both the PTP web app and the desktop app, follow these steps:

Step 1.   Open this book's companion website, as shown earlier in this Introduction under the heading "The Companion Website for Online Content Review."

Step 2.   Click the **Practice Exams** button.

Step 3.   Follow the instructions listed there both for installing the desktop app and for using the web app.

Note that if you want to use the web app only at this point, just navigate to https://www.pearsontestprep.com, establish a free login if you do not already have one, and register this book's practice tests using the registration code you just found. The process should take only a couple of minutes.

NOTE   Amazon eBook (Kindle) customers: It is easy to miss Amazon's email that lists your PTP access code. Soon after you purchase the Kindle eBook, Amazon should send an email. However, the email uses very generic text and makes no specific mention of PTP or practice exams. To find your code, read every email from Amazon after you purchase the book. Also do the usual checks for ensuring your email arrives, such as checking your spam folder.

NOTE   Other eBook customers: As of the time of publication, only the publisher and Amazon supply PTP access codes when you purchase their eBook editions of this book.

Customizing Your Exams

Once you are in the exam settings screen, you can choose to take exams in one of three modes:

- **Study mode:** Allows you to fully customize your exams and review answers as you are taking the exam. This is typically the mode you would use first to assess your knowledge and identify information gaps.

- **Practice Exam mode:** Locks certain customization options, as it is presenting a realistic exam experience. Use this mode when you are preparing to test your exam readiness.

- **Flash Card mode:** Strips out the answers and presents you with only the question stem. This mode is great for late-stage preparation when you really want to challenge yourself to provide answers without the benefit of seeing multiple-choice options. This mode does not provide the detailed score reports that the other two modes do, so you should not use it if you are trying to identify knowledge gaps.

In addition to these three modes, you will be able to select the source of your questions. You can choose to take exams that cover all of the chapters, or you can narrow your selection to just a single chapter or the chapters that make up specific parts in the book. All chapters are selected by default. If you want to narrow your focus to individual chapters, simply deselect all the chapters and then select only those on which you wish to focus in the Objectives area.

You can also select the exam banks on which to focus. Each exam bank comes complete with a full exam of questions that cover topics in every chapter. You can have the test engine serve up exams from all test banks or just from one individual bank by selecting the desired banks in the exam bank area.

There are several other customizations you can make to your exam from the exam settings screen, such as the time of the exam, the number of questions served up, whether to randomize questions and answers, whether to show the number of correct answers for multiple-answer questions, and whether to serve up only specific types of questions. You can also create custom test banks by selecting only questions that you have marked or questions on which you have added notes.

Updating Your Exams

If you are using the online version of the Pearson Test Prep practice test software, you should always have access to the latest version of the software as well as the exam data. If you are using the Windows desktop version, every time you launch the software while connected to the Internet, it checks whether there are any updates to your exam data and automatically downloads any changes that were made since the last time you used the software.

Sometimes, due to many factors, the exam data may not fully download when you activate your exam. If you find that figures or exhibits are missing, you may need to manually update your exams. To update a particular exam you have already activated and downloaded, simply click the **Tools** tab and click the **Update Products** button. Again, this is an issue only with the desktop Windows application.

If you wish to check for updates to the Pearson Test Prep exam engine software, Windows desktop version, simply click the **Tools** tab and click the **Update Application** button. This ensures that you are running the latest version of the software engine.

CHAPTER 1

Introduction to the Cisco Expressway Solution

This chapter covers the following topics:

VCS to Expressway Migration: Provides a brief history of the evolution of the Expressway and an introduction to the key functions of this product.

SIP on the Expressway: Provides a brief introduction to the SIP protocol and how it is used in a Cisco Expressway environment.

H.323 on the Expressway: Provides a brief introduction to the H.323 standard and how it is used in a Cisco Expressway environment.

Describe Expressway Licensing: Identifies the different licensing options available on the Cisco Expressway and how these licenses can be consumed.

When it comes to call control, most people think about the **Cisco Unified Communications Manager (Unified CM)**, as they should. The Unified CM offers an extensive set of options that can be configured for an extensive number of scenarios. However, the Unified CM is not the only call control option in a Cisco collaboration solution. This chapter will introduce you to the Cisco Expressway solution, which can be used in conjunction with the Unified CM or independently as the primary call control device.

This chapter covers the following objectives from the Implementing Cisco Collaboration Cloud and Edge Solutions (CLCEI) exam 300-820:

- 1.5.a Describe Expressway Licensing: Option keys

- 1.5.b Describe Expressway Licensing: Release key

- 1.5.c Describe Expressway Licensing: License consumption

"Do I Know This Already?" Quiz

The "Do I Know This Already?" quiz enables you to assess whether you should read this entire chapter thoroughly or jump to the "Exam Preparation Tasks" section. If you are in doubt about your answers to these questions or your own assessment of your knowledge of the topics, read the entire chapter. Table 1-1 lists the major headings in this chapter and their corresponding "Do I Know This Already?" quiz questions. You can find the answers in Appendix A, "Answers to the 'Do I Know This Already?' Quizzes and Review Questions."

Table 1-1 "Do I Know This Already?" Section-to-Question Mapping

Foundation Topics Section	Questions
VCS to Expressway Migration	1
SIP on the Expressway	2
H.323 on the Expressways	3
Describe Expressway Licensing	4–8

CAUTION The goal of self-assessment is to gauge your mastery of the topics in this chapter. If you do not know the answer to a question or are only partially sure of the answer, you should mark that question as wrong for purposes of the self-assessment. Giving yourself credit for an answer you correctly guess skews your self-assessment results and might provide you with a false sense of security.

1. What is the main difference between the Cisco VCS and the Cisco Expressway?

   a. The VCS supports both SIP and H.323 but the Expressway supports SIP only.

   b. The VCS supports direct registration, whereas the Expressway supports only MRA.

   c. The VCS uses device-based licenses, whereas the Expressway uses user-based licenses.

   d. There are no differences between these two servers.

2. Which of the following statements about SIP registration to the Cisco Expressway is true?

   a. Alias and SIP server settings must be manually configured on the endpoint first.

   b. SIP settings can be provisioned to the endpoint using TFTP.

   c. CDP is required for SIP registration to the Expressway.

   d. DHCP is required for SIP registration to the Expressway.

3. Which of the following is an example of an E.164 address?

   a. john@cisco.com

   b. john

   c. 4001@cisco.com

   d. 4001

4. Which license model includes Webex Conferencing as an included feature?

   a. CUWL Meetings

   b. UCL Enhanced

   c. CUWL Standard

   d. All CUWL license models

   e. All of the above

5. Which of the following options on a Cisco Expressway is used as a call forwarding feature for users?

   a. RMS

   b. FindMe

   c. MRA

   d. Interworking

   e. Single Number Reach

   f. Extension Mobility

6. What are the two ways a release key can be added to a Cisco Expressway?

   a. Via the Option Keys window in the web interface and via the API

   b. Via the Option Keys window in the web interface and via the console

   c. Via the Option Keys window and via the upgrade window in the web interface

   d. Via the Release Key window and via the upgrade window in the web interface

7. Which of the following endpoints will consume a desktop system registration license on a Cisco Expressway?

   a. Webex Board

   b. Webex Room Kit Mini

   c. Cisco Jabber client

   d. Webex Desk Pro

8. How many simultaneous video calls are supported through the Cisco Expressway with a Medium VM deployment?

   a. 100

   b. 200

   c. 250

   d. 500

Foundation Topics

VCS to Expressway Migration

Cisco Expressway is designed specifically for comprehensive collaboration services. It features established firewall-traversal technology and helps redefine traditional enterprise collaboration boundaries, supporting Cisco's vision of any-to-any collaboration. As its primary features and benefits, Cisco Expressway offers proven and highly secure firewall-traversal technology to extend an organization's reach. It helps enable business-to-business, business-to-consumer, and business-to-cloud-service-provider connections. It provides session-based access to comprehensive collaboration for remote workers, without the need for a separate **Virtual Private Network (VPN)** client. It supports a wide range of devices with Cisco Jabber for smartphones, tablets, and desktops. Finally, it complements bring-your-own-device (BYOD) strategies and policies for remote and mobile workers. As a side note, while this book was being written, Cisco began a migration plan to move customers from the Jabber client to the Webex client. All other mentions about Jabber in this book can be interchanged with the Webex client as well.

The Expressway is often deployed as a pair: an Expressway-C (Core) with a trunk and line-side connection to Unified CM, and an Expressway-E (Edge) deployed in the DMZ and configured with a traversal zone connection to an Expressway-C. Optional packages that you can deploy include registrations for Telepresence Rooms or Desktop systems (includes FindMe and Device Provisioning), Microsoft Interoperability, and Advanced Networking (Expressway-E only). The Expressway was available on a dedicated appliance (CE1100), but that server was marked End-of-Sale August 14, 2018. Now the Expressway only runs on VMware on a range of Cisco UCS and third-party servers.

The Cisco Expressway Series call control components are based upon the Cisco Telepresence **Video Communications Server (VCS)**. In May 2010, Cisco completed the acquisition of Tandberg, the developers of a key product in call control known as the VCS. This call control system is different from the Cisco Unified Communications Manager in many ways, namely that VCS provides call control only for video devices, whereas the Unified CM provides call control for both voice and video endpoints. However, the VCS solution possesses a capability that does not exist in the Unified CM: the VCS is capable of true firewall and NAT traversal between the internal network and the public Internet.

In an effort to capitalize on this capability, Cisco came out with the Expressway Series starting with version X8.1, which is built on the same OS as the VCS. The big difference between the Expressway Series and the VCS in this version was that endpoints could not register directly to the Expressway Series servers. The Expressway Series existed to proxy registration requests from endpoints outside of the corporate network to the Unified CM inside the network without the use of a VPN. This function is known as **Mobile and Remote Access (MRA)**, and it is available on both the VCS and Expressway server solutions.

With the release of version X8.6 in August 2016, Cisco announced that the Expressway Series servers will support direct registration with appropriate licenses. This meant that direct registration was no longer a distinction between these two server solutions. Although registration is allowed on both products, there is still a significant distinction between these solutions that pertains to licensing. The Cisco VCS allows for device-based licensing, whereas the Expressway allows for user-based licensing. Endpoints can register directly to the Cisco VCS Control or the Cisco VCS Expressway via Session Initiation Protocol (SIP) or H.323. The Expressway Core and Expressway Edge can now also support endpoint registrations directly via SIP or H.323, but the Expressway Edge can also proxy registration requests to the Expressway Core or the Unified CM. However, it can only proxy SIP registration requests, not H.323 requests.

At the time of this writing, Cisco recently announced the End-of-Life and End-of-Sale for the Cisco VCS. The last sale date for the VCS was December 29, 2020. Cisco will continue to support the VCS for customers who use this product until December 31, 2023; the Expressway Series servers are Cisco's preferred and recommended go-forward product. Everything discussed throughout this book can be applied to either product, but for simplicity we will only be mentioning the Expressways from this point forward.

SIP on the Expressway

Session Initiation Protocol (SIP) is a communication protocol that is created and managed by the **Internet Engineering Task Force (IETF)**. By design, SIP requires the use of a **SIP server** to function as the center of all call control activities, and endpoints that are configured to operate using SIP cannot function without this SIP server. The SIP server performs two functions, registrar and proxy.

The **SIP Registrar** maintains a table that is composed of IP addresses and **Uniform Resource Identifier (URI)** addresses taken from devices at the time of registration. URI addresses are the only type of alias SIP uses for communication other than IP addresses. Because a URI must be in the format of *user@FQDN*, where **FQDN** is the **fully qualified domain name**, the domain must exist within the SIP Registrar for successful registration to occur. The **SIP proxy** uses the table created by the registrar to match URI addresses to IP addresses so that calls can be forwarded, or proxied, to the appropriate destinations at the time of call setup.

SIP does not specify what codecs must be used in a video communication. This is accomplished with **Session Description Protocol (SDP)**, a protocol used with SIP to transfer capability sets between two SIP-capable units.

The registration process to the Cisco Expressway is different than the registration process to the Unified CM in many different ways. All Cisco Telepresence endpoints obtain local power from the power cube rather than through Power over Ethernet (PoE), as Cisco Unified IP Phones obtain power. As a Cisco Telepresence endpoint is powering on, it loads the locally stored image.

Cisco **Collaboration Endpoint (CE)** software-based endpoints can use **Cisco Discovery Protocol (CDP)** for **virtual local-area network (VLAN)** discovery, but this option is not necessary when registering to the Expressway as it is when registering to the Unified CM. When VLAN discovery is complete, or if the endpoint does not use CDP, the endpoint goes through the **Dynamic Host Configuration Protocol (DHCP)** discovery process. This process is only required if static IP address assignment is not being used on the endpoint. Also, this process is the same when registering to the Expressway as it is when registering to the Unified CM, except that the TFTP server address cannot be used by endpoints to register to the Expressway.

The endpoint initiates the DHCP discovery process by sending a DHCP Discovery message to the DHCP server. When the DHCP server receives the DHCP Discovery message, it responds with a DHCP Offer message. The DHCP Offer includes an IP address, subnet mask, default gateway address, and possibly one or more DNS addresses. The endpoints respond to the DHCP Offer with a DHCP Request for the specific information that is sent in the DHCP Offer. The DHCP server then sends a DHCP Acknowledgment authorizing the use of the DHCP information that is exchanged and ends the DHCP session.

The SIP URI and Expressway IP address are typically configured locally on the endpoint. These configurations can also be provisioned through Cisco Telepresence Management Suite (TMS). Once these settings have been configured, the final step in the process is for the endpoint to register to the Cisco Expressway. The endpoint sends its IP address with its alias information to the Cisco Expressway and requests registration. The alias must be in the form of a URI (*name@domain*) and the domain of the alias must match one of the domains that are configured in the Domains menu of the Expressway. If there are no configured restrictions on the Expressway, it responds with a SIP message 200 OK. The registration process is now complete. Figure 1-1 illustrates the registration process to the Cisco Expressway using SIP.

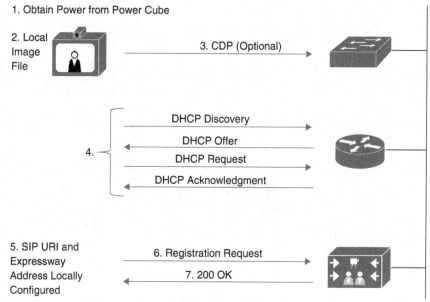

1. Obtain Power from Power Cube

2. Local Image File

3. CDP (Optional)

DHCP Discovery

DHCP Offer

4.

DHCP Request

DHCP Acknowledgment

5. SIP URI and Expressway Address Locally Configured

6. Registration Request

7. 200 OK

Figure 1-1 *SIP Registration to the Cisco Expressway*

Once an endpoint is registered, a different process is used for call processing. The Unified CM and the Cisco Expressway process SIP calls in a similar fashion. Both call control servers have **Call Admission Control (CAC)** elements that can be leveraged, although what these elements are and how they are leveraged mark the differences between each call control server. There are two methods of processing a SIP call: early offer and delayed offer. Early offer is the method that is used in the Cisco Expressway and thus is the only method described in this section. The differences between these two methods have to do with when SDP is sent. Refer to *CCNP and CCIE Collaboration CLCOR 350-801 Official Cert Guide* (Cisco Press, 2020) for a deeper explanation of the differences between SIP early offer and delayed offer. SDP is the mechanism SIP uses to exchange codec capabilities and identify the **User Datagram Protocol (UDP)** ports that are needed for Real-time Transport Protocol (RTP) media.

When a user dials the destination alias using SIP early offer, the source endpoint sends an Invite message to the SIP server with its SDP information. The SIP Proxy function examines the table that was created by the SIP Registrar to determine the destination endpoint's IP address using the alias that is dialed. The SIP server then proxies the Invite message with the SDP packets to the destination endpoint. At the same time, the SIP server responds to the source endpoint with a Trying message, which contains the destination endpoint's IP information. When the source endpoint receives the Trying message, it now possesses the source (itself) and destination IP addresses.

When the destination endpoint receives the Invite message, that endpoint now has the source and destination (itself) IP address information as well. It then responds with two messages. The first message is the Ringing message. This Ringing communication tells the destination endpoint to ring, and sends a ring-back tone to the source endpoint. Once the user of the destination endpoint answers the call, the destination endpoint sends an OK message. The OK message contains call connection status, acknowledgment that SDP information has been received, and the destination endpoint's SDP information. Because the destination

Key Topic

endpoint is now aware of the ports specified by the source endpoint for the media communication, which were identified in the SDP communication, these ports are opened and the destination endpoint can now receive audio and video media over these UDP ports.

When the source endpoint receives the OK message from the destination endpoint, the UDP ports that are specified by the destination endpoint are opened so audio and video media can be received from the destination endpoint. An Acknowledgment is sent from the source endpoint to the destination endpoint and the call is now set up. Figure 1-2 illustrates the SIP early offer call setup process.

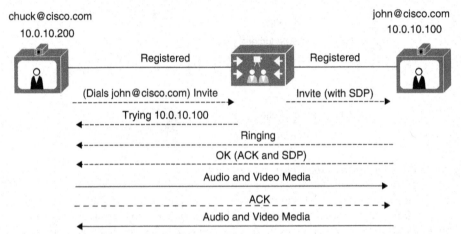

Figure 1-2   *SIP Early Offer Call Setup Process*

H.323 on the Expressways

H.323 is an "umbrella" standard developed and maintained by the International Telecommunications Union (ITU) for packet-switched communication (communication over IP). It is referred as an umbrella standard because it encompasses many sub-standards. To be H.323 compliant, the device must support a minimum set of sub-standards. Many of the standards included in the H.323 umbrella standard are taken from the **H.320** umbrella standard for circuit-switched communication, like Integrated Services Digital Network (ISDN), public switched telephone network (PSTN), and plain old telephone service (POTS).

Unlike SIP, H.323 devices can place calls without a central call control device by dialing an IP address of another system. However, a central call control device, which is known as a **gatekeeper,** can be used to extend the management functions of an H.323 environment in three capacities: registration, security, and call control.

Registration allows the use of **E.164 aliases, H.323 IDs,** and **Routing Prefixes** in addition to IP address dialing. E.164 aliases are numeric-only values containing 1 to 15 digits that are assigned to an endpoint. They work in the same manner as any phone number would in a typical telephony environment. H.323 IDs can use any combination of numbers, letters, and/or special characters. Because of this ability, an H.323 ID can be in the form of a URI. Prefixes are a feature of an H.323 dial plan architecture that allows easy access to services such as multipoint control units (MCUs) and gateways.

Security regarding the gatekeeper does not refer to call encryption. That type of security is a function that is built into endpoints and can be used with or without a gatekeeper. Security within the context of a gatekeeper refers to securing a networked environment so that device registration to the gatekeeper can be controlled. This function helps secure access and control features within the video network.

Call control is the ability to determine which devices can call each other within the video network, and administer the bandwidth that can be utilized when calling between different devices and/or locations. More advanced call control policies can be configured, such as changing (transforming) the dialed aliases, redirecting call traffic, and restricting calls through ISDN gateways from an outside source (known as *hair-pinning*).

The registration process to a gatekeeper using H.323 begins with settings on an endpoint. **Call Setup Mode** is a setting that is configured on an endpoint that can be set to either Direct or Gatekeeper. If Call Setup mode is set to *Direct*, the endpoint never attempts to register to a gatekeeper and is only able to dial by IP address. When *Gatekeeper* mode is used, the endpoint is completely subservient to a gatekeeper and performs no function until it has registered. Once registration has occurred, the device must request permission before it attempts any action. Therefore, the ITU created the communication protocol that is known as **Registration, Admission, and Status (RAS)** that identifies all messaging schemes between any device and a gatekeeper.

Gatekeeper Discovery is another setting configured on an endpoint that affects to which gatekeeper an endpoint will register by determining how an endpoint locates the gatekeeper to which it will attempt to register. *Gatekeeper Discovery Mode* can be configured to either Automatic or Manual. If it is set to *Automatic*, the endpoint sends out a broadcast message that is known as a **Gatekeeper Request (GRQ)** to the entire network broadcast domain to which the device belongs. The first gatekeeper to respond with a Gatekeeper Confirmation (GCF) is where that endpoint will try to register. If the Gatekeeper Discovery Mode is set to Manual, then the address of the gatekeeper must be entered into the endpoint manually before a registration attempt will be made. This address becomes the address to which the endpoint will direct a **Registration Request (RRQ)**.

The gatekeeper that receives the RRQ responds with a **Request in Progress (RIP)** while processing though various security policies to assess whether the endpoint is allowed to register. If a security policy prohibits registration, the gatekeeper responds to the device with a Registration Reject (RRJ). If there are no configurations prohibiting the registration, the Gatekeeper responds with a Registration Confirmation (RCF). Figure 1-3 illustrates the registration process to a gatekeeper using H.323.

Because H.323-capable endpoints are not required to register before placing calls, there are two slightly different call setup processes that can be used: one for unregistered H.323 endpoints, and one for registered H.323 endpoints. The only difference between them is that if no gatekeeper is being used, then there is no RAS. Just as SIP has an early offer and a delayed offer, H.323 has an early start and a late start. Only the late start is used on the Expressways, so that is all we will include in the following call setup process explanation.

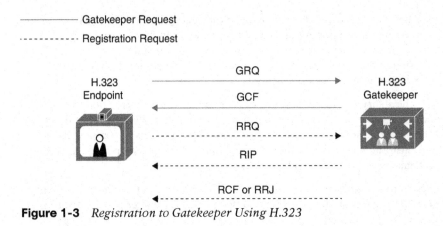

Figure 1-3   *Registration to Gatekeeper Using H.323*

During an H.323 call setup involving a gatekeeper, a call admission process must occur. When the calling endpoint dials the alias of the called endpoint, it sends an **Admission Request (ARQ)** to the gatekeeper. The gatekeeper responds with a RIP message because there may be call control policies that prohibit or restrict the call or certain aspects to the call. If the policies restrict access to the dialed alias, or the gatekeeper cannot locate the dialed alias, the return message will be an Admission Reject (ARJ). Provided the destination endpoint is located and there are no restrictions in place prohibiting the call, the return message will be an Admission Confirmation (ACF), which also includes the IP address of the destination endpoint since the calling user probably dialed the alias of the called endpoint, not the IP address.

The calling endpoint then uses this IP address to send the H.225 call setup message to the destination endpoint. This call setup message contains the source and destination IP addresses (in hexadecimal format) and any crypto-hash token if the call is to be encrypted. Both **Q.931** and RAS messaging are part of the **H.225** control standard for call setup.

When the called endpoint receives the call setup message, it must first request permission from the gatekeeper to answer the call. Therefore, the destination endpoint sends an ARQ message to the gatekeeper. The gatekeeper responds with a RIP message and proceeds to check if there are any bandwidth restrictions. Provided there are no restrictions, the gatekeeper responds with an ACF. The called endpoint can now respond to the H.225 call setup message it received. The first response this endpoint sends out is the Alerting message. This process allows the system to ring and sends a ring-back tone to the source endpoint. Once the call is answered, either manually or automatically, a Connect message is sent to the originating endpoint. Both the Alerting and Connect messages are part of the Q.931 messaging system.

After the call setup messaging is complete, the two endpoints must now go through an **H.245** negotiation process to ensure that the most appropriate codecs are being used. First, each endpoint must send a Terminal Capabilities Set (sometimes called Capabilities Exchange, or CapEx) containing all the codecs that they are capable of using. These codecs are the audio and video compression algorithms, such as G.711 and H.261, and other capabilities like dual video, far-end camera control, chair control, and so on. Because this communication is all **Transmission Control Protocol (TCP)** communication, there will be acknowledgments for each communication sent. Once this process is completed, the primary/responder determination needs to be made.

The primary is simply the endpoint that initiates communications requiring a response. Based on several checkpoints, it can be either endpoint. The primary initiates the next step—opening logical channels. These logical channels are the UDP ports that will be used for sending the media packets between each endpoint. The primary will decide which video and audio codecs to use as well. Audio ports will always be opened first, then video, then ports for each additional capability. The primary will also open the **Real-time Transport Control Protocol (RTCP)** ports first (which will always be odd-numbered), then the **Real-time Transport Protocol (RTP)** ports (even-numbered). RTCP is used for signaling, and RTP is used for the actual media. Once each set of ports has been opened, the endpoints begin to exchange media. Figure 1-4 illustrates the call setup process for H.323.

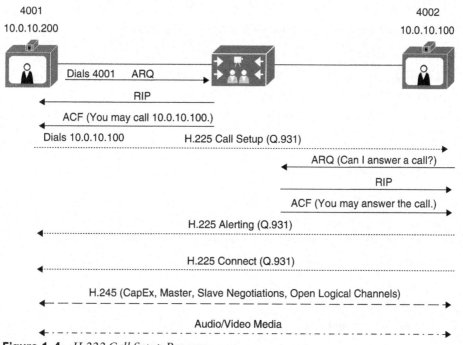

Figure 1-4   *H.323 Call Setup Process*

Describe Expressway Licensing

Like any Cisco product, it is important to understand the requirements for licensing your product at the time of installation. Historically, the Cisco VCS used "device-based" licenses, where licenses were purchased based on the number of devices registered and the number of concurrent calls the VCS would allow and the type of call (traversal versus non-traversal). With the Cisco Expressway Series, the recommended program is to use the **Cisco Unified Workspace Licensing (CUWL)** model or **Cisco Collaboration Flex Plan** licensing. Bear in mind that Cisco announced on August 3, 2020, that the CUWL and UCL licensing models will be End-of-Sale and End-of-Life soon. The End-of-Sale date for these products was February 1, 2021. Cisco will continue to support customer accounts that use these licensing models until February 29, 2024. The go-forward product is Flex licensing. All CUWL and UCL licenses can be converted to Flex automatically with a simple Flex subscription. However, understanding these older license types may be prudent.

CUWL licenses are broken down into two varieties, with a third possibility being the **Cisco User Connect Licensing (CUCL)**, which are designed for voice-only solutions on the Cisco Expressway. This licensing model is based on users rather than devices and allows the customer to simply purchase licenses based on the number of users they wish to service, with each user having access to multiple devices or services as part of the program. The CUWL and Cisco UCL licensing options are as follows:

- CUWL Standard
    - This option supports multiple endpoints per user. For example, this license allows for two desktop endpoints under a single user license, allowing for a single user to have an endpoint both at the office and at home.
    - This option also includes Cisco Unity Connection services.
- CUWL Meetings
    - This package includes everything the CUWL Standard provides plus access to multiparty and Webex options.
    - Personal Multiparty Plus (PMP): These licenses are applied to the Cisco Meeting Server specifically.
    - Webex Conferencing: These licenses are applied to the **Cisco Meeting Server (CMS)** and Webex Meeting Center accounts for Webex-enabled conferencing.
- Cisco UCL Enhanced/Enhanced Plus
    - This package is designed for voice-only solutions where the Expressway Series is only used to provide VPN-less traversal services for voice endpoints.
    - Prime collaboration services are also provided with this license model.
    - UCL licenses typically support one device per user, but they can support up to two devices per user.
- Cisco UCL Basic and UCL Essentials
    - This package is designed for voice-only solutions with no Expressway Series support and only one device supported per user.
    - Prime collaboration services and Jabber IM/P services are provided with this license model.
    - Unity Connection and Web Conferencing are the only add-on services allowed.

Figure 1-5 breaks down the various quantities of licenses that are contained in these various packages. It should be noted that these licenses are purchased and implemented in the same way on the Expressway Series as they would be used when purchasing them for a Unified CM solution, while "zeroing out" the inapplicable features.

	CUWL Meetings	CUWL Standard	UCL Enhanced/ Enhanced Plus	UCL Basic	UCL Essentials
Number of Devices Supported	Multiple	Multiple	Two/One	One	One
Cisco Prime Collaboration	Included	Included	Included	Included	Included
Jabber IM/P	Included	Included	Included	Included	Included
Jabber UC	Included	Included	Included	N/A	N/A
Expressway Firewall Traversal	Included	Included	Included	N/A	N/A
Unity Connection	Included	Included	Add-On	Add-On	Add-On
Webex Conferencing	Included	Add-On	Add-On	Add-On	Add-On
PMP Basic	Included	Add-On	Add-On	N/A	N/A
PMP Advanced	Add-On	Add-On	Add-On	N/A	N/A

Cisco Prime Collaboration Standard Is Included with the CUCM

Firewall Traversal for Voice and Video; Included with UCL Advanced and Above

One Named User License for Webex Meeting Center

Enables Up to Four Participants to Join a Conference

Allows Multiple Participants to Join a Conference

Figure 1-5 *Quantity Comparison of CUWL and UCL License Models*

There are some other differences between CUWL and UCL licenses that should be noted. CUWL Standard and Professional licenses support multiple endpoints. For example, all CUWL licenses permit two desktop endpoints for a single user license, allowing for a single user to have an endpoint both at the office and at home. UCL packages are designed for voice-only solutions, so the endpoints will not be able to register to the Expressways directly. The Expressway Series is only used to provide VPN-less traversal services for voice endpoints. Video can be used over UCL using Jabber or video UC phones, such as Cisco IP Phone models 8845 or 8865, but this is not the designed purpose of these licenses. Telepresence endpoints cannot register under the UCL model. Notice that UCL supports only one or two devices per user. The idea here is that a user may need to register a VoIP phone and Jabber, or that user may just use a VoIP phone.

Cisco has been using CUWL and UCL licenses for many years because it has led the market in on-premises infrastructure. In more recent years, a new market has opened up in cloud-based offerings, and Cisco has been working diligently to dominate this market as well. With the need to be able to deliver collaboration services cost-effectively, using on-premises infrastructure or cloud-based services, depending on the needs of employees, Cisco has added the previously mentioned Flex layer to its licensing model.

The Cisco Collaboration Flex Plan entitles customers to use Cisco's industry-leading collaboration tools with one simple subscription-based offer. It helps with transitions to the cloud, and investment protection, by including cloud, premises, hosted, and hybrid deployments, with the flexibility to use them all. Companies can choose to equip employees with meetings, calling, or both, and add more licenses at the time they're needed. Companies can also easily add Contact Center capabilities, which are also included in the Collaboration Flex Plan. One agreement covers software, entitlements, and technical support for cloud-based and on-premises services. Companies simply choose the services they need today and grow at their own pace. There is no need to manage complex agreements. And you can mix and match Meetings and Calling subscriptions for flexibility and value. With the Flex Plan, you can choose the right subscription based on your business size and needs. Each option includes technical support. Choose from the following purchasing models:

■ For enterprise-wide deployments, Cisco Enterprise Agreement customers can purchase services via the Cisco Collaboration Flex Plan. You can gain maximum value by enabling services for everyone in your organization for meetings or calling or both.

- To purchase meetings according to usage, choose Cisco Collaboration Flex Plan – Active User Meetings. Anyone can host a meeting, and you pay only for those who use the entitlement.

- To provide meetings or calling services to individuals, teams, or departments, choose Cisco Collaboration Flex Plan – Named User. Your purchase is based on the number of people who need services, which allows you to grow at your own pace.

- To provide contact center services to your service agents, choose Cisco Collaboration Flex Plan – Concurrent Agent. Your purchase is based on the number of agents simultaneously using services at your peak busy hour. Again, you can grow at your own pace.

At the same time, you can seamlessly drive enhanced team collaboration with Cisco Webex, which is included at no additional charge. Cisco Webex is a great tool to collaborate with other coworkers for ongoing work. Webex can be used on every device, in every place, to move work forward. You can enable services for selected individuals, teams, or departments, or for your entire organization. And you have the flexibility to add services as adoption grows. To learn more about the Cisco Collaboration Flex Plan, visit https://cisco.com/go/collaborationflexplan.

Cisco introduced a new way to add licenses to on-premises collaboration products called Smart Licensing. Smart Licensing was introduced as an option with Cisco Unified Communication product version 11.5, but it is required for licensing products from version 12.0 onward. Cisco is transforming the end-to-end software lifecycle to make the customers' experience better and easier. A major part of this change is a move away from *Product Activation Key (PAK)* licenses to Smart Licensing to make the license registration process faster and more flexible. At the heart of the transformation is Smart Licensing and Smart Accounts, which offer streamlined purchasing and software administration. Smart Licensing is a flexible software licensing model that simplifies the way you activate and manage licenses across your organization. The Smart Licensing model makes it easier for you to procure, deploy, and manage your Cisco software licenses. To use Smart Licensing, you must first set up a Smart Account.

A Smart Account is a central repository where you can view, store, and manage licenses across the entire organization. Comprehensively, you can get access to your software licenses, hardware licenses, and subscriptions through your Smart Account. Smart Accounts are required to access and manage Smart License–enabled products. Creating a Smart Account is easy and takes less than five minutes. You can create a Smart Account on Cisco.com. Smart Accounts offer a simple-to-use, centralized, and organized solution to license management. With a Smart Account, you get full visibility and insight into all of your Cisco software assets deposited into the Smart Account, including PAK licenses and Enterprise Agreements. When Smart Accounts are used with Smart Licenses, the benefits include the following:

Key Topic

- **Real-Time visibility:** You can view all of your software licenses, entitlements, and users across the organization.

- **Centralized management:** A single location enables authorized users to see all license entitlements and move licenses freely through the network as needed.

- **Cost-effectiveness:** You can drive down the cost of license management with reduced overhead, better utilization management, and more efficient planning.

- **Organization:** Virtual Accounts provide the flexibility to organize licenses by department, product, geography, or other designation, whatever makes the most sense for your company.

Option Keys

All of the previous talk about CUWL, UCL, Flex, and Smart Licensing is important to any component used in a Cisco Collaboration solution. However, let's move the conversation back to the Expressways specifically. As previously mentioned, the difference between a Cisco VCS and a Cisco Expressway is the licensing. To register endpoints to a VCS you simply decide how many devices you want to register and that is how many licenses you purchase, plus about 10% more for planned growth. Because the Expressway follows the user-based licensing model, you must first assess what types of devices you will register and consider how these devices will be used. Then you can apply CUWL licenses as either Room System or Desktop System licenses. *Room System* licenses are used for common endpoints not assigned to a specific user. This might include a Cisco Webex Room Kit Pro set up in a conference room, or a Webex Board on a cart so that it can be wheeled around to different classrooms. These types of licenses can be applied to only one system at a time. *Desktop System* licenses are associated with a specific user and can be applied to only a specific type of device, such as the Cisco Webex DX80 or the new Webex Desk Pro. The advantage to using CUWL licenses instead of the VCS device-based licenses is that you only need to order the quantity you need today. If you need more tomorrow, you just add them on with the Flex Plan, and they are available immediately for you to use.

Another big licensing difference between the VCS and Expressway relates to call licenses. On the VCS you have to purchase both traversal and non-traversal call licenses. These licenses are used for any call placed, regardless of whether the call is between two locally registered endpoints or is going out across the public network to another company's endpoint system. A *non-traversal call* is defined as any call that uses a common protocol and occurs within the same network, either on the same **local-area network (LAN)** or on the same **wide-area network (WAN)**. A *traversal call* is defined as any call that does not use a common protocol, such as H.323 to SIP or IPv4 to IPv6, or that does not occur within the same network, such as a firewall traversal call out across the public Internet. By contrast, the Expressway includes local call licenses between any devices within the same network. These are equivalent to non-traversal call licenses, but they come with the Expressway at no additional cost. However, these call licenses cannot be used for **business-to-business (B2B)** calling, or interworking calls. **Rich Media Services (RMS)** licenses are used where B2B, **business-to-customer (B2C)**, SIP to H.323, IPv4 to Ipv6, and Microsoft Interop calls are required.

The Microsoft Interop function requires a special option key before it can be integrated on the VCS. However, only RMS licenses are needed to use this feature on the Expressway. FindMe is another feature on a VCS that must be enabled with an option key before it can be used. This feature comes standard on the Cisco Expressway. **FindMe** is a call forwarding tool with some enhanced capabilities. An overview of FindMe is provided in Chapter 7, "Cisco Expressway Call Processing Order." Table 1-2 compares the differences between the Cisco Expressway and the Cisco VCS.

Table 1-2   Comparison of the Cisco Expressway and the Cisco VCS

Feature	Cisco Expressway	Cisco VCS
Server components	Expressway Core Expressway Edge	VCS Control VCS Expressway
Registration licensing	Included with CUWL user licenses (registration supported on X8.9 or later)	Device registration licenses required (2500 max per server)
Call licensing	Internal and mobile calling included Rich Media Session (RMS) Licenses required for B2B and B2C calling and interworking calls	Non-traversal call licenses required Traversal call licenses required
Microsoft Interop license	Requires RMS licenses	Requires option key
FindMe license	Available	Requires option key
Clustering capabilities	Up to six servers	Up to six servers

Release Key

When you are first setting up an Expressway, after you have entered all the network settings and have rebooted the system, you must enter a release key before that server can support any of the option keys for regular use. Hardware appliance Expressway servers may already have the release keys and option keys installed. Virtual deployments will not because the serial number has not been generated yet, and release keys are tied to the system's serial number. If you built the Expressway as a virtual machine (VM), then you need to go to the web interface of the Expressway and identify what your serial number is, so that you can subscribe for the release key using your PAK. Once you have navigated to the web interface of the Expressway and logged in, you can find the serial number along with the version number in the bottom-right corner of any page. The PAK is a Product Authorization Key, not the license key itself. This key allows you to register your product through the Smart Licensing portal. Once registered, your product Release Key and Option Keys will be provided. After you obtain the release key and option keys, simply use the following steps to enter them through the web interface of the Expressway.

Step 1.   Access the web interface of the Expressway with a web browser. Once you are logged in with an admin account, the Expressway Status screen will appear.

Step 2.   Navigate to **Maintenance > Option Keys**.

Step 3.   If this is a new install, the Release Key section will be available as a blank field. The Release Key field for an existing Expressway installation will not appear on this page. You can use the **Upgrade** option to set the release key in the event an upgrade is required.

The release key does not change between minor version upgrades. The release key only changes between major version upgrades such as moving from x8.X to x12.X.

Step 4.   Copy and paste your release key into the Release Key field, and then click the **Set Release Key** button.

Step 5.   A prompt will appear at the top of the page with a hyperlink to restart the Cisco Expressway. Restart the Expressway at this time.

Step 6.   After the system reboots, you can log back in to the Expressway and use the **Maintenance > Option Keys** page to add your option keys to the Expressway. A restart is not required after adding option keys.

A release key is also required for major upgrades, because the release key will change with each major version. So long as your company has a current service contract, you will be able to generate a new release key when an upgrade is needed. If the Expressway already has an active release key installed, you can add a new release key from the Upgrade menu in the web interface. Figure 1-6 illustrates the Option Keys page from the Cisco Expressway web interface.

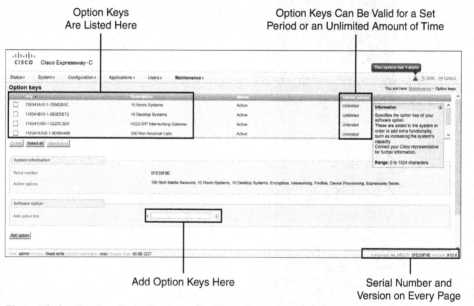

Figure 1-6   *Option Keys Page on the Cisco Expressway*

License Consumption

Now that it has been established how licensing works on the Cisco Expressways, and the licenses available have been discussed, it is important to also understand how these licenses are consumed so that ordering and support for these licenses can be planned out for customers. This section outlines the number of registrations and calls that can be supported on a single Expressway, then describes how registration licenses are consumed, followed by an explanation of how call licenses are consumed.

A virtual installation of the Cisco Expressway can be supported over three different capacity points: small, medium, and large. Each of these capacity points requires different hardware specifications and supports a different number of registrations and calls through the Expressway. Table 1-3 identifies the three capacity points for a virtual Expressway installation, along with hardware requirements and supported server platform information.

Table 1-3 Server Specifications for Cisco Expressway Virtualization

Component and Capacity Point	vCPU	vRAM	vDisk	vNIC	XS TRC	BE6000M S TRC	BE6000H S+ TRC	BE7000M M TRCs	BE7000H L TRCs	Full UC Pref. CPUs	Restricted UC Pref. CPUs
										UCS or Third-Party Spec-Based on Intel Xeon	
Small Expressway-C or Expressway-E	2	4 GB	Total 132 GB	2	No	Yes	Yes	No	No	Yes	Yes 1.80+ GHz Only
Medium Expressway-C or Expressway-E	2	6 GB	Total 132 GB	2	No	No	No	Yes	Yes	Yes	Yes 2.40+ GHz Only
Large Expressway-C or Expressway-E	8	8 GB	Total 132 GB	2	No	No	No	No	No	Yes 3.20+ GHz Only	No

The hardware appliance server CE1200 has the same capacity limitations as the large VM. The capacity limitations of a Cisco Expressway can be broken down into five categories: registration licenses, call licenses, RMS licenses, MRA registrations (proxied), and **Traversal Using Relays around NAT (TURN)** relays.

As previously described, two types of endpoints can register to the Cisco Expressway: Room Systems and Desktop Systems. Cisco has made it really easy to identify what endpoint is considered a Room System endpoint and a Desktop System endpoint by identifying four or five different Desktop System endpoints. All other endpoints would be categorized as a Room System endpoint. These endpoints include the following:

- Cisco EX60 (end-of-sale)

- Cisco EX90 (end-of-sale)

- Cisco DX70 (end-of-sale)

- Cisco Webex DX80

In addition to these endpoints, the legacy Cisco Jabber Video for Telepresence soft client, which has also been marked end-of-sale, would also register as a Desktop System to the Cisco Expressway if a business was still using this client. To register one of these endpoints as a Desktop System using SIP, DX endpoints must be running version CE8.2 or later, and EX systems must be running TC7.3.6 or later. DX and EX systems running earlier versions of software that still register using SIP will consume a Room System license. All endpoints that register using H.323 consume a Telepresence Room System License. This is due to a limitation in H.323, which does not determine the difference between desktop and room type endpoints. Therefore, Cisco recommends using SIP as the preferred signaling protocol. H.323 is available as a fallback for legacy endpoints that do not support SIP.

Some time was spent earlier in this chapter explaining the different licenses and calling types that can occur through the Cisco Expressway. So let's take a look now at how these licenses are consumed when the Expressways are used for different types of calls. The first type of call license mentioned earlier was the standard call license that comes with the Cisco Expressway. This type of license supports local calls that do not require interworking. To better understand the standard call license, the term interworking must be defined within the scope of the Expressway. **Interworking** is a gateway function of the Expressway when two dissimilar protocols are trying to communicate. The three types of interworking calls that could be experienced through the Expressway include SIP to H.323, IPv4 to IPv6, or NAT to NAT, although the last example is rarely seen anymore, if ever. Interworking is categorized as a type of traversal call, but not all traversal calls are considered interworking. There are two other types of traversal on the Expressways that can support the standard call license, firewall traversal and dual NIC. These will be explained in more detail in Chapter 10, "Multisite and Business-to-Business (B2B) Collaboration Solutions."

Getting back to the standard call license, any call within a corporate network that does not require interworking can use a standard call license. That means any SIP endpoint calling another SIP endpoint within the company is allowed. The same is true for calls between two H.323 endpoints. All of the following call scenarios fall into this category:

- Two H.323 endpoints registered to the Expressway

- Two SIP endpoints registered to the Expressway

- One SIP endpoint registered to the Unified CM and one SIP endpoint registered to the Expressway

- One SIP endpoint registered directly to the Unified CM and one SIP endpoint registered to the Unified CM through the Expressway using MRA

- One SIP endpoint registered to the Unified CM and one SIP endpoint registered to the Webex Control Hub (through a verified domain within the same company)

- One SIP endpoint registered to the Expressway and one SIP endpoint registered to the Webex Control Hub (through a verified domain within the same company)

- One SIP endpoint registered to the Unified CM through the Expressway using MRA and one SIP endpoint registered to the Webex Control Hub (through a verified domain within the same company)

- One SIP endpoint registered to the Expressway Core and one SIP endpoint registered to the Expressway Edge

- One H.323 endpoint registered to the Expressway Core and one H.323 endpoint registered to the Expressway Edge

- Any SIP endpoint registered to the Unified CM through MRA or registered to the Expressway calling out through Cisco Unified Border Element (CUBE) or a Cisco IOS XE gateway with PRI

- Any SIP endpoint (registered to the Expressway or Unified CM) calling into CMS

- Any SIP endpoint (registered to the Expressway or Unified CM) calling into Webex Meeting Center

- Any SIP endpoint (registered to the Expressway or Unified CM) calling into Video Mesh Node

- Any H.323 endpoint registered to the Expressway calling into CMS when H.323 gateway is enabled on CMS (H.323 gateway is not supported on CMS version 3.0 or later)

If we spent some time thinking about it, we could probably come up with a few more scenarios, but hopefully you have the general idea at this point. The other type of call that can be placed through an Expressway is a call that requires an RMS license before the call can be placed. RMS is required for interworking calls, traversal calls to other businesses or customers over IP, Jabber Guest calls, and Microsoft Interoperability calls. One RMS license is consumed per active call leg on the exit node of the Expressway. This means that in a firewall traversal call, the Expressway Edge is considered the exit node, and so should have adequate RMS licenses to support this type of call in the volume of the business using this service. Once a call is disconnected that was using an RMS license, that license is free to be used for another call. If you have ten RMS licenses and ten calls are active that require this license type, then an eleventh call attempt would fail, the caller would hear a fast-busy tone, and the logs would show a specific error message. If that caller attempted the call again after one of the ten connections was disconnected, then the call would go through at that time.

MRA registration capacity limitations are the same as the direct registration limitations to the Expressway. The difference is which devices are allowed to register. Only Cisco Telepresence endpoints can register directly to the Expressway, whereas both Cisco Unified IP Phones and Cisco Telepresence endpoints can register through MRA, as well as the Cisco Jabber soft client.

TURN relays are used with specific deployment scenarios involving Microsoft integrations and CMS. We will not be going very deep into TURN relays, because most scenarios can use the firewall traversal solution that is purpose-built into the Expressway Core and Edge servers. This solution is more secure and easier to manage. However, Chapter 10 offers a short discussion on TURN relays.

Table 1-4 identifies the license limitations for the different capacity points of the Cisco Expressways.

Key Topic

Table 1-4 Cisco Expressway License Limitations

Platform	Registrations (Room\ Desktop)	Calls (Video or Audio Only)	RMS Licenses	MRA Registrations (Proxied)	TURN Relays
CE1200	5000	500 video or 1000 audio	500	5000	6000
Large VM	5000	500 video or 1000 audio	500	2500	6000
Medium VM	2500	100 video or 200 audio	100	2500	1800
Small VM	2500	40 non-MRA video, or 20 MRA video, or 40 audio	75	200	1800

Exam Preparation Tasks

As mentioned in the section "How to Use This Book" in the Introduction, you have a couple of choices for exam preparation: the exercises here, Chapter 22, "Final Preparation," and the exam simulation questions in the Pearson Test Prep practice test software.

Review All Key Topics

Review the most important topics in this chapter, noted with the Key Topics icon in the outer margin of the page. Table 1-5 lists a reference of these key topics and the page numbers on which each is found.

Table 1-5 Key Topics for Chapter 1

Key Topic Element	Description	Page Number
Paragraph	Difference in licensing between the VCS and the Expressway	5
Paragraph	Contents of the OK message in a SIP early offer call setup from the recipient	7
Paragraph	Three functions of a gatekeeper	8
List	CUWL and UCL licensing options	12
List	Cisco Collaboration Flex Plan licensing options	13
List	Benefits of a Smart License account	14
Table 1-2	Comparison of the Cisco Expressway and the Cisco VCS	16
Step list	Steps to enter the release key on a new Cisco Expressway	16
Table 1-3	Server Specifications for Cisco Expressway Virtualization	18
Table 1-4	Cisco Expressway License Limitations	21

Complete Tables and Lists from Memory

Print a copy of Appendix C, "Memory Tables" (found on the companion website), or at least the section for this chapter, and complete the tables and lists from memory. Appendix D, "Memory Tables Answer Key," also on the companion website, includes completed tables and lists to check your work.

Define Key Terms

Define the following key terms from this chapter and check your answers in the glossary:

Admission Request (ARQ), business-to-business (B2B), business-to-customer (B2C), Call Admission Control (CAC), Call Setup Mode, Cisco Collaboration Flex Plan, Cisco Discovery Protocol (CDP), Cisco Meeting Server (CMS), Cisco Unified Communications Manager (Unified CM), Cisco Unified Workspace Licensing (CUWL), Cisco User Connect Licensing (CUCL), Collaboration Endpoint (CE), Dynamic Host Configuration Protocol (DHCP), E.164 alias, FindMe, fully qualified domain name (FQDN), gatekeeper, Gatekeeper Request (GRQ), H.225, H.245, H.323, H.323 ID, H.320, Internet Engineering Task Force (IETF), interworking, local-area network (LAN), Mobile and Remote Access (MRA), Q.931, Real-time Transport Control Protocol (RTCP), Real-time Transport Protocol (RTP), Registration, Admission, and Status (RAS), Registration Request (RRQ), Request in Progress (RIP), Rich Media Services (RMS), Routing Prefix, Session Description Protocol (SDP), Session Initiation Protocol (SIP), SIP Proxy, SIP Registrar, SIP server, Transmission Control Protocol (TCP), Traversal Using Relays around NAT (TURN), Uniform Resource Identifier (URI), User Datagram Protocol (UDP), Video Communications Server (VCS), virtual local-area network (VLAN), Virtual Private Network (VPN), wide-area network (WAN)

Q&A

The answers to these questions appear in Appendix A. For more practice with exam format questions, use the Pearson Test Prep practice test software.

1. What are the seven registration steps to the Cisco Expressway using SIP?

2. List the four subscription models for Flex licensing.

3. What are the three capacity points for deploying the Cisco Expressway as a VM along with the hardware requirements?

CHAPTER 2

Configure Key Cisco Expressway Settings

This chapter covers the following topics:

> **Cisco Expressway Deployment on VM:** Provides an overview and requirements of the virtual machine deployment of the Cisco Expressway.
>
> **Service Setup Wizard Through Web Interface:** Covers the Service Setup Wizard for the Cisco Expressway performed through the web interface.
>
> **Expressway System Configuration:** Explains the key setup settings required for the Cisco Expressway, including DNS, network interfaces, and network firewall rules.
>
> **Expressway Backup and Restore Procedure:** Provides the backup and restore procedures for the Cisco Expressway in both standalone and with cluster deployments.

This chapter focuses on the initial Service Setup Wizard for the Cisco Expressway via a web browser. During the Service Setup Wizard, you will apply menu settings that are crucial to initializing Cisco Expressway within the network environment it is intended for. This chapter also covers the Cisco Expressway backup and restore procedures, both standalone and cluster backup and restore procedures.

This chapter covers the following objectives from the Implementing Cisco Collaboration Cloud and Edge Solutions (CLCEI) exam 300-820:

- 1.8.a Describe key Expressway settings: DNS

- 1.8.b Describe key Expressway settings: Network interfaces

- 1.8.d Describe key Expressway settings: QoS

- 1.8.f Describe key Expressway settings: Network firewall rules

- 1.9 Describe Expressway backup and restore procedure (standalone and cluster)

- 2.1 Configure key Expressway settings

- 2.1.a Configure key Expressway settings: DNS

- 2.1.b Configure key Expressway settings: Network interfaces

- 2.1.d Configure key Expressway settings: QoS

- 2.1.e Configure key Expressway settings: Clustering

"Do I Know This Already?" Quiz

The "Do I Know This Already?" quiz enables you to assess whether you should read this entire chapter thoroughly or jump to the "Exam Preparation Tasks" section. If you are in doubt about your answers to these questions or your own assessment of your knowledge of the topics, read the entire chapter. Table 2-1 lists the major headings in this chapter and their corresponding "Do I Know This Already?" quiz questions. You can find the answers in Appendix A, "Answers to the 'Do I Know This Already?' Quizzes and Review Questions."

Table 2-1 "Do I Know This Already?" Section-to-Question Mapping

Foundation Topics Section	Questions
Cisco Expressway Deployment on VM	1
Service Setup Wizard Through Web Interface	2–3
Expressway System Configuration	4–5
Expressway Backup and Restore Procedures	6–7

CAUTION The goal of self-assessment is to gauge your mastery of the topics in this chapter. If you do not know the answer to a question or are only partially sure of the answer, you should mark that question as wrong for purposes of the self-assessment. Giving yourself credit for an answer you correctly guess skews your self-assessment results and might provide you with a false sense of security.

1. What is the minimum virtual hardware required to host virtual Expressway deployments?
   a. ESXi 6.5
   b. ESXi 7.0
   c. ESXi 6.7
   d. ESXi 6.0

2. Through what interface can the Service Setup Wizard be utilized?
   a. HTTP(S)
   b. CLI
   c. API
   d. TMS

3. What licensing does Cisco Expressway utilize? (Choose two.)
   a. VLSC
   b. APSL
   c. PAK
   d. CUWL
   e. Smart Licensing

   4. How many DNS servers can be added to the Cisco Expressway?

   a. Four

   b. Six

   c. Eight

   d. Five

   5. Which two of the following are correct regarding resolvable DNS addresses? (Choose two.)

   a. The Expressway-C is configured with DNS servers that are located on the external network.

   b. The Expressway-C is configured with DNS servers that are located on the internal network.

   c. The Expressway-C is configured with DNS servers that are publicly routable.

   d. The Expressway-E is configured with DNS servers that are publicly routable.

   6. What default file extension is the Cisco Expressway backup?

   a. sql.gz.enc

   b. .crx

   c. tar.gz.enc

   d. .bak

   7. In what situation should you perform a backup for the Cisco Expressway?

   a. Before performing an upgrade

   b. Before powering off

   c. Before performing a system restore

   d. Before applying licenses

   e. Before firewall traversal

Foundation Topics

Cisco Expressway Deployment on VM

The Expressway Open Virtualization Format (OVA) virtual appliances are designed to meet the minimum deployment requirements. Do not change the .ova configuration after installation, as Cisco may no longer be able to support your deployment. The minimum virtual hardware required to host virtual Expressway deployments is VMware ESXi 6.5. Cisco does not support Expressway VMs hosted on ESXi 6.0 or earlier (these versions are no longer supported by VMware). New installations of Expressway OVAs will not run on any host version before ESXi 6.5.

The following are the ESXi supported versions for release X12.7. For new Expressway VM deployments, the Expressway OVAs must be installed on any of the following versions. If you have existing VM deployments running on an ESXi 6.0 or earlier versions, upgrade the host to any of the following versions before you install the new Expressway software.

- ESXi 6.5 Update 2

- ESXi 6.7 Update 1 from X12.5.2, and Update 2—for Large VMs only—from X12.5.4

- ESXi 6.7 Update 3 from X12.6.1 for Large and Medium VMs

- ESXi 6.7 Update 3 from X12.6.3 for Small VMs

- ESXi 7.0

Make sure that the following requirements are in place:

- Virtualization Technology (VT) is enabled in the BIOS before you install VMware ESXi.

- The VM host "Virtual Machine Startup/Shutdown" setting is configured to "Allow Virtual machines to start and stop automatically with the system," and the VM Expressway has been moved to the Automatic startup section.

The Expressway can co-reside with applications (any other VMs occupying the same host) subject to the following conditions:

- No oversubscription of CPU. You need one-to-one allocation of vCPU to physical cores.

- No oversubscription of RAM. You need one-to-one allocation of vRAM to physical memory.

- No oversubscription of NIC. The Expressway handles large volumes of data, much of which is for real-time communications, and it needs dedicated access to all the bandwidth specified for its interfaces.

  For example, you should not assume that four co-resident small Expressway VMs can handle the expected load if there is only a 1-Gbps physical interface on the host. In this case none of the VMs meet the required minimum specification.

- Sharing disk storage subsystem is supported, subject to correct performance (latency, bandwidth) characteristics.

If you use a UCS Tested Reference Configuration or specifications-based system, the minimum requirements are listed in Table 2-2.

Table 2-2 Requirements for UCS Tested Reference Configuration or Specifications-based System

Deployment Size	vCPU	Reserved CPU Resource	Reserved RAM	Disk Space	NIC
Small	Two cores	3600 MHz (2 × 1.8 GHz)	4 GB	132 GB	1 Gb
Medium	Two cores	4800 MHz (2 × 2.4 GHz)	6 GB	132 GB	1 Gb
Large	Eight cores	25600 MHz (8 × 3.2 GHz)	8 GB	132 GB	1 Gb

Two Large Expressway VMs can co-reside on a UCS server with two eight-core 3.2-GHz processors all dedicated to Expressway when hyperthreading is enabled. To allow for hypervisor overhead, the CPU reservation is set to 16000 MHz, but the full allocation of 8 × 3.2-GHz CPU cores must be made available to each Large Expressway VM. The reservation does not limit maximum Expressway CPU speed, as the Expressway can use the headroom provided by the higher-specification host.

Increasing the capacity of a VM-based Expressway from a smaller deployment size to a larger deployment (Small -> Medium -> Large) or decreasing the capacity from a larger deployment to a smaller one (Large -> Medium -> Small) cannot be done by simply increasing or decreasing the underlying vCPUs and memory hardware resources of the VM. The correct method to upgrade or downgrade is to deploy a new VM of the required deployment size, and then restore the existing configuration (smaller VM for upgrade and larger VM for downgrade) onto the new one.

Do not change the MAC address of the VM. The serial number of a virtual Expressway is based on the virtual machine's MAC address. The serial number is used to validate Expressway licenses and to identify Expressways that are registered to the Cisco Webex cloud. Do not change the MAC address of the Expressway virtual machine when using VMware tools, or you risk losing service.

The VM Expressway is licensed using information that is generated at the time of the .ova file installation. If the .ova file was installed a second time, new licensing information would be created, and to use the new VM, new release and license keys would need to be purchased. After the VM installation is complete, Cisco recommends that you take a backup of the configuration. Do not take VMware snapshots of Cisco Expressway systems. The process interferes with database timing and negatively impacts performance.

Please follow the *Cisco Expressway on Virtual Machine Installation Guide* (for your specific version) on cisco.com for the exact installation steps relative to your organization's deployment.

Service Setup Wizard Through Web Interface

The Service Setup Wizard makes it easier to configure the Expressway system for its chosen purpose in your environment. It also simplifies the user interface for the administrator applying configurations. The wizard starts when you first launch the web user interface. In the wizard, you select the system series, either Expressway series or **Video Communications Server (VCS)** series, and system type, Expressway-C or Expressway-E. Based on the series and type, you select the services. Note, if you use **Product Authorization Key (PAK)**-based licensing, you also apply the relevant option keys for your licenses.

You can use the wizard to review and edit the Expressway basic network settings (typically already configured during initial installation). When you restart, the user interface is tailored to match your service selections and you only see menus and pages for the services you chose. Examples of Cisco Expressway services include the following:

- Cisco Webex Hybrid Services (renamed from Cisco Spark Hybrid Services)
- **Mobile and Remote Access (MRA)** including Meeting Server Web Proxy

- Jabber Guest Services

- Microsoft gateway service

- Registrar

- Collaboration Meeting Rooms (CMR) Cloud

- Business-to-business (B2B) calling

Note that the Microsoft gateway service is only for when you want this system to adapt between Microsoft SIP and standards-based **Session Initiation Protocol (SIP)** variants. If a different system (such as Cisco Meeting Server) is doing that adaptation in your deployment, you do not need this service.

Some services are incompatible and cannot be selected together. Table 2-3 provides a matrix of compatible services. The matrix specifies which services you can use together on the same system or cluster.

Table 2-3   Services That Can Be Hosted Together

	Cisco Webex Hybrid Services (Connectors)	Mobile and Remote Access	Jabber Guest Services	Microsoft gateway service	Registrar	CMR Cloud	Business to Business calling (includes Hybrid Call Service)
Cisco Webex Hybrid Services (Connectors)	Y	N	N	N	N	Y	Y
Mobile and Remote Access and/ or (from X8.9) Meeting Server Web Proxy	N	Y	N	N	Y	Y	Y*
Jabber Guest Services	N	N	Y	N	Y	Y	Y
Microsoft gateway service	N	N	N	Y	N	N	N
Registrar	N	Y	Y	N	Y	Y	Y
CMR Cloud	Y	Y	Y	N	Y	Y	Y

	Cisco Webex Hybrid Services (Connectors)	Mobile and Remote Access	Jabber Guest Services	Microsoft gateway service	Registrar	CMR Cloud	Business to Business calling (includes Hybrid Call Service)
Business to Business calling (includes Hybrid Call Service)	Y	Y*	Y	N	Y	Y	Y

Rules for Table 2-3:

- Hybrid Services connectors may co-reside with the Expressway-C of a traversal pair used for Call Service, subject to user number limitations.

* If your Hybrid Call Service, or **business-to-business (B2B)**, traversal pair is also used for MRA, then the Hybrid Services connectors must be on a separate Expressway-C. This is because Cisco does not support the connectors being hosted on the Expressway-C that is used for MRA.

- Microsoft gateway service requires a dedicated VCS Control or Expressway-C (called "Gateway VCS" or "Gateway Expressway" in the help and documentation).

- Jabber Guest cannot work with MRA (technical limitation).

- MRA is currently not supported in IPv6-only mode. If you want IPv6 B2B calling to co-reside with IPv4 MRA on the same Expressway traversal pair, the Expressway-E and Expressway-C must both be in dual-stack mode.

Before we begin describing the configurations, we assume that you have the basic prerequisites in place. These include that the static IP address has been assigned, the default passwords have been changed, and an Ethernet connection has been made to an existing Local Area Network (LAN), which is able to route **Hypertext Transport Protocol (HTTP)** and **Hypertext Transport Protocol Secure (HTTPS)** traffic to the Expressway. Also, if you prefer to not utilize the Service Setup Wizard, a skip option does exist. If you change your mind later, you can go back and run the wizard at any time on the **Status > Overview** page. If you opt to skip the wizard, you need to deal with the Expressway licensing setup requirements manually before you start the configuration tasks in this guide. Also, the user interface is not customized to reflect your specific service selections.

System configuration is normally carried out through the web interface. To use the web interface:

Step 1.   Open a browser window and in the address bar type the IP address or the FQDN of the Cisco Expressway system.

Step 2.   Enter a valid administrator username and password and click **Login.** The Overview page is displayed.

If you receive a warning message regarding Expressway's security certificate, you can ignore this until you are ready to secure the system.

The first time you log in to the Expressway web user interface you automatically see the Service Setup Wizard. (For subsequent logins you see the **Status > Overview** page, and from that page you can click Run Service Setup at any time.) To navigate the wizard:

- Click Continue to save and move to the next wizard page.

- Click Back to return to the previous wizard page.

- Click Skip Service Setup Wizard if you want to back out of the wizard completely.

If you use Smart Licensing, you cannot change the Select Series setting on the Service Selection page/wizard (to convert an Expressway to a VCS product) as shown in Figure 2-1. Instead, this process must start with a factory reset (to disable Smart Licensing because it is not supported on VCS). Some of the other settings shown in this example are unnecessary with Smart Licensing and do not appear in the wizard on Expressways that use Smart Licensing.

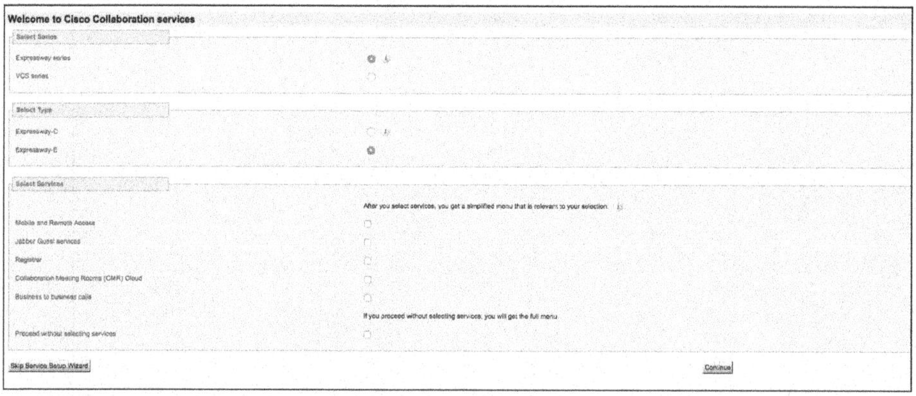

Figure 2-1 *Service Selection Page*

While we are on the topic of licensing, the process varies depending on whether the system uses the classic (PAK-based) licensing or Smart Licensing. Both processes are described in this section, but ultimately you should use the appropriate process for your deployment's licensing method.

This process applies for deployments that use classic (PAK-based) licensing:

Step 1.   In the Select Series section of the Service Selection page, click the **Expressway Series** radio button.

Step 2.   In the Select Type section, click either the **Expressway-C** radio button or the **Expressway-E** radio button. Cisco recommends that you select Expressway-C first and run the wizard for it. Then run the wizard on the Expressway-E.

The list of services changes to match what is available on your chosen Series and Type.

Step 3.   In the Select Services section, check the boxes next to the services you want to use on this system. For the compatible services that you can use together on the same system or cluster, refer to Table 2-3.

If you want to keep all the menu options, or if you want to use the wizard to apply licenses but do not want to choose services yet, check the **Proceed Without Selecting Services** check box.

Step 4.   Click **Continue** to move to the Option Keys page of the wizard, shown in Figure 2-2. This page helps you to identify and acquire the appropriate licenses for your chosen selections. The Licensing Help section at the top of the page explains how to use the Product Authorization Key (PAK) in the Cisco Product License Registration Portal. The License Status section lists the actual licenses that you need and their status (loaded/not loaded). The exact entries vary by deployment; the example shown in Figure 2-2 is for the Cisco Expressway-C Registrar service.

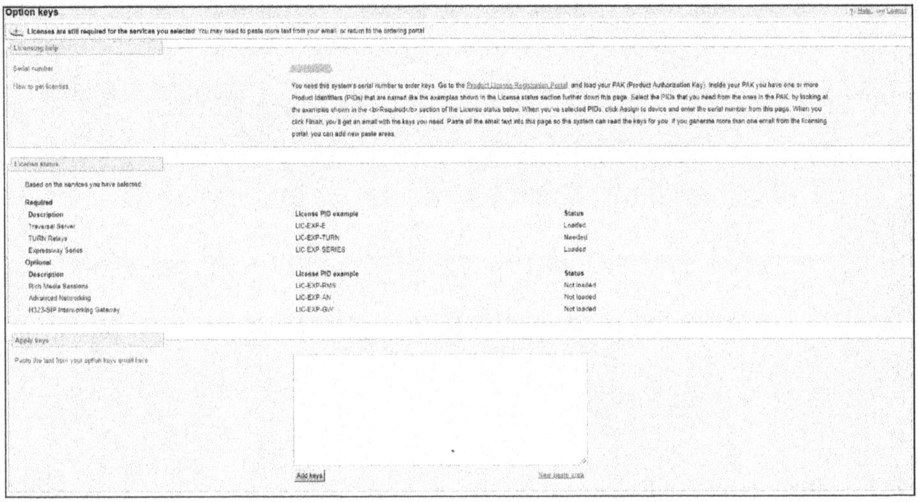

Figure 2-2   *Option Keys Page*

Step 5.   On the Option Keys page:

a.   Copy the serial number, which you need for the next step.

b.   Click the **Product License Registration Portal** link to go to the licensing portal. (For this step you need to work away from the wizard to obtain the necessary licenses.) In the licensing portal, enter the necessary details for the required licenses. For example, if you want to register desktop systems like the EX90, you need to add Desktop System registration licenses.

Detailed information about using the licensing portal is in the online help and the *Cisco Expressway Administrator Guide*. An ordering guide for Cisco products is available on the Cisco Collaboration Ordering Guides page.

Step 6.   Paste the text from the option keys email into the text area in the Apply Keys section. The system reads the option keys in the pasted text and displays them next to the text area.

Step 7.   Add new text areas if you have more email text to paste in, such as your room or desktop system registration license keys.

Step 8.   Click **Add Keys.**

The table in the License Status section groups the keys that are possible on this system and indicates whether they are loaded or not loaded. The keys are grouped as follows:

- **Required:** If any keys in this section are not yet loaded, you see the status Required and will not be able to continue through the wizard.

- **Optional:** Shows keys that may or may not be useful but are not strictly required for the services you chose.

- **Unrelated:** These keys will not harm the system if they are loaded but will not provide any benefit for the services you chose.

- **Incompatible:** These keys cannot work with the selected services. You must remove them or choose different services before you can continue.

Step 9.   Click **Continue.**

Step 10. Review the network configuration and modify the settings if necessary. Save any changes before you continue the wizard.

Step 11. Click **Finish.**

Step 12. Restart the system when prompted.

Result: When you log in, the user interface is tailored to match your service selections. You only see menus and pages for the services you chose.

This process applies for deployments that use Smart Licensing:

Step 1.   In the Select Series section of the Service Selection page, click the **Expressway Series** radio button.

Step 2.   In the Select Type section, click either the **Expressway-C** radio button or **Expressway-E** radio button. Cisco recommends that you select Expressway-C first and run the wizard for it. Then run the wizard on the Expressway-E.

The list of services changes to match what is available on your chosen Series and Type.

Step 3.   In the Select Services section, check the boxes next to the services you want to use on this system. For the compatible services that you can use together on the same system or cluster, refer to Table 2-3.

If you want to keep all the menu options, or if you want to use the wizard to apply licenses but do not want to choose services yet, check the **Proceed Without Selecting Services** check box.

Step 4.   You now need to configure Smart Licensing for the Expressway. To do this, please follow the instructions in the *Cisco Expressway Administrator Guide* section "Configure Smart Licensing."

Step 5.   Click **Continue**.

Step 6.   Review the network configuration and modify the settings if necessary. Save any changes before you continue the wizard.

Step 7.   Click **Finish**.

Step 8.   Restart the system when prompted.

Result: When you log in, the user interface is tailored to match your service selections. You only see menus and pages for the services you chose.

Once the wizard is complete for the Expressway-C system, you need to run it on the Expressway-E. For typical deployments with the Expressway-E, the services you are most likely to select with the wizard include Mobile and Remote Access and Business to Business Calls.

Expressway System Configuration

After completing the Service Setup Wizard for both the Expressway-C and the Expressway-E, you then can complete the System Configuration settings. This begins with setting the system name, which defines the name of the Expressway. The system name appears in various places in the web interface and is also used by Cisco **Telepresence Management Suite (TMS)**. Cisco recommends using a name that lets you easily and uniquely identify the Expressway. Note that the following bolded, italicized text is sample user input.

To configure the system name:

Step 1.   Go to **System > Administration**.

Step 2.   Configure the System Name field similar to the following example for unique identification (see Figure 2-3):

	Expressway-C	Expressway-E
System Name	*EXPc*	*EXPe*

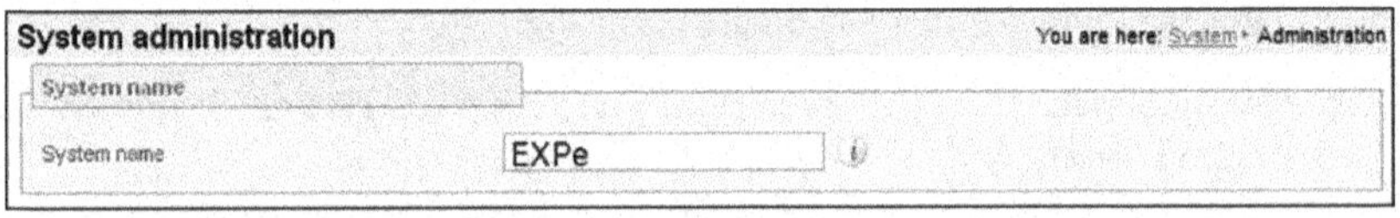

Figure 2-3 *Specifying the System Name*

Step 3.   Click **Save**.

Next, you will configure the **Domain Name System (DNS)** settings for the Cisco Expressway. The system host name defines the DNS host name that this system is known by. This is not the fully qualified domain name (FQDN), just the host label portion. Note that <system host name>.<domain name> = FQDN of this Expressway. To configure the system host name:

Step 1.   Go to **System > DNS**.

Step 2.   Configure the System Host Name field similar to the following example for unique identification:

	Expressway-C	Expressway-E
System Host Name	*expc*	*expe*

Step 3.   Click **Save**.

Continuing the DNS settings, next apply the domain name, which is the name to append to an unqualified host name before querying the DNS server. To configure the domain name:

Step 1.   Go to **System > DNS**.

Step 2.   Configure the Domain Name field similar to the following example for unique identification:

	Expressway-C	Expressway-E
Domain Name	*internal-domain.net*	*example.com*

Step 3.   Click **Save**.

The FQDN for the Expressway-C is now *expc.internal-domain.net*.

The FQDN for the Expressway-E is now *expe.example.com*.

To finish the DNS settings, you must specify the IP addresses of up to five domain name servers to be used for resolving domain names. In either of the following cases, you must specify at least one default DNS server for address resolution:

- To use FQDNs instead of IP addresses when specifying external addresses. For example, for **Lightweight Directory Access Protocol (LDAP)** and **Network Time Protocol (NTP)** servers, neighbor zones, and peers.

- To use features such as **Uniform Resource Indicator (URI)** dialing or ENUM dialing.

The Expressway queries one server at a time. If that server is unavailable, the Expressway tries another server from the list. In the example deployment, two DNS servers are configured for each Expressway, which provides a level of DNS server redundancy. The Expressway-C is configured with DNS servers located on the internal network. The Expressway-E is configured with DNS servers that are publicly routable.

To configure the default DNS server addresses:

Step 1.   Go to **System > DNS**.

Step 2.   Configure the DNS server addresses similar to the following example:

	Expressway-C	Expressway-E
Address 1	**10.0.0.11**	**194.72.6.57**
Address 2	**10.0.0.12**	**194.73.82.242**

Step 3.   Click **Save**.

Expressway-C has an FQDN of *expc.internal-domain.net*.

Expressway-E has an FQDN of *expe.example.com*.

Following the DNS settings, you can configure the NTP settings. The NTP server Address fields set the IP addresses or FQDNs of the NTP servers to be used to synchronize system time. The Time Zone field sets the local time zone of the Expressway.

NOTE   You can synchronize the Expressway-C and Expressway-E with different NTP servers, if the result is that the Expressway traversal pair is synchronized.

To configure the NTP server addresses and time zone:

Step 1.   Go to **System > Time**.

Step 2.   Configure the fields similar to the following example, on both Expressway-C and Expressway-E:

	Expressway-C	Expressway-E
Address 1	**pool.ntp.org**	**pool.ntp.org**
Address 2	**GMT**	**GMT**

Step 3.   Click **Save**. Your configuration should be similar to the example shown in Figure 2-4.

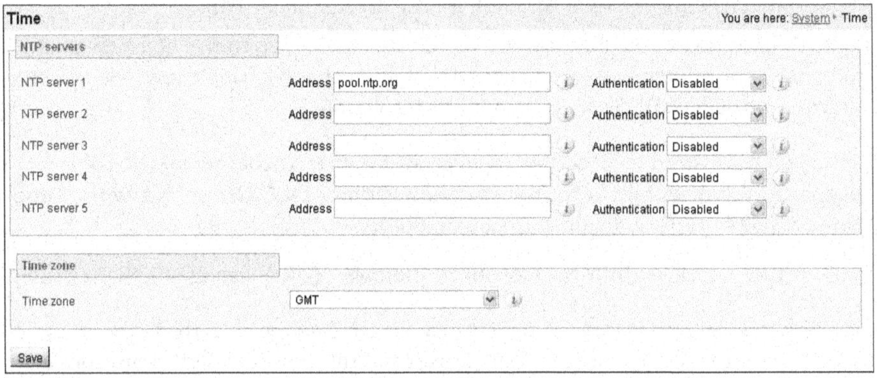

Figure 2-4   *NTP Configuration Page*

The last step of the Cisco Expressway system configuration we will cover is the configuration of SIP domains. The Expressway acts as a SIP registrar for configured SIP domains, accepting registration requests for any SIP endpoints attempting to register with an alias that includes these domains. To configure a SIP domain:

Step 1.   Go to **Configuration > Domains**.

Step 2.   Click **New**.

Step 3.   Enter the domain name into the Name field (on both Expressway-C and Expressway-E):

	Expressway-C	Expressway-E
Name	**example.com**	**example.com**

Step 4.   Click **Create Domain**.

Step 5.   The Domains page displays all configured SIP domain names (see Figure 2-5).

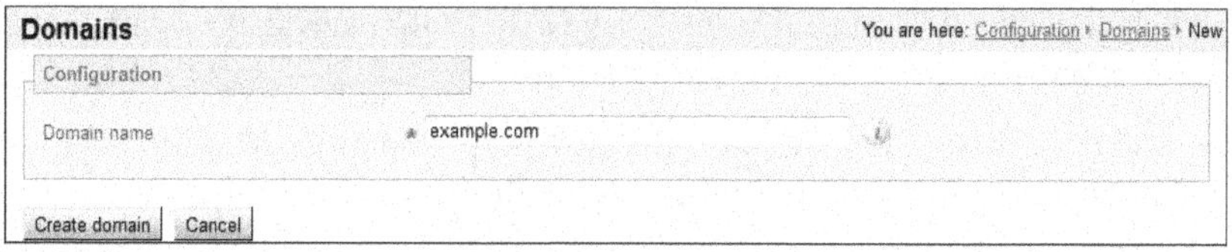

Domains   You are here: Configuration ▸ Domains ▸ New

Configuration

Domain name   ∗ example.com

Create domain   Cancel

Figure 2-5 *SIP Domain Page*

In addition to the system configurations previously covered, there are potentially more configuration steps, depending on the complexity of the deployment. These configuration tasks may include the following:

- Configuring routes to a Neighbor Zone
- Configuring Cisco TMS
- Configuring logging
- Configuring registration restriction policy
- Configuring device authentication policy
- Configuring registration by remote endpoints
- Configuring B2B federation for video calls
- Restricting access to ISDN gateways

Starting with release X8.9, the Expressway supports improved Differentiated Service Code Point (DSCP) packet marking for traffic passing through the **firewall**, including Mobile and Remote Access. DSCP is a measure of the **Quality of Service (QoS)** level of the packet. To provide more granular control of traffic prioritization, DSCP values are set (marked) for these individual traffic types, as shown in Table 2-4.

Table 2-4 Set DSCP Values

Traffic Type	Supplied Default Value	Web UI Field
Video	34	QoS Video
Audio	46	QoS Audio
XMPP	24	QoS XMPP
Signaling	24	QoS Signaling

Before X8.9 you had to apply DSCP values to all signaling and media traffic collectively. You can now optionally change the default DSCP values from the **System > Quality of Service** web page or from the **command line interface (CLI)**.

Note the following for QoS/DSCP:

- DSCP value 0 specifies standard best-effort service.
- DSCP marking is applied to SIP and H.323 traffic.

- DSCP marking is applied to Traversal Using Relay NAT (TURN) media, providing the TURN traffic is actually handled by the Expressway.

- Traffic type Video is assigned by default if the media type cannot be identified (for example, if different media types are multiplexed on the same port).

- From X8.9, support no longer exists for the previous methods to specify QoS/DSCP values. The former web GUI settings QoS Mode and QoS Value, CLI commands **xConfiguration IP QoS Mode** and **xConfiguration IP QoS Value**, and corresponding API are now discontinued. Do not use these commands.

  - If you are currently using these commands, then when you upgrade the Expressway, any existing QoS value you have defined is automatically applied to the new fields and replaces the supplied defaults. For example, if you had a value of 20 defined, all four DSCP settings (QoS Audio, QoS Video, QoS XMPP, QoS Signaling) are set to 20 also.

  - Cisco doesn't support downgrades. If you need to revert to your pre-upgrade software version, the QoS settings are reset to their original supplied defaults. So QoS Mode is set to None and QoS Value is set to 0. You will need to manually redefine the values you want to use.

With the current networks positioned with more security through the years, Cisco also wants to make their Expressway not just secure, but functional with firewalls. Here are some points to keep in mind when you are configuring your firewalls to permit the connections described in this chapter:

- If you have a cluster of Expressways, ensure that the destination ports to the public IP address of each Expressway peer are open on the external firewall.

- Sometimes there are different connection types that could be used to achieve the same task. You do not need to always open every port shown in the diagrams and tables. We recommend that you close any applications that you are not using.

  For example, if your web administration port is TCP 7443 but you only ever use SSH to configure the Expressway, you can close 7443 and leave TCP 22 open. Management ports should only be open to connections originating from inside the network.

- Some firewalls actively close connections that appear inactive, which could interfere with the operation of your video infrastructure.

  For example, TCP port 1720 is used for H.323 call signaling but may be inactive during the call. If this is prematurely closed by the firewall, the H.323 endpoint could interpret that as a dropped call and respond by tearing down the call.

  Cisco recommends extending inactivity timeouts on the known ports to at least two hours, particularly if you are seeing calls fail after a specific duration.

- Firewalls that contain Application Layer Gateway (ALG) for SIP/H.323 protocols may not work as expected with Expressway-E.

Cisco strongly recommends that you disable SIP or H.323 ALG inspection/awareness on the **Network Address Translation (NAT)** firewall. Cisco might not be able to support your configuration if you cannot make this change.

■ In some deployments, media packets can hairpin on the Expressway-E external NIC. Some firewalls cannot allow for hairpinning, and mistrust packets that are destined to their own source.

Cisco recommends configuring an exception to allow hairpinning on the Expressway-E public interface, if your deployment requires it.

■ If you want to use the static NAT feature of Expressway-E, Cisco strongly recommends using two NICs. Dedicating one NIC to the external interface and the other to the internal interface is much better for your network than using one NIC with the static NAT enabled.

Related to this discussion is the Advanced Networking deployment. This begins with enabling the Advanced Networking option to allow static NAT or two LAN interfaces. This is available on the Expressway-E (not on the Expressway-C). In the recommended dual NIC deployment, configure the External LAN Interface setting on the IP configuration page (**System > Network Interfaces > IP**) to LAN2.

Figure 2-6 illustrates the recommended deployment. It shows the typical **demilitarized zone (DMZ)** configuration where the internal and external firewalls cannot route directly to each other, and dual-NIC devices such as Expressway-E are required to validate and forward the traffic between the isolated subnets. The Expressway-E has both NICs enabled, and static NAT enabled on its outward-facing LAN interface. The Expressway-C inside the network is a traversal client of the Expressway-E in the DMZ.

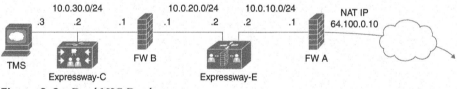

Figure 2-6   *Dual NIC Deployment*

This deployment consists of the following:

■ DMZ subnet 1, 10.0.10.0/24, containing

  ■ The internal interface of Firewall A: 10.0.10.1

  ■ The LAN2 interface of the Expressway-E: 10.0.10.2

■ DMZ subnet 2, 10.0.20.0/24, containing

  ■ The external interface of Firewall B: 10.0.20.1

  ■ The LAN1 interface of the Expressway-E: 10.0.20.2

■ LAN subnet, 10.0.30.0/24, containing

  ■ The internal interface of Firewall B: 10.0.30.1

- The LAN1 interface of the Expressway-C: 10.0.30.2

- The network interface of the Cisco TMS server: 10.0.30.3

- Firewall A is the outward-facing firewall; it is configured with a NAT IP (public IP) of 64.100.0.10, which is statically NATed to 10.0.10.2 (the LAN2 interface address of the Expressway-E).

- Firewall B is the internally facing firewall.

- Expressway-E LAN1 has static NAT mode disabled.

- Expressway-E LAN2 has static NAT mode enabled with static NAT address 64.100.0.10.

- Expressway-C has a traversal client zone pointing to 10.0.20.2 (LAN1 of the Expressway-E).

- Cisco TMS has Expressway-E added with IP address 10.0.20.2.

With the preceding deployment, there is no regular routing between the 10.0.20.0/24 and 10.0.10.0/24 subnets. The Expressway-E bridges these subnets and acts as a proxy for SIP/H.323 signaling and **Real-time Transport Protocol (RTP)/Real-time Transport Control Protocol (RTCP)** media.

With this dual NIC Deployment, you would typically configure the private address of the external firewall (10.0.10.1 in Figure 2-6) as the default gateway of the Expressway-E. Traffic that has no more specific route is sent out from either Expressway-E interface to 10.0.10.1. Use the following list based on whether the internal firewall is performing NAT for traffic from the internal network:

- If the internal firewall (B) is doing NAT for traffic from the internal network (subnet 10.0.30.0 in Figure 2-6) to LAN1 of the Expressway-E (such as traversal client traffic from the Expressway-C), that traffic is recognized as being from the same subnet (10.0.20.0 from Figure 2-6) as it reaches LAN1 of the Expressway-E. The Expressway-E can therefore reply to this traffic through its LAN1 interface. Due to Expressway-E security mechanisms, Mobile and Remote Access is not compatible with this scenario. If there is source NAT on the packets from the Expressway-C, then edge login requests will fail (destination NAT is unaffected).

- If the internal firewall (B) is not doing NAT for traffic from the internal network (subnet 10.0.30.0 in Figure 2-6) to LAN1 of the Expressway-E (such as traversal client traffic from the Expressway-C), that traffic still has the originating IP address (for example, 10.0.30.2 for traffic from the Expressway-C in Figure 2-6). You must create a static route toward that source from LAN1 on the Expressway-E, or the return traffic will go to the default gateway (10.0.10.1). You can do this on the web UI (**System > Network Interfaces > Static Routes**) or by using **xCommand RouteAdd** at the CLI. If the Expressway-E needs to communicate with other devices behind the internal firewall (for example, to reach network services such as NTP, DNS, LDAP/AD, and syslog servers), you also need to add static routes from Expressway-E LAN1 to those devices/subnets.

In the example configuration in Figure 2-6, we want to tell the Expressway-E that it can reach the 10.0.30.0/24 subnet behind the 10.0.20.1 firewall (router), which is reachable via the LAN1 interface. This is accomplished using the Static Routes configuration page, shown in Figure 2-7, or by using the following **xCommand RouteAdd** syntax (the **Interface** parameter could also be set to **Auto** as the gateway address, 10.0.20.1, is only reachable via LAN1):

```
xCommand RouteAdd Address: 10.0.30.0 PrefixLength: 24 Gateway:
   10.0.20.1 Interface: LAN1
```

Static routes	You are here: System > Network interfaces > Static routes
Create a static route	
IP address	* 10.0.30.0
Prefix length	* 24
Address range	10.0.30.0 - 10.0.30.255
Gateway	* 10.0.20.1
Interface	LAN 1 ▼

Create route

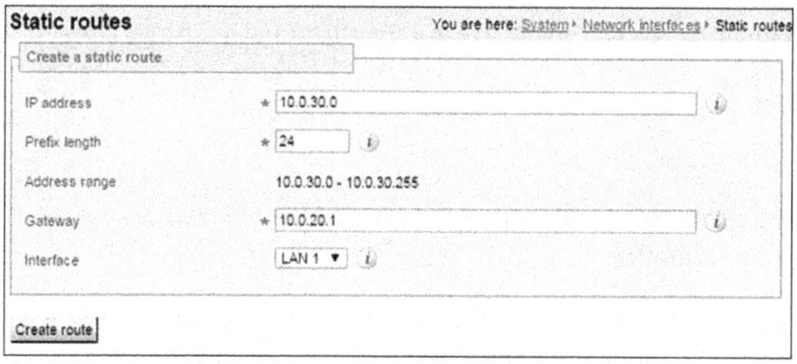

Figure 2-7 *Web UI for Creating Static Route*

Some routers and firewalls have SIP and H.323 ALG capabilities. ALG is also referred to as Fixup, Inspection, Application Awareness, Stateful Packet Inspection, Deep Packet Inspection, and so forth. This means that the router/firewall is able to identify SIP and H.323 traffic as it passes through and inspect, and in some cases modify, the payload of the SIP and H.323 messages. The purpose of modifying the payload is to help the H.323 or SIP application from which the message originated to traverse NAT; that is, to perform a similar process to what the Expressway-E does. The challenge with router/firewall-based SIP and H.323 ALGs is that these were originally intended to aid relatively basic H.323 and SIP applications to traverse NAT, and these applications had, for the most part, very basic functionality and often only supported audio. Over the years, many H.323 and SIP implementations have become more complex, supporting multiple video streams and application sharing (H.239, BFCP), encryption/security features (H.235, DES/AES), firewall traversal (Assent, H.460), and other extensions of the SIP and H.323 standards.

For a router/firewall to properly perform ALG functions for SIP and H.323 traffic, it is therefore of utmost importance that the router/firewall understands and properly interprets the full content of the payload it is inspecting. Because H.323 and SIP are standards/recommendations that are in constant development, it is not likely that the router/firewall will meet these requirements, resulting in unexpected behavior when using H.323 and SIP applications in combination with such routers/firewalls. There are also scenarios where the router/firewall normally will not be able to inspect the traffic at all, such as when using SIP over **Transport Layer Security (TLS)**, where the communication is end-to-end secure and encrypted as it passes through the router/firewall. You should disable SIP and H.323 ALGs on routers/firewalls carrying network traffic to or from an Expressway-E. Cisco does not support this functionality because, when enabled, it is frequently found to negatively affect the built-in firewall/NAT traversal functionality of the Expressway-E itself.

Cisco strongly recommends that you use the recommended dual NIC static NAT deployment, although other deployment models do exist, such as single subnet DMZ using single Expressway-E LAN interface and static NAT or 3-port firewall DMZ using single Expressway-E LAN interface, which will not be covered.

Expressway Backup and Restore Procedure

Use the Backup and Restore page (**Maintenance > Backup and Restore**) to create backup files of Expressway data and to restore the Expressway to a previous, saved configuration.

Cisco recommends creating regular backups, and always in the following situations:

- Before performing an upgrade
- Before performing a system restore
- In demonstration and test environments, if you want to be able to restore the Expressway to a known configuration

Backup files are always encrypted, as of release X8.11. In particular, they are encrypted because they include the bootstrap key, authentication data, and other sensitive information. Backups can only be restored to a system that is running the same version of software from which the backup was made. You can create a backup on one Expressway and restore it to a different Expressway (for example, if the original system has failed). Before the restore, you must install the same option keys on the new system that were present on the old one. If you try to restore a backup made on a different Expressway, you receive a warning message, but you will be allowed to continue. If you use FIPS 140-2 cryptographic mode, you can't restore a backup made on a non-FIPS system to a system that's running in FIPS mode. You can restore a backup from a FIPS-enabled system to a non-FIPS system. Do not use backups to copy data between Expressways. If you do so, system-specific information will be duplicated (like IP addresses). Because backup files contain sensitive information, you should not send them to Cisco in relation to technical support cases. Use snapshot and diagnostic files instead.

All backups must be password protected. If you restore to a previous backup, and the administrator account password has changed since the backup was done, you must also provide the old account password when you first log in after the restore. Active Directory credentials are not included in system backup files. If you use NTLM device authentication, you must provide the Active Directory password to rejoin the Active Directory domain after any restore. For backup and restore purposes, emergency account passwords are handled the same as standard administrator account passwords.

To create a backup of the Expressway system data:

Step 1. Go to **Maintenance > Backup and Restore.**

Step 2. Enter an encryption password to encrypt the backup file. (The password will be required in the future if you ever want to restore the backup file.)

Step 3. Click **Create System Backup File.**

Step 4. Wait for the backup file to be created. This may take several minutes. Do not navigate away from this page while the file is being prepared.

Step 5. When the backup is ready, you are prompted to save it. The default filename uses the format <software version>_<hardware serial number>_<date>_<time>_backup.tar.gz.enc. Or if you use Internet Explorer, the default extension is .tar. gz.gz. (These different filename extensions have no operational impact, and you can create and restore backups using any supported browser.)

Step 6. Save the backup file to a secure location.

To restore a previous backup, you need the password for the backup file from which you intend to restore. If you are restoring a backup file from a different Expressway, you need to apply the same set of license keys as exist on the system from which you intend to restore. Cisco recommends that you take the Expressway unit out of service before doing a restore. The restore process involves doing a factory reset back to the original software version and then upgrading to the same software version that was running when you took the backup. If the backup is out of date (made on an earlier version than the version you want), these extra steps are needed after the restore:

- Upgrade the software version to the required later version.

- Manually redo any configuration changes made since the backup was taken.

To restore the Expressway to a previous configuration of system data:

Step 1. First do a factory reset. This removes your configuration data and reverts the system to its original state. The reset maintains your current software version if you have upgraded since the system was first set up.

Step 2. Upgrade the system to the software version that was running when you made the backup.

Step 3. Now you can restore the system from the backup, as follows:

    a. Go to **Maintenance > Backup and Restore**.

    b. In the Restore section, click **Browse** and navigate to the backup file that you want to restore.

    c. In the Decryption Password field, enter the password used to create the backup file.

    d. Click **Upload System Backup File**.

    e. The Expressway checks the file and takes you to the Restore Confirmation page.

        i. If the backup file is invalid or the decryption password was entered incorrectly, an error message is displayed at the top of the Backup and Restore page.

        ii. The current software version and the number of calls and registrations are displayed.

    f. Read the warning messages that appear, before you continue.

g. Click **Continue with System Restore to Proceed with the Restore.** This restarts the system, so make sure that no active calls exist.

h. When the system restarts, the Login page is displayed.

Step 4. This step only applies if the backup file is out of date; that is, the software version was upgraded, or system configuration changes were made after the backup was done. In this case:

a. Upgrade the system again, this time to the required software version for the system.

b. Redo any configuration changes made after the backup (assuming you still need them on the restored system).

Use the backup and restore process to save cluster configuration information. The backup process saves all configuration information for the cluster, regardless of the Expressway used to make the backup.

Do not take VMware snapshots of Cisco Expressway systems. The process interferes with database timing and negatively impacts performance.

It is important to know that you cannot restore data to an Expressway that is part of a cluster. As described here, first remove the Expressway peer from the cluster. Then do the restore. (After the restore, you need to build a new cluster.) To restore previously backed-up cluster configuration data, follow this process:

Step 1. Remove the Expressway peer from the cluster so that it becomes a standalone Expressway.

Step 2. Restore the configuration data to the standalone Expressway.

Step 3. Build a new cluster using the Expressway that now has the restored data.

Step 4. Take each of the other peers out of their previous cluster and add them to the new cluster.

No additional steps are required if you are using FQDNs and have a valid cluster address mapping configured. Mappings will be configured on a restore action.

Exam Preparation Tasks

As mentioned in the section "How to Use This Book" in the Introduction, you have a couple of choices for exam preparation: the exercises here, Chapter 22, "Final Preparation," and the exam simulation questions in the Pearson Test Prep practice test software.

Review All Key Topics

Review the most important topics in this chapter, noted with the Key Topics icon in the outer margin of the page. Table 2-5 lists a reference of these key topics and the page numbers on which each is found.

Table 2-5 Key Topics for Chapter 2

Key Topic Element	Description	Page Number
Step list	DNS settings for the Cisco Expressway	34
List	Network firewall rules	38
Paragraph	Dual NIC Deployment	39
Step list	Back up Expressway	42
Step list	Restore a backup on the Expressway	43

Complete Tables and Lists from Memory

There are no memory tables or lists for this chapter.

Define Key Terms

Define the following key terms from this chapter and check your answers in the glossary:

business-to-business (B2B), command line interface (CLI), demilitarized zone (DMZ), Domain Name System (DNS), firewall, Hypertext Transport Protocol (HTTP), Hypertext Transport Protocol Secure (HTTPS), Lightweight Directory Access Protocol (LDAP), Mobile and Remote Access (MRA), Network Address Translation (NAT), Network Time Protocol (NTP), Product Authorization Key (PAK), Quality of Service (QoS), Real-time Transport Protocol (RTP), Real-time Transport Control Protocol (RTCP), Session Initiation Protocol (SIP), Telepresence Management Suite (TMS), Transport Layer Security (TLS), Uniform Resource Indicator (URI), Video Communications Server (VCS)

Q&A

The answers to these questions appear in Appendix A. For more practice with exam format questions, use the Pearson Test Prep practice test software.

1. What does the dual NIC Deployment consist of?

2. What are the steps to restore an Expressway that is part of a cluster?

CHAPTER 3

Initial Configuration Settings on the Cisco Expressway

This chapter covers the following topics:

> **H.323 Settings:** Explains the H.323 settings for the Cisco Expressway.
>
> **SIP and Domain Settings:** Explains how to apply required SIP and domain settings for the Cisco Expressway.
>
> **Protocol Interworking on the Cisco Expressway:** Focuses on interworking of H.323 and SIP signaling protocols via the Cisco Expressway.
>
> **Verifying Registration on the Cisco Expressway:** Spotlights the registration process and verification of registration to the Cisco Expressway.

This chapter focuses on the initial configurations needed for the Cisco Expressway. It covers both the H.323 and SIP settings and includes interworking on the Expressway. You will also confirm these settings with the verification of registration.

This chapter covers the following objectives from the Implementing Cisco Collaboration Cloud and Edge Solutions (CLCEI) exam 300-820:

- 1.4.a Describe protocol interworking on the Expressway: SIP <-> H.323
- 1.4.b Describe protocol interworking on the Expressway: IPv4 and IPv6

"Do I Know This Already?" Quiz

The "Do I Know This Already?" quiz enables you to assess whether you should read this entire chapter thoroughly or jump to the "Exam Preparation Tasks" section. If you are in doubt about your answers to these questions or your own assessment of your knowledge of the topics, read the entire chapter. Table 3-1 lists the major headings in this chapter and their corresponding "Do I Know This Already?" quiz questions. You can find the answers in Appendix A, "Answers to the 'Do I Know This Already?' Quizzes and Review Questions."

Table 3-1   "Do I Know This Already?" Section-to-Question Mapping

Foundation Topics Section	Questions
H.323 Settings	1
SIP and Domain Settings	2
Protocol Interworking on the Cisco Expressway	3–4
Verifying Registration on the Cisco Expressway	5–6

1. Registration, Admission, and Status (RAS), which is used between an H.323 endpoint and a gatekeeper to provide address resolution and admission control services, uses which ITU-T recommendation?

   a. H.320

   b. H.225.0

   c. H.245

   d. H.264

2. Which of the following is considered a SIP URI? (Choose three.)

   a. username@domain

   b. 123username

   c. username @domain.com

   d. 8088675309

   e. +18088675309

   f. username@172.16.0.50

3. Which of the following is *not* an H.323 <-> SIP Interworking Mode setting on the Cisco Expressway?

   a. Off

   b. On

   c. Registered only

   d. Gateway

4. Calls that utilize the interworking functionality are considered what type of call?

   a. Registered

   b. Rich Media Session

   c. B2B

   d. Audio-only

5. When registering an endpoint to the Cisco Expressway, what functions are the devices registering to? (Choose two.)

   a. SIP registrar

   b. SIP AOR

   c. H.323 gateway

   d. H.323 gatekeeper

   e. H.320 gatekeeper

6. Which of the following are able to register to the Cisco Expressway? (Choose three.)

   a. H.323 ID

   b. SIP ZRTP

   c. E.164 number

   d. SIP URI

   e. H.320 URI

Foundation Topics

H.323 Settings

As we move into the essential functions of the Cisco Expressway, we begin with the multimedia communications over the packet-based network. Deriving from the ITU Telecommunication Standardization Sector (ITU-T) **H.320** that was utilized over **Integrated Services Digital Network (ISDN)**-based networks, **H.323** was published by the **International Telecommunications Union (ITU)** in November 1996 with an emphasis on enabling videoconferencing capabilities over a local-area network (LAN), but was quickly adopted by the industry as a means of transmitting voice communication over a variety of IP networks, including wide-area networks (WANs) and the Internet. H.323 also provides a framework that uses other protocols to describe the actual protocol:

- **H.225.0: Registration, Admission, and Status (RAS)**, which is used between an H.323 **endpoint** and a **gatekeeper** to provide address resolution and admission control services

- **H.225.0:** Call signaling, which is used between any two H.323 entities to establish communication based on Q.931

- **H.245:** Control protocol for multimedia communication, describes the messages and procedures used for capability exchange, opening and closing logical channels for audio, video, data, and various control and indication signals

- **Real-time Transport Protocol (RTP)/Real-time Transport Control Protocol (RTCP):** Protocols for sending or receiving multimedia information (voice, video, or text) between any two entities

The Cisco Expressway supports the H.323 protocol and it is also an H.323 gatekeeper. As an H.323 gatekeeper, the Expressway accepts registrations from H.323 endpoints and provides call control functions such as address translation and admission control. For an endpoint to use the Expressway as its H.323 gatekeeper or **SIP registrar**, the endpoint must first register with the Expressway.

To enable the Expressway as an H.323 gatekeeper, ensure that the H.323 Mode setting is set to On (**Configuration > Protocols > H.323**), as shown in Figure 3-1. H.323 mode is a powerful option that enables or disables functionality of the Cisco Expressway as an H.323 gatekeeper.

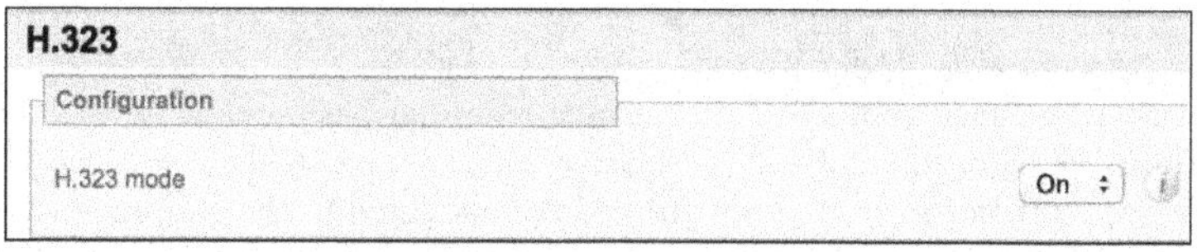

H.323

Configuration

H.323 mode   On ⌄ ⓘ

Figure 3-1 *H.323 Mode*

There are two ways an H.323 endpoint can locate an Expressway with which to register: manually or automatically. The option is configured on the endpoint itself under the Gatekeeper Discovery setting:

- If the mode is set to automatic, the endpoint tries to register with any Expressway it can find. It does this by sending out a Gatekeeper Discovery Request, to which eligible Expressways will respond.

- If the mode is set to manual, you must specify the IP address or the **fully qualified domain name (FQDN)** of the Expressway with which you want your endpoint to register, and the endpoint will attempt to register with that Expressway only.

You can prevent H.323 endpoints from being able to register automatically with the Expressway by disabling Auto Discovery on the Expressway (**Configuration > Protocols > H.323**).

While you are on the Configuration > Protocols > H.323 page, you can also configure the H.323 settings on the Expressway to fit your organization by utilizing Table 3-2 as a reference.

Table 3-2 H.323 Settings

Field	Description	Usage Tips
H.323 mode	Enables or disables H.323 on the Expressway. H.323 support is set to Off by default.	You must enable H.323 mode if you are clustering the Expressway, even if there are no H.323 endpoints in your deployment.
Registration UDP port	The listening port for H.323 UDP registrations.	The default Expressway configuration uses standard port numbers so you can use H.323 services out of the box without having to first set these up. The default port is 1719.
Registration conflict mode	Determines how the system behaves if an endpoint attempts to register an alias currently registered from another IP address. Reject: Denies the new registration. This is the default.	An H.323 endpoint may attempt to register with the Expressway using an alias that has already been registered on the Expressway from another IP address. The reasons for this could include: Two endpoints at different IP addresses are attempting to register using the same alias.

Field	Description	Usage Tips
	Overwrite: Deletes the original registration and replaces it with the new registration.	A single endpoint has previously registered using a particular alias. The IP address allocated to the endpoint then changes, and the endpoint attempts to re-register using the same alias.
		Reject is useful if your priority is to prevent two users registering with the same alias.
		Overwrite is useful if your network is such that endpoints are often allocated new IP addresses, because it will prevent unwanted registration rejections.
		Note that in a cluster, a registration conflict is only detected if the registration requests are received by the same peer.
Call signaling TCP port	The listening port for H.323 call signaling.	Default port: 1720.
Call signaling port range start and end	Specifies the port range used by H.323 calls after they are established.	The call signaling port range must be great enough to support all the required concurrent calls. Default start and end: 15000–19999.
Time to live	The interval (in seconds) at which an H.323 endpoint must re-register with the Expressway to confirm that it is still functioning. The default is 1800.	Some older endpoints do not support the ability to periodically re-register with the system. In this case, and in any other situation where the system has not had a confirmation from the endpoint within the specified period, it will send an IRQ to the endpoint to verify that it is still functioning.
		Note that by reducing the registration time to live too much, you risk flooding the Expressway with registration requests, which will severely impact performance. This impact is proportional to the number of endpoints, so you should balance the need for occasional quick failover against the need for continuous good performance.

Field	Description	Usage Tips
Call time to live	The interval (in seconds) at which the Expressway polls the endpoints in a call to verify that they are still in the call. The default is 120.	If the endpoint does not respond, the call is disconnected. The system polls endpoints in a call, whether the call type is traversal or non-traversal.
Auto discover	Determines whether the Expressway responds to Gatekeeper Discovery Requests sent out by endpoints. The default is On.	To prevent H.323 endpoints being able to register automatically with the Expressway, set Auto Discover to Off. This means that endpoints can only register with the Expressway if their Gatekeeper Discovery setting is Manual and they have been configured with the Expressway's IP address or FQDN.
Caller ID	Specifies whether the prefix of the ISDN gateway is inserted into the caller's **E.164** number presented on the destination endpoint.	Including the prefix allows the recipient to directly return the call.

SIP and Domain Settings

Session Initiation Protocol (SIP) is an ASCII-based, application-layer control protocol that can be used to establish, maintain, and terminate calls between two or more endpoints. SIP is an alternative protocol developed by the Internet Engineering Task Force (IETF) for multimedia conferencing over IP. SIP was originally standardized with IETF **Request for Comments (RFC)** 2543, "SIP: Session Initiation Protocol," published in March 1999. The current RFC 3261 (July 2002) makes the original RFC 2543 obsolete and has had many updates. The Cisco SIP implementation enables supported Cisco platforms to signal the setup of voice and multimedia calls over IP networks. SIP can be carried by several transport layer protocols including **Transmission Control Protocol (TCP)** and **User Datagram Protocol (UDP)**. SIP clients typically use TCP or UDP on port numbers 5060 or 5061 for SIP traffic to servers and other endpoints. Port 5060 is commonly used for nonencrypted signaling traffic, whereas port 5061 is typically used for traffic encrypted with Transport Layer Security (TLS). Normally SIP over UDP is not recommended because SIP messages for video systems are too large to be carried on a packet-based (rather than stream-based) transport.

Like other **Voice over IP (VoIP)** protocols, SIP is designed to address the functions of signaling and session management within a packet telephony network. Signaling allows call information to be carried across network boundaries. Session management provides the ability to control the attributes of an end-to-end call.

The Cisco Expressway supports SIP. It can act as a SIP registrar, as a SIP proxy, and as a SIP Presence Server. The Expressway can also provide **interworking** between SIP and H.323, translating between the two protocols to enable endpoints that only support one of the protocols to call each other.

To support SIP:

- SIP mode must be enabled.

- At least one of the SIP transport protocols (UDP, TCP, or TLS) must be active. Note that the use of UDP is not recommended for video because SIP message sizes are frequently larger than a single UDP packet.

For a SIP endpoint to be contactable via its alias, it must register its Address of Record (AOR) and its location with a SIP registrar. The SIP registrar maintains a record of the endpoint's details against the endpoint's AOR. The AOR is the alias through which the endpoint can be contacted; it is a SIP Uniform Resource Indicator (URI) and always takes the form *username@domain*. When a call is received for that AOR, the SIP registrar refers to the record to find its corresponding endpoint. (Note that the same AOR can be used by more than one SIP endpoint at the same time, although to ensure that all endpoints are found, they must all register with the same Expressway or Expressway cluster.)

A SIP registrar only accepts registrations for domains for which it is authoritative. The Expressway can act as a SIP registrar for up to 200 domains. To make the Expressway act as a SIP registrar, you must configure it with the SIP domains for which it will be authoritative. It will then handle registration requests for any endpoints attempting to register against that domain. Note that the Expressway will also accept registration requests where the domain portion of the AOR is either the FQDN or the IP address of the Expressway. Whether or not the Expressway accepts a registration request depends on its registration control settings.

In a Cisco Unified Communications deployment, endpoint registration for SIP devices may be provided by **Cisco Unified Communications Manager (Unified CM)**. In this scenario, the Expressway provides secure firewall traversal and line-side support for Unified CM registrations. When configuring a domain, you can select whether Unified CM or Expressway provides registration and provisioning services for the domain.

There are two ways a SIP endpoint can locate a registrar with which to register: manually or automatically. The option is configured on the endpoint itself under the SIP Server Discovery option (consult your endpoint user guide for how to access this setting; it may also be referred to as Proxy Discovery).

- If the Server Discovery mode is set to automatic, the endpoint sends a REGISTER message to the SIP server that is authoritative for the domain with which the endpoint is attempting to register. For example, if an endpoint is attempting to register with a URI of *john.smith@example.com*, the request will be sent to the registrar that is authoritative for the domain *example.com*. The endpoint can discover the appropriate server through a variety of methods including DHCP, Domain Name System (DNS), or provisioning, depending upon how the video communications network has been implemented.

- If the Server Discovery mode is set to manual, the user must specify the IP address or FQDN of the registrar (Expressway or Expressway cluster) with which the user wants to register, and the endpoint will attempt to register with that registrar only.

The Expressway is a SIP server and a SIP registrar:

- If an endpoint is registered to the Expressway, the Expressway will be able to forward inbound calls to that endpoint.

- If the Expressway is not configured with any SIP domains, the Expressway will act as a SIP server. It may proxy registration requests to another registrar, depending upon the SIP Registration Proxy Mode setting.

The Expressway acts as a SIP proxy server when SIP mode is enabled. The role of a proxy server is to forward requests (such as REGISTER and INVITE) from endpoints or other proxy servers on to further proxy servers or to the destination endpoint. If the Expressway receives a registration request for a domain for which it is not acting as a registrar (the Expressway does not have that SIP domain configured), then the Expressway may proxy the registration request onwards. This depends on the SIP Registration Proxy Mode setting, as follows:

- **Off:** The Expressway does not proxy any registration requests. They are rejected with a "403 Forbidden" message.

- **Proxy to known only:** The Expressway proxies the request in accordance with existing call processing rules, but only to known neighbor, traversal client, and traversal server zones.

- **Proxy to any:** This is the same as Proxy to Known Only but for all zone types (i.e., it also includes ENUM and DNS zones).

If the Expressway receives a proxied registration request, in addition to the Expressway's standard registration controls, you can also control whether the Expressway accepts the registration depending upon the zone through which the request was received. You do this through the Accept Proxied Registrations setting when configuring a zone. Proxied registrations are classified as belonging to the zone they were last proxied from. This is different from non-proxied registration requests, which are assigned to a subzone within the Expressway.

The Expressway, as a SIP Presence Server, supports the SIP-based SIMPLE protocol. It can act as a Presence Server and Presence User Agent for any of the SIP domains for which it is authoritative. The Presence Server can manage the presence information for locally registered endpoints whose information has been received via a SIP proxy (such as another Expressway).

The SIP page (**Configuration > Protocols > SIP**) is used to configure SIP settings on the Expressway, including:

- SIP functionality and SIP-specific transport modes and ports

- Certificate revocation checking modes for TLS connections

- Registration controls for standard and outbound registrations

Table 3-3 outlines the configurable settings for enabling SIP functionality and for configuring the various SIP-specific transport modes and ports.

Table 3-3   SIP Settings

Field	Description	Usage Tips
SIP mode	Enables and disables SIP functionality (SIP registrar and SIP proxy services) on the Expressway. The default is Off.	This mode must be enabled to use either the Presence Server or the Presence User Agent.
SIP protocols and ports	The Expressway supports SIP over UDP, TCP, and TLS transport protocols. Use the Mode and Port settings for each protocol to configure whether incoming and outgoing connections using that protocol are supported and, if so, the ports on which the Expressway listens for such connections. The default modes are ■ UDP mode: Off ■ TCP mode: Off ■ TLS mode: On ■ Mutual TLS mode: Off	At least one of the transport protocol modes must be set to On to enable SIP functionality. If you use both TLS and MTLS, Cisco recommends that you enable them on different ports. If you must use port 5061 for MTLS, you should avoid engaging the B2BUA, by switching Media Encryption mode to Auto on all zones in the call path.
TCP outbound port start/ end	The range of ports the Expressway uses when TCP and TLS connections are established.	The range must be sufficient to support all required concurrent connections.
Session refresh interval	The maximum time allowed between session refresh requests for SIP calls. The default is 1800 seconds.	This is the time period after processing a request for which any session-stateful proxy must retain its state for this session.
Minimum session refresh interval	The minimum value the Expressway will negotiate for the session refresh interval for SIP calls. Default is 500 seconds.	This is the time period after processing a request for which any session-stateful proxy must retain its state for this session.
TLS handshake timeout	The timeout period for TLS socket handshake. The default is 5 seconds.	You might want to increase this value if TLS server certificate validation is slow (e.g., if OCSP servers do not provide timely responses) and thus cause connection attempts to timeout.
Certificate revocation checking mode	Controls whether revocation checking is performed for certificates exchanged during SIP TLS connection establishment.	Cisco recommends enabling revocation checking.

The Domains page (**Configuration > Domains**) lists the SIP domains managed by this Expressway. A domain name can comprise multiple levels. Each level's name can only contain letters, digits, and hyphens, with each level separated by a period (dot). A level name cannot start or end with a hyphen, and the final level name must start with a letter. An example valid domain name is *100.example-name.com*. You can configure up to 200 domains. (Note that you cannot configure domains on an Expressway-E.)

When the Expressway-C has been enabled for Unified Communications mobile and remote access, you must select the services that each domain will support. The options are as follows:

- **SIP registrations and provisioning on Expressway:** The Expressway is authoritative for this SIP domain. The Expressway acts as a SIP registrar for the domain (and Presence Server in the case of Video Communication Server (VCS) systems) and accepts registration requests for any SIP endpoints attempting to register with an alias that includes this domain. The default is On.

- **SIP registrations and provisioning on Unified CM:** Endpoint registration, call control, and provisioning for this SIP domain are serviced by Unified CM. The Expressway acts as a Unified Communications gateway to provide secure firewall traversal and line-side support for Unified CM registrations. The default is Off.

- **IM and Presence Service:** Instant messaging and presence services for this SIP domain are provided by the Unified CM **Instant Messaging and Presence (IMP)** service. The default is Off.

- **XMPP federation:** Enables **Extensible Messaging and Presence Protocol (XMPP)** federation between this domain and partner domains. The default is Off.

- **Deployment:** Associates the domain with the selected deployment, if there are multiple deployments. This setting is absent if there is only one deployment (there is always at least one).

Any domain configuration changes, when one or more existing domains are configured for IM and Presence services on Unified CM or XMPP federation, will result in an automatic restart of the **Universal Measurement and Calibration Protocol (XCP)** router on both Expressway-C and Expressway-E.

Protocol Interworking on the Cisco Expressway

The Interworking page (**Configuration > Protocols > Interworking**) lets you configure whether or not the Expressway acts as a gateway between SIP and H.323 calls. The translation of calls from one protocol to the other is known as *interworking*.

By default, the Expressway acts as a SIP–H.323 and H.323–SIP gateway but only if at least one of the endpoints that are involved in the call is locally registered. You can change this setting so that the Expressway acts as a SIP–H.323 gateway regardless of whether the endpoints involved are locally registered. You also have the option to disable interworking completely.

The options for the H.323 <-> SIP Interworking Mode setting are as follows:

- **Off:** The Expressway does not act as a SIP–H.323 gateway.

- **Registered only:** The Expressway acts as a SIP–H.323 gateway but only if at least one of the endpoints is locally registered.

- **On:** The Expressway acts as a SIP–H.323 gateway regardless of whether the endpoints are locally registered.

Cisco recommends that you leave this setting as Registered Only. Unless your network is correctly configured, setting it to On (where all calls can be interworked) may result in unnecessary interworking, for example, where a call between two H.323 endpoints is made over SIP, or vice versa.

Calls for which the Expressway acts as a SIP to H.323 gateway are **Rich Media Session (RMS)** calls. The Expressway always takes the media for SIP–H.323 interworked calls so that it can independently negotiate payload types on the SIP and H.323 sides, and Expressway will rewrite these as the media passes. Also, in a SIP SDP negotiation, multiple codec capabilities can be agreed (more than one video codec can be accepted) and the SIP device is at liberty to change the codec it uses at any time within the call. If this happens, because Expressway is in the media path, it will close and open logical channels to the H.323 device as the media changes (as required) so that media is passed correctly.

When searching a zone, the Expressway first performs the search using the protocol of the incoming call. If the search is unsuccessful, the Expressway may then search the zone again using the alternative protocol, depending on where the search came from and the H.323 <-> SIP Interworking Mode setting. Note that the zone must also be configured with the relevant protocols enabled (SIP and H.323 are enabled on a zone by default).

- If the request has come from a neighboring system and Interworking Mode is set to Registered Only, the Expressway searches the Local Zone using both protocols, and all other zones using the native protocol only (because it will interwork the call only if one of the endpoints is locally registered).

- If Interworking Mode is set to On, or the request has come from a locally registered endpoint, the Expressway searches the Local Zone and all external zones using both protocols.

SIP endpoints can only make calls in the form of URIs, such as *name@domain*. If the caller does not specify a domain when placing the call, the SIP endpoint automatically appends its own domain to the number that is dialed. If you dial 123 from a SIP endpoint, the search will be placed for 123@*domain*. If the H.323 endpoint being dialed is just registered as 123, the Expressway will not be able to locate the alias 123@*domain* and the call will fail. The solution is to do either of the following:

- Ensure all your endpoints, both H.323 and SIP, register with an alias in the form *name@domain*.

- Create a pre-search transform on the Expressway that strips the @*domain* portion of the alias for those URIs that are in the form of *number@domain*.

You will dive into pre-search Transforms in Chapter 7, "Cisco Expressway Call Processing Order," for more depth on how to accomplish this.

For SIP calls, the Expressway implements RFC 4733 (obsoletes RFC 2833) for **dual-tone multifrequency (DTMF)** signaling in RTP payloads. For H.323 calls, the Expressway implements H.245 **UserInputIndication** for DTMF signaling. **dtmf** is the only supported **User InputCapability**. Expressway does not support any other H.245 user input capabilities (e.g., **basicString, generalString**). When the Expressway is interworking a call between SIP and

H.323, it also interworks the DTMF signaling, but only between RFC 4733 DTMF and the H.245 user input indicators **dtmf** and **basicString**.

The Expressway can also act as a gateway for calls between IPv4 and IPv6 devices. To enable this feature, select Both for the IP protocol on the IP page (**System > Network Interfaces > IP**). Calls for which the Expressway is acting as an IPv4 to IPv6 gateway are traversal calls and require a Rich Media Session license.

Verifying Registration on the Cisco Expressway

For an endpoint to use the Expressway as its H.323 gatekeeper or SIP registrar, the endpoint must first register with the Expressway. The Expressway can be configured to control which devices are allowed to register with it by using the following mechanisms:

- A device authentication process based on the username and password supplied by the endpoint

- A registration restriction policy that uses either Allow Lists or Deny Lists or an external policy service to specify which aliases can and cannot register with the Expressway

- Restrictions based on IP addresses and subnet ranges through the specification of subzone membership rules and subzone registration policies

You can use these mechanisms together. For example, you can use authentication to verify an endpoint's identity from a corporate directory and use registration restriction to control which of those authenticated endpoints may register with a particular Expressway. You can also control some protocol-specific behavior, including:

- The Registration Conflict Mode and Auto Discover settings for H.323 registrations

- The SIP registration proxy mode for SIP registrations

In a Cisco Unified CM deployment, endpoint registration for SIP devices may be provided by Unified CM. In this scenario, the Expressway provides secure firewall traversal and line-side support for Unified CM registrations. When configuring a domain, you can select whether Unified CM or Expressway provides registration and provisioning services for the domain.

H.323 systems such as gateways, multipoint control units (MCUs), and content servers can also register with an Expressway. They are known as locally registered services. These systems are configured with their own prefix, which they provide to the Expressway when registering. The Expressway then knows to route all calls that begin with that prefix to the gateway, MCU, or content server as appropriate. These prefixes can also be used to control registrations. SIP devices cannot register prefixes. If your dial plan dictates that a SIP device should be reached via a particular prefix, then you should add the device as a neighbor zone with an associated Search Rule using a pattern match equal to the prefix to be used.

When registering, the H.323 endpoint presents the Expressway with one or more of the following:

- **H.323 IDs**

- E.164 aliases

- URIs

Users of other registered endpoints can then call the endpoint by dialing any of these aliases. Note the following recommendations:

- Register your H.323 endpoints using a URI. This facilitates interworking between SIP and H.323, as SIP endpoints register using a URI as standard.

- Do not use aliases that reveal sensitive information. Due to the nature of H.323, call setup information is exchanged in an unencrypted form.

When registering, the SIP endpoint presents the Expressway with its contact address (IP address) and logical address (Address of Record). The logical address is considered to be its alias and generally is in the form of a URI.

An endpoint may attempt to register with the Expressway using an alias that is already registered to the system. How this is managed depends on how the Expressway is configured and whether the endpoint is SIP or H.323:

- **H.323:** An H.323 endpoint may attempt to register with the Expressway using an alias that has already been registered on the Expressway from another IP address. You can control how the Expressway behaves in this situation by configuring the Registration Conflict Mode setting on the H.323 page (**Configuration > Protocols > H.323**).

- **SIP:** A SIP endpoint will always be allowed to register using an alias that is already in use from another IP address. When a call is received for this alias, all endpoints registered using that alias will be called simultaneously. This SIP feature is known as *forking*.

All endpoints must periodically re-register with the Expressway to keep their registration active. If you do not manually delete the registration, the registration could be removed when the endpoint attempts to re-register, but this depends on the protocol being used by the endpoint:

- H.323 endpoints may use "light" re-registrations that do not contain all the aliases presented in the initial registration, so the re-registration may not get filtered by the restriction policy. If this is the case, the registration will not expire at the end of the registration timeout period and must be removed manually.

- SIP re-registrations contain the same information as the initial registrations, so they will be filtered by the restriction policy. This means that, after the list has been activated, all SIP registrations will disappear at the end of their registration timeout period.

The frequency of re-registrations is determined by the Registration Controls setting for SIP (**Configuration > Protocols > SIP**) and the Time to Live setting for H.323 (**Configuration > Protocols > H.323**).

Check that all endpoints that are expected to be registered are actually registered to the relevant Expressway and that they are registering the expected aliases. All successfully registered endpoints are listed on **Status > Registrations > By Device**. If the expected endpoints are not registered, review the following items:

- The endpoint's registration configuration. Is it configured to register with the Expressway-E if located on the external network/Internet, and to register with the Expressway-C if located on the internal network?

- The SIP domains.

- Any registration restriction configuration applied to the Expressway.

In some cases, home endpoints may fail to register when using **Service (SRV) records**. This can happen if the endpoint uses the home router for its DNS server and the router's DNS server software doesn't support SRV records lookup. (This also applies to the DNS server being used by a PC when Jabber Video is running on it.) If registration failure occurs, do either of the following:

- Change the DNS server on the endpoint to use a publicly available DNS server that can resolve SRV record lookups; for example, Google - 8.8.8.8.

- Change the SIP server address on the endpoint to use the FQDN of a node in the Expressway cluster and not the cluster SRV record, so that the device performs an AAAA or A record lookup.

Exam Preparation Tasks

As mentioned in the section "How to Use This Book" in the Introduction, you have a couple of choices for exam preparation: the exercises here, Chapter 22, "Final Preparation," and the exam simulation questions in the Pearson Test Prep Software Online.

Review All Key Topics

Review the most important topics in this chapter, noted with the Key Topics icon in the outer margin of the page. Table 3-4 lists a reference of these key topics and the page number on which each is found.

Table 3-4   Key Topics for Chapter 3

Key Topic Element	Description	Page Number
List	Interworking modes	55
Paragraph	IPv4 to IPv6 interworking	57
List	Registration aliases	58

Complete Tables and Lists from Memory

There are no memory tables or lists for this chapter.

Define Key Terms

Define the following key terms from this chapter and check your answers in the glossary:

Cisco Unified Communications Manager (Unified CM), dual-tone multifrequency (DTMF), E.164, endpoint, Extensible Messaging and Presence Protocol (XMPP), fully qualified domain name (FQDN), gatekeeper, H.225.0, H.245, H.320, H.323, H.323 ID, Instant Messaging and Presence (IMP), Integrated Services Digital Network (ISDN), International Telecommunications Union (ITU), interworking, Registration, Admission, and Status (RAS), Request for Comments (RFC), Rich Media Session (RMS), Service record (SRV), SIP registrar, Transmission Control Protocol (TCP), Universal Measurement and Calibration Protocol (XCP), User Datagram Protocol (UDP), Voice over IP (VoIP)

Q&A

The answers to these questions appear in Appendix A. For more practice with exam format questions, use the Pearson Test Prep practice test software.

1. Define the ITU-T H.323 standard and its core protocols.

2. What are the option modes of interworking on the Cisco Expressway and what do they imply?

CHAPTER 4

Regular Expressions on the Cisco Expressway

This chapter covers the following topics:

> **Overview and Use Cases for Regular Expressions:** Provides an overview of the use of regular expressions within the Cisco Expressway.

> **Verifying Regular Expression Using the Check Pattern Tool:** Recapitulates the use and validation of expressions using the Check Pattern Tool.

This chapter focuses on describing the use case of regular expressions within the Cisco Expressway and their ways of being utilized.

This chapter covers the following objectives from the Implementing Cisco Collaboration Cloud and Edge Solutions (CLCEI) exam 300-820:

- 1.7.d Describe Expressway Core dial plan elements: Regular expressions

- 2.2.d Configure Expressway Core dial plan elements: Regular expressions

"Do I Know This Already?" Quiz

The "Do I Know This Already?" quiz enables you to assess whether you should read this entire chapter thoroughly or jump to the "Exam Preparation Tasks" section. If you are in doubt about your answers to these questions or your own assessment of your knowledge of the topics, read the entire chapter. Table 4-1 lists the major headings in this chapter and their corresponding "Do I Know This Already?" quiz questions. You can find the answers in Appendix A, "Answers to the 'Do I Know This Already?' Quizzes and Review Questions."

Table 4-1 "Do I Know This Already?" Section-to-Question Mapping

Foundation Topics Section	Questions
Overview and Use Cases for Regular Expressions	1–4
Verifying Regular Expression Using the Check Pattern Tool	5

1. Which regular expression syntax does the Cisco Expressway utilize?

    a. Perl

    b. Python

    c. PCRE

    d. POSIX

2. Which of the following string would the expression ([^@]*) match?

    a. 123@company.com

    b. user@company.com

    c. 12345

    d. user123@company.com

3. Which of the follow regular expression patterns would match the alias string of user123@company.com? (Choose two.)

    a. (\.*)@company\.com

    b. (.{7})@company\.com

    c. \d{3}@company\.com

    d. (.{6})@company\.com

    e. (.+)@company\.com

4. Which of the following would match the regular expression pattern of (.*)(\.)(.*)([0-9]{3}@comany\.com?

    a. user.name123@company.com

    b. user.name1234@company.com

    c. username123@company.com

    d. user.name123@company.net

5. Which of the following is the correct location of the Check Pattern Tool?

    a. Maintenance > Tools > Check Pattern

    b. Status > Tools > Check Pattern

    c. Maintenance > Diagnostics > Check Pattern

    d. Status > Diagnostics > Check Pattern

Foundation Topics

Overview and Use Cases for Regular Expressions

A **regular expression (regex)**, sometimes referred to as a rational expression, is a sequence of symbols and characters expressing a string or pattern to be searched for within a longer piece of text. Many software application and programming languages support regular expressions (such as Python, Java, Oracle, etc.) and, as usual in the software world, different regular expression engines are not fully compatible with each other. The Cisco Expressway uses **Portable Operating System Interface (POSIX)** format for regular expression syntax.

Regular expressions can be used in conjunction with several Expressway features such as allow or deny lists for registration, subzone membership, alias transformations, zone transformations, **Call Processing Language (CPL)** policy, and **E.164 Number Mapping (ENUM)**. Table 4-2 provides a list of commonly used special characters in regular expression syntax. This is only a subset of the full range of expressions available.

Table 4-2 Regular Expressions

Character	Description	Example
.	Matches any single character.	. matches any alphabetical character and digit.
\d	Matches any decimal digit.	\d matches against any single digit (0–9) but not alphabetical character.
*	Matches 0 or more repetitions of the previous character expression.	.* matches against any sequence of characters including none.
+	Matches 1 or more repetitions of the previous character expression.	.+ matches against any sequence of characters.
?	Matches 0 or 1 repetition of the previous character expression.	9?123 matches both 9123 and 123 strings.
{n}	Matches n repetitions of the previous character expression.	\d{3} matches three-digit strings.
{n,m}	Matches n or m repetitions of the previous character expression.	\d{3,5} matches three-, four-, or five-digit strings.
[]	Matches a set of specified characters. Each character in the set can be specified individually, or a range can be specified by giving the first character in the range followed by the - character and then the last character in the range. You cannot use special characters within the [] because they will be taken literally.	[abc] matches only a, b, or c. [a-z] matches any alphabetical character. [0-9#*] matches any single E.164 number. The E.164 character set is made up of the digits 0–9 plus the hash key (#) and the asterisk key (*).

Character	Description	Example
[^]	Matches anything except the set of specified characters. Each character in the set can be specified individually, or a range can be specified by giving the first character in the range followed by the - character and then the last character in the range. You cannot use special characters within the [] because they will be taken literally.	[^abc] matches any nonalphabetical character and any alphabetical character except a, b, or c. [^a-z] matches any nonalphabetical character. [^0-9#*] matches anything other than the digits 0–9, the hash key (#), and the asterisk key (*).
(...)	Groups together a set of matching characters. Groups can then be referenced in order using the characters \1, \2, etc. as part of a replace string.	A regex can be constructed to transform a URI containing a user's full name to a URI based on the user's initials. The regex (.).*_(.).*(@example.com) would match against the user john_smith@example.com, and with a replace string of \1\2\3 would transform it to js@example.com.
|	Matches against one expression or an alternate expression.	.*@example.(net|com) matches against any URI for the domain example.com or the domain example.net.
\	Escapes a regular expression special character.	172\.1\.. matches 172.1.10.10 but not 172.12.0.0. \. allows a period to be matched as a period.
^	Signifies the start of a line. When used immediately after an opening brace, negates the character set inside the brace.	[^abc] matches any single character that is *not* a, b, or c.
$	Signifies the end of a line.	^\d\d\d$ matches any string that is exactly three digits long.
(?!...)	Negative lookahead. Defines a subexpression that must not be present.	(?!.*@example.com$).* matches any string that does not end with @example.com (?!alice). * matches any string that does not start with alice.
(?<!...)	Negative lookbehind. Defines a subexpression that must not be present.	.*(?<!net) matches any string that does not end with net.

With that overview of what regular expressions are and the syntax to utilize them, the following are some examples of regular expression manipulations that you can perform on the Cisco Expressway:

- Add domain to E.164 number

Alias	Pattern	Replace	Resulting Pattern
123	(\d+)	\1@company.com	123@company.com

■ Remove a domain

Alias	Pattern	Replace	Resulting Pattern
6002@company.com	(.*)@.+	\1	6002

■ Add a prefix to a numerical string

Alias	Pattern	Replace	Resulting Pattern
12345	(\d{5})	52\1	5212345

■ Reverse the order of a string

Alias	Pattern	Replace	Resulting Pattern
123	(\d) (\d) (\d)	\3\2\1	321

■ Match either 123@company.com or 123@company.net

Alias	Pattern	Leave	Resulting Pattern
123@company.com	123@company.(com|net)		123@company.com 123@company.net

The regular expression examples in this chapter will become useful in later chapters when discussing registration, subzone membership, alias transformations, and zone topics.

Verifying Regular Expression Using the Check Pattern Tool

The Check pattern tool (**Maintenance > Tools > Check Pattern**) lets you test whether a pattern or transform you intend to configure on the Expressway will have the expected result. You can use patterns when configuring the following:

■ Transforms to specify aliases to be transformed before any searches take place

■ Search rules to filter searches based on the alias being searched for, and to transform an alias before the search is sent to a zone

To use the Check pattern tool:

Step 1. In the Alias field, enter an alias against which you want to test the transform.

Step 2. In the Pattern section, enter the pattern string being tested and choose the combination of pattern type and pattern behavior from the respective drop-down lists.

■ If you select Replace from the Pattern Behavior list, you also need to enter a replace string in the Replace field that appears.

■ If you select Add Prefix or Add Suffix from the Pattern Behavior list, you also need to enter an additional text string to append/prepend to the pattern string.

■ The Expressway has a set of predefined pattern matching variables that you can use to match against certain configuration elements.

Step 3.   Click **Check Pattern** to test whether the alias matches the pattern.

The Result section shows whether the alias matches the pattern, and displays the resulting alias (including the effect of any transform if appropriate).

Exam Preparation Tasks

As mentioned in the section "How to Use This Book" in the Introduction, you have a couple of choices for exam preparation: the exercises here, Chapter 22, "Final Preparation," and the exam simulation questions in the Pearson Test Prep practice test software.

Review All Key Topics

Review the most important topics in this chapter, noted with the Key Topics icon in the outer margin of the page. Table 4-3 lists a reference of the key topic in this chapter and the page number on which it is found.

Table 4-3   Key Topic for Chapter 4

Key Topic Element	Description	Page Number
Table 4-2	Regular Expressions	64

Complete Tables and Lists from Memory

Print a copy of Appendix C, "Memory Tables" (found on the companion website), or at least the section for this chapter, and complete the tables and lists from memory. Appendix D, "Memory Tables Answer Key," also on the companion website, includes completed tables and lists to check your work.

Define Key Terms

Define the following key terms from this chapter and check your answers in the glossary:

Call Processing Language (CPL), E.164 Number Mapping (ENUM), Portable Operating System Interface (POSIX), regular expression (regex)

Q&A

The answer to this question appears in Appendix A. For more practice with exam format questions, use the Pearson Test Prep practice test software.

1.   Which regular expression strings would match the alias user123@company.com?

CHAPTER 5

Security Overview on the Cisco Expressway

This chapter covers the following topics:

> **Describe SIP Media Encryption Mode:** Explains how signaling and media is encrypted and sent through its call legs and covers the encryption policy options.

> **Certificates:** Describes how certificates are used and applied regarding the Cisco Expressway.

> **Administrator Authentication:** Summarizes the security approach from an administrative level and defines Advanced Account Security and FIPS 140-2 relative to the Cisco Expressway.

This chapter focuses on the security aspects of the Cisco Expressway and other security-related topics to include the SIP media encryption modes and certificate Expressway settings.

This chapter covers the following objectives from the Implementing Cisco Collaboration Cloud and Edge Solutions (CLCEI) exam 300-820:

- 1.6.a Describe SIP media encryption mode: Auto

- 1.6.b Describe SIP media encryption mode: Force encrypted

- 1.6.c Describe SIP media encryption mode: Force unencrypted

- 1.6.d Describe SIP media encryption mode: Best effort

- 1.8.c Describe key Expressway settings: Certificates

- 2.1.c Configure key Expressway settings: Certificates

- 2.4.b Configure a Business-to-Business (B2B) collaboration solution: Certificates (focus on Microsoft CA)

"Do I Know This Already?" Quiz

The "Do I Know This Already?" quiz enables you to assess whether you should read this entire chapter thoroughly or jump to the "Exam Preparation Tasks" section. If you are in doubt about your answers to these questions or your own assessment of your knowledge of the topics, read the entire chapter. Table 5-1 lists the major headings in this chapter and their corresponding "Do I Know This Already?" quiz questions. You can find the answers in Appendix A, "Answers to the 'Do I Know This Already?' Quizzes and Review Questions."

Table 5-1 "Do I Know This Already?" Section-to-Question Mapping

Foundation Topics Section	Questions
Describe SIP Media Encryption Mode	1–2
Certificates	3–4
Administrator Authentication	5–6

CAUTION The goal of self-assessment is to gauge your knowledge of the topics in this chapter. If you do not know the answer to a question or are only partially sure of the answer, you should mark that question as wrong for purposes of the self-assessment. Giving yourself credit for an answer you correctly guess skews your self-assessment results and might provide you with a false sense of security.

1. When using encryption signaling for SIP, what protocol is Transport Layer Security (TLS) implemented on?

   a. UDP

   b. TCP

   c. RTP

   d. RTMT

2. Which encryption policy delegates the encryption decision to the endpoints?

   a. Forced encryption

   b. Forced unencryption

   c. Best effort

   d. Auto

3. Which component of the certificate process issues the certificates?

   a. Expressway

   b. Certificate authority

   c. Firewall

   d. Certificate policy

4. Which of the following web pages allows you to manage the list of certificates for the certificate authorities trusted by an Expressway?

   a. Trusted CA Certificate page

   b. Server Certificate page

   c. Certificate-based Authentication Configuration page

   d. CRL Management page

5. When in secure mode, which of the following changes and limitations to standard Expressway functionality apply? (Choose two.)

   a. Access over SSH and through the serial port is disabled and cannot be turned on (the pwrec password recovery function is also unavailable).

   b. The CLI and API access are unavailable.

   c. The Administrator Account Authentication Source field is set to Local Only and cannot be changed.

   d. Only the administrator account may change the emergency account.

   e. The CLI and API access are available.

6. FIPS 140-2 compliance requires which of the following restrictions? (Choose two.)

   a. System-wide SIP transport mode settings must be TCP: On, and UDP: On.

   b. All SIP zones must use UDP.

   c. System-wide SIP transport mode settings must be TLS: On, TCP: Off, and UDP: Off.

   d. All SIP zones must use TLS.

Foundation Topics

Describe SIP Media Encryption Mode

With more services extending beyond the internal network, and with internal networks potentially subject to internal attacks, encryption and authentication are becoming increasingly critical. Encryption protects against attacks such as eavesdropping, tampering, and session replay. If an unauthorized user is able to capture the traffic, that user would not be able to decrypt the contents of the communication or modify it without knowing the encryption keys. Encryption can also provide authentication through digital certificates when the encrypted communication is set up. Cisco Collaboration solutions use **Transport Layer Security (TLS)** and **Secure Real-time Transport Protocol (SRTP)** for signaling and media encryption.

The TLS protocol is designed to provide authentication, data integrity, and confidentiality for communications between two applications. TLS operates in a client/server mode with one side acting as the "server" and the other side acting as the "client." TLS requires TCP as the reliable transport layer protocol to operate over. TLS is used to secure the **Session Initiation Protocol (SIP)** signaling protocol in Cisco Collaboration devices to the call controls such as the Cisco Expressway or **Cisco Unified Communications Manager (Unified CM)**.

SRTP, defined in IETF RFC 3711, details the methods of providing confidentiality and data integrity for both **Real-time Transport Protocol (RTP)** voice and video media, as well as their corresponding **Real-time Transport Control Protocol (RTCP)** streams. SRTP accomplishes this through the use of encryption and message authentication headers.

In SRTP, encryption applies only to the payload of the RTP packet. Message authentication, however, is applied to both the RTP header and the RTP payload. Because message authentication applies to the RTP sequence number within the header, SRTP indirectly provides protection against replay attacks as well. SRTP ciphers include Authentication Encryption with

Associated Data (AEAD) with **Advanced Encryption Standard (AES)** 256 or 128 and with Secure Hash Algorithm (SHA) 2. SRTP cipher based on Hash-based Message Authentication Code (HMAC) with AES 128 and SHA-1 could also be negotiated if it is not disallowed in the configuration.

Signaling and media encryption is important for business-to-business calls, but it needs to be deployed carefully so as not to restrict or limit the ability to receive calls. There is a variety of older SIP and H.323 systems that you may be communicating with that do not support signaling or media encryption.

Key Topic

Based on zone configuration, encryption policies might be set as forced (**force encrypted**), desirable (**best effort**), not allowed (**force unencrypted**), or left to the endpoint decisions (**auto**).

If **force encrypted** is configured on a target zone and the Expressway is receiving a call for an endpoint on that remote zone, then Expressway will set up an encrypted call. If the remote party accepts only unencrypted calls, the call will be dropped. If the calling endpoint is using the **Transmission Control Protocol (TCP)** and sending unencrypted media, and **force encrypted** is configured on the target zone, Expressway will terminate the call leg and set up another call leg to the destination with TLS and encryption.

When the Expressway performs RTP to SRTP, it uses a **back-to-back user agent (B2BUA)** for business-to-business calls. The B2BUA terminates both signaling and media and sets up a new call leg to the destination. The B2BUA is engaged anytime the media encryption mode is configured to a setting other than **auto**. Note that SIP TLS to TCP interworking requires the B2BUA only if the media is sent encrypted; otherwise it does not require the B2BUA. Exception occurs only in the following scenario affecting the Expressway-E: if the inbound zone and outbound zone are set to the same encryption media type and one of those zones is a traversal server zone, the Expressway-E checks the value of the associated traversal client zone. If all three of these zones are set to the same value, the Expressway-E will not engage the B2BUA. In this case, the B2BUA will be engaged only on the Expressway-C. With **best effort**, if the Expressway cannot set up an encrypted call, it will fall back to unencrypted.

Depending on the requirements, different media encryption policies might be configured. If a corporate enforcing policy is not in place, the recommendation is to set up zones with **auto** specified as the media encryption mode. A setting of **auto** delegates the encryption decisions to endpoints, and the Expressway does not perform any sort of RTP-to-SRTP conversion.

When the encryption policy is enforced on the Expressway, the call will be divided into many call legs due to B2BUA engagement, as in the following scenario:

- Expressway-C neighbor zone to Unified CM set to **auto**
- Expressway-C traversal client zone set to **best effort**
- Expressway-E traversal server zone set to **best effort**
- Expressway-E DNS zone set to **auto**
- Calling endpoint on Unified CM configured for encryption, and Unified CM configured in mixed mode
- Called endpoint or system does not support encryption

5

For example, consider a scenario where Unified CM is in mixed mode and the calling endpoint is configured for encryption. In this scenario, a secure endpoint on Unified CM calls an unencrypted endpoint on the Internet. The call consists of the following call legs:

1. The Unified CM endpoint to the Expressway-C B2BUA, encrypted

2. The Expressway-C B2BUA to the Expressway-E B2BUA, encrypted

3. The Expressway-E B2BUA to the Internet, up to unknown remote edge or final destination, unencrypted

4. Remote edge to final destination, encrypted or unencrypted depending on the called partner's settings

If call legs 1 through 3 are encrypted, the lock icon will display correctly. If one of these legs is not encrypted, the lock icon will not display. Note that the last call leg is under the control of another company and, as such, does not influence the lock status.

Every company has the control of encryption up to the other company's edge, thus allowing an endpoint to establish an encrypted call from the endpoint to the remote edge. Encryption policy protects media on the Internet if **force encrypted** is configured on the Expressway; but once the call hits the remote edge, the call might be decrypted at the edge level before sending media to the called endpoint.

Certificates

For TLS encryption to work successfully in a connection between a client and server:

- The server must have a certificate installed that verifies its identity, which is issued by a **certificate authority (CA)**.

- The client must trust the CA that signed the certificate used by the server.

Expressway lets you install a certificate that can represent the Expressway as either a client or a server in TLS connections. Expressway can also authenticate client connections (typically from a web browser) over **Hypertext Transfer Protocol Secure (HTTPS)**. You can upload **certificate revocation lists (CRLs)** for the CAs used to verify **Lightweight Directory Access Protocol (LDAP)** server and HTTPS client certificates. Expressway can generate server **certificate signing requests (CSRs)**, so there is no need to use an external mechanism to do this. Use Table 5-2 to assist in identifying who acts as the TLS server or client. Certificate and CRL files are managed via the web interface and cannot be installed using the CLI.

Table 5-2 Expressway Role in Different Connection Types

Connection Type	Expressway Role
To an endpoint	TLS server
To an LDAP server	Client
Between two Expressway systems	Either Expressway may be the client; the other Expressway is the TLS server
Over HTTPS	Web browser is the client; Expressway is the server

For all secure communications (HTTPS and SIP/TLS), it is strongly recommended that you replace the Expressway default certificate with a certificate generated by a trusted CA. TLS can be difficult to configure. So, if you are using TLS with an LDAP server, for example, we recommend verifying that the system works correctly over TCP before you attempt to secure the connection with TLS. We also recommend using a third-party LDAP browser to verify that your LDAP server is correctly configured for TLS.

CAUTION   Certificates must be RFC 5280 compliant. Do not allow CA certificates or CRLs to expire, as this may cause certificates signed by those CAs to be rejected.

Configuring Certificate-Based Authentication

The Certificate-based Authentication Configuration page (**Maintenance > Security > Certificate-based Authentication Configuration**) is used to configure how the Expressway retrieves authorization credentials (the username) from a client browser's certificate. This configuration is required if the Client Certificate-based Security option (defined on the System page) is set to Certificate-based Authentication. This setting means that the standard login mechanism is no longer available and that administrators (and FindMe accounts, if accessed via the Expressway) can log in only if they present a valid browser certificate—typically provided via a smart card (also referred to as a Common Access Card, or just CAC)—and the certificate contains appropriate credentials that have a suitable authorization level.

Enabling Certificate-Based Authentication

The following recommended procedure describes how to enable certificate-based authentication:

Step 1.   Add the Expressway's trusted CA and server certificate files (on the Trusted CA Certificate and Server Certificate pages, respectively).

Step 2.   Configure certificate revocation lists (on the CRL Management page).

Step 3.   Use the Client Certificate Testing page to verify that the client certificate you intend to use is valid.

Step 4.   Set Client Certificate-based Security option to **Certificate Validation** (on the System Administration page).

Step 5.   Restart the Expressway.

Step 6.   Use the Client Certificate Testing page again to set up the required **regular expression (regex)** and format patterns to extract the username credentials from the certificate.

Step 7.   Only when you are sure that the correct username is being extracted from the certificate, set the Client Certificate-based Security option to **Certificate-based Authentication**.

Authentication Versus Authorization

When the Expressway is operating in certificate-based authentication mode, user authentication is managed by a process external to the Expressway.

When a user attempts to log in to the Expressway, the Expressway requests a certificate from the client browser. The browser may then interact with a card reader to obtain the certificate from the smart card (or alternatively the certificate may already be loaded into the browser). To release the certificate from the card/browser, the user typically is requested to authenticate by entering a PIN. If the client certificate received by the Expressway is valid (signed by a trusted CA, in date, and not revoked by a CRL), then the user is deemed to be authenticated.

To determine the user's authorization level (read-write, read-only, and so on), the Expressway must extract the user's authorization username from the certificate and present it to the relevant local or remote authorization mechanism.

Note that if the client certificate is not protected (by a PIN or some other mechanism), then unauthenticated access to the Expressway may be possible. This lack of protection may also apply if the certificates are stored in the browser, although some browsers do allow you to password protect their certificate store.

Obtaining the Username from the Certificate

The username is extracted from the client browser's certificate according to the patterns defined in the Regex and Username Format fields on the Certificate-based Authentication Configuration page:

- In the Regex field, use the **(?<name>regex)** syntax to supply names for capture groups so that matching subpatterns can be substituted in the associated Username Format field, for example: **/(Subject:.*, CN=(?<Group1>.*))/m.**

  - The regex defined here must conform to PHP regex guidelines.

- The Username Format field can contain a mixture of fixed text and the capture group names used in the Regex field. Delimit each capture group name with **#**, for example, **prefix#Group1#suffix**. Each capture group name will be replaced with the text obtained from the regular expression processing.

You can use the Client Certificate Testing page (**Maintenance > Security > Client Certificate Testing**) to test the outcome of applying to a certificate different combinations in the Regex and Username Format fields.

Emergency Account and Certificate-based Authentication

Advanced account security mode requires that you use only remote authentication but also mandates that you have an emergency account in case the authentication server is unavailable. If you are using certificate-based authentication, the emergency account must be able to authenticate by presenting a valid certificate with matching credentials. You should create a client certificate for the emergency account, make sure that the CN matches the Username Format field on the certificate-based authentication configuration page, and load the certificate into the emergency administrator's certificate store.

Managing the Trusted CA Certificate List

The Trusted CA Certificate page (**Maintenance > Security > Trusted CA Certificate**) enables you to manage the list of certificates for the CAs trusted by the Expressway. When a TLS connection to the Expressway mandates certificate verification, the certificate presented to the Expressway must be signed by a trusted CA in this list and there must be a full chain of trust (intermediate CAs) to the root CA.

- To upload a new file containing one or more CA certificates, click Browse to locate the required PEM file and click Append CA Certificate. This appends any new certificates to the existing list of CA certificates. If you are replacing existing certificates for a particular issuer and subject, you have to manually delete the previous certificates.

- To replace all of the currently uploaded CA certificates with the system's original list of trusted CA certificates, click Reset to Default CA Certificate.

- To view the entire list of currently uploaded trusted CA certificates, click Show All (Decoded) to view it in a human-readable form, or click Show All (PEM File) to view the file in its raw format.

- To view an individual trusted CA certificate, click View (Decoded) in the row for the specific CA certificate.

- To delete one or more CA certificates, check the box(es) next to the relevant CA certificate(s) and click Delete.

Note that if you have enabled CRL checking for TLS-encrypted connections to an LDAP server (for account authentication), you must add the PEM-encoded CRL data to your trusted CA certificate file.

Expressway X12.6 and later includes these trusted root CAs, which are installed as part of the Cisco Intersection CA Bundle by default:

- O=Internet Security Research Group, CN=ISRG Root X1

- O=Digital Signature Trust Co., CN=DST Root CA X3

Managing the Expressway Server Certificate

Use the Server Certificate page (**Maintenance > Security > Server Certificate**) to manage the Expressway server certificate, which identifies the Expressway when it communicates with client systems using TLS encryption and with web browsers over HTTPS. You can view details of the currently loaded certificate, generate a CSR, upload a new certificate, and configure the ACME service. These tasks are described in the *Cisco Expressway Certificate Creation and Use Deployment Guide* available on the Expressway Configuration Guides page. We *strongly recommend* using certificates based on RSA keys. Other types of certificate, such as those based on Digital Signature Algorithm (DSA) keys, are not tested and may not work with Expressway in all scenarios.

Using the ACME Service

Starting with release X12.5, the Cisco Expressway Series supports the **Automated Certificate Management Environment (ACME)** protocol, which enables automatic certificate signing and deployment to the Expressway-E from a certificate authority such as Let's Encrypt.

Server Certificates and Clustered Systems

When a CSR is generated, a single request and private key combination is generated for that peer only. If you have a cluster of Expressways, you must generate a separate certificate signing request (CSR) on each peer. Those requests must then be sent to the CA and the returned server certificates must be uploaded to each relevant peer. Make sure that the correct server certificate is uploaded to the appropriate peer, because otherwise the stored private key on each peer will not correspond to the uploaded certificate.

Managing Certificate Revocation Lists

Certificate revocation list files are used by the Expressway to validate certificates presented by client browsers and external systems that communicate with the Expressway over TLS/HTTPS. A CRL identifies those certificates that have been revoked and can no longer be used to communicate with the Expressway.

We recommend that you upload CRL data for the CAs that sign TLS/HTTPS client and server certificates. When enabled, CRL checking is applied for every CA in the chain of trust.

Certificate Revocation Sources

The Expressway can obtain certificate revocation information from multiple sources:

- Automatic downloads of CRL data from CRL distribution points

- Through **Online Certificate Status Protocol (OCSP)** responder URIs in the certificate to be checked (SIP TLS only)

- Manual upload of CRL data

- CRL data embedded within the Expressway's Trusted CA certificate file

The following limitations and usage guidelines apply:

- When establishing SIP TLS connections, the CRL data sources are subject to the Certificate Revocation Checking settings on the SIP configuration page.

- Automatically downloaded CRL files override any manually loaded CRL files (except for when verifying SIP TLS connections, when both manually uploaded or automatically downloaded CRL data may be used).

- When validating certificates presented by external policy servers, the Expressway uses manually loaded CRLs only.

- When validating TLS connections with an LDAP server for remote login account authentication, the Expressway only uses CRL data that has been embedded into the Trusted CA certificate (**Tools > Security > Trusted CA Certificate**).

For LDAP connections, the Expressway does not download the CRL from CRL Distribution Point (CDP) URIs in the server or issuing CA certificates. Also, it does not use the manual or automatic update settings on the CRL Management page.

Automatic CRL Updates

Cisco recommends that you configure the Expressway to perform automatic CRL updates. This ensures that the latest CRLs are available for certificate validation.

To configure the Expressway to use automatic CRL updates:

Step 1.   Go to **Maintenance > Security > CRL Management.**

Step 2.   Set Automatic CRL Updates to **Enabled.**

Step 3.   Enter the set of HTTP(S) distribution points from which the Expressway can obtain CRL files.

NOTE   Follow these guidelines:

- You must specify each distribution point on a new line.
- Only HTTP(S) distribution points are supported; if HTTPS is used, the distribution point server itself must have a valid certificate.
- PEM- and DER-encoded CRL files are supported.
- The distribution point may point directly to a CRL file or to ZIP and GZIP archives containing multiple CRL files.
- The file extensions in the URL or on any files unpacked from a downloaded archive do not matter because the Expressway will determine the underlying file type for itself; however, typical URLs could be in the following formats:
  - http://example.com/crl.pem
  - http://example.com/crl.der
  - http://example.com/ca.crl
  - https://example.com/allcrls.zip
  - https://example.com/allcrls.gz

Step 4.   Enter in the Daily Update Time field the approximate time of day (in UTC) that the Expressway should attempt to update its CRLs from the distribution points.

Step 5.   Click **Save.**

Manual CRL Updates

You can upload CRL files manually to the Expressway. Certificates presented by external policy servers can only be validated against manually loaded CRLs.

To upload a CRL file:

Step 1.   Go to **Maintenance > Security > CRL Management.**

Step 2.   Click **Browse** and select the required file from your file system. It must be in PEM-encoded format.

Step 3.   Click **Upload CRL File.** This uploads the selected file and replaces any previously uploaded CRL file.

Click Remove Revocation List if you want to remove the manually uploaded file from the Expressway. If a certificate authority's CRL expires, all certificates issued by that CA are treated as revoked.

Online Certificate Status Protocol

The Expressway can establish a connection with an OCSP responder to query the status of a particular certificate. The Expressway determines the OCSP responder to use from the responder URI listed in the certificate being verified. The OCSP responder sends a status of **good**, **revoked**, or **unknown** for the certificate. The benefit of OCSP is that there is no need to download an entire CRL.

Outbound communication from the Expressway-E is required for the connection to the OCSP responder. Check the port number of the OCSP responder you are using (typically this is port 80 or 443) and ensure that outbound communication is allowed from the Expressway-E.

Configuring Revocation Checking for SIP TLS Connections

You must also configure how certificate revocation checking is managed for SIP TLS connections.

Step 1.   Go to **Configuration > SIP**.

Step 2.   Scroll down to the Certificate Revocation Checking section and configure the settings according to Table 5-3.

Table 5-3   Certificate Revocation Settings

Field	Description	Usage Tips
Certificate revocation checking mode	Controls whether revocation checking is performed for certificates exchanged during SIP TLS connection establishment.	We recommend enabling revocation checking.
Use OCSP	Controls whether OCSP may be used to perform certificate revocation checking.	To use OCSP: The X.509 certificate to be checked must contain an OCSP responder URI. The OCSP responder must support the SHA-256 hash algorithm. If it is not supported, the OCSP revocation check and the certificate validation will fail.
Use CRLs	Controls whether CRLs are used to perform certificate revocation checking.	CRLs can be used if the certificate does not support OCSP. CRLs can be loaded manually onto the Expressway, downloaded automatically from preconfigured URIs, or downloaded automatically from a CRL distribution point (CDP) URI contained in the X.509 certificate.

Field	Description	Usage Tips
Allow CRL downloads from CDPs	Controls whether the download of CRLs from the CDP URIs contained in X.509 certificates is allowed.	
Fallback behavior	Controls the revocation checking behavior if the revocation status cannot be established; for example, if the revocation source cannot be contacted. The options are as follows: Treat As Revoked (default): Treats the certificate as revoked (and thus does not allow the TLS connection). Treat As Not Revoked: Treats the certificate as not revoked.	Choosing Treat As Not Revoked ensures that your system continues to operate in a normal manner if the revocation source cannot be contacted, but it does potentially mean that revoked certificates will be accepted.

The Client Certificate Testing page (**Maintenance > Security > Client Certificate Testing**) is used to check client certificates before enabling client certificate validation. You can test the following:

- Whether a client certificate is valid when checked against the Expressway's current trusted CA list and, if loaded, the revocation list

- The outcome of applying the regex and template patterns that retrieve a certificate's authorization credentials (the username)

You can test against a certificate on your local file system or the browser's currently loaded certificate. To test if a certificate is valid:

Step 1. Select the certificate source. You can choose to

- Upload a test file from your file system in either PEM or plaintext format; if so click **Browse** to select the certificate file you want to test

- Test against the certificate currently loaded into your browser (only available if the system is already configured to use certificate validation and a certificate is currently loaded)

Step 2. Ignore the Certificate-based Authentication Pattern section, which is relevant only if you are extracting authorization credentials from the certificate.

Step 3. Click **Check Certificate**; the results of the test are shown in the Certificate Test Results section.

To retrieve authorization credentials (username) from the certificate:

Step 1. Select the certificate source as described in the previous list.

Step 2. Configure the Regex and Username Format fields as required. Their purpose is to extract a username from the nominated certificate by supplying a regular expression that will look for an appropriate string pattern within the certificate.

The fields default to the currently configured settings on the Certificate-based Authentication Configuration page, but you can change them as required.

- In the Regex field, use the **(?<name>regex)** syntax to supply names for capture groups so that matching subpatterns can be substituted in the associated Username Format field; for example, **/(Subject:.*, CN=(?<Group1>.*))/m.**

- The regex defined here must conform to PHP regex guidelines.

- The Username Format field can contain a mixture of fixed text and the capture group names used in the Regex field. Delimit each capture group name with **#**; for example, **prefix#Group1#suffix**. Each capture group name will be replaced with the text obtained from the regular expression processing.

Step 3.   Click **Check Certificate**. The results of the test are shown in the Certificate Test Results section. The Resulting String item is the username credential that would be checked against the relevant authorization mechanism to determine that user's authorization (account access) level.

Step 4.   If necessary, you can modify the Regex and Username Format fields and repeat the test until the correct results are produced. Note that if the certificate source is an uploaded PEM or plaintext file, the selected file is temporarily uploaded to the Expressway when the test is first performed:

- If you want to keep testing different Regex and Username Format field combinations against the same file, you do not have to reselect the file for every test.

- If you change the contents of your test file on your file system, or you want to choose a different file, you must click **Browse** again and select the new or modified file to upload.

Step 5.   If you have changed the Regex and Username Format fields from their default values and want to use these values in the Expressway's actual configuration (as specified on the Certificate-based Authentication Configuration page), then click **Make These Settings Permanent**.

> **NOTE**   Consider this while testing:
>
> - Any uploaded test file is automatically deleted from the Expressway at the end of your login session.
> - The regex is applied to a plaintext version of an encoded certificate. The system uses the command **openssl x509 -text -nameopt RFC2253 -noout** to extract the plaintext certificate from its encoded format.

Administrator Authentication

Next, we will cover a security overview specifically geared toward the authentication of an administrator.

Configuring SSH

The Expressway pair uses SSH tunnels to securely transfer data from the Expressway-E to the Expressway-C without requiring the Expressway-E to open the connection. The Expressway-C opens a TCP session with the Expressway-E that is listening on a fixed TCP port. The pair then uses the selected cipher and algorithms to establish an encrypted tunnel for securely sharing data.

Configure the cipher and algorithms that the pair uses to encrypt SSH tunnels as follows:

Step 1.   Go to **Maintenance > Security > SSH Configuration.**

Step 2.   Modify the following settings, only if necessary:

Setting	Description
Ciphers	aes256-ctr: Advanced Encryption Standard using the CTR (counter) mode to encipher 256 bit blocks (Default)
Public Key Algorithms	X509v3-sign-rsa (Default)
	X509v3-ssh-rsa
Key Exchange Algorithms	ecdh-sha2-nistp256
	ecdh-sha2-nistp384 (Default)

Step 3.   Click **Save.**

Advanced Security

The Advanced Security page (**Maintenance > Advanced Security**) is used to configure the Expressway for use in highly secure environments. You need to install the Advanced Account Security option key to see this page.

You can configure the system for the following modes:

■ Advanced account security mode

■ FIPS140-2 cryptographic mode

Enabling advanced account security limits login access to remotely authenticated users using the web interface only, and also restricts access to some system features. To indicate that the Expressway is in advanced account security mode, any text specified in the Classification Banner field is displayed on every web page.

A system reboot is required for changes to the advanced account security mode to take effect.

HTTP Methods

The Expressway web server allows the **Hypertext Transfer Protocol (HTTP)** methods outlined in Table 5-4.

Table 5-4   HTTP Methods

Method	Used by Web UI?	Used by API?	Used to...
GET	Yes	Yes	Retrieve data from a specified resource; for example, to return a specific page in the Expressway web interface.
POST	Yes	Yes	Apply data to a web resource; for example, when an administrator saves changes to a setting using the Expressway web interface.
OPTIONS	No	Yes	Return, for a specified URL, the HTTP methods supported by the server. For example, the Expressway can use OPTIONS to test a proxy server for HTTP/1.1 compliance.
PUT	No	Yes	Send a resource to be stored at a specified URI. Cisco REST API commands use this method to change the Expressway configuration.
DELETE	No	Yes	Delete a specified resource. For example, the REST API uses DELETE for record deletion.

Administrators have **application programming interface (API)** access by default. This can be disabled in two ways:

■ If the Expressway is running in advanced account security mode, then API access is automatically disabled for all users.

■ API access for individual administrators can be disabled through their user configuration options.

Before you can enable advanced account security mode, the following items are required:

■ The system must be configured to use remote account authentication for administrator accounts.

■ The Advanced Account Security option key must be installed.

■ You must create a local administrator account and nominate it as the emergency account, so that you can get in if remote authentication is unavailable. You cannot use a remote account for this purpose. Do not use the built-in admin account.

CAUTION   The Expressway disallows local authentication by all accounts except the emergency account. Ensure that the remote directory service is working properly before you enable the mode.

You are also recommended to configure your system so that

- SNMP is disabled.

- The session timeout period is set to a non-zero value.

- HTTPS client certificate validation is enabled.

- User account LDAP server configuration uses TLS encryption and has CRL checking set to All.

- Remote logging is disabled.

- Incident reporting is disabled.

- Any connection to an external manager uses HTTPS and has certificate checking enabled.

Alarms are raised for any non-recommended configuration settings.

Enabling Advanced Account Security

To enable advanced account security:

Step 1.   Go to **Maintenance > Advanced Security**.

Step 2.   Enter a classification banner message in the Classification Banner field. The text entered here is displayed on every web page.

Step 3.   Set Advanced Account Security Mode to **On**.

Step 4.   Click **Save**.

Step 5.   Reboot the Expressway (**Maintenance > Restart Options**).

Expressway Functionality: Changes and Limitations

When in secure mode, the following changes and limitations to standard Expressway functionality apply:

- Access over SSH and through the serial port is disabled and cannot be turned on (the pwrec password recovery function is also unavailable).

- Access over HTTPS is enabled and cannot be turned off.

- The CLI and API access are unavailable.

- The Administrator Account Authentication Source field is set to Remote Only and cannot be changed.

- Local authentication is disabled. There is no access using the root account or any local administrator account except the emergency account.

- Only the emergency account may change the emergency account.

- If you are using certificate-based authentication, the emergency account must be authenticated by credentials in the client's certificate.

- If there are three consecutive failed attempts to log in (by the same or different users), login access to the Expressway is blocked for 60 seconds.

- Immediately after logging in, the current user is shown statistics of when they previously logged in and details of any failed attempts to log in using that account.

- Administrator accounts with read-only or read-write access levels cannot view the Event Log, Configuration Log, and Network Log pages. These pages can be viewed only by accounts with Auditor access level.

- The Upgrade page only displays the System Platform component.

The Event Log, Configuration Log, Network Log, call history, search history, and registration history are cleared whenever the Expressway is taken out of advanced account security mode. Note that if intrusion protection is enabled, this will cause any existing blocked addresses to become unblocked.

Disabling Advanced Account Security

This operation wipes all configuration. You cannot maintain any configuration or history when exiting this mode. The system returns to factory state.

Step 1.   Sign in with the emergency account.

Step 2.   Disable the Advanced Account Security Mode option (**Maintenance > Advanced Security**).

Step 3.   Sign out.

Step 4.   Connect to the console.

Step 5.   Sign in as **root** and run **factory-reset**.

Configuring FIPS140-2 Cryptographic Mode

FIPS 140 is a joint U.S. and Canadian government standard that specifies security requirements for cryptographic modules. FIPS 140-1 became a mandatory standard for the protection of sensitive data in 1994 and was superseded by FIPS 140-2 in 2001. Expressway X8.8 or later implements FIPS 140-2 compliant features. When in FIPS140-2 cryptographic mode, system performance may be affected due to the increased cryptographic workload. You can also cluster Expressways that have FIPS140-2 mode enabled.

Before you enable FIPS140-2 mode:

- Ensure that the system is not using NTLM protocol challenges with a direct Active Directory service connection for device authentication; NTLM cannot be used while in FIPS140-2 mode.

- If login authentication via a remote LDAP server is configured, ensure that it uses TLS encryption if it is using Simple Authentication and Security Layer (SASL) binding.

- The Advanced Account Security option key must be installed.

FIPS 140-2 compliance also requires the following restrictions:

- System-wide SIP transport mode settings must be TLS: On, TCP: Off, and UDP: Off.

- All SIP zones must use TLS.

- SNMP and NTP server connections should use strong hashing and encryption. Use these settings:

  - System > SNMP > v3 Authentication > Type = **SHA**

  - System > SNMP > v3 Privacy > Type = **AES**

  - System > Time > NTP Server *n* > Authentication = **Symmetric key**

  - System > Time > NTP Server *n* > Hash = **SHA-1**

If your system is running as a virtualized application and has never been through an upgrade process, perform a system upgrade before you continue. You can upgrade the system to the same software release version that it is currently running. If you do not complete this step, the activation process described in the next section will fail.

Enable FIPS140-2 Cryptographic Mode

The transition to FIPS140-2 cryptographic mode requires a system reset to be performed. This removes all existing configuration data. To preserve your data, you should make a backup immediately prior to performing the reset, and then restore the backup file when the reset has completed. The reset removes all administrator account information and reinstates the default security certificates. To log in after the reset has completed, you will have to first complete the Install Wizard.

To turn your system into a compliant FIPS 140-2 cryptographic system:

Step 1.   Enable FIPS140-2 cryptographic mode:

    a.   Go to **Maintenance > Advanced Security**.

    b.   Set FIPS140-2 Cryptographic Mode to **On**.

    c.   Click **Save**.

Step 2.   Fix any alarms that have been raised that report noncompliant configuration.

Step 3.   Make a system backup if you want to preserve your current configuration data. Note that all backups require password protection.

Step 4.   Reset the system and complete the activation of FIPS140-2 mode:

    a.   Log in to Expressway as **root**.

    b.   Type **fips-activate**; the reset takes up to 30 minutes to complete.

Step 5.   Follow the prompts to complete the Install Wizard.

Step 6.   When the system has applied the configuration and restarted, log in as **admin** using the password you set. You may see alarms related to noncompliance with FIPS 140-2. Ignore these alarms if you intend to restore the backup that you made prior to the reset. You must take action if the alarms persist after restoring the backup.

Step 7.   Restore your previous data, if required. Note that while in FIPS140-2 mode, you can only restore backup files that were taken when FIPS140-2 Cryptographic Mode was set On. Any previous administrator account information and passwords will be restored, but the previous root account password will not be restored. If the data you are restoring contains untrusted security certificates, the restart that occurs as part of the restore process may take up to 6 minutes to complete.

Step 8.   Starting with release X12.6, you must manually change the SIP TLS Diffie-Hellman key size from the default 1024 bits to at least 2048 bits. To do this, type the following command in the Expressway CLI (change the value in the final element if you want a key size higher than 2048): **xconfiguration SIP Advanced SipTlsDhKeySize: "2048"**

The following Expressway features are FIPS 140-2 compliant (i.e., use FIPS 140-2 compliant algorithms):

- Administration over the web interface
- Clustering
- XML and REST APIs
- SSH access (restricted to only use AES or 3DES ciphers)
- Login authentication via a remote LDAP server (must use TLS if using SASL binding)
- Client certificate verification
- SIP certificate revocation features
- SNMP (SNMPv3 authentication is restricted to SHA-1, and SNMPv3 privacy is restricted to AES)
- NTP (NTP server authentication using symmetric key is restricted to SHA-1)
- Device authentication against the local database
- SIP connections to/from the Expressway providing they use TLS
- H.323 connections to/from the Expressway
- Delegated credential checking
- SRTP media encryption
- SIP/H.323 interworking
- Cisco Unified Communications Mobile and Remote Access (MRA)
- TURN server authentication
- Backup/restore operations
- Connections to an external manager
- Connections to external policy services
- Remote logging
- Incident reporting
- CSR generation

Other Expressway features are not FIPS 140-2 compliant, including

- SIP authentication over NTLM/Active Directory

- SIP/H.323 device authentication against an H.350 directory service

- Microsoft Interoperability service

- Use of Cisco TelePresence Management Suite Provisioning Extension (TMSPE)

Managing Domain Certificates and Server Name Indication for Multitenancy

Multitenancy is part of Cisco Hosted Collaboration Solution (HCS) and allows a service provider to share an Expressway-E cluster among multiple tenants.

Using the **Server Name Indication (SNI)** protocol extension within TLS, the Expressway can now store and use domain-specific certificates that can be offered to a client during the TLS handshake. This capability allows seamless integration of endpoints registering through MRA in a multitenant environment and ensures the certificate domain name matches the client's domain. During a TLS handshake, the client includes an SNI field in the ClientHello request. The Expressway looks up its certificate store and tries to find a match for the SNI hostname. If a match is found, the domain-specific certificate is returned to the client.

Note that in multitenant mode, you must configure the system hostname on the **System > DNS** page of the Expressway-E to match the hostname configured in DNS (case-sensitive before X8.10.1, case-insensitive from X8.10.1). Otherwise, Cisco Jabber clients will be unable to register successfully for MRA.

The following is the SNI call flow:

1. On the MRA client being registered, the user enters bob@example.com, where example.com is the user's service domain (customer domain).

2. The client does a DNS resolution:

   a. It sends a DNS SRV request for _collab-edge._tls.example.com.

   b. The DNS replies to the request:

      - In a single tenant setup, the DNS reply usually includes the hostname within the service domain (for example, mra-host.example.com).

      - In a multitenant setup, DNS may instead return the service provider's MRA hostname in the service provider's domain, which is different from the user's service domain (for example, mra-host.sp.com).

3. The client sets up the SSL connection:

   a. The client sends an SSL ClientHello request with an SNI extension:

      - If the DNS-returned hostname has the same domain as the user's service domain, the DNS hostname is used in SNI server_name (unchanged).

      - Otherwise, in the case of a domain mismatch, the client sets the SNI server_name to the DNS hostname plus the service domain (for example, instead of the DNS-returned mra-host.sp.com, it changes to mra-host.example.com).

b. The Expressway-E searches its certificate store to find a certificate matching the SNI hostname.

- If it finds a match, the Expressway-E sends back the certificate (SAN/dnsName=SNI hostname).

- Otherwise, MRA returns its platform certificate.

c. The client validates the server certificate:

- If the certificate is verified, SSL setup continues and SSL setup finishes successfully.

- Otherwise, a certificate error occurs.

4. Application data starts. Note, for SIP and HTTPS, the application starts SSL negotiation immediately. For XMPP, the SSL connection starts after the client receives XMPP StartTLS.

Managing the Expressway's Domain Certificates

You manage the Expressway's domain certificates through the Domain Certificates page (**Maintenance > Security > Domain Certificates**). These certificates are used to identify domains when multiple customers (in a multitenant environment) are sharing an Expressway-E cluster to communicate with client systems using TLS encryption and with web browsers over HTTPS. You can use the Domain Certificates page to

- View details about the currently loaded certificate

- Generate a CSR

- Upload a new domain certificate

- Configure the ACME service to automatically submit a CSR to an ACME provider and automatically deploy the resulting server certificate

Note that using certificates based on RSA keys is highly recommended. Other types of certificate, such as those based on DSA keys, are not tested and might not work with the Expressway in all scenarios. Use the Trusted CA Certificate page to manage the list of certificates for the CAs trusted by this Expressway.

When you click a domain, the Domain Certificate Data section shows information about the specific domain certificate currently loaded on the Expressway. To view the currently uploaded domain certificate file, click Show (Decoded) to view it in a human-readable form, or click Show (PEM File) to view the file in its raw format. To delete the currently uploaded domain, click Delete. Do not allow your domain certificate to expire, as this may cause other external systems to reject your certificate and prevent the Expressway from being able to connect to those systems.

The following steps are for adding a new domain:

Step 1.   Go to **Maintenance > Security > Domain Certificates**.

Step 2.   Click **New**.

Step 3.   Under New Local Domain, enter the name of the domain you wish to add. An example valid domain name is 100.example-name.com.

Step 4.   Click **Create Domain**.

Step 5.   The new domain is added on the Domain Certificates page and you can proceed to upload a certificate for the domain.

The Expressway can generate domain CSRs, which removes the need to use an external
mechanism to generate and obtain certificate requests. To generate a CSR:

Step 1.   Go to **Maintenance > Security > Domain Certificates**.

Step 2.   Click the domain for which you wish to generate a CSR.

Step 3.   Click **Generate CSR** to go to the Generate CSR page.

Step 4.   Enter the required properties for the certificate.

Step 5.   Click **Generate CSR**. The system produces a signing request and an associated
private key. The private key is stored securely on the Expressway and cannot be
viewed or downloaded. *Never* disclose your private key, not even to the certificate authority.

Step 6.   You are returned to the Domain Certificate page, from which you can

- Download the request to your local file system so that it can be sent to a
  CA. You are prompted to save the file (the exact wording depends on your
  browser).

- View the current request. Click **Show (Decoded)** to view it in a human-
  readable form, or click **Show (PEM File)** to view the file in its raw format.

NOTE   The following are guidelines to generating a certificate signing request:

- Only one signing request can be in progress at any one time, because the Expressway
  must keep track of the private key file associated with the current request. To discard
  the current request and start a new request, click Discard CSR.

- The user interface provides an option to set the digest algorithm. The default is set to
  SHA-256, with options to change it to SHA-384 or SHA-512.

- The user interface provides an option to set the key length. Expressway supports a key
  length of 1024, 2048, or 4096 bits.

When you receive the signed domain certificate back from the certificate authority, you
need to upload it to the Expressway. Use the Upload New Certificate section to replace the
current domain certificate with a new certificate.

To upload a domain certificate:

Step 1.   Go to **Maintenance > Security > Domain Certificates**.

Step 2.   Click the **Browse** button in the Upload New Certificate section to select and
upload the domain certificate PEM file.

Step 3.   If you used an external system to generate the CSR, you must also upload the
server private key PEM file that was used to encrypt the domain certificate.

(The private key file will have been automatically generated and stored earlier if the Expressway was used to produce the CSR for this domain certificate.)

- The server private key PEM file must not be password protected.

- You cannot upload a server private key if a certificate signing request is in progress.

Step 4. Click **Upload Domain Certificate Data.**

The ACME service on the Expressway-E, starting from release X12.5, can request and deploy domain certificates (used with SNI).

When you go to **Maintenance > Security > Domain Certificates,** the list of domains has an ACME column that shows the status of the ACME service for each domain. Click View/Edit next to the domain name to enable the ACME service.

The process of configuring ACME service for domain certificates is the same as it is for the server certificate, only from a different place in the Expressway-E interface. See the *Cisco Expressway Certificate Creation and Use Deployment Guide* on the Expressway Configuration Guides page for more information.

When a CSR is generated, a single request and private key combination is generated for that peer only. If you have a cluster of Expressways, you must generate a separate signing request on each peer. Those requests must then be sent to the CA and the returned domain certificates uploaded to each relevant peer. Make sure that the correct domain certificate is uploaded to the appropriate peer, otherwise the stored private key on each peer will not correspond to the uploaded certificate.

Exam Preparation Tasks

As mentioned in the section "How to Use This Book" in the Introduction, you have a couple of choices for exam preparation: the exercises here, Chapter 22, "Final Preparation," and the exam simulation questions in the Pearson Test Prep practice test software.

Review All Key Topics

Review the most important topics in this chapter, noted with the Key Topics icon in the outer margin of the page. Table 5-5 lists a reference of these key topics and the page numbers on which each is found.

Table 5-5 Key Topics for Chapter 5

Key Topic Element	Description	Page Number
Paragraph	Encryption policies	71
Paragraph	Expressway certificates	72
List	Testing client certificates	79

Complete Tables and Lists from Memory

There are no memory tables or lists in this chapter.

Define Key Terms

Define the following key terms from this chapter and check your answers in the glossary:

Advanced Encryption Standard (AES), application programming interface (API), Automated Certificate Management Environment (ACME), back-to-back user agent (B2BUA), certificate authority (CA), certificate revocation list (CRL), certificate signing request (CSR), Cisco Unified Communications Manager (Unified CM), Hypertext Transfer Protocol (HTTP), Hypertext Transfer Protocol Secure (HTTPS), Lightweight Directory Access Protocol (LDAP), Online Certificate Status Protocol (OCSP), Real-time Transport Control Protocol (RTCP), Real-time Transport Protocol (RTP), regular expression (regex), Secure Real-time Transport Protocol (SRTP), Server Name Indication (SNI), Session Initiation Protocol (SIP), Transmission Control Protocol (TCP), Transport Layer Security (TLS)

Q&A

The answers to these questions appear in Appendix A. For more practice with exam format questions, use the Pearson Test Prep practice test software.

1. If adding a cluster, will you need to generate two CSRs for each server?

2. What will happen if the time stamp for the certificate has expired?

CHAPTER 6

Registration on Cisco Expressway

This chapter covers the following topics:

Registration Conflict Policy: Explains how to use the Registration Conflict Policy on the Cisco Expressway to control H.323 endpoint registration.

Registration Restriction Policy: Explains how to use the Registration Restriction Policy on the Cisco Expressway to control which endpoints are allowed or denied registration for both H.323 and SIP.

Registration Authentication: Describes how to control registration to the Cisco Expressway using MD5 encryption and authentication.

Subzones and Membership Rules: Recapitulates all the policies mentioned throughout this chapter by reviewing the registration process, examining how each of these policies fits into the bigger registration picture, and concluding with an explanation of the Subzones and Membership Rules.

Before calls can be made, endpoints must first register to the call control server. When it comes to registration to the Cisco Expressway, there are many differences from registration to the Cisco Unified Communications Manager (Unified CM). Out of the box there is very little that must be configured before endpoints will be able to register with either SIP or H.323. However, the Expressway has several policies that enable an administrator to control which endpoints are allowed to register. This extra layer of security can affect many other aspects within the Expressway environment.

Although this chapter does not cover any objectives from the Implementing Cisco Collaboration Cloud and Edge Solutions (CLCEI) exam 300-820, it does establish a foundation for other topics you will be required to know for the exam.

"Do I Know This Already?" Quiz

The "Do I Know This Already?" quiz enables you to assess whether you should read this entire chapter thoroughly or jump to the "Exam Preparation Tasks" section. If you are in doubt about your answers to these questions or your own assessment of your knowledge of the topics, read the entire chapter. Table 6-1 lists the major headings in this chapter and their corresponding "Do I Know This Already?" quiz questions. You can find the answers in Appendix A, "Answers to the 'Do I Know This Already?' Quizzes and Review Questions."

Table 6-1 "Do I Know This Already?" Section-to-Question Mapping

Foundation Topics Section	Questions
Registration Conflict Policy	1–2
Registration Restriction Policy	3–4
Registration Authentication	5–6
Subzones and Membership Rules	7–8

CAUTION The goal of self-assessment is to gauge your mastery of the topics in this chapter. If you do not know the answer to a question or are only partially sure of the answer, you should mark that question as wrong for purposes of the self-assessment. Giving yourself credit for an answer you correctly guess skews your self-assessment results and might provide you with a false sense of security.

1. Which of the following settings can affect how long an H.323 registration remains in the database of the Expressway?

    a. Call Time to Live

    b. Registration Time to Live

    c. Time to Live

    d. Registration Conflict Policy

2. What setting does Cisco recommend configuring the Registration Conflict Policy to when endpoints are configured with static IP addresses?

    a. Overwrite

    b. Reject

    c. Allow

    d. Deny

3. The Restriction Policy option is set to Deny List on the Expressway, and an Allow List rule is created using Regex for 55/d/d.* Which of the following statements is true when an endpoint tries to register with the alias 5401@cisco.com?

    a. The registration will fail because the Allow List rule requires 55 to precede any alias registering.

    b. The registration will fail because the Deny List has been enabled.

    c. The registration will succeed because the Allow List ends in .*, which allows anything to register.

    d. The registration will succeed because the Deny List is enabled but there is not a rule in the Deny List to prevent registration.

4. When enabling the Registration Restriction Policy on the Expressway, what options exist?

    a. Allow List, Deny List, or both

    b. Allow List or Deny List only

    c. Allow List, Deny List, or Policy Service

    d. Allow List, Deny List, External Policy Service, or Internal Policy Service

5. What protocol is used for authentication over SIP endpoints?

    a. Digest

    b. MD5

    c. H.235

    d. NTP

6. Which of the following statements is true regarding configuring Registration Authentication on the Expressway?

    a. Authentication can be enabled universally across the Expressway or based on individual Subzones.

    b. Authentication requires signed certificates to secure communications between the endpoint and the Expressway.

    c. The Expressway can use the Local Database and an LDAP server for authentication credentials at the same time.

    d. The Expressway can use either the Local Database or an LDAP server for authentication credentials, but only one can be enabled at a time.

7. Which of the following logical components that make up the Cisco Expressway can be used to connect a call to an endpoint not registered to the Expressway?

    a. Local Zone

    b. Default Subzone

    c. Traversal Subzone

    d. Default Zone

    e. Link

    f. Subzone

8. What number does the binary value 11000000 represent?

    a. 192

    b. 128

    c. 224

    d. 144

Foundation Topics

Registration Conflict Policy

One of the security features the Cisco Expressway offers is the **Registration Conflict Policy**. This policy does not ever need to be enabled because it is always operational in one of two modes: Reject or Overwrite. However, the Registration Conflict Policy is only operational within the H.323 standard for communication. The reason the Expressway includes this policy is that duplicate aliases cannot exist within the H.323 standard. This behavior can be contrasted with SIP, which does support the use of duplicate aliases. A SIP server routes a call request out to every device that is registered with an alias that matches the dialed alias. The H.323 gatekeeper only routes a call request out to a single alias match; therefore, if duplicate aliases attempt to register from different endpoints, an error message is generated and the call attempt fails.

Because the Registration Conflict Policy does not need to be enabled, the administrator only needs to configure it to enact the desired behavior. If the Conflict Policy is configured to Reject, which is the default setting, any device that tries to register to the Expressway with an H.323 alias that conflicts with another device already registered with the same alias information will be rejected. For example, if endpoint 1 has an IP address of 192.168.1.101 and is registered to the Expressway with the H.323 **E.164 alias** 6501 and endpoint 2 with the IP address of 192.168.1.102 tries to register with the H.323 E.164 alias 6501, the Expressway will send a **Registration Reject (RRJ)** message to endpoint 2 rejecting the registration attempt. The error message that would be logged in the Cisco Expressway would be Expressway: Event="Registration Rejected" Reason="duplicate alias".

If an organization wants to use H.323, then Cisco recommends that the endpoints be configured with static IP addresses and the Conflict Policy be left at the default value of Reject. The reason for this recommendation is that H.323 registrations do not drop out of the gatekeeper registration database immediately after the endpoint loses connection to the gatekeeper. The Expressway has a **Time to Live** setting that determines how long an H.323 registration remains in the database before the endpoint is required to renew the registration. The default value for this setting is 1800 seconds, or 30 minutes, and it can be changed to as little as 60 seconds or as much as 65534 seconds. Assume for a moment that DHCP is used for endpoint addressing instead of statically assigned IP addresses. Endpoint 1 has been assigned a DHCP address of 192.168.1.101 and registers to the Expressway with an H.323 E.164 alias of 6501. After a reboot of the endpoint, the DHCP server assigns a new IP address of 192.168.1.103 and the endpoint tries to register again to the Expressway with the H.323 E.164 alias of 6501. This time the Expressway sends a RRJ to the endpoint because there is already a registration entry with a different IP address using the same alias, and the Time-to-Live counter has not yet expired. Therein lies the problem that can be easily resolved with statically assigning IP addresses to the endpoints. However, if the enterprise environment requires DHCP addresses to be used on the endpoints, there is another setting that can be used with the Conflict Policy.

If the Registration Conflict Policy is configured as Overwrite, and any device tries to register to the Expressway with an alias that already exists within the registration database, the entry that is registered will be unregistered and the device trying to register will receive a **Registration Confirm (RCF)** message from the Expressway confirming the registration request. Using the same example that was previously described, the address record of 6501 associated to IP address 192.168.1.101 would be unregistered and the new RRQ for the alias 6501 associated with IP address 192.168.1.103 would be allowed to register. With that said, the limitation of configuring the Expressway with the Registration Conflict Policy set to Overwrite should be obvious. Should a different endpoint try to register via H.323 with the same E.164 alias as an endpoint already registered to the same Expressway while the

6

Conflict Policy is set to Overwrite, the endpoint currently registered will be unregistered. After unregistering from the Expressway, that endpoint would immediately attempt to register again, causing the second endpoint to unregister. This cycle would continue, causing potentially serious call routing issues. The Cisco Expressway has no built-in mechanism to contend with this issue. For this reason, Cisco recommends that H.323 endpoints registering to the Expressway use static IP addresses and the Registration Conflict Policy be left at the default value of Reject. Keep in mind that this setting is an H.323 setting and has no bearing on SIP registrations. Additionally, multiple SIP endpoints can register with the same alias on an Expressway without any routing issues.

To set the Registration Conflict Policy, follow these steps:

Key Topic

Step 1.   From the web interface of the Cisco Expressway, navigate to **Configuration > Protocols > H.323.**

Step 2.   In the Registration Conflict Mode field, choose a value from the drop-down list (**Overwrite** or **Reject**), as shown in Figure 6-1.

Step 3.   Click **Save.**

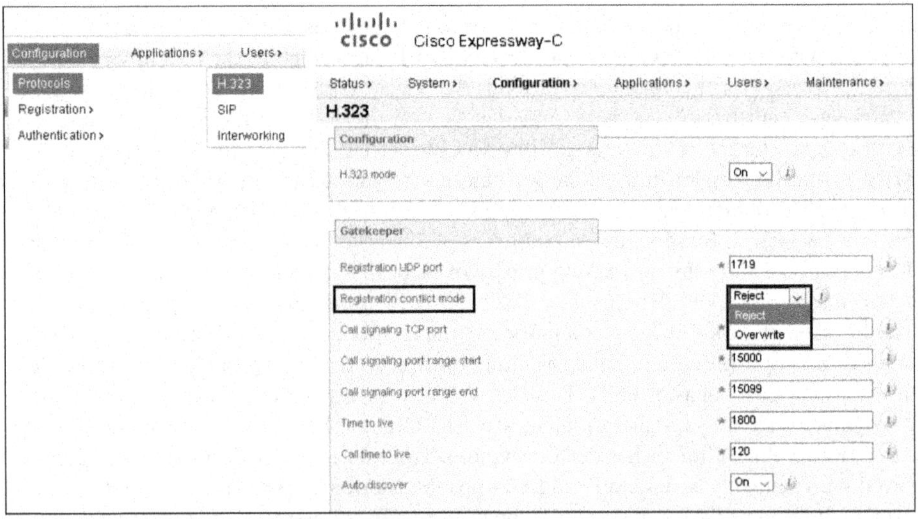

Figure 6-1   *Configuring the Registration Conflict Policy on the Cisco Expressway*

Registration Restriction Policy

Chapter 3, "Initial Configuration Settings on the Cisco Expressway," discusses SIP and H.323 settings on the Expressway for registration. As that chapter mentioned, SIP needs to be enabled and at least one domain must be established within the database before SIP endpoints can register to the Expressway. No settings have to be configured for H.323 endpoints to register to the Expressway. The only security policy that exists preconfigured out of the box on the Expressway that affects how endpoints register is the Registration Conflict Policy, and that only impacts H.323 endpoint registration. We mention all this to emphasize that there is no security enabled on the Expressway that will limit or control endpoint registration out of the box. Any endpoint that is pointed to the Expressway for registration will be allowed to register without restriction. You have to manually and purposefully enable and configure any limitations you want to enforce. The good news is that there are two very good policies that can be configured to control registration, and they both affect SIP and H.323 equally and without bias.

The first of these policies is the **Registration Restriction Policy**. This policy service controls which endpoints are allowed to register to the Expressway, and you can configure it to use an *Allow List* or a *Deny List*. There are two settings that you must configure when configuring the Registration Restriction Policy. You must first enable the service by selecting Allow List or Deny List from the Configuration drop-down menu. Note that the only way to enable this policy is to choose the list type you want to use, allow or deny, meaning both the Deny List and Allow List cannot be enabled simultaneously. You must choose one or the other. Once enabled, you must then configure the policies themselves to determine what endpoints will be allowed or denied registration based on their alias. If the Expressway is configured to use the Allow List but no Allow List policies are configured, all endpoints will be *forbidden* to register to the Expressway, because no alias pattern is "allowed" to register. In like manner, if the Expressway is configured to use the Deny List and no Deny List policies are configured, all endpoints attempting to register to the Expressway will be allowed, because no alias pattern is "denied" from registration.

To enable the Registration Restriction Policy, follow these steps:

Step 1. From the web interface of the Expressway, navigate to **Configuration > Registration > Configuration.**

Step 2. In the Restriction Policy field, choose a value from the drop-down list. The options include

- Allow List

- Deny List

- Policy Service

Step 3. Click **Save.**

Step 4. Assuming you have selected either Allow List or Deny List, next you need to navigate to either **Configuration > Registration > Allow List** or **Configuration > Registration Deny List** depending on which policy is being used.

Step 5. Click **New.**

Step 6. In the Pattern Type field, enter the type of pattern you are allowing or denying.

Step 7. In the Pattern String field, enter the characters and wildcards you are using as the criteria to allow or deny.

Step 8. Click **Add Allow List** pattern or **Add Deny List** pattern.

There are four pattern types that can be used when configuring registration restriction policies: exact match, prefix, suffix, and regular expression. Exact match refers to the entire alias and no part can be left out. Prefix and suffix have no limit on the length of characters they can represent. However, they can only represent a part of the alias, not the whole thing. Let's say we were matching the alias 6501@cisco.com using the previously mentioned methods.

Obviously, the entire alias would have to be used for an exact match to work. Using just 6501 or just cisco.com would not be adequate for an exact match. If prefix were used, then you could get away with just 6501. In fact, you could use any alias pattern from 6 to 6501@cisco.co (leaving the "m" off the end). So long as the complete alias is not included in the match, any part of it can be used. Likewise, suffix can be used in the same manner. Anything from m (the last character) to 501@cisco.com (everything except the first character) can be used.

Chapter 4, "Regular Expressions on the Cisco Expressway," covered how to use regular expressions. This is the first place in the Expressway these expressions can be used. The nice part about using regular expressions in registration restriction policies is that they can be used to represent the middle part of an alias pattern. Using the same alias example previously described, a regular expression such as 650[^0]@cisco\.com could be used to match alias patterns based on the fourth number of the first numeric part of the alias. Basically, this pattern will match all aliases starting at 6501@cisco.com through 6509@cisco.com, but will not match 6500@cisco.com. Figure 6-2 illustrates the menus used to enable an Allow List on the Expressway and configure patterns for that Allow List.

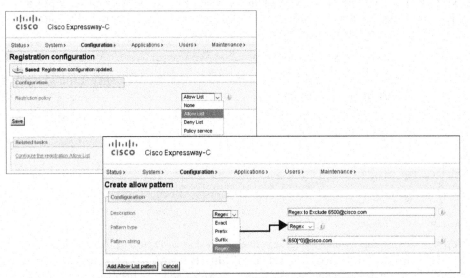

Figure 6-2 *Registration Restriction Policy Allow List on the Cisco Expressway*

The same method can be used to create deny policies within the Expressway. However, an alternative method to add devices to the Deny List also exists whereby endpoints already registered to the Expressway can be unregistered and blocked from registering again. From the web interface of the Expressway, navigate to **Status > Registration > By Device**, check the box beside registered devices you want to add to the Deny List, and then click the Unregister and Block button at the bottom of the screen. This process unregisters the devices from the Expressway and adds their entire alias information to the Deny List so they cannot register to the Expressway again. Bear in mind that this option only exists if the Deny List has been enabled. If not, then the only option available from the **Registration > By Device** menu would be to Unregister an endpoint without the "block" option.

When enabling the Registration Restriction Policy from the **Configuration > Registration > Configuration** menu, there is a third option apart from Allow List and Deny List that is rarely discussed: Policy Service. The Policy Service option is used if you want to refer all Registration Restriction Policy decisions out to an external service. If you select this option, an extra set of configuration fields appears so that you can specify the connection details of the external service.

The Expressway has built-in support for registration policy and call policy configuration. Call policy will be discussed more in Chapter 7, "Cisco Expressway Call Processing Order." It also supports **Call Processing Language (CPL)** for implementing more complex policy decisions. CPL is designed as a machine-generated language and is not immediately intuitive; while the Expressway can be loaded with CPL to implement advanced call policy decisions, complex CPL is difficult to write and maintain. The Expressway's external policy feature allows policy decisions to be made by an external system, which can then instruct the Expressway on the course of action to take, such as whether to accept a registration, fork a call, and so on. The external policy server can make routing decisions based on data available from any source that the policy server has access to, allowing companies to make routing decisions based on their specific requirements. When the Expressway is configured to use an external policy server, the Expressway sends the external policy server a service request (over HTTP or HTTPS), and the service sends a response back containing a CPL snippet, which the Expressway then executes.

To configure the registration policy to refer all Registration Restriction Policy decisions to an external service, use the following steps:

Step 1. From the web interface of the Expressway, navigate to **Configuration > Registration > Configuration**.

Step 2. From the Restriction Policy drop-down list, choose **Policy Service**.

Step 3. Configure the fields identified in Table 6-2.

Table 6-2   External Policy Service Configuration Information for Registration Restriction Policy

Field	Description	Usage Tips
Protocol	The protocol used to connect to the policy service. The default is HTTPS.	The Expressway automatically supports HTTP to HTTPS redirection when communicating with the policy service server.
Certificate verification mode	When connecting over HTTPS, this setting controls whether the certificate presented by the policy server is verified. If set to On, for the Expressway to connect to a policy server over HTTPS, the Expressway must have a root CA certificate loaded that authorizes that server's server certificate. Also, the certificate's Subject Common Name or Subject Alternative Name must match one of the Server Address fields.	The Expressway's root CA certificates are loaded via **Maintenance > Security > Trusted CA Certificate**.

Field	Description	Usage Tips
HTTPS certificate revocation list (CRL) checking	Enable this option if you want to protect certificate checking using CRLs and you have manually loaded CRL files, or you have enabled automatic CRL updates.	Go to **Maintenance > Security > CRL Management** to configure how the Expressway uploads CRL files.
Server address 1–3	Enter the IP address or fully qualified domain name (FQDN) of the server hosting the service. You can specify a port by appending :<port> to the address.	If an FQDN is specified, ensure that the Expressway has an appropriate DNS configuration that allows the FQDN to be resolved. For resiliency, up to three server addresses can be supplied.
Path	Enter the URL of the service on the server.	
Status path	Identifies the path from where the Expressway can obtain the status of the remote service. The default is Status.	The policy server must supply return status information.
Username	The username used by the Expressway to log in and query the service.	
Password	The password used by the Expressway to log in and query the service.	The maximum plaintext length is 30 characters (which is subsequently encrypted).
Default CPL	This is the fallback CPL used by the Expressway if the service is not available.	You can change it, for example, to redirect to an answer service or recorded message.

Step 4.   Click **Save.**

The Expressway should connect to the policy service server and start using the service for registration policy decisions. Any connection problems will be reported on this page. Check the Status area at the bottom of the page and check for additional information messages against the Server Address fields.

As mentioned before, Registration Restriction Policy operates for both SIP and H.323. You can also control registrations at the **subzone** level. Each subzone can be configured to allow or deny registrations assigned to it via the subzone **Membership Rules**. This means, for example, that you can deny the registration of endpoints with specific IP addresses or sub-net ranges by setting up Membership Rules for those addresses/ranges and setting the target subzone to deny those registration requests. Subzones and Membership Rules are covered in more depth in the last section of this chapter. The error message the Expressway will report for all devices that are blocked by this restriction policy service will state **Expressway: Event="Registration Rejected" Reason="not permitted by policy"**.

Registration Authentication

Registration Authentication is the other form of security that has the ability to control which endpoints can register to the Expressway. Registration Authentication should not be confused with administrator authentication or user authentication. Although they operate in a similar manner, administrator and user authentication are a different service of the Expressway and as such are configured from different menus within the Expressway web interface.

When Authentication is enabled, it affects all devices no matter if they're registered H.323 or SIP. However, each of these communication protocols uses different encryption standards for authentication. SIP uses an encryption process known as **Digest**, and H.323 uses an encryption standard known as **H.235**. Both H.235 and Digest use a system that is called **Message Digest Algorithm 5 (MD5)**, which is a messaging system that uses a time stamp from a time server as part of its encryption key. Therefore, no matter whether you are using H.323 or SIP with authentication, it is critical that both the Expressway and the device registering to it are pointed to the same **Network Time Protocol (NTP)** server or synced cluster.

Key Topic

Authentication policy is applied by the Expressway at the zone and subzone levels. We will discuss more about how authentication is used at the zone level in Chapter 9, "Multisite Collaboration Solutions." Authentication controls how the Expressway challenges incoming messages for provisioning, registration, phone books, and calls from the subsequent zone or subzone and whether those messages are rejected, treated as authenticated, or treated as unauthenticated within the Expressway. The primary authentication policy configuration options and their associated behavior are as follows:

- **Check credentials:** Verifies the credentials using the relevant authentication method. Note that in some scenarios, messages are not challenged.

- **Do not check credentials:** Does not verify the credentials and allows the message to be processed.

- **Treat as authenticated:** Does not verify the credentials and allows the message to be processed as if having been authenticated.

This might be a little confusing to some readers as to why enabling authentication is not as simple as toggling a switch on or off. There are numerous types of endpoints from many different vendors, and many different scenarios by which authentication may or may not be used. A company may need to cater to endpoints from third-party suppliers that do not support authentication within their registration mechanism. Some companies may want to use authentication for endpoint registration in more secure areas, and not use authentication in less secure areas. Additionally, there are certain features within the Expressway that cannot operate unless packets are marked as authenticated. Whatever the reason authentication may or may not be used is only the justification as to why this policy service exists within the Expressway. With all that said, an explanation of how these three settings operate can be rationalized through a simple analogy.

Imagine walking into a club. The bouncer at the entrance to the club checks your ID to verify you are over the legal drinking age limit and then stamps your hand. When you walk up to the bar, the bartender simply needs to see your stamp to serve you an alcoholic beverage. This is the same as the Check Credentials setting. Once the bouncer verified your identity and age, the stamp was all you needed to fully utilize the services within the club.

6

Now imagine walking up to that same club. This time there is no bouncer at the door, so you just walk in. This time when you go up to the bar, the bartender cannot serve you any alcoholic drinks because you don't have the stamp. You can go into the club; you just can't drink. This is the same as the Do Not Check Credentials option. Endpoints can register to the Expressway with this type of encryption, but there are some services they just can't use.

In a third scenario you walk up to the same club as before. The bouncer is not there this time either, but the stamp and ink pad are sitting on his chair at the entrance. So, you stamp your own hand and go into the club. No one actually checks your credentials. But you can now order drinks at the bar because you have the stamp. This is the same as the Treat As Authenticated option. Messages sent through the Expressway will be marked as authenticated even though they never actually had their credentials checked. However, because these endpoints have the authenticated stamp, they can utilize all the services available through the Expressway.

The first step to setting up Registration Authentication is to enable the authentication policy at the subzone level. All Subzones support authentication. Because we have not yet discussed Subzones on the Expressway, we will use the Default Subzone to illustrate how authentication can be enabled. From the web interface of the Expressway, navigate to **Configuration > Local Zone > Default Subzone**. In the Policy section at the top of the screen, change the Authentication Policy field to Check Credentials. Scroll to the bottom of the page and click Save. You have now enabled Registration Authentication. The next step is to configure the authentication credential in the database.

The database type used to verify credentials for Registration Authentication can be local or remote through **Microsoft Active Directory (AD)** or an **OpenLDAP** server. The default is to use the Local Database located on the Expressway itself. If Local Database is the database type being used, the administrator needs to go into the Local Database and create a username and password. Multiple credentials can be created, and SIP and H.323 can use the same set of credentials. They are not protocol specific. However, both the username and password are case-sensitive, so pay attention to syntax when creating the credentials. All letters, numbers, and special characters can be used. To configure the Local Database, navigate to **Configuration > Authentication > Devices > Local Database**. You should see a list of usernames with the source that created the credentials. They can be created locally on the Expressway itself, or through TMS. Click New to create a new set of credentials, enter the name and password you want to use in the respective fields, and click Create Credentials. This creates the authentication credentials that endpoints must use to register to the Expressway.

You can configure the Expressway to use both the Local Database and an **H.350** directory.

If an H.350 directory is configured, the Expressway will always attempt to verify any Digest credentials presented to it by first checking against the Local Database before checking against the H.350 directory. If an LDAP database is used, then you need to configure the LDAP settings and download and configure appropriate schemas on the LDAP server itself. If you navigate to **Configuration > Authentication > Devices** in the Expressway, you will see three additional menu options to the Local Database:

- **Active Directory Service:** Should be enabled and configured to communicate with a Microsoft Active Directory service.

- **H.350 directory service:** Should be enabled and configured to communicate with an OpenLDAP directory service.

- **H.350 directory schemas:** Regardless of which LDAP service you choose to use, there are schemas that you need to download so that you can configure the LDAP service for use in this capacity.

Each LDAP service type has four schema files that can be downloaded. Table 6-3 identifies these four types of schemas along with the ITU specification for these schemas and their descriptions.

Table 6-3   LDAP Schemas for Registration Authentication on Cisco Expressway

ITU Specification	Schema	Description
H.350	commObject schema	Directory services architecture for multimedia conferencing; an LDAP schema to represent endpoints on the network.
H.350.1	H323Identity schema	Directory services architecture for H.323; an LDAP schema to represent H.323 endpoints.
H.350.2	H235Identity schema	Directory services architecture for H.235; an LDAP schema to represent H.235 elements.
H.350.4	SIPIdentity schema	Directory services architecture for SIP; an LDAP schema to represent SIP endpoints.

After you download the schemas from the Expressway, you need to install them on the LDAP Directory server of your choosing. To install the schemas on a Microsoft Active Directory server, open an elevated command prompt from the onscreen display of the Microsoft Windows Server hosting this service. You can do so by right-clicking Command Prompt and selecting Run As Administrator. Enter the following command in the command prompt:

```
Ldifde -i -c DC=X <ldap_base> -f filename.ldf
```

where *<ldap_base>* is the base DN for your Active Directory server.

After you have installed the schemas on the AD server, you need to create an organizational hierarchy by adding H.350 objects. First, use the following steps to create an organizational hierarchy:

Step 1.   Open the Active Directory **Users and Computers** MMC snap-in.

Step 2.   Under your BaseDN, right-click and select **New Organizational Unit**.

Step 3.   Create an organizational unit called **h350**.

It is good practice to keep the H.350 directory in its own organizational unit to separate H.350 objects from other types of objects. This allows access controls to be set up, which will only allow the Expressway read access to the BaseDN and therefore limit access to other sections of the directory. Next you need to add the H.350 objects.

Step 4.   Create an LDIF file with the following contents:

```
# MeetingRoom1 endpoint
dn: commUniqueId=comm1,ou=h350,DC=X
objectClass: commObject
objectClass: h323Identity
objectClass: h235Identity
objectClass: SIPIdentity
commUniqueId: comm1
h323Identityh323-ID: MeetingRoom1
h323IdentitydialedDigits: 626262
h235IdentityEndpointID: meetingroom1
h235IdentityPassword: mypassword
SIPIdentityUserName: meetingroom1
SIPIdentityPassword: mypassword
SIPIdentitySIPURI: sip:MeetingRoom@X
```

Step 5.   Add the LDIF file to the server using the following command:

```
ldifde -i -c DC=X <ldap_base> -f filename.ldf
```

where *<ldap_base>* is the base DN of your Active Directory server.

This example adds a single endpoint with an H.323 ID alias of MeetingRoom1, an E.164 alias of 626262, and a SIP URI of MeetingRoom@X. The entry also has H.235 and SIP credentials of ID meetingroom1 and password mypassword, which are used during authentication. H.323 registrations look for the H.323 and H.235 attributes; SIP looks for the SIP attributes. Therefore, if your endpoint is registering with just one protocol, you do not need to include elements relating to the other. Take special note that the SIP URI in the LDIF file must be prefixed by sip:.

As you can see, the process for using Registration Authentication through LDAP directory services is quite complex. For this reason, most people use only the Local Database for Registration Authentication. Installing schemas for OpenLDAP is even more complicated and less commonly used. Therefore, we will not be covering this procedure in the book. Refer to the *Cisco Expressway Administrator Guide* for information on how to install and configure schemas using OpenLDAP.

The last task in configuring the Expressway for Registration Authentication is to ensure the NTP settings have been configured and that there is at least one active server. You can verify this setting under the **System > Time** menu from the Expressway web interface. Up to five different NTP servers can be specified, and the synchronization status for each NTP server is shown on the same page. Once this process is accomplished, the Expressway sends a "get time" message to the NTP server, and receives from the NTP server a "sent time" message. This time stamp will be used for each authentication sequence. Figure 6-3 illustrates the settings that must be configured on the Expressway to use Registration Authentication.

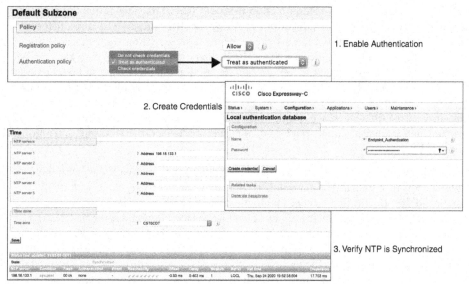

Figure 6-3 *Registration Authentication Settings on the Cisco Expressway*

Once the Expressway has been configured for authentication, the registering devices need to be configured for authentication as well. It is necessary to turn on authentication for H.323 but not for SIP. Digest is built into SIP as an automatic feature that's used when required and therefore does not need to be enabled. With H.323, it is a separate standard completely and must be enabled to operate. Configure the same username and password combo that exists in the Local Database of the Expressway, or on the LDAP server if LDAP is being used instead. Finally, do not forget to configure NTP on the endpoint. The time stamp the endpoint receives from the NTP server must match exactly to the time stamp received by the Expressway, or else registration will fail. Therefore, the same NTP server should be used on both the endpoint and the Expressway. All other settings required on the endpoint for registration must still be configured. Once the endpoint is configured and ready for registration, it attempts to communicate immediately with the Expressway.

After all the configuration settings are correct on the endpoint, it initiates a handshake with the Expressway to perform a key exchange so that data shared between the endpoint and the Expressway can be securely encrypted and decrypted. Once the encryption is established, the device must first send authentication credentials to the Expressway for authentication. The Expressway then performs an authentication challenge in order to verify if the username and password are valid. The Expressway first verifies the information against the Local Database. If the credentials are determined invalid and remote authentication is enabled through an LDAP server, the Expressway sends an H.350 request to that server to verify the credentials. If the credentials are still not valid, then the Expressway returns an Authentication Failure message back to the endpoint and registration fails. If the credentials do check out, then the Expressway sends an Authentication OK message and the registration process can continue. This part of the process is the same for both H.323 and SIP. After this point they follow a slightly different process for registration. We will begin by explaining the H.323 registration process.

In H.323, the endpoint sends a **Registration Request (RRQ)** message to the Expressway. The Expressway responds with a **Request in Progress (RIP)** message because, before it can allow any device to register, it must check the other security policies in place. Those policies, as have already been discussed, are the Registration Conflict Policy, which can be set to Reject or Overwrite, and the Registration Restriction Policy, which can be set to Allow List or Deny List. Finally, the Expressway checks Membership Rules (discussed in the next section). Provided everything to this point has passed, the Expressway responds with a Registration Confirm (RCF) message and the endpoint is registered. If there were any issue with these policies, the Expressway would send a Registration Reject (RRJ) message and registration would fail.

With a SIP endpoint, although the messaging is slightly different, the process within the Expressway is very similar. The endpoint sends a "Register" message, along with its IP address and the SIP URI that has been configured on the endpoint. The Expressway checks the Registration Restriction Policy for an Allow List or Deny List, and it verifies that the domain in the URI matches the domain that is configured in the Domains section of the Expressway. Like with the H.323 endpoint, the Expressway also checks the Membership Rules. Provided all this passes the test, the Expressway sends a SIP 200OK message and the endpoint is registered. If any of this fails, then the Expressway sends a 40x error code and registration fails. Figure 6-4 illustrates the registration process with all the registration security components mentioned throughout this chapter.

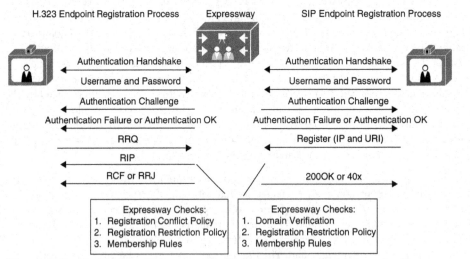

Figure 6-4   *Registration Process on the Cisco Expressway with Security Components*

Subzones and Membership Rules

Examining the registration process previously described, the last component that is verified before an endpoint is allowed to register is the Membership Rules. To best understand what Membership Rules are and how they work, you first need to understand the basic logical components that make up the Expressway. The Cisco Expressway can be divided into five logical components, which can be categorized by two main classes: Subzones and Zones.

Subzones and Zones exist within the Expressway for different purposes; they are not used for the same purpose, so it is critical to not confuse them with one another.

The **Local Zone** is the first logical component we will define for you, because it is representative of the Expressway itself. The Expressway is the Local Zone, and the Local Zone is the Expressway. All other logical components that make up the Expressway are defined in how they relate back to the Local Zone. Out of the box, the Local Zone contains by default one Default Zone, one Default Subzone, and one Traversal Subzone. Additional Subzones and additional Zones can be created within the Local Zone, but we will talk about those more later. First, we need to define the default components that come preconfigured on the Expressway.

The **Default Subzone** is a logical group within the Local Zone that all endpoints register to by default. This Subzone does not discriminate based on protocol. Both H.323 and SIP endpoints can register here so long as the Expressway has been configured to support that type of registration. This may be the only Subzone needed so long as you have uniform bandwidth and authentication requirements available between all your devices within the organization. If different bandwidth provisions or security authentication requirements are needed for different endpoints within your organization, you should create a new Subzone for each pool of devices. More on that momentarily.

The **Traversal Subzone** is another logical component of the Expressway. This Subzone is different from all other Subzones, because it is only used to manage and throttle bandwidth for any traversal calls through the Expressway. Devices registering to the Expressway will never register to the Traversal Subzone. There are four types of traversal calls on the Cisco Expressway, all of which must navigate through the Traversal Subzone: interworking, IPv4 to IPv6 traversal, firewall traversal, and dual network interface traversal, which is only available on the Expressway Edge servers.

The **Default Zone** is the default logical connection into and out of the Local Zone. If Subzones were the interior doors of a building that separate different rooms, then Zones would be the exterior doors that allow people to enter and exit the building itself. Based on this analogy, the Default Zone would be the front door to the Expressway. Devices can only register to the Default Subzone. The Default Zone and Traversal Subzone do not accept any device registration. None of these logical components—the Default Subzone, Default Zone, and Traversal Subzone—can be deleted from the Expressway. However, additional Subzones and Zones can be created and deleted.

Different types of Zones can be created on the Expressway for various network routing requirements. Neighbor Zones are used to connect to other parts of the same network. This could be within the same LAN or across the WAN. Traversal Zones are for routing into and out of a network through a firewall. Common applications of this usage include business-to-business (B2B) communication. DNS Zones are used when DNS plays a role in call routing. This zone could be on an internal or external network. We will discuss Zones more in Chapters 9 and 10.

The fifth and last default logical component that needs to be mentioned here is the humble **Link**, a logical connection between two Subzones or between a Subzone and a Zone. In the building analogy previously described, Links would be the corridors between rooms within the building. Without Links, access to these different rooms would not be possible. Consider a scenario where a SIP endpoint and an H.323 endpoint are both registered to the

Default Subzone. If Links did not exist, then these two endpoints could not call each other, even though they are registered to the same Subzone. That traversal call must be able to navigate through the Traversal Subzone in order to connect, which is rendered impossible without Links. Out of the box, the Expressway comes with a Link preconfigured between the Default Subzone and Traversal Subzone, a Link between the Default Subzone and the Default Zone, and a Link between the Default Zone and the Traversal Subzone. Unlike these other default logical components, the default Links can be deleted and created again. In fact, you can enter the command **xCommand DefaultLinksAdd** from the CLI of the Cisco Expressway to create these default Links for you. If you create other Subzones and Zones, you can create and delete Links for connecting to those logical components as well. Figure 6-5 illustrates the logical components that make up the Cisco Expressway, along with additional Subzones that can also be created for registration.

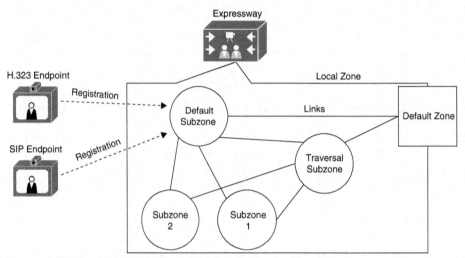

Figure 6-5 *Logical Components That Make Up the Cisco Expressway*

Continuing to build on the logical components that have already been defined, additional Subzones can be created within the Local Zone. Subzones are logical groupings of registered devices, such as endpoints, conference bridges, gateways, and so on, for the purposes of bandwidth management and access control. As seen in the previous section, Subzones allow authentication requirements to be set for endpoints attempting to register. By creating multiple Subzones, you can create an environment where some endpoints are required to present credentials before being allowed to register, while other endpoints may not be required to authenticate due to the setting on their respective Subzone. Subzones also determine the bandwidth restrictions to be applied on calls between endpoints, and whether calls are established between endpoints within the same Subzone or several different Subzones. When a new Subzone is created, two Links are also created automatically at the same time. One of those Links connects the new Subzone to the Default Subzone, and the other Link connects the new Subzone to the Traversal Subzone. Like all other Links within the Expressway, these Links can be deleted, and other Links can be created.

To create a Subzone on the Cisco Expressway, use the following steps:

Step 1. From the web interface of the Cisco Expressway, navigate to **Configuration > Local Zone > Subzones**. An easy way to remember this is that a Subzone is a logical component of the Local Zone.

Step 2. Click **New** and configure the following parameters:

- **Name:** We like to use a name like Accounting_SZ or Raleigh_SZ, depending on whether we are identifying a department or physical location.

- **Authentication Policy:** The options are Do Not Check Credentials, Treat As Authenticated, or Check Credentials

Step 3. Click the **Create Subzone** button at the bottom of the page.

We have already established that, by default, all devices register to the Default Subzone. When you create additional Subzones, you must also create Membership Rules to determine where a device will register. Membership Rules can be created using either a subnet mask or an alias pattern match. An alias pattern match can be configured as an exact match, prefix, suffix, or a regular expression.

To use the subnet function of Membership Rules, you do not have to be a master at subnetting. There is a calculator built into the Expressway that will identify the subnet ranges you are entering based on an IP address you enter and the cyber mask you associate with it. To understand these concepts, however, a basic understanding of subnetting is required. The purpose of this book is not to teach you networking principles; however, we will cover some basics to subnetting at this time.

An IPv4 address is a 32-bit address divided into four octets of 8 bits. Each bit in these addresses has a binary value, which is a base-2 numeral system represented in a zero or a one. It is often easier to think of these binary values as on or off; a one represents on and a zero represents off. A byte is made up of 8 bits, and each bit position in a byte holds a specific numeric value. If the bit is on, then you add the value of that bit to the total for the byte. If the bit is off, then you do not add the value of that bit to the total for the byte. The bit values in an octet from left to right are 128, 64, 32, 16, 8, 4, 2, and 1. Table 6-4 illustrates the binary values that total 1–7 and 255. If you were to add up all the bit values, the byte would total 255.

Table 6-4   Binary Values for 1 Byte

128	64	32	16	8	4	2	1	Byte Total
0	0	0	0	0	0	0	1	1 = 1
0	0	0	0	0	0	1	0	2 = 2
0	0	0	0	0	0	1	1	2 + 1 = 3
0	0	0	0	0	1	0	0	4 = 4
0	0	0	0	0	1	0	1	4 + 1 = 5
0	0	0	0	0	1	1	0	4 + 2 = 6
0	0	0	0	0	1	1	1	4 + 2 + 1 = 7
1	1	1	1	1	1	1	1	128 + 64 + 32 + 16 + 8 + 4 + 2 + 1 = 255

6

Understanding how values are calculated for each byte within an IPv4 address is important to understanding how Subnet masks work. A **Subnet mask** is a networking parameter that defines a range of IP addresses. Subnet masks define this range based on a number of bits that are considered static within that range, leaving the rest of the bits to dynamically change. That is the range allowed within the Subnet. Because we now know that an IPv4 address is made up of 4 bytes with 8 bits per byte, and 1 byte can have a total value of 255, a Subnet mask may look something like 255.255.255.0. This mask identifies the first 3 bytes as static, meaning they cannot change. The last byte value is zero, meaning this mask allows for 255 total addresses. If you combine this Subnet mask with the IP address of 192.168.1.0, then the total addresses within this Subnet range from 192.168.1.0 to 192.168.1.255. Because there are 8 bits per byte, the Subnet mask does not have to make the cutoff at each full byte value. For example, you could have an IP address of 192.168.1.0 and a Subnet mask of 255.255.255.128 and now the IP address range is from 192.168.1.0 to 192.168.1.127. If you change the IP address to 192.168.1.128 but leave the Subnet mask the same, then the IP address range is now from 192.168.1.128 to 192.168.1.255.

Another way of representing the Subnet mask is to use a CIDR notation, which is a suffix that follows an IP address. This number is based on the static number of bits within a Subnet mask. Therefore, if we had an IP address of 192.168.1.100 and a Subnet mask of 255.255.255.0, then we could write it using a CIDR notation of 192.168.1.100/24. The first 3 bytes are considered static in the Subnet mask, and there are 8 bits per byte; 8 times 3 is 24, hence the /24. The other example we gave previously of an IP address 192.168.1.128 and a Subnet mask of 255.255.255.128 could be written as 192.168.1.128/25. All 8 bits of the first 3 bytes are static, plus 1 bit from the fourth byte, totaling 25 bits.

Now let's bring this back to the Membership Rules on the Expressway. When you create a Membership Rule and select Subnet as the Type, you must provide two important pieces of information in that rule regarding the subnet. You must first provide the Subnet address, which can be any IP address that exists within the subnet being identified for this Membership Rule. That IP address does not have to be the starting IP address of the subnet range. It can exist anywhere within the range of the Subnet mask. The second piece of information is the Prefix length, which is the CIDR notation for the Subnet mask being configured. Once these two pieces of information have been entered into the Expressway, the calculator built into the Membership Rule automatically provides the range of IP addresses associated with the IP address and CIDR notation you configured.

For those of you reading this book who already understand how subnetting works, notice that we did not mention the network address or the broadcast address. That's because this is not true subnetting, like what you'd configure on a router. This tool only uses the basic principles of subnetting to create a range of addresses that determines which endpoints are allowed or not allowed to register to the designated Subzone based on that endpoint's IP address. Also remember from earlier in this chapter that Subzones can be configured to allow or deny registrations in the same manner as the Registration Restriction Policy. When the Subzone is configured to Allow or Deny, it is based on the Membership Rule created here. However, if an endpoint is denied registration because of this Membership Rule, that only denies registration to this Subzone, not to the Expressway. If an endpoint cannot register to any of the created Subzones based on a Membership Rule match, then it will automatically register to the Default Subzone. Figure 6-6 illustrates how Membership Rules can be configured using a Subnet mask.

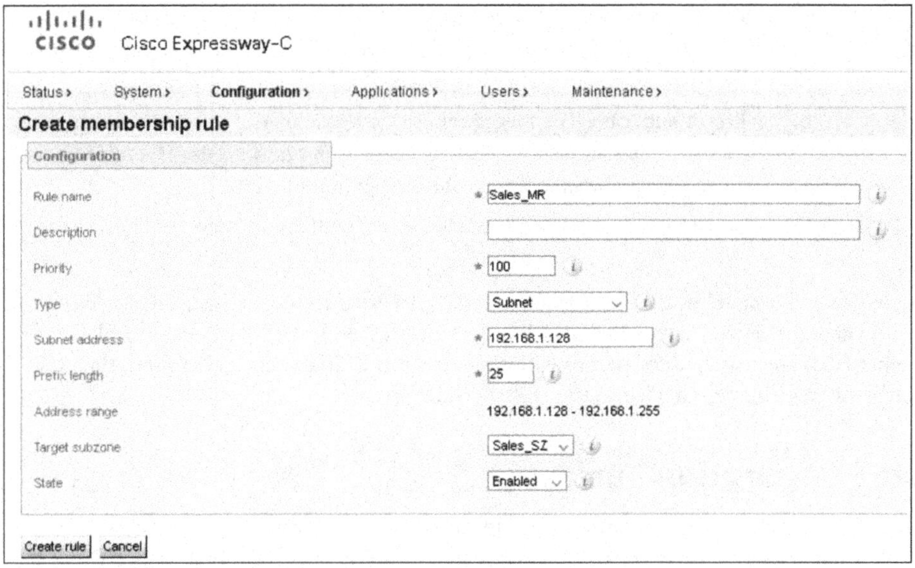

Figure 6-6 *Membership Rules Based on a Subnet Mask*

The other method by which Membership Rules can determine whether endpoints are allowed or denied registration to a Subzone is using an Alias Pattern Match. Alias Pattern Matches are based on an exact match, prefix, suffix, or regular expression. This should seem familiar to you, because these are the same methods used to create Allow List and Deny List patterns.

To create Membership Rules, use the following steps:

Step 1. From the web interface of the Cisco Expressway, navigate to **Configuration > Local Zone > Subzone Membership Rules.**

Step 2. Click **New** and configure the following Setting:

    a. **Rule name:** This is the identifying name for the rule. We like to use a naming convention similar to the Subzone it corresponds with. For example, if the Subzone is called Accounting_SZ, then the Membership Rule may be called Accounting_MR.

    b. **Description:** This is an optional setting that describes the reason this Membership Rule exists.

    c. **Priority:** The Expressway looks at all the available rules in the order of their priority. The priority can be anywhere between 1 and 65534, 1 being the highest priority, and 100 is the default priority value.

    d. **Type:** There are two types that can be selected, as previously described. The settings that follow will change based on the type selected.

        i. Subnet: If this type is selected, then the next three settings will be Subnet Address, Prefix Length, and Address Range. Address Range is not a configurable value; it displays the range of IP addresses based on how the first two settings are configured.

        ii. Alias pattern match: If this type is selected, then the next two settings will be Pattern Type and Pattern String. The Pattern Type setting can be configured as Exact, Prefix, Suffix, or Regex.

    e. **Target subzone:** The target cannot be the Traversal Subzone, because no endpoints are allowed to register there, nor can it be the Default Subzone. It can only be a Subzone created by an administrator.

Step 3. Click the **Create Rule** button to create the Membership Rule.

The first rule that matches the credentials of a device trying to register is used, the Expressway registers the device in the Subzone that is associated with the Membership Rule, and no other rules are searched for that registration attempt. If no matches are found, then the Expressway registers the device to the Default Subzone.

Exam Preparation Tasks

As mentioned in the section "How to Use This Book" in the Introduction, you have a couple of choices for exam preparation: the exercises here, Chapter 22, "Final Preparation," and the exam simulation questions in the Pearson Test Prep practice test software.

Review All Key Topics

Review the most important topics in this chapter, noted with the Key Topics icon in the outer margin of the page. Table 6-5 lists a reference of these key topics and the page numbers on which each is found.

Table 6-5   Key Topics for Chapter 6

Key Topic Element	Description	Page Number
Steps	Registration Conflict Policy steps	96
Steps	Registration Restriction Policy steps	97
Table 6-2	External Policy Service Configuration Information for the Registration Restriction Policy	99
Paragraph and List	Authentication policy configuration options	101
Table 6-3	LDAP Schemas for Registration Authentication on Cisco Expressway	103
Paragraph	H.323 registration process in Expressway	106
Paragraph	SIP registration process in Expressway	106
Steps	Subzone creation steps	109
Table 6-4	Binary Values for 1 Byte	109
Steps	Membership Rules creation steps	111

Complete Tables and Lists from Memory

Print a copy of Appendix C, "Memory Tables" (found on the companion website), or at least the section for this chapter, and complete the tables and lists from memory. Appendix D, "Memory Tables Answer Key," also on the companion website, includes completed tables and lists to check your work.

Define Key Terms

Define the following key terms from this chapter and check your answers in the glossary:

Call Processing Language (CPL), Default Subzone, Default Zone, Digest, E.164 alias, H.235, H.350, Link, Local Zone, Membership Rules, Message Digest Algorithm 5 (MD5), Microsoft Active Directory (AD), Network Time Protocol (NTP), OpenLDAP, Registration Authentication, Registration Confirm (RCF), Registration Conflict Policy, Registration Reject (RRJ), Registration Request (RRQ), Registration Restriction Policy, Request in Progress (RIP), Subnet mask, Time to Live, subzone, Traversal Subzone

Q&A

The answers to these questions appear in Appendix A. For more practice with exam format questions, use the Pearson Test Prep practice test software.

1. What are the three configuration options for the Registration Restriction Policy?

2. List the three configuration options for the Registration Authentication policy.

3. What are the three main steps to configure Registration Authentication on the Expressway?

4. List the five default logical components of the Cisco Expressway.

CHAPTER 7

Cisco Expressway Call Processing Order

This chapter covers the following topics:

Transforms: Introduces the Call Processing Order and the first of the pre-search call processing components, Transforms (two types on the Cisco Expressway).

Call Policy: Examines the second pre-search component of the Call Processing Order, Call Policy (aka Admin Policy), which uses CPL scripts to control call behavior.

User Policy: Explores the third pre-search component of the Call Processing Order, User Policy (aka FindMe), which is a call forwarding service similar to Single Number Reach.

Search History and the Locate Tool: Demonstrates how to use a log and a tool on the Cisco Expressway to monitor how the Call Processing Order is being executed for each call attempt, and how they can be used to troubleshoot call routing issues.

There is a logic built into the Cisco Expressway that is applied to every call attempt processed by the Expressway. That logic is called the **Call Processing Order.** The first three components of the Call Processing Order are referred to as the pre-search components, because they are each a call processing policy with the ability to modify the dialed alias from its originally dialed form. These three components are Transforms, Call Policy, and User Policy. This chapter delves into each of these components to build an understanding of why they exist, how they operate, and when they can be used to maximize how the Expressway can be leveraged within a Cisco collaboration environment.

This chapter covers the following objectives from the Implementing Cisco Collaboration Cloud and Edge Solutions (CLCEI) exam 300-820:

- 1.7.a Describe Expressway Core dial plan elements: Transforms

- 2.2.a Configure Expressway Core dial plan elements: Transforms

- 2.3 Configure toll fraud prevention on Expressway series (no custom CPL scripts)

"Do I Know This Already?" Quiz

The "Do I Know This Already?" quiz enables you to assess whether you should read this entire chapter thoroughly or jump to the "Exam Preparation Tasks" section. If you are in doubt about your answers to these questions or your own assessment of your knowledge of the topics, read the entire chapter. Table 7-1 lists the major headings in this chapter and their corresponding "Do I Know This Already?" quiz questions. You can find the answers in Appendix A, "Answers to the 'Do I Know This Already?' Quizzes and Review Questions."

Table 7-1 "Do I Know This Already?" Section-to-Question Mapping

Foundation Topics Section	Questions
Transforms	1–2
Call Policy	3–4
User Policy	5–6
Search History and the Locate Tool	7

CAUTION The goal of self-assessment is to gauge your mastery of the topics in this chapter. If you do not know the answer to a question or are only partially sure of the answer, you should mark that question as wrong for purposes of the self-assessment. Giving yourself credit for an answer you correctly guess skews your self-assessment results and might provide you with a false sense of security.

1. Which of the following is the correct order to the Call Processing Order on the Cisco Expressway?

   a. Transforms, Call Policy, User Policy, Zone search, bandwidth management

   b. Admin Policy, FindMe, Transforms, Zone search, bandwidth management

   c. Transforms, Admin Policy, Call Policy, Zone search, bandwidth management

   d. Transforms, User Policy, FindMe, Zone search, bandwidth management

2. Which of the following regular expressions can be used to match only aliases that do not have a domain?

   a. (.*)(^@)*

   b. ({^@}*)

   c. ([^@]*)

   d. (.*)(^@cisco\.com)

3. Which of the following can be used to create a custom Call Policy?

   a. JavaScript

   b. JSON

   c. CPL scripts

   d. Python

4. How is Call Policy prioritized in the Expressway?

   a. Between 1–65534, with 1 being the highest priority.

   b. From the top down.

   c. There are no priority assignments with Call Policy.

   d. Between 1–65534, with 1 being the lowest priority.

5. What is the purpose of User Policy on the Cisco Expressway?

   a. User Policy is used to add additional administrators to the Cisco Expressway.

   b. User Policy is used to provision and manage users and user phones from the Cisco Expressway.

   c. User Policy is used to control how users call one another through the Cisco Expressway.

   d. User Policy is used to reroute a call to different aliases based on a set of user settings.

6. Where can FindMe be configured for and by specific users?

   a. FindMe portal on the Cisco Expressway

   b. User portal on the Cisco Expressway

   c. TMSPE FindMe user portal screen

   d. TMSPE portal on the Cisco Expressway

7. Under which of the following Cisco Expressway menus can an administrator access the Locate tool?

   a. Status

   b. System

   c. Configuration

   d. Applications

   e. Users

   f. Maintenance

Foundation Topics

Transforms

The Cisco Expressway has been designed with a systematic process used to gauge incoming call requests against a series of criteria that can be fashioned by an administrator. This process is known as the Call Processing Order, which consists of five main components. Listed in the order each component is executed, they are Transforms, Call Policy, User Policy, Zone search, and bandwidth management.

The first three components are known as the pre-search components, because each of these elements contains the ability to permanently change the destination alias from its originally dialed form. If the alias is going to be changed, then this action should take place before the alias is searched, hence the name pre-search components.

The next step in the Call Processing Order is the Zone search. All Zones are searched based on Search Rules configured within the Expressway itself, including the Local Zone. Search Rules are searched based on priority, and the priorities can be set between 1 and 65534 (1 is the highest priority, so the larger the number the lower the priority). There is one Search Rule created by default on the Expressway for the Local Zone with a priority of 50 that is set to match any alias. This allows for all local calls on the Expressway to match and connect without having to configure any other settings on the Expressway.

Assuming a match is found, the next criteria that must be corroborated by the Call Processing Order relates to bandwidth management. Bandwidth can be controlled by the

Expressway through two means. As mentioned in Chapter 6, "Registration on Cisco Expressway," Subzones can be used to control bandwidth. Another option is to use a mechanism call Pipes, which are applied to Links. These bandwidth management tools can also be used in such a way that they can offer a level of call control as well. Bandwidth management on the Cisco Expressway deserves a much deeper critique, so we will save the intricacies until Chapter 8, "Bandwidth Management." After bandwidth settings have been checked, provided the call is allowed to proceed, the Expressway returns communication back to the initiating endpoint and allows the call setup process to proceed. For H.323 endpoints, this communication will be an Admission Request (ARQ), and for SIP endpoints this communication will be a Trying message. Figure 7-1 illustrates the flow of the Call Processing Order.

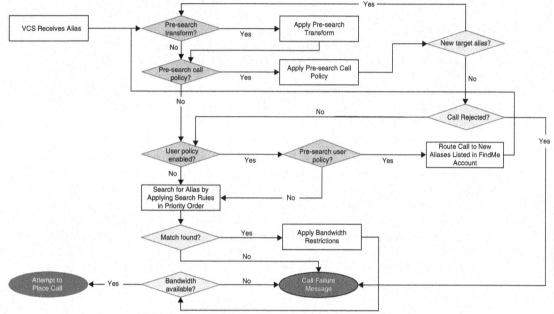

Figure 7-1 *Call Processing Order Flow*

Keep a marker on the page with Figure 7-1, because you will want to refer back to it as we explain the process of the Call Processing Order throughout the next several sections. Circling back to the first step in the Call Processing Order, the pre-search components will be the focus for the rest of this chapter. When the Expressway receives the dialed alias, whether the call was initiated by an H.323 endpoint or a SIP endpoint, the pre-search components are applied starting first with Transforms. These are better defined as Pre-Search Transforms, because there are actually two types of Transforms that can be applied in the Expressway. If a Pre-Search Transform rule applies, the alias will be changed, or "transformed," for the entire duration of the call setup. The other type of Transform can be applied at the Search Rule and will apply only to that search. If there is no match, then the alias will revert to the previous form it assumed, which could be the Pre-Search Transform identity.

Whether an alias is changed using a Pre-Search Transform or a Search Rule Transform, the function of the transform is the same. So, what exactly is a Transform? A **Transform** is a rule that, when applied, changes an alias based on the criteria it has been configured to change. This rule could include changing an alias of one type to an alias of another type. For example, a Transform could change an E.164 alias to a full URI address. Transforms are the first step in the pre-search process and have a priority between 1 and 65534, 1 being the highest priority. Best practice suggests that if you are going to create multiple Transforms, the increments should be larger than 1 (for example, 10, 20, 30, and so on). Once a match is made with a Pre-Search Transform, no other Transform will be applied, and the alias never returns to its original dialed state during the search. Transforms can be created using an exact match, prefix, suffix, or regular expression.

A great scenario where transforms are commonly used revolves around interworking between SIP and H.323 endpoints. When a SIP endpoint dials another endpoint, it must always dial the full URL. If the full URL is not created at the time the user launches the call, the endpoint automatically adds its own domain to the end of the dialing string before sending the Invite message off to the Expressway. For instance, if the user of a SIP endpoint dials 4721 and the URI of the endpoint the user is dialing from is 4724@cisco.com, the endpoint appends the @cisco.com domain to the end of 4721 and sends 4721@cisco.com to the Expressway. Herein lies the first interworking dialing issue. In this example, the called endpoint is an H.323 endpoint that is registered with the E.164 alias of 4721. The alias being searched in the Expressway is 4721@cisco.com, so without a rule to correct the dial string and strip the domain, the call will fail.

Alternatively, H.323 endpoints dial exactly what the user inputs to the endpoint. When a user dials 4724 and presses Send, only the digits 4724 are presented to the Expressway. Because the previously mentioned SIP endpoint is registered as 4724@cisco.com, the call will fail. You must take care to create a set of Transforms that allows interworking between SIP and H.323 endpoints. These transforms must be able to strip a domain when it is not needed and add a domain when it is needed. The call attempts that must be supported with this type of deployment include the following call scenarios:

- H.323 endpoint calling an H.323 endpoint

- H.323 endpoint calling a SIP endpoint

- SIP endpoint calling a SIP endpoint

- SIP endpoint calling an H.323 endpoint

The good news is that all you need to configure to support these four call scenarios is one Pre-Search Transform and one Search Rule Transform, plus use the one preexisting Search Rule already in the Expressway. The Pre-Search Transform that you create should be designed to add a domain to any alias dialed that does not already have a domain. This will bring all dialed aliases to the same plane so that they can all be treated the same way moving forward. The only way to achieve this behavior is with the use of a **regular expression (regex)**. Table 7-2 identifies the settings that you need to configure for this Pre-Search Transform to function correctly.

Key Topic

Table 7-2 Pre-Search Transform for Interworking on the Cisco Expressway

Field	Value
Priority	100
Description	Add a Domain

Field	Value
Pattern Type	Regex
Pattern String	([^@]*)
Pattern Behavior	Replace
Replace String	\1@cisco.com
State	Enabled

Sometimes when reading a regular expression, it is easier to understand it if you read it backward. To understand this expression ([^@]*), let's start by ignoring the parentheses for now. Working backward on the regular expression, the asterisk represents "anything." The square brackets with the caret symbol inside mean "does not include." Because there is an @ symbol inside the square brackets as well, together it means "does not include @." Couple that with the asterisk, and this expression represents anything that does not include an @. Because this whole expression is in parentheses, it represents one group. If there were more than one group of parentheses then each group would be numbered from left to right. When you look at the replacement string, \1 identifies that group 1 should be used in the transformed alias. The replacement string takes the whole value represented by the regular expression and appends @domain to the end of it, @cisco.com in this case. True to its purpose, this Pre-Search Transform takes any alias dialed that is not in the form of a URI and adds a domain to the end of it to make it a URI format. This Transform ignores any alias dialed that is already in the form of a URI.

After you create the Transform, you need to create two Search Rules. The first Search Rule transforms the alias and should be configured as indicated in Table 7-3.

Key Topic

Table 7-3   Search Rule Transform for Interworking on the Cisco Expressway

Field	Value
Rule Name	Local Zone—Strip Domain
Description	Interworking Search Rule Transform
Priority	45
Protocol	Any
Source	Any
Request must be authenticated	Yes (only if authentication is being used for applicable Subzones)
Mode	Alias Pattern Match
Pattern Type	Regex
Pattern String	(.*)@cisco\.com
Pattern Behavior	Replace
Replace String	\1
On Successful Match	Stop
Target	Local Zone
State	Enabled

7

Remember that when this rule is applied to an alias, it affects only this one search. If there is a match, then the On Successful Match setting causes the search to stop and the Call Processing Order can continue to the next step, which is bandwidth management. However, if no match is found, then the called alias reverts to its previous form and continues on to the next Search Rule. Understanding this regular expression is fairly straightforward: (.*) is a common catchall wildcard. The parentheses create group 1, while the dot asterisk represents anything. @cisco\.com is just the domain @cisco literally dot com. The backslash is just the literalization of the dot, which would mean any one number, character, or letter without the backslash. The \1 in the Replace String field represents the first group. So, this rule performs in exactly the opposite way as the Pre-Search Transform. This rule says that for anything that has a domain, strip it off at the @ symbol.

The second Search Rule you should not have to create, because it is the default Local Zone rule, and it should already be configured as identified in Table 7-4.

Table 7-4 Default Search Rule on the Cisco Expressway

Field	Value
Rule Name	LocalZoneMatch
Description	Default rule: queries the Local Zone for any alias
Priority	50
Protocol	Any
Source	Any
Request must be authenticated	Yes (only if authentication is being used for applicable Subzones)
Mode	Any Alias
On Successful Match	Continue
Target	Local Zone
State	Enabled

Once the appropriate Pre-Search Transform and Search Rules have been configured, calls between all devices will work regardless of the alias type that is dialed.

If an H.323 endpoint dials another H.323 endpoint using the E.164 alias 4722, that endpoint sends an ARQ to the Expressway. The Expressway then invokes the Call Processing Order, beginning with Transforms. There is one Transform that states if there is no domain on an alias dialed, append @cisco.com to the end of the alias. Because 4722 does not have a domain, the alias is transformed to 4722@cisco.com. When the process comes to the Search Rules, the lowest priority rule is 45, which states that if an alias has a suffix of @cisco.com, strip it. Because the transformed alias is 4722@cisco.com, the alias is changed back to 4722 and the Expressway performs a search for that alias. A match is made and call setup can proceed.

If an H.323 endpoint attempts to dial a SIP endpoint but only dials 4723, then the calling endpoint sends an ARQ to the Expressway. The Expressway invokes the Call Processing Order, beginning with Transforms. The presearchTransform changes the alias to 4723@cisco.com. Then the Search Rule with the lowest priority of 45 changes the alias back to 4723. The

Expressway performs a search for that alias on this search only, but a match is not made. So, the Expressway proceeds to the next priority Search Rule, which has a priority of 50. Remember that at this point, the alias reverts to its previous value, 4723@cisco.com. This default rule states that if any alias is dialed, it must be searched for in its current state without any changes. The alias is left as 4723@cisco.com, and when the Expressway performs the search again, a match is made and the call can proceed.

If a SIP endpoint attempts to dial another SIP endpoint, but the user only dials 4724 and presses Send, an Invite message is sent to the Expressway. This creates a bit of a different scenario, because SIP endpoints behave differently than H.323 endpoints. Any time a SIP endpoint dials an alias, if the domain was not added in the dialed string, the endpoint automatically appends its own domain to the end of it. Even though the alias dialed was 4724, the alias the endpoint sends to the Expressway is 4724@cisco.com. The Expressway then invokes the Call Processing Order, beginning with Transforms. The one Transform is ignored because 4724@cisco.com does in fact have a domain. When the process comes to the Search Rules, the lowest priority rule of 45 changes the alias to 4724 and the Expressway performs a search for that alias. A match is not made, so the Expressway proceeds to the next priority Search Rule, which is 50. This time the alias is left as 4724@cisco.com, and when the Expressway performs the search again, a match is made and the call can proceed.

If a SIP endpoint attempts to dial an H.323 endpoint using the E.164 alias 4721, it still sends an Invite message to the Expressway. Again, because a SIP endpoint initiated the call, the alias sent to the Expressway is 4721@cisco.com. The Expressway invokes the Call Processing Order, beginning with Transforms, but because 4721@cisco.com already has a domain, the alias is not transformed. When the process comes to the Search Rules, the lowest priority rule of 45 will change the alias to 4721. When the Expressway performs a search for that alias, a match is made and the call can proceed.

As you can see, by creating one Pre-Search Transform, creating one Search Rule Transform, and using the existing default Search Rule in the Expressway, you can quickly and easily create a full interworking environment for SIP and H.323 endpoints. Users can continue to dial aliases the same way regardless of the type of endpoint they're dialing from, and all calls will connect. Another common use of Transforms is for interoperability with the Cisco Unified Communications Manager (Unified CM). Cisco Unified CM will sometimes send alias to the Expressway in the form of DN@<IP_of_Expressway>:Port (for example, 4721@192.168.1.40:5060). Obviously, this is not how any endpoint is going to be registered to the Expressway, so a Transform can be used to change this alias to a dialable alias. Figure 7-2 illustrates what that Transform might look like.

To configure Transforms, follow these steps:

Step 1.   Choose **Configuration > Dial Plan > Transforms**.

Step 2.   Click **New**.

Step 3.   In the Priority field, enter the priority number.

Step 4.   In the Pattern Type field, choose a value from the drop-down list.

Step 5.   Enter values for any remaining fields as applicable.

Step 6.   Click Create Transform.

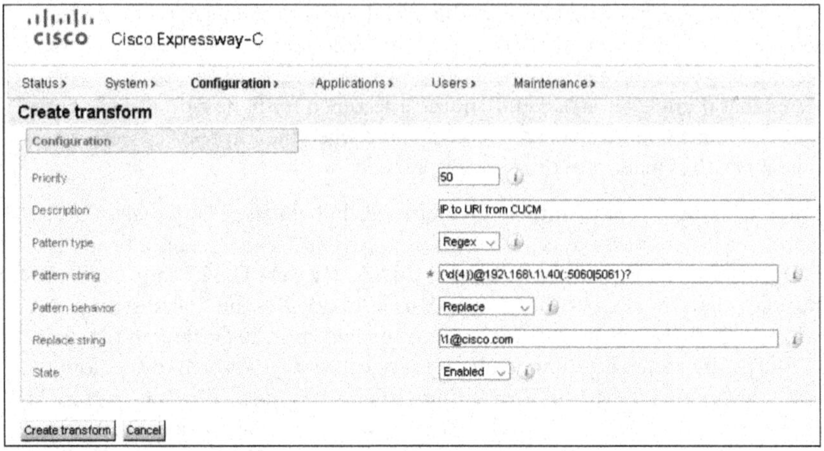

Figure 7-2 *Transform on the Cisco Expressway*

Call Policy

Whether a transform is applied or not, the next pre-search component that is applied to a call attempt through the Expressway is **Call Policy**. Another name for Call Policy is Administrator Policy (or Admin Policy). When an administrator goes to configure this service, the menu to search for is called Call Policy. However, when using the Search History log and other logging tools, this service is referred to as Admin Policy. Expressway administrators should be able to identify this service by either name.

If there are any network engineers reading this book, you'll understand the comparison of Call Policy to access control lists (ACLs). I, Jason, began my career as an AV engineer, and had to learn the networking side later in my career, so I actually learned about Call Policy before I learned about ACLs. However, as I was learning about ACLs, it made perfect sense to me because the behavior is essentially the same between these two different policy services. Call Policy is essentially a list of rules that are used to control call behavior through the Expressway. With Call Policy there is an explicit allow rule for all calls that do not meet the criteria for any specific allowance or denial of access. Specific Call Policy rules can be created easily using a tool built into the Expressway that will allow or reject a call based on a source pattern and destination pattern alias match, and these patterns can be matched using regular expressions.

All Call Policy is implemented using a programming language designed to control Internet telephony services called **Call Processing Language (CPL) Script**. CPL Script is an XML-based language for defining call handling. So, when the built-in tool is used to create rules, the Expressway is creating a CPL Script on behalf of the administrator within the database itself. Programmers who understand CPL Scripts can create even more intricate rules beyond "allow" or "reject" that change the dialed alias completely from its originally dialed form. However, for administrators who want to create custom scripts but are less familiar with programming, there are some prewritten script templates that can be found in the *Cisco Expressway Administrator Guide*. Example 7-1 illustrates one of these custom CPL Scripts.

Example 7-1   *CPL Script Example: Allow Calls from Locally Registered Endpoints Only*

```
<?xml version="1.0" encoding="UTF-8" ?> <cpl xmlns="urn:ietf:params:xml:ns:cpl"
xmlns:taa="http://www.tandberg.net/cpl-extensions" xmlns:xsi="http://www.w3.org/
2001/XMLSchema-instance" xsi:schemaLocation="urn:ietf:params:xml:ns:cpl
cpl.xsd"> <taa:routed>
<address-switch field="registered-origin"> <not-present>
<reject status="403" reason="Only local endpoints can use this Expressway"/>
</not-present>
</address-switch> </taa:routed>
</cpl>
```

I remember teaching a class on the Expressway several years ago for some Cisco engineers. One of the attendees approached me on a break and inquired about how to configure the Expressway for a specific customer scenario. This customer used a combination of personal Telepresence endpoints and conference room systems for calling within the organization, but often hosted meetings with participants from outside the organization as well. These hosted meetings were on a Cisco Telepresence MCU MSE 8510. The customer did not like participants from outside the company being able to dial into the meetings before internal personnel joined the meeting. The customer's short-term solution was to give all attendees outside the organization a number assigned to an auto attendant, and then have a conference administrator monitor and move participants to the appropriate meetings at the appropriate times. Unfortunately, this was not foolproof, and some attendees were still able to obtain the alias to dial into the meeting directly. The Cisco engineer asked me if there was a way to redirect all external participants to the auto attendant regardless of the alias dialed but allow internal participants to dial any alias they want without inhibition. We worked up a plan together that used Call Policy with a custom CPL Script that identified the caller by the server the call originated through. If the call came from the Expressway Edge, then the destination alias was changed to the auto attendant alias and the call was routed to the Telepresence MCU. If the call originated from anywhere else, then the destination alias was ignored, and call routing could commence.

This is just one example of how a custom CPL Script could be used in a Cisco Expressway deployment. In cases where an administrator does create a custom CPL script for Call Policy that changes the destination, the new alias must start the Call Processing Order over, beginning with Transforms, as previously shown in Figure 7-1. If Call Policy Rules created with the built-in tool are used instead of a custom CPL, the only behavior configurable is to allow or reject a call that is based on source and destination aliases. If reject is the applied behavior, then the call will fail at this point and "Forbidden" will be the cause reflected in the logs. If allow is the applied behavior, then no change will be implemented, and the call will progress to the next pre-search component of the Call Processing Order.

Because all Call Policy uses CLP Scripts, the priority of Call Policy is unlike any other setting in the Expressway. A script, like an English book, is read from the top down and from left to right. Therefore, policy matches listed first are applied and no other policy will be searched. When using the built-in tool to create Call Policy, the top of the list is highest priority and therefore searched first. Each additional Call Policy in order from top to bottom assumes its position in the search order because this is how the script will be created in the Expressway database. Once you create Call Policy rules, you can rearrange their order by using the arrow keys beside each rule. Rules can only be moved one line at a time, and the web page refreshes after each rule position change. If you create a lot of rules, it could take some time to move a rule at the bottom of the list to the top. Therefore, it makes sense to plan how and what rules you will create before implementing them. But at least they don't have to be deleted and re-created if the order is wrong.

Call Policy service must be enabled before it can be used, but enabling Call Policy is not as simple as turning it on. Prior to enabling Call Policy, the administrator needs to decide how these policies will be implemented within the collaboration environment. You can use a local policy service or an external policy service. You can create and upload custom CPL Scripts or use the built-in tool to create Rules. All of these decisions impact how this service will be enabled. The following are the basic steps required to enable Call Policy:

Step 1.   From the web interface of the Expressway, navigate to **Configuration > Call Policy > Configuration.**

Step 2.   Use the drop-down menu to set the Call Policy Mode to one of the following settings:

    a.   **Off:** Call Policy is not in use (default).

    b.   **Local CPL:** Uses locally defined Call Policy.

    c.   **Policy Service:** Uses an external policy service.

Step 3.   Click **Save.**

The Local CPL option uses the Call Policy that is configured locally on the Expressway. If you choose Local CPL, you must do one of the following:

- Configure basic Call Policy through the Call Policy rules page, which only lets you allow or reject specified calls

- Upload a Call Policy file that contains CPL Script, which includes a level of complexity to writing CPL scripts

Only one of these two methods can be used at any one time to specify Call Policy. If a CPL script has been uploaded, this takes precedence and you will not be able to use the Call Policy Rules page. To use the Rules page, you must first delete the CPL script that has been uploaded. If Local CPL is enabled but no policy is configured or uploaded, then a default policy is applied that allows all calls, regardless of source or destination.

Use the Policy Service option if you want to refer all Call Policy decisions to an external service. If you select this option, an extra set of configuration fields appears so that you can specify the connection details of the external service. Figure 7-3 illustrates the Call Policy Configuration page.

Step 4.   To configure rules using the built-in tool, navigate to **Configuration > Call Policy > Rules.**

Step 5.   Click **New** and configure the following fields:

    a.   Source Type: Choose From Address or Zone

    b.   Rule Applies To: Choose Authenticated Callers or Unauthenticated Callers (only available if From Address is selected in the Source Type field)

    c.   Originating Zone: Select Zone from the drop-down list (only available if Zone is selected in the Source Type field)

    d.   Source Pattern: Enter a source alias or regex pattern (only available if From Address is selected in the Source Type field)

    e.   Destination Pattern: Enter a destination alias or regex pattern

    f.   Action: Choose Allow or Reject

Step 6.   Click **Add** when finished.

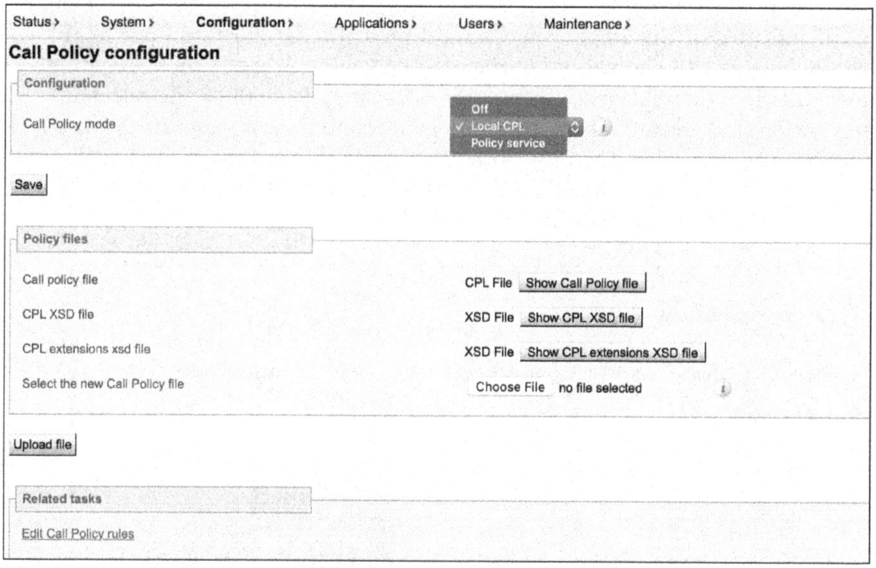

Figure 7-3 *Call Policy Configuration on the Cisco Expressway*

A lot about these Rule settings needs to be explained. Cisco introduced a significant change in the Expressway running version X7.0 or later. Prior to this version, registration authentication was a universal setting that was either enabled for all endpoints or disabled for all endpoints. With version X7.0 or later, authentication can be configured on the Subzone level or Zone level, as described in Chapter 6. As part of this change to authentication, a dependency was added to several other services within the Expressway, such as Call Policy. When these changes were first implemented, Call Policy would not work unless the Subzone or Zone was configured to Check Credentials or Treat As Authenticated, even if this service was enabled. Since then Cisco added the Rule Applies To option so that Call Policy can be applied to *unauthenticated callers.* However, there are still other services that can be impacted by the Authentication setting. All the services this new authentication requirement impacts on the Expressway include the following:

- All Call Policy

- Registration Restriction Policy using the Policy Service

- Search Rules using the Policy Service

As seen in the previous steps, changing the Source Type field changes the other field options available. You can have a mixture of rules using different source types. Define and order them to implement your Call Policy or protect your conferencing resources from toll fraud. If the Source Type field is set to From Address, then the subsequent fields available include Rule Applies To (just explained), Source Pattern, Destination Pattern, and Action. If the Source Type field is set to Zone, the subsequent fields available include Originating Zone, Destination Pattern, and Action. Both the Source Pattern and Destination Pattern fields can be an exact match or use regular expressions to formulate the pattern necessary to encompass a broader range of aliases. If the Source Pattern field is left blank, the policy rule applies to all incoming calls from the selected type of caller, whether Authenticated or Unauthenticated was selected. The Originating Zone field allows the administrator to choose any of the existing Zones on the Expressway from a drop-down list. This rule then inspects all calls originating from the Zone selected. Finally, the Action field setting determines what happens to the call requests that are matched by one of these rules. The only options available through the built-in tool are to allow or reject the call request. Figure 7-4 illustrates the configuration options available on the Expressway through the built-in Call Policy Rule tool.

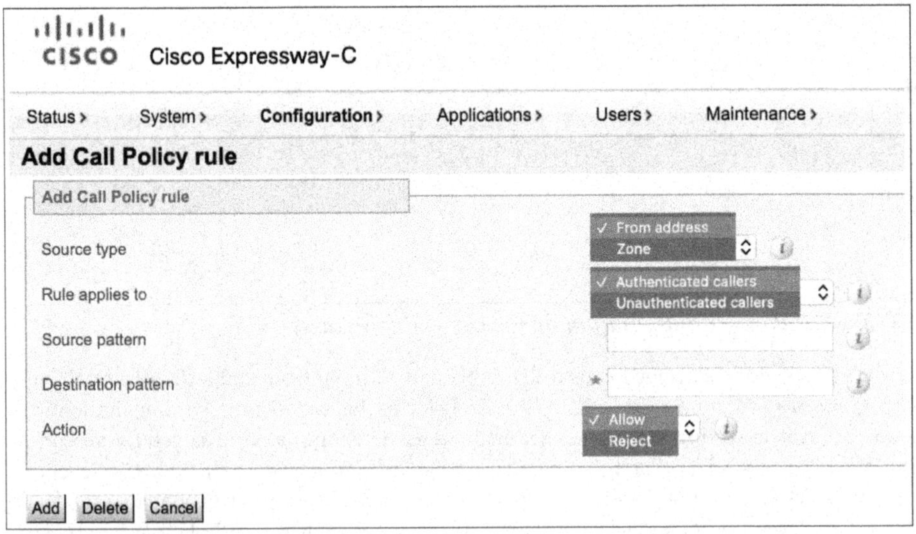

Figure 7-4 *Call Policy Rules on the Cisco Expressway*

Once two or more Call Policy rules have been created, remember that you can rearrange the order using the arrows that appear on the Rules page. If you needed to move the last rule to become the first rule, you would have to click the arrow repeatedly, moving that rule up one position with each click, allowing the screen to refresh in between clicks. This process could be cumbersome; therefore, it is best practice to plan all the rules before creating them so that you can insert them in the order in which they are to be searched.

One common use for Call Policy on the Cisco Expressway is to prevent **hair pinning**, otherwise known as toll fraud. The way this works is someone outside your organization first identifies they can call into your network via an IP-based call. Then they scan your dial plan to discover a prefix to reach an outside line through the **Public Switched Telephone Network (PSTN)** gateway. All they have to do at that point is dial the PSTN number they want to call using your Expressway IP address as the domain, and the PSTN prefix in front of their number, and your dial plan will do the rest. They can then place PSTN calls at your expense, and this often goes undiscovered until the enormous phone bill comes in. Restricting access to the local gateway is the best way to implement toll fraud prevention.

You can configure this behavior using Call Policy Rules, so you don't need to do it using a CPL script. However, you cannot use a combination of UI configured rules and uploaded CPL script, so if you have any CPL requirements that you cannot implement using the UI rules, you must use a script for all of your rules. You can find examples of how to create CPL scripts for toll fraud prevention in the *Cisco Expressway Administrator Guide 12.6*: https://www.cisco.com/c/dam/en/us/td/docs/voice_ip_comm/expressway/admin_guide/ Cisco-Expressway-Administrator-Guide-X12-6.pdf.

Steps to configure toll fraud prevention using just the Rules from the built-in tool could be performed in several ways, and each method is influenced by your dial plan. The outline we provide here offers one possible method as an example of how these rules can be configured. Start by creating a reject rule for all unauthenticated users by entering the following information:

- Source type: From address
- Rule applies to: Unauthenticated callers
- Source pattern: .*
- Destination pattern: .*
- Action: Reject

The source and destination patterns listed use a regular expression that encompasses all aliases. This rule says that all calls from anyone to anyone who is not an authenticated caller will be rejected. Obviously, this rule will not work properly if you do not register your endpoints with either Check Credentials or Treat As Authenticated. No one will be able to call in that case. These rules assume you have enabled Treat As Authenticated at a minimum.

Another rule you may want to create is an allow rule for outbound calls over IP. Instead of using a from address as the source type for this rule, you could use a zone type. The following rule will allow any call originating from the Traversal Zone going out to any alias to pass through the Expressway:

- Source type: Zone
- Outgoing Zone: Traversal_Zone
- Destination pattern: .*
- Action: Allow

There is as least one more rule you may want to allow that pertains to incoming calls from outside the network. Someone from another organization, whether they be another business or a customer, will need to be able to call in. Their call will likely be tagged as an *unauthenticated caller*, and currently all unauthenticated callers are rejected by the first rule. You can create a rule to allow these calls to come in if they are targeted to a specific destination:

- Source type: From address

- Rule applies to: Unauthenticated callers

- Source pattern: .*

- Destination pattern: ([3-5]\d{3})@cisco.com

- Action: Allow

To explain this rule, we need to explain the dial plan we are accommodating with this destination pattern. Imagine a network topology that uses a Cisco Unified CM for registering Cisco Unified IP Phones, an Expressway for Firewall Traversal and Telepresence endpoint registration, and a Cisco Meeting Server for hosting multipoint conference meetings. All aliases are four digits followed by the domain @cisco.com. Everything registering to the Unified CM begins with a 3, everything registering to the Expressway begins with a 4, and all our conferencing spaces begin with a 5. We also use 9 for an outside line to the PSTN, so we want to be specific in what the first number is within our dialing plan. The regular expression used in the destination pattern matches any four-digit number that begins with a 3, 4, or 5 and ends with @cisco.com. This rule applies to unauthenticated callers and allows these types of calls to go through.

Now that we have identified several rules that can be created to control our environment and prevent toll fraud, the order of these rules is equally important. If the reject rule is listed first, then the last rule allowing unauthenticated users in specific circumstances will never be matched because all unauthenticated users will be rejected first, and no other rule will be searched. Therefore, it is a good rule of thumb to list all the allow rules first, and then list your explicit reject all rules last. Figure 7-5 illustrates these three rules mentioned for preventing toll fraud from the Cisco Expressway using Call Policy.

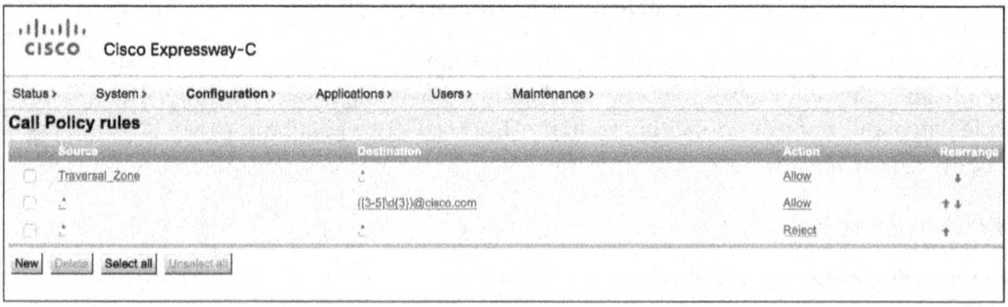

Figure 7-5   *Toll Fraud Prevention Using Call Policy Rules on the Cisco Expressway*

User Policy

Before we delve into the third pre-search component of the Call Processing Order, let's review the first two components. When a call request comes into the Expressway, the Expressway invokes the Call Processing Order. The first pre-search component executed, before the Expressway ever tries to locate the destination alias, is Transforms. This component may change the destination alias from its originally dialed form before continuing on to the next pre-search component, Call Policy. This service may just allow or reject the call based on Call Policy Rules, or it may change the destination alias altogether based on a more complex CPL script. If the alias is changed, then that alias starts the Call Processing Order all over again, beginning with Transforms. Assuming the call attempt makes it past Transforms and Call Policy, the next pre-search component is User Policy. This policy service also has the ability to change the alias from its originally dialed form, and each changed alias must go back through the Call Processing Order again from the beginning, starting with Transforms, then Call Policy, and then User Policy again. So, what is User Policy?

User Policy, also known as FindMe, is an option on the Expressway that works similarly to call forward or Single Number Reach, where a call can be rerouted to other aliases based on a set of user-defined settings. A **FindMe ID** is created for a user. The user account associated with the FindMe ID can then be used to configure what aliases should be dialed, as well as the order and circumstances surrounding when each alias is dialed. Unlike Transforms and Call Policy, User Policy can be enabled or disabled. If it is disabled, the Expressway skips it altogether and continues in the Call Processing Order to search for the alias. If it is enabled but there is no match within the FindMe configurations, the call still progresses to the search function of the Expressway. However, if FindMe is enabled and there is a match to a user's FindMe account, then each alias that is defined within the FindMe user account must begin the Call Processing Order again, starting with Transforms.

As of Cisco Expressway version X12.5, the FindMe option has been deprecated. Support for this feature will be withdrawn in a subsequent release. Therefore, we won't spend too much time going over this feature. However, if you work for an organization that is running the Cisco Expressway prior to version X12.5 and want to understand how the FindMe feature functions, this section offers a short explanation.

User accounts are created locally on the Expressway or on **Telepresence Management Suite (TMS)**. The **Telepresence Management Suite – Provisioning Extension or TMSPE** option is required for FindMe to be remotely managed. Authentication can be either local on the Expressway or remote through an LDAP integration. Once a user account has been configured, the FindMe address can be used. Figure 7-6 illustrates how the FindMe solution can be executed.

In Figure 7-6, User Alice dials john@cisco.com. Notice that the FindMe ID dialed does not match any of the endpoint aliases. When the Expressway receives the call request from Alice's endpoint, it invokes the Call Processing Order. After checking Transforms and Call Policy, the Expressway checks to see if FindMe is enabled and, if so, checks whether the dialed alias matches a FindMe ID.

In this scenario john@cisco.com does match a FindMe ID in the Expressway. The alias is then changed from john@cisco.com to 3001 and John.office@cisco.com. Notice that FindMe has the ability to match more than one alias at a time. The Expressway must then start the pre-search Call Processing Order again for each of these aliases. Once the pre-search process is complete, the Expressway searches for those devices and attempts to connect the call. Figure 7-6 signifies these two searches with the number 1.

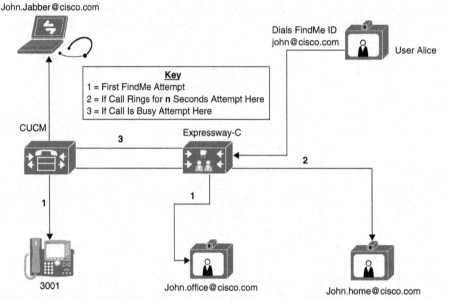

Figure 7-6   *FindMe on the Cisco Expressway*

With FindMe, the profile can be configured to behave differently, depending on the options that are configured in the user profile. For instance, if the call is not answered after a set number of seconds, then the Expressway can change the alias again. In Figure 7-6 the number 2 indicates that the alias was changed again to John.home@cisco.com. Again, because the alias changed again, it must be sent back through the pre-search components of the Call Processing Order. The Expressway then checks the Search Rules and tries to connect the call again.

The call can also be redirected through FindMe if the call is busy. Figure 7-6 illustrates with the number 3 how the Expressway changes the alias again to John.Jabber@cisco.com and repeats the pre-search process with this new alias. The Expressway then checks the Search Rules and tries to connect the call again. If the user answers, the call connects.

FindMe used to be configured from the web interface of the Expressway, but bulk provisioning practices led to using TMS for the management of this service. Now FindMe is only enabled in the Expressway but is fully configured in TMS. The administrator can create user accounts and edit them from TMS. The user can only edit their assigned user account once it has been created. For the user to access their user account, the user must navigate to the URL of the TMSPE FindMe user portal screen. Once logged in, the user can make changes to their account, such as adding and removing devices, and create locations with different call routing behaviors.

To access the FindMe portal as an administrator, select a specific account from the TMS and then click the Edit in FindMe User Portal link. This opens the FindMe portal page without the need to supply user credentials. Figure 7-7 illustrates the configuration settings for FindMe through the TMS portal. Although the GUI is different from the legacy Expressway configuration portal, the options of the menu are the same.

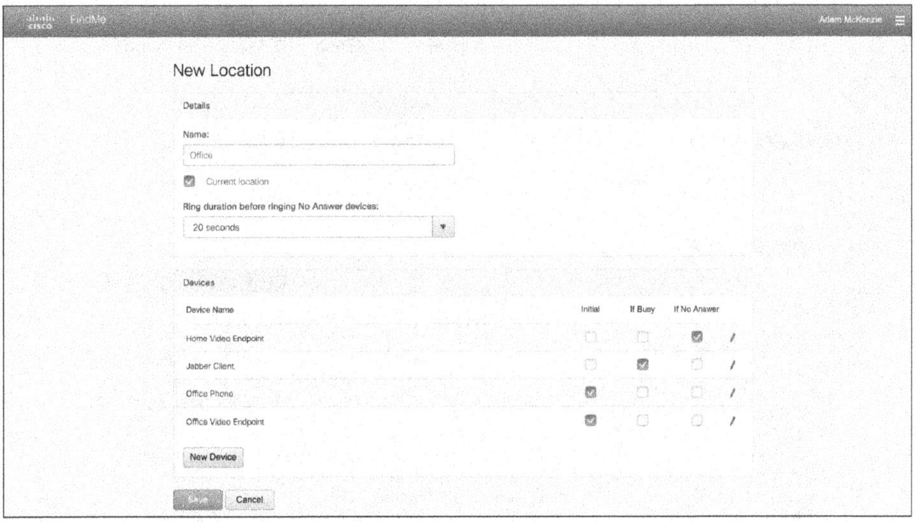

Figure 7-7   *FindMe Configuration on Cisco TMS*

Search History and the Locate Tool

Search History is a log that aids in troubleshooting call setup issues. This log displays all the pre-search Call Processing Order information for each call or call attempt and the Zone searches in order of priority, even if the call attempt fails. This allows the Expressway administrator to use the Search History log with failed call attempts to pinpoint exactly where the issue resides. The log flows with the Call Processing Order. The source and destination node information is identified first. Then the Expressway invokes the pre-search checklist:

1. Are there any Pre-Search Transform matches?

2. Are there any Admin Policy matches? Even though it is called Call Policy when you configure it, the Search History log refers to it as Admin Policy.

3. Are there any FindMe matches? Although this policy service is called User Policy, it does not appear by that name anywhere within the Expressway or TMS.

After the pre-search components are checked, the Cisco Expressway performs the Zone search. The first zone that should be searched is the Local Zone. If there is no match, then the Expressway searches External Zones. The only part of the Call Processing Order that is not displayed here is the Bandwidth search. However, there are other logs available on the Expressway that allow the administrator to monitor bandwidth consumption. We discuss those logs in Chapter 12, "Troubleshoot a Business-to-Business (B2B) Collaboration Solution." Figure 7-8 illustrates how a call might appear in the Search History log.

To access the Search History information, follow these steps:

Step 1.   From the web interface of the Cisco Expressway, navigate to **Status > Search History.**

Step 2.   Click the **View** link next to the call attempt you want to review.

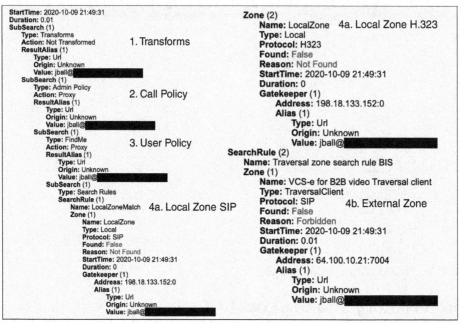

Figure 7-8   *Search History Log on the Cisco Expressway*

Cisco has built a tool into the Expressway that allows administrators to qualify a network and troubleshoot calling issues related to the dial plan the same way Search History is used without actually placing a call. This tool is called the **Locate** tool. When you use this tool, Search History information is displayed as if a call was actually placed. This allows you to assess the information and deduce whether a call could have been placed successfully, what the behavior would be, and, if not possible, what problems would be encountered connecting the call.

To access the Locate tool, follow these steps:

Step 1.   From the web interface of the Expressway, navigate to **Maintenance > Tools > Locate**.

Step 2.   In the Alias field, enter the destination alias of the device you want to research. All other information can be left at its default values, but you might want to change some of the settings for a more honed search. The following is a list of the optional fields:

    a.   Hop count: Number of hops to use in the search; default is 5

    b.   Protocol: SIP or H.323

    c.   Source: The Zone or Subzone from which to simulate the search request; Default Zone is the default setting

    d.   Authenticated: Yes or No

    e.   Source Alias: Enter a source alias to use in the search

Step 3.   Click **Locate**. The information displays below the locate criteria.

Exam Preparation Tasks

As mentioned in the section "How to Use This Book" in the Introduction, you have a couple of choices for exam preparation: the exercises here, Chapter 22, "Final Preparation," and the exam simulation questions in the Pearson Test Prep practice test software.

Review All Key Topics

Review the most important topics in this chapter, noted with the Key Topics icon in the outer margin of the page. Table 7-5 lists a reference of these key topics and the page numbers on which each is found.

Key Topic

Table 7-5 Key Topics for Chapter 7

Key Topic Element	Description	Page Number
Table 7-2	Pre-Search Transform for Interworking on the Cisco Expressway	118
Table 7-3	Search Rule Transform for Interworking on the Cisco Expressway	119
Table 7-4	Default Search Rule on the Cisco Expressway	120
Steps	Steps to configure Transforms on the Expressway	121
Steps	Steps to enable Call Policy	124
List	Toll fraud prevention using Rules in Expressway	127
Steps	Accessing Search History logs	131
Steps	Accessing the Locate tool	132

Complete Tables and Lists from Memory

7

Print a copy of Appendix C, "Memory Tables" (found on the companion website), or at least the section for this chapter, and complete the tables and lists from memory. Appendix D, "Memory Tables Answer Key," also on the companion website, includes completed tables and lists to check your work.

Define Key Terms

Define the following key terms from this chapter and check your answers in the glossary:

Call Policy, Call Processing Language (CPL) Script, Call Processing Order, FindMe ID, hair pinning, Locate, Public Switched Telephone Network (PSTN), regular expression (regex), Search History, Telepresence Management Suite (TMS), Telepresence Management Suite – Provisioning Extension (TMSPE), Transform, User Policy

Q&A

The answers to these questions appear in Appendix A. For more practice with exam format questions, use the Pearson Test Prep practice test software.

1. List the five main components of the Call Processing Order.
2. List the three services in the Cisco Expressway that require an authentication setting of Treat As Authenticated or Check Credentials.

CHAPTER 8

Bandwidth Management

This chapter covers the following topics:

Subzone Bandwidth Management: Explains how Subzones can be used to manage bandwidth for calls through the Cisco Expressway.

Links and Pipes Bandwidth Management: Describes how to use an alternative means of managing bandwidth using Pipes to throttle calls across Links on the Cisco Expressway.

Call Control Using Pipes: Examines how Pipes can be used for call control across an Expressway, and not just for bandwidth management.

Chapter 7, "Configure Expressway Call Processing Order," examined how call control on the Cisco Expressway can be managed using pre-search tools, such as Transforms, Call Policy, and User Policy. That chapter also briefly discussed how call control can be implemented using Transforms within Search Rules. However, one of the most significant means of administering call control is through bandwidth management. While the Cisco Unified CM uses Regions and Locations to administer bandwidth management, the Cisco Expressway uses Subzones and Pipes. This chapter will provide you with a thorough understanding of what these tools are, how they work, and how you can configure them to control **bandwidth** from within the Cisco Expressway.

This chapter covers the following objectives from the Implementing Cisco Collaboration Cloud and Edge Solutions (CLCEI) exam 300-820:

- 1.7.e Describe Expressway Core dial plan elements: Pipes and Links

- 2.2.e Configure Expressway Core dial plan elements: Pipes and Links

"Do I Know This Already?" Quiz

The "Do I Know This Already?" quiz enables you to assess whether you should read this entire chapter thoroughly or jump to the "Exam Preparation Tasks" section. If you are in doubt about your answers to these questions or your own assessment of your knowledge of the topics, read the entire chapter. Table 8-1 lists the major headings in this chapter and their corresponding "Do I Know This Already?" quiz questions. You can find the answers in Appendix A, "Answers to the 'Do I Know This Already?' Quizzes and Review Questions."

Table 8-1 "Do I Know This Already?" Section-to-Question Mapping

Foundation Topics Section	Questions
Subzone Bandwidth Management	1–3
Links and Pipes Bandwidth Management	4–6
Call Control Using Pipes	7

1. With which of the following methods can bandwidth be applied to calls from the Cisco Expressway?

   a. Total bandwidth only

   b. Within and total bandwidth

   c. In and Out and total bandwidth

   d. Per call and total bandwidth

2. In which of the following scenarios would the In and Out bandwidth restriction be used in Subzones?

   a. Calls between two H.323 endpoints within the same Subzone

   b. Calls between two SIP endpoints within the same Subzone

   c. Calls between an H.323 endpoint and a SIP endpoint within the same Subzone

   d. Calls between an H.323 endpoint and a SIP endpoint within the same Traversal Subzone

3. Which of the following best describes the purpose of the Default Call Bandwidth setting on the Cisco Expressway?

   a. Sets the maximum bandwidth allowed per call across the Expressway by default

   b. Sets the maximum total bandwidth allowed across the Expressway by default

   c. Applies a default bandwidth rate to all calls that don't request a limit

   d. Applies bandwidth settings to all calls by default regardless of the requested limit when enabled

4. Which of the following can be used to restrict bandwidth within the Cisco Expressway?

   a. Links

   b. Pipes

   c. Zones

   d. Default Zone

5. How many Links can a single Pipe be applied to on the Cisco Expressway?

   a. No limit

   b. One Link

   c. Two Links

   d. Ten Links

6. How many Pipes can be applied to a single Link on the Cisco Expressway?

   a. No limit

   b. One Pipe

   c. Two Pipes

   d. Ten Pipes

7. Which of the following statements is true regarding how the Cisco Expressway processes calls?

   a. If a call between two Subzones is blocked, the call reroutes along another path.

   b. If a call between a Zone and a Subzone is blocked, the call reroutes along another path.

   c. All calls follow the shortest path. If that path is blocked, the call reroutes to the next shortest path.

   d. All calls follow the shortest path. If that path is blocked, the call fails.

Foundation Topics

Subzone Bandwidth Management

Chapter 7 began by introducing you to the Call Processing Order, which is the order in which every call attempt through Expressway will be executed. Before the Expressway begins to search for the dialed alias, it goes through a pre-search checklist. The first things the Expressway checks are Transforms, then Call Policy, and finally User Policy. Once the Expressway has completed the pre-search criteria, it begins the search through Zones. Searches are performed based on the priority of the search rules. If endpoints are registered to the Expressway, the first Zone that the Expressway searches is the Local Zone. If no match is found, then external Zones should be searched. After the Expressway locates the dialed endpoint, the last item the Expressway checks within the Call Processing Order is whether any bandwidth restrictions have been configured that need to be applied to this call and, if so, if there's any available bandwidth to allow the call to proceed. Figure 8-1 illustrates the two ways that bandwidth restrictions can be applied to calls through the Expressway.

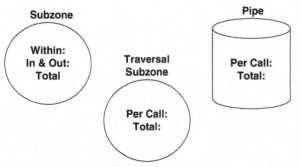

Figure 8-1　*Bandwidth Restriction Options on the Expressway*

As shown in Figure 8-1, there are two methods for implementing bandwidth restrictions on an Expressway: using Pipes or using Subzones. Using either of these methods, bandwidth restrictions can be applied to the call in two ways: on a per-call basis and on a total-bandwidth basis. Per-call restrictions are applied to every call attempt on an independent basis. Total-bandwidth restrictions take the culmination of all concurrent calls in progress and allow or restrict calls based on that total accumulative value. This per-call and total-bandwidth value is evident in the Traversal Subzone, because no devices will ever register to this Subzone.

Because the default Subzone, or any other created Subzone, possesses the capability to host device registration, the per-call bandwidth restriction is divided into two categories: Within and In and Out. Within restrictions control the bandwidth that is used between two devices that are registered to the same Subzone. In and Out restrictions control the bandwidth that is used when the call flow must travel outside of the Subzone.

The following list provides examples of when In and Out restrictions are used:

- When a call is placed between two endpoints that are registered to different Subzones in the same Expressway.

- When a call is placed between an endpoint registered to the Expressway and another call control device such as the Cisco Unified CM. This would also include business-to-business (B2B) and business-to-consumer (B2C) calls.

- When a call is placed between two endpoints that are registered to the same Subzone, but the call must be interworked using the Traversal Subzone, such as a call between a SIP endpoint and an H.323 endpoint.

When configuring the bandwidth restrictions, there are three restriction modes:

- **No Bandwidth:** No bandwidth is allocated and therefore no calls can be made.

- **Limited:** Limits are applied according to the value set in the [Total|Per call] Bandwidth Limits (kbps) field.

- **Unlimited:** No restrictions will be applied to the amount of bandwidth being used.

Now that basic parameters have been established for how bandwidth restrictions need to be configured for Subzones, the following scenarios will explain the behavior of the Cisco Expressway when executing Subzone bandwidth restrictions. Figure 8-2 illustrates how bandwidth restrictions can be applied to Subzones. This figure will be used to explain several call scenarios.

In Figure 8-2, there are three Subzones, and each Subzone has been assigned various bandwidth restrictions with endpoints registered to it. Obviously, you would not use bandwidth restrictions this low in a production environment; we are using low bandwidth rates for the sake of easier calculations to better illustrate how bandwidth restrictions work within Subzones. For example, if endpoint 4001 calls endpoint 4002 at 768 kbps, the call goes through as dialed without issues. Both the endpoints are registered to the same Subzone and the bandwidth limitation for calls within the Default Subzone is 768 kbps.

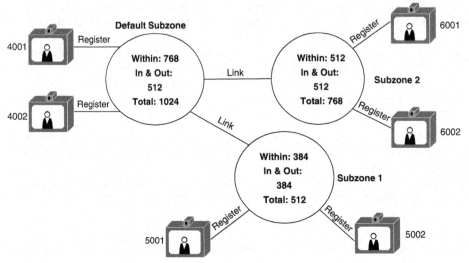

Figure 8-2 *Bandwidth Restrictions Using Subzones*

Now let's examine call behavior for a call attempt outside the allowed bandwidth restrictions illustrated in Figure 8-2. Imagine endpoint 4001 calls endpoint 4002 at 2 Mbps. As examined previously, both endpoints are registered to the same Subzone but the bandwidth limitation for calls within that Subzone is 768 kbps. Therefore, the call would either fail or down speed, depending on how the downspeed settings are configured within the Cisco Expressway. To configure the **Downspeed Mode** settings, navigate to **Configuration > Bandwidth > Configuration**. Figure 8-3 illustrates these bandwidth settings on the Cisco Expressway.

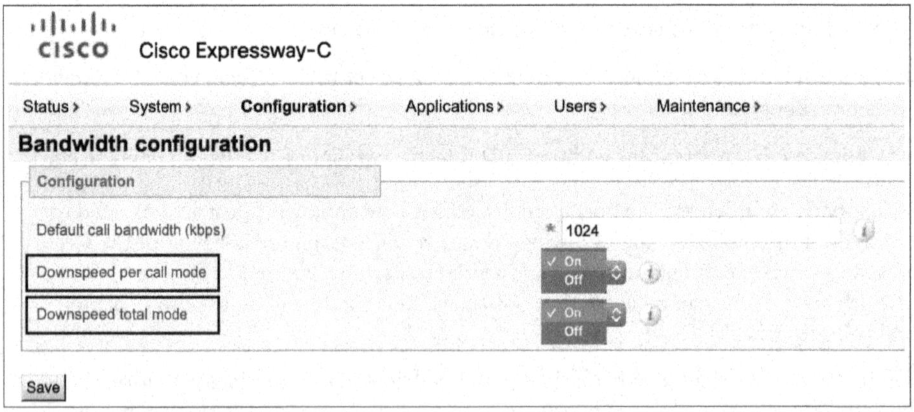

Figure 8-3 *Bandwidth Downspeed Mode*

The three settings in Figure 8-3 need some explanation. The first and often the most confusing setting is **Default Call Bandwidth**. This bandwidth setting is not a limitation. Some endpoints allow the internal bandwidth setting to be auto-negotiated. If one of those endpoints places a call but does not specify the desired bandwidth, the Expressway implements whatever limit has been established here. The default value is 384 kbps, but this setting can be changed to whatever limit is desired. If this limit is set to a high rate, such as 2048 Mbps, and there are bandwidth restrictions set in Subzones or Pipes that would restrict the per-call rate to a lower limit, such as 768 kbps, then that restricted rate of 768 kbps takes precedence over the Default Call Bandwidth rate.

The two settings that are used to down speed calls are somewhat self-explanatory. **Downspeed Per Call Mode** pertains to each individual call attempt. **Downspeed Total Mode** refers to all calls occurring concurrently. Each mode has two configuration settings, On or Off, with the default being On. Now let's apply these default settings to the last call scenario we were examining where endpoint 4001 calls endpoint 4002 at 2 Mbps. Obviously, this call attempt cannot continue at this bandwidth rate because the per-call bandwidth limit within the Default Subzone is 768 kbps, which is the rate to which this call would down speed.

Now let's imagine another call scenario that assumes the downspeed setting is on. If endpoint 5001 calls endpoint 6001 at 2 Mbps, the call would down speed. However, there are several aspects to this topology that must be considered. First, the two endpoints involved with this call attempt are registered to different Subzones. Endpoint 5001 is registered to Subzone 1 and endpoint 6001 is registered to Subzone 2. So, when examining the bandwidth limitations, the In and Out limit is the one to examine most closely. Second, these two Subzones are not connected together with a direct link. Each Subzone is connected to the Default Subzone, so the bandwidth limitations of the Default Subzone must also be considered when examining the limitations of this call attempt. The In and Out limitations from the source endpoint toward the destination endpoint are 384 kbps for Subzone 1, 512 kbps for Default Subzone, and 512 kbps for Subzone 2. The lowest restrictive rate for bandwidth is 384 kbps, so that is the rate to which the call will down speed.

One final call scenario to consider with Subzone bandwidth limitations pertains to call behavior when the total bandwidth limitation is exceeded. First imagine endpoint 4001 calls endpoint 4002 at 768 kbps. The call would go through as dialed because both endpoints are registered to the same Subzone and the bandwidth limitation for calls within that Subzone is 768 kbps. Now imagine, with that call still connected, endpoint 5002 calls endpoint 6002 at 384 kbps. As stated in the previous call scenario, the In and Out limitations from the source endpoint toward the destination endpoint are 384 kbps for Subzone 1, 512 kbps for Default Subzone, and 512 kbps for Subzone 2. So on the surface it would seem that this call would proceed without needing to down speed. However, the Total Bandwidth Available setting in the Default Subzone is 1024 kbps, and there is already a call up at 768 kbps. Subtract 768 from 1024 and you come up with 256 kbps. Therefore, the call attempt from endpoint 5002 to 6002 would down speed to 256 kbps even though neither endpoint involved in the call is registered to the Default Subzone.

Subzone bandwidth settings are configured in the Subzones themselves, and Subzones are configured in the Local Zone. Therefore, it is easy to remember what menu to use to configure Subzone bandwidth settings. In the Expressway web interface, navigate to **Configuration > Local Zone** and then either select the Default Subzone, Traversal Subzone, or Subzone menu, depending on which Subzone you want to configure. Remember that the Traversal Subzone shows only two menu options for configuring bandwidth restrictions, because endpoints cannot register to this Subzone. Alternatively, the Default Subzone, or other subsequent Subzones you may have created, offer three menu options for configuring bandwidth restrictions. Figure 8-4 illustrates the bandwidth configuration menus on both the Default Subzone and Traversal Subzone.

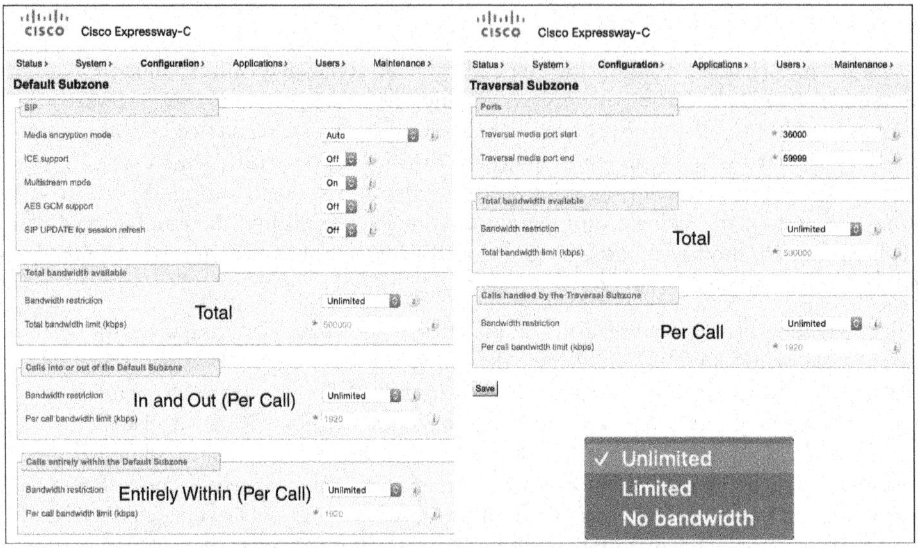

Figure 8-4 *Bandwidth Restriction Menus Using Subzones*

Links and Pipes Bandwidth Management

As mentioned in the previous section, there is another bandwidth restriction method in the Cisco Expressway called Pipes that can be used in conjunction with or as an alternative to the Subzone bandwidth restriction method. A **Pipe** is a bandwidth restriction that is applied to Links. Remember that Links have no bandwidth restriction capability in and of themselves. Links are simply logical connections between two Subzones, or between a Subzone and a Zone. However, a Link can have zero, one, or two Pipes applied to it. Additionally, a single pipe can be applied to more than one link, in which case that total bandwidth limit is the single total for calls across all Links that Pipe is applied to. We will explain this in more detail in a moment.

First, we want to answer the question "Why use Pipes with Subzones?" When the VCS was created, there were always endpoints registered to it. Therefore, Subzones were used to group endpoints together so that they could be managed the same way, such as with bandwidth restrictions. Some of these endpoints were even soft clients, so they were not always central to one location, and didn't have a set bandwidth rate applied to them. This created a need to control them more restrictively than endpoints that live in a single location. Additionally, there were bandwidth restrictions that needed to control calls outside the local zone, such as neighboring VCSs. This is where Pipes comes into the picture. Zones do not have a bandwidth restriction setting like Subzones do. Therefore, a Pipe can be applied to the Link connected to the Zone, and all calls out that Zone will be restricted by the bandwidth rates defined within that Pipe.

With all that stated, let's examine scenarios in which Pipes are used instead of Subzones. When Cisco first introduced the Expressway series, no endpoints could register directly to the Expressway Core or Edge. Therefore, Subzones and the bandwidth restrictions they contain were not needed on these servers. However, Pipes did still exist and were commonly used to control bandwidth. Even though the Expressways can now support direct registration, in many deployments they still only serve to proxy the registration requests to the Unified CM. If this is how the Expressways are used within your production environment, then you don't need Subzone bandwidth management. Pipes would be the only logical mechanism to use for controlling bandwidth from within the Expressway.

You should now have a better understanding of when to use Pipes, so let's examine the characteristics of Pipes. Because Links are defined as logical connections between two Subzones or between a Subzone and a Zone, and Pipes are applied to Links, Pipes can be defined as bandwidth limitations between two Subzones or between a Subzone and a Zone. They restrict bandwidth over a link in order to model any physical network limitations. Pipe bandwidth restrictions can be configured "per call" and "total bandwidth" between endpoints, just as they are configured in the Traversal Subzone. Pipes can be applied to one or more Links. Consider the following scenarios where Pipes can be used:

- When calls are placed between endpoints in different Subzones, it is possible to control the bandwidth used on the link between them.

- After creating a Pipe, it must be assigned to a link. Calls traversing the link will take the pipe's bandwidth allocation into consideration.

- Pipes may be shared between one or more Links. This configuration is used to model the situation where a site communicates with several other sites over the same broadband connection to the Internet. Each link may have up to two Pipes that are associated with it. This setup is useful for modeling two sites, each with its own broadband connection to the Internet backbone.

- A single call can be limited by bandwidth restrictions within Subzones and any Pipes at the same time if these restrictions are within the path of the call.

One Pipe, One Link:

- Applying a single pipe to a single link is useful when you want to apply specific limits to calls between a Subzone and another specific Subzone or zone. When a pipe is applied to a link, it restricts the bandwidth of calls that are made between the two nodes of the link. These restrictions apply to calls in either direction. Normally a single pipe would be applied to a single link. However, one or more Pipes may be applied to one or more Links, depending on how you want to model your network.

One Pipe, Two or More Links

- As illustrated in Figure 8-5, one Pipe can be applied to more than one link. Notice that there are two distinct Links: one connecting the Default Subzone to Subzone 1 and another connecting the Default Subzone to Subzone 2. However, the Pipe applied to both Links is called *Pipe 1*. Because this is the same pipe, the bandwidth limits apply the same on both Links. If calls between endpoints in the Default Subzone and Subzone 1 consume all the total bandwidth within Pipe 1, then no calls are possible between endpoints in Subzone 2 to any other Subzone.

Key
Topic

8

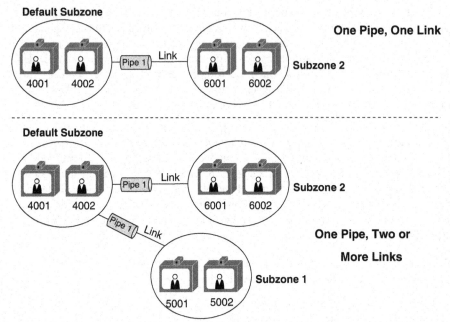

Figure 8-5   *Pipes Applied to One or More Links*

■ Each pipe may be applied to multiple Links. There is no limit to the number of Links to which a Pipe can be applied.

■ This solution is used to model the situation where one site communicates with several other sites across a **wide-area network (WAN)** connection.

■ A pipe should be configured to represent the WAN connection, and then applied to all the Links.

■ This solution allows you to configure the bandwidth options for calls in and out of that site.

Figure 8-5 illustrates the first two applications of Pipes within the Cisco Expressway.

Two Pipes, One Link:

■ Each link may have up to two Pipes that are associated with it.

■ This scenario is used to model the situation where two nodes of a link use different connection rates across the WAN.

■ Each location should then have its own pipe limitations based on its own connection rates, resulting in the link between the two nodes being subject to the bandwidth restrictions of both Pipes.

This third application of Pipes on the Cisco Expressway is illustrated in Figure 8-6.

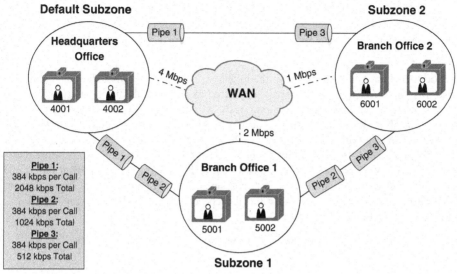

Figure 8-6   *Two Pipes Applied to One Link*

In Figure 8-6 there is a single Expressway being used to span three different office locations across a WAN. The Default Subzone represents the Headquarters Office, Subzone 1 represents Branch Office 1, and Subzone 2 represents Branch Office 2. Because each office has a different connection rate across the WAN, bandwidth restrictions need to be instituted for each site based on these bandwidth restrictions. The network is a shared network, meaning both video and data share the same network. So, when creating Pipes for each office location, only half the available bandwidth will be allocated to video. This leaves plenty of bandwidth available for day-to-day operations and important business tasks. No office can function in today's market without these capabilities. Again, we are using smaller numbers than you would normally use in a production environment, for the sake of easier math calculations.

The HQ office has a 4-Mbps connection available to the WAN. If we halve the network connection rate and allocate that to the total bandwidth limit, it will be 2048 kbps. The per-call limit will be 384 kbps for all office locations. We can create Pipes all day long and they will do no good unless they are applied to Links. Because the Default Subzone represents the HQ office, and Pipe 1 represents the bandwidth limitations of the HQ office, Pipe 1 needs to be applied to all Links that connect with the Default Subzone.

Branch office 1 has a network connection of 2 Mbps. By halving that network connection rate and allocating it to the total bandwidth limit, Pipe 2 will have 1024 kbps of total bandwidth available. Again, the per-call limit will be set to 384 kbps. Because Branch Office 1 is represented by Subzone 1 and Pipe 2 represents the bandwidth limitations of Branch Office 1, Pipe 1 needs to be applied to all the Links that connect with Subzone 1. If you examine Figure 8-6 and ignore all the Pipes except the ones mentioned up to this point, you should notice that the link between the Default Subzone and Subzone 1 now has two Links applied to it.

Finally, Branch office 2 has a network connection of 1 Mbps. By halving that network connection rate and allocating it to the total bandwidth limit, Pipe 3 will have 512 kbps of total bandwidth available. Again, the per-call limit will be set to 384 kbps. Because Branch Office 2 is represented by Subzone 2 and Pipe 3 represents the bandwidth limitations of Branch Office 2, Pipe 3 needs to be applied to all the Links that connect with Subzone 2. Now all the Pipes represented in Figure 8-6 have been explained. Each Link in this scenario will have two Pipes applied to it.

If endpoint 4001 calls endpoint 6001 at the highest bandwidth rate available, the call connects at 384 kbps. This bandwidth cost is subtracted from the totals of Pipe 1 and Pipe 3. If, while that call is still connected, endpoint 5001 calls endpoint 6002 at the highest bandwidth rate available, then the call connects at only 128 kbps. Because the first call at 384 kbps is subtracted from the 512 kbps total limit of Pipe 3, that only leaves 128 kbps. Even though the per-call rate is set to 384 kbps, there is not enough bandwidth available to support that rate. So, the call connects at 128 kbps and this bandwidth cost is subtracted from Pipe 2 and Pipe 3. No one else can call into Subzone 2 until one of the connections ends, but endpoints in Subzone 1 and Default Subzone can still call each other because there is plenty of total bandwidth left in Pipe 1 and Pipe 2.

There are basically two main steps to configuring Pipes. You need to create the Pipe and then apply the Pipe to a Link.

Step 1.   To create a Pipe, navigate to **Configuration > Bandwidth > Pipes.** Click **New** and configure the following settings:

- Name: Provide a name for the pipe that describes its purpose.

- Total Bandwidth Available section:

    - Bandwidth Restriction: Select Unlimited, Limited, or No Bandwidth.

    - Total Bandwidth Limit (kbps): Enter a numeric value to represent the total bandwidth limit in kbps that is being allowed for all concurrent calls.

- Calls Through This Pipe section (per-call bandwidth limitation):

    - Bandwidth Restriction: Select Unlimited, Limited, or No Bandwidth.

    - Per Call Bandwidth Limit (kbps): Enter a numeric value to represent the per-call bandwidth limit in kbps that is being allowed for all concurrent calls.

Step 2.   Click **Create Pipe** when finished. Figure 8-7 illustrates the Pipe configuration menus.

Step 3.   To apply the Pipe to a Link, navigate to **Configuration > Bandwidth > Links.** (Alternatively, click the **View, Edit, Add, and Delete Links** hyperlink at the bottom of the Pipes page under the Related Tasks section.)

Step 4.   Either click the Link name or click the **View/Edit** action. Do not click the Node 1 or Node 2 name. That will redirect you to that Subzone or Zone.

Step 5.   Under the Pipe 1 or Pipe 2 field, use the drop-down menu to select the Pipe(s) that should be applied to this link. The order does not matter if selecting more than one Pipe. If you are only selecting one Pipe, it does not matter which Pipe entry you enter it in either.

Step 6.   Click **Save** once finished. Your bandwidth settings are now set.

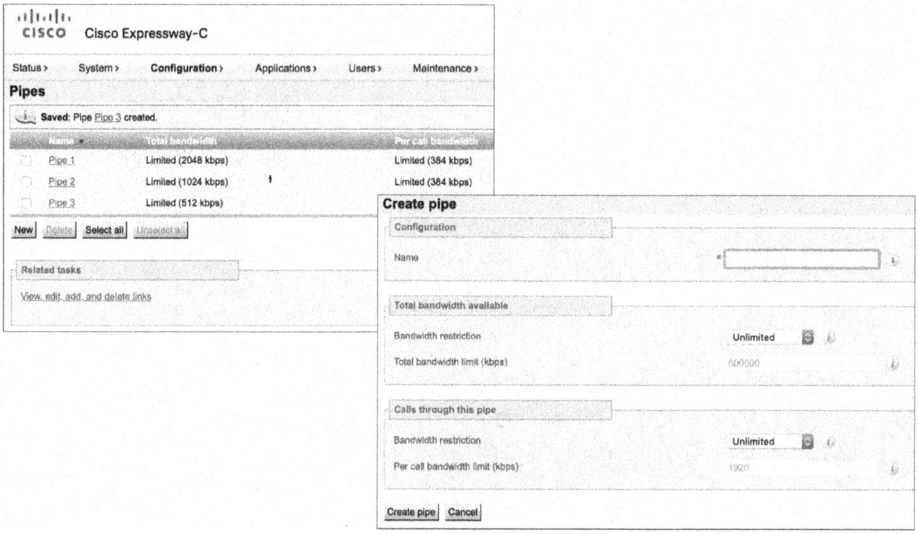

Figure 8-7 *Creating Pipes on the Cisco Expressway*

Figure 8-8 illustrates how to apply Pipes to Links on the Cisco Expressway.

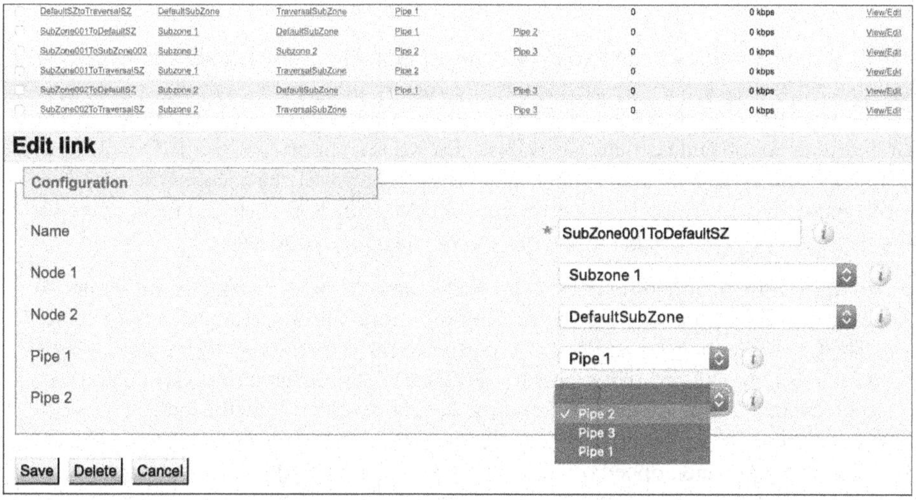

Figure 8-8 *Applying Pipes to Links on the Cisco Expressway*

Call Control Using Pipes

The primary purpose of Pipes is to limit bandwidth for calls that pass through the Cisco Expressway. Because Pipes are applied to Links, they can also be used for call control. Before we explain how they can be used in this capacity, it is important to first review a fundamental behavior of call routing within the Cisco Expressway. When a call is routed between Subzones or between a Subzone and Zone, the call will always take the shortest path. If that path is blocked, then the call will not reroute across another logical path.

The call will simply fail. Figure 8-9 illustrates a scenario that exemplifies this behavior of call control using Pipes.

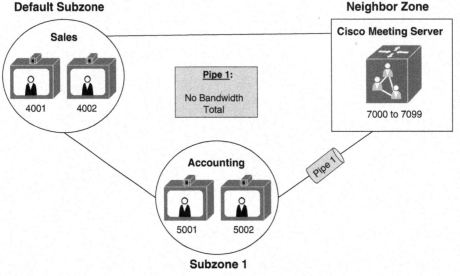

Figure 8-9   *Using Pipes for Call Control*

Imagine a company that uses the Expressway for endpoint registration. Sales associates need endpoints so that they can communicate with customers and generate sales for the company. The accounting team also needs endpoints so that they can communicate with the sales team about expense reports and account receivables. The sales team often uses the Cisco Meeting Server for conferences with customers and vendors; however, the accounting team does not need these services, so their access to the Cisco Meeting Server should be restricted to ensure the resources are available to the sales team when they need them.

To create this environment within the Cisco Expressway, the Sales endpoints are set up to register to the Default Subzone, and the Accounting endpoints are set up to register to Subzone 1. The Cisco Meeting Server does not register to the Expressway. Therefore, a Neighbor Zone needs to be created that points to the Cisco Meeting Server. An extra link also needs to be created between Subzone 1 and the Neighbor Zone. Now the magical piece to this whole solution can be applied. A Pipe needs to be created with a total bandwidth setting of No Bandwidth and applied to the link that was just created between Subzone 1 and the Neighbor Zone.

Because there are no restrictions between the Default Subzone and the shortest path to the Neighbor Zone, the Sales team will still be able to call out to the Cisco Meeting Server. Because there are no restrictions between the Default Subzone and the shortest path to Subzone 1, the Sales team will still be able to call out to the accounting team and vice versa. However, because Subzone 1 is restricted with No Bandwidth along the shortest path to the Neighbor Zone, any call attempts in that direction will fail.

Now let's change this scenario so you can see why it is important to set up this solution the way that has previously been described. Assume for a moment that the link between Subzone 1 and the Neighbor Zone was never created. Now the shortest path from Subzone 1 to the Neighbor Zone is through the Default Subzone. If we apply the No Bandwidth Pipe to the link connecting these two Subzones, then the Accounting endpoints and the Sales endpoints cannot communicate with one another, which is not the desired outcome. If the No Bandwidth Pipe is applied to the Link between the Default Subzone and the Neighbor Zone, then the Sales endpoints and Accounting endpoints can communicate with one another, but Sales will not be able to access the Cisco Meeting Server. Therefore, to use Pipes as a call control mechanism, such as has been described with this scenario, a "shortest path" must be created between Subzone 1 and the Neighbor Zone, and then the No Bandwidth Pipe needs to be applied to that link.

Exam Preparation Tasks

As mentioned in the section "How to Use This Book" in the Introduction, you have a couple of choices for exam preparation: the exercises here, Chapter 22, "Final Preparation," and the exam simulation questions in the Pearson Test Prep practice test software.

Review All Key Topics

Review the most important topics in this chapter, noted with the Key Topics icon in the outer margin of the page. Table 8-2 lists a reference of these key topics and the page numbers on which each is found.

Key Topic

Table 8-2 Key Topics for Chapter 8

Key Topic Element	Description	Page Number
List	Examples of when In and Out restrictions are used	137
List	Three bandwidth restriction modes	137
List	Criteria of applying one Pipe to two or more Links	141
List	Criteria of applying two Pipes to one Link	142

Complete Tables and Lists from Memory

There are no memory lists or tables in this chapter.

Define Key Terms

Define the following key terms from this chapter and check your answers in the glossary:

bandwidth, Default Call Bandwidth, Downspeed Mode, Downspeed Per Call Mode, Downspeed Total Mode, Pipe, wide-area network (WAN)

Q&A

The answers to these questions appear in Appendix A. For more practice with exam format questions, use the Pearson Test Prep practice test software.

1. What are the three bandwidth restriction modes?

2. List three ways Pipes can be applied to Links.

CHAPTER 9

Multisite Collaboration Solutions

This chapter covers the following topics:

Dial Plan Elements: Describes two specific elements of a Cisco Expressway dial plan: zones and Search Rules.

Simple Video Network with a Flat Dial Plan: Examines the advantages and disadvantages of a simple video network with a flat dial plan.

Complex Video Network with a Flat Dial Plan: Examines the advantages and disadvantages of a complex video network with a flat dial plan.

Complex Video Network with a Structured Dial Plan: Examines the advantages and disadvantages of a complex video network with a structured dial plan.

Hierarchical Video Network with a Structured Dial Plan: Examines the advantages and disadvantages of a hierarchical video network with a structured dial plan.

Configuring Neighbor Zones: Explains how to deploy Neighbor Zones and Search Rules on an Expressway Core between two Expressway Cores and between an Expressway Core and Cisco Unified CM.

All the elements discussed in the previous two chapters are components of the Call Processing Order. After the pre-search components are exhausted, the next successive function is to search zones. There are a lot of different zones that can be configured within the Cisco Expressway. The order these zones should be searched and how they are searched require more explanation than one chapter can contain. Therefore, this chapter examines zones as whole, and then focuses on Neighbor Zones specifically.

This chapter covers the following objectives from the Implementing Cisco Collaboration Cloud and Edge Solutions (CLCEI) exam 300-820:

- 1.7.c Describe Expressway Core dial plan elements: zones

- 2.2.c Configure Expressway Core dial plan elements: zones

- 2.4.d Configure a Business to Business (B2B) collaboration solution: Neighbor Zones

- 2.4.g Configure a Business to Business (B2B) collaboration solution: SIP trunk integration with Cisco Unified Communications Manager

"Do I Know This Already?" Quiz

The "Do I Know This Already?" quiz enables you to assess whether you should read this entire chapter thoroughly or jump to the "Exam Preparation Tasks" section. If you are in doubt about your answers to these questions or your own assessment of your knowledge of the topics, read the entire chapter. Table 9-1 lists the major headings in this chapter and their corresponding "Do I Know This Already?" quiz questions. You can find the answers in Appendix A, "Answers to the 'Do I Know This Already?' Quizzes and Review Questions."

Table 9-1 "Do I Know This Already?" Section-to-Question Mapping

Foundation Topics Section	Questions
Dial Plan Elements	1–3
Simple Video Network with a Flat Dial Plan	4
Complex Video Network with a Flat Dial Plan	5
Complex Video Network with a Structured Dial Plan	6
Hierarchical Video Network with a Structured Dial Plan	7
Configuring Neighbor Zones	8–10

CAUTION The goal of self-assessment is to gauge your mastery of the topics in this chapter. If you do not know the answer to a question or are only partially sure of the answer, you should mark that question as wrong for purposes of the self-assessment. Giving yourself credit for an answer you correctly guess skews your self-assessment results and might provide you with a false sense of security.

1. Which of the following is a zone type on the Cisco Expressway?

    a. MGCP Zone

    b. SIP Zone

    c. H.323 Zone

    d. Neighbor Zone

    e. Transversal Zone

2. Which of the following is the correct way to set up the Incoming Calls to Unknown IP Addresses setting on the Cisco Expressway?

    a. Set the Expressway Core to Indirect and set the Expressway Edge to Direct.

    b. Set the Expressway Core to Direct and set the Expressway Edge to Direct.

    c. Set the Expressway Core to Indirect and set the Expressway Edge to Indirect.

    d. Set the Expressway Core to Direct and set the Expressway Edge to Indirect.

3. How are zones searched on the Cisco Expressway?

    a. Zones are searched by type. The order in which they are searched is Local Zone first and DNS Zone last.

    b. Zones are searched by the order in which the Search Rules are listed in the Cisco Expressway.

    c. Zones are searched by priority, and the higher the number, the higher the priority.

    d. Zones are searched by priority, and the lower the number, the higher the priority.

4. Which of the following scenarios requires media and signaling to move through the Cisco Expressway?

    a. SIP to SIP calls.

    b. SIP to H.323 calls.

    c. H.323 to H.323 calls.

    d. All calls require signaling and media to move through the Cisco Expressway.

    e. Call setup signaling always goes through the Cisco Expressway, but media is always point-to-point.

5. What component is used in Call Loop Detection Mode to prevent loopbacks from occurring?

    a. Call Signaling Optimization

    b. Call serial number

    c. Call tag

    d. Destination endpoint alias

6. What is the main distinguishing factor of a complex video network with a structured dial plan on an Expressway?

    a. Unique suffixes

    b. Site codes

    c. Unique prefixes

    d. Unique aliases

7. What setting should be used on the Cisco Expressway when more than two Expressways are being used in a video network in order to limit the number of hops for call setup signaling?

    a. Call Loop Detection Mode

    b. Call Signaling Optimization

    c. Optimal Call Routing

    d. Neighbor Zone

8. Which of the following is an appropriate use for Neighbor Zones?

    a. Neighboring a Unified CM to an Expressway Core

    b. Neighboring an Expressway Core to an Expressway Edge

    c. Neighboring an Expressway Edge to an Expressway Edge

    d. Neighboring an Expressway Edge to a DNS server

9. While creating a Neighbor Zone from an Expressway Core to another Expressway Core, the engineer decides to change the SIP Transport setting to TLS. What should the engineer change the SIP port to so that TLS can be used over the appropriate port?

   a. 5060

   b. 5061

   c. 5062

   d. No change is necessary because the port will change automatically when the Transport setting is changed.

10. An engineer just finished building a Neighbor Zone on the Expressway Core to the Unified CM, but the zone status is showing that it is inactive. Which of the following is most likely the cause of this issue?

    a. The Unified CM needs a SIP trunk to the Expressway Core before the Neighbor Zone will become active.

    b. The wrong port is being used for SIP on the Neighbor Zone.

    c. H.323 was not disabled before creating the zone.

    d. The wrong peer address was entered for the Expressway.

Foundation Topics

Dial Plan Elements

The Call Processing Order, discussed extensively in Chapter 7, "Cisco Expressway Call Processing Order," is an important process to understand because it affects every call through the Cisco Expressway. Knowing all the components involved with the Call Processing Order and understanding how they work will help administrators troubleshoot calling issues when they arise within the Expressway.

As a refresher, the Call Processing Order begins with the pre-search components. When a call request enters the Cisco Expressway, it first checks the alias dialed against Transforms, Call Policy, and User Policy. Once the pre-search components have all been checked, the next step in the Call Processing Order is to perform a zone search to locate the destination alias. The first zone that should be searched is the Local Zone. If a match is not found, then external zones should be searched. Zones are pointers or trunks to other servers, and there are several types of external zones that exist. **Search Rules** determine the order in which zones are searched within the Expressway.

Zones

Chapter 6, "Registration on Cisco Expressway," introduced the logical components that make up the Cisco Expressway, including the Local Zone, which was defined as the Expressway itself. So, when the Local Zone is searched, what the Expressway is actually searching for are endpoints registered locally to that Expressway. Because endpoints register to subzones, it is logical to think of a Local Zone search as a search within the subzones.

Beyond the Local Zone, additional zones can be configured and used on Expressways to establish communication with other servers and organizations outside the corporate network. Other zones that exist within the Expressway include the Default Zone, Neighbor Zones, Traversal Zones, and DNS and **ENUM Zones**.

As defined in Chapter 6, the *Default Zone* is the default path into and out from the Local Zone. It always exists on the Expressway and cannot be deleted. The Default Zone is used for sending call media out from the Local Zone and receiving call media into the Local Zone after external destinations have been established using other zones. It is also used for broadcast traffic if the appropriate zone has not been configured. An example of the type of broadcast traffic that's sent would be calls to unknown IP addresses. This type of call is not allowed by default on the Expressway. However, if the Calls to Unknown IP Addresses setting is enabled, and appropriate Search Rules are created, then the Default Zone can be used to send a broadcast communication throughout the broadcast domain of the network to locate an unknown IP address. Figure 9-1 illustrates how calls to unknown IP addresses work in a Cisco Expressway environment.

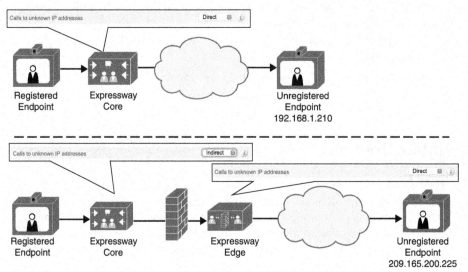

Figure 9-1 *Calls to Unknown IP Addresses Operation*

In the top illustration of Figure 9-1, the Expressway Core has the Calls to Unknown IP Addresses setting set to Direct. This allows the Expressway to send a broadcast search out the Default Zone to locate the endpoint that is not registered. The Expressway Core should have the Calls to Unknown IP Addresses setting set to Direct only if the unregistered endpoint exists within the same broadcast network. However, this is almost never the case. In most cases a call to an unknown IP address exists outside a corporate network and therefore is not within the local broadcast domain.

In this type of scenario, the Calls to Unknown IP Addresses setting on the Expressway Core should be set to Indirect. This allows the Expressway Core to forward the call request across the Traversal Zone to the Expressway Edge. The Calls to Unknown IP Addresses setting on the Expressway Edge should then be set to Direct. This allows the call to traverse through the firewall in order to connect to the endpoint that exists outside the corporate network. You can configure the Calls to Unknown IP Addresses setting in the Expressway by navigating to **Configuration > Dial Plan > Configuration**.

Incoming calls using IP addresses can also be allowed by using the Expressway IP address. However, an alias should be included with the dialed alias, such as john@192.168.1.40 or 6501@192.168.1.40, assuming the IP address in both these examples is the IP address of the Expressway. In the event that an incoming call to the Expressway IP address does not include a callee alias, a fallback alias can be configured in the Expressway. This alias will be used to forward all incoming calls that used only the Expressway IP address. Figure 9-2 shows the Dial Plan Configuration page on the Cisco Expressway.

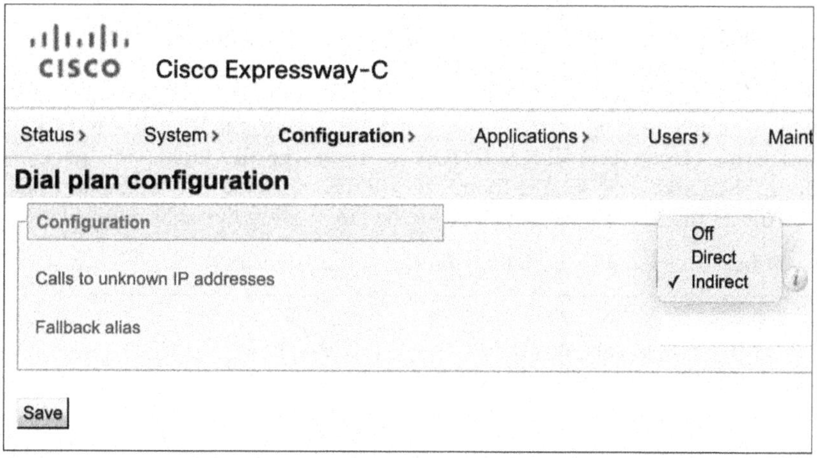

Figure 9-2 *Dial Plan Configuration Page of the Cisco Expressway*

Another zone type on the Cisco Expressway is the **Neighbor Zone**, which is used to communicate with other communication servers within the same LAN or WAN. These servers could include other Cisco Expressway Cores, Cisco Unified CMs, Cisco Meeting Servers, a Microsoft unified communications server, or some other third-party gatekeeper or SIP server. Because the rest of this chapter delves into Neighbor Zones with more depth, we will save this discussion until later.

Traversal zones are used for communication through a firewall. Two Expressways are required to set up a traversal communication. The Expressway Core needs to be located inside the firewall, while the Expressway Edge needs to be located outside the firewall. The Expressway Core supports a **Traversal Client Zone**, while the Expressway Edge can support both a Traversal Client Zone and a **Traversal Server Zone**. The Traversal Client Zone must communicate with the Traversal Server Zone to establish a traversal connection. Another type of traversal zone that exists within the Expressway is the **Unified Communications Traversal Zone**. This type of traversal zone is only used in conjunction with a Mobile Remote Access (MRA) deployment, which will be discussed more in Part 3 of this book. There are two communication protocols that can be used with the firewall traversal solution. **Assent** is a Cisco proprietary protocol that supports both SIP and H.323 communication. **H.460.18 and H.460.19** are ITU standards that are used only for H.323 firewall traversal communication.

DNS Zones are used for communication between the Expressway and a Domain Name System (DNS) server. Appropriate Service (SRV) records and A records need to be set up in DNS for routing to be established between communication servers. ENUM (Enumerated Dialing) can also be used for routing calls between E.164 aliases and URIs. An ENUM Server can be built in any DNS server or can be configured as a separate entity.

Cisco introduced a new type of DNS Zone on the Cisco Expressway Edge servers called the **Webex Zone** beginning in version X8.11.4. The Webex Zone not only automates and simplifies Hybrid Call Service configuration, but is also a single zone entry that ensures that all calling and meetings solutions under the Webex banner precisely route to the correct cloud microservices and are handled accordingly.

The decision-making for call routing and protocols is offloaded from the Expressway itself (manual configuration by you, the admin) onto DNS (automated configuration, managed by Cisco). The decisions are made by a Name Authority Pointer (NAPTR) DNS record that is able to pinpoint call and meeting paths that are then advertised to the DNS SRV record. The two entries in the record's ANSWER SECTION determine the SRV lookup that gets advertised back to the Expressway-E. The Expressway-E then does the SRV lookup as usual. Example 9-1 illustrates the NAPTR lookup made by the Expressway through a public DNS.

Example 9-1 *Webex NAPTR DNS Lookup from Cisco Expressway*

```
;; ANSWER SECTION:
example.call.ciscospark.com. 300 INNAPTR 50 50 "S" "SIPS+D2T" ""
_sips._tcp.call.ciscospark.com.
example.call.ciscospark.com. 300 INNAPTR 30 50 "S" "SIPSM+D2T" ""
_sips._tcp.callservice.ciscospark.com.
```

All of this happens behind the scenes, and all you have to do is create the Webex Zone on the Expressway with preconfigured settings; no further zones-per-service are required. A further benefit is that your deployment is future-proofed as more services are added to Cisco's Webex cloud and more complex routing decisions need to be made.

Search Rules

For all zone types, including the Local Zone, Search Rules must be configured before any calls can be routed. Search Rules can be configured to search Any Alias, search Any IP Address, or perform a search based on an Alias Pattern Match. This last option allows patterns to be configured based on Exact Match, Prefix, Suffix, or Regex. The previous section mentioned that calls to unknown IP addresses must have the corresponding setting configured as Direct or Indirect and have the appropriate rules configured. In addition to changing the Calls to Unknown IP Addresses setting, a Search Rule must be configured to allow Any IP Address calling. If the Expressway Core has been configured as Indirect, then the Any IP Address rule should point to the appropriate traversal zone. If the Expressway Edge has been configured as Direct, then the Any IP Address rule should point to the Local Zone. From there the call will find its way out the Default Zone because of the Calls to Unknown IP Addresses setting.

Zones are searched based on the priority of the Search Rules. Priority values can be set between 1 and 65,534. 1 is the highest priority, so the higher the number, the lower the priority. The first zone that should be searched is the Local Zone. Therefore, there is a default Search Rule that comes preconfigured on the Expressway with a priority of 50 that matches Any Alias and points to the Local Zone. This rule can be modified, changed, inactivated or deleted if needed. When the Expressway searches a rule for an alias pattern match and that alias is not found, the Expressway proceeds to search all the applicable rules for all zones based on this priority until a match is found or all available options have been exhausted. Because there are different types of zones available on the Expressway, there is a preferred search order of these zones that should be followed. Understand that this is not a hard-and-fast rule, and different circumstances may determine following a different search order of zones. Best practice suggests that the Neighbor Zones are searched after the Local Zone, followed by Traversal Zones, and last the DNS/ENUM Zones should be searched. A suggested way of grouping the priorities to create this manner of searches could be as follows:

Local Zone: 1–19,999

Neighbor Zone: 20,000–29,999

Traversal Zone: 30,000–39,999

DNS and ENUM Zones: 40,000–49,999

Webex Zone: 50,000–59,999

The actual priority values used do not matter so long as you keep in mind that lower numbers are searched first, and higher numbers are searched last. Each administrator should adjust priority groupings based on enterprise needs. There are some other settings that are less commonly used when configuring Search Rules on an Expressway, but they do warrant a brief explanation. These settings are shown in Figure 9-3 and described here:

Key Topic

- Rule Name is simply the name given to a rule. It is important to provide a name that describes the purpose of the rule.

- Description is an optional setting that can be used to better describe the purpose of a rule. This allows administrators to keep rule names shorter and put longer details in the description.

- The Protocol setting allows the administration to specify a protocol with which this rule can be used. If SIP is selected, then H.323 calls cannot use this Search Rule, and vice versa. The default value is Any, and it can be changed to SIP or H.323.

- The Source setting determines the zone from which a call must originate. Options include the following:

  - **Any:** Locally registered devices, neighbor or traversal zones, and any nonregistered devices

  - **All Zones:** Locally registered devices plus neighbor or traversal zones

  - **Local Zone:** Locally registered devices only

  - **Named:** A specific zone or subzone; if selected, a drop-down menu is presented with all available options

- Request Must Be Authenticated indicates whether this Search Rule applies only to authenticated search requests. The default value is No.

- Mode describes the pattern used to match a destination alias, as described previously. Mode can be set to Any Alias, Any IP Address, or Alias Pattern Match. When Alias Pattern Match is selected, three additional fields appear:

  - Pattern Type can be set to Exact, Prefix, Suffix, or Regex.

  - Pattern String is the pattern that should be matched based on the pattern type selected previously.

9

- Pattern Behavior determines what the Expressway should do with the alias once a match has been made. The Pattern Behavior options include

  - **Strip:** Commonly used with a Pattern Type setting of either Prefix or Suffix, this behavior removes whatever pattern string was matched.

  - **Leave:** Commonly used with Exact Match, but any of the Pattern Type settings could be used here. The alias matched by this pattern will be searched for in its exact form.

  - **Replace:** This behavior opens another configuration option where a Replace String value can be entered. This new string will be used to try and locate the destination endpoint. This one is most commonly used with Regex, but can be used with Prefix or Suffix too.

- On Successful Match is a behavior that determines if the Expressway should continue to search for alternative paths to a destination should a match be found. If no match is found, the Expressway continues the search regardless of how this setting is configured. The two configuration options are Continue and Stop. Using the Stop option helps to prevent loopback issues when searching external zones.

- Target is the destination zone the call will be forwarded to when the Expressway finds a successful match. Local Zone is always one of the options, although any additional zones that have been created will be listed as viable options as well.

- State determines whether this Search Rule is active or inactive. This setting can be configured as Enabled or Disabled. Disabling a rule is better than deleting the rule in case the rule needs to be used again in the future. This will prevent having to re-create the rule. Disabling a rule also helps in isolating issues while troubleshooting calls.

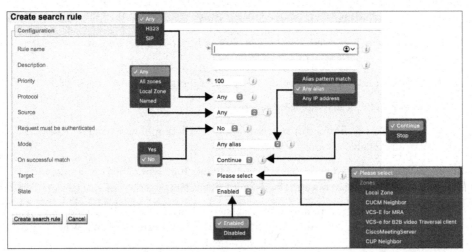

Figure 9-3   *Search Rule Menu Options*

It is important to note that if the Expressway changes an alias using the mechanisms under Mode, then the changes are applied only for the search under this particular Search Rule. If a match is not found, then the alias reverts to the state in which it existed prior to this search.

Simple Video Network with a Flat Dial Plan

Four different deployment models can be used in a Cisco Expressway architectural design. Each of these models has merits and limitations, and there are circumstances that would warrant using each of these models depending on the customer environment. Up to this point in the book only one of these deployment models has been discussed, which is the simple video network with a flat dial plan. A single Expressway Core is used, and all signaling and media traffic is linked through that one Expressway. Each endpoint is using a unique alias and registers to the single Expressway; therefore, no neighboring is required between Expressway Core peers. If a simple video network with a flat dial plan model is used for a company that spans multiple locations linked across a WAN, then subzones can be used to represent each physical location respectively. A simple video network with a flat dial plan could involve a single cluster of Expressway Cores and could also involve an Expressway Edge for firewall traversal calls or MRA. Figure 9-4 illustrates a single combined deployment model that supports four locations interconnected across a WAN.

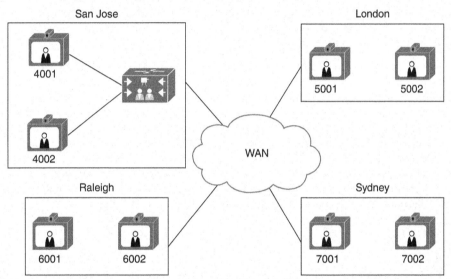

Figure 9-4 *Simple Video Network with a Flat Dial Plan*

There are some advantages and disadvantages to using the simple video network with a flat dial plan. The advantages to this type of deployment model are that it is a simple concept to configure and a simple model to maintain. This is an ideal model for a customer environment that has only one location, or only a few endpoints spread out across multiple locations, as illustrated in Figure 9-4.

On the other side of the coin, there are many disadvantages to this type of deployment model. All signaling and media traffic is linked through the same Expressway, so if that Expressway ceases to function, no calls are possible. This single point of failure can be overcome by implementing a cluster of Expressways, but there is still another limitation to funneling all the media and signaling through a single location.

When a non-traversal call is set up through the Expressway, the signaling for call setup must travel through the Expressway before it is sent to the destination endpoint. However, the actual UDP media and signaling for the audio and video are direct between the endpoints. This works well in this scenario because bandwidth will only be consumed at the locations involved with the call. This is true so long as the call is not a traversal call. With traversal calls, the media must always traverse through the Expressway. As mentioned in Chapter 6, "Registration on Cisco Expressway," the Expressway supports four types of traversal calls: firewall traversal, SIP/H.323 interworking, IPv4/IPv6 interworking, and dual network traversal. The last type is only available on the Expressway Edge server. In the illustration of Figure 9-4, if an H.323 endpoint in Raleigh is trying to communicate with a SIP endpoint in Sydney, the media must travel through San Jose. Therefore, bandwidth at the San Jose site must be robust enough to support calls at all locations simultaneously, including San Jose itself. This could potentially create an issue with other calls connecting, even if they are not traversal calls. If the hosting site of San Jose runs out of bandwidth, signaling for call setup will not even get through this site. This is why this type of deployment model is not suitable for medium or large-sized organizations.

Complex Video Network with a Flat Dial Plan

As companies grow, the need for larger networks becomes inevitable. A simple means of scaling a network would be to add Expressways to each location. This creates a complex video network with a flat dial plan that would definitely overcome the limitations of the previously described deployment model.

This deployment model is complex for two main reasons. There are now more than one Expressway that need to be managed, and communication between the two or more Expressways needs to be established and maintained. However, the dial plan doesn't change. You can continue to use the same flat dial plan used in the previous deployment model. Assume the same customer represented in Figure 9-4 simply adds an Expressway Core to each location, and then neighbors the Expressways together using Neighbor Zones. Because this model uses a flat dial plan, the Any Alias Search Rule could be used for each Neighbor Zone created. When an Expressway receives a call for an endpoint that is not registered locally, it sends out a **Location Request (LRQ)** to all the other Expressways it is neighbored to where there is a matching Search Rule. Figure 9-5 illustrates how this complex video network with a flat dial plan might look.

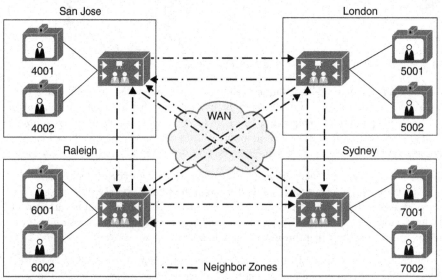

Figure 9-5   *Complex Video Network with a Flat Dial Plan*

There are several advantages to this type of deployment model. Even though it is called a complex video network, it is still a pretty simple concept to configure and maintain. So, the advantage of the simple video network holds true for this video network design as well. Additionally, the disadvantages of the simple video network become advantages within the complex video network model. Each Expressway is neighbored to all other Expressways in a full-mesh model. Therefore, there are three Neighbor Zones on each respective Expressway. Any calls between locations will consume bandwidth only within the involved locations regardless of the type of call, traversal or non-traversal. There is no longer a single point of failure either. If the Expressway in San Jose fails, calls are still possible between the other three locations.

Unfortunately, this deployment model is not impervious to disadvantages. All Expressways must know about all other peers. This means that this is not a very scalable solution. Adding or removing an Expressway requires changing the configuration of every Expressway. Already, there are three Neighbor Zones on each Expressway. If the customer with the network shown in Figure 9-5 decided to add a location in Paris, it would have to create four Neighbor Zones on the Paris Expressway plus one additional Neighbor Zone on each of the existing Expressways. That's eight Neighbor Zones, plus corresponding Search Rules, that must be created just to add one location. Then for each location added after that, the number of Neighbor Zones grows exponentially. This is definitely not a very scalable deployment model.

Another disadvantage is that one call attempt can result in many LRQs being sent out. As mentioned previously, when calling an endpoint that is not registered on the same local Expressway, a LRQ will be sent to every Expressway with a matching Search Rule. Because this deployment model uses a flat dial plan, all the Search Rules use the Any Alias pattern match. This will result in an external LRQ going out to every neighbored Expressway. This can create a call routing error called **Loopback**, which results in the call failing. Figure 9-6 illustrates how loops can occur in a full-mesh topology between Expressways.

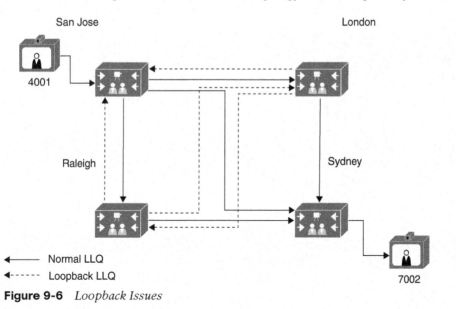

Figure 9-6 *Loopback Issues*

In Figure 9-6, endpoint 4001 in San Jose is attempting to call endpoint 7002 in Sydney. Because the alias 7002 is not registered to the San Jose Expressway, the Expressway sends out an LRQ to the London, Raleigh, and Sydney Expressways. Following the logical path, the Sydney Expressway identifies the endpoint registered locally and replies with a **Location Confirm (LCF)**. However, there are still two more searches out that must complete their cycle.

Because the destination endpoint is not found in Raleigh, that Expressway sends out its own set of LRQs to try and locate the endpoint. The request originated from San Jose, so the Raleigh Expressway does not send an LRQ back to the San Jose Expressway. However, it does send an LRQ to the London and Sydney Expressways. Likewise, the London Express-way continues the search from the San Jose LRQ by sending its own LRQ to Raleigh and Sydney. This is where the issue begins to propagate. Neither Raleigh nor London sent an LRQ back to San Jose from the original LRQ sent to these locations. However, Raleigh does send the LRQ from London to San Jose and Sydney. Likewise, London sends the LRQ from Raleigh to San Jose and Sydney. Even though the endpoint was located in Sydney, the call fails because the San Jose Expressway received a loopback LRQ on the original request it sent out.

Key Topic

The **Call Loop Detection Mode** setting on the Expressway prevents search loops from occurring. Each search has a call serial number and a call tag. The serial number is unique to the search, but the call tag information is passed with an LRQ. The Expressway uses the tag to identify a call that has already been received and hence ignored, preventing loopback errors. This is not a foolproof method for preventing loopbacks. However, customers for whom using a complex video network with a flat dial plan makes sense can still be protected from being crippled from this loopback issue. Figure 9-7 shows the Call Loop Detection Mode setting on the Cisco Expressway and the menu path to access it.

Figure 9-7   *Cisco Expressway Call Loop Detection Mode Setting*

Complex Video Network with a Structured Dial Plan

Because the Call Loop Detection Mode setting does not always work to prevent loopbacks, there is another deployment model that can be used as a foolproof method for preventing loopbacks. The complex video network with a structured dial plan introduces a more complex and structured dial plan that allows Search Rules to target specific locations based on the alias patterns that are matched. Figure 9-8 illustrates how a complex video network with a structured dial plan can be configured.

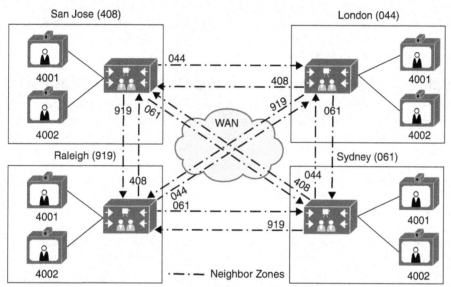

Figure 9-8   *Complex Video Network with a Structured Dial Plan*

In Figure 9-8, notice first that all the endpoints use the same four-digit numbers as their local extensions regardless of their location. In a production environment, it would not be necessary to use the same numbers on all endpoints. It is done in this example only to illustrate that the structure of this dial plan allows for this type of overlap in extensions. This in turn allows for up to 10,000 phones to be supported within each location while still using four-digit extensions. Using the flat dial plan exemplified in previous figures, only 1000 phones could be supported per location using a four-digit extension.

The real key to this structured dial plan is the use of a site code of sorts. These are not "site codes" like you would configure on the Unified CM. The Search Rules that would coincide with Figure 9-8 would actually use a prefix pattern match. A suffix could also be used for domain routing, if SIP URIs are being used as the alias type without a numeric host portion of the URI. In the case of Figure 9-8, a site code, or prefix, is assigned to each location. San Jose is 408, London is 044, Raleigh is 919, and Sydney is 061. These prefixes are not configured on the Expressways for the site they are assigned to. Rather, the Search Rules on the other three Expressways are configured with the prefix of the fourth Expressway. For example, a Search Rule on the London Expressway will be configured with the 408 prefix and applied to the San Jose Neighbor Zone. The default Any Alias rule for the Local Zone could be changed to use a regular expression that allows local dialing to include the London prefix or not. That regular expression would look something like this:

```
(044)?\d{4}
```

The **(044)?** indicates that the dialed number can start with 044, or not. The **\d{4}** indicates there must be four numbers at least in this pattern match. If any endpoint in London dials 4084002, the call will be routed only to San Jose. It will not search the Local Zone, nor will it send an LRQ to Raleigh or Sidney. In this manner, the structure of this dial plan will prevent loopback errors from occurring. This is the greatest advantage of the complex video network with a structured dial plan.

Because this is still a complex video network, however, this solution still possesses most of the disadvantages of the complex video network with a flat dial plan. The greatest disadvantage is the lack of scalability. The complexity of this solution grows exponentially as each additional location with an Expressway is added.

Hierarchical Video Network with a Structured Dial Plan

The scalability issue of the previous two deployment models is resolved in the hierarchical video network with a structured dial plan. There is no need to neighbor all the Expressways with each other in a full-mesh pattern. One Expressway is nominated as the **directory Expressway** for the hierarchical deployment. The "directory" designation is in name only based on the network positioning and function this Expressway will serve. No actual settings or licensing determines if an Expressway is the directory Expressway or not. Each additional Expressway is neighbored to that directory Expressway, and the structured dial plan on the directory Expressway determines how calls are routed. Different directory Expressways can also serve as sub-directory Expressways by using a global directory Expressway between them. Figure 9-9 illustrates a hierarchical video network with a structured dial plan that uses a global directory Expressway with regional sub-directory Expressways.

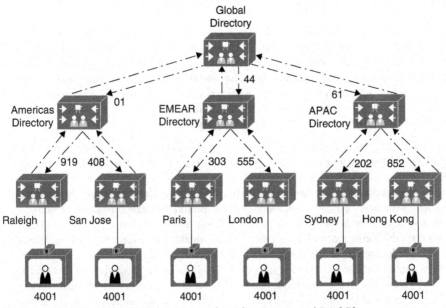

Figure 9-9 *Hierarchical Video Network with a Structured Dial Plan*

Obviously, this type of video network design would be best suited for a large enterprise corporation with a wide footprint that spans multiple locations. Each location possesses its own Expressway that can support the local registration of endpoints. In the example provided in Figure 9-9, there are three geographical regions, each represented with an Expressway acting as the directory for that region. The local Expressway for each location is neighbored to the regional directory Expressway and vice versa. Each regional directory Expressway is also neighbored to a global directory Expressway, and vice versa, so that communication can be shared globally. A structured dial plan accompanies this design so that loopbacks can be avoided, and calls can be routed quickly and easily between endpoints located in different locations.

As with each of the deployment models discussed previously, there are certain advantages and disadvantages to this model. We mentioned the first of these advantages at the beginning of this section. The hierarchical video network with a structured dial plan resolves the scalability issue of the complex video network designs. Adding a location only requires building two Neighbor Zones with corresponding Search Rules. Using the example in Figure 9-9, if the company wanted to add a location in Los Angeles, it would need to build a Neighbor Zone between the LA Expressway and the Americas Directory Expressway and vice versa. Now any endpoint from any location can call to an endpoint in LA and an LA endpoint can call to any endpoint at any other location. The company can add a location in Berlin, Germany, and only need to create two Neighbor Zones and corresponding Search Rules. It can add a location in Tokyo, Japan, and only need to create two Neighbor Zones and corresponding Search Rules. This deployment model is very scalable, only requiring the same minimum effort to add an unlimited number of locations each time.

Another series of advantages to the hierarchical video network with a structured dial plan is closely related to the scalability advantage:

- No fully connected mesh of Expressways is required. All local Expressways do not need to know all other Expressways. Each Expressway only needs to know how to reach its own directory Expressway.

- A minimized number of LRQs need to be issued when a call is attempted.

- Calls consume bandwidth only within the local Expressway locations.

The reason these advantages exist and are all so closely related has to do with a function of the Cisco Expressways called **optimal call routing**, which should be used anytime more than one Expressway is used. Figure 9-10 illustrates how optimal call routing operates.

9

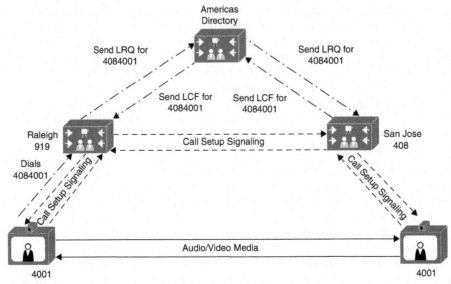

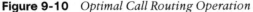

Figure 9-10   *Optimal Call Routing Operation*

In Figure 9-10, the Raleigh Expressway is neighbored to the Americas Expressway, the Americas Expressway is neighbored to the Raleigh and San Jose Expressways, and the San Jose Expressway is neighbored to the Americas Expressway. There is no Neighbor Zone between the Raleigh and San Jose Expressways. The Raleigh endpoint on the left side of the figure tries to call the San Jose endpoint on the right side of the figure by dialing 4084001. When the call request reaches the Raleigh Expressway, no match is found locally, so this Expressway sends an LRQ to its neighbor, the Americas Directory Expressway. The Americas Directory Expressway cannot locate the endpoint locally either, so the LRQ is forwarded to the San Jose Expressway. Because the San Jose Expressway can locate the endpoint locally, it responds to the Americas Directory Expressway with a Location Confirm (LCF) that includes the IP address of the Expressway the endpoint is registered to. The Americas Directory Expressway then sends the LCF to the Raleigh Expressway with the destination IP address of the San Jose endpoint. The Raleigh Expressway and the San Jose Expressway can now communicate directly with one another to send the rest of the call setup messaging without involving the Americas Directory Expressway in the rest of the call. So long as the call is not a traversal call, the media can be direct between the Raleigh endpoint and the San Jose endpoint. Only the Raleigh and San Jose Expressways will consume a call license. Optimal call routing prevents calls being passed through more Expressways and consuming more licenses than are needed.

Optimal call routing can be configured the same way the Call Loop Detection Mode setting is configured, because its setting, Call Signaling Optimization, is under the same menu on the Cisco Expressway (refer to Figure 9-7). Just remember that **Call Signaling Optimization** is the setting on a Cisco Expressway that allows for optimal call routing. Optimal call routing is the function of limiting hops between Expressways for call setup signaling when more than two Expressways are being used in a video network. On the Cisco Expressway web interface, navigate to **Configuration > Call Routing**. Change the Call Signaling Optimization setting to On and click Save.

There is one additional advantage to the hierarchical video network with a structured dial plan design that is worth mentioning. There is a layer of resiliency that exists in this design without having to cluster Expressways. If an Expressway were to go down, the video network as a whole is not down. There are still other call scenarios that are possible. Building off the design example in Figure 9-9, if the Global Directory Expressway were to go down, calls are still possible within each of the three regions. If one of the regional Expressways were to go down, such as the Americas Directory Expressway, calls are still possible in each location under the Americas directory, Raleigh and San Jose respectively, and calls are still possible between any other location globally outside of the Americas directory. Obviously, it would make sense to cluster the global and regional directory Expressways, but this network design still has a level of resiliency built into it without clusters due to its nature by design.

There is but one disadvantage to this network design, but it is big enough to prohibit many companies from using it. That disadvantage is cost. The infrastructure investment that a company must make to host all the Expressways, plus licenses and service contracts, for this solution may outweigh the advantages it brings to the table. Not to mention this network design is overkill for what smaller companies even need. However, for those larger companies that can afford the investment and possess the need, this solution is a perfect fit.

Configuring Neighbor Zones

Now that the four network designs for Expressways using Neighbor Zones have been explained, it's time to turn the focus to how these Neighbor Zones can be configured. Notice in Figures 9-5, 9-8, and 9-9 that each pair of Expressways has two Neighbor Zones, one pointing in each direction. All zones on the Cisco Expressway are unidirectional; therefore, for calls to be placed in each direction, Neighbor Zones must exist on both Expressways.

Neighbor Zones have several notable characteristics. A Neighbor Zone is essentially a trunk that can be used to connect like devices over the same network type. The other device the Neighbor Zone points to is referred to as a neighbor. These Zones can be used to connect two Expressway Cores on an internal network or two Expressway Edges in a DMZ or on a public network. Neighbor Zones are not used to connect an Expressway Core with an Expressway Edge. Even though the devices are essentially the same, the network parameters they operate within are not. Traversal zones should be used in this type of scenario, which will be discussed in Chapter 10, "Multisite and Business-to-Business (B2B) Collaboration Solutions." You can also use a Neighbor Zone to connect an Expressway Core to a Cisco Unified CM or a Cisco Meeting Server. Neighbor Zones can also support either H.323 calls, SIP calls, or both.

As mentioned at the beginning of this chapter, you create a neighbor relationship with another server by creating a new Neighbor Zone on your local Expressway. Similar to creating new subzones on a Cisco Expressway, when a new zone is created, two Links are automatically created as well. One Link connects the new zone with the Default Subzone and the other Link connects the zone with the Traversal Subzone. These Links can be deleted, and additional Links can be created. There are no bandwidth restriction settings inherent to zones as there are with subzones, but Pipes can be applied to Links associated with zones in order to control bandwidth. Search Rules are needed to match destination aliases to determine which zone should be used to forward the call request. For the Expressway to support SIP encryption over a Traversal or Neighbor Zone, TLS must be configured as the transport type. When configuring TLS on a Neighbor Zone, the port needs to be manually changed to 5061 from 5060.

Expressway to Expressway Neighbor Zones

The way in which you create a Neighbor Zone to another Expressway is different than how you create a Neighbor Zone to a Unified CM. The following steps will first examine how to build a Neighbor Zone from an Expressway Core to another Expressway Core. These steps will also explain how to build the necessary Search Rules on an Expressway Core.

Let's begin by creating a Neighbor Zone from an Expressway Core to another Expressway Core. Figure 9-11 shows the initial menu option to select the zone type on the Cisco Expressway.

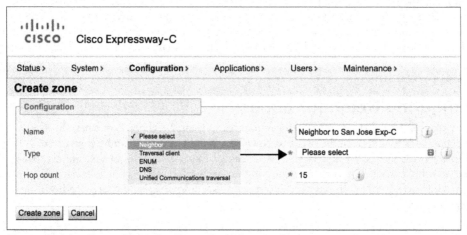

Figure 9-11 *Create Zone Configuration Menu on Expressway Core*

Step 1. Log in to the web interface of the Expressway Core and navigate to **Configuration > Zones > Zones.**

Step 2. Click **New** and enter the following information:

Name: Create something logical, such as Neighbor to San Jose Exp-E.

Type: Choose **Neighbor.**

Hop Count: Leave at the default, **15.**

Once you select Neighbor in the Type field, additional menu options appear. Figure 9-12 shows the H.323 and SIP menu options for a Neighbor Zone.

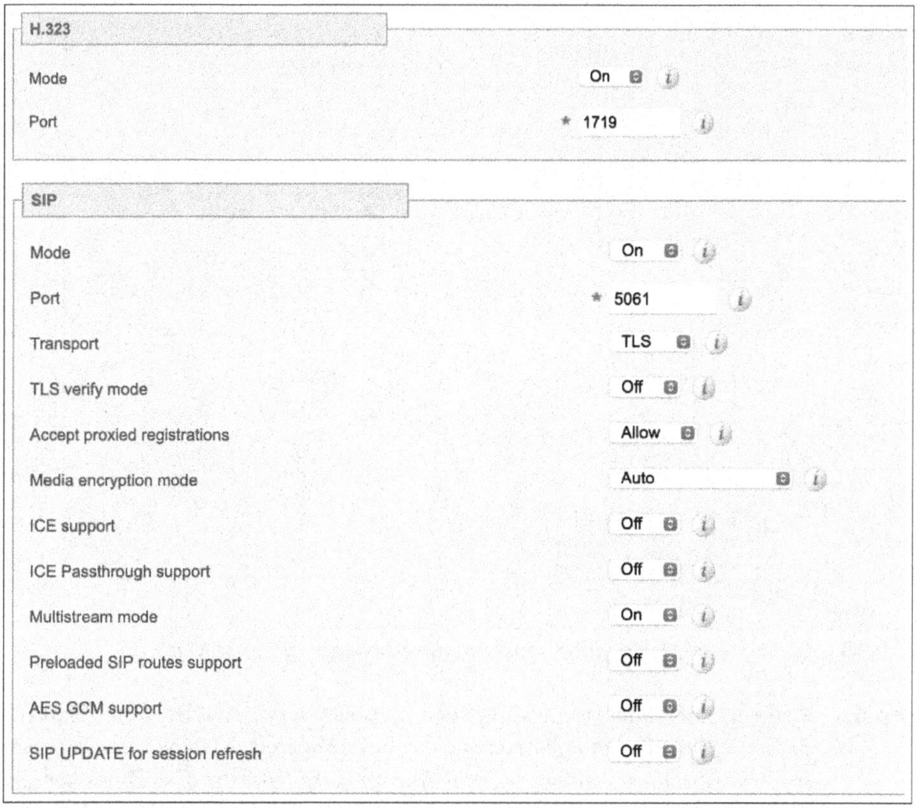

H.323		
Mode	On	
Port	* 1719	

SIP		
Mode	On	
Port	* 5061	
Transport	TLS	
TLS verify mode	Off	
Accept proxied registrations	Allow	
Media encryption mode	Auto	
ICE support	Off	
ICE Passthrough support	Off	
Multistream mode	On	
Preloaded SIP routes support	Off	
AES GCM support	Off	
SIP UPDATE for session refresh	Off	

Figure 9-12 *H.323 and SIP Neighbor Zone Menus*

Step 3. If you do not plan to support H.323, set the Mode option to **Off**. Otherwise, leave the Mode and Port settings at their default values.

Step 4. Most of the SIP settings can be left at their default values as well. However, if you change the SIP Transport setting, then you need to change the Port setting as well. TCP uses port 5060 and TLS uses port 5061.

You need to configure three other sections for a Neighbor Zone: Authentication, Location, and Advanced. Figure 9-13 shows the menu options for these sections.

9

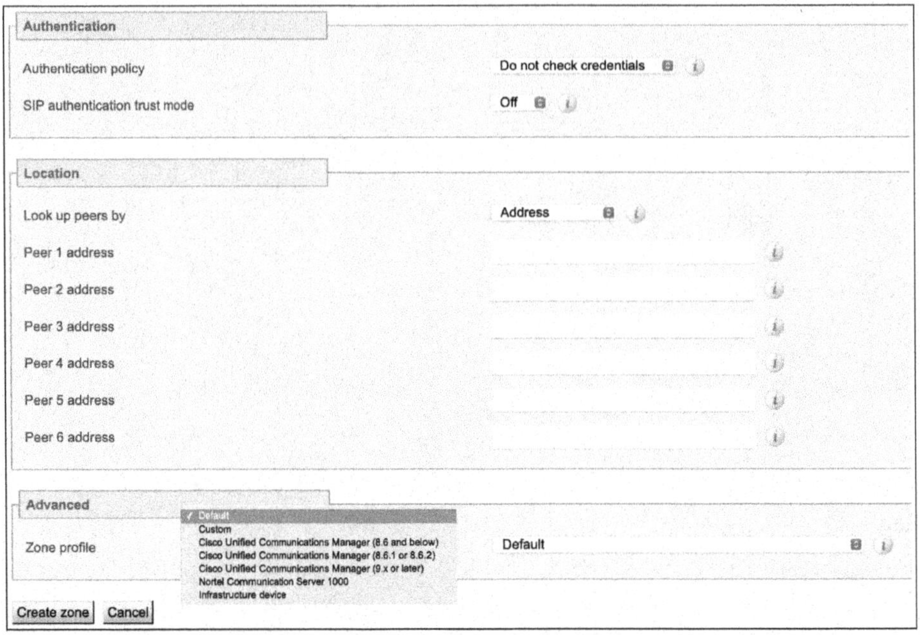

Figure 9-13 *Authentication, Location, and Advanced Neighbor Zone Menus*

Step 5. Authentication refers to the same security policy service described in Chapter 6. The Authentication Policy setting can be configured as Do Not Check Credentials, Check Credentials, or Treat As Authenticated. How Call Policy can be configured to impact this zone is in part determined by how Authentication Policy is configured. As with subzones, best practice is to set Authentication Policy to either **Check Credentials** or **Treat As Authenticated**.

Step 6. The Location section is where you enter the address of the destination server. You can use either the address or the SRV record of the destination. The address could be the URL or the IPv4 address. There are six Peer Address fields that can be configured. If you were trying to neighbor a local Expressway to two other Expressways that were disparate from one another, you would not want to use two Peer Address slots in one Neighbor Zone for those two neighbor relationships. You would want to create two different Neighbor Zones, one for each peer respectively. Because Expressways can be clustered with up to six peers in a cluster, there is an entry slot for each of the peer addresses within the cluster. You would not use the cluster FQDN; rather, you would use the six unique addresses of each peer in the cluster.

Step 7. The last section is Advanced. If you are establishing Neighbor Zones between two Cisco Expressway servers, you can leave the zone Profile setting as **Default.** If the Neighbor Zone points to a different server type, such as the Cisco Unified CM or Cisco Meeting Server, then changes may be required.

Step 8. Click **Create Zone.** This step takes you back to the Zones page. The zone that you created should show active for both H.323 and SIP, assuming you left both protocols active.

Step 9. The last step is to create at least one Search Rule for the Neighbor Zone. Refer to the subsection "Search Rules" earlier in this chapter to review the components and menu options for creating Search Rules.

Expressway to Cisco Unified CM Neighbor Zone

As mentioned in the previous section, creating a Neighbor Zone to the Cisco Unified CM from an Expressway Core is similar to creating a Neighbor Zone to another Expressway Core. However, there are a few differences. H.323 must be disabled because the Unified CM does not support H.323 communication. Some of you reading this book may say, "That's not true. The Unified CM can support H.323 because I can create an H.323 gateway." However, there are big differences between supporting an *H.323 gateway* and supporting *H.323*. H.323 endpoints cannot register directly to the Unified CM without another device standing between the Unified CM and the H.323 endpoint. Also, the Unified CM has no H.323 gatekeeper functions.

The Location section is not treated differently, per se, for the Unified CM. However, you can support more than six peers within a Unified CM cluster. Therefore, Cisco recommends that if you're creating a Neighbor Zone on an Expressway Core to a Unified CM cluster, you use only the peer addresses of the Unified CMs running the CallManager service.

The third difference to creating a Neighbor Zone from an Expressway Core to the Unified CM was mentioned in the previous section. Under the Advanced section, the zone Profile setting needs to be changed. To ease changing these settings, Cisco has some preconfigured template settings you can choose from based on the version of Cisco Unified CM you are running. The custom template options of the Unified CM for the zone Profile include the following:

- Cisco Unified Communications Manager (8.6 or earlier)
- Cisco Unified Communications Manager (8.6.1 or 8.6.2)
- Cisco Unified Communications Manager (9.*x* or later)

Beyond those three differences, creating a Neighbor Zone on the Expressway Core to the Unified CM is the same as creating a Neighbor Zone to another Expressway Core. Do not forget to create the Search Rule. No zone will be searched on any Expressway without at least one Search Rule. Unfortunately, the Neighbor Zone to a Unified CM will not show up as active unless an active SIP trunk exists on the Unified CM that points to the Expressway Core. However, a Unified CM SIP trunk to an Expressway Core will show active without a Neighbor Zone ever being created. Therefore, it is best practice to create the SIP trunk on the Unified CM first, then go back and create the Neighbor Zone on the Expressway Core. Creating a SIP trunk from a Unified CM is a complicated process that includes four basic steps:

Step 1. Configure a SIP Trunk Security Profile.

Step 2. Configure a SIP trunk.

Step 3. Configure a Route Pattern.

Step 4. Transform the pattern once it arrives at the Cisco VCS.

9

The first step is to create a SIP Trunk Security Profile on the Unified CM, as shown in Figure 9-14 and described here:

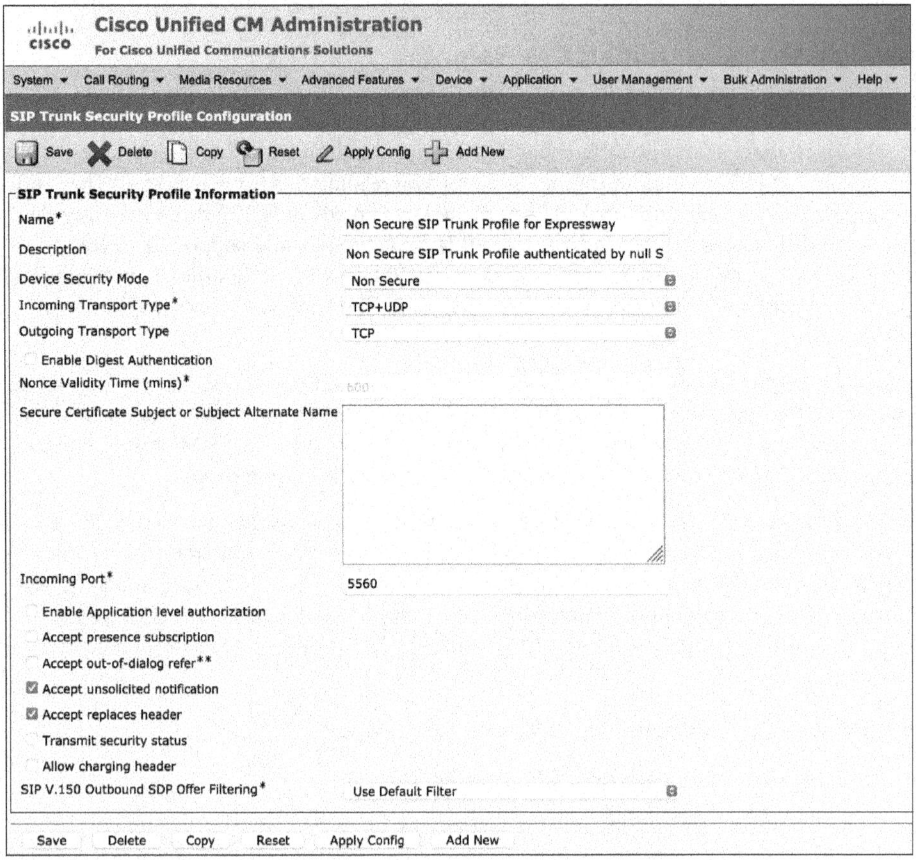

Figure 9-14 *SIP Trunk Security Profile on Cisco Unified CM*

Step 1. Log in to the web interface of the Unified CM and navigate to **System > Security > SIP Trunk Security Profile**.

Step 2. Click **Add New** and configure the following fields:

- **Name:** Enter **Non Secure SIP Trunk Profile for Expressway**.

- **Device Security Mode:** Choose **Non Secure**.

- **Incoming Transport Type:** Choose **TCP+UDP**.

- **Outgoing Transport Type:** Choose **TCP**.

- **Incoming Port:** You can use **5060** for SIP communication if it hasn't been used by another SIP Trunk Security Profile. Otherwise, you might need to use a different port, such as **5560**. If you use a different port, be sure to change the SIP port of the Neighbor Zone on the Expressway to match.

■ Check the **Accept Unsolicited Notifications** check box.

■ Check the **Accept Replaces Header** check box.

Step 3.   Click **Save**.

The second step of creating a SIP trunk from a Unified CM is to create a SIP trunk on the Unified CM. There are many different settings that can be configured on a SIP trunk. Which settings must be configured is entirely dependent on the customer environment, and will vary greatly from customer to customer. The following steps merely outline the most basic settings, shown in Figure 9-15, that must be configured to support an active SIP trunk to an Expressway Core.

Step 1.   From the Unified CM web interface, navigate to **Device > Trunk**.

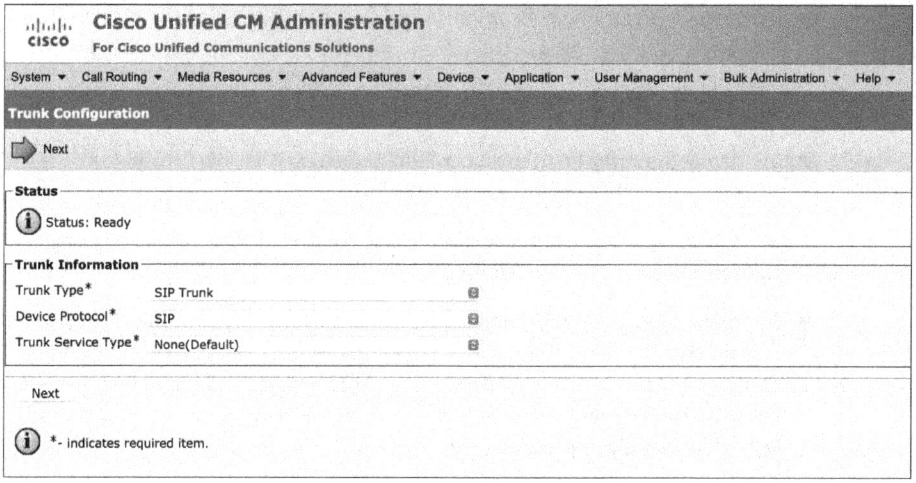

Figure 9-15   *SIP Trunk Configuration on the Cisco Unified CM*

Step 2.   Click **Add New** and enter the following information:

■ **Trunk Type:** Choose **SIP Trunk**. This will populate the following two fields.

■ **Device Protocol:** Leave the setting as **SIP**.

■ **Trunk Service Type:** Leave the setting as **None (Default)**.

Step 3.   Click **Next**, which opens several other sections and fields that you need to configure for this SIP trunk.

Step 4.   In the Device Information screen, enter the following criteria:

■ **Device Name:** Choose a descriptive name for the SIP trunk. You can't use spaces, but you can use underscores or dashes to replace spaces.

■ **Device Pool:** You must choose a Device Pool for every trunk. If you have not created a Device Pool, you can choose **Default**, which is preconfigured on the Unified CM.

There are numerous settings between Device Pool and Step 5 that won't be covered here. Remember, the objective here is limited to identifying the most basic settings that must be configured on a SIP trunk to an Expressway Core.

Step 5. In the SIP Information section, enter the following criteria:

- Destination Address Is an SRV check box:

  - Enable if SRV records are used by the Unified CM to locate the Expressway Core. This setting is required when TLS is being used.

  - Do not enable if IP addresses are used. This is typical for TCP communication.

- Destination Address: Enter the appropriate IP address.

- Destination Port: Enter the appropriate port number. Use **5060** for TCP and **5061** for TLS. Do not use the inbound port configured on the SIP Trunk Security Profile. This is an outbound port, not an inbound port. If SRV records are used, the Destination Port field displays 0.

- SIP Trunk Security Profile: Select **Non Secure SIP Trunk Profile for Expressway**, which you created previously.

- SIP Profile: Choose **Standard SIP Profile for Cisco VCS**, which is a preconfigured SIP profile on the Unified CM.

- Normalization Script: SIP normalization and transparency is an optional feature that handles SIP interoperability issues between the Unified CM and endpoints, service providers, PBXs, or gateways that implement SIP differently. The Expressway is no exception to this list. Therefore, you should select the **vcs-interop** normalization script.

Step 6. Click **Save**. Once the page refreshes, click **Reset**. A popup window will appear, at which time you should click **Reset** again and then click **Close**.

Every trunk on the Unified CM must be reset, whether you are creating the trunk for the first time or making a change to an existing trunk. Without a reset, the trunks will not come up properly and could cause communication issues. Figure 9-16 shows the basic settings that must be configured on a SIP trunk to an Expressway Core from a Unified CM.

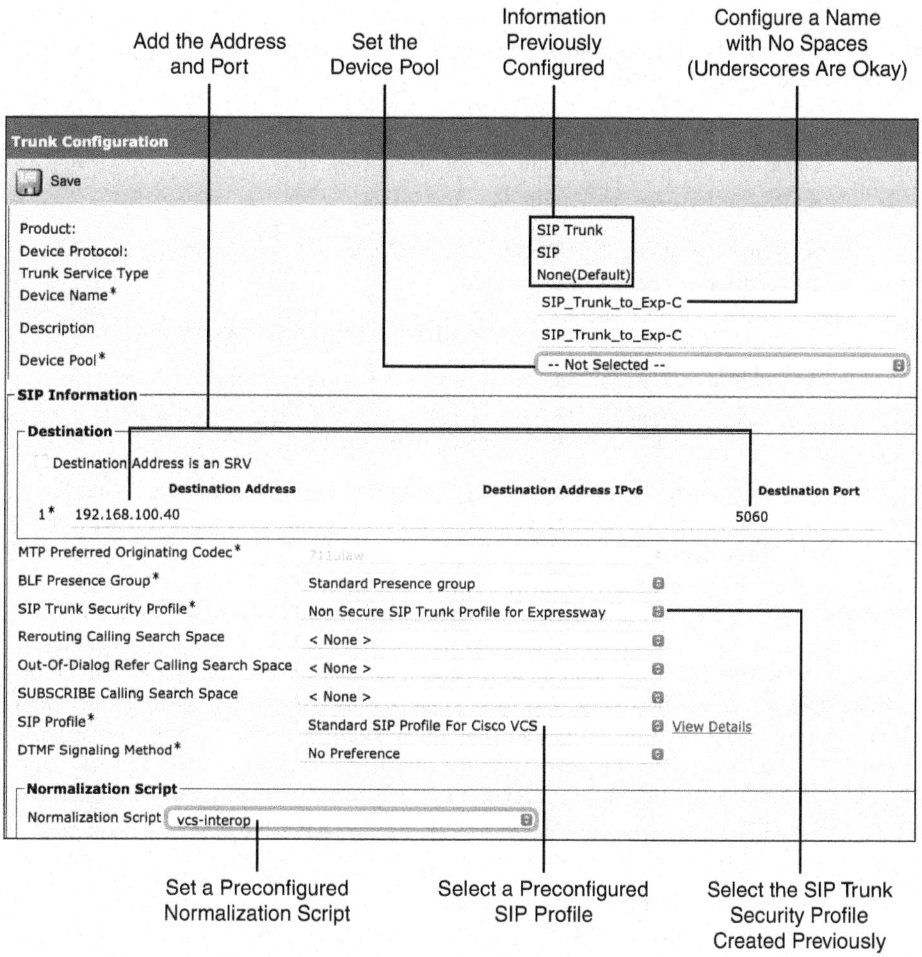

Add the Address and Port

Set the Device Pool

Information Previously Configured

Configure a Name with No Spaces (Underscores Are Okay)

Trunk Configuration

Save

Product:	SIP Trunk
Device Protocol:	SIP
Trunk Service Type	None(Default)
Device Name*	SIP_Trunk_to_Exp-C
Description	SIP_Trunk_to_Exp-C
Device Pool*	-- Not Selected --

SIP Information

Destination

Destination Address is an SRV

	Destination Address	Destination Address IPv6	Destination Port
1*	192.168.100.40		5060

MTP Preferred Originating Codec*	711ulaw
BLF Presence Group*	Standard Presence group
SIP Trunk Security Profile*	Non Secure SIP Trunk Profile for Expressway
Rerouting Calling Search Space	< None >
Out-Of-Dialog Refer Calling Search Space	< None >
SUBSCRIBE Calling Search Space	< None >
SIP Profile*	Standard SIP Profile For Cisco VCS View Details
DTMF Signaling Method*	No Preference

Normalization Script

Normalization Script   vcs-interop

Set a Preconfigured Normalization Script

Select a Preconfigured SIP Profile

Select the SIP Trunk Security Profile Created Previously

Figure 9-16 *Basic SIP Trunk Settings on the Cisco Unified CM*

The third step of creating a SIP trunk from a Unified CM is to create dialing rules that will match alias patterns so that the Unified CM knows when to route calls across this trunk to the Expressway Core. These dialing rules perform the same function on the Unified CM as Search Rules perform on the Expressway Core. However, how these rules are created is quite different. Two different types of patterns can be created: Route Patterns and SIP Route Patterns. These two pattern types can be used exclusively or in tandem with one another to match any trunk. You can also create multiple patterns of each type for any one trunk.

Route Patterns are routing rules that match numeric digits. Because the primary phone extension used on the Unified CM is a **Directory Number (DN)**, which is the same as an E.164 alias, it makes sense to use Route Patterns for routing to and from DNs. An "x" represents a single digit. This allows for patterns to be created that match multiple aliases.

For example, if the alias of every endpoint registered to the Expressway Core starts with the number 4, and is four digits long, you could create a Route Pattern of 4xxx. Use the following steps to create a Route Pattern:

Step 1.   On the Unified CM, navigate to **Call Routing > Route Hunt > Route Pattern**.

Step 2.   Click **Add New** and configure the following parameters:

- **Route Pattern:** Enter something like **4xxx**.

- **Route Partition:** The default value is **<None>**, but you can choose another partition if one has been created.

- **Gateway/Route List:** Select the SIP trunk you created previously.

- **Call Classification:** This can be set to OnNet or OffNet. OffNet is used for toll charges that are routed across the PSTN. Because calls to the Expressway Core are over IP, change this setting to **OnNet**.

Step 3.   There are other settings that can be configured under Route Patterns, but the preceding settings are all the basic settings you need to configure. Once you are finished, click **Save**.

Where Route Patterns are used for numeric-only digits, SIP Route Patterns are used for SIP URI dialing. You can perform SIP URI dialing within the Unified CM without ever creating a SIP Route Pattern. Therefore, SIP Route Patterns are designed to match the second part of the URI. This can be a little bit confusing, so let us explain some terminology. The IETF defines a SIP URI as having two parts: the host portion and the domain, or FQDN, portion. For example, in the URI john@cisco.com, john would be the host and cisco.com would be the domain or FQDN. Within the Unified CM, the parts of a URI are defined a little bit differently. The first part is called the user portion and the second part is called the host portion. Thus, for the same URI john@cisco.com, john would be the user and cisco.com would be the host.

The reason this is so important to understand relates to how a SIP Route Pattern is configured. When you enter the string in the IPv4 Pattern field in the following steps, you should only enter the host portion of the URI, which is to say the domain or FQDN. The @ sign is not a recognizable character and the user portion will not result in a successful search. With all that said, use the following steps to configure a SIP Route Pattern, as shown in Figure 9-17:

Step 1.   From the Cisco Unified CM, navigate to **Call Routing > SIP Route Pattern**.

Step 2.   Click **Add New** and configure the following settings:

- **Pattern Usage:** Leave this setting at **Domain Routing**.

- **Ipv4 Pattern:** Enter the host (domain or FQDN) portion of the URI.

- **Route Partition:** The default value is **<None>**, but you can choose another partition if one has been created.

- **SIP Trunk/Route List:** Select the SIP trunk you created previously.

Step 3.   Again, there are other settings that can be configured under SIP Route Patterns, but these are all the basic settings you need to configure. Once you are finished, click **Save**.

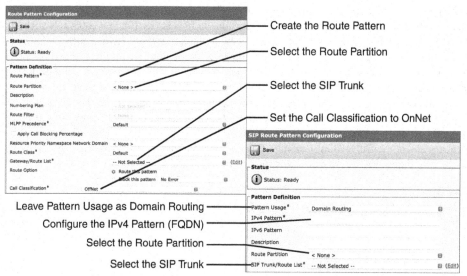

Figure 9-17 *Route Patterns and SIP Route Patterns on the Cisco Unified CM*

Everything you have configured up to this point on the Unified CM will enable calls to be forwarded to the Expressway Core. How the aliases are presented when sent to the Expressway is determined by other settings on the Unified CM. So long as the Unified CM is set up to use DNS, a domain configured on the Unified CM will be appended at the end of all aliases, even if a DN is dialed. For example, if the domain on the Unified CM is cisco.com and a phone registered to the Unified CM dials 4001, then the Route Pattern previously described would make the match and send the alias 4001@cisco.com to the Expressway Core. So long as this is how the endpoint alias appears, the phones should connect and the call will go through. However, if the Unified CM is not set up to use DNS, then the IP address of the destination will be appended to every DN along with the port. Using the same scenario as before, if a phone on the Unified CM dials 4001, then the Route Pattern previously described would make the match, but the alias that would be sent to Expressway Core would look more like 4001@192.168.100.40:5060. This is clearly not how the endpoint is registered to the Expressway Core; therefore, one more step must be completed to enable calls from the Unified CM to the Expressway Core.

The fourth step in building a peer relationship between the Unified CM and Expressway Core is to create a Transform on the Expressway Core to handle incoming calls from the Unified CM. Transforms were already covered in Chapter 7, "Configure Expressway Core Dial Plan Elements," so we will only demonstrate a pattern you can use to make this transformation. Assuming the destination alias is registered to the Expressway via SIP with the domain cisco.com, we would recommend using a regular expression pattern match that looks something like this:

Pattern type: Regex

Pattern string: ([4]\d{3})@192\.168\.100\.40(:5060|:5061)?

Pattern behavior: Replace

Replace string: \1@cisco.com

The first part of this pattern matches anything that begins with a 4 followed by three more digits and an @. The next part is a pattern match for the IP address 192.168.100.40. Notice that each dot has a backslash preceding it. This is a literalization that clarifies each dot is literally a dot. In regular expressions, a dot by itself could be any one number, letter, or character. Therefore, it is best practice to literalize the dot when it should represent a literal dot. The last part matches either port :5060 or :5061 or neither. The question mark at the end signifies the contents of the last set of parentheses could exist in the pattern match or not. Once the pattern match is made, only the contents of the first set or parentheses should be kept followed by the domain @cisco.com. This is why the replace string is stated as \1, which represents the first group designated by the first parentheses set, followed by the @cisco.com. Figure 9-18 shows how this transform should be configured.

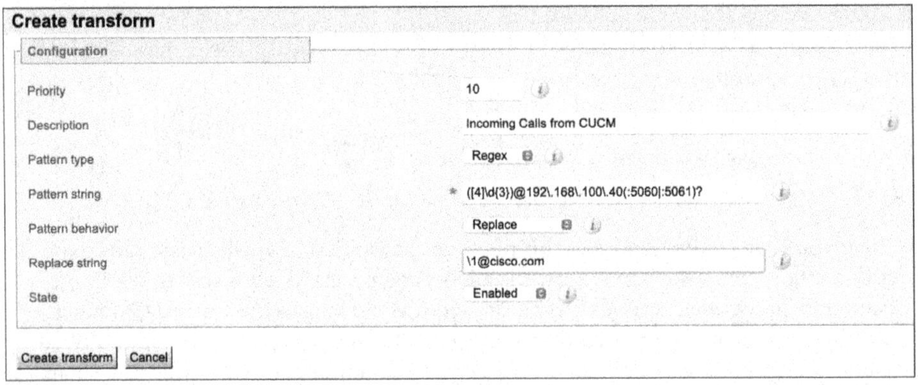

Create transform

Configuration	
Priority	10
Description	Incoming Calls from CUCM
Pattern type	Regex
Pattern string	* ([4]\d{3})@192\.168\.100\.40(:5060|:5061)?
Pattern behavior	Replace
Replace string	\1@cisco.com
State	Enabled

Create transform Cancel

Figure 9-18 *Transform on Expressway for Incoming Calls from the Cisco Unified CM*

Exam Preparation Tasks

As mentioned in the section "How to Use This Book" in the Introduction, you have a couple of choices for exam preparation: the exercises here, Chapter 22, "Final Preparation," and the exam simulation questions in the Pearson Test Prep practice test software.

Review All Key Topics

Review the most important topics in this chapter, noted with the Key Topics icon in the outer margin of the page. Table 9-2 lists a reference of these key topics and the page numbers on which each is found.

Table 9-2 Key Topics for Chapter 9

Key Topic Element	Description	Page Number
Paragraph	Zone types on the Cisco Expressway	151
Paragraph	Calls to Unknown IP Addresses settings	152
Paragraph	Traversal Zone Types	153
Paragraph	Webex Zone	154
List	Search Rule components	155
Paragraph	Call Loop Detection Mode	160

Key Topic Element	Description	Page Number
List	Advantages to a hierarchical video network with a structured dial plan	163
Steps	Configuring Neighbor Zone	166
List	Custom template options of the Unified CM for the zone profile	169
Steps	Four basic steps to creating a SIP trunk from the Unified CM to the Expressway	169

Complete Tables and Lists from Memory

There are no memory tables or lists for this chapter.

Define Key Terms

Define the following key terms from this chapter and check your answers in the glossary:

Assent, Call Loop Detection Mode, Call Signaling Optimization, directory Expressway, Directory Number (DN), DNS Zone, ENUM Zone, H.460.18 and H.460.19, Location Confirm (LCF), Location Request (LRQ), Loopback, Neighbor Zone, optimal call routing, Search Rule, Traversal Client Zone, Traversal Server Zone, Traversal Zone, Unified Communications Traversal Zone, Webex Zone

Q&A

The answers to these questions appear in Appendix A. For more practice with exam format questions, use the Pearson Test Prep practice test software.

1. List the three different Traversal Zones that can be configured on the Cisco Expressway.

2. List the recommended order in which Zones should be searched on the Cisco Expressway.

3. List five advantages of a hierarchical video network with a structured dial plan.

4. What are the four basic steps to creating a SIP trunk from the Unified CM to the Expressway Core?

9

CHAPTER 10

Multisite and Business-to-Business (B2B) Collaboration Solutions

This chapter covers the following topics:

Firewall Issues in a Collaboration Environment: Examines firewall issues that could prevent UDP media packets from routing through a corporate firewall, whereby preventing audio and video calls from connecting.

NAT Issues in a Collaboration Environment: Examines NAT issues that could prevent UDP media packets from routing through a network edge NAT server, thereby preventing audio and video calls from connecting.

Purpose of STUN, TURN, and ICE: Describes the IETF solutions to NAT traversal, identifying the strengths and weaknesses of each solution, and the limitations of the solution as a whole.

Expressway Media Traversal: Identifies two highly secure and very effective firewall and NAT traversal solutions that work in a Cisco collaboration deployment using Expressway Core and Edge servers. This topic also outlines the steps needed to configure this solution and provides an overview of different deployment options pertaining to firewall traversal.

DNS Zones: Explains how DNS can be used for both internal routing and external routing for business-to-business communications. This topic also outlines how to configure DNS Zones on the Cisco Expressway Edge server.

Chapter 9, "Multisite Collaboration Solutions," introduced Zones and then focused on Neighbor Zones. This chapter examines two other types of Zones that can be used to extend IP communications outside the organization's network to other businesses or customers. To achieve this goal, there are some firewall and NAT obstacles that must be overcome first. Traversal Zones are used to aid in overcoming these issues. Once outside the network, DNS Zones can be used to resolve publicly registered domains to routable IP addresses.

This chapter covers the following objectives from the Implementing Cisco Collaboration Cloud and Edge Solutions (CLCEI) exam 300-820:

- 1.1 Describe the complications of NAT in a Collaboration environment

- 1.2 Describe the purpose of ICE, TURN and STUN

- 1.3 Describe Expressway media traversal

- 2.4.a Configure a Business to Business (B2B) collaboration solution: DNS records (focus on Microsoft DNS)

- 2.4.c Configure a Business to Business (B2B) collaboration solution: Traversal Zones

"Do I Know This Already?" Quiz

The "Do I Know This Already?" quiz enables you to assess whether you should read this entire chapter thoroughly or jump to the "Exam Preparation Tasks" section. If you are in doubt about your answers to these questions or your own assessment of your knowledge of the topics, read the entire chapter. Table 10-1 lists the major headings in this chapter and their corresponding "Do I Know This Already?" quiz questions. You can find the answers in Appendix A, "Answers to the 'Do I Know This Already?' Quizzes and Review Questions."

Table 10-1 "Do I Know This Already?" Section-to-Question Mapping

Foundation Topics Section	Questions
Firewall Issues in a Collaboration Environment	1
NAT Issues in a Collaboration Environment	2
Purpose of STUN, TURN, and ICE	3–5
Expressway Media Traversal	6–9
DNS Zones	10

CAUTION The goal of self-assessment is to gauge your mastery of the topics in this chapter. If you do not know the answer to a question or are only partially sure of the answer, you should mark that question as wrong for purposes of the self-assessment. Giving yourself credit for an answer you correctly guess skews your self-assessment results and might provide you with a false sense of security.

1. In which of the following circumstances will a firewall typically allow communications packets into a network from an outside source?

    a. A firewall will never allow an outside source to send packets into a private network.

    b. A firewall will always allow an outside source to send packets into a private network.

    c. When sending UDP packets in response to communication originating from inside the network.

    d. When sending TCP packets in response to communication originating from inside the network.

2. Which of the following is a Class B private IP address?

    a. 10.1.1.10

    b. 172.32.1.10

    c. 172.28.1.10

    d. 192.168.168.10

3. Which of the following NAT traversal solutions is recommended for asymmetric networks?

    a. ICE

    b. TURN

    c. STUN

    d. ASSENT

    e. H.460.18/19

4. Which of the following is the only IETF service available on the Expressway Edge server for traversal?

   a. ICE

   b. TURN

   c. STUN

   d. ASSENT

   e. H.460.18/19

5. Which of the following IETF traversal solutions will always enable a connection regardless of the number of NATs involved?

   a. ICE

   b. TURN

   c. STUN

   d. ASSENT

   e. H.460.18/19

6. What ports does H.460.18 use for RTP and RTCP packets?

   a. 2776 and 2777

   b. 36,000 and 36,001

   c. 36,000 to 59,999

   d. 1024 to 34,545

7. What type of Traversal Zones can be configured on the Expressway Edge server?

   a. Traversal Client Zone

   b. Traversal Server Zone

   c. Unified Communications Traversal Zone

   d. All Zone types

   e. Only Unified Communications Traversal Zones and Traversal Server Zones

8. What type of Traversal Zones can be configured on the Expressway Core server?

   a. Traversal Client Zone

   b. Traversal Server Zone

   c. Unified Communications Traversal Zone

   d. All Zone types

   e. Only Unified Communications Traversal Zones and Traversal Client Zones

9. Which of the following deployment scenarios for firewall traversal through a DMZ does Cisco recommend?

   a. Single-subnet DMZ deployment scenario

   b. Three-port firewall DMZ deployment scenario

   c. Dual NIC DMZ deployment scenario

   d. Triple Expressway deployment scenario

10. Which of the following is a Zone type on the Cisco Expressway that allows E.164 aliases to be mapped to URIs for domain routing?

    a. ENUM Zone

    b. DNS Zone

    c. Traversal Server Zone

    d. Traversal Client Zone

Foundation Topics

Firewall Issues in a Collaboration Environment

Communication over IP has come a long way in a short time. One huge obstacle that had to be overcome before companies could really start migrating away from PSTN-based communication to IP-based communication was how to securely route network traffic through firewalls and across NAT servers.

Allowing uninhibited traffic into and out from a corporate network allows hackers unconstrained access to private information. Therefore, a **firewall** exists to protect the inside of a corporate network from outside attacks by controlling IP traffic entering your network. Firewalls can be a software solution or a hardware device designed to block unsolicited incoming requests from outside a private networked environment, meaning that any communication originating from outside your network will be prevented. However, firewalls can be configured to allow outgoing requests to certain trusted destinations, and to allow responses from those destinations.

Most firewalls use ports to mark TCP outgoing traffic so that reply messages from outside the network coming in on the same ports will be allowed back into the private corporate network. This means that any two-way communication must be started by an internal system. An example of this type of communication is when a user within an enterprise network browses to Google.com from a web browser. A TCP communication is sent through the firewall, which marks the packets and then forwards the request to the Google web server. When the Google server sends back the response, the firewall is already expecting this response, so the firewall allows the communication to come in and redirects it to the requesting application.

In a similar manner, a video call made from an endpoint inside a network through a firewall to an outside endpoint begins with a TCP communication. The firewall allows the exchange of TCP call setup information and allows UDP media packets originating from an inside endpoint to be sent to an outside endpoint. However, the media traffic in the opposite direction does not come back on the same ports. The firewall observes these communication packets as originating from outside the network and blocks those packets from ever reaching the internal endpoint. This is a common issue, and it is referred to as one-way-audio and one-way-video. Notice also that to even get to this point in the call setup process, the call had to originate from inside the network. Inbound calls originating from outside the network are out of the question. Two endpoints located behind two different firewalls would never be able to call each other. The seemingly obvious resolution to this issue would be to open the ports needed for two-way communication; however, this will not work for two reasons. First, opening the ports on the firewall would leave the network vulnerable to attacks from outside the network. The very reason for the firewall's existence would be negated by this action. Second, there is another issue related to NAT that could still prevent endpoints from communicating with each other even if there was no firewall.

10

NAT Issues in a Collaboration Environment

The Institute of Electrical and Electronic Engineers (IEEE) first introduced communication using packet-switched technology in 1974. Several Internet Protocol versions were experimented with (IPv1 through IPv3) until the predominant protocol was established circa 1981, called **Internet Protocol version 4 (IPv4)**. At that time engineers couldn't imagine the 4 billion addresses made available with IPv4 would ever run out. Initially anyone could purchase IP addresses in pools, and they would own them for life. Telco companies and universities were some of the main consumers of these IP addresses. As the number of devices that required an IP address greatly increased, and the World Wide Web began to expand, it was realized that the number of people and devices requiring an IP address would soon eclipse the finite number of IPv4 addresses available. One solution to this problem was the introduction of **Internet Protocol version 6 (IPv6)**, which contains 340 undecillion addresses. Some say you could assign an IPv6 address to every grain of sand on earth and still not run out of addresses. However, IPv6 introduces other issues, like how to migrate hundreds of millions of devices over to an IPv6 network that are already established under IPv4.

Another resolution that came about around the same time as IPv6 was **Network Address Translation (NAT)**. The IETF published RFC 2663 outlining the basic use of NAT. In order for NAT to work, IP addresses first had to be divided into two pools: public IP addresses and private IP addresses. The Internet Corporation for Assigned Names and Numbers (ICANN) was created in 1998 to assume responsibility for managing IP addresses and domains. Private IP addresses are designated in the following categories, which anyone can use, but are not routable across the public Internet:

Key Topic

- **Class A addresses:** 10.0.0.0–10.255.255.255, with 16,777,216 available addresses

- **Class B addresses:** 172.16.0.0–172.31.255.255, with 1,048,576 available addresses

- **Class C addresses:** 192.168.0.0–192.168.255.255, with 65,536 available addresses

Public IP addresses are routable across the public Internet and can be leased from an Internet service provider. Today there are different versions of NAT that can be used based on many different factors. However, the basis of how NAT works is a private IP address is masqueraded with a public IP address when a device needs to route across the public Internet. For example, if a computer assigned a private IP address of 10.10.1.14 tries to navigate to Google.com, the edge router masquerades that private IP address with its assigned public IP address of 209.165.201.1. When the Google server returns communication to the edge router at the public IP address, the router then changes the destination address from 209.165.201.1 to the private IP address of the endpoint, 10.10.1.14, and routes the packets sent from Google to the computer that initiated the communication. A limitation to this type of NAT solution could arise from the number of outgoing communication devices exceeding the number of public IP addresses available. A simple resolution could be to use **Port Address Translation (PAT)**.

Sometimes NAT and PAT can be used together. Similar to the previous scenario, the router masquerades the IP address and marks the packets going out with a virtual port number to enable routing return traffic to the desired destination. For example, if a computer assigned a private IP address of 10.10.1.14 tries to navigate to Google.com, the edge router masquerades that private IP address with its assigned public IP address of 209.165.201.1:12345. Notice the port tagged on to the end of the IP address. When the Google server returns communication to the computer, return traffic goes to the edge router, but the port :12345 tagged at the end of the IP address indicates to the router where to send the return traffic based on a table the router keeps. The router then changes the destination address from 209.165.201.1:12345 to the private IP address of the endpoint, 10.10.1.14, and routes the packets sent from Google to the computer that initiated the communication. In this manner a single public IP address can be used to masquerade private IP addresses from multiple devices by simply using a different port for each device.

NAT becomes an issue with collaboration devices for two reasons. First, NAT doesn't allow communication to be initiated from outside the private network because the virtual ports can change with each new transmission that is created. So, if two video endpoints behind different NATs wanted to communicate, one will never be able to discover the other. For example, if a device were to try and route to the private IP address of another endpoint, the transmission would fail at the source router, because private IP addresses are not publicly routable. Alternatively, if the source device tried to route to the public IP address of the far end router, once the packets arrived, the far end router wouldn't know to which device the packets should be routed within the private network.

The second issue that comes with NAT has to do with UDP (User Datagram Protocol) transmissions. Where TCP communications require a response, UDP communications are unidirectional. Once video calls are set up using TCP, the audio and video packets are sent using UDP. Because each UDP packet sent is essentially a new transmission, a different virtual port is used, and transmissions will never reach their targeted destination.

Purpose of STUN, TURN, and ICE

The IETF, who came up with the SIP communications protocol and NAT, also created the first solution that allowed communication between private networks through a NAT server. That protocol is known as **Session Traversal Utilities for NAT (STUN)**. After creating the RFC for STUN, the IETF produced two related RFC protocols known as **Traversal Using Relays around NAT (TURN)** and **Interactive Connectivity Establishment (ICE)**.

STUN, TURN, and ICE are methods that assume certain behavior from the NAT and firewall and do not work in all scenarios. The control is removed from the firewall, which has to be sufficiently opened to allow clients to create the pinholes needed to let the communication through. Therefore, STUN, TURN, and ICE only offer a NAT traversal solution, and are not a firewall traversal solution at all. Also, these solutions can only operate within the SIP communications protocol, so they offer no solution for H.323 communications.

STUN

STUN requires a STUN client, which could be the phone or some other device, and a STUN server. The client initiates communication to the STUN server by sending a port request packet to the STUN server, which should be located outside the NAT server. The NAT server masquerades the IP address and port before forwarding the information to the STUN server. The STUN server then maps that assigned port to the client and sends back a reply. Both the NAT server and client record the port assignment so that all future inbound packets sent on this port will be forwarded to the client. Once the STUN server assigns a port, it is no longer involved in the line of communication.

STUN requires that the NAT server allow all traffic that is directed to a particular port to be forwarded to the client on the inside. This means that STUN only works with less-secure NATs, so-called "full-cone" NATs, exposing the internal client to an attack from anyone who can capture the STUN traffic. STUN may be useful within **asymmetric network**

10

environments but is generally not considered a viable solution for enterprise networks. In addition, STUN cannot be used with symmetric NATs. This may be a drawback in many situations because most enterprise-class firewalls are symmetric. For more information about STUN, see RFC 8489. Figure 10-1 illustrates how STUN works within a network.

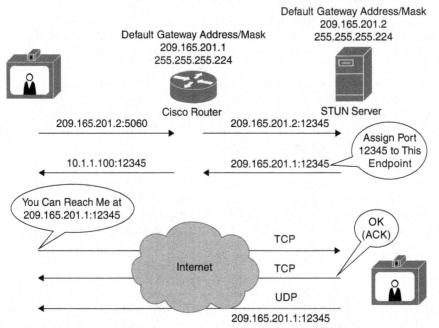

Figure 10-1 *STUN Operation Within an Asymmetric Network*

TURN

Key Topic

TURN operates similarly to STUN, but it allows a client behind a firewall to receive SIP traffic on either TCP or UDP ports. This solves the problem of clients behind symmetric NATs, which cannot rely on STUN to solve the NAT traversal issue. TURN connects clients behind a NAT to a single peer. Its purpose is to provide the same protection as that created by symmetric NATs and firewalls. Symmetric NATs use dynamic ports that often change. Therefore, the TURN server acts as a relay so that any data received is forwarded on to the client, and port allocation can be updated on the fly. The client on the inside can also be on the receiving end of a connection that is requested by a client on the outside.

This method is appropriate in some situations, but because it essentially allows inbound traffic through a firewall, with only the client in control, it has limited applicability for enterprise environments. It also scales poorly because the media must traverse through the TURN server. Also, because all media must traverse the TURN server, the server supporting TURN must be robust enough to handle high volumes of traffic. For more information about TURN, see RFC 8656. Figure 10-2 illustrates how TURN works within a network.

TURN relay services are the only IETF services available on the Expressway-E. To use TURN services, the TURN Relay option key is needed. This controls the number of TURN relays that can be simultaneously allocated by the TURN server. The TURN configuration page on the Expressway web interface is located at **Configuration > Traversal > TURN**. The settings on this page are used to configure the Expressway-E's TURN settings. Table 10-2 identifies the configurable options for TURN on the Cisco Expressway.

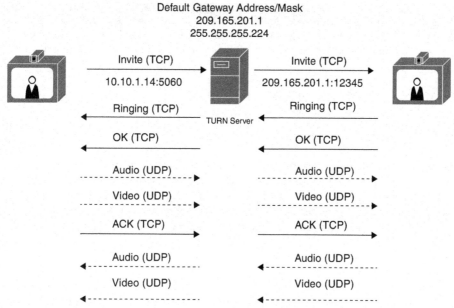

Figure 10-2 *TURN Operation Within a Symmetric Network*

Table 10-2 Configurable Options for TURN on the Cisco Expressway

Field	Description	Usage Tips
TURN Services	Determines whether the Expressway offers TURN services to traversal clients.	
TURN requests port	The listening port for TURN requests. The default is 3478. On large VM deployments you can configure a range of TURN request listening ports. The default range is 3478–3483.	To allow endpoints to discover TURN services, you need to set up DNS Service (SRV) records for _turn._udp. and _turn._tcp. (either for the single port or a range of ports as appropriate). If you need to change the TURN requests port (or range, for large systems) while the TURN services are already On: 1. Change Turn Services to Off and Save. 2. Edit the port number/range. 3. Change Turn Services to On and Save. This is because changes to the port numbers do not come into effect until the TURN services are restarted.

Key Topic

10

Field	Description	Usage Tips
Authentication realm	This is the realm sent by the server in its authentication challenges.	Ensure that the client's credentials are stored in the local authentication database.
Media port range start/end	The lower and upper port in the range used for the allocation of TURN relays. The default TURN relay media port range is 24000–29999.	

A summary of the TURN server status is displayed at the bottom of the TURN page. When the TURN server is active, the summary also displays the number of active TURN clients and the number of active relays. Click the active relay links to access the TURN relay usage page, which lists all the currently active TURN relays on the Expressway. Further details of each TURN relay can be reviewed, including permissions, channel bindings, and counters.

ICE

ICE provides a mechanism for SIP client NAT traversal. ICE is not a protocol but rather a framework that pulls together a number of different techniques such as TURN and STUN. ICE allows clients residing behind NAT devices to discover paths through which they can pass media, verify peer-to-peer connectivity via each of these paths, and then select the optimum media connection path. The available paths typically depend on any inbound and outbound connection restrictions that have been configured on the NAT device. Such behavior is described in RFC 4787. ICE essentially incorporates all of the methods proposed for NAT traversal of SIP that do not rely on the firewall or NAT device. ICE is a complex solution to the problem of NAT traversal, but because it encompasses multiple solutions, it is regarded as one that will always enable the connection, regardless of the number of NATs involved. However, ICE still relies on client/server-based approaches and removes control from the enterprise. Due to its complexity, there is very limited client support for ICE today.

When a client reaches out to the ICE server, the server has the capability to determine what type of NAT is being used, whether it's in an asymmetric or **symmetric network** environment. The ICE server then establishes a connection with the client using STUN or TURN, depending on what the situation calls for. If STUN is used, then the ICE server assigns a port to the client and steps out of the line of communication. If TURN is used, then the ICE server acts as the relay between client communications. For more information about ICE, see RFC 8445. Figure 10-3 illustrates how ICE works within a network.

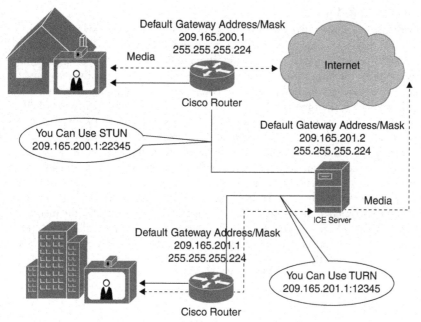

Figure 10-3 *ICE Operation Within Asymmetric and Symmetric Networks*

Expressway Media Traversal

The IETF overcame many problems, such as NAT traversal issued in both synchronous and asynchronous networked environments. However, there were still many more to overcome. Their solutions, although good, were incomplete. As mentioned before, the IETF solutions only support SIP communication and they only traverse NATs. To account for the firewall, many ports need to be opened for the media flows. In fact, most IETF NAT traversal solutions require over 30,000 UDP ports to be open. Some of the more conservative TURN solutions still require over 2000 ports to be open for media to tunnel through the firewall. This creates huge security vulnerabilities.

Tandberg was a company that had been a leader in video telepresence for many years prior to the acquisition by Cisco. Tandberg climbed this ladder to success much the same way as Cisco, by acquiring key companies that possessed the technology Tandberg needed for the time. In 2004 Tandberg acquired a company called Ridgeway Systems and Software, which was a UK-based software company specializing in firewall and NAT traversal. Ridgeway had developed a unique proprietary solution that is known today as Assent. This protocol has revolutionized the way IP communication traverses firewalls and NATs and has become the paradigm used by the International Telecommunication Union (ITU) for creating a traversal standard all companies can incorporate.

10

Assent and H.460.18/19

The way **Assent** works requires two components, a traversal server and a traversal client. The traversal server resides outside the firewall or in a demilitarized zone (DMZ). The traversal client resides inside the firewall and initiates communication with the traversal server. In a Cisco environment, the Expressway Core is the traversal client, and the Expressway EcPorts do need to be opened on the firewall, but they cannot be used unless a communication is initiated from inside the firewall. This is where the magic happens. The traversal client sends a keep-alive message to the traversal server, essentially asking, "Do you have any calls for me?" Should someone initiate a call from outside the firewall through the traversal server, that server can respond to the keep-alive message sent from the traversal client. As far as the firewall is concerned, the communication initiated from inside the firewall with the keep-alive message. Now the ports allocated to this solution can be used once the call setup has completed. Even better, though, are the ports needed for media using Assent. Only two ports are required to be opened on the firewall, because Assent will multiplex the media so all RTP traffic uses one port, and all RTCP traffic uses a second port. In addition to the firewall traversal capabilities of Assent, NAT traversal is built into the protocol as well. Also, Assent can be used with both the SIP and H.323 communication standards. Figure 10-4 illustrates the process used by Assent for firewall traversal.

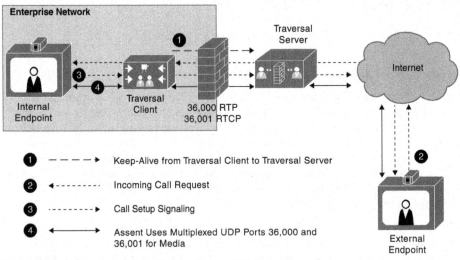

Figure 10-4   *Assent Operation for Firewall Traversal*

Assent is such a powerful tool that the ITU used it as the basis to develop H.323 traversal standards. By summer of 2005 the standards were completed and in full use. H.460.17 was the traversal standard used prior to the Assent-based standards. H.460.17 performs firewall traversal by carrying the media over TCP ports instead of UDP. H.460.18 works just like Assent, except it requires de-multiplexed ports 36,000 to 59,999 to be opened on the firewall. H.460.19 works as a layer on H.460.18 to allow multiplexing the media ports so only two ports need to be opened for RTP and RTCP media streams. In this, H.460.18 and H.460.19 accomplish together what Assent is capable of independently. It is important to note that the ITU standards for firewall traversal only support the H.323 communication standard. Table 10-3 compares all the ports required for Assent to all the ports required for **H.460.18/19**.

Table 10-3 *Ports Used with Assent and H.460.18/19*

	Assent	H.460.18 Only	H.460.18/19
SIP Registration	5060 UDP/TLS	N/A	
H.323 Registration	1719 UDP	1719 UDP	
SIP Call Setup	5060 TCP/TLS	N/A	
H.323 Call Setup	2776 TCP	1720 TCP (Q.931/H.225) 2777 TCP (H.245)	
SIP Media RTP	36,000 (UDP)	N/A	N/A
SIP Media RTCP	36,001 (UDP)	N/A	N/A
H.323 Media RTP	2776 (UDP)	36,000–59,999 (UDP)	2776 (UDP)
H.323 Signaling RTCP	2777 (UDP)		2777 (UDP)

Configuring Traversal Zones on Expressway Core and Edge

When building Traversal Zones between your Expressway Core and your Expressway Edge, it is best practice to configure the Expressway Edge first. This is not a requirement, but the nature of how these servers communicate will warrant a faster initial connection if this procedure is followed accordingly. The Zone on the Expressway Edge will await for a communication from the Expressway Core an infinite amount of time once that Zone is configured. However, the Zone on the Expressway Core will only send a keep-alive message for 120 seconds. If a connection is not established within that time frame, then the server stops sending the keep-alive messages altogether. If the Zone on the Expressway Core were created first, then this final timeout could occur before the administrator has had time to create the Zone on the Expressway Edge. Even if the final timeout had not occurred, an instantaneous connection between the Expressway Core and Expressway Edge is not likely to happen. However, we live in a day and age where we want things to happen instantly. Without that instantaneous result we tend to think something went wrong. If you build the Zone on the Expressway Edge first, then once you create and save the Zone on the Expressway Core, the connection between the two servers is usually instantaneous.

Because we're talking about firewall traversal, it is necessary to have a secure connection between the Expressway Core and Edge servers, reducing as much as possible the ability for any other server to mimic that communication. Therefore, before you create the **Traversal Server Zone** on the Expressway Edge, you must first create authentication credentials that the Expressway Core will use to authenticate the connection between the two nodes. This is the same authentication process used with endpoint registration, which was discussed in Chapter 6, "Registration on Cisco Expressway." Traversal Zones always require authentication, so no setting exists that enables authentication for this process; it is enabled automatically. Because the Expressway Edge is acting as the Traversal Server, it will do the authenticating. Therefore, these credentials should be configured in the authentication database on this server. Keep in mind that both the Name and Password settings you create for authentication are case sensitive. Pay attention to syntax because they must match exactly when configured in the **Traversal Client Zone** on the Expressway Core. The following steps explain how to configure the authentication credentials:

10

Step 1. Log in to your Expressway Edge, and then navigate to **Configuration > Authentication > Devices > Local Database**.

Step 2. Click **New** and enter the following information:

   a. **Name:** Create a username that will be used for this Traversal Zone relationship.

   b. **Password:** Create a corresponding password for the previously created username.

Step 3. Click **Create Credential**.

Once you have created these authentication credentials, the next step is to create the first Zone. The Zone type to choose on the Expressway Edge for this type of deployment is the Traversal Server Zone. Other options include the Traversal Client Zone and the Unified Communications Traversal Zone. For this deployment scenario, the Traversal Client Zone will be used on the Expressway Core. There is a scenario where you may want to configure a Traversal Client Zone on the Expressway Edge, but that scenario will be discussed further in the next section of this chapter. The Unified Communications Traversal Zone is used for Mobile Remote Access (MRA) deployments, which will be discussed in Part 2 of this book.

The following steps explain how to configure a Traversal Server Zone on the Expressway Edge:

Step 1. From the web interface of the Expressway Edge, navigate to **Configuration > Zones > Zones**.

Step 2. Click **New** and configure the following fields:

   a. Name: Provide a logical name for the Zone you're creating.

   b. Type: **Traversal Server**

   c. Hop Count: **15** (default value)

   The three previously mentioned settings are all that will display at first, because additional menu options are based on the Zone Type that's selected. Once you choose Traversal Server in the Type field, the following menu options appear. Continue to configure these settings as described:

   d. Connection Credentials (section) > Username: Specify the "Name" you configured in the authentication database.

   Syntax matters as much here as it does when the credentials were created. Notice you are only configuring the Username field and not the Password field. That's because the password already exists in the database. Specifying the username ties that username to this Zone specifically. If credentials were used on the Traversal Client Zone that exist in the database on the Expressway Edge, but the username was not specified here, then authentication would fail, resulting in the Traversal Zones being inactive. This provides another layer of security between the Expressway Core and Expressway Edge. Under the **Password** menu option, you will see a link entitled Add/Edit Local Authentication Database. If you forgot to create the authentication credentials, or if you want to modify the credential, clicking this link will open a pop-up window to the credential database. This way, you do not lose where you are in creating this Traversal Server Zone.

e.   H.323 > Mode: **On** (default). You can disable this service if you know H.323 will not be used.

f.   H.323 > Protocol: **Assent** (default). You can change this value to **H46018** per your preferences.

g.   H.323 > Port: **6001** (default)

This is the listening port used to maintain the H.323 connection between the Expressway Core and Edge servers once active. This setting is generated by the Expressway automatically and is set to 6001 for the first Traversal Server Zone you create. Should you create more than one Traversal Zones, each subsequent Zone you create will use the next number in sequential order. You can change this port number to any number between 1024 and 65534, but whatever number you use must be configured on the Traversal Client Zone to match.

h.   H.323 > H.460.19 Demultiplexing Mode: **Off** (default). Enable this setting only if you changed the Protocol field to H46018 and you want to use the multiplexing mode. Figure 10-5 illustrates this first set of settings for the Traversal Server Zone.

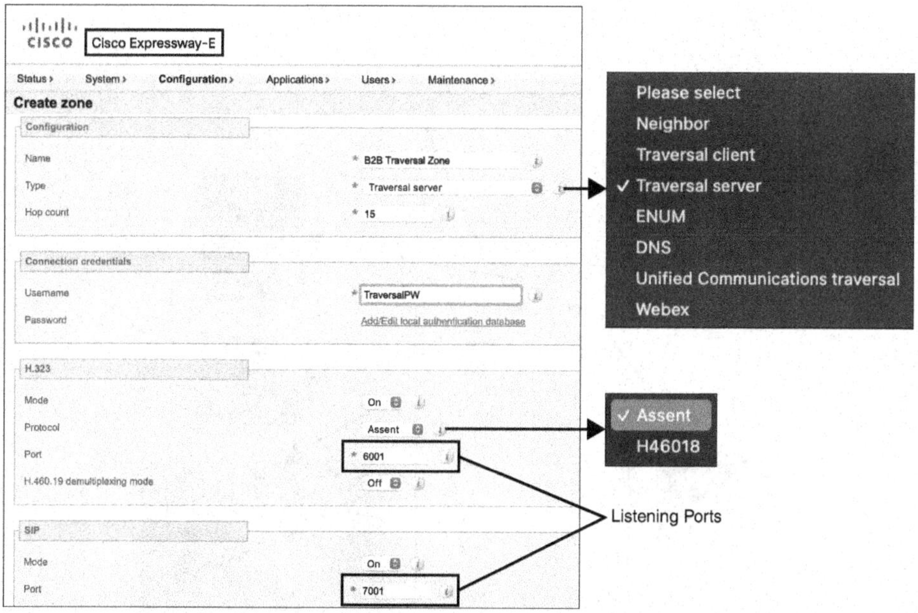

Figure 10-5   *Connection Credentials and H.323 Settings for a Traversal Server Zone*

i.   SIP > Mode: **On** (default)

j.   SIP > Port: **7001** (default). This is the listing port for SIP. The same rules apply as previously described for the H.323 port.

k.   SIP > Transport: **TLS** (default)

l.   SIP > TLS Verify Mode: **Off** (default). Enable this setting only if certificates are being used to mutually authenticate the Expressway Core and the Expressway Edge. TLS Verify is synonymous with Mutual TLS.

10

m.   SIP > Accept Proxied Registrations: **Allow** (default). This setting is dependent on other settings in the Expressway.

n.   SIP > Media Encryption Mode: **Auto** (default)

o.   SIP > ICE Support: **Off** (default)

p.   SIP > ICE Passthrough Support: **Off** (default)

q.   SIP > Multistream Mode: **On** (default)

r.   SIP > SIP Poison Mode: **Off** (default)

s.   SIP > Preload SIP Routes Support: **Off** (default)

t.   SIP > SIP Parameter Preservation: **Off** (default)

u.   SIP > AES GCM Support: **Off** (default)

v.   SIP > SIP UPDATE for Session Refresh: **Off** (default)

Obviously, there are a lot of settings that pertain to SIP. We have included some instruction as to how each of these settings should be configured, but most of these settings can be left at their default values for a basic Traversal Server Zone configuration, as is being described here. Figure 10-6 illustrates the previously described SIP settings on a Traversal Server Zone.

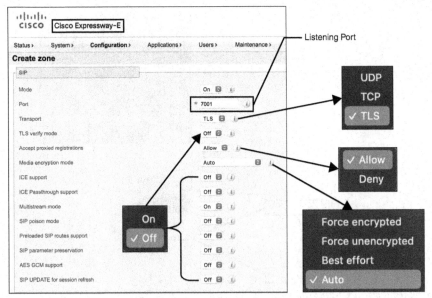

Figure 10-6   *SIP Settings for a Traversal Server Zone*

w.   Authentication > Authentication Policy: **Do Not Check Credentials** (default). Remember that authentication must occur with Traversal Zones no matter what. Therefore, this setting has nothing to do with whether the Zone will use authentication to establish a connection. This setting has to do with how traffic across this Zone will be treated. Use the same standard to set this setting as described in Chapter 6.

x.   UDP/TCP Probes settings: There are six probe settings, three for UDP and three for TCP. These have to do with keep-alive messages sent between the client and server Zones (UDP), and keep-alives for call setup to keep the firewall's NAT bindings open (TCP). There is no reason to change these settings, so leave them at their default values.

Step 3. Click **Create Zone** to complete the Traversal Server Zone configuration.

Notice that there is no place to enter the address of the Expressway Core. This is because the Expressway Edge, which lives outside the firewall, will never be able to initiate a communication to the Expressway Core, which lives inside the firewall. However, when the Expressway Core does initiate a communication with the Expressway Edge, the Core server address will be provided to the Edge at the same time. Once the connection is saved, the web portal will return you to the main Zones page. You should see a line item for the Zone you just created, and the status for both H.323 and SIP will show On (No Active Connections). This is the indication we mentioned at the beginning of this section that the Expressway Edge is waiting for a communication from the Expressway Core. This status will persist, unchanging, until the Expressway Core establishes a successful connection to the Expressway Edge. Figure 10-7 illustrates the final settings that need to be configured on the Traversal Server Zone and the saved Zone results from the Zones page.

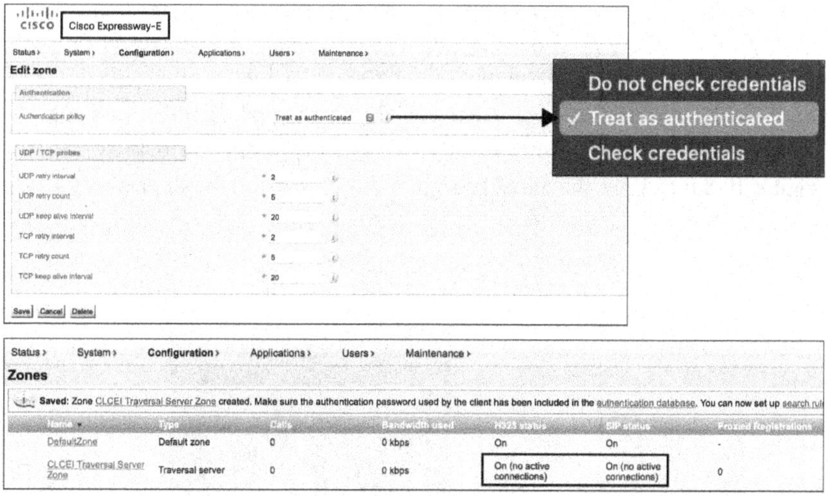

Figure 10-7 *Authentication Settings and Saved Results for a Traversal Server Zone*

There is still one final step that must be completed on the Expressway Edge to complete the configuration. Remember that anytime you create a Zone of any type on an Expressway, you must also create at least one corresponding Search Rule, or else the Zone can never be searched. Search Rules are configured the same way for Traversal Zones as they are configured for any other Zone. Review the information from Chapter 9 pertaining to Search Rules if you need a refresher on how to configure them.

Once you have finished configuring the Traversal Server Zone on the Expressway Edge, you can now turn your attention to configuring the Traversal Client Zone on the Expressway Core. Use the following steps to configure this Zone:

Step 1. Log in to the Expressway Core and then navigate to **Configuration > Zones > Zones**.

Step 2.   Click **New** and enter the following information:

a.   Name: Provide a logical name for the Zone you're creating.

b.   Type: **TraversalClient**

c.   Hop count: **15** (default)

There are only two types of Traversal Zones available on the Expressway Core: the Unified Communications Traversal Zone, which is used for MRA, and the Traversal Client Zone, which you will use in this type of deployment. The Expressway Core cannot ever act as a Traversal Server; therefore, the Traversal Server Zone is not available on this server. Similar to the Zone creation on the Expressway Edge, only the first three configuration options appear until select a type in the Type field. Then the following configuration options appear:

d.   Username: Enter the name configured in the authentication database on the Expressway Edge.

e.   Connection Credentials > Password: Enter the password configured in the authentication database on the Expressway Edge.

f.   H.323 > Mode: **On** (default)

g.   H.323 > Protocol: **Assent** (default). You can change this setting to **H46018**, but notice there is not an H.460.19 option. This part of the ITU protocol is only configured on the Expressway Edge.

h.   H.323 > Port: Be sure to use the H.323 listening port number that you configured on the Traversal Server Zone on the Expressway Edge.

Figure 10-8 illustrates the initial configuration settings on the Expressway Core for the Traversal Client Zone.

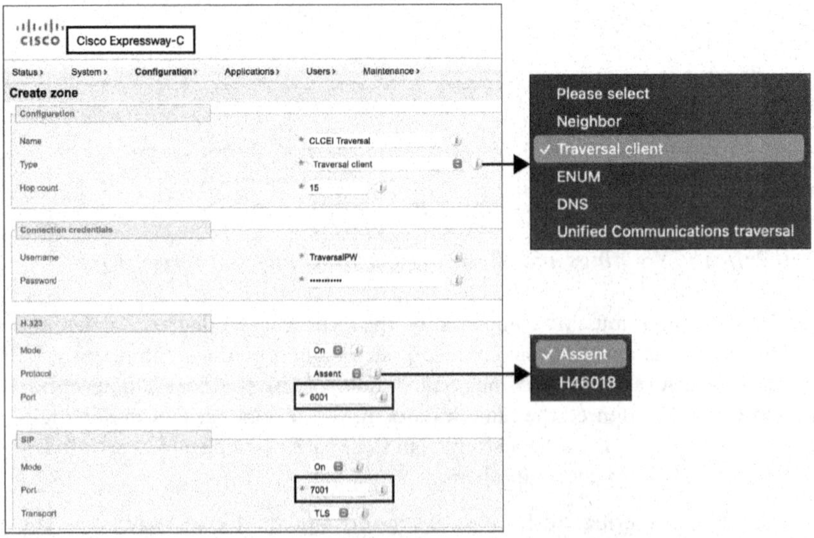

Figure 10-8   *Connection Credentials and H.323 Settings for a Traversal Client Zone*

i.   SIP > Mode: **On**

j.   SIP > Port: Use the same SIP listening port number that you configured while building the Traversal Server Zone on the Expressway Edge.

k. All remaining SIP settings are the same as previously described under the Traversal Server Zone configuration steps. These settings should be configured the same way on the Traversal Client Zone.

l. Authentication > Authentication Mode: **Do Not Check Credentials** (default). Again, configure this setting per your environment and as to how you want devices using this Zone to be treated. This setting does not have anything to do with the authentication that must be set up between this Zone and the Traversal Server Zone.

m. Client Settings > Retry Interval: **120** (default). This is the time parameter mentioned at the beginning of this section whereby the Expressway Core will attempt to establish a connection with the Expressway Edge through the Traversal Client and Server Zones.

n. Client Settings > Disconnect on Fail Interval: **0** (default). This setting defines the number of times the retry interval will attempt to establish a connection before it stops trying.

o. Location > Peer <1–6> Address: This is where you would configure the IP address or URL of the Expressway Edge. There are six peer addresses, but peer addresses 2 through 6 should only be used when traversing to a cluster of Expressway Edges. Clustering will be covered in more detail in Chapter 11, "Clustering Expressways."

Step 3. Click **Create Zone**. This takes you back to the main Zones page. The Zone that you created should show as Active. Figure 10-9 illustrates the Location section settings for the Traversal Client Zone and the active connection after the Zone is saved. Bear in mind that this figure shows H.323 as disabled so only SIP will show up as Active.

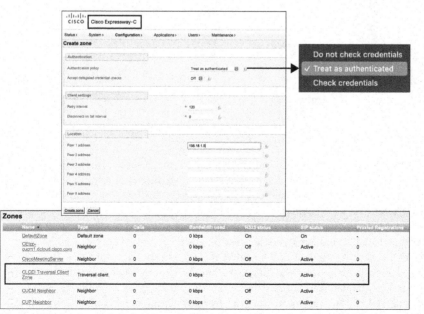

Figure 10-9 *Location Settings and an Active Status for a Traversal Client Zone*

As with any Zones created on the Expressway servers, the final step is to create at least one Search Rule on the Expressway Core for the Traversal Client Zone. Refer to Chapter 9 for a refresher on configuring Search Rules should you need it. Your traversal configuration on the Expressway Core and Edge servers is complete. Before using this solution in a production environment, it is prudent to test calls in both directions first to ensure the network is behaving as it should. If calls fail, or if you experience one-way audio and one-way video, then you should check that the appropriate ports are open on the firewall.

Deployment Scenarios for Traversal Zones

Up to this point we have covered the basic mechanics of creating Traversal Zones on Expressway servers. However, different networked environments require different techniques be used to successfully and securely traverse into and out from these networks. One network component that many companies incorporate into their network topologies to add another layer of security is a **demilitarized zone (DMZ)**. The DMZ is a perimeter network that exists outside an organization's main corporate network and acts as a buffer for services that are public facing, such as the Expressway Edge. Therefore, the Cisco Expressway solution supports several deployment scenarios for networked environments that utilize the DMZ.

In a deployment scenario where a DMZ exists between two firewalls, there is a way to route traffic through an Expressway Edge located within this DMZ. This single-subnet DMZ scenario involves using a single LAN interface with static NAT. In this scenario, firewall A can route traffic to firewall B and vice versa. The Expressway Edge allows video traffic to be passed through firewall B without pinholing firewall B from outside to inside. The Expressway Edge also handles firewall traversal on its public side. Figure 10-10 illustrates the single-subnet DMZ deployment scenario.

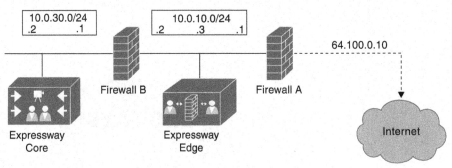

Figure 10-10   *Single-Subnet DMZ Deployment Scenario*

The name of this deployment scenario is derived from the single subnet that exists within the DMZ. Notice in Figure 10-10 that this subnet consists of an internal interface for Firewall A with the IP address of 10.0.10.1, and an external interface for Firewall B with an IP address of 10.0.10.2. There's also a LAN interface for the Expressway Edge with an IP address of 10.0.10.3. The LAN subnet for the internal corporate network includes an internal IP address for Firewall B of 10.0.30.1 and a network address for the Expressway Core of 10.0.30.2. A static 1:1 NAT has been configured on Firewall A, NATing the public address 64.100.0.10 to the LAN address of the Expressway Edge. Within the Expressway Edge web interface, Static NAT mode is enabled for the LAN the Expressway Edge is on, with the same static NAT address of 64.100.0.10. This means that the Traversal Client Zone configured on the

Expressway Core should have the 64.100.0.10 address configured as the Peer 1 address. However, the Expressway Edge should use 10.0.10.1 as the default gateway address in the network settings. The 10.0.10.3 address is used exclusively for management.

Similar to the single-subnet DMZ deployment scenario is the three-port firewall DMZ deployment using a Single Expressway Edge LAN interface. Although both scenarios use a single interface on the Expressway-E, the three-port firewall DMZ uses three ports on a single firewall to create two subnets. The first interface is used to create a DMZ subnet of 10.0.10.0/30. The DMZ interface on the firewall should be configured as 10.0.10.1 and the interface for the Expressway Edge should be configured as 10.0.10.2. The second interface on the firewall is used to create the internal LAN subnet of 10.0.30.0/24. The LAN interface should be configured as 10.0.30.1, and the Expressway Core should be configured as 10.0.30.2. The third interface is configured with the public IP address of 64.100.0.10 for public Internet access. A static 1:1 NAT has been configured on the firewall, NATing the public address 64.100.0.10 to the LAN address of the Expressway Edge. Static NAT mode on the Expressway Edge is enabled for the LAN with a static NAT address of 64.100.0.10. The Expressway Edge should be configured with a default gateway of 10.0.10.1. Because this gateway must be used for all traffic leaving the Expressway Edge, no static routes are needed in this type of deployment. Again, the Traversal Client Zone on the Expressway Core should be configured with a Peer 1 address of 64.100.0.10. Figure 10-11 illustrates the three-port firewall DMZ deployment scenario.

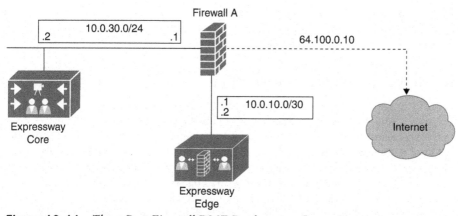

Figure 10-11   *Three-Port Firewall DMZ Deployment Scenario*

Neither the single-subnet DMZ deployment scenario nor the three-port firewall DMZ deployment scenario is recommended by Cisco for a production environment. For all the deployments that use only one **network interface card (NIC)** on the Expressway Edge but also require static NAT for public access, the media must "hairpin" or reflect on the external firewall whenever media is handled by the Expressway Edges **Back-to-Back User Agent (B2BUA)**. In these deployments, the B2BUA sees the public IP address of the Expressway Edge instead of its private IP address, so the media stream must go through the network address translator to get to the private IP address. Not all firewalls allow this reflection, and it is considered by some to be a security risk. Each call where the B2BUA is engaged will consume three times as much bandwidth as it would using the recommended dual NIC deployment. This could adversely affect call quality.

10

This brings us to the dual NIC DMZ deployment scenario, which is the method Cisco recommends using for most DMZ deployments. This deployment requires the Advanced Networking option key be installed on the Expressway Edge that lives within the DMZ. This option key enables the use of two NICs on the Expressway Edge to connect to two autonomous networks. This option key comes as a $0.00 item with the purchase of a basic license package for Expressway series, but it can only be installed on the Expressway Edge. The Expressway Core will not support the Advanced Networking option key. Figure 10-12 illustrates the dual NIC DMZ deployment scenario.

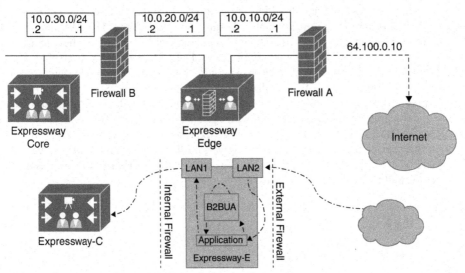

Figure 10-12 *Dual NIC DMZ Deployment Scenario*

In a dual NIC deployment, configure the External LAN Interface setting on the IP Configuration page to LAN2. This setting determines where the Expressway Edge TURN server allocates TURN relays. If any routers are being used within your network that support **Application Layer Gateways (ALGs)**, be sure to disable the settings for SIP and H.323. The Cisco Expressway solution does not support this functionality on firewalls when deploying the Expressway Edge behind a NAT. The Expressway Edge must perform the static NAT on its own Interface. The LAN1 and LAN2 interfaces must be located in nonoverlapping subnets. This ensures traffic is sent through the correct interface. Figure 10-11 illustrates how this solution should be deployed. In a typical DMZ deployment, the internal firewall and external firewall cannot route directly between one another. Therefore, dual-NIC devices, such as the Expressway Edge, are required to validate and forward the traffic between the isolated subnets. This is the security of this solution. No traffic can pass through the network without traversing through the Expressway Edge. The Expressway Edge will only allow voice and video signaling and media through, so hackers will have to find another path into the network. The outward-facing interface on the Expressway Edge, LAN2, has static NAT configured. The Traversal Client Zone on the Expressway Core will point to the internal-facing interface on the Expressway Edge, LAN1, using the address 10.0.20.2.

One final deployment scenario for Traversal Zones through a DMZ that is worth mentioning involves an Expressway Core that exists inside the corporate network, an Expressway Edge that exists in the DMZ, and a second Expressway Edge that exists on the network edge outside the DMZ on the public-facing side. The public-facing Expressway Edge should be configured with a Traversal Server Zone. The Expressway Edge that exists inside the DMZ is configured with a Traversal Client Zone pointing to the IP address of the public-facing Expressway Edge. The Expressway Edge that exists in the DMZ is also configured with a Traversal Server Zone. The Expressway Core that exists within the corporate network is configured with a Traversal Client Zone that points to the Expressway Edge in the DMZ. In this manner, the two firewalls never talk to one another, so the security from the dual NIC DMZ deployment scenario is still in play. Additionally, TURN is not required to achieve access through the external firewall, so there is a higher level of security where this firewall is concerned. The downside to this deployment scenario comes with the cost of supporting a third Expressway. Additionally, MRA cannot be supported though this type of deployment either. For these reasons, most corporations will not use this deployment scenario. However, for networked environments that require the highest level of security, such as with government and military, this is the only approved deployment solution for firewall traversal. Figure 10-13 illustrates the triple Expressway deployment scenario.

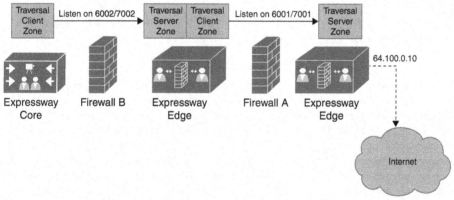

Figure 10-13 *Triple Expressway Deployment Scenario*

DNS Zones

Another Zone type that can be used on the Expressway Series is the **Domain Name System (DNS)** Zone. This Zone type allows the Expressway to query a DNS server for domain lookup. Due to the nature of how DNS works, and where DNS servers typically live within an enterprise network, DNS Zones have two applications within a Cisco collaboration solution: to route calls between Expressways within an enterprise network, and to route calls between corporations through the public Internet space.

Chapter 9 discussed the use of Neighbor Zones to route traffic between Cisco Expressways. The Complex Video Network with a Hierarchical Dial Plan was also discussed in that chapter as an efficient method of routing calls across an enterprise network. In a similar fashion to the Hierarchical Dial Plan using Neighbor Zones, DNS Zones can be used to route calls between Expressways within an enterprise network. An advantage to using DNS Zones versus using Neighbor Zones is that the number of Zones needed to support this solution is greatly reduced by leveraging DNS. A potential disadvantage to using DNS Zones is that DNS only allows for URI dialing. Figure 10-14 illustrates what a network topology would look like when DNS Zones are used for internal dialing.

10

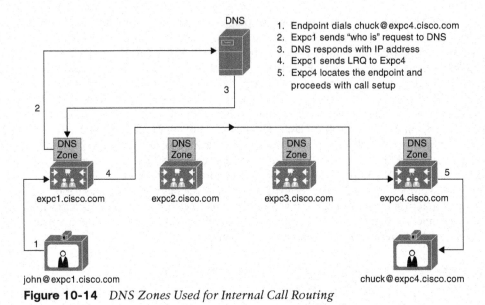

Figure 10-14 *DNS Zones Used for Internal Call Routing*

Based on the scenario outlined in Figure 10-14, the endpoint on the left dials chuck@expc4.cisco.com and sends the call request to its local Expressway Core, which is expc1.cisco.com for this example. Like all other Zones in an Expressway, DNS Zones need Search Rules too. Based on the Search Rule configured for the DNS Zone, this Expressway knows it needs to query the DNS server before proceeding with the call setup. So, expc1.cisco.com sends a WHOIS request to the DNS server to find the location of expc4.cisco.com. Notice that the query to the DNS server is not for chuck@expc4.cisco.com; the query is only for the domain part of the URI, which is expc4.cisco.com. The DNS server looks up the **A record** for expc4.cisco.com to discover the associated IP address, and then returns this information to the requesting server. Now that the Expressway has the IP address of the destination server, it sends a Location Request (LRQ) to the destination IP address searching for chuck@expc4.cisco.com. Because this Expressway is able to locate the endpoint using this alias, the call setup continues so that John and Chuck can communicate with one another.

Notice that the alias used for DNS dialing is a URI address, which resembles an email address. With SIP this is an organic method of dialing because the SIP URI is already in the proper format for dialing using DNS. With H.323, the H.323 ID should be used in the form of a URI, or else Transforms should be used to format aliases appropriately.

ENUM Zones on the Cisco Expressway work on the same principle as DNS Zones. **ENUM** stands for E.164 Number Mapping. It is a way of using DNS **Name Authority PoinTeR (NAPTR) records** to convert E164 numbers into routable URIs. ENUM is defined in RFC 6116. A DNS server must be configured with NAPTR records that do the following:

- Define (using regular expressions) how a presented E.164 number is converted to a routable URI

- Define the transport protocol to be used for the call, such as SIP or H.323

Therefore, an E164 alias such as 25677809 could be translated to SIP:auser@Cisco.com or H323:auser@Cisco.com. The NAPTR record needs to exist in the name server that is specified in the DNS suffix, such as enum.search.com. When searching an ENUM Zone, the Expressway transforms an E164 alias from 1234 into 4.3.2.1@enum.org. This alias is looked up as a DNS lookup, and the enum.org server replies with a service and a URI. The URI can then be contacted through a DNS lookup.

Three settings must be configured on the Cisco Expressway before DNS Zones can be used. Obviously, you must configure a DNS Zone and at least one Search Rule. The third setting actually is a group of settings, the DNS settings. The settings are not configured in the DNS Zone as you might expect. Rather, you configure the DNS server address and Expressway URL under the Systems menu of the Cisco Expressway. To create a DNS Zone and configure the DNS settings, follow these steps:

Step 1.   Log in to the Cisco Expressway and navigate to **Configuration > Zones > Zones**.

Step 2.   Click **New** and configure the following information:

  a.   Name: Enter the name of the DNS Zone you are creating.

  b.   Type: Select **DNS**. As with other Zones, this will expand the menu options based on the Zone Type you selected.

Step 3.   Notice that the menu options are quite different than those for other Zones you have created on the Expressway. There is no place to enter the DNS server address, and few other options that can be configured at all. Leave all the settings at their default values, and click **Create Zone**, which is located at the bottom of the page.

Step 4.   Create the appropriate Search Rules after the zone creation is complete. Figure 10-15 illustrates the menu options for configuring DNS Zones on the Cisco Expressway.

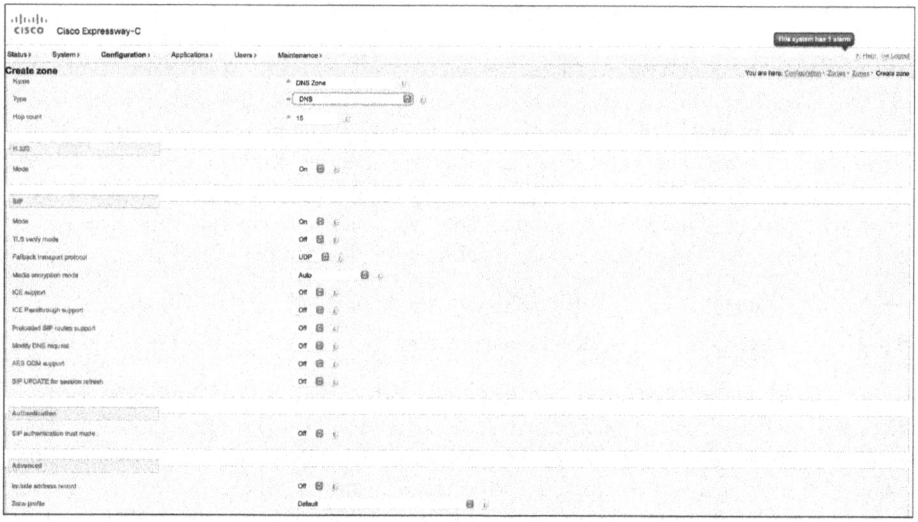

Figure 10-15   *DNS Zone Menus on Cisco Expressway*

To configure DNS settings on the Cisco Expressway, follow these steps:

Step 1. Navigate to **System > DNS**.

Step 2. In the System Host Name field, enter the host name as it appears in the DNS.

Step 3. In the Domain Name field, enter the domain name as it appears in the DNS.

Step 4. In the Address 1 field, enter the IP address of the DNS server. You can enter up to five DNS addresses here. There is also a section at the bottom of this page where you can enter a different address for up to five unique domains.

Step 5. Click **Save** once you have configured all the appropriate fields. Figure 10-16 illustrates the DNS settings on a Cisco Expressway.

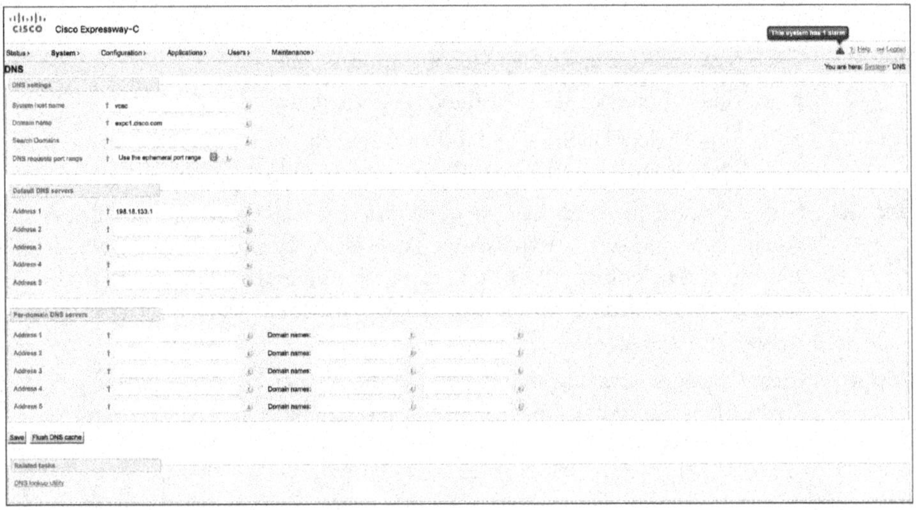

Figure 10-16 *DNS Settings on Cisco Expressway*

All the settings just covered on the Cisco Expressway will only get a WHOIS request to the DNS server. There are still settings that must be configured on the DNS server so that URI addresses can be resolved to IP addresses. If you are only planning to use an internal DNS server to route calls between Expressway Core servers, then the only DNS record you need to create is an A record. DNS A records are the most basic type of any DNS records. They are simply a mapping of a domain or subdomain to an IP address. The following is an A record example, where Target is an A record defining the destination:

Host	Domain	URL (DNS puts them together)	IP address
expc1	cisco.com	expc1.company.com	10.1.1.40

There are a multitude of DNS servers on the market today that can be used to host these services. Although the basic elements of an A record are the same, how you should configure these settings depends on the model of the DNS server being used. For the purpose of this book, we will show you how to create a DNS A record using the Microsoft DNS service running on a Microsoft Windows Server 2012 R2 Standard platform. Note that DNS is a service that runs on the server, and as such it must be enabled and configured prior to creating any address records of any type. This book will not go into how to initially configure any part of a Microsoft Windows Server. Use the following steps to configure A records on a Microsoft DNS server:

Step 1.   Open the Server Manager, and then navigate to **Tools > DNS**.

Step 2.   Depending on how DNS was set up to begin with, there may be several folders in the hierarchical tree structure. Right-click the folder in which you want to create the A record and select **New Host (A or AAAA)**.

Step 3.   In the pop-up window, enter the following information, as shown in Figure 10-17:

    a.   Name (uses parent domain name if blank): This is the *host* part of the URL specified previously.

    b.   Fully Qualified Domain Name (FQDN): This is the full URL, and this field is automatically populated. Notice there is nowhere to enter the domain. That's because the folder this A record is being added to already operates under a specific domain.

    c.   IP Address: This is the IP address of the server to which the URL will map.

    d.   Create Associated Pointer (PTR) Record: Check this box if you want the DNS server to create a reverse DNS record, or Pointer record, in association with this A record. Generally, it is a good idea to check this box.

    e.   Allow Any Authenticated User to Update DNS Records with the Same Owner Name: For security reasons, you probably do not want to check this box. Only administrators should be allowed to update DNS records.

Step 4.   Click **Add Host** to complete the creation of this A record.

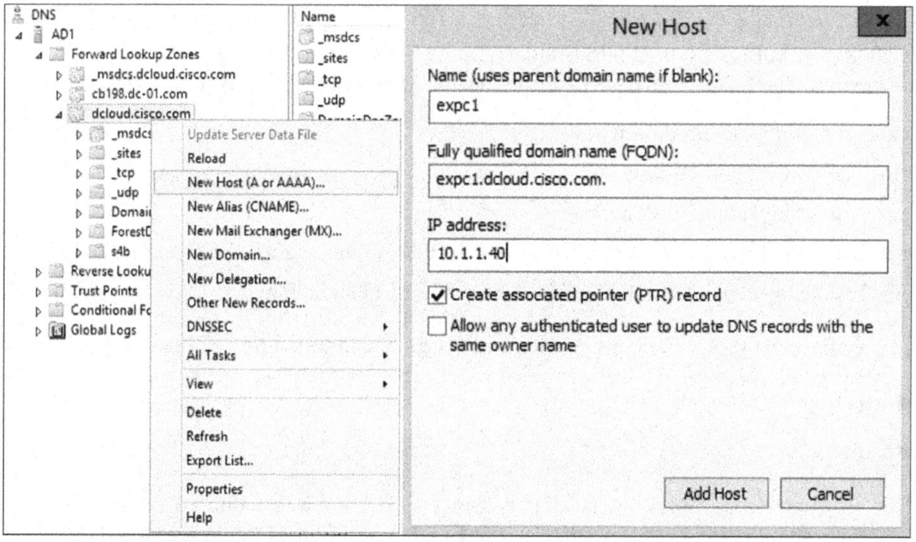

Figure 10-17   *Creating A Records on a Microsoft DNS Server* (Image is copyright of Microsoft Corporation)

For locally registered endpoints to be reached via DNS routing, the dialed alias must be in the form of a URI. The easiest way to achieve this outcome is to have both SIP and H.323 endpoints register using a URI; otherwise they will only be discoverable by the local Expressway to which they are registered. H.323 endpoints should register with the Expressway using an H.323 ID in the form of a URI address to be reachable via DNS routing. SIP endpoints always register with an **Address of Record (AOR)** in the form of a URI, so no change is needed for these aliases.

An alternative solution would be to create transforms on the Search Rule for the DNS Zone that changes aliases to a full URI if they are not already in that form. Additional Transforms must also be configured to strip domains from a URI for incoming calls. The interworking Transform and Search Rule, which was explained in Chapter 7, "Configure Expressway Call Processing Order," could be implemented to prevent the need for H.323 IDs to take the form of URI addresses. E.164 aliases could be dialed through DNS as well, as long as the source endpoint originally dialed E.164@domain.

The other application for using a DNS Zone in a Cisco collaboration solution centered on the Expressway series is to use it for business-to-business (B2B) or business-to-consumer (B2C) communication. This is the more common application for how DNS is used in a current Cisco collaboration solution. Where an internal DNS server is used for routing within an enterprise network, a public DNS server must be used for routing across the public Internet. Internal routing can be achieved by simply creating an A record as previously explained, but routing across the public Internet requires both an A record and **Service (SRV) records**. The DNS SRV response is a set of records in the following format:

_service. _protocol.<fqdn>.	TTL	Priority	Weight	Port	Target
_sip._tcp.company.com	7200	20	5	5060	vcs1.company.com

An SRV record is primarily used to handle incoming service requests over specific ports. If both SIP and H.323 are being used, an SRV record must be created for every port that is associated with these two protocols. H.323 uses UDP port 1719 and TCP port 1720. SIP uses UDP port 5060, TCP port 5060, and TLS port 5061. Therefore 5 SRV records will need to be created. The formats of DNS SRV queries for SIP and H.323 used by Expressway are

_sips._tcp.<fully.qualified.domain>

_sip._tcp.<fully.qualified.domain>

_sip._udp.<fully.qualified.domain>

_h323ls._udp.<fully.qualified.domain> —for UDP RAS messaging, for example: LRQ

_h323cs._tcp.<fully.qualified.domain> —for H.323 call signaling

When configuring TLS for SIP, the service and protocol can be configured two ways:

- sip._tls.

- sips._tcp.

Within an enterprise network where DNS is used for B2B and B2C calling, DNS Zones and DNS servers should only be configured on the Expressway Edge. DNS A records should be configured on a public DNS server using the IP address and URL of the Expressway Edge as the authoritative proxy for the enterprise. Figure 10-18 illustrates a network set up for B2B communications using a DNS Zone on the Expressway Edge.

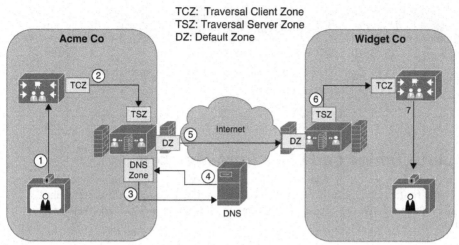

Figure 10-18 *DNS Zohe Used for B2B Communication*

Exam Preparation Tasks

As mentioned in the section "How to Use This Book" in the Introduction, you have a couple of choices for exam preparation: the exercises here, Chapter 24, "Final Preparation," and the exam simulation questions in the Pearson Test Prep practice test software.

Review All Key Topics

Review the most important topics in this chapter, noted with the Key Topics icon in the outer margin of the page. Table 10-4 lists a reference of these key topics and the page numbers on which each is found.

Table 10-4   Key Topics for Chapter 10

Key Topic Element	Description	Page Number
Paragraph	One-way audio/video issue caused by firewalls	181
List	Classes for private IP addresses	182
Paragraphs	Two issues NAT causes with AV communication over IP	183
Paragraph	How STUN works	183
Paragraph	How TURN works	184
Table 10-2	Configurable Options for TURN on the Cisco Expressway	185
Paragraph	How ICE works	186
Paragraph	How Assent works	188
Paragraph	How the H.460 protocols work	188
Table 10-3	Ports Used with Assent and H.460.18/19	189
Paragraph	Authentication requirements for Traversal Zones	189
Paragraph	Zone options on the Expressway Edge	190
Paragraph	Zone options on the Expressway Core	194

Key Topic Element	Description	Page Number
Paragraph	Dual NIC DMZ deployment scenario explained	198
Paragraph	DNS Zones used for internal routing between Expressways	199
List	A record format and example	202
Paragraph	DNS Zones used for B2B/B2C communication	204
List	SRV record format and example	204

Complete Tables and Lists from Memory

Print a copy of Appendix C, "Memory Tables" (found on the companion website), or at least the section for this chapter, and complete the tables and lists from memory. Appendix D, "Memory Tables Answer Key," also on the companion website, includes completed tables and lists to check your work.

Define Key Terms

Define the following key terms from this chapter and check your answers in the glossary:

A record, Application Layer Gateway (AKG), Address of Record (AOR), Assent, asymmetric network, back-to-back user agent (B2BUA), demilitarized zone (DMZ), Domain Name System (DNS), Enumerated Dialing (ENUM), firewall, H.460.18/19, Interactive Connectivity Establishment (ICE), Internet Protocol version 4 (IPv4), Internet Protocol version 6 (IPv6), Name Authority Pointer (NAPTR) record, Network Address Translation (NAT), Network Interface Card (NIC), Port Address Translation (PAT), Service (SRV) record, Session Traversal Utilities for NAT (STUN), symmetric network, Traversal Using Relays around NAT (TURN), traversal, Traversal Client Zone, Traversal Server Zone

Q&A

The answers to these questions appear in Appendix A. For more practice with exam format questions, use the Pearson Test Prep practice test software.

1. List the three classes of private IP addresses with the IP ranges.

2. List all the components (broad scope) that must be configured on the Expressway Core and Edge servers to support a firewall traversal connection.

3. List the A record format with an example and the SRV record formats with examples for SIP and H.323.

CHAPTER 11

Clustering Expressways

This chapter covers the following topics:

Clustering Requirements: Reviews the prerequisites that must be met before clustering Cisco Expressways.

DNS and Clustering: Discusses the role DNS should play in Expressway clusters.

Zones and Clustering: Examines different scenarios where Neighbor Zones and Traversal Zones are used with Expressway clusters.

Clustering is certainly not a new concept. Ever since people began to store data on digital servers, the architects of those servers have been working on solutions to provide redundancy so that information will not be lost in the event of a server failure. Live content during an audio or video meeting is no exception to the vulnerability of servers going down. For this reason, the architects of the Cisco Expressway server have built redundancy into the solution through clustering. This chapter will provide you with the knowledge and skills to understand clustering for the use of redundancy on the Cisco Expressway. This knowledge includes understanding the requirements and limitations, integration with DNS, and how clustering functions with Neighbor Zones and Traversal Zones.

This chapter covers the following objectives from the Implementing Cisco Collaboration Cloud and Edge Solutions (CLCEI) exam 300-820:

- 1.8.e Describe key Expressway settings: Clustering
- 2.1.e Configure key Expressway settings: Clustering

"Do I Know This Already?" Quiz

The "Do I Know This Already?" quiz enables you to assess whether you should read this entire chapter thoroughly or jump to the "Exam Preparation Tasks" section. If you are in doubt about your answers to these questions or your own assessment of your knowledge of the topics, read the entire chapter. Table 11-1 lists the major headings in this chapter and their corresponding "Do I Know This Already?" quiz questions. You can find the answers in Appendix A, "Answers to the 'Do I Know This Already?' Quizzes and Review Questions."

Table 11-1 "Do I Know This Already?" Section-to-Question Mapping

Foundation Topics Section	Questions
Clustering Requirements	1–3
DNS and Clustering	4
Zones and Clustering	5

1. When using clustering to increase the capacity of an Expressway, how many registrations can a cluster of six Expressways support?

    a. 2500

    b. 10,000

    c. 15,000

    d. 40,000

2. Which of the following settings is true when setting up a cluster?

    a. Federation and dual-homed domain spaces are supported within an Expressway cluster.

    b. Major versions on Expressways being clustered must be the same, but minor versions do not matter.

    c. Room System and Desktop System licenses must be the same on all peers within the cluster.

    d. Rich Media session licenses do not have to be the same on all peers within the cluster.

3. What round-trip-delay time must be maintained between all peers within a cluster of Expressways to support the sending and receiving of information?

    a. 30 ms

    b. 40 ms

    c. 80 ms

    d. 300 ms

4. Which of the following statements is true about using DNS with an Expressway cluster?

    a. The DNS server does replicate, so only one cluster member needs to be created in DNS.

    b. Reverse lookup is not used with clustering, so no PTR records need to be created.

    c. SRV records are never required when setting up DNS to operate with Expressway clusters.

    d. The cluster FQDN must be used with the unique IP address of each Expressway when creating the A records.

5. When creating Neighbor or Traversal Zones between clustered and single Expressways, which of the following combinations is allowed?

    a. Three Expressway Cores neighbored to six Expressway Cores

    b. Two Expressway Cores traversing to four Expressway Edges

    c. One Expressway Core neighbored to three Expressway Cores

    d. Six Expressway Cores traversing to one Expressway Edge that is also traversing to another cluster of three Expressway Edges

    e. Three Expressway Cores neighbored to three Expressway Cores

    f. All choices

Foundation Topics

Clustering Requirements

Clustering is achieved by establishing a logical group of up to six identical peer Expressways. This allows the systems to work together as one large Local Zone. Clustering Expressways can add both increased capacity and resiliency.

Clustering can increase the capacity of an Expressway deployment by a maximum factor of four, compared with a single Expressway. There is no capacity gain after four peers. So, if you deploy a maximum six-peer cluster, the fifth and sixth Expressways do not add extra call capacity to the cluster. Resilience is improved with the extra peers, but not capacity. Also, the Small Expressway VMs are intended for Cisco Business Edition 6000 customers, so clustering of Small VMs only provides redundancy and does not provide any additional scale benefit. Capacity licensing is done on a per-cluster basis, and all capacity licenses installed on a cluster peer are available to any peer in the cluster. This includes Rich Media Session licenses and Room System and Desktop System registration licenses. Table 11-2 identifies the capacity limitations within a cluster of Cisco Expressways.

Key Topic

Table 11-2   Expressway Cluster Registration and Call Capacity Limitations

Licenses on Expressway	Single Expressway Deployment	Cluster with Maximum Six Expressways
Room System and Desktop System registrations	2500	10,000
Rich Media Sessions (small/medium or large deployment)	100 small/medium deployment 500 large deployment	500 small/medium deployment 2000 large deployment
TURN Relays (small/medium or large deployment)	1800 small/medium deployment 6000 large deployment	7200 small/medium deployment 24,000 large deployment

Clustering can provide redundancy while an Expressway is in maintenance mode, or in case it becomes inaccessible due to a network or power outage, or other reason. The Expressway peers in a cluster share bandwidth usage as well as routing, zones, FindMe, and other configuration settings. All peers within the cluster are always active; there is no hot-standby. Therefore, endpoints can register to any of the peers in the cluster. If an endpoint loses connection to its initial peer, it can re-register to another node within the cluster.

Requirements for setting up a cluster of Expressways have changed over the years. Therefore, to ensure that all the requirements are met, you will want to check the *Cisco Expressway Cluster Creation and Maintenance Deployment Guide* for the version you are clustering before setting up the cluster. However, for an X12.5 Expressway cluster, ensure that the following requirements are met.

Common settings that must be configured the same across all peers in a cluster include the following:

Key Topic

- Only Expressway Cores can be clustered with Expressway Cores, and only Expressway Edges can be clustered with Expressway Edges. Likewise, a legacy VCS Control cannot be clustered with an Expressway Core or Edge, nor can a legacy VCS Expressway be clustered with an Expressway Edge or Core.

- All settings under the Configuration menu must be configured the same way. In a green-field deployment, it is best to leave these settings at their default values until after the cluster is created. Then configure these settings on the primary Peer. The settings will be replicated to all other peers in the cluster. Brown-field deployments require only the primary peer be configured, because it will replicate the settings once the cluster is active. Any settings configured on other Peer Expressways will be replaced with the settings on the Primary Peer once the cluster is initiated.

- All peers in the cluster must operate within the same domain. No federation or dual-homed domain spaces are supported within an Expressway cluster.

- All peers must be running the same version of firmware, because how you configure a cluster may diverge between different versions. Therefore, if the firmware version is different, the cluster may not work.

- All peers within the cluster must have the same set of option keys installed. Exceptions to this rule include Rich Media Session (RMS) licenses and Room System and Desktop System registration licenses.

- H.323 mode is enabled on each peer. This setting can be enabled under the **Configuration > Protocols > H.323** menu by setting the H.323 mode to On. The cluster uses H.323 signaling between peers to determine the best route for calls, even if all endpoints are SIP endpoints.

- The firewall rules on each peer must be configured to block connections to the clustering TLS ports from all IP addresses except those of its peers. Within the external network firewall itself, policies should be set up to block access to the clustering TLS ports as well.

Common settings that must be configured differently across all peers in a cluster include the following:

- Each peer must have a different System Name to all other peers.

- Each peer must have a different LAN address configured. There must be no NAT between cluster peers.

These LAN addresses can be within the same subnet or in different subnets. As far as the network is concerned, there are only two other requirements that must be met. First, all peers within the cluster must be able to route to all other peers within the cluster. Second, each peer within the cluster must be able to support a round-trip-delay of up to 80 ms. This is an improvement over previous versions of the Expressway that required a 30-ms round-trip-delay time. This means that each Expressway in the cluster must be within a 40-ms hop to any other peer within the cluster.

In addition to all the requirements previously mentioned, there are some other considerations that must be taken into account regarding security certificates. Each peer in the cluster should have a certificate that identifies it to other peers. The minimum requirement regarding certificates is to set the TLS Verification Mode to the default value of Permissive. If you want to have authenticated TLS connections, the certificate must also be valid and be issued by an authority that is trusted by all peers. This requires the TLS Verification Mode be set to Enforce. Cisco recommends populating the CN of all peer certificates with the same cluster fully qualified domain name (FQDN), and populating each peer certificate's SAN with that peer's FQDN. Although using one certificate for multiple Expressways in one cluster is supported, this is not recommended due to the security risk. That is, if one private key is compromised on one device, it means all devices in the cluster are compromised.

Once an Expressway has been determined as the primary, Configuration menu settings must be configured only on the primary. Any attempt to configure these settings on any other peer will result in those settings being overwritten by the primary immediately. When these settings are configured on the primary, they will be applied to all peers within the cluster. The password for the default admin account is not replicated. Each Peer can have a different password for this one account. However, any other administration accounts and passwords created on Expressway peers will be replicated from the Master Peer to all other peers.

Some settings within an Expressway cluster can be configured on any peer within the cluster, and these settings will be replicated out to all other peers. Peers share information with each other about their use of bandwidth, registrations, and FindMe users. This process is part of what allows the cluster to act as one large Expressway Local Zone. The Event Log and Configuration Log on each Peer will only report activity for that particular Expressway. It is recommended that you set up a remote Syslog server to which the logs of all peers can be sent. This log will allow you to have a global view of activity across all peers in the cluster. Figure 11-1 illustrates how an Expressway cluster operates as one large Local Zone.

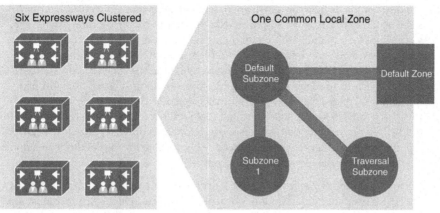

Figure 11-1 *Expressway Cluster Operation as One Large Local Zone*

DNS and Clustering

Clustering Expressways managed by Cisco Telepresence Management Suite (TMS) is heavily dependent on DNS. However, whether TMS is being used or not, DNS can be used with Expressway clusters for many other purposes. A profound fundamental use of DNS with clusters is the use of round-robin DNS. This process allows for load distribution between all devices registering to the Expressway. Figure 11-2 illustrates how DNS can be used to create a load distribution of registered endpoints using the round-robin method.

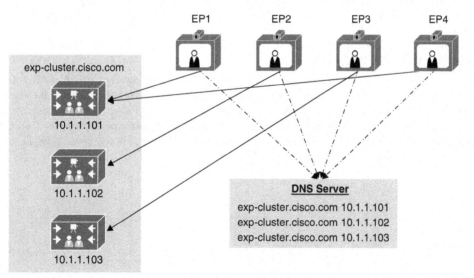

Figure 11-2 *Expressway Cluster Using DNS for Round Robin*

Figure 11-2 shows a cluster of three Expressways that each have a unique IP address. The cluster uses the FQDN of exp-cluster.cisco.com, and there are three A records created in DNS, each using this cluster FQDN and the respective unique IP address of each Expressway. When endpoint 1, indicated by EP1 in the figure, sends a WHOIS request to the DNS server for exp-cluster.cisco.com, the DNS server returns the IP address from the A record matching this URL using a weighted scale. If the weight of each entry is the same, a round-robin distribution using a top-down approach is implemented. Therefore, endpoint 1 receives the IP address 10.1.1.101 and proceeds to register to the first Expressway in the cluster. When endpoint 2 queries DNS for exp-cluster.cisco.com, it receives the IP address 10.1.1.102 in response and proceeds to register to the second Expressway in the cluster. When endpoint 3 queries DNS for exp-cluster.cisco.com, it receives the IP address 10.1.1.103 in response and proceeds to register to the third Expressway in the cluster. So, what happens when endpoint 4 queries DNS for exp-cluster.cisco.com? Because there are no more Expressways listed in DNS for this cluster, round robin returns to the first A record. The IP address 10.1.1.101 is sent to endpoint 4 in response, and that endpoint proceeds to register to the first Expressway in the cluster. This process will continue for each additional endpoint that tries to register using the exp-cluster.cisco.com URL.

To use DNS with a cluster of Expressways, the cluster name must be created in DNS as an FQDN. The DNS server configuration does not replicate, so each cluster member must also be created in DNS with both forward and reverse A records. The DNS servers must also provide address lookup for any other DNS functionality required, such as NTP servers or the External Manager address if they are configured using DNS names. A Microsoft Front-End (FE) server FQDN lookup may be required, as well as an LDAP server forward and reverse lookup. Reverse lookups are frequently provided through Pointer (PTR) records.

SRV records may also be required for the cluster. Multiple entries for each service with equal weights can be entered to cover each peer in the cluster. This configuration is advised for video interoperability and business-to-business (B2B) video calling but is not required for Mobile and Remote Access (MRA). For MRA, create a collab-edge SRV record for each peer in the Expressway Edge cluster. For B2B-only calls, the Expressway Edge cluster has a DNS SRV record that defines all cluster peers. Part 3 of this book will delve deeper into the MRA solution.

Zones and Clustering

A cluster of Expressway Cores can be neighbored to a single Expressway Core. A cluster of Expressway Cores can also be neighbored to another cluster of Expressway Cores. Likewise, a cluster of Expressway Cores can traverse to a single Expressway Edge. A single Expressway Core can traverse to a cluster of Expressway Edges. And a cluster of Expressway Cores can traverse to a cluster of Expressway Edges. Figure 11-3 illustrates how Expressway clusters can communicate using zones.

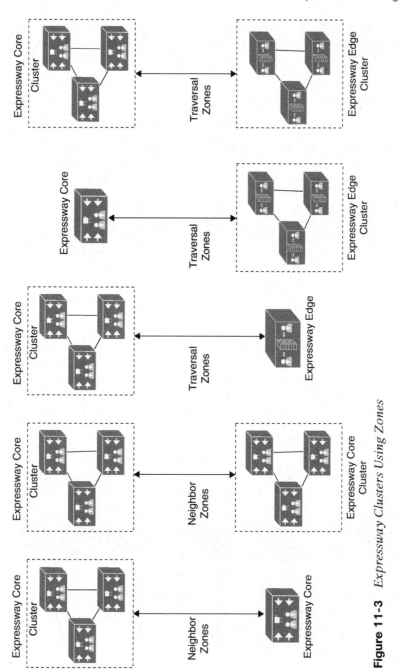

Figure 11-3 *Expressway Clusters Using Zones*

In each of these cases, when a call is received on your local Expressway and is passed via the relevant zone to the remote cluster, it will be routed to whichever peer in that neighboring cluster that has the lowest resource usage. That Peer will then forward the call as appropriate to one of the following:

- To one of its locally registered endpoints, if the endpoint is registered to that Peer

- To one of its peers, if the endpoint is registered to another Peer in that cluster

- To one of its external zones, if the endpoint has been located elsewhere

When configuring a connection to a remote cluster, you should configure the relevant zone with details of all the peers in the cluster. Adding this information to the zone will ensure that the call is passed to the cluster regardless of the status of the individual peers. You need to enter the IP address of all peers only when configuring Neighbor or Traversal Client Zones. As you may recall, the Traversal Server Zones do not allow you to configure any IP addresses. Also, zones are only configured on the primary Peer within the cluster. Do not try to configure zone settings on any of the alternate peers. When you are configuring a zone between two clusters, it is not necessary to have the same number of peers in each cluster. For example, a cluster of three Expressway Cores can traverse to a cluster of six Expressway Edges.

Exam Preparation Tasks

As mentioned in the section "How to Use This Book" in the Introduction, you have a couple of choices for exam preparation: the exercises here, Chapter 22, "Final Preparation," and the exam simulation questions in the Pearson Test Prep practice test software.

Review All Key Topics

Review the most important topics in this chapter, noted with the Key Topics icon in the outer margin of the page. Table 11-3 lists a reference of these key topics and the page numbers on which each is found.

Table 11-3 Key Topics for Chapter 11

Key Topic Element	Description	Page Number
Table 11-2	Expressway Cluster Registration and Call Capacity Limitations	210
List	Common settings in an Expressway cluster	211
List	Different settings in an Expressway cluster	212
Paragraph	Using DNS for round-robin distribution	213
List	Call forwarding between peers within a cluster	216
Paragraph	Common rules when using Zones with clusters	216

Complete Tables and Lists from Memory

Print a copy of Appendix C, "Memory Tables" (found on the companion website), or at least the section for this chapter, and complete the tables and lists from memory. Appendix D, "Memory Tables Answer Key," also on the companion website, includes completed tables and lists to check your work.

Define Key Terms

There are no new key terms for Chapter 11.

Q&A

The answers to these questions appear in Appendix A. For more practice with exam format questions, use the Pearson Test Prep pratice test software.

1. List the six common settings that must be configured the same on each Expressway Peer within a cluster.

2. List the two common settings that must be configured differently on each Expressway Peer within a cluster.

3. List the three ways a cluster of Expressways will forward incoming call requests when using Zones.

CHAPTER 12

Troubleshooting a Business-to-Business (B2B) Collaboration Solution

This chapter covers the following topics:

Troubleshooting Registration Issues: Identifies four main reasons registration would fail on the Cisco Expressway, and how to easily identify these issues using the Event Log.

Troubleshooting Calling Issues: Explains how to use different tools on the Cisco Expressway to identify call setup issues. These issues may be impacted by Neighbor Zones, Traversal Zones, Transforms, Search Rules, or a variety of other misconfigured components. These troubleshooting tools and techniques can even support troubleshooting issues with the SIP trunk integration from the Cisco Unified Communications Manager.

Troubleshooting DNS Issues: Presents DNS tools available on the Cisco Expressway to help troubleshoot DNS-related issues.

Troubleshooting Certificate Issues: Identifies common issues with certificates used on the Cisco Expressway and how to identify these issues.

Other Troubleshooting Tools: Provides an overview of other troubleshooting tools available on the Cisco Expressway that can aid in resolving many other potential issues.

Automobiles are complex machines that have many different moving parts. As such, they often require a specialist to troubleshoot and fix issues that come up. There are even several different types of specialists that may be required to work on a single automobile because the machine is so complex. Anything that has a lot of moving parts could experience many different issues, and the more moving parts there are, the more difficult it could become to isolate the issue that needs to be fixed. So, too, the Cisco Expressway is a complex machine that has many different moving parts, as has been explained in the first half of this book. Therefore, having the right tools to troubleshoot issues when they inevitably come up is essential to isolating and fixing these issues. This chapter explains the troubleshooting tools available on the Cisco Expressway, and how these tools can be used to support this server within your networked environment.

This chapter covers the following objectives from the Implementing Cisco Collaboration Cloud and Edge Solutions (CLCEI) exam 300-820:

- 2.5.a Troubleshoot a Business to Business (B2B) collaboration solution: DNS records (focus on Microsoft DNS)

- 2.5.b Troubleshoot a Business to Business (B2B) collaboration solution: Certificates (focus on Microsoft CA)

- 2.5.c Troubleshoot a Business to Business (B2B) collaboration solution: Traversal Zones

- 2.5.d Troubleshoot a Business to Business (B2B) collaboration solution: Neighbor Zones

- 2.5.e Troubleshoot a Business to Business (B2B) collaboration solution: Transforms

- 2.5.f Troubleshoot a Business to Business (B2B) collaboration solution: Search rules

- 2.5.g Troubleshoot a Business to Business (B2B) collaboration solution: SIP trunk integration with Cisco Unified Communications Manager

"Do I Know This Already?" Quiz

The "Do I Know This Already?" quiz enables you to assess whether you should read this entire chapter thoroughly or jump to the "Exam Preparation Tasks" section. If you are in doubt about your answers to these questions or your own assessment of your knowledge of the topics, read the entire chapter. Table 12-1 lists the major headings in this chapter and their corresponding "Do I Know This Already?" quiz questions. You can find the answers in Appendix A, "Answers to the 'Do I Know This Already?' Quizzes and Review Questions."

Table 12-1 "Do I Know This Already?" Section-to-Question Mapping

Foundation Topics Section	Questions
Troubleshooting Registration Issues	1
Troubleshooting Calling Issues	2–3
Troubleshooting DNS Issues	4
Troubleshooting Certificate Issues	5
Other Troubleshooting Tools	6

CAUTION The goal of self-assessment is to gauge your mastery of the topics in this chapter. If you do not know the answer to a question or are only partially sure of the answer, you should mark that question as wrong for purposes of the self-assessment. Giving yourself credit for an answer you correctly guess skews your self-assessment results and might provide you with a false sense of security.

1. An engineer is troubleshooting a registration issue on the Cisco Expressway. When reviewing the Event Log, the engineer comes across an error message that says "Registration Rejected – Unknown Domain." Which of the following is the possible cause of this issue?

   a. The SIP endpoint cannot register because the URI domain does not match the domain in the gatekeeper.

   b. The domain in the Allow List does not match the URI domain.

   c. The domain was not used to set up authentication.

   d. The URI domain does not match anything in the Expressway domain database.

2. Which of the following is a tool used to troubleshoot call setup issues on the Cisco Expressway?

   a. Search History

   b. Check Pattern

   c. Configuration Log

   d. Alarms

3. When using the Locate tool on the Cisco Expressway, which of the following fields should be used when CPL scripts are used with the Call Policy?

   a. Alias

   b. Source

   c. Source Alias

   d. Authenticated

4. When performing a DNS lookup on the Cisco Expressway, if the host is not a fully qualified domain name, how is DNS queried first?

   a. *Host*

   b. *Host.<system_domain>*

   c. Neither, only FQDN hosts can be queried

   d. Both queried at the same time

5. What two tools exist on the Cisco Expressway that can be used for troubleshooting certificate-related issues? (Choose two.)

   a. Client Certificate Testing

   b. Server Certificate Testing

   c. Server Traversal Test

   d. CRL Management

   e. Certificate-based authentication configuration

   f. Trusted CA certificate

6. Which of the following is a way to view alarms on the Cisco Expressway?

   a. Navigate to **System** > **Alarms**.

   b. Navigate to **Maintenance** > **Diagnostics** > **Alarms**.

   c. Enter the command **show alarms** from the CLI.

   d. Click the red triangle in the top-right corner of the web interface.

Foundation Topics

Troubleshooting Registration Issues

Before we delve into troubleshooting registration issues, we'll first review the registration process on the Cisco Expressway and all the parts that impact registration. Remember there are some tools and settings that affect SIP and H.323 individually, and there are other tools that affect all registrations, regardless what protocol is being used. For example, SIP registration requires at least one domain to be configured in the Expressway, and H.323 uses the

Registration Conflict Policy to prevent duplicate aliases from registering to the same gate-keeper. Domains do not affect H.323 registrations, and Conflict Policy does not affect SIP registrations. In fact, you can have duplicate aliases register using SIP on the Cisco Express-way. Other settings, such as Authentication and Registration Restriction Policy, affect both SIP and H.323 registrations.

To configure authentication on the Expressway, first change the Authentication setting to On. This authentication is performed on a per subzone level by setting the Authentication Mode to Check Credentials for Expressways running version X6.0 or higher. Next, go into the Local Database and create a username and password. Multiple credentials can be created, but SIP and H.323 can use the same credentials as well. Note that both the Username and Password are case sensitive. All letters, numbers, and special characters can be used. The last setting to configure on the Expressway is the NTP setting. Once NTP has been configured, the Expressway sends a client request timestamp to the NTP server and receives a server reception timestamp from the NTP server. This timestamp will be used for each authentication sequence.

Once the Expressway has been configured for authentication, the registering devices can be configured as well. It is necessary to turn on authentication for H.323 but not for SIP. The SIP Digest Authentication Scheme is built into the SIP protocol and therefore does not need to be enabled. With H.323, it is a separate standard altogether and must be enabled to operate. Configure the same username and password that exist in the Local Database of the Expressway, making sure the syntax matches exactly. Finally, do not forget to configure the NTP. Once the NTP settings have been configured the Device will send a client request time-stamp to the NTP Server and receive a server reception timestamp from the NTP server. This timestamp will be used for each authentication sequence.

Once the other registration settings are configured, the endpoint initiates a handshake with the Expressway to establish an MD5 encryption key used to exchange information securely. Then the endpoint sends the username and password to the Expressway for authentication. The Expressway verifies the username and password against the credentials in the Local Database. If the credentials do not match, registration fails. If the credentials do match, then the endpoint can now attempt to register to the Expressway.

To register, the endpoint sends the registration request to the Expressway. The Express-way then checks the Registration Conflict Policy settings for H.323 endpoints, which can be configured as Overwrite or Reject. For SIP endpoints, the Expressway checks to ensure the domain used with the alias attempting to register matches the domain config-ured in the database of the Expressway. Then the Expressway checks the Registration Restriction Policy settings, which can be configured as Allow or Deny. This policy is applied to both SIP and H.323. Finally, the Expressway checks Membership Rules, which determine what subzone a device will register to. As long as everything checks out, the endpoint will then be allowed to register. Figure 12-1 illustrates all the steps required to register to the Cisco Expressway.

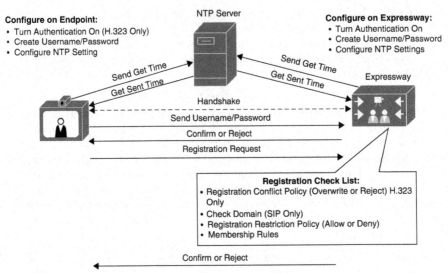

Figure 12-1   *Registration Steps on the Cisco Expressway*

All submenus under the Status menu on the Expressway are logs that can be used to support the video network. The registration logs can be used to verify if endpoints are registered. The registration logs are divided into three categories: By Device, By Alias, and History.

From the web interface of the Cisco Expressway, navigate to **Status > Registration > By Device**. This page lists all the devices that are currently registered to the Expressway. Moving from left to right, the Name column lists the name of the endpoint, if one was assigned. If a name was not assigned, then the alias will be used as the endpoint name. If the device has an E.164 alias, it is listed next in the Number column. Obviously, this column would only be populated for H.323 registered endpoints because SIP does not support E.164 aliases. The next column is Type, which identifies the device that is registering, specifically whether it's an MCU, Gateway, or Endpoint. SIP devices all register as a SIP UA (User Agent). The Protocol column reflects whether the device has registered as a SIP device or H.323 device. If the device has registered as both, two separate registrations are listed for this one endpoint. The next column, Creation Time, provides the time that particular alias for a device was registered to the Expressway. The Address column lists the IP address and the port of the device that is used for the registration. Figure 12-2 illustrates the registration menus and Registration by Device categories.

It is possible that some devices could register to the Expressway with up to three different aliases, as shown in Figure 12-2: E.164, H323ID, and a SIP URI. CE software-based endpoints do not support dual registration between SIP and H.323, but legacy TC software-based endpoints or third-party endpoints support this function. In such an example, the Registration by Device page might not reflect all these aliases. To ensure that all the aliases have registered to the Expressway, navigate to **Status > Registration > By Alias**. This page displays a different line for each of the aliases that are registered to the Expressway. This tool can be useful if you are encountering any alias conflicts for H.323 registrations. Notice in Figure 12-2 that one endpoint with the IP address 192.168.160.101 is registered with three different aliases.

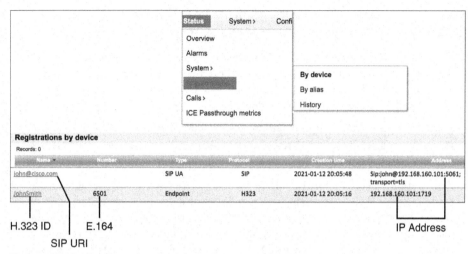

Figure 12-2 *Registration by Device Menu on the Cisco Expressway*

The third menu under **Status > Registration** is History. From this log you can view what devices are no longer registered to the Expressway and the reason they are no longer registered. The information provided under the History menu is very limited: the reason for an endpoint being unregistered is often vague, and there is no information provided for a failed registration. The information provided in this log only pertains to endpoints that were once registered and are no longer registered. If you are trying to troubleshoot why endpoints are not registering to the Cisco Expressway, then the Event Log is the best tool to troubleshoot these registration-related issues.

To access the Event Log, navigate to **Status > Logs > Event Log**. The Event Log provides a lot of useful information pertaining to both registration and calls. Some examples of the type of information the Event Log provides include

- Call disconnected

- Call connected

- Search completed

- Call answer attempted

- Call attempted

- Search attempted

- Call rejected

- Search canceled

There are four error messages that could appear in the Event Log that identify the top reasons endpoint registrations would fail on the Cisco Expressway:

- **Registration Rejected – Unknown Domain:** This error message pertains only to SIP registration attempts. To resolve this issue, check the domain configured on both the endpoint and the Expressway to ensure they match. The issue could be as simple as a fat-fingered character in either of the domains.

- **Registration Rejected – Alias Conflicts with an Existing Registration:** This error message pertains only to H.323 registration attempts. To resolve this issue, check the **Status > Registrations > By Alias** page to find the endpoint with the duplicate alias.

- **Registration Rejected – Not Permitted by Policy:** This error message could pertain to either SIP or H.323 registration attempts. To resolve this issue, check the Allow or Deny list policies on the Expressway to identify why the registration attempt would fail. Be sure to also check how the Registration Configuration is set up. If the policy service is set to Allow List, then any Deny List Rules will not affect registration failures.

- **Registration Rejected – Received from Unauthenticated Source:** This error message could also pertain to either SIP or H.323 registration attempts. To resolve this issue, check the Authentication settings on the Expressway and on the endpoints. Also, check the NTP settings in both locations. NTP is the most common reason authentication fails.

Figure 12-3 illustrates how these four error messages would appear in the Event Log on the Cisco Expressway.

tvcs: Event="Registration Rejected" Reason="Unknown domain"

SIP only. Check the Domain on the endpoint and the Cisco Expressway.

tvcs: Event="Registration Rejected" Reason="Alias conflicts with an existing registration"

H.323 only. Check **Status > Registrations > By Alias** to find the endpoint with the duplicate alias.

tvcs: Event="Registration Rejected" Reason="Not permitted by policy"

Check the Allow/Deny list policies on the Cisco Expressway.

tvcs: Event="Registration Rejected" Reason="Received from unauthenticated source"

Check the Authentication settings and the NTP settings on the Cisco Expressway and on the endpoint(s).

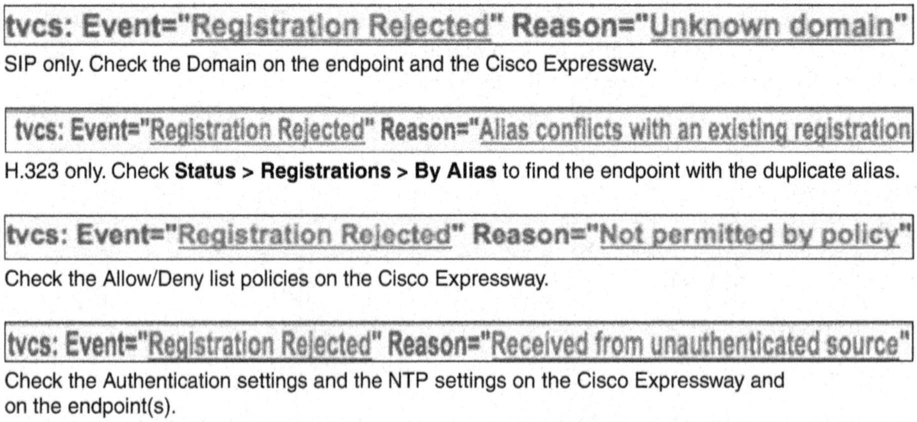

Figure 12-3 *Registration Rejected Messages in the Event Log*

Obviously, other issues could affect registration to the Cisco Expressway other than the four issues identified previously. However, using these four notices in the Event Log to troubleshoot registration issues could help you isolate other problems with registration. If an endpoint were to fail to register to the Expressway and you could not find any of these error messages in the Event Log, that would be a clear indication that the issue lies somewhere else. For example, the issue could be network related. You may try using a ping tool on the endpoint to see if it has network connectivity to the Expressway.

You can change the level of information that can be captured in the Event Log by navigating to **System > Logging**. There are four levels of logging, 1 being the lowest level. If this setting is changed to a higher level, be warned that the information is captured to the local disk space on the Expressway. If that space fills up, then the oldest information will be deleted and cannot be recovered. The information can also be sent to an external syslog server by simply entering the IP address of the syslog server in the space provided. Should a remote syslog server be used, information will be stored both locally on the Expressway and on the remote syslog server. Best practice suggests keeping the log level at the default value of 1, unless this log is being used to troubleshoot issues that require a deeper log trace. Then set the level back to 1 after the issue is resolved. Table 12-2 identifies the information captured at each log level.

Table 12-2   Event Log Levels

Level	Assigned Events
1	High-level events such as registration requests and call attempts. Easily readable. For example: ■ Call attempt/connected/disconnected ■ Registration attempt/accepted/rejected
2	All Level 1 events, plus logs of protocol messages sent and received (SIP, H.323, LDAP, etc.) excluding noisy messages such as H.460.18 keep-alives and H.245 video fast updates
3	All Level 1 and Level 2 events, plus: ■ Protocol keep-alives ■ Call-related SIP signaling messages
4	The most verbose level, with all Level 1, Level 2, and Level 3 events, plus network-level SIP messages

Troubleshooting Calling Issues

The previous section demonstrated how to use the registration process on the Cisco Expressway to identify where potential issues could occur that may prevent endpoints from registering. In like manner, the Call Processing Order on the Expressway can be used to identify where potential issues could occur that may prevent endpoints from calling one another. Therefore, before we delve into troubleshooting calling issues, we'll first review the Call Processing Order used on the Expressway to process all call attempts. (See Chapter 7, "Cisco Expressway Call Processing Order," for complete details.)

First, there are three components of the Call Processing Order that occur pre-search; that is, before the Expressway searches for the destination endpoint. They are as follows:

1. Transforms (pre-search)

2. Call Policy or Admin Policy (pre-search)

3. User Policy or FindMe (pre-search)

Each of these pre-search components has the capability to change a dialed alias from its original form. Each time the alias is changed pre-search, that change is permanent for the duration of the call attempt. Should the Call Policy or User Policy change the alias, then the Call Processing Order must start over with the new alias, beginning with Transforms.

The call will proceed in the Call Processing Order only after all of the pre-search components have been exhausted and the alias is not changed anymore. The Call Policy also has the ability to reject the call.

After the pre-search components have finished their purpose, the next part of the Call Processing Order is used to search for the destination endpoint. There are two different types of searches that can occur during this part of the Call Processing Order:

1. Local Zone Search
2. External Zone Search

Remember from Chapter 6 that the Local Zone is the Cisco Expressway itself. Although the Local Zone is listed first, all zones are searched based on the priority assigned to the Search Rule associated with that zone. Also, Search Rules have the ability to transform the destination alias as well, but that transform will only affect that one search. If a rule is matched but a connection is not established, then the alias returns to its previous form and the Expressway continues searching for another match.

Three types of External zones exist within the Cisco Expressway:

- Neighbor Zones
- Traversal Zones
- DNS/ENUM Zones

Once a match is made, the Expressway executes the fifth component of the Call Processing Order, which is bandwidth management. Bandwidth management can be assigned to subzones and Pipes, and Pipes are applied to Links. These bandwidth restrictions can be controlled on a per-call and total-bandwidth management basis.

Search History is a log that aids in troubleshooting call setup issues. It captures all search events of every call attempt on the Expressway as it utilizes this Call Processing Order, except for bandwidth consumption. This display of the Call Processing Order information for each call pinpoints exactly where the issue occurred in failed call attempts so that engineers can more easily identify the problem area and resolve the issue quickly.

To access the Search History information, navigate to **Status > Search History**. This page displays some basic information to help you assess where problem areas occur. Each call attempt is listed with the following information from left to right:

- **Start time:** The date and time at which the search was initiated.
- **Search type:** The type of message being sent.
- **Source:** The alias of the endpoint that initiated the call.
- **Destination:** The alias that was dialed from the endpoint. This may be different from the alias to which the call was actually placed, as the original alias may have been transformed either locally or before the neighbor was queried.
- **Status:** Indicates whether or not the search was successful.
- **Actions:** Click View to go to the Search Details page, which lists full details of this search.

To limit the list of searches, enter one or more characters in the Filter field and click Filter. Only those searches that contain the filtered information of the characters you entered in any of the displayed fields are shown. Click the View link next to the call attempt you want to review. Figure 12-4 illustrates a Search History log of a call attempt.

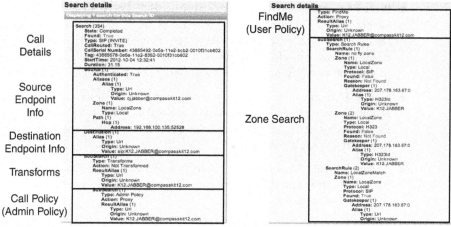

Figure 12-4   *Details Page of the Search History Log*

This is where the Search History log begins to show its greatest value. Notice in Figure 12-4 how the log flows with the Call Processing Order. The Source and Destination aliases are identified first. Then the Expressway performs the pre-search check list:

1. Are there any Transforms?

2. Are there any Call Policies (called admin policies in the Search History tool)?

3. Are there any User Policies (called FindMe in the Search History tool)?

4. Then the Cisco Expressway performs the zone search.

The first zone searched is the Local Zone. In the Figure 12-4 example, the destination alias is matched and connected in the Local Zone, so no other zones are searched. If a connection was not made, then the Search History log would have shown the Expressway continue to search External zones. The only part of the Search History log that is not displayed here is the Bandwidth management search. There are other logs available on the Expressway that cover bandwidth utilization. We will cover those logs soon as well.

First, there is another tool that operates similarly to the Search History tool that needs mentioning. The Locate tool can be used for troubleshooting call connections without actually placing a call. When the tool is used, Search History information is displayed as if a call were placed. This allows administrators to deduce whether a call placed would have connected, how the call would be routed, and, if not possible, what problems would be encountered connecting the call. To access the Locate tool, follow these steps:

Step 1.   Navigate to **Maintenance > Tools > Locate**.

Step 2.   In the Alias field, enter the destination alias of the endpoint to which you need to test a call.

Step 3.   Technically, the Alias field is the only field required to use the Locate tool. However, there are some other fields that you can use to narrow down the search result:

■ **Hop Count:** Enter the maximum number of hops allowed during this search. The default value is **5.**

■ **Protocol:** Used to initiate the search as either H.323 or SIP. The search may be interworked during the search process, but the Expressway always uses the native protocol first to search those target zones and policy services associated with Search Rules at the same priority, before searching those zones again using the alternative protocol. H.323 is the default value.

■ **Source:** Determines where the simulated search will originate. Choose **Default Zone** for an unknown remote system (the default value), choose **Default Subzone** for a locally registered endpoint, or choose any other configured zone or subzone.

■ **Authenticated:** Choose whether the request should be treated as authenticated or not. Search rules can be restricted so that they only apply to authenticated messages.

■ **Source Alias:** Typically, this optional field is only relevant if the routing process uses Call Processing Language (CPL) that has rules dependent on the source alias. (If no value is specified, a default alias of **xcom-locate** is used.)

Step 4.   Click **Locate.**

The status bar will show Searching... followed by Search Completed. The results will display below the Locate section and will look identical to the Search History details page. Figure 12-5 illustrates the menus and search results of the Locate tool.

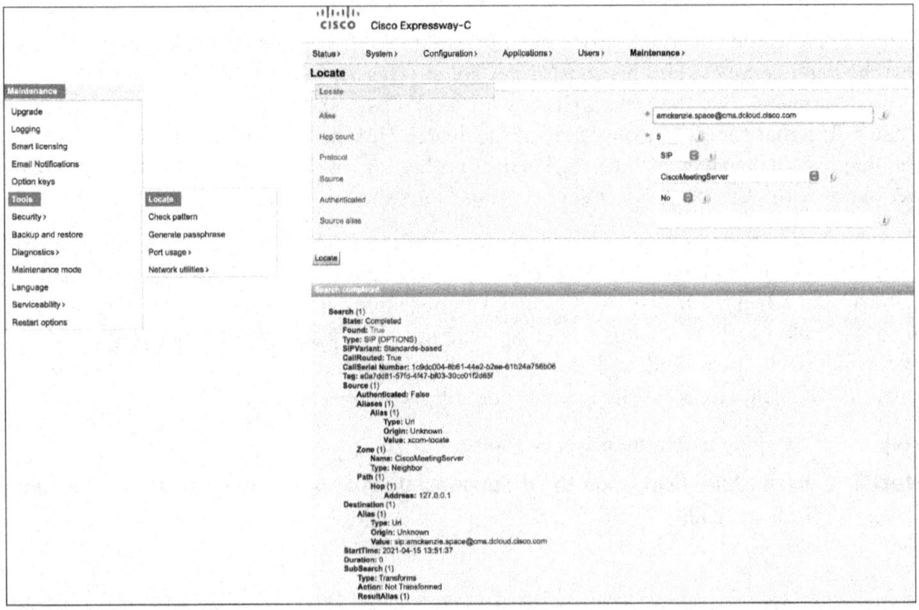

Figure 12-5   *Locate Tool*

The Network Log is similar to the Event Log, in that they both show SIP and H.323 messaging. However, the Network Log also shows the call routing decisions that were made based on the Expressway search rules.

This brings us to the Calls logs. These logs provide useful information when troubleshooting various call setup and call media issues. There are two logs available under the Calls logs: Calls and History. Go to **Status > Calls > Calls** for useful information regarding calls that connected successfully and are currently still connected. Go to **Status > Calls > History** for the same information about calls that have disconnected and call attempts that have failed. To access a Calls log under either of these menus, click the View link located in the right column. A general information screen opens, providing some basic information about the call or call attempt. To access more information concerning this call, click the Local Call Serial Number link.

More extensive call details are listed on the Call Details page. Scroll down to see more information. At the bottom of the Call Details page are several hyperlinks that can take you to other pages full of valuable troubleshooting information, all of which have been previously discussed:

- **View summary of this call:** Takes you to the previous summary details page.

- **View media statistics for this call component:** Takes you to another layer of the Calls log where you can view information about the media flow for the call. For traversal calls where the Expressway transmitted the media, it also lists the individual media channels, such as audio, video, data, etc., that made up the call.

- **View search details for this call component:** Takes you to the Search History record for this particular call.

- **View all events associated with this call:** Takes you to the Events Log page with filters in place to only display the relevant events for this call.

As you can see, the Calls logs are designed to provide administrators a single log location that provides all the tools needed to easily assess issues, with links to all the other relevant logs that could also provide troubleshooting assistance. Figure 12-6 illustrates the various levels of the Calls log.

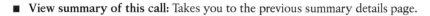

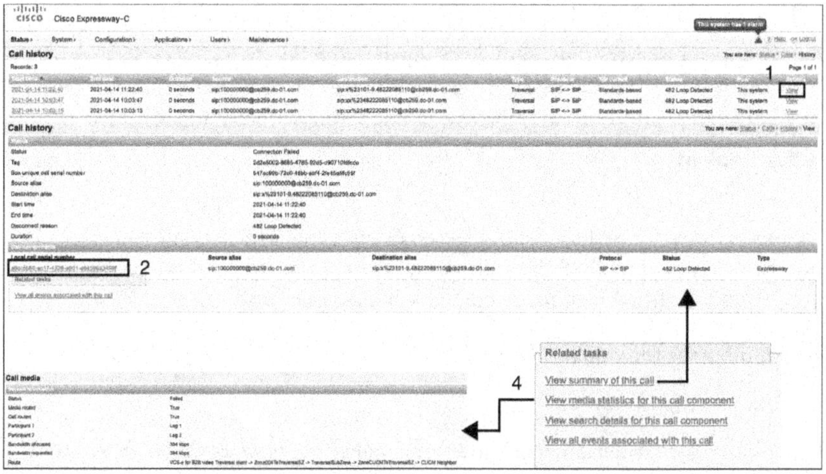

Figure 12-6 *Calls Log Information*

Troubleshooting DNS Issues

When DNS is involved with a video network topology, there are some unique issues that can occur. Cisco provides a tool in the Cisco Expressway to aid administrators in troubleshooting DNS-related issues. You can access the DNS Lookup tool by navigating to **Maintenance > Tools > Network Utilities > DNS Lookup.**

You can use this tool to assist in troubleshooting system issues. It allows you to query DNS for a supplied host name and display the results of the query if the lookup was successful. The following steps explain how to use this tool.

Step 1. In the Host field, enter either:

   ■ The name of the host you want to query

   ■ An IPv4 or IPv6 address if you want to perform a reverse DNS lookup

Step 2. In the Query Type field, select the type of record for which you want to search. For reverse lookups, the Query Type field is ignored and the search automatically looks for PTR records. Table 12-3 identifies the different options that you can select in this field and what each selection will search.

Key Topic

Table 12-3 Query Types on the DNS Lookup Tool

Option	What It Searches For
All	Any type of record
A (IPv4 address)	A record that maps the host name to the host's IPv4 address
AAAA (IPv6 address)	A record that maps the host name to the host's IPv6 address
SRV (services)	SRV records (which include those specific to H.323, SIP, Unified Communications, and TURN services)
NAPTR (Name Authority Pointer)	A record that rewrites a domain name (into a URI or other domain name, for example)

Step 3. By default, the system submits the query to all of the system's default DNS servers, which you can find on the **System > DNS** page on the Expressway. To query specific servers only, set Check Against the Following DNS Servers to **Custom** and then select the DNS servers you want to use. Note that this feature has been removed from the Expressway beginning with version X12.0.

Step 4. Click **Lookup.**

A separate DNS query is performed for each selected query type. The domain that is included within the query sent to DNS depends upon whether the supplied host is fully qualified or not. A fully qualified host name contains at least one "dot."

   ■ If the supplied host is fully qualified:

      ■ DNS is queried first for *host*.

      ■ If the lookup for *host* fails, then an additional query for *host.<system_domain>* is performed, where *<system_domain>* is the domain name as configured on the DNS page of the Expressway.

- If the supplied host is not fully qualified:

    - DNS is queried first for *host.<system_domain>*.

    - If the lookup for *host.<system_domain>* fails, then an additional query for *host* is performed.

For SRV record type lookups, multiple DNS queries are performed. An SRV query is made for each of the following *_service._protocol* combinations:

- _h323ls._udp.*<domain>*

- _h323rs._udp.*<domain>*

- _h323cs._tcp.*<domain>*

- _sips._tcp.*<domain>*

- _sip._tcp.*<domain>*

- _sip._udp.*<domain>*

- _collab-edge._tls

- _cisco-uds._tcp

- _turn._udp.*<domain>*

- _turn._tcp.*<domain>*

In each case, as for all other query types, either one or two queries may be performed for a *<domain>* of either *host* or *host.<system_domain>*. A new section will appear showing the results of all of the queries. Table 12-4 identifies the various fields of information that are displayed if the query is successful.

Table 12-4   Successful Returned Data from DNS Lookup

Query Type	Type of Query Sent by the Expressway
Name	The host name contained in the response to the query.
TTL	The length of time (in seconds) that the results of this query will be cached by the Expressway.
Class	IN (Internet) indicates that the response was a DNS record involving an Internet host name, server, or IP address.
Type	The record type contained in the response to the query.
Response	The content of the record received in response to the query for this name and type.

The Expressway uses UDP and TCP to do DNS resolution, and DNS servers usually send both UDP and TCP responses. If the UDP response exceeds the UDP message size limit of 512 bytes, then the Expressway cannot process the UDP response. This is not usually a problem, because the Expressway can process the TCP response instead. However, if you block TCP inbound on port 53, and if the UDP response is greater than 512 bytes, then the Expressway cannot process the response from the DNS server. In this case you won't see the results using the DNS Lookup tool, and any operations that need the requested addresses will fail. Figure 12-7 illustrates the DNS Lookup tool on the Cisco Expressway.

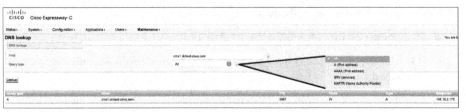

Figure 12-7   *DNS Lookup Tool on the Cisco Expressway*

Troubleshooting Certificate Issues

Certificate-related issues can be very complex. Certificates can fulfill many different purposes in a Cisco Expressway deployment, and several different types of certificates can be used. Entire volumes have been dedicated to creating, supporting, and troubleshooting certificates and security. However, Cisco provides two troubleshooting tools on the Cisco Expressway that can aid administrators in troubleshooting certificate issues: the Client Certificate Testing page and the Server Traversal Test page.

Client Certificate Testing Tool

To access the Client Certificate Testing page, navigate to **Maintenance > Security > Client Certificate Testing.** You can use this tool to check client certificates before enabling client certificate validation. The client certificate validation service is part of the Web Server Configuration under the **System > Administration** menu. The Client Certificate Testing tool enables you to test whether a client certificate is valid when checked against the Expressway's current trusted CA list and, if loaded, the certificate revocation list. The tool also allows you to test the outcome of applying the regex and template patterns that retrieve a certificate's authorization credentials.

You can test against a certificate on your local file system or the browser's currently loaded certificate. Use the following steps on the Client Certificate Testing page (see Figure 12-8) to test if a certificate is valid:

Step 1.   Click the **Certificate Source** list box and choose one of the following options:

■ Uploaded Test File (PEM Format)

■ Uploaded Test File (Plain Text)

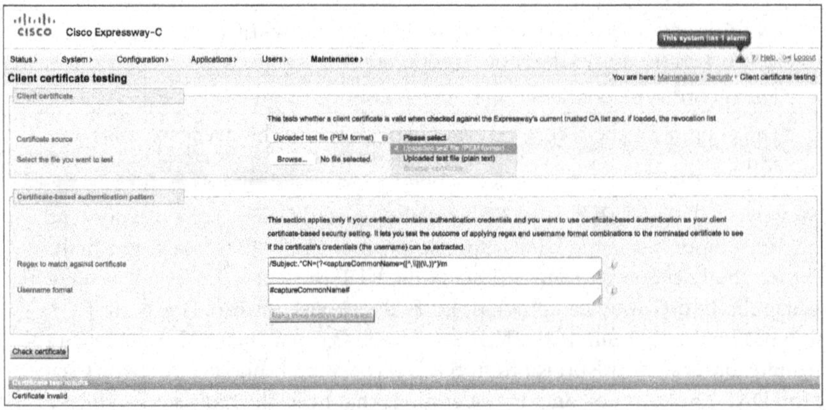

Figure 12-8   *Client Certificate Testing Tool*

Step 2.   Click **Browse** to select the certificate file you want to test. You can test against the certificate currently loaded into your browser. This option is only available if the system is already configured to use certificate validation and a certificate is currently loaded.

Step 3.   Ignore the Certificate-based Authentication Pattern section, which is relevant only if you are extracting authorization credentials from the certificate.

Step 4.   Click **Check Certificate**.

The results of the test are shown in the Certificate Test Results section.

There is a way to retrieve authorization credentials from the certificate using this Client Certificate Testing tool. Select the certificate source as previously described and then configure the Regex to Match Against Certificate field and Username Format field as required. Their purpose is to extract a username from the nominated certificate by supplying a regular expression that will look for an appropriate string pattern within the certificate itself. These fields default to the currently configured settings on the Certificate-based Authentication Configuration page, but you can change them as required.

In the Regex field, use the *(?<name>regex)* syntax to supply names for capture groups so that matching sub-patterns can be substituted in the associated Username Format field, such as /(Subject:.*, CN=(?<Group1>.*))/m. The regex defined here must conform to PHP regex guidelines, which you can review at the following link: https://www.php.net/manual/en/book.pcre.php.

The Username Format field can contain a mixture of fixed text and the capture group names used in the Regex field. Delimit each capture group name with #; for example, *prefix#Group1#suffix*. Each capture group name will be replaced with the text obtained from the regular expression processing. The results of the test are shown in the Certificate Test Results section. The resulting string item is the username credential that would be checked against the relevant authorization mechanism to determine that user's authorization account access level.

If necessary, you can modify the Regex to Match Against Certificate and Username Format fields and repeat the test until the correct results are produced. Note that if the certificate source is an uploaded PEM or plain text file, the selected file is temporarily uploaded to the Expressway when the test is first performed. If you want to keep testing different regex and username format combinations against the same file, you do not have to reselect the file for every test. If you change the contents of your test file on your file system, or you want to choose a different file, you must click the Browse button again and select the new or modified file to upload. If you have changed the Regex to Match Against Certificate and Username Format fields from their default values and want to use these values in the Expressway's actual configuration as specified on the Certificate-based Authentication Configuration page, then click the Make These Settings Permanent button.

Server Traversal Test Tool

Another tool that you can use to troubleshoot certificate-related issues on the Cisco Expressway is the Secure Traversal Test tool. This utility tests whether a secure connection can be made from the Expressway-C to the Expressway-E. A secure connection is required for a Unified Communications Traversal Zone and is optional for a normal traversal zone.

If the secure traversal test fails, the utility raises a warning with appropriate resolution where possible.

To use the Secure Traversal Test tool on the Expressway (shown in Figure 12-9):

Step 1.   On the Expressway-C, navigate to **Maintenance > Security > Secure Traversal Test.**

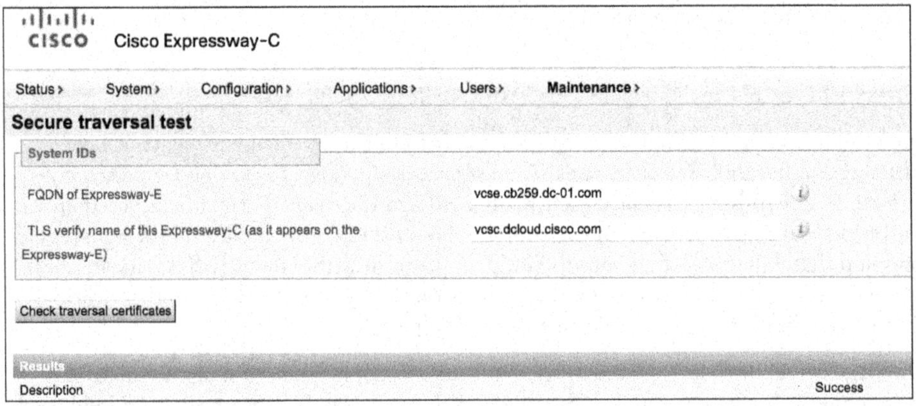

---

cisco   Cisco Expressway-C

| Status › | System › | Configuration › | Applications › | Users › | **Maintenance ›** |

Secure traversal test

System IDs

FQDN of Expressway-E   vcse.cb259.dc-01.com   *i*

TLS verify name of this Expressway-C (as it appears on the   vcsc.dcloud.cisco.com   *i*
Expressway-E)

Check traversal certificates

Results
Description   Success

Figure 12-9   *Secure Traversal Test Tool*

Step 2.   In the FQDN of Expressway-E field, enter the FQDN that is paired with this Expressway-C.

Step 3.   In the TLS Verify Name of This Expressway-C field, enter the name as it appears on the paired Expressway-E. This setting is in the SIP section of the Expressway-E's Traversal Zone Configuration page.

Step 4.   Click **Test Connection.**

The Secure Traversal Test utility checks whether the hosts on either side of the traversal zone recognize each other and trust each other's certificate chains.

Other Troubleshooting Tools

There are many other tools and logs available on the Cisco Expressway that can be used for various troubleshooting tasks. These tools may not be used as frequently as the previously mentioned tools, but that does not diminish the function these tools serve.

A log mentioned while discussing the Search History log pertains to bandwidth utilization. If you navigate to **Status > Local Zone,** you can monitor the number of concurrent calls and all bandwidth utilization across any subzone within the Expressway. In like manner, if you navigate to **Status > Bandwidth > Links,** or **Status > Bandwidth > Pipes,** you can monitor the number of concurrent calls and bandwidth utilization across all Links and Pipes. Figure 12-10 illustrates the bandwidth monitoring logs on the Cisco Expressway.

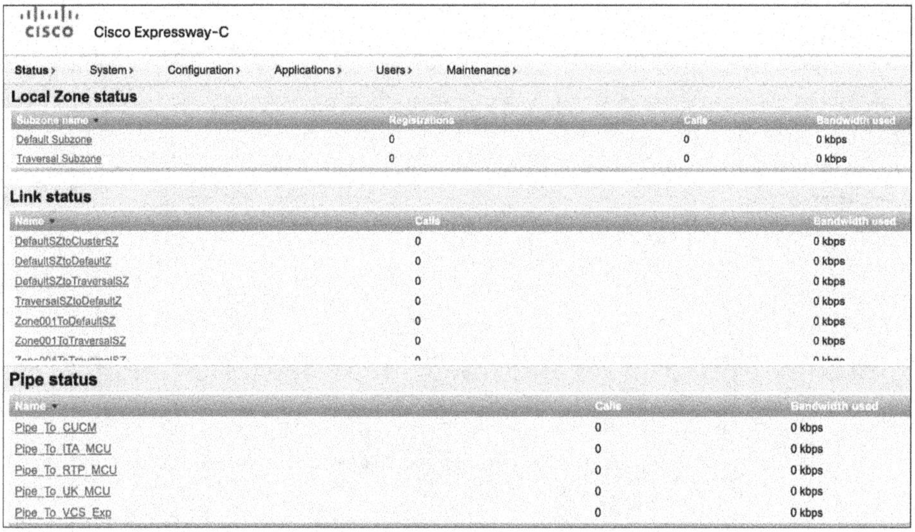

Figure 12-10 *Bandwidth Monitoring Logs on Cisco Expressway*

The Configuration Log provides a list of changes that are made to the Expressway configuration by the system administrator through the web interface or CLI. It also shows from which IP address and user the changes were made. This log is useful when reviewing a system that has started to behave unexpectedly. Any changes that are made to the system can be reviewed to see if they may have had an impact on the state of the system. For this reason, Cisco recommends that you create a unique administrator account for each individual who is to be granted access to the Cisco Expressway. In this manner, each user's activity can be monitored with accountability.

There are three ways to view alarms on the Expressway, as shown in Figure 12-11:

- A red triangle appears at the top right corner when there is an alarm, with a banner identifying how many alarms exist on the system. Clicking the triangle takes you to the Alarms page. If there are no alarms, or the alarms have been dismissed, then the triangle no longer appears.

- Navigate to **Status > Alarms**, which takes you to the same menu.

- Log in using SSH through IP or a serial connection. After successfully logging in, all open alarms are listed in text at the top of the console window. You can also use the CLI to display alarms by typing xStatus Alarm.

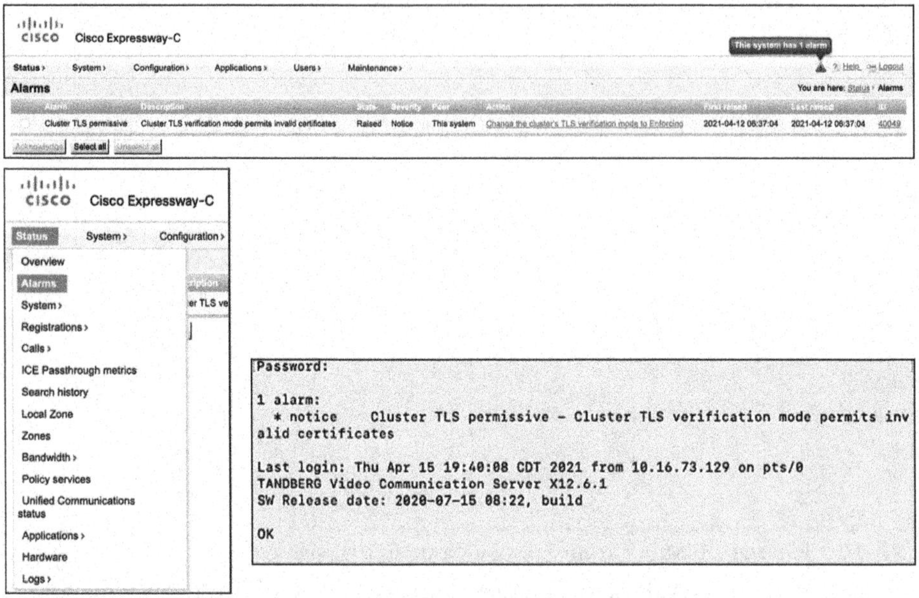

Figure 12-11 *Viewing Alarms on the Cisco Expressway*

Two levels of alarms exist on the Cisco Expressway. First there are warnings. These alarms are not critical to the day-to-day operation of the Expressway. There is even a way to acknowledge an alarm without resolving the issue. Using the Acknowledge option keeps the alarm in the Alarms page, but the alerts to the alarm go away. In other words, the red triangle in the top right corner will no longer alert you to this alarm. The second type of alarm is an Error. These alarms are critical to the day-to-day operation of the Expressway and should be resolved immediately. The good news is that the Alarms page will provide an explanation of the issue and will either provide a link to where you need to go to resolve the issue or provide instructions on how to resolve the problem.

In most scenarios, the logs and tools described in this chapter up to this point are all you will need to troubleshoot and resolve all your collaboration issues on the Cisco Expressway. However, on rare occasions an engineer will need to take a deeper look into what might be causing an issue. Therefore, Cisco provides the Diagnostic Logging tool, which is capable of creating a deep-level log trace of all communication to and from the Expressway. You can generate a diagnostic log of system activity over a period of time and download it to send to your Cisco customer support representative. You can also obtain and download a tcpdump while logging is in progress. To access the Diagnostic Logging tool, navigate to **Maintenance > Diagnostics > Diagnostic logging**. This log supports three different log levels:

- Setting Network Log Level to Debug is equivalent to the legacy Expressway **netlog 2** logging from the console. It provides protocol-level logs for analyzing call signaling flows.

- Setting both Network Log Level and Interworking Log Level to Debug is equivalent to the legacy Expressway IWF tracing. These logs provide protocol-level logs for analyzing call signaling flows, together with additional information about decisions the Expressway makes when interworking calls between SIP and H.323, including codec conversion.

■ Setting B2BUA Log Level to Debug enables protocol logging for the B2BUA. This log level may be used on its own, or together with the Network Log Level and/or Interworking Log Level fields.

Exam Preparation Tasks

As mentioned in the section "How to Use This Book" in the Introduction, you have a couple of choices for exam preparation: the exercises here, Chapter 22, "Final Preparation," and the exam simulation questions in the Pearson Test Prep practice test software.

Review All Key Topics

Review the most important topics in this chapter, noted with the Key Topics icon in the outer margin of the page. Table 12-5 lists a reference of these key topics and the page numbers on which each is found.

Key Topic

Table 12-5   Key Topics for Chapter 12

Key Topic Element	Description	Page Number
List	Four main issues related to registration	224
Table 12-2	Event Log Levels	225
List	Locate tool menu options	227
List	Calls log hyperlinks to other logs	229
Table 12-3	Query Types on the DNS Lookup Tool	230
List	_service._protocol SRV queries made through Expressway	231
Table 12-4	Successful Returned Data from DNS Lookup	231
Steps	Steps to using the Secure Traversal Test	234

Complete Tables and Lists from Memory

Print a copy of Appendix C, "Memory Tables" (found on the companion website), or at least the section for this chapter, and complete the tables and lists from memory. Appendix D, "Memory Tables Answer Key," also on the companion website, includes completed tables and lists to check your work.

Define Key Terms

Define the following key term from this chapter and check your answer in the glossary:

Name Authority Pointer (NAPTR)

Q&A

The answers to these questions appear in Appendix A. For more practice with exam format questions, use the Pearson Test Prep practice test software.

1. List the four main issues that could prevent endpoints from registering to the Cisco Expressway.

2. List the ten different SRV queries made in the _service._protocol combinations.

CHAPTER 13

Introduction to Mobile and Remote Access (MRA)

This chapter covers the following topics:

Purpose of MRA: Introduces the MRA solution and the purpose behind why Cisco developed this solution.

Components of MRA: Identifies the six main components that make up the MRA solution, and the purpose each of these components serves.

Considerations for MRA Deployment: Explains the different considerations that should be deliberated upon prior to deploying this solution.

Virtual private networks have a long-time tradition of connecting remote locations with an enterprise network. However, VPNs are very complex and require a lot of resources to operate. Additionally, the modern workplace is not always located in an office environment. Companies are now encouraging their employees to work from home, which complicates how these employees communicate with each other and the outside world. Cisco's out-of-the-box thinking has brought about a solution to many of the problems created by the modern workplace mindset. The Mobile and Remote Access (MRA) solution is a unique deployment that incorporates many facets of the more traditional traversal solution discussed in Chapter 10, "Multisite and Business-to-Business (B2B) Collaboration Solutions." Communication devices can operate from any network at any location without the use of VPNs. Employees can leverage these communication devices from a home office without the need to set up and store another router in their home. Additionally, all the features and capabilities that employees would have from a communications device located in an office are still at their disposal from their remote location using the MRA solution.

This chapter does not cover any of the objectives from the Implementing Cisco Collaboration Cloud and Edge Solutions (CLCEI) exam 300-820. It only serves to establish the foundation for Chapters 14 and 15.

"Do I Know This Already?" Quiz

The "Do I Know This Already?" quiz enables you to assess whether you should read this entire chapter thoroughly or jump to the "Exam Preparation Tasks" section. If you are in doubt about your answers to these questions or your own assessment of your knowledge of the topics, read the entire chapter. Table 13-1 lists the major headings in this chapter and their corresponding "Do I Know This Already?" quiz questions. You can find the answers in Appendix A, "Answers to the 'Do I Know This Already?' Quizzes and Review Questions."

Table 13-1 "Do I Know This Already?" Section-to-Question Mapping

Foundation Topics Section	Questions
Purpose of MRA	1
Components of MRA	2–3
Considerations for MRA Deployment	4–5

CAUTION The goal of self-assessment is to gauge your mastery of the topics in this chapter. If you do not know the answer to a question or are only partially sure of the answer, you should mark that question as wrong for purposes of the self-assessment. Giving yourself credit for an answer you correctly guess skews your self-assessment results and might provide you with a false sense of security.

1. Which of the following statements best describes the MRA solution?

   a. MRA is a call control solution designed to replace the Cisco Unified CM.

   b. MRA is a firewall traversal solution that allows the Cisco Unified CM to call outside the network.

   c. MRA is a VPN solution that allows endpoints outside the network to register to the Cisco Unified CM.

   d. MRA is a VPN-less solution that allows endpoints outside the network to register to the Cisco Unified CM.

2. Which of the following statements is true regarding MRA?

   a. MRA only supports SIP.

   b. MRA only supports H.323.

   c. MRA supports either SIP or H.323.

   d. MRA is not based on any communications protocol.

3. Which of the following certificate requirements must be established when configuring MRA?

   a. MTLS must be established between the Cisco Unified CM and Expressway Core, as well as between the Expressway Core and the Expressway Edge.

   b. MTLS is not required between the Cisco Unified CM and the Expressway Core, but it is required between the Expressway Core and the Expressway Edge.

   c. MTLS must be established between the Cisco Unified CM and the Expressway Core, but it is not required between the Expressway Core and the Expressway Edge.

   d. MTLS is recommended but not required between the Cisco Unified CM and the Expressway Core, nor is it required between the Expressway Core and the Expressway Edge. Standard TLS can be used instead.

4. Which outbound port must be open on the internal firewall to allow XMPP traffic between the Expressway-C and the Expressway-E?

   a. TCP 7001

   b. TCP 7400

   c. UDP 7001

   d. UDP 7400

5. Which of the following settings is required on the Cisco Unified CM in every MRA deployment?

   a. Cisco AXL Web Service running on the publisher node

   b. MRA Access Policy enabled for Jabber users

   c. OAuth Refresh Logins

   d. Denial of Service Thresholds

Foundation Topics

Purpose of MRA

No matter what line of business is being evaluated, extending to branch offices is a fundamental approach to reaching a wider market. Cisco's next-gen routers offer incredible routing capabilities across network borders. However, these complicated network deployments can falter, leaving communication gaps at critical times. Additionally, not all companies use a modern IP solution for communications. Yet companies that have moved to an IP-based communications solution still need to be able to communicate with businesses and consumers who have not yet made this move. The Cisco Edge products allow communications to be unified and uninterrupted regardless of location or disruption.

In today's ever-changing workplace, businesses are no longer tied to the four walls of the office space. Employees are now allowed and encouraged to work from home, which reduces company overhead expenses and increases employee productivity. However, with these changes to the corporate environment, there are many challenges to overcome as well. One such challenge pertains to how employees communicate with one another from many different remote locations. Cisco has designed a solution to this communications dilemma called **Mobile and Remote Access (MRA).** This distinctive platform allows employees to leverage the same great Cisco collaboration solution from anywhere in the world without a VPN while maintaining the same level of security that employees experience within the corporate network. MRA is a core part of the Cisco Collaboration Edge architecture. MRA allows endpoints, such as Cisco Jabber, UC phones, and CE software-based Telepresence endpoints, to securely utilize registration, call control, provisioning, messaging, and presence services that are provided by Cisco Unified Communications Manager when the endpoints are not within the enterprise network. Cisco Expressway Series components are used to provide secure access and firewall traversal to the endpoints that register with the Cisco Unified CM. The Cisco Expressway Series product portfolio is an evolved solution that originated in the Tandberg **Video Communications Server (VCS)** products.

Cisco first launched the Expressway Series in version X8.1. The Cisco Expressway solution was originally designed to offer a low-cost solution for existing Cisco Unified CM customers, providing them with a traversal solution without the need to buy expensive servers and licenses. Because these servers could be virtualized, customers who were already running the Unified CM could install the Expressway Series for free, gaining the ability to do secure firewall traversal for IP communications. The X8.1 version of the Expressway could not support registrations directly, but MRA allowed for endpoints outside the firewall to register to an internal Unified CM from anywhere outside the corporate network through a proxied registration rather than through a VPN. This limits the need for small and medium-sized businesses to install complex VPN routers and improves the media flow of calls between internal endpoints and external endpoints. In August 2016, Cisco released version X8.9, which allows for registrations directly to the Expressway Core and Edge servers. At the writing of this book, the current version of the Expressway is 14.0.

Key Topic

Components of MRA

Although the MRA solution operates in a similar fashion to a standard firewall traversal solution for B2B communications, there are some significant differences between them. First, MRA is only supported for SIP; there is no H.323 support in the MRA solution. Second, certificates are required for MRA between the Expressway Core and Edge servers; there is no way to build the Traversal Zones with a basic TLS or TCP SIP connection. TLS Verify is required for MRA. Third, some specific settings must be configured to enable MRA on the Expressway servers. Fourth, the zones created between the Cisco Expressway Core and Cisco Expressway Edge servers are not the same Traversal Client Zone and Traversal Server Zone used in a standard firewall traversal solution. Finally, the DNS SRV records that need to be created are different from what are required for a traditional firewall traversal solution.

MRA consists of six main components. One of the components is a set of DNS records. Internal and external DNS records are essential to enable endpoints to detect whether they should register directly with Cisco Unified CM or proxy registration through the MRA deployment.

Certificates are another component of MRA. This solution provides secure communication over Transport Layer Security (TLS). Mutual TLS (MTLS) authentication, or TLS Verify, is required between the Expressway Core and Edge servers. Trust between TLS entities is established based on certificates. Implementing the necessary certificates for a **public key infrastructure (PKI)** is an important part of Cisco Collaboration MRA implementation.

Another component is Firewall Traversal Services. MRA supports internal firewalls between the Expressway Core and the Expressway Edge, and an external firewall between the Expressway Edge and the Internet. The firewall traversal capabilities of MRA use the same Assent traversal protocol of standard firewall traversal, but traversal chaining is not supported with MRA. There is a specific type of Traversal Zone that must be created in association with MRA, called Unified Communications Traversal.

There are other settings that must be configured to initiate MRA on the Expressways. These Unified Communications configuration settings are an essential component to MRA. Enabling these services will open additional configuration fields, such as Domain settings. These services will also create necessary Neighbor Zones and Search Rules to the Unified CM for MRA functionality and allow communication to be established between the Unified CM and the Expressway Core. If the customer plans to use IM and presence services through the Jabber client, or any voice messaging services from endpoints through MRA, the Expressway will use these settings to establish communication with the IM and Presence server or Unity Connection server, as well as the CUCM.

The fifth component in an MRA solution is reverse HTTPS proxy. To support secure data services, such as visual voicemail, contact photo retrieval, Cisco Jabber custom tabs, and so on, a reverse HTTPS proxy runs on the Cisco Expressway Edge server. If these services are not needed in an enterprise deployment of MRA, this component does not need to be set up.

The final component that needs to be mentioned regarding the MRA solution is the SIP Trunk Security Profile on the Unified CM that will be used in connection with the Expressway Core. Mutual TLS (MTLS) is not required between these two servers. However, if MTLS is used, then a trust needs to be established between the Unified CM and Expressway Core certificates, and the subject alternative names (SANs) in the Expressway Core certificate need to be included in the SIP Trunk Security Profile. Once these components are set up, the MRA deployment can support two main features:

■ **Off-premises access:** MRA offers a consistent experience to clients, such as Cisco Jabber; UC phones; and Cisco DX, MX, SX, and Webex series endpoints, regardless of whether they are in the internal network or on an external network.

■ **Business-to-business communications:** MRA offers secure communications to other businesses.

Considerations for MRA Deployment

Before you begin setting up the MRA solution, there are some requirements and prerequisites you will want to examine first. Refer to the *Mobile Remote Access Through Cisco Expressway Deployment Guide* for the version of Expressway you are running for a more accurate and detailed list of these prerequisites and requirements. For MRA port information, consult the *Cisco Expressway IP Port Usage Configuration Guide*, which describes the ports that you can use between the Expressway-C in the internal network, the Expressway-E in the DMZ, and the public Internet. Also, assign separate IP addresses to the Expressway-C and the Expressway-E. Do not use a shared address for both elements, as the firewall cannot distinguish between them.

Ensure that the relevant ports are configured on your firewalls between your internal network where the Expressway-C is located, and the DMZ where the Expressway-E is located, and between the DMZ and the public Internet. No inbound ports are required to be opened on the internal firewall. The internal firewall must allow the following outbound connections from the Expressway-C to the Expressway-E:

Key Topic

■ **SIP:** TCP 7001

■ **Traversal media:** UDP 2776 to 2777 (or 36000 to 36011 for large VM/appliance)

■ **XMPP:** TCP 7400

■ **HTTPS (tunneled over SSH between C and E):** TCP 2222

The external firewall must allow the following inbound connections to the Expressway-E:

■ **SIP:** TCP 5061

■ **HTTPS:** TCP 8443

13

- **XMPP:** TCP 5222

- **Media:** UDP 36002 to 59999

The ideal scenario for MRA is to have a single domain with a split DNS configuration, and this is the recommended approach. This is not always possible, so the following list also provides some other approaches to deal with various alternative scenarios. The domain to which the calls are routed must match with the MRA domain to which the endpoints were registered. For example, if endpoints are registered with the domain exp.example.com, the calls must be routed to this domain, and it must not be routed to the subdomain cluster1.exp.example.com.

Key Topic

- **Single domain with split DNS (recommended):** A single domain means that you have a common domain (*example.com*) with separate internal and external DNS servers. This allows DNS names to be resolved differently by clients on different networks depending on the DNS configuration, and aligns with basic Jabber service discovery requirements.

- **Dual domain without split DNS:** Starting with X12.5, the Cisco Expressway Series supports the case where MRA clients use an external domain to look up the _collab-edge SRV record, and the _cisco-uds SRV record. That same external domain cannot be resolved by the Expressway-C. This is typically the case when split DNS is not available for the external domain. Prior to X12.5 this required a pinpoint subdomain or some other DNS workaround on the Expressway-C, to satisfy the client requirements for resolving the _cisco-uds record.

  Limitation: This case is not supported for Unified CM nodes identified by IP addresses, only for FQDNs.

  This feature also supports a secondary case, for MRA deployments that only allow Jabber access over MRA even if users are working on premises. In this case, only one domain is required and typically the DNS records are publicly resolvable (although this is not required if MRA access is disallowed for users when off premises). The change in X12.5 means that there is no need to have a _cisco-uds._tcp.<*external-domain*> DNS SRV record available to the Expressway-C or to the Jabber clients.

- **Single domain without split DNS:** Deployments that require Jabber clients to always connect over MRA also benefit from the X12.5 update that no longer requires the Expressway-C to resolve the _cisco-uds DNS SRV record. So, administrators only need to configure the _collab-edge DNS SRV record, and Jabber clients using service discovery will only have the option of connecting over MRA.

- **URL for Cisco Meeting Server Web Proxy and MRA domain cannot be the same:** If you use both the CMS Web Proxy service and MRA on the same Expressway, the following configuration items must be assigned different values per service. If you try to use the same value, the service that was configured first will work, but the other one will fail:

  - **MRA domain(s):** The domain(s) configured on the Expressway and enabled for Unified CM registration

- **CMS Web Proxy URL link:** Defined in the Expressway Guest Account Client URI setting on the **Expressway > Configuration > Unified Communications > Cisco Meeting Server** page

- **Multiple external domains for MRA:** Cisco Expressway supports MRA with multiple external domains. With this deployment, you have more than one external domain where your MRA clients may reside. The Expressway-E must be able to connect to all of them. To configure this deployment, do the following:

  - For the Expressway-E:

    - On the Expressway-E, configure _collab-edge._tls.<*domain*> and _sips_tcp.<*domain*> DNS SRV records for each Edge domain.

    - Configure A records that point the Expressway-E host name to the public IP address of the Expressway-E.

  - For the Expressway-C:

    - For internal DNS, add A and PTR records that point to the Expressway-E FQDN. Add these records to all Expressway-C nodes.

    - Configure the _cisco_uds SRV record for every domain to point to your Unified CM clusters.

    - On the Domains page of the Expressway-C, add each of the internal domains that point to the Unified CM cluster.

The Maximum Session Bit Rate for Video Calls setting on Unified CM for the default region is 384 kbps by default. The Default Call Bandwidth setting on the Expressway-C is also 384 kbps by default. These settings may be too low to deliver the expected video quality for MRA-connected devices.

The following Cisco Unified Communications Manager configuration requirements exist for deploying Mobile and Remote Access:

Key Topic

- **IP addressing:** Unified CM must be using IPv4 addressing.

- **Cisco AXL Web Service:** This service must be running on the publisher node.

- **Multiple CUCM clusters:** If you have multiple Unified CM clusters, configure Home Cluster Discovery. End users must have the Home Cluster field assigned in End User Configuration so that the Expressway-C can direct MRA users to the correct Unified CM cluster. Use either of the following configuration methods:

  - **Option 1: ILS network:** Configure an Intercluster Lookup Service (ILS) network between your remote Unified CM clusters. ILS completes cluster discovery automatically, populating the Cluster View for each cluster, connecting your clusters into an intercluster network. ILS can also replicate your enterprise dial plan across all Unified CM clusters, although this functionality is not required by MRA. ILS is the recommended approach, particularly for large intercluster networks.

■ **Option 2: manual connections:** Configure each Unified CM cluster manually with connections to the other remote clusters. From Cisco Unified CM Administration, navigate to **Advanced Features > Cluster View** and add the remote clusters. Note that this option does not allow for dial plan replication.

■ **MRA Access Policy:** If you have Cisco Jabber clients using OAuth authentication over MRA, make sure that your Jabber users' User Profiles allow MRA. Check that the following settings exist within the User Profile Configuration of the Unified CM:

■ The Enable Mobile and Remote Access check box must be checked (the default setting is checked).

■ The Jabber Desktop Client Policy and Jabber Mobile Client Policy fields must be set to allow the appropriate Jabber services for your deployment (the default setting is IM & Presence, Voice and Video Calls).

■ **Push notifications:** If you are deploying Cisco Jabber or Webex on iOS or Android clients over MRA, you must configure Push Notifications and Cisco Cloud Onboarding in Unified CM. For configuration details, see the *Push Notifications Deployment Guide.*

■ **OAuth:** If you are using OAuth on the Expressway, you must also enable OAuth Refresh Logins on Unified CM as well. This can be turned on in Cisco Unified CM Administration by setting the OAuth with Refresh Login Flow enterprise parameter to Enabled.

If you want to deploy SAML single sign-on (SSO) for MRA users and clients, you must configure it on Unified CM before you configure it on the Expressway.

■ For video calling over MRA, it's recommended that you reconfigure the Maximum Session Bit Rate for Video Calls setting within the Region Configuration, as the default value of 384 kbps is not enough for video.

If Unified CM and the Expressway are in different domains, you must use either IP addresses or FQDNs for the Unified CM server address.

■ **Denial of service thresholds:** High volumes of MRA calls may trigger denial of service thresholds on Unified CM when all calls arrive at the Unified CM from the same Expressway-C (cluster). If necessary, Cisco recommends that you increase the level of the SIP Station TCP Port Throttle Threshold service parameter to 750 KB/second. You can access the parameter from the **System > Service Parameters** menu by selecting the Cisco CallManager service.

In addition to everything covered in this section, you may also want to check the IM and Presence service requirements and the Cisco Unity Connection service requirements if you plan to use these services. There are also certificate requirements specific to the MRA solution, including certificate signing request (CSR) requirements for Expressway servers. Finally, you may also want to check any endpoint requirements, including validating all compatible endpoints and soft clients that can be used with the MRA solution.

Exam Preparation Tasks

As mentioned in the section "How to Use This Book" in the Introduction, you have a couple of choices for exam preparation: the exercises here, Chapter 22, "Final Preparation," and the exam simulation questions in the Pearson Test Prep practice test software.

Review All Key Topics

Review the most important topics in this chapter, noted with the Key Topics icon in the outer margin of the page. Table 13-2 lists a reference of these key topics and the page numbers on which each is found.

Table 13-2   Key Topics for Chapter 13

Key Topic Element	Description	Page Number
Section	Components of MRA	241
Lists	Inbound and outbound ports for MRA	242
List	Domain configuration list	243
List	Cisco Unified CM prerequisites for MRA	244

Complete Tables and Lists from Memory

There are no memory tables or lists in this chapter.

Define Key Terms

Define the following key terms from this chapter and check your answers in the glossary:

Mobile and Remote Access (MRA), public key infrastructure (PKI), Video Communications Server (VCS)

Q&A

The answers to these questions appear in Appendix A. For more practice with exam format questions, use the Pearson Test Prep practice test software.

1. List the six main components required to deploy the MRA solution.

2. List the five different approaches to domain configuration with MRA.

CHAPTER 14

Configure an MRA Solution

This chapter covers the following topics:

DNS Records: Introduces the different DNS records required for MRA, and how to configure these records.

Certificates: Identifies the certificates allowed on a Cisco Expressway, what certificates are needed to deploy MRA, and what steps to follow when creating these certificates.

Cisco Unified CM Settings for MRA: Explains all the different components required on the Unified CM to support MRA, and how to configure these settings.

Unified Communications Configuration on Expressways: Explains how to configure the Unified Communications settings on the Expressway Core and Edge servers.

HTTP Allow List: Describes what the HTTP allow list is on the Cisco Expressway, why it may need to be updated, and how it can be accessed and modified.

Unified Communications Traversal Zones: Describes how to configure the Unified Communications Traversal Zones on the Cisco Expressway Core and Edge servers.

Cisco Collaboration Mobile and Remote Access (MRA) is a core part of the Cisco Collaboration Edge architecture. MRA allows endpoints, such as Cisco Jabber, UC phones, and CE software-based Telepresence endpoints, to securely utilize registration, call control, provisioning, messaging, and presence services that are provided by Cisco Unified CM when the endpoint is not within the enterprise network. Cisco Expressway Series components are used to provide secure access and firewall traversal to the endpoints that register with the Unified CM. This chapter identifies how to configure the six main components of the MRA solution defined in Chapter 13, "Introduction to Mobile and Remote Access (MRA)."

This chapter covers the following objectives from the Implementing Cisco Collaboration Cloud and Edge Solutions (CLCEI) exam 300-820:

- 3.1.a Configure a Mobile and Remote Access (MRA) solution: DNS records types (not platform-specific)

- 3.1.b Configure a Mobile and Remote Access (MRA) solution: Certificates (not platform specific, covers Unified Communications Manager, IM&P, Expressways, Unity Connection)

- 3.1.c Configure a Mobile and Remote Access (MRA) solution: Unified Communications Traversal Zones

- 3.1.d Configure a Mobile and Remote Access (MRA) solution: Unified Communications configuration on Expressway

- 3.1.e Configure a Mobile and Remote Access (MRA) solution: HTTP allow list

- 3.1.f Configure a Mobile and Remote Access (MRA) solution: SIP trunk security profile on Cisco Unified Communications Manager

"Do I Know This Already?" Quiz

The "Do I Know This Already?" quiz enables you to assess whether you should read this entire chapter thoroughly or jump to the "Exam Preparation Tasks" section. If you are in doubt about your answers to these questions or your own assessment of your knowledge of the topics, read the entire chapter. Table 14-1 lists the major headings in this chapter and their corresponding "Do I Know This Already?" quiz questions. You can find the answers in Appendix A, "Answers to the 'Do I Know This Already?' Quizzes and Review Questions."

Table 14-1 "Do I Know This Already?" Section-to-Question Mapping

Foundation Topics Section	Questions
DNS Records	1–2
Certificates	3–6
Cisco Unified CM Settings for MRA	7
Unified Communications Configuration on Expressways	8–9
HTTP Allow List	10
Unified Communications Traversal Zones	11

CAUTION The goal of self-assessment is to gauge your mastery of the topics in this chapter. If you do not know the answer to a question or are only partially sure of the answer, you should mark that question as wrong for purposes of the self-assessment. Giving yourself credit for an answer you correctly guess skews your self-assessment results and might provide you with a false sense of security.

1. Which of the following is an SRV record that's needed on the public DNS for an enterprise MRA deployment?

   a. _collab-edge._tls.*<domain>*

   b. _cisco-uds._tcp.*<domain>*

   c. _cuplogin._tcp.*<domain>*

   d. _sip._tcp.*<domain>*

2. When an endpoint located outside the corporate network is configured to register to the Cisco Unified CM using MRA, what is the first communication sent by that endpoint?

   a. TLS handshake with the Expressway Edge to establish a trusted certificate verification

   b. Registration request sent to the Unified CM through the Expressway Core and Edge servers

   c. DNS SRV lookup for _collab-edge._tcp.*<domain>*

   d. DNS SRV lookup for _cisco-uds._tcp.*<domain>*

3. Which of the following certificate pairs are required for an MRA deployment? (Choose two.)

   a. Public or enterprise CA certificate chain used to sign the Expressway Core certificate

   b. Public or enterprise CA certificate chain used to sign the Expressway Edge certificate

   c. Unified CM Tomcat certificates or CA chain

   d. Unified CM CallManager certificates or CA chain

   e. IMP Tomcat certificate or CA chain

   f. Unified CM CAPF certificates

4. Which of the following certificate options should be used on the Cisco Expressways for an MRA deployment?

   a. Self-signed certificates

   b. Single host/domain certificate

   c. Multiple subdomain wildcard certificates

   d. All of the above

5. What Cisco Unified CM certificates are significant for Mobile and Remote Access? (Choose two.)

   a. Public or enterprise CA certificate chain used to sign Expressway Core certificate

   b. Public or enterprise CA certificate chain used to sign Expressway Edge certificate

   c. Cisco Unified CM Tomcat certificates or CA chain

   d. Cisco Unified CM CallManager certificates or CA chain

   e. IMP Tomcat certificate or CA chain

   f. Cisco Unified CM CAPF certificates

6. What is the recommended format for certificates on the Expressway servers for an MRA deployment?

   a. .cer or .crt format

   b. DER-encoded or Base64-encoded format

   c. DER-encoded format

   d. Base64-encoded format

7. What bandwidth rate does Cisco recommend changing the SIP Station TCP Port Throttle Threshold to on the Cisco Unified CM for MRA calls across the network?

   a. 480 kbps

   b. 750 kbps

   c. 1020 kbps

   d. 2400 kbps

8. Which of the following statements is true when configuring an MRA solution?

   a. Enabling MRA on the Expressway-C involves turning it on and configuring MRA Access Control settings, but enabling MRA on the Expressway-E only involves turning it on.

   b. Enabling MRA on the Expressway-E involves turning it on and configuring MRA Access Control settings, but enabling MRA on the Expressway-C only involves turning it on.

   c. MRA needs to be enabled only on the Expressway-C, not the Expressway-E.

   d. MRA needs to be enabled only on the Expressway-E, not the Expressway-C.

   e. Enabling MRA is exactly the same on both the Expressway-C and the Expressway-E.

9. When nodes are being discovered on the Expressway-C for an MRA deployment, which of the following statements is true?

   a. The Unified CM and Unified CM IM and Presence nodes will not show Active until the Traversal Zones are configured and active.

   b. The Unified CM IM and Presence nodes will not show Active until the Traversal Zones are configured and active.

   c. The Unified CM node will not show Active until the Traversal Zones are configured and active.

   d. The Unified CM and Unified CM IM and Presence nodes will show Active immediately after they are discovered.

10. What two ports are used with reverse proxy to allow inbound authenticated HTTPS requests for TFTP file download and SOAP API requests on the Cisco Unified CM?

    a. TCP 2222 and TCP 8443

    b. TCP 6970 and TCP 8443

    c. TCP 7400 and TCP 8443

    d. TCP 5222 and TCP 8443

11. What zone type should be selected on the Cisco Expressway Edge server when setting up the traversal component of the MRA solution?

    a. Traversal Client Zone

    b. Neighbor Zone

    c. Traversal Server Zone

    d. Unified Communications Traversal Zone

    e. DNS Zone

    f. ENUM Zone

Foundation Topics

DNS Records

The DNS **A records** and **Service (SRV) records** required for a **Mobile and Remote Access (MRA)** deployment are different from those required for a traditional **firewall** traversal solution. Additionally, different records need to be configured on an internal **Domain**

Name Service (DNS) server and an external DNS server. Before deploying an MRA solution, you need to set up DNS. Certificates cannot be created until DNS is configured because the **public key infrastructure (PKI)** certificates depend on the DNS records of the different servers.

Cisco endpoints, especially Jabber, are programmed to use DNS so that they always search for the Cisco Unified CM SRV record first. If the Unified CM cannot be reached, the endpoints search for the Expressway-E. The Expressway-E can be located with an SRV lookup whether the endpoint is internal or external to the network, but the endpoint should not search for the Expressway unless it's external to the corporate network. The endpoint should be able to locate the Unified CM using an SRV lookup only if the endpoint is located within the corporate network. This is the reason that the endpoint will always search for the Unified CM first. If that path fails, there is an alternative path for the endpoint to register through the Expressway servers using MRA.

The external DNS server must be configured with a _collab-edge._tls.<domain> SRV record so that external endpoints can discover that they should use the Expressway-E for Mobile and Remote Access. Service records for secure SIP are also required, not specifically for MRA but for deploying a secure SIP service on the Internet. The SRV records must point to each cluster member of the Cisco Expressway-E server. Table 14-2 provides examples of the SRV records needed on a public DNS for two Cisco Expressway Edge servers clustered together.

Table 14-2 Public DNS SRV Records for Expressway-E Cluster

Service	Protocol	Domain	Priority	Weight	Port	Target
_Collab-edge.	_tls.	Cisco.com	10	10	8443	Exp-e1.cisco.com
_Collab-edge.	_tls.	Cisco.com	10	10	8443	Exp-e2.cisco.com
_sips.	_tcp.	Cisco.com	10	10	5061	Exp-e1.cisco.com
_sips.	_tcp.	Cisco.com	10	10	5061	Exp-e2.cisco.com

The internal DNS server must be configured with a _cisco-uds._tcp.<domain> SRV record so that internal endpoints can discover that they should use Unified CM for direct registration. When using Unified CM IM and Presence (IM&P) services, a _cuplogin._tcp.<domain> SRV record is also required on the internal DNS server. Just as the public DNS SRV records must refer to the Cisco Expressway-E servers, the internal DNS SRV records must refer to all call processing nodes of a Unified CM cluster, as well as with all Unified CM IM and Presence server SRV records. The internal DNS records must be available to all internal endpoints and to the Cisco Expressway Core. The Unified CM and Unified CM IM and Presence server SRV records must not be resolvable from outside the internal network. Otherwise, Cisco endpoints and soft clients will not use the necessary Mobile and Remote Access registration via the Cisco Expressway-E. Table 14-3 provides examples of the SRV records needed on a private DNS for two Unified CMs and two Unified CM IM and Presence servers clustered together.

14

Table 14-3   Private DNS SRV Records for Cisco Unified CM and Cisco Unified CM IMP Clusters

Service	Protocol	Domain	Priority	Weight	Port	Target
_cisco-uds.	_tcp.	Cisco.com	10	10	8443	cucm1.cisco.com
_cisco-uds.	_tcp.	Cisco.com	10	10	8443	cucm2.cisco.com
_cuplogin.	_tcp.	Cisco.com	10	10	5061	imp1.cisco.com
_cuplogin.	_tcp.	Cisco.com	10	10	5061	imp2.cisco.com

Before explaining how to configure an MRA solution, it is a good idea to more closely examine the MRA service discovery operation. This discussion will help administrators deploying this solution fully understand the dependencies between the components involved with an MRA solution. Figure 14-1 illustrates the way Cisco MRA service discovery operates on the public network. This example is for a Cisco Jabber client in phone-only mode. Additional steps involving the Unified CM IM and Presence services would need to be included if additional Cisco Jabber services were being utilized.

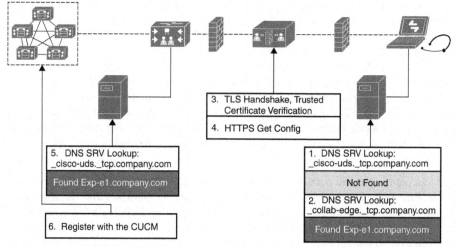

Figure 14-1   *Cisco MRA Service Discovery Operation*

Figure 14-1 assumes that the initiating endpoint, or Jabber client in this case, does not connect to the corporate network over a VPN. This is the reason that the initial DNS SRV lookup for the _cisco-uds._tcp.domain record fails. The service discovery occurs as follows. First, a Cisco Jabber client located outside the corporate network, and without a VPN connection, sends a DNS SRV record lookup for _cisco-uds._tcp.company.com to a public DNS server. The public enterprise DNS that manages company.com should not have such an SRV record and, therefore, the lookup fails. Next, the Cisco Jabber client sends another DNS SRV record lookup for _collab-edge._tls.company.com. This time the lookup is successful, and the address of the Cisco Expressway Edge is provided to the Jabber client in the DNS response.

Now the Cisco Jabber client can start the Mobile and Remote Access negotiation with the Cisco Expressway Edge server. A certificate is presented to Cisco Jabber and may need to be manually trusted by the user if it is not signed by a certificate authority server that the client PC already trusts. A TLS handshake is exchanged to establish a secure connection. The Cisco Expressway Edge then acts as a proxy for the Cisco Jabber client by passing messages that it receives from Cisco Jabber to Cisco Expressway Core through the firewall traversal connection and returns messages from the Expressway Core to the Jabber client.

When a trusted connection between Cisco Jabber and the Cisco Expressway Edge is established, Cisco Jabber tries to register to the services that are enabled on the Cisco Expressway Core, which in this case is the Unified CM. The Cisco Expressway Core sends a DNS SRV record lookup for _cisco-uds._tcp.company.com to the internal DNS server. The internal DNS server responds with the address of the Unified CM. The Cisco Expressway Core then forwards the registration request from the Cisco Jabber client to the Unified CM. The Cisco Expressway Core acts as the proxy for messages between the Unified CM and the Expressway Edge.

Certificates

Six different certificate pairs can be configured in an MRA deployment. However, only two pairs are required to set up the solution. The other four exist in an ideal environment for absolute security pertaining to registration and calling. The first certificate required is a public or enterprise **certificate authority (CA)** certificate chain used to sign the Expressway-C. This is required to establish the traversal zone for the client connection. The second certificate required is a public or enterprise CA certificate chain used to sign the Expressway-E. This is also required to establish the traversal zone for the server connection. Both are absolutely required for **TLS Verify** to operate successfully. The **Traversal Zones** used for an MRA deployment will not work without these two certificate pairs. The **root CA certificate** for the Expressway-C certificate should be added to both the Expressway-C and the Expressway-E. The root CA certificate for the Expressway-E certificate should be added to both the Expressway-E and the Expressway-C. If both servers were signed by the same CA, then they will use the same root CA certificate; therefore, it needs to be added to each server only once.

The next optional certificate is the Unified CM Tomcat certificate or CA chain. The Tomcat certificate is for Tomcat trust. This certificate is used for MRA only when the Expressway-C is configured to use TLS Verify mode on Unified CM discovery. The Tomcat CA should be added to the Expressway-C, and the root CA certificate for the Expressway-C should be added to the Unified CM. If TLS Verify is not used on the Expressway-C for Unified CM discovery, this certificate is not needed.

Another optional certificate is the Unified CM certificate or CA chain used when the Unified CM is in mixed mode for end-to-end TLS. If this certificate is used, the Unified CM CA should be added to the Expressway-C, and the certificate CA for the Expressway-C should be added to the Unified CM.

The Unified CM IM and Presence Tomcat certificate or CA chain is similar to the Unified CM Tomcat certificate or CA chain. This certificate is used only when the Expressway-C is configured to use TLS Verify mode on Unified CM IM and Presence discovery. The Tomcat CA should be added to the Expressway-C, and the certificate CA for the Expressway-C should be added to the Unified CM IM and Presence server. If TLS Verify is not used on the Expressway-C for Unified CM IM and Presence discovery, this certificate is not needed.

The last optional certificate is the Unified CM Certificate Authority Proxy Function (CAPF) certificate. This certificate is used when remote endpoints authenticate using a Locally Significant Certificate (LSC). By default, the LSC is signed by the CAPF, so the CAPF is the CA for phones in this scenario. However, when the CAPF is signed by an external CA, then the CAPF in this scenario acts as a subordinate CA or intermediate CA. The difference between a self-signed CAPF and CA-signed CAPF is that the CAPF is the **root CA** to the LSC when doing a self-signed CAPF, but the CAPF is the subordinate or intermediate CA to the LSC when doing a CA-signed CAPF. Table 14-4 identifies each of the six certificate pairs used in an MRA deployment.

Key Topic

Table 14-4 Certificate Pairs Used in an MRA Deployment

Certificate Type	Core	Edge	Required
Public or enterprise CA certificate chain used to sign Expressway Core certificate	Yes	Yes	Yes
Public or enterprise CA certificate chain used to sign Expressway Edge certificate	Yes	Yes	Yes
Unified CM Tomcat certificates or CA chain	Yes	No	No
Unified CM CallManager certificates or CA chain	Yes	No	No
IMP Tomcat certificate or CA chain	Yes	No	No
Unified CM CAPF certificates	No	Yes	No

TLS Verify Requirements

Transport Layer Security (TLS) and its predecessor, **Secure Sockets Layer (SSL)**, both frequently referred to as "SSL," are cryptographic protocols that provide communications security over a computer network. This TCP protocol aims primarily to provide privacy and data integrity between two communicating hosts or applications.

Client/server applications such as web browsers, email, and VoIP commonly use the TLS protocol to prevent eavesdropping and tampering of information. The protocols these applications use must choose to use or not to use TLS. The easiest way to segregate the information is to use different port numbers for unencrypted traffic, such as port 80 for HTTP, and TLS-encrypted traffic, such as port 443 for HTTPS. The connection is secure because **symmetric cryptography** is used to encrypt the transmitted data. The keys for this symmetric encryption are generated uniquely for each connection and are based on a shared secret negotiation at the start of the session. The server and client negotiate the details of which encryption algorithm and cryptographic keys to use before the first byte of data is transmitted. Identification is usually in the form of digital "certificates" that contain the server name, the trusted CA, and the server's public encryption key. The identity of the communicating parties can be authenticated using this public-key cryptography (**asymmetric cryptography**) to ensure only the intended recipient can decrypt the traffic. The negotiation of a shared secret is both secure and reliable against eavesdroppers and attacks, including man-in-the-middle attacks. The connection ensures integrity because each message transmitted includes a message integrity check using a message authentication code to prevent undetected loss or alteration of the data during transmission.

14

Once the client and server have agreed to use TLS, they negotiate a stateful connection by using a handshake procedure. The handshake begins when a client connects to a TLS-enabled server requesting a secure connection and presents a list of supported ciphers and hash functions. From this list, the server picks a cipher and hash function that it also supports, and it informs the client of the decision. The server then identifies itself with its digital certificate, which can contain the server name, the trusted CA, and the server's public encryption key. The client then validates the certificate before proceeding. Public-key encryption is used to share the pre-master secret via the use of **Rivest-Shamir-Adleman (RSA)** or **Diffie-Hellman key exchange.** This process generates a random and unique session key for encryption and decryption that has the additional property of forward secrecy, which protects past sessions against future compromises of secret keys or passwords.

Remember that the server is validated because the client initiates the secure connection. The client side confirms that the server is who it claims to be and whether it can be trusted with the use of certificates. The client receives the digital certificate from the server side of the TLS negotiation, but the identity must be verified before proceeding. The server certificate may contain the name of the certificate holder. This name is checked against the Common Name (CN) or the Subject Alternative Name (SAN). The server certificate may also include additional information such as a serial number, expiration dates, revocation status, a copy of the certificate holder's public key (which is used for encrypting messages and digital signatures), and the digital signature of the certificate-issuing authority. This information identifies to the client that the certificate is signed by a certificate authority. If you trust this CA, you can verify using the CA's public key that it really did sign the server's certificate. To sign a certificate yourself, you need the private key, which is only known to the CA of your choice. This way an attacker cannot sign a certificate himself and falsely claim to be the server. When the certificate has been modified, the signature will be incorrect, and the client will reject it. Figure 14-2 illustrates the steps involved with a security handshake between a client and a server.

Mutual TLS authentication is also an option that can be chosen. In this type of authentication, both parties authenticate each other through verifying the provided digital certificate so that both parties are assured of the other's identity. Mutual TLS is very similar to the normal process of the client handling the verification of the server's certification but including the additional step of the client providing a certificate. This process allows the server side to authenticate the client, allowing for both parties to trust each other.

Server-to-server connections rely on mutual TLS for mutual authentication. In the Cisco Collaboration infrastructure, some examples would be a secure connection between endpoints and the Unified CM, Unified CM SIP trunks to other clusters, and even Unified CM SIP trunks with a Cisco Expressway Core.

To secure voice and video traffic, you must understand multiple technologies. Remember, the most common VoIP communication used today is SIP. For secure transmissions of SIP messages, the protocol may be encrypted with TLS. Media identification and negotiation are achieved with the Session Description Protocol (SDP). SDP can also be used for the master key exchange. For the transmission of media streams, SIP employs the Real-time Transport Protocol (RTP) or Secure Real-time Transport Protocol (SRTP). Unencrypted SIP generally uses port 5060, whereas TLS-encrypted SIP utilizes port 5061.

14

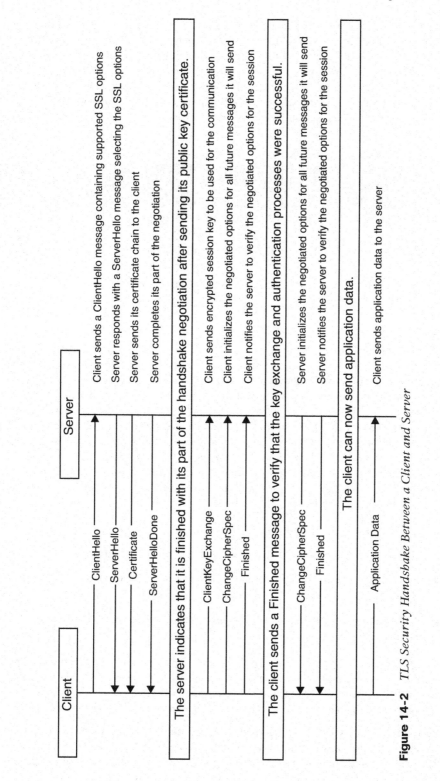

Figure 14-2 *TLS Security Handshake Between a Client and Server*

The diagram shows a message sequence between a **Client** and a **Server**:

ClientHello	Client sends a ClientHello message containing supported SSL options
ServerHello	Server responds with a ServerHello message selecting the SSL options
Certificate	Server sends its certificate chain to the client
ServerHelloDone	Server completes its part of the negotiation

The server indicates that it is finished with its part of the handshake negotiation after sending its public key certificate.

ClientKeyExchange	Client sends encrypted session key to be used for the communication
ChangeCipherSpec	Client initializes the negotiated options for all future messages it will send
Finished	Client notifies the server to verify the negotiated options for the session

The client sends a Finished message to verify that the key exchange and authentication processes were successful.

ChangeCipherSpec	Server initializes the negotiated options for all future messages it will send
Finished	Server notifies the server to verify the negotiated options for the session

The client can now send application data.

Application Data	Client sends application data to the server

Trusted certificates are very important to create secure connections. This part of the process is where the CA comes into the solution. CAs are widely used both on the public Internet and private networks to issue digital certificates containing identity credentials binding them to SSL or TLS cryptography keys. However, because these CAs are trust anchors, they must conduct several checks into the identity of the applicant. The checks corrolate to the class and type of certificate for which it is being applied. Table 14-5 identifies each of these classes of certificates available and which of these certificates are supported on Cisco Collaboration servers.

Key Topic

Table 14-5 *Classes of Certificates on Cisco Collaboration Servers*

Options	Types			Support Info
	DV	OV	EV	
Single Host/Domain	Yes	Yes	Yes	Supported on all Cisco Collaboration servers
UCC/Multiple SAN/Cert	Yes	Yes	Yes	Supported on all Cisco Collaboration servers
Multiple Subdomain Wildcard Cert	Yes	Yes	No	Not supported at all on Cisco Expressways

For **Domain Validation (DV) certificates**, the CA checks only the right of the applicant to use a specific domain name. No company identity information is vetted, and no information is displayed other than encryption information within the Secure Site Seal. For **Organization Validation (OV) certificates**, the CA checks the right of the applicant to use a specific domain name and conducts some vetting of the organization. Additional vetted company information is displayed to customers when clicking the Secure Site Seal, giving enhanced visibility into who is behind the site and associated enhanced trust. For **Extended Validation (EV) certificates**, the CA checks the right of the applicant to use a specific domain name and, additionally, conducts a thorough vetting of the organization. The issuance process of EV certificates is strictly defined in the EV guidelines, as formally ratified by the CA/Browser Forum in 2007, that specify all the steps that are required for a CA before issuing a certificate. They include

- Verifying the legal, physical, and operational existence of the entity

- Verifying that the identity of the entity matches official records

- Verifying that the entity has exclusive rights to use the domain that is specified in the EV SSL certificate

- Verifying that the entity has properly authorized the issuance of the EV SSL certificate

EV certificates are available for all types of businesses, including government entities and both incorporated and unincorporated businesses. A second set of guidelines, the EV Audit Guidelines, specify the criteria under which a CA needs to be successfully audited before issuing EV certificates. The audits are repeated yearly to ensure the integrity of the issuance process.

Because people are constantly searching the Internet, the browsers constantly are checking the websites that are visited against a CA to authenticate web pages. As an example, web browsers like Google Chrome, Firefox, and Internet Explorer maintain lists of certificate authorities they consider trustworthy. When you access what should be a secure website, the site presents its security certificate to your browser. If the certificate is up to date and from a trusted CA, you will see the trusted secure connection. If the certificate lacks any of the requirements, you will see that your web browser will not establish a connection until you accept the risks and proceed.

With the Cisco Collaboration products, only certain certificate options are supported. The Expressway-E requires a public certificate because it is the most public-facing part of the Cisco Collaboration solution and needs to be trusted by outside sources such as clients and other businesses. A single host/domain certificate option will suffice with any type of validation desired. If multiple hosts, domains, or subdomains need to be covered, multiple SAN certificates are required. Note that the wildcard certification is not supported on the Cisco Expressway Series.

In the Cisco Collaboration architecture, it is easy to secure all enterprise network information simply by creating a private network behind the security of a firewall. However, companies may need to work with other businesses or clients for their day-to-day operations. To place voice and video calls outside the network and connect to other networks securely, Cisco offers the Expressway Series. This robust and secure solution comes equipped with Cisco's proprietary Assent protocol that allows secure firewall-traversal technology for any-to-any collaboration.

Cisco Expressway Certificates

Best practice for setting up the Expressway Series begins with the Expressway Edge, which is usually placed in between two firewalls in a separate network from the private enterprise network and the public outside network. This subnetwork is known as a demilitarized zone (DMZ). First, you can add authentication credentials and build a **Traversal Server Zone** on the Expressway Edge. All zones also require search rules that determine when and how they are searched. Next, you can configure the Expressway Core to use a **Traversal Client Zone**. This zone initiates a secure traversal connection through the firewall on a specific keep-alive port and authenticates against the authentication database configured on the Expressway Edge. Once a connection is established, the Expressway Core preserves the connection by continuously sending UDP keep-alive packets over that same port to the Expressway Edge. This allows endpoints to both place calls out of the network and receive incoming calls. When a call comes into the network, the call setup is forwarded from the Expressway Edge to the Expressway Core and ultimately to the Unified CM to search for a user or endpoint. Once call setup has completed, both the call signaling and media will securely traverse through the firewall using the traversal zones previously created.

The process described here can use a standard TLS verification, which uses a single self-signed certificate on the Expressway Edge, or it can use the more secure TLS Verify mode where both Expressways have to validate each other's certificates. The TLS Verify mode can be set to enabled or disabled on the Zone Settings page, which will decide which mode is used. When the zone is configured with the TLS Verify mode set to Off, the Expressway Edge declines to verify the host name and signature of a certificate from the Expressway Core. The Expressway Core still verifies the certificate of the Expressway Edge's self-signed certificate, but this certificate does not use domain verification; therefore, this configuration also allows for the use of IP addresses for the peers. With TLS Verify mode set to On, Mutual TLS (MTLS) is activated, and both client and server will match the CN or SAN against the peer address.

When using the TLS Verify mode in the On configuration on an Expressway-E, the CA and SAN must match the TLS Verify Subject Name field in the zone configuration. As a result, this configuration is commonly used in closed or federated systems. For open B2B searches to other nonfederated enterprises, TLS Verify mode on the Expressway-E needs to be in the Off mode. When you are setting up traversal zones for MRA, TLS Verify mode is required to be turned On. MRA will not work if TLS Verify mode is set to Off.

Cisco Unified CM Certificates

Two Unified CM certificates are significant for Mobile and Remote Access: the CallManager certificate and the Tomcat certificate. These certificates are automatically installed on the Unified CM, and by default, they are self-signed and have the same Common Name (CN). Cisco recommends using CA-signed certificates. However, if self-signed certificates are used, the two certificates must have different Common Names. The Expressway does not allow two self-signed certificates with the same CN. If the CallManager and Tomcat self-signed certificates have the same CN in the Expressway's trusted CA list, the Expressway can trust only one of them. This means that either secure HTTP or secure SIP between the Expressway-C and the Unified CM will fail.

Two IM and Presence Service certificates are significant if you use Extensible Messaging and Presence Protocol (XMPP): the cup-xmpp certificate and Tomcat certificate. Cisco recommends using CA-signed certificates. However, if self-signed certificates are used, these two certificates must also have different CNs. Again, the Expressway does not allow two self-signed certificates with the same CN. If the cup-xmpp and Tomcat (self-signed) certificates have the same CN, Expressway trusts only one of them, and some TLS attempts between Cisco Expressway-E and IM and Presence Service servers will fail.

Although Expressway certificates were discussed in the previous section, some important settings on the Unified CM can affect how the Expressway Core certificates are set up. The Expressway Core server certificate needs to include the following elements in its list of SANs:

- **Unified CM phone security profile names:** The names of the phone security profiles in the Unified CM that are configured for encrypted TLS and are used for devices requiring remote access. Use the FQDN format and separate multiple entries with commas. Having the secure phone profiles as alternative names means that the Unified CM can communicate via TLS with the Expressway-C when it is forwarding messages from devices that use those profiles.

- **IM and Presence chat node aliases (federated group chat):** The chat node aliases that are configured on the IM and Presence Service servers. These are required only for Unified Communications XMPP federation deployments that intend to support group chat over TLS with federated contacts. The Expressway-C automatically includes the chat node aliases in the CSR, providing it has discovered a set of IM and Presence Service servers. Cisco recommends using DNS format for the chat node aliases when generating the CSR. The same chat node aliases must be used in the Expressway Edge server certificate's alternative names (SANs).

The Expressway Edge server certificate needs to include the following elements in its list of SANs:

- **Unified CM registrations domains:** All of the domains that are configured on the Expressway Core for Unified CM registrations. Required for secure communications between endpoint devices and the Expressway Edge.

- **XMPP federation domains:** The domains used for point-to-point XMPP federation. These are configured on the IM and Presence Service servers and should also be configured on the Expressway-C as domains for XMPP federation. Select the DNS format and manually specify the required FQDNs. Separate the FQDNs with commas if you need multiple domains. Do not use the *XMPPAddress* format because your CA may not support it, and it may be discontinued in future versions of the Expressway software.

- **IM and Presence chat node aliases (federated group chat):** The same set of chat node aliases as entered on the Expressway-C's certificate. They are required only for voice and presence deployments that will support group chat over TLS with federated contacts. Note that you can copy the list of chat node aliases from the equivalent Generate CSR page on the Expressway-C.

The Unified CM registration domains used in the Expressway configuration and Expressway-E certificate are used by Mobile and Remote Access clients to look up the _collab-edge DNS SRV record during service discovery. They enable MRA registrations on the Unified CM and are primarily for service discovery. These service discovery domains may or may not match the SIP registration domains. It depends on the deployment, and they don't have to match. One example is a deployment that uses a .local or similar private domain with Unified CM on the internal network and public domain names for the Expressway-E FQDN and service discovery. In this case, you need to include the public domain names in the Expressway-E certificate as SANs. There is no need to include the private domain names used on the Unified CM. Only the edge domain needs to be listed as a SAN. Select the DNS format and manually specify the required FQDNs. Separate the FQDNs with commas if you need multiple domains. You may select CollabEdgeDNS format instead, which simply adds the prefix collab-edge to the domain that you enter. This format is recommended if you do not want to include your top-level domain as a SAN.

Creating Certificates for MRA

The Cisco Unified CM does not require an MTLS connection to the Expressway Core for the MRA deployment; therefore, this section covers only the detailed steps on how to sign and load certificates on the Expressway Core and Edge servers. Once all MRA settings have been configured on the Expressway-C, Traversal Zones can be configured between the Expressway-E and the Expressway-C. TLS Verify is required for these zones, so certificates must be used. If the certificates come from the same CA, the root CA will be the same on both Expressway servers. However, if a different CA is used for the Expressway Core than what is used on the Expressway Edge, the root CA certificate must be uploaded to both Expressways to identify where the certificates were signed. Information required when signing certificates is the same regardless of the CA being used. The instructions provided in this book on how to sign certificates are through a Microsoft certificate server.

The Expressway-C and Expressway-E have a tool built into them that can generate a **certificate signing request (CSR)**. The CSR contains all the information the CA needs to sign the certificate. When the CA signs the certificate, it's important that it is done with a template that contains the server and client authentication extensions. The certificate generation process seems to confuse a lot of customers and engineers. The basic requirement to get this set up is fairly straightforward. The first consideration is what to use for a CA. There are two commonly used approaches. One method is to use OpenSSL, and the other is to use **Active Directory Certificate Services (ADCS)**. Setting up ADCS in a Microsoft environment is very complex and would warrant discussion that goes beyond the scope of this book. The OpenSSL method is well defined in the *Cisco VCS Certificate Creation and Use Deployment Guide*; therefore, this section focuses only on how to use an ADCS after it has already been configured on a Windows server.

Step 1. On the Expressway, generate a CSR. For the most part, the following steps pertain to both the Expressway-C and Expressway-E servers.

    a. On the Expressway, navigate to **Maintenance > Security > Server Certificate**.

    b. Click **Generate CSR** to access the Generate CSR page.

    c. Fill out the appropriate details, and then click the **Generate CSR** button:

        ■ Key Length (in Bits): Recommended to use 2048 or higher

        ■ Country: (Optional) Abbreviations OK

        ■ State or Province: (Optional) Abbreviations OK

        ■ Locality (Town Name): (Optional)

        ■ Organization (Company Name): (Optional)

        ■ Organization Unit: (Optional)

Make a note of the Common Name that is auto-populated on the Generate CSR page. This is automatically created using the DNS settings, so the DNS settings on the Expressway must be accurate. The Common Name on the Expressway-C will be used as the Subject Name when the traversal zone is configured on the Expressway-E. The Common Name on the Expressway-E will be used as the Peer address when the traversal zone is configured on the Expressway-C. There are a few points of interest for the Expressway-C certificate. If the IM and Presence Service has already been added to the Expressway-C, a prepopulated Chat Node Alias will appear. This is required for XMPP federation deployments that intend to use both TLS and group chat, such as conference-2-StandAloneCluster5ad9a.%yourdomain%. Also, if the solution is being deployed using TLS between the Expressway-C and the Unified CM, ensure that the Subject Alternate Name on the certificate contains the names in FQDN format of all the phone security profiles in the Unified CM that are configured for encrypted TLS, such as CSFJabber.tftp.com.

d. Under the Certificate Signing Request section, click **Show (PEM file)**. Copy the entire contents of the PEM file to a notepad. Be sure to include the -----**Begin Certificate Request**----- and -----**End Certificate Request**----- lines. The contents of this PEM file will be used to sign the Expressway-C certificate using Microsoft ADCS. Figure 14-3 illustrates the settings that need to be configured when generating a CSR.

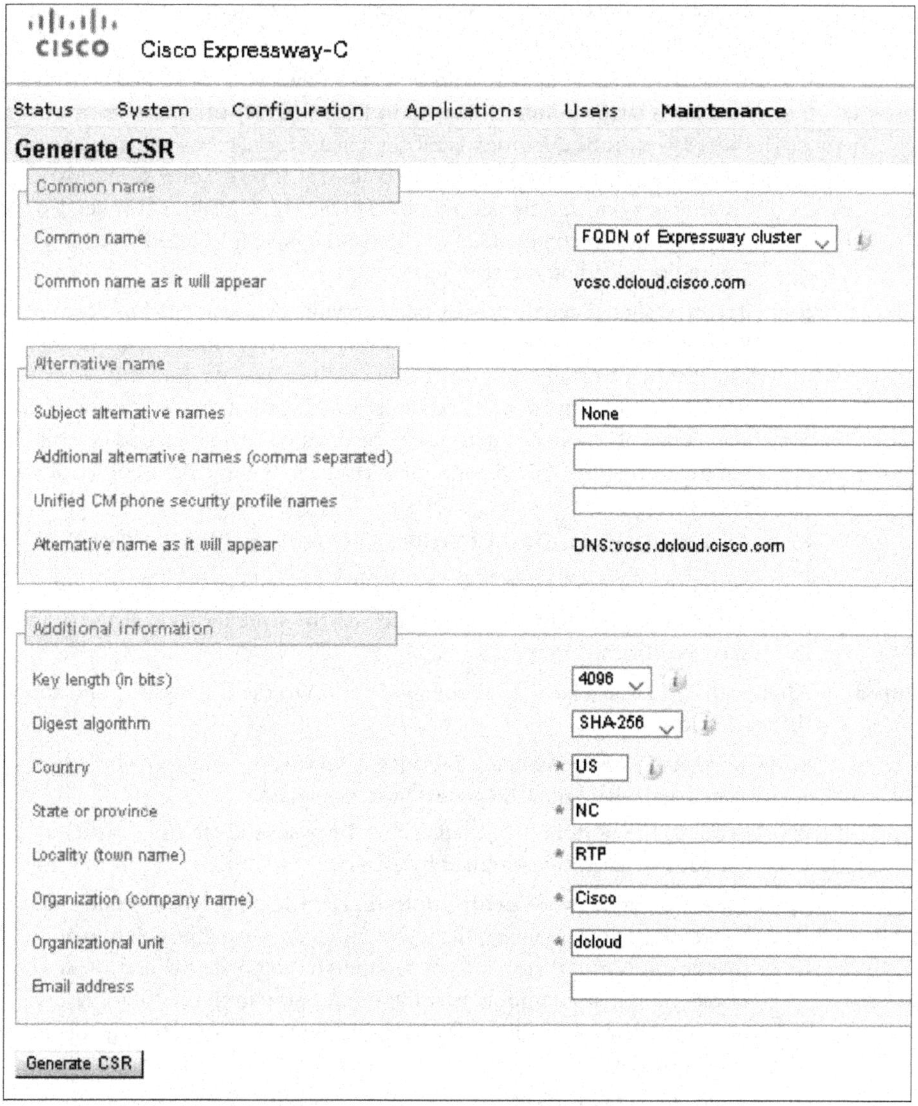

Figure 14-3 *Generate CSR Page in an Expressway Server*

Step 2.   Sign the CSR with the Microsoft ADCS.

a. Browse to the ADCS web interface at **https://<IP_address>/certsrv**.

b. Log in and select **Request a Certificate**.

    c.   Click the **Submit a Certificate Request by Using a Base-64-Encoded CMC or PKCS #10 File, or Submit a Renewal Request by Using a Base-64-Encoded PKCS #7 File** option.

    d.   Paste the copied contents from the Expressway-C Server PEM file into the Base-64-Encoded Certificate Request box.

    e.   Some ADCS servers have a Certificate Template field. If this option is available, choose the most appropriate one for your certificate purpose, and then click **Submit**.

    f.   The next page that appears allows you to download the signed certificate in either a **Distinguished Encoding Rules (DER)-encoded format** or **Base64-encoded format**. DER is a binary format. Base64 is an encoding method that converts binary to plain ASCII text. Some scenarios prevent copying and transferring data in binary, so plain text is needed. Therefore, it is recommended to choose the **Base 64 Encoded** option before downloading the certificate.

    g.   After the signed certificate has been downloaded, you need to download a copy of the root CA certificate as well. The root CA certificate establishes a trusted chain that begins at the root CA, or in this case the ADCS, through the root CA certificate, and ends at the certificate that was signed. The use of the root CA certificate provides an added level of security. From the ADCS page, click **Home** in the top-right corner of the screen.

    h.   Click the **Download a CA Certificate, Certificate Chain or CRL** link.

    i.   Select the **Base 64** radio button and click **Download CA Certificate**.

    j.   When prompted, save the certificate into the same location as the signed server certificate.

Step 3.   After both certificates have been obtained, return to the Expressway and apply the certificates.

    a.   Navigate to **Maintenance > Security > Server Certificate**. This is the same page where the CSR request was generated.

    b.   Scroll to the bottom of the page, click **Browse**, and choose the server certificate that was just signed by ADCS.

    c.   Click **Upload Server Certificate Data**. Depending on what version of Expressway you are using, the web browser may prompt you to reauthenticate. A restart may also be required to complete the certificate installation. If so, do not restart the Expressway until the root CA has been installed. Figure 14-4 illustrates the Server Certificate page on an Expressway-C.

    d.   Navigate to **Maintenance > Security > Trusted CA Certificate**.

    e.   Click **Browse** and choose the root CA certificate that you downloaded from ADCS.

Server certificate

Server certificate data

Server certificate   Show (decoded)   Show (PEM file)

Currently loaded certificate expires on   Sep 30 2037

Reset to default server certificate

Certificate signing request (CSR)

Certificate request   There is no certificate signing request in prog

Generate CSR

Upload new certificate

Select the server private key file   Browse...   No file selected.   i

Select the server certificate file   Browse...   No file selected.   i

Upload server certificate data

Figure 14-4 *Expressway-C Server Certificate Page*

f.   Click the **Append CA Certificate** button. A restart of the server may be required.

g.   Navigate to **Maintenance > Restart Options** and click **Restart.** When prompted to confirm, click **OK.** The restart will take two to three minutes on the Expressways. Figure 14-5 illustrates the Trusted CA Certificate page.

Now you need to repeat all these steps on the other Expressway. There are some points of interest for the Expressway-E certificate. If multiple domains are being used, be sure that each domain configured for the Unified CM is a part of the SAN on the certificate. As with the Expressway-C certificate, if you are deploying the solution with XMPP federation, the same chat node aliases will be required. For successful validation of received certificates, the Cisco Expressway servers must trust the CA that issued certificates and will be exchanged during the TLS handshake. Therefore, if a different CA was used for the Expressway Core and the Expressway Edge, the root CA certificate must be added to the counterpart server. For example, if an ADCS was used to sign the Expressway-C CSR, and a public CA was used to sign the Expressway-E CSR, the public root CA certificate will need to be loaded on both servers, as well as the ADCS root CA certificate.

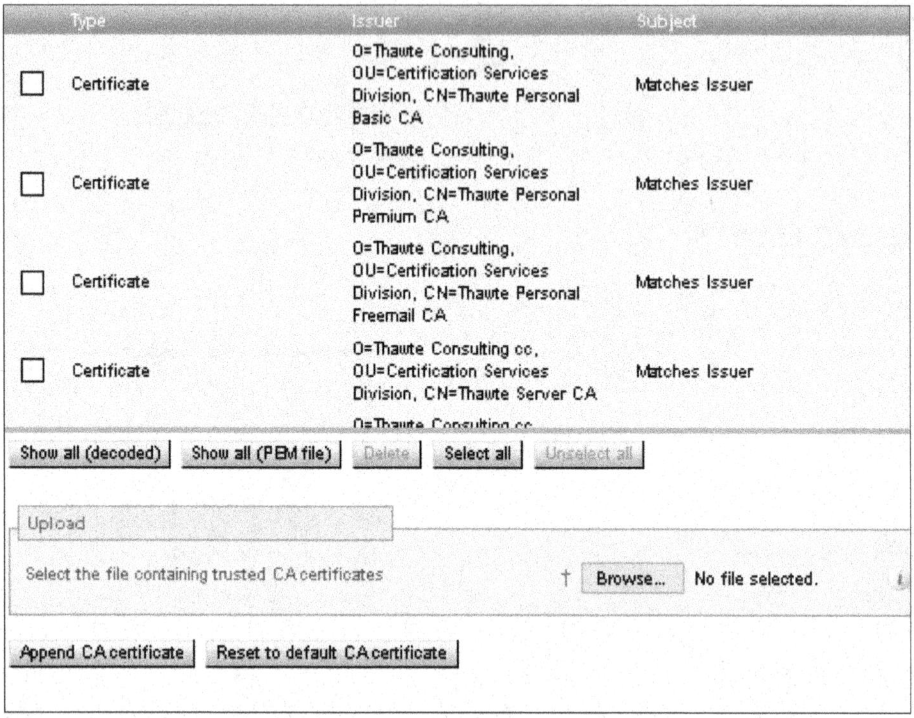

Type	Issuer	Subject
☐ Certificate	O=Thawte Consulting, OU=Certification Services Division, CN=Thawte Personal Basic CA	Matches Issuer
☐ Certificate	O=Thawte Consulting, OU=Certification Services Division, CN=Thawte Personal Premium CA	Matches Issuer
☐ Certificate	O=Thawte Consulting, OU=Certification Services Division, CN=Thawte Personal Freemail CA	Matches Issuer
☐ Certificate	O=Thawte Consulting cc, OU=Certification Services Division, CN=Thawte Server CA	Matches Issuer
	O=Thawte Consulting cc	

Show all (decoded)   Show all (PEM file)   Delete   Select all   Unselect all

Upload

Select the file containing trusted CA certificates   † Browse...   No file selected.

Append CA certificate   Reset to default CA certificate

Figure 14-5 *Expressway-C Trusted CA Certificate Page*

Cisco Unified CM Settings for MRA

After you have ensured that all the prerequisite components have been configured, which were covered in the first two sections of this chapter and in Chapter 13, the process for configuring MRA in a corporate network begins on the Cisco Unified CM. The seven steps presented in this section must be completed to deploy Mobile and Remote Access endpoints.

The first requirement on the Unified CM that you must configure before you set up MRA on the Expressway Core is to create an application user that has been assigned the *AXL API Access* role. The Cisco Expressway Core will need this level of access into the Unified CM; otherwise, communication will fail. You can use the default administrator account, but Cisco recommends creating a new application user account for each application service that's set up with the Unified CM. The same is also true for MRA deployments that include the Unified CM IM and Presence services. The corresponding IM and Presence user must have the *Standard AXL API Access* role assigned.

Step 1.   Make sure that the Cisco AXL Web Service is activated on the publisher node.

    a.   Log into the Cisco Unified CM and select **Cisco Unified Serviceability** from the Navigator menu in the top-right corner of the screen, and click **Go.** When that page loads, navigate to **Tools > Service Activation.**

    b.   From the Server drop-down menu, select the publisher node and click **Go.**

> **c.** Under the Database and Admin Services section, confirm that the Cisco AXL Web Service status is Activated.
>
> **d.** If the service is not activated, check the corresponding check box and click **Save** to activate the service.

Step 2. Optionally, configure region-specific settings for MRA endpoints. The default settings may be sufficient in many cases, but if you expect MRA endpoints to use video, you may want to increase the Maximum Session Bit Rate for Video Calls within your region configuration. The default setting of 384 kbps may be too low for some video endpoints, such as the DX series.

> **a.** Use the Navigator menu in the top-right corner of the screen to select **Cisco Unified CM Administration**. When that page loads, navigate to **System > Region Information > Region**.
>
> **b.** Perform any one of the following:
>
> - Click **Find** and select a region to edit the bit rates.
>
> - Click **Add New** to create a new region.
>
> **c.** In the Modify Relationship to Other Regions section, configure a new setting for the Maximum Session Bit Rate for Video Calls, such as 6000 kbps.
>
> **d.** Configure other fields in the Region Configuration window as necessary. For more information on the fields and their configuration options, see the system's online help.
>
> **e.** Click **Save**.

Step 3. After you have created a new region, assign your region to the device pool that your MRA endpoints use.

> **a.** From the Cisco Unified CM Administration page, navigate to **System > Device Pool**.
>
> **b.** Do either of the following:
>
> - Click **Find** and select the existing device pool to edit.
>
> - Click **Add New** to create a new device pool.
>
> **c.** Enter a device pool Name.
>
> **d.** Select a redundant CUCM Group.
>
> **e.** Assign a Date/Time Group. This group includes the Phone NTP references that may have been set up for MRA endpoints.
>
> **f.** Click the **Region** drop-down menu and assign a region to the device pool that MRA endpoints will use.
>
> **g.** Complete the remaining fields in the Device Pool Configuration window as necessary. For more information on the fields and their configuration options, see the system's online help.
>
> **h.** Click **Save**.

14

Step 4. Use this procedure to set up a phone security profile to be used by MRA endpoints. You must apply this profile to the phone configuration for each of your MRA endpoints.

    a. From Cisco Unified CM Administration, navigate to **System > Security > Phone Security Profile**.

    b. Click **Add New**.

    c. Click the **Phone Security Profile Type** drop-down list and select your device type, such as the **Cisco Unified Client Service Framework** for a Jabber application.

    d. Click **Next**.

    e. Enter a Name for the profile. For MRA, the name must be in FQDN format and must include the enterprise domain.

    f. Click the **Device Security Mode** drop-down list and select **Encrypted**. This field must be set to Encrypted; otherwise, Expressway will reject the communication.

    g. Set the Transport Type to **TLS**.

    h. Leave the TFTP Encrypted Config check box unchecked for the following phones because MRA will not work for these phones with this option enabled: DX Series, IP Phone 7800, or IP Phone 8811, 8841, 8845, 8861, and 8865.

    i. Complete the remaining fields in the Phone Security Profile Configuration window. For more information on the fields and their configuration options, see the system's online help.

    j. Click **Save**.

Step 5. This step is for Cisco Jabber only. Set up an MRA Access Policy for Cisco Jabber users. Cisco Jabber users must be enabled with MRA access within their user profiles to use the MRA feature. The Jabber desktop client includes Cisco Jabber for Windows users and Cisco Jabber for Mac users. The Jabber mobile client includes Cisco Jabber for iPad and iPhone users and Cisco Jabber for Android users.

    a. In Cisco Unified CM Administration, navigate to **User Management > User Settings > User Profile**.

    b. Click **Add New**.

    c. Enter a Name and Description for the user profile.

    d. Assign a Universal Device Template to apply to users' desk phones, mobile and desktop devices, and remote destination/device profiles.

    e. Assign a Universal Line Template to apply to the phone lines for users in this user profile.

    f. If you want the users in this user profile to be able to use the self-provisioning feature to provision their own phones, do the following:

        ■ Check the **Allow End User to Provision Their Own Phones** check box.

- In the Limit Provisioning Once End User Has This Many Phones field, enter a maximum number of phones the user is allowed to provision. The maximum is 20.

g. If you want Cisco Jabber users associated with this user profile to be able to use the Mobile and Remote Access feature, check the **Enable Mobile and Remote Access** check box. By default, this check box is selected. When you uncheck this check box, the Jabber Policies section is disabled, and the No Service Client Policy option is selected by default. This setting is mandatory only for Cisco Jabber users. Non-Jabber users do not need this setting to be able to use MRA.

h. Assign the Jabber policies for this user profile. From the Jabber Desktop Client Policy and Jabber Mobile Client Policy drop-down list, choose one of the following options:

- **No Service:** This policy disables access to all Cisco Jabber services.

- **IM & Presence Only:** This policy enables only instant messaging and presence capabilities.

- **IM & Presence, Voice and Video Calls:** This policy enables instant messaging, presence, voicemail, and conferencing capabilities for all users with audio or video devices. This is the default option.

i. Click **Save**.

Step 6. This step is also for Cisco Jabber users only. The user policy that was set up previously must be applied to the appropriate end user. End users can be set up manually, from an import using LDAP or using BAT. Setting up LDAP and BAT on a Unified CM is outside of the scope of this book, so we will not cover the steps to apply the user policy to the end user in the book. Refer to *CCNP and CCIE Collaboration Core CLCOR 350-801 Official Cert Guide* (Cisco Press, 2020) for instructions on how to configure these settings.

Step 7. Configure and provision endpoints that will use the MRA feature. This step is achieved by ensuring the corresponding settings above are applied to the phone through TFTP when registration is attempted. Again, refer to *CCNP and CCIE Collaboration Core CLCOR 350-801 Official Cert Guide* for instructions on how to configure these settings.

High volumes of Mobile and Remote Access calls may trigger denial-of-service thresholds on the Unified CM. The reason is that all the calls arriving at the Unified CM are from the same Expressway-C cluster. If necessary, Cisco recommends that you increase the level of the SIP Station TCP Port Throttle Threshold to 750 kbps. To make this change from Cisco Unified CM Administration, navigate to **System > Service Parameters**, and select the Cisco CallManager service.

Unified Communications Configuration on Expressways

Before configuring a Cisco MRA solution, make sure certain settings are already configured within the Collaboration environment. All endpoints being used with the MRA solution need to be running a version of software that supports this feature. Cisco Jabber 9.7 or later must be used. Starting with this version, Cisco Collaboration Mobile and Remote Access functionality is enabled by default, and the client can identify that it must connect through the Cisco Expressway Edge when there is no response to the _cisco-uds._tcp.*<domain>* DNS SRV record lookup request. Administrators should also ensure that the local DNS and public DNS servers are configured with the required SRV records for MRA functionality. The _cisco-uds._tcp.*<domain>* and _cuplogin._tcp.*<domain>* SRV records must not be resolvable from outside the internal network. The Cisco Expressway-C and Cisco Expressway-E should be configured with initial configurations, such as system name, DNS, and NTP at a minimum. The Cisco Unified CM should be configured to allow registrations from Cisco Jabber clients.

Most of the configuration steps to deploy an MRA solution are performed on the Cisco Expressway Core and Cisco Expressway Edge servers. The Unified CM Tomcat certificate that must be installed on the Cisco Expressway Core must be obtained from the Unified CM server or servers. These certificates are required only if MTLS is being used between the Expressway Core and the Unified CM. The following is an overview of the steps to configure MRA on the Expressway servers:

Step 1. Enable MRA on both Cisco Expressways (Core and Edge).

Step 2. Configure MRA on the Cisco Expressway Core.

    a. Configure a SIP domain to route registrations to the Unified CM.

    b. Install the Unified CM Tomcat certificate (if TLS Verify is being used).

    c. Discover the Unified CM from the Expressway Core.

Step 3. Configure a secure Traversal Zone connection between the Cisco Expressway Edge and the Cisco Expressway Core.

    a. Generate a CSR on both Expressways.

    b. Sign both CSRs.

    c. Install the signed CA and root CA on each respective Cisco Expressway (Core and Edge).

    d. Configure a Unified Communications Traversal (Server) Zone on the Expressway Edge.

    e. Configure a Unified Communications Traversal (Client) Zone on the Expressway Core.

To enable the Cisco Collaboration Mobile and Remote Access on the Expressway-C, navigate to **Configuration > Unified Communications > Configuration**. Change the Unified Communications Mode to Mobile and Remote Access. All other settings can be left at their defaults. Click Save when finished. On the Expressway-E, the menu path is the same to enable MRA, but the menu options are slightly different. Change the Unified

Communications Mode to Mobile and Remote Access and leave all other settings at their defaults. Figure 14-6 illustrates some of the settings available when MRA is enabled on the Expressway-C. Figure 14-7 illustrates the settings available when MRA is enabled on the Expressway-E. Use these figures to compare and contrast the differences between the settings.

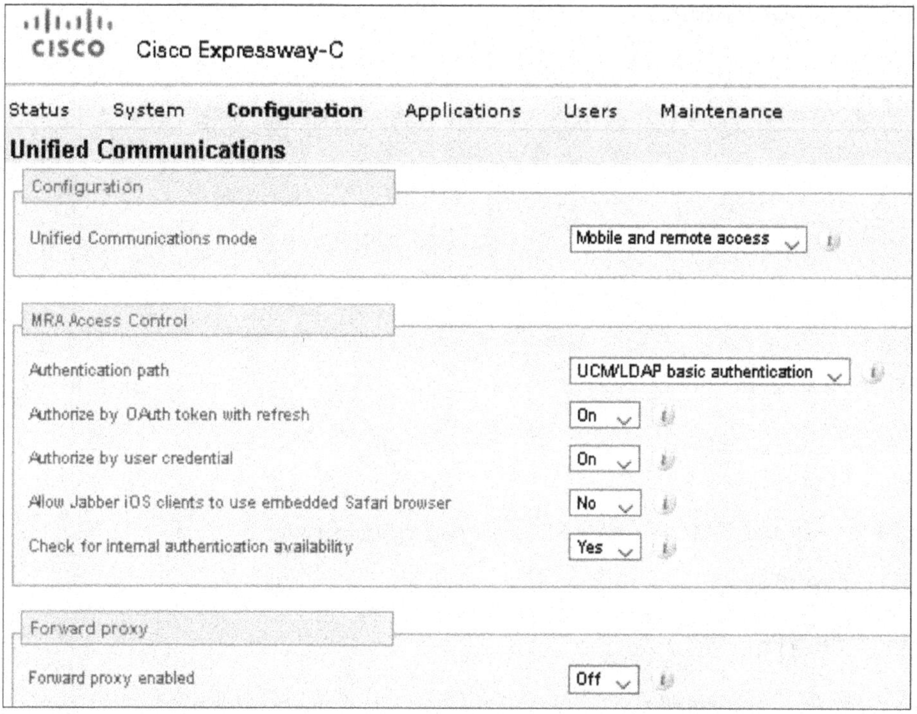

Figure 14-6 *Settings Used to Enable MRA on the Expressway-C*

No more MRA-specific settings have to be configured on the Expressway-E. However, several settings need to be configured on the Expressway-C. First, navigate to **Configuration > Domains**. If a domain was configured previously, you can click that domain to edit the settings. If not, you need to create a new domain by clicking the New button. When MRA is not in use, there is only one field to configure in the Domains menu, which is the domain itself. When MRA is enabled, several settings need to be configured. First, configure the domain in the Domain Name field. In the next section, you need to enable all the services for this domain that will need to be supported using MRA. The options include SIP Registrations and Provisioning on Expressway, SIP Registrations and Provisioning on Unified CM, IM and Presence Service, and XMPP Federation. Figure 14-8 illustrates the DNS settings related to MRA on the Expressway-C.

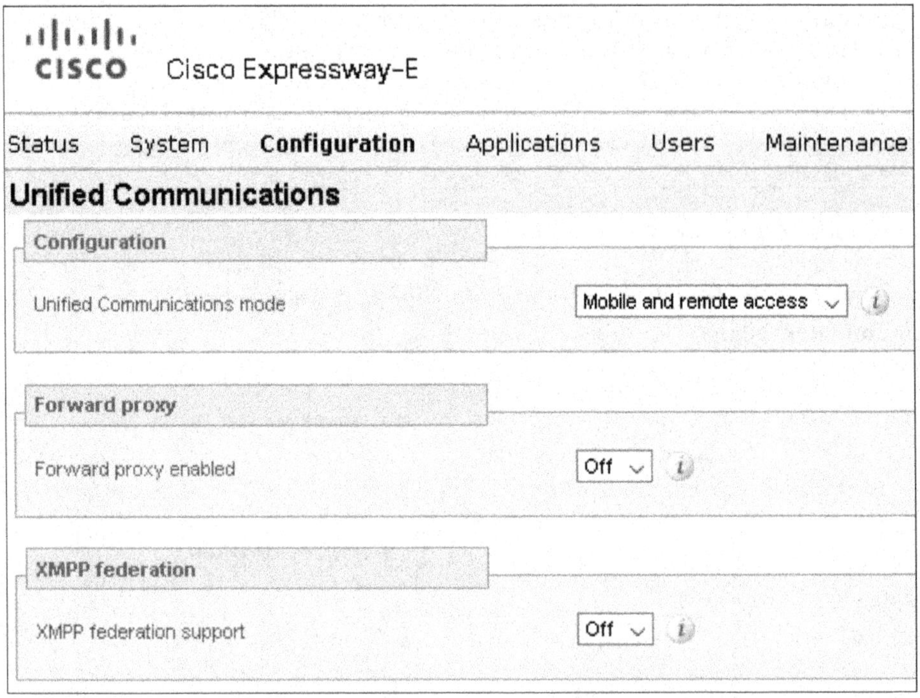

Figure 14-7   *Settings Used to Enable MRA on the Expressway-E*

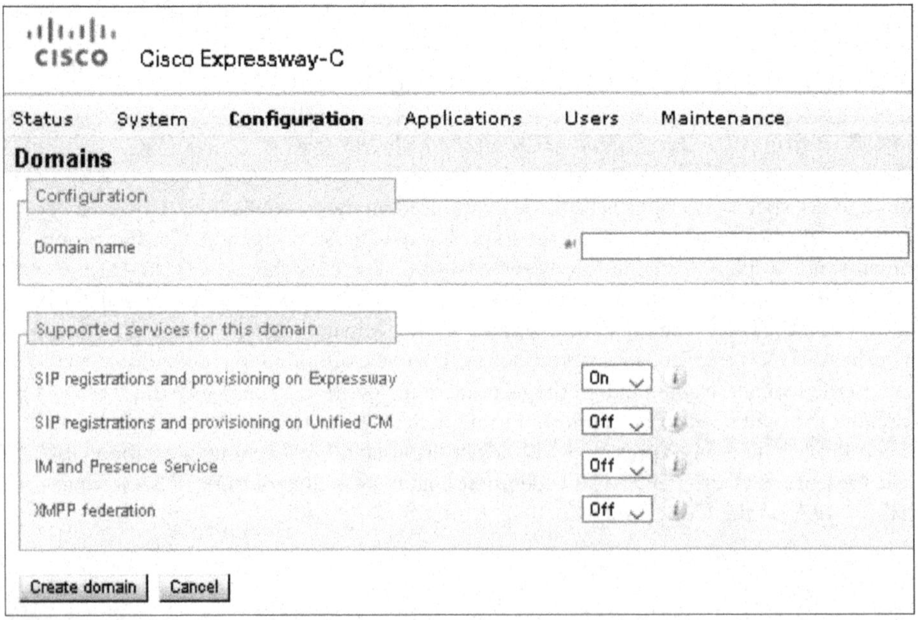

Figure 14-8   *DNS Settings on the Expressway-C for MRA*

Before adding any servers to the Expressway-C, such as the Unified CM, you need to add the Tomcat certificate. You need to add this certificate only if TLS Verify is being used for communication between the Unified CM and the Expressway-C. Navigate to **Maintenance > Security > Trusted CA Certificate**. Under the Upload section, click Browse and select the Tomcat certificate that's intended for this server. Click Open to return to the Trusted CA Certificate page and click the Append CA Certificate button to load the certificates. Check the list of certificates to ensure the Tomcat certificate was uploaded successfully.

Now the Unified CM can be discovered by the Expressway-C. Navigate to **Configuration > Unified Communications > Unified CM Servers.** Click the Add button and enter the following parameters:

- If TLS Verify is being used, the Unified CM Publisher Address must be the URL of the Unified CM publisher. If TLS Verify is not being used, this address can be the URL or the IP address of the Unified CM Publisher.

- The Username and Password settings should correspond to the AXL application user credentials created on the Unified CM.

- Verify TLS Verify Mode is set to On if TLS Verify is being used. If not, change this setting to Off.

- When these settings are saved, the Expressway-C will automatically create a Neighbor Zone to the Unified CM. The last setting on this page is the AES GCM Support setting. If it is enabled, the Neighbor Zone generated for the Unified CM will support AES GCM algorithms to encrypt and decrypt media passing through the zone. The default is Off but can be switched to On depending on how the Unified CM is configured to handle media encryption.

When finished, click the Add Address button. This returns you to the Unified CM Servers page. In the Currently Found Unified CM Nodes section, verify that the discovery status is displayed as Active. Figure 14-9 illustrates the settings that need to be configured when adding a Unified CM to the Expressway-C for discovery.

You can navigate to **Configuration > Zones > Zones** and verify that the Neighbor Zone to the Unified CM has been created. Clicking into this zone will display all the settings, but they will be grayed out and cannot be changed. There is also a search rule associated with this zone that was automatically created. Navigate to **Configuration > Dial Plan > Search Rules** to verify this rule exists. These settings will also be grayed out. The Unified CM IM and Presence Service and Cisco Unity Connections servers can also be discovered by the Expressway-C if these servers are being used. However, be aware that the status will not show Active on these until the Traversal Zones are configured and active. Navigate to **Configuration > Unified Communications > IM and Presence Service Nodes** or **Configuration > Unified Communications > Unity Connection Servers** to configure the discovery settings for these servers in the same manner as the Unified CM.

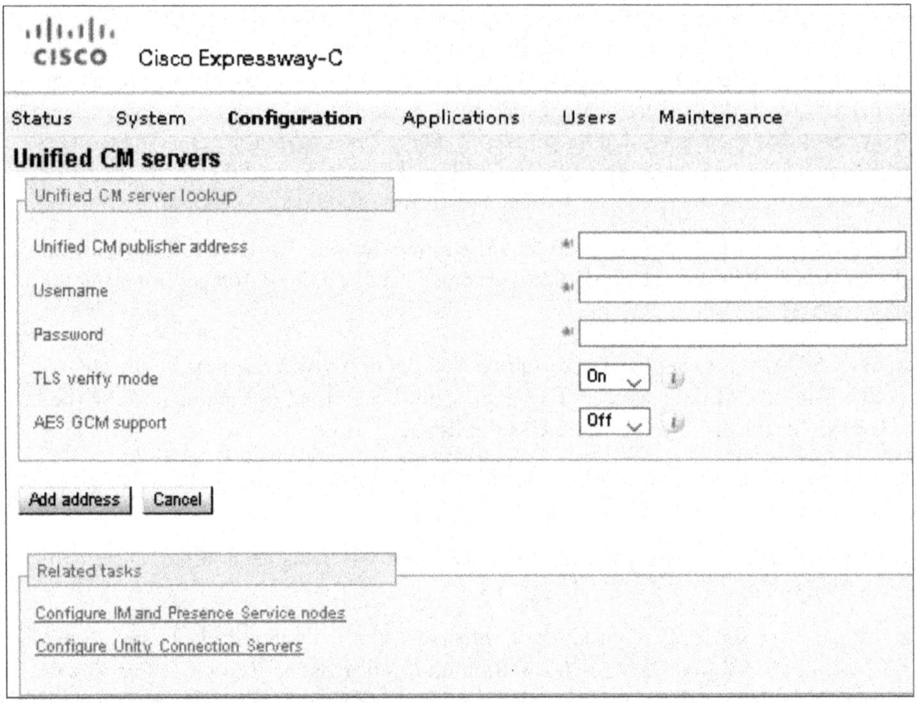

Figure 14-9 *Unified CM Discovery Settings in the Expressway-C*

HTTP Allow List

Cisco MRA uses a firewall traversal connection to allow inbound and outbound-initiated packet exchange, such as registration and call setup messages. MRA uses the Cisco Expressway Edge as the traversal server that is installed in a demilitarized zone (DMZ), and the Expressway Core is the traversal client that is installed on the internal network. Firewall traversal offers secure communication across firewalls as follows:

1. The Cisco Expressway-C initiates an outbound traversal connection through the internal firewall to specific ports on the Cisco Expressway-E with secure authentication credentials to establish a connection between the two servers.

2. Once the connection has been established, the Expressway-C sends keep-alive packets periodically to the Expressway-E to maintain the connection.

3. When the Expressway-E receives an incoming message, whether it's a registration or call setup message, from an outside endpoint, it sends the request to the Expressway-C through the existing traversal connection.

4. The Expressway-C then sends the message, such as a call setup request, to the Unified CM.

5. The Unified CM processes the call, and media streams are set up over the same existing traversal connection.

Key Topic

For communication to flow through the firewall, appropriate ports must be opened to allow the flow of packets. The following ports must be opened on the internal firewall between the Expressway Core and the Expressway Edge:

- SIP: TCP 7001

- Traversal Media: UDP 36000 to 36001 (for small to medium VM deployments)

- Extensible Messaging and Presence Protocol (XMPP): TCP 7400

- HTTPS (Tunneled over Secure Shell [SSH] between Expressway-C and Expressway-E): TCP 2222

The following ports must be opened on the external firewall between the public Internet and the Cisco Expressway Edge in the DMZ:

- SIP: TCP 5061

- HTTPS: TCP 8443

- XMPP: TCP 5222

- TURN Server Control and Media: UDP 36012 to 59999 (if TURN relays are being used only)

The firewall administrator should open all of the ports from the preceding lists before Traversal Zones are set up between the Expressway-C and the Expressway-E. Certificates must also be set up before Traversal Zones are created. Whether firewall ports are opened or certificates are established first doesn't matter as long as both tasks are competed before configuring the Traversal Zones.

The Cisco MRA reverse proxy settings provide a mechanism to support visual voicemail access, contact photo retrieval, Cisco Jabber custom tabs, and other data applications. **HTTPS reverse proxy** is a function that is provided by the Cisco Expressway-E using port TCP 8443 for HTTPS traffic. Initial MRA configuration allows inbound authenticated HTTPS requests to the following destinations:

- TCP 6970 (TFTP file download) and TCP 8443 (SOAP API) to all discovered Unified CM nodes

- TCP 7400 (XCP router) and TCP 8443 (SOAP API) to all Unified CM IM and Presence nodes

Additional hosts can be added to the HTTP allow list on the Cisco Expressway-C. The HTTP allow list is a type of access list for HTTP services. The Expressway-C adds both inbound and outbound rules automatically. For example, the Expressway adds inbound rules automatically that allow external clients to access the Unified Communications nodes that were discovered during MRA configuration. These include Unified CM nodes (running CallManager and TFTP service), IM and Presence Service nodes, and Cisco Unity Connection nodes.

However, in some cases, you may need to edit the inbound rules to allow certain types of access. You cannot edit outbound rules. To view inbound rules from the web interface of the Expressway-C, navigate to **Configuration > Unified Communications > HTTP Allow List >**

14

Automatic Inbound Rules. To view outbound rules, go to **Configuration > Unified Communications > HTTP Allow List > Automatic Outbound Rules.**

You can add your own inbound rules to the HTTP allow list if remote clients need to access other web services inside the enterprise. For example, the following services may require you to configure the allow list:

- Jabber Update Server

- Cisco Extension Mobility

- Directory Photo Host

- Managed File Transfer

- Problem Report Tool server

- Visual Voicemail

You cannot add outbound rules to the HTTP allow list. In addition, you can't edit or delete auto-added rules in the list. For the Managed File Transfer feature to work across Expressway, make sure that all Unified CM IM and Presence Service nodes appear on the allow list, whether manually or automatically added. Expressway automatically edits the HTTP allow list when you discover or refresh Unified Communications nodes. This page shows the discovered nodes and the rules that apply to those nodes. The first list is Discovered nodes and contains all the nodes currently known to this Expressway-C. For each node, the list contains the node's address, its type, and the address of its publisher. The second list is the rules that have been added for you to control client access to the different types of Unified Communications nodes. For each type of node in your MRA configuration, you'll see one or more rules in this list. They are shown in the same format as the editable rules, but you cannot modify these rules. Table 14-6 identifies the properties of automatically added allow list rules.

Key Topic

Table 14-6   Properties of Automatically Added Allow List Rules

Property	Description
Type	This rule affects all nodes of the listed type: ■ Cisco Unified CM servers ■ IM and Presence Service nodes ■ Unity Connection servers ■ TFTP nodes
Protocol	The protocol on which the rule allows clients to communicate with these types of nodes.
Ports	The ports on which the rule allows clients to communicate with these types of nodes.
Match Type	Exact or Prefix. Depends on the nature of the service the clients access with the help of this rule.
Path	The path to the resource that clients access with the help of this rule. This may not be present or may only be a partial match of the actual resource, if the rule allows Prefix match.
Methods	The HTTP methods that will be allowed through by this rule (such as GET).

The following steps outline how to edit HTTP allow list rules:

Step 1.   From the web interface of the Expressway-C, navigate to **Configuration > Unified Communications > HTTP Allow List > Editable Inbound Rules** to view, create, modify, or delete HTTP allow list rules.

The page has two areas: one for controlling the default HTTP methods, and the other showing the editable rules.

Step 2.   (Optional) Use the check boxes to modify the set of default HTTP methods, then click **Save**.

You can override the defaults while you're editing individual rules. If you want to be as secure as possible, clear all methods from the default set and specify methods on a per-rule basis. When you change the default methods, all rules that you previously created with the default methods will use the new defaults.

Step 3.   It is recommended that you delete any rules you don't need by checking the boxes in the left column, then clicking **Delete**.

Step 4.   Click **New** to create a rule.

Step 5.   Configure the rule to your requirements.

Table 14-7 identifies properties of manually added HTTP allow list rules, with some advice for each of the fields.

Table 14-7   Properties of Manually Added Allow List Rules

Field	Description
URL	Specify a URL that MRA clients are allowed to access. For example, to allow access to http://www.example.com:8080/resource/path, just type it in exactly like that.
	The protocol the clients are using to access the host must be http:// or https://.
	Specify a port when using a non-default port; e.g., :8080. Default ports are 80 (HTTP) and 443 (HTTPS).
	Specify the path to limit the rule scope (more secure); e.g., /resource/path.
	If you select Prefix Match for this rule (in the Match Type field), you can use a partial path or omit the path. Be aware that this could be a security risk if the target resources are not resilient to malformed URLs.
Allowed Methods	Select Use Defaults or Choose Methods.
	If you choose specific HTTP methods for this rule, they will override the defaults you chose for all rules.
Match Type	Select Exact Match or Prefix Match.
	Your decision here depends on your environment. It is more secure to use exact matches, but you may need more rules. It is more convenient to use prefix matches, but there is some risk of unintentionally exposing server resources.
Deployment	If you are using multiple deployments for your MRA environment, you also need to choose which deployment uses the new rule. You won't see this field unless you have more than one deployment.

Key Topic

14

Step 6. Click **Create Entry** to save the rule and return to the editable allow list.

Step 7. (Optional) Click **View/Edit** to change the rule.

In addition to automatically created rules and manually created rules, there is also a way to upload rules to the HTTP allow list. However, you cannot upload outbound rules. Follow these steps to upload rules to the HTTP allow list:

Step 1. Navigate to **Configuration > Unified Communications > HTTP Allow List > Upload Rules.**

Step 2. Browse to and select the CSV file containing your rule definitions.

Step 3. Click **Upload.** The Expressway responds with a success message and displays the Editable Inbound Rules page.

Unified Communications Traversal Zones

After you have configured the MRA settings and exchanged the certificates, the next step is to create Traversal Zones between the Expressway servers. Traversal Zones should always be configured on the Traversal Server first, in this case the Cisco Expressway-E. As mentioned before, you will need to use a different type of Traversal Zone from the types used for a basic firewall traversal connection. The type you must use for MRA is called Unified Communications Traversal. The **Unified Communications Traversal Zones** cannot be used with the **Traversal Chaining** deployment method discussed in Chapter 10, "Multisite and Business to Business (B2B) Collaboration Solutions."

Step 1. Configure the Unified Communications Traversal Zone on the Expressway E.

    a. On the web interface of the Expressway-E, navigate to **Configuration > Authentication > Local Database** and create new authentication credentials.

    b. Navigate to **Configuration > Zones > Zones** and add a new zone. Because this zone is specifically for MRA, the zone Type should be set to **Unified Communications Traversal.**

    c. In the Username field, supply the username from the authentication database. Notice that no H.323 settings are available under this zone type. The reason is that H.323 is not supported using MRA. If H.323 calls are to be supported, another Traversal Zone must be established using the standard Traversal Zone setup outlined in Chapter 10.

To enable Unified Communications Services on this Traversal Zone, the SIP settings must use TLS with TLS Verify Mode enabled, and Media Encryption Mode must be set to Force Encrypted. All of these settings default to the aforementioned parameters, and should not be changed. Therefore, these settings will not appear in the Unified Communications Traversal Zone settings page.

    d. Supply the SIP TLS Verify Subject Name. The Subject Name must match the subject name, or the alternative subject name specified in the Cisco Expressway Core server security certificate. This is the Common Name you should have noted from the CSR of the Expressway Core. If you did not write it down, it is the full URL of the Expressway Core.

e.   Set the Accept Proxied Registrations setting to **Allow**.

f.   Set the Authentication Policy to **Treat as Authenticated**.

g.   Click **Create Zone** when finished.

Step 2.   To route calls from the Expressway Edge to the Expressway Core through this Traversal Server Zone, you need to configure a search rule as well.

a.   Navigate to **Configuration > Dial Plan > Search Rules**.

b.   Click **New**, configure the settings, and then click **Create Search Rule**. Figure 14-10 illustrates some of the Unified Communications Traversal Zone settings on the Expressway-E.

Configuration	
Name	* Exp-C for MRA (i)
Type	Unified Communications traversal
Hop count	* 15 (i)

Connection credentials	
Username	* cisco (i)
Password	Add/Edit local authentication database

SIP	
Port	* 7001 (i)
TLS verify subject name	* vcsc.dcloud.cisco.com
Accept proxied registrations	Allow ⌄ (i)

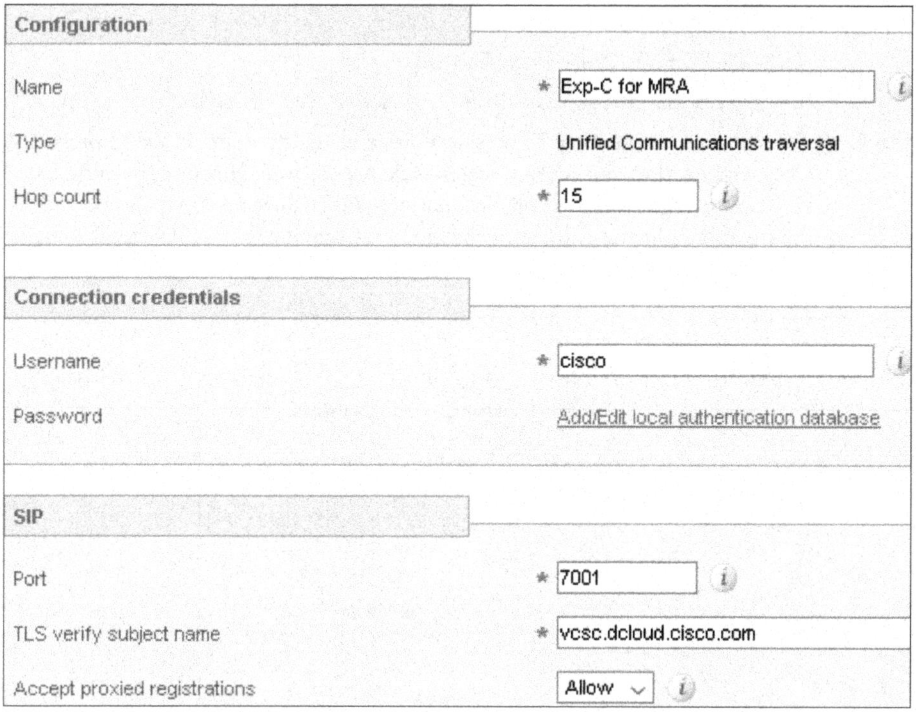

Figure 14-10   *Unified Communications Traversal Zone Settings on the Expressway-E*

Once you've configured the Expressway Edge with the appropriate zone, you can configure the Cisco Expressway-C with a zone to initiate communication between the two servers.

Step 3.   Configure the Unified Communications Traversal Zone on the Expressway Core.

a.   On the Expressway-C, navigate to **Configuration > Zones > Zones** and add a new zone. Again, because this zone is specifically for MRA, you should set Zone Type to **Unified Communications Traversal**.

b.   In the Username and Password fields, supply the username and password that were configured in the Authentication database on the Expressway-E.

c.   In the Port field, enter the port that will be used to establish a connection and keep the connection alive. This port needs to match the SIP keep-alive port that was configured on the Expressway Edge.

d.   Set the Accept Proxied Registrations setting to **Allow**.

e.   Set the Authentication Policy setting to **Treat As Authenticated**.

f.   In the Peer 1 Address field, enter the URL of the Expressway Edge.

Because TLS Verify is being used, this setting must be in the URL format. It must also match the Common Name you should have noted from the CSR of the Expressway Edge. If the IP address of the Expressway-E is used, communication will fail between the Traversal Zones on the Expressway-C and the Expressway-E.

g.   Click **Create Zone** when finished.

h.   Verify that the state of the zone is Active after saving the zone settings.

Step 4.   To route calls through the Expressway Edge using this zone on the Expressway Core, you need to configure a Search Rule here as well. However, because calls may be routed to any possible destination, you can use an Any Alias rule. Figure 14-11 illustrates some of the Unified Communications Traversal Zone settings on the Expressway-C.

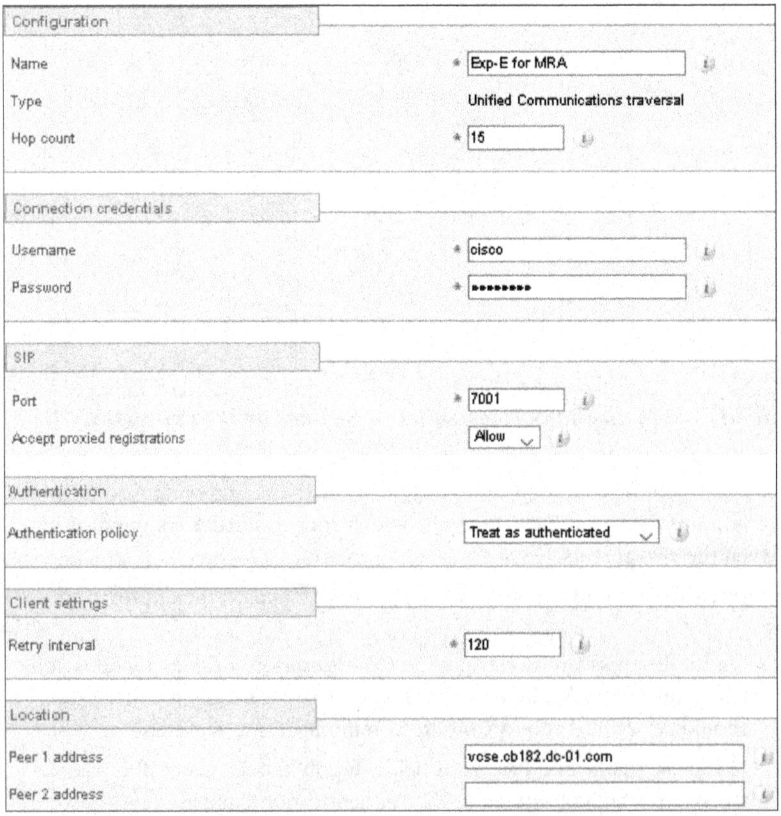

Figure 14-11   *Unified Communications Traversal Zone Settings on the Expressway-C*

The MRA deployment is now complete. You can test these settings by trying to register endpoints located both inside the enterprise network and outside the network. If the zones created will support calls as well, test the deployment by trying to place a few calls. Try calling between an internally registered endpoint and an externally registered endpoint. Then try calling between an internally registered endpoint and an endpoint located in another business network. Also, try calling between an externally registered endpoint and an endpoint located in another business network. You should try all call attempts from both directions: initiated from inside out, and initiated from outside in.

Exam Preparation Tasks

As mentioned in the section "How to Use This Book" in the Introduction, you have a couple of choices for exam preparation: the exercises here, Chapter 22, "Final Preparation," and the exam simulation questions in the Pearson Test Prep practice test software.

Review All Key Topics

Review the most important topics in this chapter, noted with the Key Topics icon in the outer margin of the page. Table 14-8 lists a reference of these key topics and the page numbers on which each is found.

Table 14-8   Key Topics for Chapter 14

Key Topic Element	Description	Page Number
Table 14-2	Public DNS SRV records for Expressway-E cluster	252
Table 14-3	Private DNS SRV records for Unified CM and Unified CM IMP clusters	253
Table 14-4	Certificate pairs used in an MRA deployment	255
Table 14-5	Classes of certificates on Cisco Collaboration servers	258
Paragraph	Pre-populated fields in a CSR on Expressway	262
Step 2-f (Certificates: Creating Certificates for MRA)	DER and Base64-encoded certificate formats	264
Step 2-g (Certificates: Creating Certificates for MRA)	Root CA certificate	264
Paragraph	Certificate considerations for Expressway-E	265
Paragraph	AXL API user needed on Unified CM for MRA	266
Paragraph	Tomcat certificate requirements for MRA	270
Paragraph	Additional settings on the Expressway-C for MRA	273
Two lists	Expressway-C and Expressway-E ports used for MRA firewall traversal	275
Table 14-6	Properties of automatically added allow list rules	276
Table 14-7	Properties of manually added allow list rules	277

Complete Tables and Lists from Memory

Print a copy of Appendix C, "Memory Tables" (found on the companion website), or at least the section for this chapter, and complete the tables and lists from memory. Appendix D, "Memory Tables Answer Key," also on the companion website, includes completed tables and lists to check your work.

Define Key Terms

Define the following key terms from this chapter and check your answers in the glossary:

A record, Active Directory Certificate Service (ADCS), asymmetric cryptography, Base64-encoded format, certificate authority (CA), certificate signing request (CSR), Diffie-Hellman key exchange, Distinguished Encoding Rules (DER)-encoded format, Domain Name Service (DNS), Domain Validation (DV) Certificate, Extended Validation (EV) Certificate, firewall, HTTPS reverse proxy, Mobile and Remote Access (MRA), Organization Validation (OV) Certificate, public key infrastructure (PKI), Rivest-Shamir-Adleman (RSA), root CA, root CA certificate, Secure Sockets Layer (SSL), Service (SRV) record, symmetric cryptography, TLS Verify, Transport Layer Security (TLS), Traversal Chaining, Traversal Client Zone, Traversal Server Zone, Traversal Zone, Unified Communications Traversal Zone

Q&A

The answers to these questions appear in Appendix A. For more practice with exam format questions, use the Pearson Test Prep practice test software.

1. List the six certificate types that can be used in an MRA deployment.

2. List the seven steps to configure the Cisco Unified CM for MRA preparation.

3. List three settings on the Expressway Core that must be configured after MRA is enabled.

CHAPTER 15

Troubleshoot an MRA Solution

This chapter covers the following topics:

MRA Troubleshooting General Techniques: Provides a litany of tools that can be used to identify issues with an MRA setup, and explains how to examine logging errors more closely when troubleshooting MRA issues.

Registration and Certificate Issues: Identifies common reasons endpoints cannot register over MRA and the cause of common certificate and TLS connectivity issues.

Cisco Jabber Sign-In Issues: Identifies the most common reasons the Cisco Jabber client cannot sign in over MRA.

Other Specific Issues: Describes several other common issues that can occur when setting up an MRA solution, as well as common error codes engineers could encounter.

Each of the components outlined in Chapter 14, "Configure an MRA Solution," that must be configured when deploying a Mobile and Remote Access (MRA) solution could also cause issues if not set up correctly. This chapter systematically walks you through how to identify and correct the most common issues encountered when deploying MRA.

This chapter covers the following objectives from the Implementing Cisco Collaboration Cloud and Edge Solutions (CLCEI) exam 300-820:

- 3.2.a Troubleshoot a Mobile and Remote Access (MRA) solution: DNS records (focus on Microsoft DNS)

- 3.2.b Troubleshoot a Mobile and Remote Access (MRA) solution: Certificates (focus on Microsoft CA, covers Unified Communications Manager, IM&P, Expressways, Unity Connection)

- 3.2.c Troubleshoot a Mobile and Remote Access (MRA) solution: Unified Communications traversal zones

- 3.2.d Troubleshoot a Mobile and Remote Access (MRA) solution: Unified Communications configuration on Expressway

- 3.2.e Troubleshoot a Mobile and Remote Access (MRA) solution: HTTP allow list

- 3.2.f Troubleshoot a Mobile and Remote Access (MRA) solution: SIP trunk security profile on Cisco Unified Communications Manager

"Do I Know This Already?" Quiz

The "Do I Know This Already?" quiz enables you to assess whether you should read this entire chapter thoroughly or jump to the "Exam Preparation Tasks" section. If you are in doubt about your answers to these questions or your own assessment of your knowledge of the topics, read the entire chapter. Table 15-1 lists the major headings in this chapter and their corresponding "Do I Know This Already?" quiz questions. You can find the answers in Appendix A, "Answers to the 'Do I Know This Already?' Quizzes and Review Questions."

Table 15-1 "Do I Know This Already?" Section-to-Question Mapping

Foundation Topics Section	Questions
MRA Troubleshooting General Techniques	1–3
Registration and Certificate Issues	4
Cisco Jabber Sign-In Issues	5
Other Specific Issues	6

CAUTION The goal of self-assessment is to gauge your mastery of the topics in this chapter. If you do not know the answer to a question or are only partially sure of the answer, you should mark that question as wrong for purposes of the self-assessment. Giving yourself credit for an answer you correctly guess skews your self-assessment results and might provide you with a false sense of security.

1. An engineer built an MRA solution but was receiving invalid services errors. Which of the following steps should the engineer take to resolve these errors?

   a. Check that the traversal zones are active.

   b. Restart the Expressway-C and Expressway-E servers.

   c. Check the connection from the Expressway-C to the Cisco Unified CM is active.

   d. Check that the certificates are valid.

2. How can an engineer access the Collaboration Solutions Analyzer tools?

   a. From the Expressway-C, navigate to Maintenance > Tools > CSA.

   b. From the Expressway-E, navigate to Maintenance > Tools > CSA.

   c. From the Expressway-C or the Expressway-E, navigate to Maintenance > Tools > CSA.

   d. From the Cisco Unified Serviceability portal on the Cisco Unified CM, navigate to Tools > CSA.

   e. CSA is a tool set provided by TAC.

3. Which three of the following logging levels should be set to Debug before starting the diagnostics log on the Expressway to troubleshoot MRA? (Choose three.)

   a. developer.edgeconfigprovisioning

   b. developer.edgemanager

   c. developer.edgemanager.conn

   d. developer.edgemanager.domaindata

   e. developer.trafficserver

   f. developer.xcp

   g. developer.framework.applicationobjectcontroller

   h. developer.xmlapi.cdr

4. A Cisco Unified CM in an existing customer environment has already been deployed with an Expressway-C and Expressway-E, so that B2B calls can be placed through the network over IP. The customer wanted to deploy MRA for new remote workers, but when the engineer set up the solution, communication between the Expressway-C and the Unified CM failed. Which of the following could the engineer do to resolve the situation?

   a. Create a new SIP Trunk Security Profile for the SIP trunk to the Expressway-C that uses a different listening port than 5060 or 5061.

   b. Verify that the Expressway-C and Expressway-E have an active traversal zone between them, and that TLS Verify is used to secure communications between those two zones.

   c. Verify that the SIP trunk from the Unified CM to the Expressway-C and the Neighbor Zone from the Expressway-C to the Unified CM are configured to use TLS Verify.

   d. Verify that the SIP Trunk Security Profile on the Unified CM and the listening port on the Expressway-C are configured to use either 5060 or 5061.

5. An engineer set up an MRA solution, but when he tested the settings with a Jabber client, the client did not register for any phone services. Which of the following is the likely cause of this issue?

   a. This is a symptom of an incorrectly configured server certificate on the Cisco Expressway-E.

   b. This can occur if the Cisco Expressway-E DNS host name contains underscore characters.

   c. This can occur when there is inconsistency of the DNS domain name between Cisco Expressway-E peers in a cluster.

   d. There is a case-handling mismatch between the Cisco Expressway and the User Data Service.

6. Which of the following error codes would you see on the Expressway-E if an MRA connection failed due to exceeding the hop count to the next node?

   a. 403

   b. 407

   c. 502

   d. 500

   e. 401

Foundation Topics

MRA Troubleshooting General Techniques

There are many tools that can be used to troubleshoot issues in a Mobile and Remote Access (MRA) deployment solution. This section will walk you through a troubleshooting process using many of these different tools.

When troubleshooting, first check whether any alarms have been raised. On the Cisco Expressway Core and Edge servers, you can access the Alarm menu by navigating to **Status > Alarms.** If alarms exist, follow the instructions in the Action column to try and resolve the issue. Check the alarms on both the Cisco Expressway-C and Cisco Expressway-E.

Next, review the status summary and configuration information. Navigate to **Status > Unified Communications Status** and check the status on both the Expressway-C and Expressway-E. If any required configuration is missing or invalid, an error message and a link to the relevant configuration page are shown. Figure 15-1 illustrates some of the information that you can find on the Unified Communications Status page of an Expressway-C.

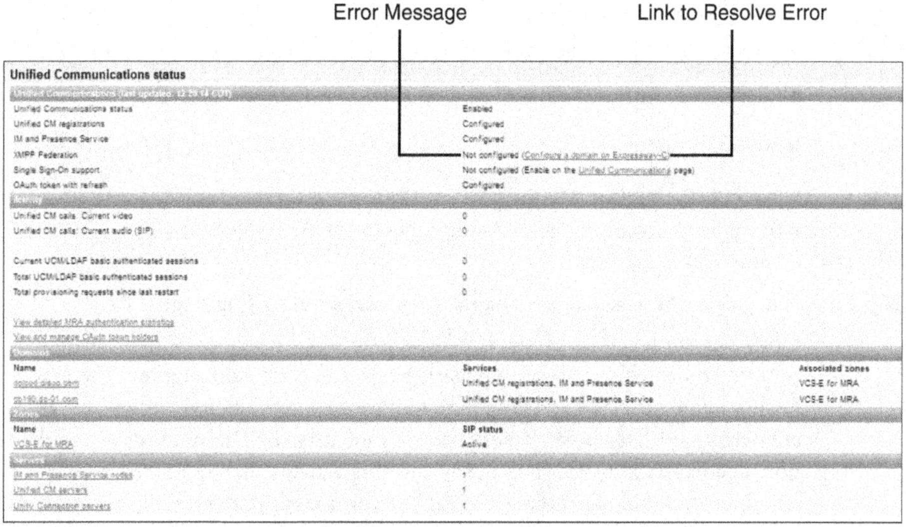

15

Error Message   Link to Resolve Error

Status > Unified Communications Status

Figure 15-1 *Unified Communications Status Page on Expressway-C*

You might see invalid services errors if you changed any of the following items on the Cisco Expressway. A system restart is required to be sure the configuration changes take effect.

Key Topic

■ Server or CA certificates

■ DNS configuration

■ Domain configuration

The **Collaboration Solutions Analyzer (CSA)** is a tool set provided by Cisco TAC. It can be used to help with deploying and troubleshooting MRA. The Cisco Expressway release notes provide instructions on how to access the CSA. This tool set is composed of a validator tool and a **log analysis tool**. The **CollabEdge validator tool** should be used first to validate your MRA deployment. It simulates a Jabber client sign-in process and provides feedback on the result. If the CollabEdge validator cannot identify the issue, Cisco suggests that you collect logs from the Cisco Expressway while attempting to sign in. Then use the log analysis tool in the CSA to analyze the logs.

Two different diagnostic logs can be used to troubleshoot MRA issues: one is available on the computer hosting the Cisco Jabber client and the other is activated from the Expressway Core or Edge server. You can access the Jabber for Windows Diagnostic Logs file in the C:\Users\<*UserID*>\AppData\Local\Cisco\Unified Communications\JabberCSF\Logs folder. The file is listed as csf-unified.log.

The diagnostic logging tool in the Cisco Expressway can be used to assist in troubleshooting system issues. It allows you to generate a diagnostic log of system activity over a period of time, and then to download the log. Before generating a diagnostic log, you must configure the log level of the relevant logging modules for MRA related services.

Step 1. To configure the diagnostic log level from the Expressway web interface, navigate to **Maintenance > Diagnostics > Advanced > Support Log configuration**. Select the following logs:

- developer.edgeconfigprovisioning

- developer.trafficserver

- developer.xcp

Step 2. Click **Set to Debug**.

After you configure the Expressway diagnostic log levels, you can start the diagnostic log capture.

Step 3. Navigate to **Maintenance > Diagnostics > Diagnostic Logging**.

Optionally, you can check the box beside the Take Tcpdump While Logging option. You can also enter some marker text and click **Add Marker**. The marker facility can be used to add comment text to the log file before certain activities are performed. This helps to subsequently identify the relevant sections in the downloaded diagnostic log file. You can add as many markers as required, at any time while the diagnostic logging is in progress. Marker text is added to the log with a **"DEBUG_MARKER"** tag.

Step 4. Click **Start New Log**.

Step 5. Reproduce the system issue you want to trace in the diagnostic log.

Step 6. Click **Stop Logging**.

Step 7. Click **Collect Log**.

Step 8. When the log collection completes, click **Download Log** to save the diagnostic log archive to your local file system.

Step 9. When prompted, you can save your log file or open it.

If you want to download the logs again, you can recollect them by clicking the **Collect Log** button. If the button is grayed out, try refreshing the page in your browser.

Step 10. After you have completed your diagnostic logging, return to the Support Log configuration page and reset the modified logging modules back to **INFO** level.

You can use the Cisco Expressway's DNS lookup tool to assist in troubleshooting system issues. From the web interface of the Expressway, navigate to **Maintenance > Tools > Network Utilities > DNS Lookup.** The SRV record lookup includes records specific to H.323, SIP, Unified Communications, and TURN services. Performing the DNS lookup from the Expressway-C returns the view from within the enterprise. Performing the DNS lookup on the Expressway-E returns what is visible from within the DMZ, which is not necessarily the same set of records available to endpoints in the public Internet. The DNS lookup includes the following SRV services that are used for Unified Communications:

`_collab-edge._tls`

`_cisco-uds._tcp`

Another troubleshooting technique for diagnosing MRA issues is to check that the Expressway-E is reachable. Ensure that the fully qualified domain name (FQDN) of the Expressway-E is resolvable in the public DNS. On the Expressway-E, the FQDN is configured at **System > DNS** and is designated as *<System host name>.<Domain name>.*

Call status information can be displayed for both current and completed calls. The same set of call status information is also shown on the Calls by Registration page. If the Cisco Expressway is part of a cluster, all calls that apply to any peer in the cluster are shown, although the list is limited to the most recent 500 calls per peer. If you want to get information about current calls, go to the Call Status page by navigating to **Status > Calls > Calls.** The Call Status page lists all the calls currently taking place to or from devices registered with the Expressway, or that are passing through the Expressway. If you want to get information about the completed calls, navigate to the Call History page via **Status > Calls > History.** The Call History page lists all the calls that are no longer active. The list is limited to the most recent 500 calls, and only includes calls that have taken place since the Expressway was last restarted.

The Call Status and Call History pages show all call types, including Unified CM remote sessions if MRA is enabled as well as Cisco Expressway Rich Media Session (RMS) sessions. To distinguish between the call types, you must drill down into the call components. MRA calls have different component characteristics depending on whether the call is being viewed on the Expressway-C or the Expressway-E:

- On the Expressway-C, a Unified CM remote session has three components, as it uses the back-to-back user agent (B2BUA) to enforce media encryption. One of the Expressway components routes the call through one of the automatically generated Neighbor Zones with a name prefixed by either CEtcp or CEtls between the Expressway and the Unified CM.

- On the Expressway-E, there is one component, which routes the call through the Unified Communications Traversal Zone.

If both endpoints are outside of the enterprise (that is, off premises), you will see this treated as two separate calls. If your system has an RMS key installed and thus supports

15

business-to-business calls, and interworked or gatewayed calls to third-party solutions and so on, those calls are also listed on the Call Status and Call History pages.

When devices are registered to the Unified CM via the Cisco Expressways using MRA, you can identify these devices as follows:

Step 1. From the Cisco Unified CM Administration web interface, navigate to **Device > Phone** and click **Find**.

Step 2. Check the IP Address column. Devices that are registered via the Expressway display the IP address of the Expressway-C they are registered through.

From the Expressway-C, you can use the following steps to identify sessions, otherwise known as proxy requests, that have been provisioned via the Expressway-C.

Step 3. From the web interface of the Expressway-C, navigate to **Status > Unified Communications Status**.

Step 4. In the Advanced Status Information section at the bottom of the page, click the link **View Sessions Authorized by User Credentials**. This shows a list of all current and recent provisioning sessions. Figure 15-2 illustrates how to access the proxy request page.

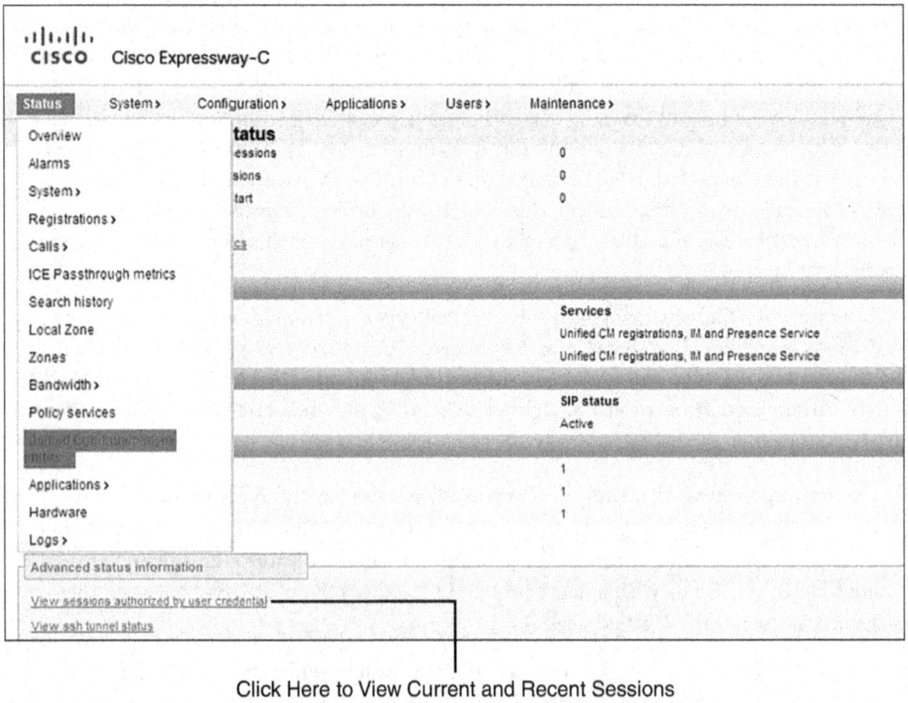

Click Here to View Current and Recent Sessions

Figure 15-2　*View Sessions from the Proxy Request Page on the Expressway-C*

Another troubleshooting technique for diagnosing MRA issues is to ensure that the Expressway-C is synchronized to the Unified CM. Changes to a Unified CM cluster or node configuration can lead to communication problems between the Unified CM and the Expressway-C. This includes changes to the following items:

Key Topic

- Number of nodes within a Unified CM cluster

- Host name or IP address of an existing node

- Listening port numbers

- Security parameters

- Phone security profiles

You must ensure that any such changes are reflected in the Cisco Expressway-C. To do this, navigate to **Configuration > Unified Communications** from the web interface of the Expressway. Rediscover all Unified CM and IM and Presence Service nodes.

The final troubleshooting technique for diagnosing MRA issues is to check the MRA authentication status and tokens. Check and clear standard OAuth user tokens from the web interface of the Expressway by navigating to **Users > OAuth Token Users**. This could help identify problems with a particular user's OAuth access. You can also check statistics for MRA authentication from the Expressway by navigating to **Status > Unified Communications > View Detailed MRA Authentication Statistics**. Any unexpected requests or responses on this page could help identify configuration or authorization issues.

Registration and Certificate Issues

Looking outside general techniques for troubleshooting MRA, the most common issues encountered with an MRA deployment pertain to registration or certificate issues. Endpoints may fail to register for various reasons. Endpoints may not be able to register to the Cisco Unified CM if there is also a SIP trunk configured between the Unified CM and the Cisco Expressway-C. If a SIP trunk is configured, you must ensure that it uses a different listening port on the Unified CM from that used for SIP line registrations to the Unified CM. Because no SIP trunk is required on the Unified CM to route calls through the Expressways for MRA-registered devices, the port used for these calls is 5060 or 5061, depending on whether TCP or TLS is used between the Unified CM and the Expressway Core. Endpoints registered to the Unified CM that are not using MRA may need to be routed through the Expressways as well. Therefore, a different port needs to be used to distinguish between these different endpoints. Note that the port used on the Unified CM in the SIP trunk that points to the Expressway core will always be 5060 or 5061. However, the Neighbor Zone on the Expressway Core should use a SIP port that matches the port identified in the SIP Trunk Security Profile on the Unified CM.

Secure registrations may fail if the server certificate on the Expressway-C does not contain in its Subject Alternate Name list the names of all of the phone security profiles in the Unified CM that are configured for encrypted TLS and are used for devices requiring remote access. The error message you will see with this issue is "Failed to establish SSL connection." Note that these names in both the Unified CM and in the Expressway's certificate must be in FQDN format.

15

It is essential to generate a certificate signing request (CSR) for the new node while adding a new Expressway-C node to an existing cluster of Expressway-Cs. It is mandated to put secure profile names as they are on the Unified CM, if secure registration of an MRA client is needed over MRA. CSR creation on the new node will fail if Unified CM phone security profile names are just names or host names on Unified CM device security profiles. This will force administrators to change the value of Unified CM Phone Security Profile Names on the Unified CM on the Secure Phone Profile page.

Starting with Expressway version X12.6, the Unified CM phone security profile name must be an FQDN. It cannot be just any name or host name or a value. Examples of acceptable Unified CM phone security profile names include jabbersecureprofile.domain.com and DX80SecureProfile.domain.com. The FQDN can be composed of multiple levels. Each level's name can contain only letters, digits, and hyphens, with each level separated by a period (dot). A level name cannot start or end with a hyphen, and the final level name must start with a letter.

Modifications to the Cisco Expressway's server certificate or trusted CA certificates require restarting the Expressway for the changes to take effect. If you are using secure profiles, ensure that the root CA of the authority that signed the Expressway-C certificate is installed as a CallManager-trust certificate by navigating to the **Security > Certificate Management** menu in the Cisco Unified OS Administration interface of the Unified CM.

If you are running version 9.x, or earlier, of the Unified CM or the IM and Presence Service, with Cisco Expressway version X8.7.2 or later, then the SSL handshake between the two systems will fail by default. The symptom is that all MRA endpoints fail to register or make calls after you upgrade to Cisco Expressway X8.7.2 or later. The cause of this issue is an upgrade of the CiscoSSL component to 5.4.3 or later. This version rejects the default 768-bit key provided by the Unified CM when using the Diffie-Hellman key exchange. You must either upgrade your infrastructure or consult Cisco TAC to check whether it is possible to modify the default configurations for the Unified CM or IM and Presence Service to support TLS. As always, the best solution is to upgrade to the latest version of the Unified CM and the Expressway.

Cisco Jabber Sign-In Issues

Although this section is specific to Jabber, remember that Cisco is phasing out Jabber and replacing it with the Webex client. However, all behavior, and therefore troubleshooting issues, is applicable regardless of which client you are using. Registration issues with the Cisco Jabber client are often very different than UC phone or Telepresence endpoint registration issues when proxied through the Expressways using MRA. First off, Jabber triggers automated intrusion protection when your MRA solution is configured for authorization by OAuth token with or without a refresh, when the Jabber user's access token has expired, or when Jabber does one of the following:

Key Topic

- Resumes from desktop hibernation

- Recovers a network connection

- Attempts fast login after it has been signed out for several hours

The result is that some Jabber clients will attempt to authorize at the Expressway-E using the expired access token. The Expressway-E will in turn correctly deny these requests. However, if there are more than five such requests from a particular Jabber client, the Expressway-E blocks that IP address for ten minutes by default. The affected Jabber client's IP address is added to the Expressway-E's Blocked Addresses list, in the HTTP Proxy Authorization Failure category. You can view this list by navigating to **System > Protection > Automated Detection > Blocked Addresses.**

There are two ways you can work around this issue. You can increase the detection threshold for that particular category, or you can create exemptions for the affected clients. We will describe the threshold option here because the exemptions may well be impractical in your environment.

Step 1.   From the web interface of the Expressway, navigate to **System > Protection > Automated detection > Configuration.**

Step 2.   Select **HTTP Proxy Authorization Failure** from the list.

Step 3.   Change the Trigger Level from 5 to **10**, which should be enough to tolerate the Jabber modules that present expired tokens.

Step 4.   Click **Save**, and the configuration changes will take effect immediately.

Step 5.   Under the Related Tasks section at the bottom of the page, click the **View Currently Blocked Addresses** link and unblock any affected clients. Figure 15-3 illustrates the HTTP proxy authorization failure menus on the Expressway-C.

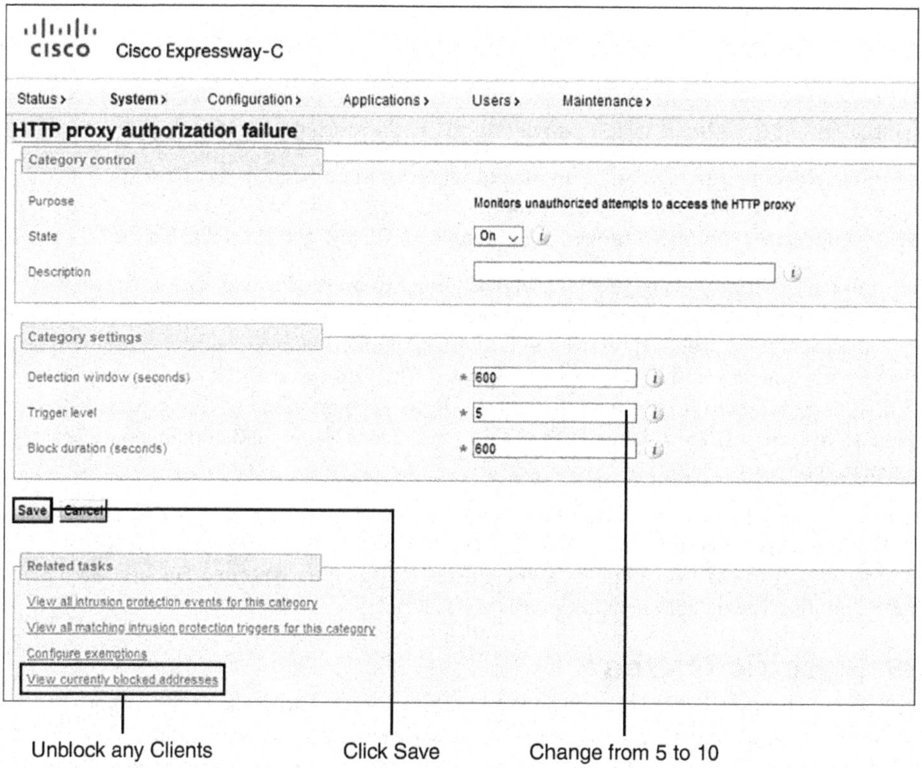

Figure 15-3   *HTTP Proxy Authorization Failure Menus on Expressway-C*

Another issue unique to Jabber that you might encounter with MRA is a Jabber popup window that warns about an invalid certificate when connecting from outside the network. This is a symptom of an incorrectly configured server certificate on the Expressway-E. The certificate could be self-signed, or it may not have the external DNS domain of your organization listed as a Subject Alternative Name (SAN). This is the expected behavior from Jabber. Cisco recommends that you install a certificate issued by a CA that Jabber trusts, and that the certificate has the domains Jabber is using included in its list of SANs.

When Jabber doesn't register for phone services, there is a case-handling mismatch between the Cisco Expressway and the **User Data Service (UDS)**. This mismatch prevents Jabber from registering for phone services if the supplied user ID does not match the case of the stored ID. In this case Jabber still signs in but cannot use phone services. Users can avoid this issue by signing in with the user ID exactly as it is stored in UDS. Users can recover from this issue by signing out and resetting Jabber.

Users might get the error "Cannot communicate with the server," which indicates that Jabber cannot sign in due to an XMPP bind failure. This will be indicated by resource bind errors in the Jabber client logs; for example:

```
XmppSDK.dll #0, 201, Recv:<iq id='uid:527a7fe7:00000cfe:00000000'
type='error'><bind

xmlns='urn:ietf:params:xml:ns:xmpp-bind'/><error code='409'
type='cancel'><conflict

xmlns='urn:ietf:params:xml:ns:xmpp-stanzas'/></error></iq>

XmppSDK.dll #0, CXmppClient::onResourceBindError

XmppSDK.dll #0, 39, CTriClient::HandleDisconnect, reason:16
```

This typically occurs if the IM and Presence Intercluster Sync Agent is not working correctly. Refer to the *Configuration and Administration of the IM and Presence Service* guide for information on fixing broken-agent issues on the IM and Presence Service.

Jabber can fail to sign in due to the SSH tunnels failing to be established. The Traversal Zone between the Expressway-C and Expressway-E will work normally in all other respects even when this issue occurs. The Expressway will report "Application failed – An unexpected software error was detected in portforwarding.pyc." This can occur if the Expressway-E DNS host name contains underscore characters. On the web interface of the Expressway-E, navigate to **System > DNS** and ensure that the System Host Name field contains only letters, digits, and hyphens.

Jabber sign-in failures have also occurred when there is inconsistency of the DNS domain name between Cisco Expressway-E peers in a cluster. The domain names must be identical, even with respect to case, on all peers in the cluster. Navigate to **System > DNS** on each peer to make sure that the domain name is identical on all peers.

Other Specific Issues

In addition to all the possible issues discussed in this chapter that could occur within an MRA deployment, there are some other issues and error codes to watch out for. A **401 Unauthorized** failure message can occur when the Cisco Expressway attempts to authenticate the credentials presented by the endpoint client. The reasons for this error may be due to the client supplying an unknown username or the wrong password. It could also be that the Cisco Intercluster Lookup Service (ILS) has not been set up on all of the Unified CM clusters. This may result in intermittent failures, depending upon which Unified CM node is being used by the Expressway for its UDS query to discover the client's home cluster.

You may see call failures due to a **407 Proxy Authentication Required** error message or a 500 Internal Server Error message. Call failures can occur if the Traversal Zones on the Expressway are configured with an Authentication Policy setting of Check Credentials. Ensure that the Authentication Policy setting on the Traversal Zones used for Mobile and Remote Access is set to Do Not Check Credentials.

If the call bit rate is restricted to 384 kbps, or video issues occur when using Binary Floor Control Protocol (BFCP) for presentation sharing, this can be caused by video bit rate restrictions within the regions configured on the Unified CM. Ensure that the Maximum Session Bit Rate for Video Calls setting between and within regions is set to a suitable upper limit for your system, such as 6000 kbps. You can check region information on the Unified CM by navigating to **System > Region Information > Region.**

Provisioning failures can occur when the IM and Presence Service realm has changed and the realm data on the Expressway-C has not been updated. For example, this could happen if the address of an IM and Presence Service node has changed, or if a new peer has been added to an IM and Presence Service cluster. The diagnostic log may contain an INFO message like "Failed to query auth component for SASL mechanisms" because the Expressway-C cannot find the realm. On the Expressway-C, navigate to **Configuration > Unified Communications > IM and Presence Service Nodes**, click Refresh Servers, and then save the updated configuration. If the provisioning failures persist, verify the IM and Presence Service node's configuration and refresh again.

If you get the error No Voicemail Service "403 Forbidden" response, then ensure that the Cisco Unity Connection (CUC) host name is included on the HTTP server allow list on the Expressway-C. A **403 Forbidden** response may also occur for any other service requests. These services may fail if the Expressway-C and Cisco Expressway-E are not synchronized to a reliable NTP server. Ensure that all Expressway systems are synchronized to a reliable NTP service.

When client HTTPS requests are dropped by the Cisco Expressway, this can be caused by the automated intrusion protection feature on the Expressway-E if it detects repeated invalid attempts, which are **404** errors, from a client IP address to access resources through the HTTP proxy. To prevent the client address from being blocked, ensure that the HTTP Proxy Resource Access Failure category is set to Off. You check this from the web interface of the Expressway by navigating to **System > Protection > Automated Detection > Configuration.** Figure 15-4 illustrates the Expressway menu for this setting.

A **502** message on the Cisco Expressway-E indicates that the next hop failed, which is typically to the Cisco Expressway-C. To identify what is causing this issue, navigate to the **Status > Unified Communications** page on the Cisco Expressway-E. Does the Cisco Expressway-E report any issues? If the status looks normal, click the SSH Tunnel Status link at the bottom of the Status page. If one (or more) of the tunnels to the Cisco Expressway-C node is down, that is probably causing the 502 error. MRA calls will also fail if the called endpoint is more than 15 hops away from the Expressway-E. The Unified Communications Traversal Zone has a default hop count of 15. If you suspect this is a contributing factor, sign in to all your MRA Expressways, raise the hop count to a significantly larger number, such as 70, and test registration or calls again.

Figure 15-4 *HTTP Proxy Resource Access Failure Setting*

Exam Preparation Tasks

As mentioned in the section "How to Use This Book" in the Introduction, you have a couple of choices for exam preparation: the exercises here, Chapter 22, "Final Preparation," and the exam simulation questions in the Pearson Test Prep practice test software.

Review All Key Topics

Review the most important topics in this chapter, noted with the Key Topics icon in the outer margin of the page. Table 15-2 lists a reference of these key topics and the page numbers on which each is found.

Table 15-2   Key Topics for Chapter 15

Key Topic Element	Description	Page Number
List	System restart for invalid services error with MRA	287
Paragraph	DNS lookup tool on the Expressway	289
List	Changes on Cisco Unified CM that can cause MRA failure	291
List	Reasons Jabber triggers automated intrusion protection	292

Complete Tables and Lists from Memory

There are no memory tables or lists for this chapter.

Define Key Terms

Define the following key terms from this chapter and check your answers in the glossary:

401 Unauthorized, 403 Forbidden, 404, 407 Proxy Authentication Required, 502, CollabEdge validator tool, Collaboration Solutions Analyzer (CSA), log analysis tool, User Data Service (UDS)

Q&A

The answers to these questions appear in Appendix A. For more practice with exam format questions, use the Pearson Test Prep practice test software.

1. List three settings that must be configured in an MRA deployment that require the Expressway to restart.

2. What two tools exist in the Collaboration Solutions Analyzer tool set?

3. List five setting changes on the Cisco Unified CM that can cause an MRA deployment to fail.

15

CHAPTER 16

Introduction to Cisco Cloud Collaboration

This chapter covers the following topics:

Cloud Collaboration Solutions: Provides an overview and understanding of Collaboration solutions, including Cisco Hosted Collaboration Solution (HCS), Cisco Webex, and Cisco Unified Communications Manager Cloud.

Cisco Webex Components: Explains the Webex components such as Meetings, Messaging, and Calling.

Cisco Webex Hybrid Services: Reviews the Webex Hybrid Services such as Hybrid Calendar Service, Hybrid Directory Service, Hybrid Call Service, Hybrid Message Service, Hybrid Security Service, and Video Mesh.

This chapter focuses on the Cisco cloud collaboration solutions that are mainly hosted in cloud environments along with the Webex components that can be additionally included. This chapter also focuses on the Webex Hybrid Services that provide integration or enhancement to the on-premises and cloud components.

This chapter covers the following objectives from the Implementing Cisco Collaboration Cloud and Edge Solutions (CLCEI) exam 300-820:

- 4.2.a Configure Webex Hybrid Services/Connector: Calendar Service (Office 365, Microsoft Exchange, One Button to Push)

- 4.2.b Configure Webex Hybrid Services/Connector: Message Service (Deployment requirements; Expressway requirements, certificates, CallManager prerequisites, IM&P prerequisites, deployment models)

- 4.2.c Configure Webex Hybrid Services/Connector: Directory Services (Deployment requirements; deployment models, infrastructure requirements, Active Directory configuration, synchronization, Webex user service assignment)

- 4.2.d Configure Webex Hybrid Services/Connector: Video Mesh (Deployment requirements including bandwidth, clustering, endpoint support, video call capacity, ports and protocols, deployment models)

"Do I Know This Already?" Quiz

The "Do I Know This Already?" quiz enables you to assess whether you should read this entire chapter thoroughly or jump to the "Exam Preparation Tasks" section. If you are in doubt about your answers to these questions or your own assessment of your knowledge of the topics, read the entire chapter. Table 16-1 lists the major headings in this chapter and their corresponding "Do I Know This Already?" quiz questions. You can find the answers in Appendix A, "Answers to the 'Do I Know This Already?' Quizzes and Review Questions."

Table 16-1 "Do I Know This Already?" Section-to-Question Mapping

Foundation Topics Section	Questions
Cloud Collaboration Solutions	1–2
Cisco Webex Components	3–4
Cisco Webex Hybrid Services	5–6

CAUTION The goal of self-assessment is to gauge your mastery of the topics in this chapter. If you do not know the answer to a question or are only partially sure of the answer, you should mark that question as wrong for purposes of the self-assessment. Giving yourself credit for an answer you correctly guess skews your self-assessment results and might provide you with a false sense of security.

1. The Cisco Hosted Collaboration Solution (HCS) is positioned with which stakeholder's cloud infrastructure?

   a. Cisco Cloud

   b. Partner cloud

   c. Customer cloud

   d. Public cloud

2. Cisco UCM Cloud supports multiple PSTN connectivity models. Which one of the following is not a supported model?

   a. Central (cloud) breakout

   b. Mixed mode

   c. Local breakout

   d. Fiber breakout

3. Which encryption standard does Webex Meetings utilize to secure its data?

   a. AES-256

   b. Triple DES

   c. RSA

   d. MD5

4. Cisco Cloudlock is utilized as what kind of integration for Webex messaging?

   a. Archiving solutions

   b. Productivity tools

   c. Pro Pack

   d. Data loss prevention solutions

5. What color is seen for the OBTP feature on enabled video devices right before an upcoming scheduled meeting?

   a. Blue

   b. Green

   c. Red

   d. Purple

6. Which of the following Webex Hybrid Services synchronizes Microsoft Active Directory users with Cisco Webex user management (creating, updating, deleting) so that users are always current in Cisco Webex?

   a. Hybrid Data Security Service

   b. Hybrid Meeting Service

   c. Hybrid Message Service

   d. Hybrid Directory Service

Foundation Topics

Cloud Collaboration Solutions

"The cloud" started off as a tech industry slang term. In the early days of the Internet, technical diagrams often represented the servers and networking infrastructure that make up the Internet as a cloud. As more computing processes moved to this servers-and-infrastructure part of the Internet, people began to talk about moving to "the cloud" as a shorthand way of expressing where the computing processes were taking place. Today, "the cloud" is a widely accepted term for this style of computing.

Today's enterprises are looking at cloud innovations to enable a digital workplace. Cloud services can enable enhanced collaboration and increase employee productivity and engagement while enhancing customer experience. Organizations are looking for a flexible deployment model to protect their existing on-premises investments while providing new innovations and features.

Cisco Hosted Collaboration Solution

Work today often requires collaboration and involves teams that are spread across continents and time zones. Organizations everywhere are seeking stronger employee engagement and customer experiences to enable more productivity and greater business agility. More effective collaboration helps organizations work smarter. To achieve such high levels of collaboration and productivity, people use a variety of collaboration tools: IP telephony for voice calling, web and video conferencing, voice mail, mobility, desktop sharing, instant messaging (IM), presence, and more. **Cisco Unified Communications (UC)** solutions deliver integration of these tools to help people work together more effectively.

The Cisco **Hosted Collaboration Solution (HCS)** incorporates industry-leading Cisco cloud collaboration applications and services to bring real-time, integrated communications from phone and conferencing solutions together with messaging, chat, and more, including everyday business applications via **application programming interface (API)** integration. Cisco HCS and the Cisco UC applications provide seamless user experiences for end customers. Cisco cloud provider partners can implement Cisco HCS for end customers as a partner-hosted or partner-managed Unified Communications-as-a-Service (UCaaS) solution. Figure 16-1 outlines the many Cisco HCS deployment options available.

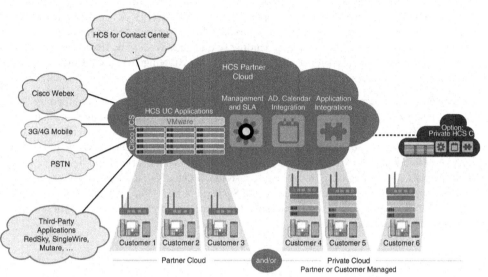

Figure 16-1 *Cisco HCS Deployment Options*

If you are already using **Cisco Unified Communications Manager (UCM)** on premises, you can maintain the same familiar user interfaces and experiences, reducing training and deployment costs as you transition to HCS to benefit from the cloud model.

Significant features and capabilities of Cisco HCS include

- **Industry-leading UC services:** Get all the capabilities of UCM hosted in the Cisco partners' clouds.

- **Endpoint choice:** Cisco HCS supports the full line of Cisco voice and video endpoints.

- **Deployment customization and flexibility:** A dedicated, virtualized instance of UCM allows you to set a class of restrictions, deploy flexibility with dial plans, and more.

- **Interoperability:** Cisco HCS is standards-based and open, enabling seamless integration with existing third-party systems and applications.

- **Data sovereignty:** Cisco HCS is hosted in over 50 countries, helping to meet compliance and regulatory requirements.

- **Proven:** Introduced in 2011, Cisco HCS is used by more than six million people and deployed at thousands of customer sites worldwide.

Cisco HCS is delivered through flexible Cisco Cloud and Data Center Validated designs. A Cisco Validated Design (CVD) is a specific bundle of Cisco products and products from Cisco partners designed to address the business needs of customers. CVDs are created based on Cisco's observation of market trends and inside knowledge of future directions of Cisco and its partners. As a complete solution, each CVD consists of both hardware and software. Implementing a CVD optimizes the capabilities of the Cisco HCS components to maximize speed, performance, stability, and reliability. Most important, each CVD has been extensively tested, validated, and documented. The CVDs were designed to facilitate faster, more reliable, and more predictable customer deployments. In addition to CVDs, employing the Cisco SAFE Security architecture bolsters the security strategy of the deployments. The Cisco SAFE security reference architecture model helps to ensure a secure infrastructure design for the edge, branch, data center, campus, cloud, and WAN. The framework encompasses operational domains such as management, security intelligence, compliance, segmentation, threat defense, and secure services.

Cisco HCS system capacity that is deployed upon these architectures is determined by system performance requirements rather than by strict limits. Overall system performance is impacted by key parameters such as customer size, network topology, subscriber feature profile, redundancy, and call profile. Dedicated virtual applications per customer and separation of network and data traffic secures the end customer's applications and helps to ensure that the traffic is coming only from trusted customers. These capabilities are delivered via a combination of the Cisco Unified Computing System (Cisco UCS), VMware vSphere, Fibre Channel SAN storage, and Cisco Nexus switching platforms. Figure 16-2 shows these components in a data center model.

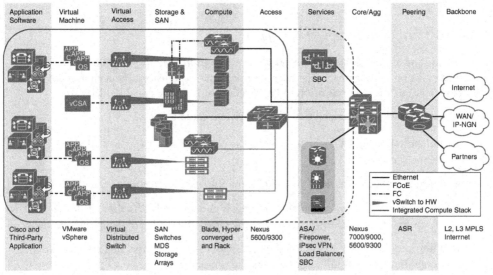

Figure 16-2 *Cisco HCS Data Center Architecture*

With hosted collaboration, Cisco partners can deliver the most up-to-date collaboration services, everywhere. Partners can employ the growing portfolio of Cisco Collaboration applications, which are delivered from a single infrastructure and architecture. As a result, partners can spend minimal time and effort deploying and upgrading applications and avoid the risk of technology obsolescence.

Cisco HCS partners use mobility solutions and a variety of deployment models, including private cloud and managed services. Enterprise service delivery is carrier-grade on a virtualized architecture that supports collaboration services and maintains high security, flexibility, and application functionality. An end-to-end validated management system, designed for cloud services, is utilized to oversee the Cisco HCS service.

Cisco Webex

In the year 2000, there were many rememberable events, from the "world-ending" Y2K bug to one of the most memorable volleyballs from the movie *Castaway*. In particular, there was a Webex Super Bowl commercial that depicted a group of folks struggling to listen to a boring presentation in what appears to be a traditional boardroom setting. Enter the fabulous RuPaul, who says: "Girl, you could be at home, sipping a latte in lingerie and still make this meeting. Don't you people have better places to be?" As everyone escaped from the boring boardroom, the commercial ended with the phrase "We've got to start meeting like this!"

Now, more than two decades later, we live in a world that continues to push the boundaries of the changing face of work: from new work styles (people collaborating and contributing from anywhere at any time), new workflows, and new workspaces, especially with the onset of the COVID-19 pandemic, which closed schools and workplaces across the world and forced all aspects of our lives into the digital realm. The new normalcy will have a stronger focus on remote work, remote education, and remote socializing as we progress into more hybrid environments.

The **Cisco Webex** platform protects user information without compromising on must-have features like secure search for stored and shared content. Cisco Webex end-to-end encryption keeps your messages, documents, and whiteboard content encrypted from one device to another. And you can integrate Webex messaging with your existing **data loss prevention (DLP)** applications to keep your sensitive information safe. This is achieved along with making the most of the management and metrics through Cisco Webex Control Hub. IT can manage users, define policies, assign meeting and calling services, and quickly configure new Cisco devices. Users get new services in a snap, so you can drive adoption, and ROI.

16

Cisco Unified Communications Manager Cloud

Cisco Unified Communications Manager Cloud (Cisco UCM Cloud) delivers enterprise-grade unified communications and collaboration as a service from the Cisco Webex cloud. Cisco UCM Cloud is hosted and operated by Cisco in North America, Europe, and Asia Pacific. The service offers voice, video, messaging, meeting, presence, and mobility solutions with the features and benefits of Cisco IP phones, mobile devices, and desktop clients. Cisco UCM Cloud for Government is a separate cloud offer that is FedRAMP-authorized. It serves the U.S. federal, state, and local governments, educational institutions, government contractors, and critical infrastructure deployments in the United States.

Cisco UCM Cloud is part of Cisco's cloud calling portfolio powered by Cisco's core call control engine, Cisco Unified Communications Manager. It provides enterprise-class call control, session management, voice, video, messaging, mobility, and conferencing services in a way that is efficient, highly secure, scalable, and reliable. Cisco UCM Cloud also offers a standards-based **IM and Presence (IM&P)** service that enables users to securely exchange presence and instant messages with others. The IM&P service enables instant messaging between individuals or groups using the Cisco **Jabber** IM client. The Jabber client supports instant messaging, presence, click-to-call, voice, video, and visual voicemail. Users can also utilize a voice messaging service that is based on the Cisco Unity technology. The voice messaging service allows users to leave, retrieve, and record voice messages from their voice mailbox, including support for voice commands, speech-to-text transcription, and even video greetings. Cisco UCM Cloud also supports video calls inbound and outbound from the enterprise to and from external video services or customers over the Internet, while traversing the corporate firewalls in a secure fashion.

Cisco Emergency Responder (CER) enhances the existing emergency 9-1-1 functionality offered in Cisco UCM Cloud. It assures that Cisco UCM Cloud will send emergency calls to the appropriate Public Safety Answering Point (PSAP) for the caller's location, and that the PSAP can identify the caller's location and return the call if necessary. In addition, the system automatically tracks and updates equipment moves and changes. Deploying this capability helps ensure more effective compliance with legal or regulatory obligations, reducing the risk of liability related to emergency calls as a result.

Mobile and Remote Access (MRA) lets endpoints (hard and soft clients) register and access calling, messaging, and presence services over the top (OTT) for those users who are outside the enterprise network. By default, endpoint registration support will be enabled for 100% of Flex 2 knowledge workers and Flex 3 professional users. For example, a customer with 10,000 knowledge workers will be enabled with an audio call registration capability for up to 10,000 endpoints. Additional endpoint registration capacity can be purchased.

Services are based on the Cisco Collaboration Flex Plan subscription model. The Flex Plan now bundles Cisco UCM Cloud with the Webex Suite. Partners can then complete the package by adding Webex devices and integrate a customer's existing **public switched telephone network (PSTN)** service, with customer support, for an end-to-end customer solution. Customers can buy the technology using the Enterprise Agreement or Named User options.

Initially, Cisco will support two calling package options:

- **Knowledge Worker:** The full-featured **private branch exchange (PBX)** replacement, with unified communications (Webex, Jabber, and all Cisco endpoints) and meetings (Webex Meetings for up to 1000 participants)

- **Common Area:** Basic dial tone for common area phones (for example, the lobby, break room, etc.)

Cisco UCM Cloud addresses the need for telephony with an opportunity to include Webex and Webex Meetings within one subscription.

Cisco UCM Cloud Direct Connect is a set of services that allow customers to connect directly to Cisco UCM Cloud in the Cisco Webex cloud. Each of these options is available on a regional basis, but mixing different Direct Connect types across regions is supported:

- Cisco Webex Edge Connect for Cisco UCM Cloud enables customers to connect dedicated, managed, redundant IP links from their premises to Cisco UCM Cloud (calling workload only). Customers connect directly to the Cisco Webex backbone via the Equinix cloud exchange.

- Virtual Peering enables customers to securely extend their private network virtually over the Internet to Cisco UCM Cloud without the need to own and support the remote infrastructure and dedicated circuits. The supported options include Cisco SD-WAN (formerly Viptela) or VPN. In both cases, Cisco hosts, manages, and assures redundant customer-dedicated routers (VPN router or SD-WAN Edge device) with Internet access, in the Cisco UCM Cloud data center region(s) where service is required. The customer is responsible for the corresponding premises equipment and SD-WAN licenses.

■ Fiber Connect enables customers to securely connect their private network via their point-to-point fiber circuit directly to Cisco UCM Cloud. Cisco provides the customer the ability to securely terminate redundant fiber connections in the Cisco UCM Cloud data center region(s) where service is required. The customer is responsible for the fiber circuit and the corresponding premises equipment.

■ MPLS Connect enables customers to securely connect their private network via their **Multiprotocol Label Switching (MPLS)** connection directly to Cisco UCM Cloud. Cisco provides the customer the ability to securely terminate redundant MPLS connections in the Cisco UCM Cloud data center region(s) where service is required. The customer is responsible for the MPLS circuit and the corresponding premises equipment.

PSTN services (telephone numbers, number porting, minutes, listings, emergency calling, etc.) and all related regulatory and commercial obligations are the explicit responsibility of Cisco's partner. Cisco will not provide, nor is responsible for, any of the underlying PSTN services or obligations. Cisco UCM Cloud supports multiple PSTN connectivity models:

■ **Central (cloud) breakout:** Partner provided and/or procured PSTN that is integrated with Cisco UCM Cloud (bring your own SIP trunk)

■ **Local breakout:** Interconnect with the customer's existing PSTN carrier via a local gateway on premises

■ **Mixed mode:** Multinational enterprises require the ability to support a complex mix of both central and local PSTN interconnects based on site locations.

Cisco UCM Cloud supports various application and third-party integrations. Developers can use the APIs provided by the collaboration applications that are hosted in Cisco UCM Cloud to develop custom solutions and extend collaboration services. You can find documentation and sample code on the dedicated technical center for each API.

APIs are available for the following:

■ Cisco UCM

  ■ Call control

  ■ Serviceability

  ■ SIP and CTI

■ Cisco IM&P

  ■ Cisco AJAX XMPP Library (CAXL)

  ■ IM&P APIs

■ Cisco Unity Connection

  ■ Provisioning

  ■ Messaging interface

16

- Telephony interface

- Notification interface

Cisco Webex Components

Businesses will rise and fall by the strength of the teams that fuel their agility. Collaboration often includes not only internal colleagues but also ecosystems of external experts and partners. To support your teams, you need tools that bring people together easily and enable them to work together productively. At the same time, you need to meet increasingly complex security and compliance requirements, which are key to keeping your information safe and secure. Webex is your secure place for connecting and getting things done in one inclusive app. It is an easy-to-use and a powerful collaboration solution that keeps people and teamwork connected anytime, anywhere, on any device.

With Webex, you can create secure virtual workspaces for everything, from completing short-term projects to solving longer-term business opportunities. You can simplify day-to-day interactions with messaging and file sharing that can be enhanced with third-party app integrations for a seamless workflow. You can start calls instantly, have high-quality video meetings with screen-sharing at the touch of a button, and stay connected after. When teamwork flows into meeting rooms, bring the Webex experience with you. Just connect the app to a Webex device to start meetings wirelessly, share your screen, capture life-size whiteboard drawings, and more.

Webex Meetings

Although the digital age has made it easier to connect across borders without the cost and hassle of travel, the human connection is still critical. Video has saturated every corner of our daily interactions, from social media to personal calls with friends and family. Strong businesses start with strong relationships. Sturdy relationships are forged on a foundation of strong communication. That is why Cisco Webex Meetings puts video at the forefront of communication and collaboration to empower hundreds of millions of people to put their best face forward. Its simple video-centric experience allows effective collaboration with an easy, consistent experience.

Cisco Webex Meetings offers highly secure integrated audio, video, and content sharing conferencing services from the Cisco Webex cloud to any device with simple joining and scheduling. No downloads and plug-ins are required. Join from the Webex web app for the best browser experience, with full meeting functionality on all major browsers. If quality is a focus, add Webex Rooms, Desk, or even third-party video devices to your meeting.

Customize how you want to view your meeting with layout options, including active speaker plus five participants. Choose a full-screen video layout with the ability to switch to a grid view that shows equal-sized windows for up to 25 video streams at once. Toggle back and forth between your content share and your video, depending on your meeting preference. Easily navigate your meeting with the centralized control bar for easy access to all your meeting controls. Lock and pin individual videos so that you can focus on the participant of your choosing and see their reactions. Chat privately or publicly with participants during a meeting and monitor interest with real-time polls. Customize your look with virtual or blurred backgrounds supported on iOS, Android, Mac, and Windows platforms.

Meet even faster in your own, always-ready personal virtual room. Schedule ahead or leave your room open, lock it, and easily admit people waiting in your virtual lobby. If you are unavailable to attend your meeting, choose an alternate host to start and run the meeting in your personal room. Save time and join Cisco Webex Meetings from your Cisco Webex app, or easily continue your discussions with messaging in the Webex app after your meeting ends. Share an application or your entire screen with remote attendees in real time. Attendees can take control and share content or annotate yours. On the go, share your content or screen from your browser, Android device, or iPhone or iPad. With the Webex desktop app, easily share your screen wirelessly via Proximity sharing.

Offer an interactive meeting experience with Cisco Webex Meetings integrated audio that is available through the Cisco Webex PSTN or Webex Cloud Connected Audio administered by your company or a certified service provider. You can also use a range of third-party audio options. Choose toll or toll-free, or call-in or call-back. Or give attendees the option to connect using **Voice over IP (VoIP)** or your computer's built-in audio. Wideband audio support using VoIP provides outstanding audio quality, even over low-bandwidth networks.

Virtual corporate training, classrooms, conferences, or just any large team can now break out into subgroups, directly from within Webex Meetings. Break out to 100 rooms with 100 participants for sidebars, brainstorming, and small group work. Breakout sessions support video, audio, and content just as in any Webex meeting. Additional features include the ability to assign people to groups automatically or manually, broadcast messages to the groups, create timed sessions, and much more.

16

Cisco Webex Assistant for Webex Meetings is the first digital in-meeting assistant for the enterprise. AI-powered and voice activated with "OK Webex" lets you automate common meeting tasks so you can focus on interacting with other participants. Webex Assistant for Meetings features real-time transcription and closed captioning with leadership word accuracy, which can be especially helpful for participants who are hearing-impaired. Ask Webex Assistant to take a note, highlight it yourself, or automatically capture the note with predetermined trigger words. Recorded transcripts make sure you never miss a meeting detail, and speaker labeling within the transcript lets you know exactly what was said by whom. Finally, post-meeting features let you edit highlights, notes, and transcripts; create and share meeting highlights and recaps with your team; and search all your recorded meetings using keyword search so you can find that exact place where something was discussed. Cisco is the only provider with in-house data management, preserving your security. Other conferencing vendors may depend on third parties for transcription, which exposes your data to additional security risks.

With People Insights for Webex Meetings, you are armed with the relevant information you need to better understand and relate to your colleagues, partners, clients, and prospects. This information includes position, contact information, location, and even reporting structure for internal colleagues. You can also review the latest company news, including an overview, market capitalization, and stock price. Make faster connections and build better relationships, right from your meeting space. Instantly learn more about your meeting participants and the company they work for with people profiles right at your fingertips. You can edit or hide your information at any time, including an overview, market capitalization, and stock price. Make faster connections and build better relationships, right from your meeting space.

Enjoy great meetings right where you work, using the tools you love. Webex Meetings has deep integrations with the leading productivity tools, including Microsoft Teams, Slack, Workplace by Facebook, Salesforce, and many others. Easily schedule meetings in Microsoft 365, Google Calendar, and Lotus Notes. Use single sign-on to access Cisco Webex. Meet where you learn in learning management systems such as Canvas, Moodle, Blackboard, Desire 2 Learn, Sakai, and Schoology. Take advantage of integration and interoperability with Cisco collaboration products such as Cisco Jabber, Cisco Webex app, and Cisco video devices.

Securely create encrypted and password-protected recordings of your meetings for future reference, training, or demonstrations. Play back meetings from mobile devices as well. Replay your recordings along with transcripts. Engage your audience by incorporating multimedia into your presentations, including PowerPoint, animations, audio, and web-based and video files. In addition, the multimedia experience supports third-party closed captioning services that offer streaming live text or a sign language interpreter video feed. Stream your Webex meeting via Facebook Live, YouTube, Twitter, Vbrick, and any platform using the Real-Time Messaging Protocol for even broader reach.

Enjoy a rich meeting experience with high-quality audio, high frame-rate video, and advanced collaboration tools across smartphones, tablets, smartwatches, and more. Whether meeting on the go or working from home, Cisco Webex Meetings on mobile delivers industry-leading collaboration for the modern enterprise. Experience amazing ways to improve and sustain your productivity with features like custom virtual backgrounds (on both Android and iOS), optimized video sharing, and 3-D augmented reality file sharing. Use voice commands, widgets, or any of your preferred calendaring apps to easily join your next meeting. Support for Apple CarPlay, Ford SYNC AppLink, and Toyota Smart Device Link lets you attend your Webex meetings hands-free in the car.

Webex Meetings is built with Cisco's industry-leading security expertise. A global architecture and network help ensure speed and performance with data centers located throughout the globe, so you will get secure, high-quality video meetings without compromise. Webex security encrypts both at the file level and at the logical volume level. The file key is a 256-bit block AES GCM key. This file key is then encrypted with a master key based on AES HMAC-SHA256 that is rotated based on policy and saved to a database. This same process is also used during the viewing, playback, or downloading of Webex data, where the encrypted media is then decrypted before, during, and after the session. In addition, industry-leading DLP and compliance capabilities also protect meeting artifacts, including recordings, Webex Assistant transcriptions, action items, and highlights. Webex Meetings helps reduce costs and allows IT to focus on core priorities. It is a cloud service on the Cisco Webex platform, making it easy to deploy and scale as your organization grows. The global, enterprise-grade Cisco Webex platform is designed specifically for highly secure delivery of real-time applications. It offers a scalable architecture, consistent availability, and multilayer tenant security validated by rigorous independent audits, including SSAE-16 and ISO 27001. For more Webex Meeting security information, please reference the *Cisco Webex Meetings Security White Paper*.

Webex Messaging

Productivity should not stop just because your meeting has finished. Webex messaging connects your team before, during, and after a meeting to create an immersive, real-time collaboration experience. Connect one to one-to-one, or as a group, and express your personality with messages, GIFs, emojis, and reactions. Easily delete or edit messages, start a conversation thread, add people to conversations, see read receipts, and more.

Share all your project files and content in a secure space that is organized, searchable, and saved right alongside all your chats, so it is easy to find what you need. Also share, open, and simultaneously edit documents sourced within SharePoint and OneDrive directly from a Webex one-to-one or team space. Whiteboard or draw with your team and share the interactive drawing in chat. Keep expressing yourself, whether you are in a live meeting or not.

Webex messaging keeps your information safe by utilizing end-to-end encryption. This means your messages, files, and whiteboard drawings are fully encrypted, all the way from your device to your recipients' devices. You can also have control over what is shared and keep teamwork private by locking spaces so only moderators can add others. Integrate with DLP tools, including Cisco Cloudlock, to protect sensitive information even when you are working with others outside your company, or to block users from sharing files, to maintain company data policies.

Webex Calling

Communication and collaboration go hand in hand. When you call on Webex, whether in the office, at home, or on the go, you will have the same calling features you expect from an enterprise-grade collaboration service to keep your business moving. You can start a voice or a video call in just one click for impromptu conversations.

Webex Calling (formally Cisco Spark Calling) is a cloud-based service that offers the benefits of traditional phone systems without the complexity of on-premises deployment. You can transfer an existing number you want to keep or get a new one. You can add phone numbers for all members of your organization as well. Control your incoming calls with an automated phone menu and intelligent call routing that directs your calls to the right destination. Connect to your voicemail and access a visual voicemail. Quickly move your call from one device to another or turn it into a video meeting without missing a word.

Get powerful cloud calling features like recording important calls to transcribe, listen to later, or share with other team members. Merge calls seamlessly or quickly go from a one-to-one call to a conference call. Easily place a call on hold and resume or transfer it to another colleague. Never miss a call with features like Call Pickup that gives the ability to answer a colleague's phone or a Hunt Group that searches for an available colleague to answer the call. Also get complete visibility and see who is calling with Call Waiting.

Webex Calling is a proven cloud calling solution that delivers enterprise-grade calling, enabling you to replace your PBX network with a globally trusted cloud calling solution. It easily extends to a complete collaboration experience that includes market-leading calling, meetings, messaging, contact center, and integrated devices for all situations. Important qualities include the following:

- Integrated collaboration
    - One application for calling, messaging, and meetings
    - Consistent and intuitive experience
    - Collaboration-enabled workflows

- Intelligent devices

  - Proximity awareness between the Webex application and Webex devices

  - Seamless call hand-off between devices

  - Designed for every workspace and every workflow

- Enterprise performance

  - Complete enterprise feature set

  - Trusted quality and reliability with geo-redundant data centers around the globe

  - End-to-end Cisco security

  - Globally available

  - Protection of existing investment in any on-premises Cisco UCM licenses, including devices, through the Cisco Collaboration Flex Plan

- Exceptional control

  - Complete, integrated service management

  - One centralized and comprehensive administrative portal

  - Advanced analytics and reporting

  - Tools and commercial licenses to enable smooth migrations from on-premises calling solutions, including UCM or hybrid deployments

Cisco Webex Hybrid Services

More and more, organizations are choosing collaboration services from the cloud. Why? Cloud services are easier and faster to deploy, they do not require the upfront capital of on-premises systems, and they can free up IT staff to focus on what matters most to the business. Many organizations, however, are unable or do not want to move all their services to the cloud. Often, they are not ready to replace everything they have on premises or they want to augment their current collaboration tools with those from the cloud. However, having tools from both the cloud and the premises can create poor user experiences with tools that do not work together as one. Webex Hybrid Services brings cloud and premises-based services together as one solution to deliver the best meeting experience from any location while maximizing the ROI of existing investments. If you like the capabilities of Webex, you can integrate those capabilities with what you currently deploy for an even better end-user and administrator experience. Hybrid Services can be deployed together or individually.

Cisco Webex Hybrid Services use Hybrid Service Connectors to securely connect Cisco Webex to an organization's premises or to the Cisco HCS in a partner cloud. The connectors are software applications that are installed on premises or in the Cisco HCS partner cloud and that enable integration with Cisco Webex. The Call Connector, Message Connector, and Calendar Connector run as modules within the Expressway. The Directory Connector runs as a service on a Microsoft Windows Server for Microsoft Active Directory synchronization. Data Security Service uses software similar to the Video Mesh software and can be installed on VMware ESXi.

Hybrid Calendar Service

Cisco Webex Hybrid Calendar Service integrates your on-premises Microsoft Exchange, Office 365, hybrid Exchange, or Google Calendar deployment to Cisco Webex. This service makes it easier to schedule and join Cisco Webex meetings from your calendar client, especially for mobile users, because no extra plugins are required.

From a calendar client, in the field where meeting location is normally added, users can

- Add @webex or their Personal Room URL to automatically share the host's Webex Personal Room and join information in the invitation.

- Add @meet to automatically create a Cisco Webex space and corresponding join link for the space.

From Microsoft Outlook, people can share their out-of-office status in Cisco Webex. As soon as someone sets an automatic reply and date range, others can see the status in Cisco Webex in these locations:

- In @mentions directed at the out-of-office user

- In the People space for that user

- In search results for that user's name

- In the expanded People roster for a space

Hybrid Calendar Service also enables Cisco Webex users to utilize **One Button to Push (OBTP)** so that when a scheduled meeting includes video devices, a green Join button appears on the devices right before the meeting begins, just as it does in the Cisco Webex app. To provide One Button to Push on video devices, you would deploy Hybrid Calendar Service. The details of the deployment depend on the type of calendar environment that you have, and on the type of device.

Hybrid Directory Service

Hybrid Directory Service utilizes the Cisco Directory Connector to automatically synchronize Microsoft Active Directory and Azure Active Directory users into the web-based management portal, Webex Control Hub, so that user account information is always current in the cloud. Active Directory remains the single source for all user account information that is mirrored in Control Hub. Simplify your day-to-day user administration and management tasks. Provide accurate and up-to-date directory content for all Cisco Webex users when they click to call, message, or add people to meetings.

Hybrid Call Service

This service is ideal for organizations that want the capabilities of Cisco Webex but already have or would prefer to use Cisco Unified Communications Manager, Business Edition 6000 or 7000, or a Cisco powered cloud service from a certified Cisco HCS partner for call control. Hybrid Call Service can enable you to use the Cisco call control you have and integrate it so tightly with Cisco Webex that your end users will never know they are not a single service. It makes Cisco Webex aware of all calls across the unified communications system and connects them, so they work together. Capabilities include instant desktop sharing, using the

Cisco Webex app as a mobile client, integration of Cisco video devices with your dial plan, and an integrated call history in the Cisco Webex app.

Hybrid Message Service

This service is ideal for organizations that have users on Cisco Webex that need to exchange messages with users on the on-premises Cisco Unified Communications Manager IM and Presence (IM&P) Service. Hybrid Message Service enables exchange of one-to-one instant messages between a Cisco Webex client and a Cisco Jabber client registered to Cisco UCM IM&P Service. Hybrid Message Service enables Cisco Jabber users to see the Presence status of Cisco Webex users based on the user's client activity.

Hybrid Data Security Service

From day one, data security has been the primary focus in designing the Cisco Webex. The cornerstone of this security is end-to-end content encryption, enabled by Cisco Webex clients interacting with the Key Management Service (KMS). The KMS is responsible for creating and managing the cryptographic keys that clients use to dynamically encrypt and decrypt messages and files.

By default, all Cisco Webex customers get end-to-end encryption with dynamic keys stored in the cloud KMS, Cisco's security realm. Cisco Webex Hybrid Data Security Service moves the KMS and other security-related functions to your enterprise data center, so only you hold the keys to your encrypted content.

Hybrid Meeting Service (Video Mesh)

Cisco Webex Video Mesh dynamically finds the optimal mix of on-premises and cloud conferencing resources. On-premises conferences stay on premises when there are enough local resources. When local resources are exhausted, conferences then expand to the cloud.

Webex Video Mesh provides these benefits:

Key Topic

- Improves quality and reduces latency by allowing you to keep your calls on premises.

- Extends your calls transparently to the cloud when on-premises resources have reached their limit or are unavailable.

- Manages your Webex Video Mesh clusters from the cloud with a single interface: Cisco Webex Control Hub.

- Optimizes resources and scale capacity, as needed.

- Combines the features of cloud and on-premises conferencing in one seamless user experience.

- Reduces capacity concerns because the cloud is always available when additional conferencing resources are needed. There is no need to do capacity planning for the worst-case scenario.

- Provides advanced reporting on capacity and usage in https://admin.webex.com.

- Uses local media processing when users dial in to a Cisco Webex meeting from on-premises standards-based SIP endpoints and clients:

    - SIP-based endpoints and clients (Cisco endpoints, Jabber, third-party SIP) registered to on-premises call control (Cisco UCM or Expressway) that call into a Cisco Webex meeting.

    - Cisco Webex apps (including paired with room devices) that join a Cisco Webex meeting.

    - Cisco Webex room and desk devices (including Cisco Webex Board) that directly join a Cisco Webex meeting.

- Provides optimized audio and video interactive voice response (IVR) to on-net SIP-based endpoints and clients.

- Cisco Webex clients (internal and external) continue to join meetings from the cloud.

- H.323, IP dial-in, and Skype for Business (S4B) endpoints continue to join meetings from the cloud.

- Supports 1080p 30fps high-definition video as an option for meetings, if meeting participants that can support 1080p are hosted through the local on-premises Hybrid Media Nodes. (If a participant joins an in-progress meeting from the cloud, on-premises users continue to experience 1080p 30fps on supported endpoints.)

- Enhanced and differentiated QoS by marking separate audio (EF) and video (AF41) values.

Exam Preparation Tasks

As mentioned in the section "How to Use This Book" in the Introduction, you have a couple of choices for exam preparation: the exercises here, Chapter 22, "Final Preparation," and the exam simulation questions in the Pearson Test Prep practice test software.

Review All Key Topics

Review the most important topics in this chapter, noted with the Key Topics icon in the outer margin of the page. Table 16-2 lists a reference of these key topics and the page numbers on which each is found.

Table 16-2   Key Topics for Chapter 16

Key Topic Element	Description	Page Number
List	HCS features and capabilities	301
Paragraph	Webex Meetings security	308
Paragraph	Webex Hybrid Services	310
Paragraph	One Button to Push (OBTP)	311
List	Webex Video Mesh features and capabilities	312

Complete Tables and Lists from Memory

There are no memory tables or lists in this chapter.

Define Key Terms

Define the following key terms from this chapter and check your answers in the glossary:

application programming interface (API), Cisco Unified Communications Manager (UCM), Cisco Webex, data loss prevention (DLP), Hosted Collaboration Solution (HCS), IM and Presence (IM&P), Jabber, Mobile and Remote Access (MRA), Multiprotocol Label Switching (MPLS), One Button to Push (OBTP), private branch exchange (PBX), public switched telephone network (PSTN), Cisco Unified Communications (UC), Voice over IP (VoIP)

Q&A

The answers to these questions appear in Appendix A. For more practice with exam format questions, use the Pearson Test Prep practice test software.

1. What is a Cisco CVD?

2. When utilizing Webex Hybrid Calendar Service, what is the difference between @webex and @meet?

CHAPTER 17

Configure Webex Hybrid Directory Service

This chapter covers the following topics:

Deployment Model: Explains the deployment model of Webex Hybrid Directory Service.

Deployment Requirements: Describes the high-level requirements prior to implementing and deploying Webex Hybrid Directory Service.

Infrastructure Requirements: Provides the infrastructure requirements and provides the proxy options available to the Cisco Directory Connector.

Active Directory Configuration and Synchronization: Provides an overview of the configuration of Microsoft Active Directory, Directory Connector, and the Cisco Webex cloud. Also covers the methods of synchronization and the behavior of adding, modifying, and deleting users.

Webex User Service Assignment: Covers the Webex users' services that can be assigned in the Webex Control Hub.

This chapter focuses on the synchronization of Microsoft Active Directory users into Webex Control Hub (creating, updating, deleting) so that user account information is always current in the cloud. Active Directory remains the single source for all user account information that is mirrored in Control Hub to simplify day-to-day administration and management tasks.

This chapter covers the following objective from the Implementing Cisco Collaboration Cloud and Edge Solutions (CLCEI) exam 300-820:

- 4.2.c Configure Webex Hybrid Services/Connector: Directory Services (Deployment requirements; deployment models, infrastructure requirements, Active Directory configuration, synchronization, Webex user service assignment)

"Do I Know This Already?" Quiz

The "Do I Know This Already?" quiz enables you to assess whether you should read this entire chapter thoroughly or jump to the "Exam Preparation Tasks" section. If you are in doubt about your answers to these questions or your own assessment of your knowledge of the topics, read the entire chapter. Table 17-1 lists the major headings in this chapter and their corresponding "Do I Know This Already?" quiz questions. You can find the answers in Appendix A, "Answers to the 'Do I Know This Already?' Quizzes and Review Questions."

Table 17-1 "Do I Know This Already?" Section-to-Question Mapping

Foundation Topics Section	Questions
Deployment Model	1
Deployment Requirements	2
Infrastructure Requirements	3
Active Directory Configuration and Synchronization	4
Webex User Service Assignment	5

CAUTION The goal of self-assessment is to gauge your mastery of the topics in this chapter. If you do not know the answer to a question or are only partially sure of the answer, you should mark that question as wrong for purposes of the self-assessment. Giving yourself credit for an answer you correctly guess skews your self-assessment results and might provide you with a false sense of security.

1. The core components for Cisco Webex Hybrid Directory Service include which of the following? (Choose two.)
   a. Key Management Service
   b. Cisco Directory Connector
   c. Cisco Unified Communications Manager
   d. Automatic Certificate Management Environment
   e. Microsoft Active Directory

2. From where can the Cisco Directory Connector software installation package be downloaded?
   a. https://admin.webex.com
   b. Cisco Expressway
   c. https://www.webex.com
   d. https://www.microsoft.com

3. What is the limit for how many Active Directory objects can be synchronized to the cloud using the Cisco Directory Connector?
   a. 5,000
   b. 10,000
   c. 500
   d. No limit

4. You can map attributes from your local Active Directory instance to corresponding attributes in the cloud. The only required field is uid, a unique identifier for each user account in the cloud identity service. What format must the attribute be presented as?
   a. Numeric
   b. Date

     c. Alphabetical

     d. Email

5. A site administrator would like to set a user's privileges. Which Webex plan is required?

     a. Enterprise Plan

     b. Business Plan

     c. Starter Plan

     d. Free Plan

Foundation Topics

Deployment Model

Deploying Cisco Webex Hybrid Directory Service simplifies the administrator's experience. It takes the hassle out of updating user information in the cloud by automatically synchronizing it with Microsoft Active Directory or Azure Active Directory instance on your premises. Cisco Webex Hybrid Directory Service supports Cisco Webex Meetings, Webex, and Webex Calling capabilities.

For administrators, Cisco Webex Hybrid Directory Service simplifies not only the Cisco Webex onboarding experience, but also the day-to-day operations. Without Hybrid Directory Service, administrators must either manually add, delete, and edit Cisco Webex users through **Cisco Webex Control Hub** or upload a **Comma-Separated Values (CSV)** file every time they need to add or change a user that has changed in the Microsoft Active Directory instance. Hybrid Directory Service automatically synchronizes an organization's on-premises Active Directory users to Cisco Webex and Hybrid Directory Service securely eliminates the need to manage multiple directory databases. When an employee leaves the company, the user is deleted from the Microsoft Active Directory instance and their Cisco Webex account will be deactivated as soon as it is replicated. The user will no longer be able to log in to Cisco Webex and will be removed from all spaces and services.

For end users, Hybrid Directory Service provides accurate and up-to-date directory content for all Cisco Webex users. And because profile data in Cisco Webex is synchronized with the premises (verified names, email addresses, and company avatars), it can help ensure that your users are communicating with the right people.

The core components for Cisco Webex Hybrid Directory Service include

■ **Cisco Directory Connector**

■ Microsoft Active Directory

Microsoft Active Directory (AD) is the enterprise resource and user repository and the single source of validation for that information. The directory administrator maintains the enterprise resource and user information contained within the directory with moves, adds, changes, and deletions. This enables synchronization not only of users but also of resources such as enterprise room systems. Any updates to this information in Active Directory are propagated to the Cisco Directory Connector (and in turn to Webex) during synchronization. The Cisco Directory Connector plays the role of synchronization agent between the corporate Active Directory and the organization's identity store in Webex. The Directory Connector initially populates Webex with user and resource information from the Active Directory and maintains this information with subsequent synchronizations to update the organization's Webex identity store with the latest moves, adds, changes, and deletions occurring on the enterprise Active Directory. The Cisco Directory Connector relies on Active Directory **application programming interfaces (APIs)** to pull user information from the Active Directory. The APIs are based on the Microsoft .NET Framework. Directory Connector uses **Hypertext Transfer Protocol Secure (HTTPS)** to push user information to the organization's Webex identity store.

Deployment Requirements

Prior to implementing and deploying Webex Hybrid Directory Service, perform the following high-level requirements:

- Deploy Microsoft Active Directory within the organization and populate it with user information.

- Make sure Cisco Unified Communications Manager (UCM) is fully integrated with Active Directory (directory synchronization and authentication).

- If the on-premises network is behind a firewall, ensure that outbound access to the Internet through HTTPS on port 443 is available either directly or by way of an HTTP proxy.

Figure 17-1 shows the high-level steps required to deploy Webex Hybrid Directory Service, described here:

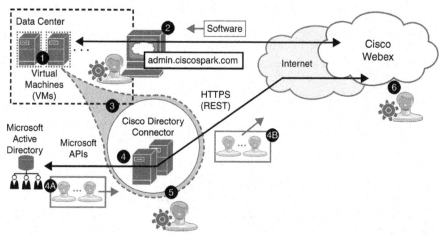

Figure 17-1 *Deployment of Webex Hybrid Directory Service*

Step 1.   Virtual Microsoft Windows Server instances are created and deployed in the enterprise data center.

Step 2.   After the Windows servers are deployed, the administrator logs in to the Webex Control Hub at https://admin.webex.com to enable directory synchronization and download the Cisco Directory Connector software installation package.

Step 3. Directory Connector is installed on the Windows servers (refer to the next section, "Infrastructure Requirements," for hardware requirements).

Step 4. After Directory Connector is installed, the administrator configures the connector, and an initial synchronization occurs between Microsoft Active Directory and the Directory Connector (step 4A) and between the Directory Connector and Webex (step 4B).

Step 5. Once the initial synchronization completes, the administrator configures the schedule for periodic incremental and full synchronizations.

Step 6. The administrator manages users and provisions them for cloud services as appropriate.

For high availability, two Cisco Directory Connectors are deployed, as shown in Figure 17-2. These Windows Server virtual machines are deployed on separate hosts in separate buildings or data centers to provide high availability and redundancy.

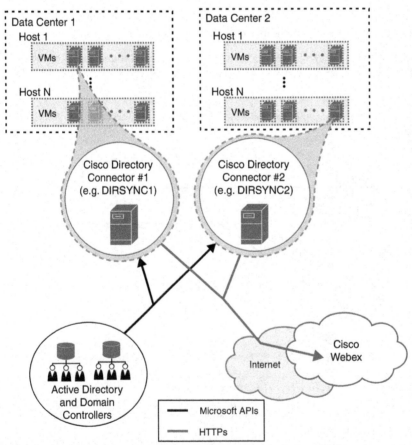

Figure 17-2 *Webex Hybrid Directory Service High Availability*

Directory Connectors are deployed as a pair, and both are capable of synchronizing directory information between the enterprise directory and the cloud. However, under normal operation, one Directory Connector (primary) handles directory synchronization while the other (backup) maintains connectivity to Webex but does not perform any synchronization. If the primary Directory Connector fails, the backup Directory Connector will continue to handle synchronization operations based on the configured failover interval.

In cases where only a single Cisco Directory Connector is deployed (nonredundant deployments), if the Directory Connector fails, user information is no longer synchronized between Active Directory and the Webex identity store. The administrator is able to manage existing users and to provision them for services while the Directory Connector is down, but no users or resources can be added or removed from the Webex identity store until the Directory Connector is returned to service.

In addition to the Cisco Directory Connector high availability considerations, also consider providing redundancy for other aspects of the integration such as the Active Directory services, connectivity to Webex (HTTPS), and availability of cloud services. Microsoft components (Active Directory, domain controllers, and other Microsoft enterprise network services) should be deployed in a redundant fashion. Consult Microsoft product documentation for information on high availability. Highly available network connectivity to the Internet is also required to ensure that Webex and other Webex services are reachable from the enterprise. Redundant physical Internet connections, preferably from different providers, are recommended. Webex services are highly available because those services and components are deployed across multiple physical data centers on elastic compute platforms.

The primary sizing and scalability consideration for Webex Hybrid Directory Service is the size of the synchronization. The larger the enterprise directory and the search base in terms of number of resources and users, the longer a synchronization will take to complete. For this reason, it is important to monitor synchronization operations initially to ensure that both incremental and full synchronizations are completing prior to the beginning of the next synchronization period. Cisco recommends running the Directory Connector on a dedicated Windows server host. Additional load on the Windows server can reduce performance and increase overall system response and synchronization times.

Infrastructure Requirements

You can install the Cisco Directory Connector on these supported Windows Server versions:

- Windows Server 2019

- Windows Server 2016

- Windows Server 2012 R2

- Windows Server 2012

- Windows Server 2008 R2

- Windows Server 2003

To address a cookie issue, Cisco recommends that you upgrade your domain controller to a release that contains the fix, either Windows Server 2012 R2 or 2016.

You must install the Cisco Directory Connector on a computer with these minimum hardware requirements:

■ 8 GB of RAM

■ 50 GB of storage

■ No minimum for the CPU

The Cisco Directory Connector is supported with the following Active Directory services:

■ Active Directory 2016

■ Active Directory 2012

■ Active Directory 2008 R2

■ Active Directory 2008

Note the following additional requirements:

■ The Cisco Directory Connector requires TLS 1.2. You must install the following:

■ .NET Framework v3.5 (required for the Cisco Directory Connector application; if you run into any issues, use the directions in the article "Enable .NET Framework 3.5 by using the Add Roles and Features Wizard," available at https://docs.microsoft.com/)

■ .NET Framework v.4.5 (required for TLS 1.2)

■ Active Directory forest functional level 2 (Windows Server 2003) or higher is required. (See "Forest and Domain Functional Levels" available at https://docs.microsoft.com/ for more information.)

If your network is behind a firewall, ensure that your system has HTTPS (port 443) access to the Internet.

To access the Cisco Directory Connector software from Cisco Webex Control Hub, you will require a Cisco Webex organization with a trial or any paid subscription. Optionally, if you want new Webex user accounts to be active before they sign in for the first time, it is recommended that you do the following:

■ Add, verify, and optionally claim domains that contain the user email addresses you want to synchronize into the cloud.

■ Perform a single sign-on (SSO) integration of your identity provider (IdP) with your Webex organization.

■ Suppress automatic email invites, so that new users will not receive the automatic email invitation and you can do your own email campaign. (This feature requires the SSO integration.)

For a multiple domain environment (either single forest or multiple forests), you must install one Cisco Directory Connector for each Active Directory domain. If you want to synchronize a new domain (B) while maintaining the synchronized user data on another existing domain (A), ensure that you have a separate supported Windows server to install Directory Connector for domain (B) synchronization. For the sign-in to the connector, Cisco does not require an administrative account in Active Directory. It requires a local user account that is the same user as a full admin account in Cisco Webex Control Hub. This local user must have privileges on that Windows machine to connect to the domain controller and read Active Directory user objects. The machine login account should be a computer administrator with privileges to install software on the local machine. This also applies to a virtual machine login. Also, make sure that Windows Safe dynamic link library (DLL) search mode is enabled. If you use **Microsoft Active Directory Lightweight Directory Services (AD LDS)** for multiple domains on a single forest, Cisco recommends that you install the Cisco Directory Connector and Active Directory Domain Service/Active Directory Lightweight Directory Services (AD DS/AD LDS) on separate machines.

The Cisco Directory Connector works as a bridge between the on-premises Active Directory and the Webex cloud. As such, the connector does not have an upper limit for how many Active Directory objects can be synchronized to the cloud. Any limits on premises directory objects are tied to the specific version of and specifications for the Active Directory environment that is being synchronized to the cloud, not the connector itself. A few factors can affect the speed of the synchronization:

- The total number Active Directory objects. (A 5000-user sync job will not take as long as a 50,000-user sync job.)

- Network speed and bandwidth.

- System workload and specifications.

If web proxy authentication is enabled in your environment, you can still use the Cisco Directory Connector. If your organization uses a transparent web proxy, it does not support authentication. The connector successfully connects and synchronizes users. You can take one of these approaches:

- Explicit web proxy through Internet Explorer (the connector inherits the web proxy settings)

- Explicit web proxy through a .pac file (the connector inherits enterprise-specific proxy settings)

- Transparent proxy that works with the connector without any changes

You can set up the Cisco Directory Connector to use a web proxy through Internet Explorer. If Cisco DirSync Service runs from a different account than that of the currently signed-in user, you also need to sign in with this account and configure the web proxy.

Step 1.   From Internet Explorer, go to **Internet Options**, click **Connections**, and then choose **LAN Settings**.

Step 2.   Point the Windows instance where the connector is installed at your web proxy. The connector inherits these web proxy settings.

Step 3.   If your environment uses proxy authentication, add these **Uniform Resource Locators (URLs)** to your allowed list:

- cloudconnector.webex.com for synchronization

- idbroker.webex.com for authentication

You may perform this either site-wide (for all hosts) or just for the host that has the connector. Note that if you add these URLs to an allowed list to completely bypass your web proxy, make sure your firewall's access control list (ACL) table is updated to permit the connector host to access the URLs directly.

You can configure a client browser to use a .pac file. This file supplies the web proxy address and port information. The Cisco Directory Connector directly inherits the enterprise-specific web proxy configuration.

Step 1.   For the connector to successfully connect and sync user information to the Cisco Webex cloud, make sure proxy authentication is disabled for cloud-connector.webex.com in the .pac file configuration for the host where the connector is installed.

Step 2.   If your environment uses proxy authentication, add these URLs to your allowed list:

- cloudconnector.webex.com for synchronization.

- idbroker.webex.com for authentication.

You may perform this either site-wide (for all hosts) or just for the host that has the connector. Note that if you add these URLs to an allowed list to completely bypass your web proxy, make sure your firewall ACL table is updated to permit the connector host to access the URLs directly.

The Cisco Directory Connector supports **NT LAN Manager (NTLM)**. NTLM is one approach to support Windows authentication among the domain devices and ensure their security. In most cases, a user wants to access another workstation's resources through a client PC, which can be difficult to do in a secure way. Generally, the technical design of NTLM is based on a mechanism of challenge and response:

1. A user signs in to a client PC through a Windows account and password. The password is never saved locally. Instead of a plaintext password, a hash value of the password is stored locally. When a user signs in through the password to the client, Windows compares the stored hash value and hash value from the input password. If both are the same, the authentication passes. When the user wants to access any resource in another server, the client sends a request to the server with the account name in plain text.

2. When the server receives the request, the server generates a 16-bit random number, which is called a challenge (or nonce). Then the server sends the challenge to the client in plain text.

3. As soon as the client receives the challenge sent from server, the client encrypts the challenge by the hash value that was mentioned in step 1. After encryption, the value is sent back to the server.

4. When the server receives the encrypted value from the client, the server sends it to the domain controller for verification. The request includes: the account name, encrypted challenge that the client sent, and the original plain challenge.

5. The domain controller can retrieve the hash values of passwords according to account name. And then the domain controller can encrypt on the original challenge. The domain controller can then compare with the received hash value and the encrypted hash value. If they are same, the verification is successful.

Windows has security authentication built into the operating system, making it easier for applications to support security authentication. As a result, you do not need to complete further configurations.

In a transparent proxy scenario, the browser is unaware that a transparent web proxy is intercepting **Hypertext Transfer Protocol (HTTP)** requests (port 80/port 443) and no client-side configuration is required.

1. Deploy a transparent proxy, so that the connector can connect and synchronize users.

2. Confirm that the proxy is successful—you see an expected browser authentication popup window when starting the connector.

If you are setting up proxy authentication, add the URL cloudconnector.webex.com to your allowed list by creating an ACL on your enterprise firewall server. Apply this ACL to the appropriate firewall interface, which is only applicable for this single connector host. For example:

```
access-list 2000 acl-inside extended permit TCP [IP of the connec-
tor] cloudconnector.webex.com eq https
```

Ensure that the rest of the hosts in your enterprise are still required to use your web proxy by configuring the appropriate implicit deny statement.

Before following the next tasks in the Cisco Directory Connector deployment, keep the following requirements and recommendations in mind if you are going to synchronize Active Directory information from multiple domains into the cloud:

■ A separate instance of the Cisco Directory Connector is required for each domain.

■ The Cisco Directory Connector software must run on a host that is on the same domain that it will synchronize.

■ Cisco recommends that you verify or claim your domains in Cisco Webex Control Hub.

■ If you want to synchronize more than 50 domains, you must open a ticket to get your organization moved to a large org list.

■ If desired, you can synchronize room resource information along with user accounts.

If you are synchronizing more than 50,000 users, it is highly recommended that you use a second connector for failover and redundancy.

17

Active Directory Configuration and Synchronization

Cisco Webex Control Hub initially shows directory synchronization as disabled. To turn on directory synchronization for your organization, you must install and configure the Cisco Directory Connector and then successfully perform a full synchronization. You must install one connector for each Active Directory domain that you want to synchronize. A single Cisco Directory Connector instance can only serve a single domain. If you authenticate through a proxy server, ensure that you have your proxy credentials. For proxy basic-auth, you will enter the username and password after you install an instance of the connector. Internet Explorer proxy configuration is also required for basic-auth. For proxy NTLM, you may see an error when you open the connector for the first time; the required steps are listed later in this section.

Step 1.   From the customer view in https://admin.webex.com, go to **Users**, click **Manage Users**, click **Enable Directory Synchronization**, and then click **Next**.

Step 2.   Click the **Download and Install** link to save the latest version of the connector installation .zip file to your VMware or Windows server. You can obtain the .zip file directly from this link, but you must have full administrative access to a Control Hub organization for this software to work. For a new installation, get the latest version of the software so that you are using the latest features and bug fixes. After you install the software, upgrades are reported through the software and automatically install when available.

Step 3.   On the VMware or Windows server, unzip and run the .msi file in the setup folder to launch the setup wizard.

Step 4.   Click **Next**, check the box to accept the license agreement, and then click **Next** until you see the account type screen.

Step 5.   Choose the type of service account that you want to use and perform the installation with an admin account:

- **Local System:** The default option. You can use this option if you have a proxy configured through Internet Explorer.

- **Domain Account:** Use this option if the computer is part of the domain. Directory Connector must interact with network services to access domain resources. You can enter the account information and click **OK**. When entering the username, use the format: *{domain}\{user_name}*.

For a proxy that integrates with AD (NTLMv2 or Kerberos), you must use the domain account option. The account used to run Directory Connector Service must have enough privilege to pass proxy and access AD.

To avoid errors, make sure the following privileges are in place:

- The server is part of the domain.

- The domain account can access the on-premises AD data and avatars data. The account must also have the local administrator role because it must be able to access files under C:\Program Files.

- For a virtual machine login, the admin account privilege must at least be able to read domain information.

Step 6.   Click **Install**. After the network test runs and if prompted, enter your proxy basic credentials, click **OK**, and then click **Finish**.

It is recommended that you reboot the server after installation. The dry run report cannot show the correct result when the data was not released. While rebooting the machine, all data is refreshed to show an exact result in the report. If you are synchronizing multiple domains, repeat these steps on a different Windows machine and install one connector per domain.

Ensure that you have your credentials for proxy basic-auth, because you will enter the username and password after you open the connector for the first time. For proxy NTLM, open Internet Explorer, click the gear icon, go to **Internet Options > Connections > LAN Settings**, ensure the proxy server information is added, and then click OK. Follow these steps:

Step 1.   Open the connector, and then add **https://idbroker.webex.com** to your list of trusted sites if you see a prompt.

Step 2.   If prompted, sign in with your proxy authentication credentials, and then sign into Cisco Webex using your admin account and click **Next**.

Step 3.   Confirm your organization and domain.

■ If you choose **AD DS**, check **LDAP over SSL** to use Secure LDAP (LDAPS) as the connection protocol, choose the domain that you want to synchronize from, and then click **Confirm**. If you do not check LDAP over SSL, DirSync will continue to use the LDAP connection protocol. **Lightweight Directory Application Protocol (LDAP)** and LDAPS are the connection protocols used between an application and the domain controller within the infrastructure. LDAPS communication is encrypted and secure.

■ If you choose **AD LDS**, enter the host, domain, and port, and then click **Refresh** to load all application partitions. Then select the partition from the drop-down list and click **Confirm**. In addition, open the CloudConnectorCommon.dll.config file and add the **ADAuthLevel** setting to the **appSetting** node, like this:

```
<appSettings>
<add key="ConnectorServiceURI"
value="https://cloudconnector.webex.com/Synchronization-
Service-v1_0/?orgId=GLOBAL" />
<add key="ADAuthLevel" value="1" />
</appSettings>
```

Step 4.   After the Confirm Organization screen appears, click **Confirm**. If you already bound AD DS/AD LDS, the Confirm Organization screen appears.

Step 5.   Click **Confirm**.

Step 6.   Choose one of the following, depending on the number of Active Directory domains you want to bind to Directory Connector:

■ If you have a single domain that is AD LDS, bind to the existing AD LDS source, and then click **Confirm**.

- If you have a single domain that is AD DS, either bind to the existing domain or to a new domain. If you choose **Bind to a New Domain**, click **Next**. Because the existing source type is AD DS, you cannot select AD LDS for the new binding.

- If you have more than one domain, choose an existing domain from the list or choose **Bind to a New Domain** and then click **Next**. Because you have more than one domain, the existing source type must be **AD DS**. If you choose Bind to a New Domain and click Next, you cannot select AD LDS for the new binding.

After you sign in, you are prompted to perform a dry run synchronization.

During the process to onboard users from different domains, you must decide whether to retain or delete the user objects that might already exist in the Cisco Webex cloud. With the Cisco Directory Connector, the goal is to have an exact match between your Active Directory instance(s) and the Cisco Webex cloud. You may already have some Cisco Webex users in Control Hub before you used the Cisco Directory Connector. Among the users in the cloud, some might match on-premises Active Directory objects and be assigned licenses for services. But some may be test users that you want to delete while doing a synchronization. You must create an exact match between your Active Directory and Control Hub.

If you have multiple domains in a single forest or multiple forests, you must do this step on each of the Cisco Directory Connector instances you have installed for each Active Directory domain.

Step 7.   Choose one:

- After first-time sign-in, click **Yes** at the prompt to perform a dry run.

- If you miss a reminder to perform a dry run, at any time from the Cisco Directory Connector, click **Dashboard**, choose **Sync Dry Run**, and then click **OK** to start a dry run synchronization.

The dry run identifies the users by comparing them with domain users. The application can identify the users if they belong to the current domain. In the next step, you must decide whether to delete the objects or retain them. The mismatched objects are identified as already existing in the Cisco Webex cloud but not existing in the on-premises Active Directory.

Step 8.   Review the dry run results and then choose an option depending on whether you use a single domain or multiple domains:

- **Single domain:** Decide whether you want to keep the mismatched users. If you want to keep them, choose **No, Retain Objects**; if you do not want to keep them, choose **Yes, Delete Objects**. After you do these steps and manually run a full sync so that there is an exact match between the premises and cloud, the Cisco Directory Connector automatically enables scheduled auto-sync tasks.

- **Multiple domains:** For an organization with Domain A and Domain B, first do a dry run for Domain A. If you want to keep mismatched users, choose **No, Retain Objects**. (These mismatched users might be members of Domain B.) If you want to delete, choose **Yes, Delete Objects**.

  If you keep the users, run a full sync for Domain A first, and then do a dry run for Domain B. If there are still mismatched users, add those users in Active Directory and then do a full sync for Domain B. When there is an exact match between the premises and cloud, the Cisco Directory Connector automatically enables scheduled auto-sync tasks.

Step 9.   At the Confirm Dry Run prompt, click **Yes** to redo the dry run synchronization and view the dashboard to see the results. Any accounts that were successfully synchronized in the dry run appear under Objects Matched. If a user in the cloud does not have a corresponding user with the same email in Active Directory, the entry is listed under Users Deleted. To avoid this delete flag, you can add a user in Active Directory with the same email address. To view the details of the items that were synchronized, click the corresponding tab for specific items or **Objects Matched**. To save the summary information, click **Save Results to File**.

Key Topic

Perform a dry run before you enable full synchronization, or when you change the synchronization parameters. If the dry run was initiated by a configuration change, you can save the settings after the dry run is complete. If you have already added users manually, performing an Active Directory synchronization may cause previously added users to be removed. You can check the Cisco Directory Connector Dry Run Reports to verify that all expected users are present before you fully synchronize to the cloud.

17

To get the latest features, bug fixes, and security updates, it is always important to keep your Cisco Directory Connector software up to date to the latest version. Cisco recommends that you use this procedure to allow new versions of the connector software to be installed silently and automatically when they are available:

Step 1.   From the Cisco Directory Connector, select **Configuration > General**, and then check the **Automatically upgrade to the new Cisco Directory Connector Version** check box.

Step 2.   Click **Apply** to save your changes.

  If for some reason you decide to not have automatic upgrades, there is a procedure to manually update the Cisco Directory Connector. It is recommended to perform an upgrade at your earliest convenience during a maintenance window. Prepare at least one hour for the upgrade and note that provisioning and deprovisioning will not work during this time.

By default, the Cisco Directory Connector synchronizes all users that are not computers and all groups that are not critical system objects for a domain. For more control over what objects get synchronized, you can select specific users to synchronize and specify LDAP filters by using the Object Selection page in the Cisco Directory Connector.

Step 1.   From the Cisco Directory Connector, go to **Configuration > Object Selection**.

Step 2. In the Object Type section, check **Users**, and consider limiting the number of searchable containers for users. If you want to synchronize just users in a certain group, for example, you must enter an LDAP filter in the **Users** LDAP filters field. If you want to sync users that are in the Example-manager group, use a filter like this one:

```
(&(sAMAccountName=*)(memberOf=cn=Example-
manager,ou=Example,ou=Security Group,dc=COMPANY))
```

Step 3. Check **Identify Room** to separate room data from user data. Click **Customize** if you want to set up additional attributes to identify user data as room data. Use this setting if you want to synchronize on-premises room information from Active Directory into the Cisco Webex cloud. After you synchronize the room information, the on-premises room devices with a configured, mapped SIP address show up as searchable entries on cloud-registered room devices.

Step 4. Check **Groups** if you want to synchronize your Active Directory user groups to the cloud. Do not add a user sync LDAP filter to the Groups field. You should only use the Groups field to sync the group data itself to the cloud. In the Cisco Directory Connector, you must check **Groups** if you are using Hybrid Data Security to configure a trial group for pilot users. See *Deployment Guide for Cisco Webex Hybrid Data Security* for guidance. This Cisco Directory Connector setting does not affect other user synchronization into the cloud.

Step 5. Configure the LDAP filters. You can add extended filters by providing a valid LDAP filter.

Step 6. Specify the **On Premises Base DNs to Synchronize** by clicking **Select** to see the tree structure of your Active Directory. From here, you can select or deselect which containers to search on.

Step 7. Check the objects you want to add for this configuration and click **Select**. You can select individual or parent containers to use for synchronization. Select a parent container to enable all child containers. If you select a child container, the parent container shows a gray check mark that indicates a child has been checked. You can then click **Select** to accept the Active Directory containers that you checked. If your organization places all users and groups in the Users container, you do not have to search other containers. If your organization is divided into organization units, make sure that you select **OUs**.

Step 8. Click **Apply**. Choose an option:

- Apply Config Changes

- Dry Run

- Cancel

You can map attributes from your local Active Directory to corresponding attributes in the cloud. The only required field is the Webex attribute name uid, a unique identifier for each user account in the cloud identity service. You can choose what Active Directory attribute to map to the cloud. For example, you can map firstName lastName in Active Directory or a custom attribute expression to displayName in the cloud. Accounts in Active Directory must have an email address as the uid maps by default to the AD field of mail (not sAMAccountName). If you choose to have the preferred language come from your Active Directory, then Active Directory is the single source of truth: users will not be able to change their language setting in Cisco Webex Settings and administrators won't be able to change the setting in Cisco Webex Control Hub.

Step 1. From the Cisco Directory Connector, click **Configuration > User Attribute Mapping.** This page shows the attribute names for Active Directory (on the left) and the Cisco Webex cloud (on the right). All required attributes are marked with a red asterisk.

Step 2. Scroll down to the bottom of Active Directory Attribute Names and then choose one of these Active Directory attributes to map to the cloud attribute **uid**:

- **mail:** Used by most deployments for email format.

- **userPrincipalName:** An alternative choice if your mail attribute is used for other purposes in Active Directory. This attribute must be in email format.

You can map any of the other Active Directory attributes to uid, but Cisco recommends that you use mail or userPrincipalName, as indicated. For the synchronization to work, you must make sure the Active Directory attribute that you choose is in email format. The Cisco Directory Connector shows a popup to remind you if you do not choose one of the recommended attributes.

Step 3. If the predefined Active Directory attributes do not work for your deployment, click the **Attribute** drop-down, scroll to the bottom, and then choose **Customize Attribute** to open a window that lets you define an attribute expression. Click the **Help** button to get more information about the expressions and see examples of how expressions work. The Cisco Directory Connector verifies the attribute value of uid in the identity service and retrieves available users under the current user filter options. The Cisco Directory Connector shows an information message reminding you to ensure that all users have a valid email format. If the attribute cannot be verified, you will see a following warning and can return to Active Directory to check and fix the user data.

Step 4. (Optional) Choose mappings for **mobile** and **telephoneNumber** if you want mobile and work numbers to appear, for example, in the user's contact card in the Webex app. The phone number data appears in Webex when a user hovers over another user's profile picture. For more information on calling from a user's contact card, see the *Deployment Guide for Calling in Webex (Unified CM)* on cisco.com.

Step 5. Choose additional mappings for more data to appear in the contact card:

- departmentNumber

- displayName

- given

- employeeType

- manager

- title

17

Once the attributes are mapped, the information appears when a user hovers over another user's profile picture. After these attributes are synchronized to each user account, you can also turn on People Insights in Control Hub. This feature allows Webex users to share more information in their profiles and learn more about each other.

Step 6. After you make your choices, click **Apply**.

Any user data that is contained in Active Directory overwrites the data in the cloud that corresponds to that user. For example, if you created a user manually in Cisco Webex Control Hub, the user's email address must be identical to the email address in Active Directory. Any user without a corresponding email address in Active Directory is deleted. Deleted users are kept in the cloud identity service for seven days before they are permanently deleted.

You can synchronize your users' directory avatars to the cloud so that each avatar appears when they sign in to the Cisco Webex app. Use this procedure to synchronize raw avatar data from an Active Directory attribute:

Step 1. From the Cisco Directory Connector, go to **Configuration**, click **Avatar**, and then check **Enable**.

Step 2. From the Get Avatar From field, choose **AD attribute**, and then choose the Avatar attribute that contains the raw avatar data that you want to synchronize to the cloud.

Step 3. To verify that the avatar is accessed correctly, enter a user's email address, and then click **Get user's avatar**. The avatar appears to the right.

Step 4. After you verify that the avatar appeared correctly, click **Apply** to save your changes.

The images that are synchronized become the default avatars for users in the Cisco Webex app. Users are not allowed to set their own avatar after this feature is enabled from the Cisco Directory Connector. The user avatars synchronize over to any matching accounts on the Webex site.

You can also synchronize your users' directory avatars to the cloud so that each avatar appears when the user signs in to the Cisco Webex app. Use this procedure to synchronize avatars from a resource server. The avatar URI pattern and the server where the avatars reside must be reachable from the Cisco Directory Connector application. The connector needs HTTP or HTTPS access to the images, but the images do not need to be publicly accessible on the Internet. The avatar data synchronization is separated from the Active Directory user profiles. If you run a proxy, you must ensure that avatar data can be accessed by NTLM authentication or basic-auth. The URI pattern and variable value in this procedure are examples. You must use actual URLs where your directory avatars are located.

Step 1. From the Cisco Directory Connector, go to **Configuration**, click **Avatar**, and then check **Enable**.

Step 2. For Get Avatar From, choose **Resource server** and then enter the avatar URI pattern in the Avatar URI Pattern field—for example, http://www.example.com/dir/photo/zoom/{mail: .*?(?=@.*)}.jpg.

Let's look at each part of the avatar URI pattern and what it means:

- http://www.example.com/dir/photo/zoom/ is the path to where all the photos that will be synced are located. It must be a URL that the Cisco Directory Connector service on your server can reach.

- mail: tells the Cisco Directory Connector to get the value of the mail attribute from Active Directory.

- .*?(?=@.*) is a regex syntax that performs these functions:

  - .* is any character, repeating zero or more times.

  - ? tells the preceding variable to match as few characters as possible.

  - (?= ...) matches a group after the main expression without including it in the result. Directory Connector looks for a match and doesn't include it in the output.

  - @.* is the "at" symbol, followed by any character, repeating zero or more times.

- .jpg is the file extension for your users' avatars.

Step 3.　(Optional) If your resource server requires credentials, check **Set user credential for avatar**, then choose either **Use current service logon user** or **Use this user** and enter the password.

Step 4.　In the Variable Value field, enter the variable value—for example, abcd@example.com.

Step 5.　Click **Test** to make sure the avatar URI pattern works correctly.

In this example, if the mail value for one AD entry is abcd@example.com and JPG images were being synchronized, the final avatar URI is http://www.example.com/dir/photo/zoom/abcd.jpg.

Step 6.　After the URI information is verified and looks correct, click **Apply**. For detailed information about using regular expressions, see the Microsoft "Regular Expression Language Quick Reference," available at https://docs.microsoft.com/.

The images that are synchronized become the default avatar for users in the Cisco Webex app. Users are not allowed to set their own avatar after this feature is enabled from the Cisco Directory Connector. The user avatars synchronize over to any matching accounts on the Webex site.

In some cases, organizations will want to synchronize on-premises room information from Active Directory into the Cisco Webex cloud. After you synchronize the room information, the on-premises room devices with a configured, mapped SIP address show up as searchable entries on cloud-registered Webex devices (Room, Desk, and Board).

Step 1.　From the Cisco Directory Connector, go to **Configuration**, and then choose **Object Selection**.

Step 2. Check **Identify Room** to separate the room data from the user data so it is identified properly. When this setting is disabled, room data is treated the same way as user synchronized data.

Step 3. Go to **User Attribute Mapping**, and then change the attribute mapping for the cloud attribute **sipAddresses;type=enterprise.**

■ Choose **MSRTCSIP-PrimaryUserAddress** if available.

■ If you don't have the MSRTCSIP-PrimaryUserAddress attribute in your Active Directory schema, use another field such as **ipPhone**.

Step 4. Create a Room Resource mailbox in Exchange. This adds the **msExchResourc eMetaData;ResourceType:Room** attribute, which the connector then uses to identify rooms.

Step 5. From Active Directory users and computers, navigate to and edit properties of the Room. Add the Fully Qualified SIP URI with a prefix of **sip:**.

Step 6. Do a dry run sync and then a full run sync in the connector. The new room objects are listed Objects Added and matched room objects appear in Objects Matched in the dry run report. Any room objects flagged for deletion are under Rooms Deleted. The dry run results show any room resources that were matched. This setting separates the Active Directory room data (including the room's attribute) from user data. After the synchronization finishes, the cloud statistics on the connector dashboard show room data that was synchronized to the cloud.

Now that you have done these steps, when you do a search on a Webex cloud-registered device, you will see the synchronized room entries that are configured with SIP addresses. When you place a call from the Webex device on that entry, a call is placed to the SIP address that has been configured for the room. Know that the endpoint cannot loop a call back to Cisco Webex. For test dialing devices, these devices must be registered as a SIP URI on-premises or somewhere other than Webex. If the Active Directory room system that you are searching for is registered to Webex and the same email address is on the Webex Room Device, Desk device, or Webex Board for Calendar Service, then the search results will not show the duplicate entry. The Room, Desk, or Board device is dialed directly in Webex, and a SIP call is not made.

By default, the organization contacts or administrators always receive email notifications. With this setting, you can customize who should receive email notifications that summarize directory synchronization reports.

Step 1. From the Cisco Directory Connector, click **Configuration**, and then choose **Notification**.

Step 2. Check **Enable Notification** if you want to override the default notification behavior and add one or more email recipients.

Step 3. Click **Add** and then enter an email address. If you enter an email address with an invalid format, a message pops up telling you to correct the issue before you can save and apply the changes.

Step 4.   If you need to edit any email addresses that you entered, double-click the email entry in the left column and then make any changes you need to.

Step 5.   After you have added all the valid email addresses, click **Apply**.

If you decide that you want to remove email addresses, you can click an email to highlight that entry and then click Remove.

While we have focused on the dry run and configurations of mapping attributes, they will not be replicated to the Webex cloud until a synchronization is performed. There are two synchronization types:

■ Do a full synchronization of Active Directory users into the cloud for when you first synchronize new users to the cloud. You do so from **Actions > Sync Now > Full**, and then users from the current domain are synchronized.

■ Set the Connector schedule and run an incremental synchronization after you run a full synchronization if you want to pick up changes after the initial synchronization. This type of synchronization is recommended to pick up on small changes made to the Active Directory user source.

By default, an incremental synchronization is set to occur every 30 minutes (on the Cisco Directory Connector versions 3.4 and earlier) or every 4 hours (on versions 3.5 and later), but you can change this value. The incremental synchronization does not occur until you initially perform a full synchronization.

When you run a full synchronization, the connector service sends all filtered objects from your Active Directory to the cloud. The connector service then updates the identity store with your AD entries. If you created an auto-assign license template, you could assign that to the newly synchronized users. If you have multiple domains, you must do this step on each of the Cisco Directory Connector instances you have installed for each Active Directory domain. The Cisco Directory Connector synchronizes the user account state in Active Directory, and any users that are marked as disabled also appear as inactive in the cloud.

If you want the Cisco Webex user accounts to be in Active status after the full synchronization and before users sign in for the first time, you must complete these requirements to bypass the email validation:

■ Integrate single sign-on with your Cisco Webex organization.

■ Use Cisco Webex Control Hub to verify and optionally claim domains contained in the email addresses.

■ Suppress automatic email invites in Control Hub, so that new users won't receive the automatic email invitation to Webex. If emails aren't suppressed, an email is sent to each user with an invite to join and download Cisco Webex. (You can do your own email campaign if desired.)

You must set up an auto-assign license template in Control Hub before you use it on new Cisco Webex users that you synchronized from Active Directory. The auto-assign license template only works on new synced users. If you update any user, you must remove those users and add them back in for the template to apply to them.

Step 1.   Choose one of the following options:

■ After first-time sign-in, if the dry run is complete and looks correct for all domains, click **Enable Now** to allow automatic synchronization to occur.

■ From the Cisco Directory Connector, go to the **Dashboard**, click **Actions**, choose **Synchronization Mode > Enable Synchronization**, and then choose **Sync Now > Full** to start the synchronization.

Step 2.   Confirm the start of the synchronization. For any changes that you make to users in Active Directory (for example, display name), Cisco Webex Control Hub reflects the change immediately when you refresh the user view, but the Cisco Webex app reflects the changes up to 72 hours after you perform the synchronization.

■ During the synchronization, the dashboard shows the synchronization progress; this may include the type of synchronization, the time it started, and the phase in which the synchronization is currently running.

■ After synchronization, the Last Synchronization and Cloud Statistics sections are updated with the new information. User data is synchronized to the cloud.

■ If errors occur during the synchronization, the status indicator ball turns red.

Step 3.   Click **Refresh** if you want to update the status of the synchronization. (Synchronized items appear under Cloud Statistics.)

Step 4.   For information about errors, select **Launch Event Viewer** from the Actions toolbar to view the error logs.

Step 5.   (Optional) To set a synchronization schedule for ongoing incremental syncs to the cloud, click **Configuration**, and then choose **Schedule**.

Step 6.   Specify the Incremental Synchronization Interval in minutes. By default, an incremental synchronization is set to occur every 30 minutes. The full incremental synchronization does not occur until you initially perform a full synchronization.

Step 7.   Change the Send Reports Per...time value if you want to change how often reports are sent.

Step 8.   Check **Enable Full Sync Schedule** to specify the days and times on which you want a full synchronization to occur.

Step 9.   Specify the Failover Interval in minutes.

Step 10. Click **Apply**.

After full synchronization is completed, the status for directory synchronization updates from Disabled to Operational on the Settings page in Cisco Webex Control Hub. When all data is matched between on premises and cloud, the Cisco Directory Connector changes from manual mode to automatic synchronization mode. Unless you integrate single sign-on, verify domains, optionally claim domains for the email accounts that you synchronized, and suppress automated emails, the Cisco Webex user accounts remain in a Not Verified state until users sign in to Cisco Webex for the first time to confirm their accounts. If you have multiple domains, do this step on any other Cisco Directory Connector that you have installed. After synchronization, the users on all domains you added are listed in Cisco Webex Control Hub. If you integrated SSO with Cisco Webex and suppressed email notifications, the email invitations are not sent out to the newly synchronized users. You cannot manually add users in Cisco Webex Control Hub after the Cisco Directory Connector is enabled. Once enabled, user management is performed from the Cisco Directory Connector and Active Directory is the single source of truth.

When you remove a user from Active Directory, the user is soft-deleted after the next synchronization. The user status becomes Inactive but the cloud identity profile is kept for seven days (to allow for recovery from accidental deletion). When you check Account is Disabled in Active Directory, the user status becomes Inactive after the next synchronization. The cloud identity profile is not deleted after seven days, in case you want to enable the user again.

Note these exceptions to an incremental synchronization (follow the full synchronization steps previously provided):

- In the case of an updated avatar but no other attribute change, incremental sync will not update the user's avatar to the cloud.

- Configuration changes on attribute mapping, base DN, filter, and avatar setting require a full synchronization.

After you complete a full user synchronization from the Cisco Directory Connector to Cisco Webex Control Hub, you can use Control Hub to assign the same Cisco Webex service licenses to all your users at once or add additional licenses to new users if you already configured an auto-assigned license template. You can make individual user account changes after this initial step.

When you assign a license to a Cisco Webex user, that user receives an email confirming the assignment, by default. The email is sent by a notification service in Cisco Webex Control Hub. If you integrated SSO with your Cisco Webex organization, you could also suppress these automatic email notifications in Control Hub if you prefer to contact your users directly.

At the time of full synchronization, the user is created in the cloud, no service assignments are added, and no activation email is sent. If emails are not suppressed, the new users receive an activation email when you assign services to users by a standard user management method in Control Hub, such as CSV import, manual user update, or through successful auto-assignment completion.

Follow these steps to suppress email notifications:

Step 1.   From the customer view in https://admin.webex.com, go to **Users**, click **Manage Users**, choose **Modify all synchronized users**, and then click **Next**.

Step 2.   If you suppressed email notifications, read the prompt that appears and then click **Next**.

Step 3.   On the Sync Status indicator, click the refresh arrow to reload the list, click **Next**.

Step 4. Check the Cisco Webex services that you want to apply initially to all the synchronized users. If the license template has already been configured and activated, Cisco Webex services from the template are applied to the newly synchronized users.

If you selected the same Cisco Webex services for all your users, afterwards you can change licenses assigned individually or in bulk in Cisco Webex Control Hub.

Webex User Service Assignment

Site administrators can manage Webex users from Cisco Webex Control Hub and can individually or bulk assign privileges to people in their organization. Take note that site administrators can only set a user's privileges if the user has Cisco Webex Enterprise Edition.

Step 1. From the customer view in https://admin.webex.com, go to **Users** and select the user whose privileges you would like to change.

Step 2. Under **Services**, select **Meeting**.

Step 3. Under **Webex Meeting Sites**, select the Webex site to update privileges.

Step 4. Select **User Privileges** and choose to

- View and adjust the user's basic privileges, such as telephony privileges for hosting a meeting, privileges for personal room, high-quality video, and high-definition video.

- Select **Advanced Settings** to configure the user's more detailed privileges and settings. Utilize Table 17-2 for advanced user privileges and click **Update** after making changes in the Advanced Settings page.

Table 17-2 Advanced User Setting Options

Privilege	Description
Additional Recording Storage	Enter the amount of extra recording space to be allocated for a user.
Contact Information	Specify the user's phone information and enable call-back teleconferencing.
Create Recording Transcripts for All of This User's MP4 Recordings	Enable recording transcripts for all this user's MP4 recordings.
Enable Facebook Live Integration	Allow this user to stream meetings with Facebook Live.
High-quality Video	Enable video settings. High-quality video must be enabled in order to turn on high-definition video.
Personal Room (Webex Meetings Only)	Enable Personal Room, when available on the site.
Personal Room URL	Create a custom URL for the user's Personal Room by entering it in the text box.
Recording and Content Management	Enable to assign recordings, programs, and categories to this user, reassign them to a different user, or delete them.

Privilege	Description
Telephony Privilege	Select the types of teleconference options you want the user to be able to select when scheduling sessions, including call-in and call-back teleconferencing and integrated VoIP.
Video Systems	List the user's video system name and video address. The site administrator can also indicate if the user's default video system.
WebACD Preferences	If enabled, WebACD is enabled for a user. A site administrator can indicate ■ If the user is an agent, manager, or both ■ The maximum number of simultaneous sessions the agent can participate in ■ If the agent can accept Webex Support inbound requests, and specifically from which or from all queues ■ If the manager can monitor specific or all Webex Support queues and Webex Support agents
Webex Events	If Webex Events is enabled for this user, select Optimize Bandwidth Usage for Attendees Within the Same Network to maximize network performance.
Webex Support	■ If Webex Support sessions are recorded by selecting Enforce Recording Automatically When Meeting Starts. Choose from Network-Based Recording (NBR) or Save Recording at Local Computer and specify a location. ■ If the default client for this user is from the Multi Session client or Single Session client. On the single session client, indicate if the user is using the New Console or Old Console in the drop-down list.
Webex Training	If Webex Training and the Hands-on Lab options are enabled for the site, select Hands-On Lab Admin (effective only when Hands-On Lab is enabled) to make this user a lab administrator.

Step 5. When complete, click **Save**.

You can leave the Display Name field empty (default) so that users' first and last names appear in meetings and reports, or you can overwrite their official names by entering their preferred names in the Display Name field. To update display names in bulk, modify user attributes with CSV File Imports. To manually update an individual user's display name in Control Hub, follow these instructions:

Step 1. From the customer view in https://admin.webex.com/, go to **Management > Users**, and select the user that you'd like to give a display name.

Step 2. Select the edit icon by the user's name to open the user details.

Step 3. Add a name in the Display Name field and click **Save**.

To edit multiple users' services:

Step 1.   Go to **Users**, click **Manage Users**, select **Export and Import Users with a CSV File**, and then click **Export.**

Step 2.   In the file that you download, simply add **True** for the services you want to assign to each of your users.

Step 3.   Import the completed file, click **Add and Remove Services**, and then click **Submit.**

Exam Preparation Tasks

As mentioned in the section "How to Use This Book" in the Introduction, you have a couple of choices for exam preparation: the exercises here, Chapter 24, "Final Preparation," and the exam simulation questions in the Pearson Test Prep practice test software.

Review All Key Topics

Review the most important topics in this chapter, noted with the Key Topics icon in the outer margin of the page. Table 17-3 lists a reference of these key topics and the page numbers on which each is found.

Key Topic

Table 17-3   Key Topics for Chapter 17

Key Topic Element	Description	Page Number
Steps	Deploy Webex Hybrid Directory Service	319
Paragraph	Configuration and synchronization of Active Directory	326
Paragraph	Cisco Directory Connector dry run	329

Complete Tables and Lists from Memory

There are no memory tables or lists in this chapter.

Define Key Terms

Define the following key terms from this chapter and check your answers in the glossary:

application programming interface (API), Cisco Directory Connector, Cisco Webex Control Hub, Comma-Separated Values (CSV), Hypertext Transfer Protocol (HTTP), Hypertext Transfer Protocol Secure (HTTPS), Lightweight Directory Access Protocol (LDAP), Microsoft Active Directory (AD), Microsoft Active Directory Lightweight Directory Services (AD LDS), NT LAN Manager (NTLM), Uniform Resource Locator (URL)

Q&A

The answers to these questions appear in Appendix A. For more practice with exam format questions, use the Pearson Test Prep practice test software.

1. What are the requirements and recommendations for synchronizing Active Directory information from multiple domains into the Webex cloud?

2. What are the high-level steps required to deploy Webex Hybrid Directory Service?

17

CHAPTER 18

Configure Webex Hybrid Calendar Service

This chapter covers the following topics:

Calendar Service Operation: Provides an overview of Hybrid Calendar Service and its operation.

Expressway-Based Calendar Connector: Describes how to deploy the Expressway-based Calendar Connector to your environment.

Google Calendar Deployment in the Cloud: Recapitulates the deployment process of the Google Calendar integration.

Office 365: Covers the deployment of cloud Office 365 with Cisco Webex Hybrid Calendar Service.

One Button to Push (OBTP): Reviews the OBTP feature and its integration with Hybrid Calendar Service.

This chapter focuses on Webex Hybrid Calendar Service and the integration of Microsoft Exchange, Office 365, or Google Calendar. It covers Hybrid Calendar Service and its operation, deployment of the Expressway-based Calendar Connector, and integration of cloud-based calendar services, and provides an overview of One Button to Push (OBTP).

This chapter covers the following objective from the Implementing Cisco Collaboration Cloud and Edge Solutions (CLCEI) exam 300-820:

- 4.2.a Configure Webex Hybrid Services/Connector: Calendar Service (Office 365, Microsoft Exchange, One Button to Push)

"Do I Know This Already?" Quiz

The "Do I Know This Already?" quiz enables you to assess whether you should read this entire chapter thoroughly or jump to the "Exam Preparation Tasks" section. If you are in doubt about your answers to these questions or your own assessment of your knowledge of the topics, read the entire chapter. Table 18-1 lists the major headings in this chapter and their corresponding "Do I Know This Already?" quiz questions. You can find the answers in Appendix A, "Answers to the 'Do I Know This Already?' Quizzes and Review Questions."

Table 18-1 "Do I Know This Already?" Section-to-Question Mapping

Foundation Topics Section	Questions
Calendar Service Operation	1
Expressway-Based Calendar Connector	2–3
Google Calendar Deployment in the Cloud	4
Office 365	5
One Button to Push (OBTP)	6

CAUTION The goal of self-assessment is to gauge your mastery of the topics in this chapter. If you do not know the answer to a question or are only partially sure of the answer, you should mark that question as wrong for purposes of the self-assessment. Giving yourself credit for an answer you correctly guess skews your self-assessment results and might provide you with a false sense of security.

1. Under the meetings list in the Cisco Webex app, how long in advance can users see upcoming meetings?

   a. 1 week

   b. 2 weeks

   c. 4 weeks

   d. 8 weeks

2. Which of the following is a micro-service on the Expressway-C that is the on-premises component of Hybrid Calendar Service?

   a. Calendar Connector

   b. Management Connector

   c. Directory Connector

   d. Call Connector

3. True or False? The Expressway-C Connector Hosts support dual NIC deployments.

   a. True

   b. False

4. How many user emails can be associated with a single Hybrid Calendar integration?

   a. Unlimited

   b. Three

   c. Ten

   d. One

5. Which API service does the Cisco Hybrid Calendar Service utilize with a Microsoft Office 365 environment?

   a. Microsoft Graph API

   b. Microsoft Edge

   c. Microsoft Stream API

   d. Microsoft Discovery Service API

6. To deploy the One Button to Push feature on video devices, what Hybrid Service is required?

   a. Webex Hybrid Directory Service

   b. Webex Hybrid Calendar Service

   c. Webex On-premises Service

   d. Webex Hybrid Message Service

Foundation Topics

Calendar Service Operation

Cisco Webex Hybrid Calendar Service leverages information from users' **Microsoft Exchange, Office 365**, or **Google Calendar** accounts to make meetings and their workflow more efficient. With one of the simplest meeting scheduling flows on the market, this service is beneficial to all users, whether they are in the office or on a mobile device. However, this service especially makes scheduling from mobile devices easier. As more and more users become mobile, they want to schedule meetings from their mobile phones. Modern built-in mobile calendar applications do not allow plug-ins. Consequently, there is no easy way to add a Cisco Webex Space or meeting join information in a mobile app. Using a web-based calendar for scheduling, such as Microsoft Outlook Web Access (OWA), is difficult and forces users to manually copy and paste the meeting join information. This problem is so significant that many users wait until they get to the office to open their laptop and schedule meetings.

Cisco Webex Hybrid Calendar Service overcomes these issues so that you can schedule meetings and create a Cisco Webex Space on any device, anywhere. Adding the phrase @webex:space to the location line of the meeting invitation automatically opens a new Cisco Webex workspace with the invitees, allowing that team to begin the conversation and share documents and ideas before the meeting even starts. It also automatically populates the body of the invitation with the meeting join information and adds an artifact to the team workspace so the team knows a meeting has been scheduled. Attendees can then join the meeting from the Cisco Webex workspace. If users do not need a workspace and just need to meet, they can add the phrase @webex to the location field of the invitation. The invitation is automatically populated with the meeting join information, allowing the users to enjoy Cisco Webex Meetings. These capabilities do not require any plug-ins. No manual cutting and pasting of information is necessary. Simply adding @webex:space or @webex to a meeting invitation allows people to schedule meetings from any device.

In addition to the scheduling keywords, Hybrid Calendar Service can parse a SIP URI or other video address from the body of a calendar invitation, even if it is not a Webex standard meeting, Webex Personal Room meeting, or Webex team meeting address. When the address matches a supported format, the meeting appears in invitees' meetings lists and meeting notifications in the Webex app. The meeting also appears in the list on any scheduled room or desk devices that are enabled for Hybrid Calendar Service, and the devices show the green Join button (One Button to Push) just before the meeting starts.

The meetings list in Cisco Webex lets users see upcoming meetings for the next 4 weeks. Users see a Join button in the meetings list and a scheduled meeting notification 5 minutes before the meeting starts.

Users can add Cisco Webex room and desk devices and Webex Boards to a meeting to make conferencing resources available. If the device is enabled for Hybrid Calendar Service, the green Join button appears on the device. (The Join button is also known as One Button to Push and is also available to devices that are registered to Cisco Unified Communications Manager and managed by Cisco Telepresence Management Suite.) Hybrid Calendar Service–enabled room and desk devices can also show meetings to which they have been invited in the meetings list.

Expressway-Based Calendar Connector

The Cisco Expressway-C Connector Host is a standard Cisco Expressway-C server deployed within the customer's organization to provide an integration point between the on-premises and cloud collaboration services. The integration between the Cisco Expressway-C server and Cisco Webex is facilitated via micro-services installed and managed on the Expressway-C Connector Host by Webex. These micro-services enable Hybrid Calendar Service.

Cisco Expressway-C Connector Host Preparation

The Management Connector is included in the Expressway-C base. You use it to register an Expressway to the cloud and link the Expressway interface with **Cisco Webex Control Hub**. The Management Connector plays an important role as the coordinator of all connectors running on the Expressway server or cluster. It provides you with a single point of control for connector activities. The Management Connector enables cloud-based management of the on-premises connectors, handles initial registration with the cloud, manages the connector software lifecycle, and provides status and alarms.

For a **Hypertext Transfer Protocol Secure (HTTPS)** connection to be established between the Management Connector and the cloud, you must update the trust list on the Expressway-C Connector Host with certificates that were signed by **certificate authorities (CAs)** in use by the **Cisco Webex cloud**. You can allow the Cisco Webex cloud to upload CA certificates to the Expressway-C trust store. Or, in the case where security policies prevent the Cisco Webex cloud from uploading trusted CA certificates on the Expressway-C, you may upload them manually.

Figure 18-1 shows the components of Hybrid Calendar Service architecture and where the Expressway-based connectors integrate the on-premises components with the cloud.

18

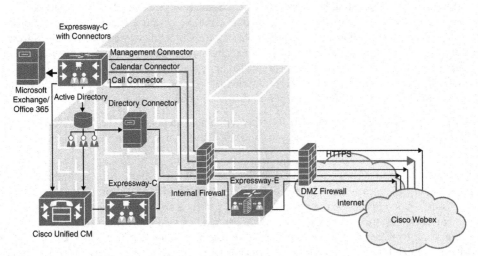

Figure 18-1 *Hybrid Calendar Service Architecture*

The Calendar Connector is the on-premises component of Hybrid Calendar Service. The connector runs on an Expressway-C host that you register to the Cisco Webex cloud. The Calendar Connector acts like a broker between the cloud and your Microsoft Exchange (on premises), Office 365 (cloud), or both (hybrid Exchange deployment). The connector acts on behalf of users, similar to the way a client application would access a user's calendar information. The connector uses the impersonation role (which you can restrict to a subset of users) and uses Exchange Web Services to

- Autodiscover where users are homed

- Listen for notifications on a user's calendar

- Retrieve information on a user's calendar items and Out-of-Office status

- Populate meeting invitations with details of Cisco Webex spaces and Webex Personal Rooms

Webex Hybrid Calendar Service is designed to minimize security concerns in a hybrid environment:

- The cloud cannot retrieve or access the Exchange credentials from the connector.

- The cloud has no direct access to Exchange through the connector.

- The connector does not access any user email or contacts.

- The connector does not create search folders or other extra folders for the user.

- The connector is not an Exchange Foreign connector.

- The connector does not interact with the Exchange Hub transport server.

- No Active Directory schema extensions are required.

In a production Exchange server, the Calendar Connector increases the CPU usage and load on the Client Access server (CAS) and Mailbox (MBX) servers. The impact on your Exchange environment depends on the following:

- Your Exchange deployment

- The number of configured users

- The number of meetings that Hybrid Calendar Service updates per user per hour

- The size of calendars

With the release of the cloud-based service for Office 365 users, you can now choose whether to deploy only the Expressway-based Calendar Connector, a combination of the Calendar Connector and the cloud-based service, or, if you have no Microsoft Exchange users, only the cloud-based service. The cloud-based service can scale beyond the 1000 user limit for Office 365 users and is simpler to deploy and maintain. It does not service Microsoft Exchange users. If you deploy it alongside the Calendar Connector, your Office 365 users automatically move to the cloud-based service (unless they are in resource groups).

The cloud-based service supports the Cisco **Telepresence Management Suite (TMS)** scheduling option. This integration allows the service to leverage your on-premises resource management and conference hosting environment for simplified meeting scheduling. The integration also extends the **One Button to Push (OBTP)** meeting join experience to a wide range of video devices. The cloud-based service links to the on-premises Cisco TMS by using the Calendar Connector. For this reason, you cannot deploy the Cisco TMS integration in the same organization with a Calendar Connector that is configured for Microsoft Exchange or Office 365.

Each user's email address in the calendar system (Microsoft Exchange or Office 365) must match their Cisco Webex login address. To use @webex, the address should also match the user's Cisco Webex account address. If it does not, users must associate their Webex Personal Room within the Cisco Webex app to use @webex. Each Webex user can have only one email address associated with only one Hybrid Calendar Service integration. In other words, Hybrid Calendar Service will only process meetings from a single address for creating spaces, decorating meetings, showing the meetings list and Join button, and sending OTBP to video devices.

The Calendar Connector integrates Cisco Webex with Microsoft Exchange 2013, 2016, 2019, or Office 365 through an impersonation account. The application impersonation management role in Exchange enables applications to impersonate users in an organization to perform tasks on behalf of the user. The application impersonation role must be configured in Exchange and is used in the Calendar Connector as part of the Exchange configuration on the Expressway-C interface. The Exchange impersonation account is Microsoft's recommended method for this task. Expressway-C administrators do not need to know the password, because the value can be entered in the Expressway-C interface by an Exchange administrator. The password is not clearly shown, even if the Expressway-C administrator has root access to the Expressway-C box. The password is stored encrypted using the same credential encryption mechanism as other passwords on the Expressway-C.

Before you begin to set up an impersonation account for on-premises Microsoft Exchange, you must choose a mail-enabled account to use as the service account. The account does not have to be an administrator, but it must have a mailbox. Do not use an impersonation account that is used by other services such as Cisco Unity Connection, Cisco TMS Extension for Microsoft Exchange (TMSXE), and so on. If you limited the set of users that are synchronized with Active Directory using LDAP filters, you may want to limit the impersonation by using a new or existing management scope in Exchange. For instructions and more detailed information from Microsoft on management scopes and impersonation, see the Microsoft Docs article "ApplicationImpersonation Role."

Step 1. Sign in to a server on which Exchange Management Shell is installed. Sign in with one of the following accounts:

■ An account that is a member of the Enterprise Admins group

■ An account that can grant permissions on Exchange objects in the configuration container

Step 2. Run the following command in Exchange Management Shell:

new-ManagementRoleAssignment -Name:*RoleName* -Role: ApplicationImpersonation -User '*ServiceUserName*'

Where:

■ *RoleName* is the name that you want to give the assignment; for example, CalendarConnectorAcct. The name that you enter for *RoleName* appears when you run **get-ManagementRoleAssignment**.

■ *ServiceUserName* is the name of the account you selected, in domain\alias format.

Next, you may set up an impersonation account for Office 365. Give impersonation permissions to the service account that the Calendar Connector will use with Office 365. Do not use an impersonation account that is used by other services such as Cisco Unity Connection, Cisco TMSXE, and so on. You must choose a mail-enabled account for this task. The account does not have to be an administrator, but it must have a mailbox. Ensure that the service account can authenticate with the authentication service or directory that is used in your deployment. For a hybrid Exchange on-premises and Office 365 integration, you can use a simplified configuration with a single impersonation account if your deployment meets all the following criteria:

■ You synchronize your on-premises Exchange accounts to the Office 365 cloud.

■ The impersonation account that you use must also be synchronized to the Office 365 cloud, and the account's userPrincipalName must match one of its SMTP addresses.

■ You administer all users in the on-premises Active Directory, including users whose mailboxes have been migrated to the Office 365 cloud.

■ You synchronize passwords or have configured a federation so that users have a single password both on-premises and in the cloud.

■ Your Exchange is configured such that all Autodiscovery service requests reach the on-premises environment. (If a mailbox has been migrated, the response indicates the relocation and provides the cloud email address.)

In the simplified configuration, you use a single impersonation account to service all users. Because **ApplicationImpersonation** privileges that you assign on premises do not automatically apply to mailboxes homed in the Office 365 cloud, you must still explicitly assign these privileges.

For a hybrid integration that does not meet these criteria, follow the procedure presented next, and use a different service account for impersonation than you used in the setup of an impersonation account for on-premises Microsoft Exchange. Later, you will set up two Exchange configuration records on the Expressway-C: one for the Exchange on-premises integration, and one for the Office 365 integration.

Step 1.   Log in to the Office 365 Admin Center using the administrator account.

Step 2.   Under **Admin**, select **Exchange**.

Step 3.   Select **Permissions**.

Step 4.   Under **Admin Roles**, create a new role group and enter a descriptive name, such as *ImpersonationGroup*.

Step 5.   Under **Roles**, add a new role. Select **ApplicationImpersonation** role.

Step 6.   Add the role to the group, and then click **OK**.

Step 7.   Add the service account to be used for impersonation to the group.

Next complete the prerequisites for Hybrid Calendar Service:

Step 1.   Ensure that users are listed in Active Directory and have a discoverable mailbox in the organization's Exchange server.

Step 2.   (Optional) Download the latest Directory Connector software from Cisco Webex Control Hub (https://admin.webex.com) and use it to import user attributes from your Active Directory.

Step 3.   Provide the following port access:

■ Port access for HTTPS or secure web sockets outbound from Expressway to *.rackcdn.com, *.ciscospark.com, *.wbx2.com, *.webex.com, and *.clouddrive.com: TCP port 443 (secure)

■ Port access for Exchange Web Services (EWS) outbound from Expressway to Exchange: TCP port 443 (secure) or TCP port 80 (nonsecure)

■ Port access for LDAP outbound from Expressway to Active Directory: TCP port 636 (secure) or TCP port 389 (nonsecure)

■ Port access for Microsoft Global Catalog search: TCP port 3269 (for Global Catalog search secured by SSL) or TCP port 3268 (for unsecured Global Catalog search)

Step 4.   For @webex functionality, configure or use a Cisco Webex Meetings site. You must enable the Personal Room feature for the site and for the individual users.

18

Step 5. To make One Button to Push available for UCM–registered endpoints managed by TMS:

- Set up Cisco TMS 15.0 and Cisco TMSXE 5.0 or higher with Microsoft Exchange integration. See the *Cisco Collaboration Meeting Rooms (CMR) Hybrid Configuration Guide (TMS 15.0 – Webex Meeting Center WBS30)*. TMS and XE require no additional configuration to support Hybrid Calendar Service.

- To make conference rooms schedulable in Microsoft Outlook/Exchange, configure them in XE as if you were using on-premises conferencing. To configure rooms in Exchange, consult the *Cisco Telepresence Management Suite Extension for Microsoft Exchange Administrator Guide*.

- Understand the licensing requirements:

  - TMS and XE licensing is the same as if using on-premises resources. You require enough licenses to cover the number of endpoints that will use OBTP. A TMS license is needed to manage the endpoint and to push the speed-dial button on the touchpad at the time of the scheduled conference. A TMSXE license is needed for the endpoint to be scheduled in Exchange.

  - For UCM–registered endpoints, OBTP works with Hybrid Calendar Service and Productivity Tools plugin for meeting invitations:

  - Hybrid Calendar Service (scheduling keywords or supported video address) populates the user attribute **TMS:ExternalConferenceData** with the SIP URI for TMS to set the OBTP dial string.

  - The Productivity Tools plugin populates the attribute **UCCapabilities** with the SIP URI for TMS to set the OBTP dial string.

- If you plan to deploy a hybrid Exchange environment with Office 365, you must enable TNEF for remote domains in Exchange Online. Having TNEF disabled causes Exchange Online to strip the TMS:ExternalConferenceData and UCCapabilities attributes, breaking OBTP for UCM–registered endpoints. For more information on TNEF, see the "Exchange Server: TNEF conversion options" located at docs.microsoft.com.

If you have on-premises conferencing, you can add OBTP with Cisco Webex Meetings and run both at the same time. Cisco supports OBTP functionality only; auto connect is not available.

For Cisco Webex Hybrid Services, Cisco recommends that the Expressway-C be dedicated to hosting connectors for Cisco Webex Hybrid Services. You can use the Expressway-C Connector Host for other purposes, but that can change the supported number of users. As an administrator of Webex Hybrid Services, you retain control over the software running on your on-premises equipment. You are responsible for all necessary security measures to protect your servers from physical and electronic attacks. Use the following checklist to prepare an Expressway-C for Cisco Webex Hybrid Services before you register it to the Cisco Webex cloud to host hybrid services connector software.

Step 1.   Obtain full organization administrator rights before you register any Expressways and use these credentials when you access the customer view in Cisco Webex Control Hub (https://admin.webex.com).

Step 2.   Deploy the Expressway-C Connector Host in a cluster to account for redundancy. Follow the supported Expressway scalability recommendations:

- For Hybrid Calendar Service (Exchange or Office 365) on a dedicated Expressway-C:

  - Calendar Connector supports a single cluster with up to two Expressway-C nodes.

  - Calendar Connector can under-provision users. If a single node fails, the system has extra capacity for all users to fail over to the working node. If one of the nodes fails in the cluster, the discovery and assignment services move users to the working node in approximately 30 seconds.

  - The service catches up on any missed notifications if there is an outage.

Hybrid Calendar Service is highly available if Exchange and Cisco Expressways are deployed in a cluster. The same guidelines apply for the Expressway-C Connector Host clustering.

Step 3.   Follow these requirements for the Expressway-C Connector Host:

- Install at least the minimum supported Expressway software version.

- Install the virtual Expressway OVA file according to the *Cisco Expressway on Virtual Machine Installation Guide* on Cisco.com, after which you can access the user interface by browsing to its IP address.

The serial number of a virtual Expressway is based on the virtual machine's MAC address. The serial number is used to validate Expressway licenses and to identify Expressways that are registered to the Cisco Webex cloud. Do not change the MAC address of the Expressway virtual machine when using VMware tools, or you risk losing service.

- You do not require a release key, or an Expressway series key, to use the virtual Expressway-C for Cisco Webex Hybrid Services. You may see an alarm about the release key. You can acknowledge it to remove it from the interface.

- Use the Expressway web interface in a supported browser. The interface may or may not work in unsupported browsers. You must enable JavaScript and cookies to use the Expressway web interface.

Step 4.   If this is your first time running the Expressway, you get a first-time setup wizard to help you configure it for Cisco Webex Hybrid Services. If this is not the first-time setup, select **Cisco Webex Hybrid Services.** This ensures that you will not require a release key.

18

Step 5.   Check that the following requirements are met for the Expressway-C Connector Host. You would normally do this during installation. See the *Cisco Expressway Basic Configuration Deployment Guide* on Cisco.com for more details.

- Basic IP configuration (**System > Network Interfaces > IP**)

- System name (**System > Administration Settings**)

- DNS settings (**System > DNS**)

- NTP settings (**System > Time**)

- New password for admin account (**Users > Administrator Accounts**, click **Admin** user, then click the **Change Password** link)

- New password for root account (log on to CLI as root and run the **passwd** command)

Note that the Expressway-C Connector Hosts do not support dual NIC deployments.

Step 6.   Configure the Expressway-C as a "cluster of one":

- Cisco recommends that you configure the Expressway as a primary peer before you register it, even if you do not currently intend to install an extra peer.

  - When you change clustering settings on X8.11 and later, be aware that removing all peer addresses from the **System > Clustering** page signals to the Expressway that you want to remove it from the cluster. This causes the Expressway to factory reset itself on its next restart. If you want to remove all peers but keep configuration on the remaining Expressway, leave its address on the clustering page and make it the primary in a "cluster of one."

- Here are the minimum clustering settings required, but the *Cisco Expressway Cluster Creation and Maintenance Deployment Guide* has more detail:

  - Enable H.323 protocol. Go to **Configuration > Protocols > H.323** page and set **H.323 Mode to On**. H.323 mode is required for clustering, even if the Expressway does not process H.323 calls. You may not see the H.323 menu item if you used the Service Select wizard to configure the Expressway for Hybrid Services. You can work around this problem by signing in to the Expressway console and issuing the command **xconfig H323 Mode: "On"**.

  - **System > Clustering > Cluster Name** should be an FQDN. Typically this FQDN is mapped by an SRV record in DNS that resolves to A/AAAA records for the cluster peers.

  - **System > Clustering > Configuration** primary should be **1**.

- **System > Clustering > TLS Verification Mode** should be **Permissive**, at least until you add a second peer. Select **Enforce** if you want cluster peers to validate each other's certificates before allowing intercluster communications.

- **System > Clustering > Cluster IP Version** should match the type of IP address of this Expressway-C.

- **System > Clustering > Peer 1 Address** should be the IP address or FQDN of this Expressway.

- Each peer FQDN must match that Expressway's certificate if you are enforcing **Transport Layer Security (TLS)** verification.

- To ensure a successful registration to the cloud, use only lowercase characters in the hostname that you set for the Expressway-C. Capitalization is not supported at this time.

Step 7.   If you have not already done so, open required ports on your firewall.

- All traffic between Expressway-C and the Cisco Webex cloud is HTTPS or secure web sockets.

- TCP port 443 must be open outbound from the Expressway-C. See the article "Network Requirements for Webex Services" located at help.webex.com for details of the cloud domains that are requested by the Expressway-C.

Step 8.   Get the details of your HTTP proxy (address, port) if your organization uses one to access the Internet. You will also need a username and password for the proxy if it requires basic authentication. The Expressway cannot use other methods to authenticate with the proxy.

- Cisco has tested and verified Squid 3.1.19 on Ubuntu 12.04.5.

- Cisco has not tested auth-based proxies.

- If your organization uses a TLS proxy, the Expressway-C must trust the TLS proxy. The proxy's CA root certificate must be in the trust store of the Expressway. You can check whether you need to add it at **Maintenance > Security > Trusted CA Certificate**.

- The details of the proxy, as configured on the primary Expressway in the connector host cluster, are shared throughout the Expressway cluster. You cannot configure different proxies for different nodes in the cluster.

Step 9.   Review the following points about certificate trust. You can choose the type of secure connection when you begin the main setup steps.

- Cisco Webex Hybrid Services requires a secure connection between the Expressway-C and Cisco Webex.

18

- You can let Cisco Webex manage the root CA certificates for you. However, if you choose to manage them yourself, be aware of certificate authorities and trust chains; you must also be authorized to make changes to the Expressway-C trust list.

- Access to the Expressway CA trust list may also be required if you want to secure the connections between the Expressway-C and Microsoft Exchange, or between the Expressway-C and Microsoft Active Directory, when configuring the Calendar Connector.

Next, we will configure a throttling policy and apply it to the impersonation account. A custom throttling policy helps the Calendar Connector work smoothly:

- The custom policy removes EWS limits from the impersonation account, to avoid issues such as maxconcurrency.

- The custom policy is tailored for an enterprise application. (The default policy is tailored for user load.)

This procedure is not required for Office 365.

Step 1.   In Exchange Management Shell, create the policy.

New-ThrottlingPolicy -Name "*CalendarConnectorPolicy*" -EWSMax Concurrency unlimited -EWSMaxBurst unlimited -EWSRechargeRate unlimited -EWSCutOffBalance unlimited -EWSMaxSubscriptions 5000

Step 2.   If the impersonation account does not have a mailbox, run the following command:

Enable-Mailbox "*impersonation account*" -Database "*database name*"

Step 3.   Apply the new policy to the impersonation account:

Set-ThrottlingPolicyAssociation -Identity "*impersonation account*" -ThrottlingPolicy "*CalendarConnectorPolicy*"

- "*impersonation account*" is the name of the impersonation account you are using as the service account for the Calendar Connector.

- *CalendarConnectorPolicy* is the name of the policy that you created in the previous steps.

Step 4.   Confirm that the mailbox is using the new policy:

Get-ThrottlingPolicyAssociation -Identity "*impersonation account*" | findstr "*ThrottlingPolicy*"

Hybrid Calendar Service Deployment

Next, we will register Expressway-C Connector Hosts to the Cisco Webex cloud. Cisco Webex Hybrid Services use software connectors hosted on the Expressway-C to securely connect Cisco Webex to your organization's environment. Use the following procedure to register Expressway-C resources to the cloud. After you complete the registration steps, the connector software is automatically deployed on your on-premises Expressway-C.

Before you begin, make sure your Expressway-C is running on a version that is supported for hybrid services. See the article "Supported Versions of Expressway for Cisco Webex Hybrid Services Connectors" located at help.webex.com for more information about which versions are supported for new and existing registrations to the cloud. Then, sign out of any open connections to the Expressway-C interface that are open in other browser tabs. Also, if your on-premises environment proxies the outbound traffic, you must first enter the details of the proxy server at **Applications > Hybrid Services > Connector Proxy** before you complete this procedure. Doing so is necessary for successful registration.

Step 1.   From the customer view in https://admin.webex.com, go to **Services** and then choose one of the following options:

■ If this is the first connector host you are registering, click **Set Up** on the card for the hybrid service you are deploying, and then click **Next**.

■ If you have already registered one or more connector hosts, click **View All** on the card for the hybrid service you are deploying, and then click **Add Resource**.

The Cisco Webex cloud rejects any attempt at registration from the Expressway web interface. You must first register your Expressway through Cisco Webex Control Hub because the Control Hub needs to hand out a token to the Expressway to establish trust between premises and cloud to complete the secure registration.

Step 2.   Choose a method to register the Expressway-C:

■ New Expressways: Choose **Register a New Expressway with Its Fully Qualified Domain Name (FQDN)**, enter your Expressway-C IP address or FQDN so that Cisco Webex creates a record of that Expressway-C and establishes trust, and then click **Next**. You can also enter a display name to identify the resource in Cisco Webex Control Hub. Caution: To ensure a successful registration to the cloud, use only lowercase characters in the host name that you set for the Expressway-C. Capitalization is not supported at this time.

■ Existing Expressways: Choose **Select an Existing Expressway Cluster to Add Resources to This Service**, and then choose from the drop-down list the node or cluster that you previously registered. You can use it to run more than one hybrid service.

If you are registering a cluster, register the primary peer. You do not need to register any other peers, because they register automatically when the primary registers. If you start with one node set up as a primary, subsequent additions do not require a system reboot.

Step 3.   Click **Next**, and for new registrations, click the link to open your Expressway-C. You can then sign in to load the Connector Management window.

Step 4.   Decide how you want to update the Expressway-C trust list. A check box on the welcome page determines whether you will manually append the required

18

CA certificates to the Expressway-C trust list or you will allow Cisco Webex to add those certificates for you. Choose one of the following options:

- When you register, the root certificates for the authorities that signed the Cisco Webex cloud certificates are installed automatically on the Expressway-C. This means that the Expressway-C should automatically trust the certificates and be able to set up the secure connection. Check the box if you want Cisco Webex to add the required CA certificates to the Expressway-C trust list. If you change your mind, you can use the Connector Management window to remove the Cisco Webex cloud CA root certificates and manually install root certificates.

- Uncheck the box if you want to manually update the Expressway-C trust list.

Step 5. Click **Register.** (When you register, you will get certificate trust errors if the trust list does not currently have the correct CA certificates.) After you are redirected to Cisco Webex Control Hub, read the onscreen text to confirm that Cisco Webex identified the correct Expressway-C.

Step 6. After you verify the information, click **Allow** to register the Expressway-C for Cisco Webex Hybrid Services.

- Registration can take up to 5 minutes depending on the configuration of the Expressway and whether it is a first-time registration.

- After the Expressway-C registers successfully, the Cisco Webex Hybrid Services window on the Expressway-C shows the connectors downloading and installing. The Management Connector automatically upgrades itself if there is a newer version available, and then installs any other connectors that you selected for the Expressway-C Connector Host.

- Each connector installs the interface pages that you need to configure and activate that connector.

This process can take a few minutes. When the connectors are installed, you can see new menu items on the **Applications > Hybrid Services** menu on your Expressway-C Connector Host. If registration fails and your on-premises environment proxies the outbound traffic, review the paragraph at the beginning of this procedure. If the registration process times out or fails (for example, you must fix certificate errors or enter proxy details), you can restart registration in Cisco Webex Control Hub.

If you want to verify the certificates presented by the Exchange Server, then the Expressway trust list must contain the certificate of the CA that signed the Exchange Server certificate. The CA certificate may already be in the trust list; use the following procedure on each Expressway cluster to check the list and append the certificate if necessary.

If you are using a custom domain, make sure that you add the CA certificate for the domain certificate issuer to the Expressways. Also, you must import certificates to each Expressway-C.

Step 1. On the Expressway-C Connector Host, go to **Maintenance > Security certificates > Trusted CA Certificate.**

Step 2.   Review the CA certificates in the trust list to check if the correct CA certificate is already trusted.

Step 3.   To append any new CA certificates:

    a.   Click **Browse** (or the equivalent in your browser) to locate and select the PEM file.

    b.   Click **Append CA Certificate**. The newly appended CA certificate appears in the list of CA certificates.

Step 4.   To replace an existing CA certificate with an updated one, for a particular issuer and subject:

    a.   Check the check box next to the issuer details.

    b.   Click **Delete**.

    c.   Append the replacement certificate as described previously.

The "Supported Certificate Authorities for Cisco Webex Hybrid Services" article located on help.webex.com lists the CAs that your on-premises or existing environment must trust when using Cisco Webex Hybrid Services. If you opted to have Cisco Webex manage the required certificates, then you do not need to manually append CA certificates to the Expressway-C trust list.

Note that the issuers used to sign the Cisco Webex host certificates may change in the future.

The Calendar Connector installs automatically after you register your Expressway-C Connector Host for Cisco Webex Hybrid Services. The connector does not start automatically and requires some configuration to link to your calendar environment.

Step 1.   From the Expressway-C Connector Host, go to **Applications > Hybrid Services > Calendar Service > Microsoft Exchange Configuration**, and then click **New**. Make sure you choose **Microsoft Exchange Configuration**, not Cisco Conferencing Services Configuration. You cannot configure the Calendar Connector for Microsoft Exchange or Office 365 in the same organization with the conferencing services (integration with Cisco Telepresence Management Suite).

Step 2.   Enter the credentials of the service account that you want the Calendar Connector to use to connect to Exchange. The service account queries calendars on behalf of your users, using the impersonation role. You can use these formats:

    ■   *username@domain.com*: The userPrincipalName. Typically, this value matches the user's primary email address, but the properties are separate. userPrincipalName consists of the User Logon Name (not always the same as sAMAccountName) and the UPN suffix, which is based on the Active Directory domain (not always the same as the NetBIOS domain). Use this format whenever possible. If you used the simplified configuration with a single impersonation account to prepare a hybrid Exchange on-premises and Office 365 integration, you must use this format. Also, make sure that the impersonation account that you use is synchronized to the Office 365 cloud, and that its userPrincipalName matches one of the account's SMTP addresses.

18

■ *DOMAIN\username*: *DOMAIN* is the NetBIOS domain (the pre-Windows 2000 domain); *username* is the sAMAccountName (the legacy username or pre-Windows 2000 username). If you are unsure about what to use for these formats, use Active Directory Users and Computers on a Windows machine to view the Account tab of the Properties pane for the user in question. The correct values to use are displayed as follows:

  ■ User logon name for the first format

  ■ User logon name (pre-Windows 2000) for the second format

Step 3. Enter in the Display Name field a unique display name for this Exchange server.

Step 4. For the Type setting:

■ Select **Exchange On-Premises** for Exchange 2013, 2016, or 2019. (Select this type even if you are preparing a hybrid Exchange on premises.)

■ Select **Office365** for Office 365 integration.

Step 5. For Need Proxy for Connection?, select **Yes** if HTTPS access goes through a web proxy to your Exchange environment.

Step 6. For Enable This Exchange Server?, select **Yes**. You can select **No** for debugging purposes, but users will not be subscribed to this Exchange.

Step 7. Check a value for the Authentication Type:

■ For added security, Cisco recommends NTLM for on-premises Exchange servers.

■ For hybrid Exchange (on-premises and Office 365) deployments, check both **NTLM** and **Basic** authentication types. If one method fails, then the other method is used.

Step 8. Leave TLS Verify Mode as the default value **On** so that this Expressway-C verifies the certificate that the Exchange Server presents. You may need to update the trust stores on both servers to ensure that each one trusts the CA that signed the other's certificate.

Step 9. Under Discovery, select **Use Autodiscover** to enable autodiscovery. The Calendar Connector queries to find one or more Exchange servers. You must use autodiscovery for deployments of Microsoft Exchange 2013 and later. Use **Provide Exchange Address Directly** only for troubleshooting or testing purposes. This option does not use the Microsoft Autodiscover service. If you select it, enter the IPv4 address, IPv6 address, or FQDN of the Exchange server.

Step 10. Configure the extra fields that are related to Autodiscover:

a. Choose whether to Enable SCP record lookup. If you set this field to **Yes**, the first autodiscover step that the Calendar Connector takes is an Active Directory Service Connection Point (SCP) record lookup to get a list of Autodiscover URLs. The Calendar Connector uses the Active Directory Domain, Active Directory Site, Query Mode, and LDAP TLS Verify Mode fields only if you enable this step. These fields provide the information necessary to find and query an LDAP server in Active Directory. Even if this step fails, autodiscovery may succeed at a later step.

b. Enter the Active Directory domain to query for the SCP record.

c. (Optional) Enter the Active Directory site that is geographically closest to the Calendar Connector, to optimize the query response time.

d. Select a query mode to control which directory access protocol that Calendar Connector uses to query Active Directory. If you select **ldaps** (secure LDAP), the domain controller must authenticate itself by presenting a server certificate to this Expressway-C.

e. Enable **LDAP TLS Verify Mode** if you want the Expressway-C to validate the certificate that the domain controller presents. This option checks the server name against the CN or SANs in the received certificate and checks that the issuing authority is in the local trusted CA list.

f. Enter an email address in the Email Address field so that Calendar Connector can test the autodiscover process (other than SCP record lookup, which uses the Active Directory domain instead). Use the email address of a user that you will enable for Webex Hybrid Calendar Service, as it appears in Cisco Webex Control Hub. If the test fails, then your settings are not saved. If you omit the email address, then your settings are saved without verifying the autodiscover process (other than SCP record lookup, if enabled).

g. (Optional) To manually configure any Autodiscover redirect URLs that the Calendar Connector should trust, click **Configure Trust List**. Once you click **Add**, the Calendar Connector automatically populates any missing Autodiscover redirect URLs that it finds while contacting the Autodiscover service. URLs from unauthenticated sources are placed in pending state and blocked unless you choose to allow them. If you skip this step now, you can still manually add URLs later, or explicitly accept or deny the pending URLs.

Step 11. Click **Add** to store the Exchange Server configuration on the Expressway-C Connector Host. The Calendar Connector tests the connection to the Exchange environment and notifies you if there are pending Autodiscover redirect URLs to review.

Step 12. (Optional) If your organization has multiple user email domains, Cisco recommends that you test the autodiscover configuration with a user address from each email domain to ensure that the process works for all of them. To test another address, change the value of the Email Address field to a different address, and then click **Save**.

After you configure the Exchange settings, configure the details for your Cisco Webex Meetings sites. If you have more than one Webex site, do these steps for each site, and set the default to the site with the most users. Users who are not on the default site, or who want to use a different site, must associate their Cisco Webex Personal Room with Cisco Webex in the app.

For the @webex functionality to work for users, verify the following:

- You have at least one Cisco Webex Meetings site, with the Personal Room feature enabled for the site and for the individual users.

- The email address in each user's Webex account matches the user's Exchange email address and Cisco Webex login address. If it does not, the user must associate their Cisco Webex Personal Room with the Cisco Webex app.

Gather the Webex user account email address of a valid user on your site. The Calendar Connector uses this account to access the Webex Personal Room details for users who schedule meetings with @webex.

Step 1. From the Expressway-C Connector Host, go to **Applications > Hybrid Services > Calendar Service > Cisco Conferencing Services Configuration**, and then click **New**.

Step 2. Under Conferencing Services Type, select **Webex**.

Step 3. In the Fully Qualified Site Name field, enter the name for this Cisco Webex Meetings site. For example, if your site is accessed at site-example.webex.com, you would enter site-example.webex.com.

Step 4. Enter a valid Webex user account email address, leave the password field blank, and then click **Test Connection** to validate the site information that you entered. If testing the connection fails, you can save the configuration with both the username and password fields blank.

Step 5. Indicate whether this site is the default. The default site is used for @webex unless the user has a different site configured in their My Personal Room setting in the Webex app (either because the user's Webex site has been linked to Webex by an administrator or because the user configured the setting with a different site).

Step 6. Click **Save** to save the configuration.

In Cisco Webex Control Hub, the Default Language setting controls the language of the join details that Hybrid Calendar Service adds to invitations. If you leave the setting at its default, the service uses the language from the **item.Culture** property of each meeting invitation. (Typically, the scheduler's operating system controls the value of **item.Culture**.)

To override choosing languages on a meeting-by-meeting basis from **item.Culture**, choose a specific language to use for join details for all meetings across your organization.

Step 1. From the customer view in https://admin.webex.com, go to **Services**.

Step 2. From the Hybrid Calendar card for Exchange, click **Edit Settings**.

Step 3. Choose a language from the **Default Language** drop-down list and click **Save**.

After you save the change, Hybrid Calendar Service uses the language you chose each time it adds joining details to a meeting. It does not change the language for existing joining details.

By default, when users add @webex to a meeting location, Hybrid Calendar Service updates the meeting with their Cisco Webex Personal Room details. When users add @meet, by default the Calendar Service updates the meeting with Cisco Webex space details. As an administrator, you can change these default actions for either keyword.

Regardless of how you set these actions, power users can add the modifier :space or :myroom to specify the action for either keyword. For example, adding @webex:space causes the service to update the meeting with Webex space details.

Step 1.   From the customer view in https://admin.webex.com, go to **Services**.

Step 2.   From the Hybrid Calendar card for your calendar environment, click **Edit Settings**. If you have Hybrid Calendar Service set up for multiple calendar environments, you can access the keywords settings from multiple pages in Control Hub, but the values that you set apply to all environments.

Step 3.   In the Keywords section, select the default action that you want for each keyword.

Step 4.   Click **Save**.

You can do this task before you configure the Calendar Connector links to your Exchange environment and Webex environment, but all tests will fail until the Calendar Connector status is Running and you may need to restart the connector after configuration.

Step 1.   From the Expressway-C, go to **Applications > Hybrid Services > Connector Management**. The Connector Management section of the page has a list of connectors and the status of each. The Management Connector status is Running and the Calendar Connector status is Not Enabled.

Step 2.   Click **Calendar Connector**.

Step 3.   Select **Enabled** from the **Active** drop-down list.

Step 4.   Click **Save**. The Calendar Connector starts and the status changes to Running.

Any of these previous tasks requires that users have signed in to the Cisco Webex app to be fully activated. To enable @webex for users who have never signed in to the app, add and verify the users' domain using the Add, Verify, and Claim Domains process located at help. webex.com. (You must own a domain for it to be verifiable. You do not need to claim the domain.) Use the following procedure to enable a small number of Cisco Webex users for Hybrid Calendar Service with Microsoft Exchange or Office 365.

Step 1.   From the customer view in https://admin.webex.com, go to **Users**.

Step 2.   Choose a specific user from the list, or use the search to narrow the list, and then click the row to open an overview of the user.

Step 3.   Click **Edit**, and then ensure that the user is assigned at least one paid service under Licensed Collaboration Services. Make necessary changes, and then click **Save**.

Step 4.   Click **Calendar Service**, toggle on **Calendar**, choose **Microsoft Exchange**, and then save your changes. After you activate the service, the user status changes from Pending Activation to Activated. The length of time for this change depends on the number of users that you are enabling for the service. Users receive an email that indicates the feature is enabled.

Google Calendar Deployment in the Cloud

Cisco Webex Hybrid Calendar Service provides a rich collaboration experience between Cisco Webex Meetings and Cisco Webex with Google's Workspace Calendar, for users and rooms. Google Calendar is a time-management and scheduling calendar service developed by Google.

Figure 18-2 shows the components of Hybrid Calendar Service and Google Calendar architecture and lists a high-level process of the scheduling flow.

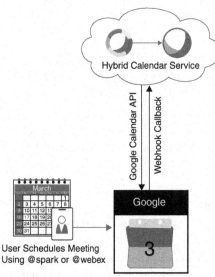

Figure 18-2   *Hybrid Calendar Service and Google Calendar Architecture*

1.   A user creates a meeting in Google Calendar, putting a scheduling keyword or video address in the location field.

2.   Google sends a notification to Hybrid Calendar Service.

3.   Hybrid Calendar Service requests and receives the encryption key, and then uses it to encrypt the meeting information.

4.   Hybrid Calendar Service validates meeting creation and recipients, and then creates a Webex team space, if applicable.

5.   Hybrid Calendar Service calls the **application programming interface (API)** service and maps the meeting to the space.

6.   Hybrid Calendar Service retrieves the meeting join information, including the Personal Room if applicable.

7. Hybrid Calendar Service updates the meeting invite with the meeting join information and, if applicable, the space ID.

8. The updated meeting information appears in Google Calendar.

For more information on how the cloud-based Hybrid Calendar Service integrates with Google's Google Workspace Calendar, see the article "Cisco Webex Hybrid Calendar Service with Google Calendar Integration Reference," available at https://help.webex.com.

Cisco does not currently support deploying both Google Calendar and Office 365 with the cloud-based Hybrid Calendar Service in the same Cisco Webex organization. As a requirement, a Google Workspace organization (formerly Google Apps for Work) with Google accounts for all users in your Webex organization. Each user in your Webex organization can have only one email address associated with only one Hybrid Calendar Service integration. In other words, Hybrid Calendar Service will only process meetings from a single address for creating spaces, decorating meetings, showing the meetings list and Join button, and sending OTBP to video devices.

Enable and configure Hybrid Calendar Service with Google Calendar by following these steps to register your Google Calendar environment to the Cisco Webex cloud, enable API access, test the connection, and set the default Webex site. The setup wizard in https://admin.webex.com will also guide you through the process.

Step 1. From https://admin.webex.com go to **Services**, and then choose one of the following options:

■ For a new environment, click **Set Up** on the Hybrid Calendar card. Choose the Google logo, and then click **Next**.

■ If you have an existing Exchange environment registered for Hybrid Calendar Service and want to add Google Calendar, click **Set Up** under the Google section of the Hybrid Calendar card, and then click **Next**.

Step 2. Follow the steps to authorize Cisco Webex cloud access on your Google Workspace account. You need to copy information from https://admin.webex.com, so keep it open in a browser tab.

a. Click the link to open https://admin.google.com, and then go to **Security > API controls**.

b. In the Domain wide delegation section, click **Manage Domain Wide Delegation**.

c. Click **Add New** to add an API client.

d. Copy the value for Client ID to the clipboard from the tab you have open on https://admin.webex.com, and paste it into the corresponding field in your Google Workspace settings tab.

e. Copy the text for Scope to the clipboard from the tab you have open on https://admin.webex.com, and paste it into the corresponding field in your Google Workspace settings tab.

f. Click **Authorize**.

g. Return to https://admin.webex.com.

18

Step 3. Enter the address of a test email account that already has a Google Workspace license, then click **Next**. This is used to test the connection with Google Calendar.

Step 4. (Optional) If you use meeting room resources, access control list (ACL) changes to their calendars may be required. For Hybrid Calendar Service to perform this change, check the box and then provide the name of an authorized account. Click **Next**.

Step 5. After the setup completed prompt appears, click **Done**.

Step 6. From the Hybrid Calendar card, go to the Google Calendar **Settings**.

Step 7. Choose or type the default Cisco Webex Meetings site that you want to use for @webex scheduling and save your changes. The default site is used for @webex unless the user has a different site configured in their My Personal Room setting in the Webex app (either because the user's Webex site has been linked to Webex by an administrator or because the user configured the setting with a different site).

Step 8. Confirm that an event called "Hybrid Calendar setup validated" was added to the test account that you provided, scheduled at the current time. You can safely remove this test event.

In Cisco Webex Control Hub, the Default Language setting controls the language of the join details that Hybrid Calendar Service adds to invitations. If you leave the setting at its default, the service uses the language from the locale setting from the user's calendar settings.

To override choosing languages on a per-user basis from the locale, choose a specific language to use for joining details for all meetings across your organization.

Step 1. From the customer view in https://admin.webex.com, go to **Services**.

Step 2. From the Hybrid Calendar card for Google, click **Edit Settings**.

Step 3. Choose a language from the **Default Language** drop-down list and click **Save**.

After you save the change, Hybrid Calendar Service uses the language you chose each time it adds joining details to a meeting. It does not change the language for existing join details.

By default, when users add @webex to a meeting location, Hybrid Calendar Service updates the meeting with their Cisco Webex Personal Room details. When users add @meet, by default the Calendar Service updates the meeting with Cisco Webex space details. As an administrator, you can change these default actions for either keyword.

Regardless of how you set these actions, power users can add the modifier :space or :myroom to specify the action for either keyword. For example, adding @webex:space causes the service to update the meeting with Webex space details.

Step 1. From the customer view in https://admin.webex.com, go to **Services**.

Step 2. From the Hybrid Calendar card for your calendar environment, click **Edit Settings**. If you have Hybrid Calendar Service set up for multiple calendar environments, you can access the keywords settings from multiple pages in Control Hub, but the values that you set apply to all environments.

Step 3.   In the Keywords section, select the default action that you want for each keyword.

Step 4.   Click **Save**.

Use the following procedure to enable a small number of Cisco Webex users for Hybrid Calendar Service with Google Calendar. Any of the previous tasks requires that users have signed in to the Cisco Webex app to be fully activated. To enable @webex for users who have never signed in to the app, add and verify the users' domain using the Add, Verify, and Claim Domains process located at help.webex.com. (You must own a domain for it to be verifiable. You do not need to claim the domain.)

Before you begin to activate a user for calendar access, the following conditions must be met to ensure success:

- The user's email address in Control Hub must match their Google Calendar account in the organization's Google Workspace tenant.

- The administrator must have verified the domain in the user's email address, *or* the user needs to have verified their email address by successfully signing in to Webex.

Successful validation is a requirement for using the Hybrid Calendar Service functionality. If the service cannot validate a user, it puts the user in error state. The service enforces a policy to access only the calendars of successfully activated users for ongoing processing.

Step 1.   From the customer view in https://admin.webex.com, go to **Users** and choose a specific user from the list. You can use the search function to narrow down the list of users.

Step 2.   Click the row to open an overview of the user.

Step 3.   Choose one of the following options and then save your changes:

- In a new environment, click **Calendar Service**, toggle on **Calendar**, and ensure that the Google Calendar is selected.

- In an existing environment with Exchange, click **Calendar Service** and, under Calendar Type, ensure that the Google Calendar is selected.

After you activate the service, the Cisco Webex user status changes from Pending Activation to Activated. The length of time for this change depends on the number of users that you are enabling for the service. Users receive an email that indicates the feature is enabled. If you want to disable email notifications, you can do so by navigating to **Services > Edit Settings > General**, scrolling to **User Email Notifications**, and then toggling on or off the email notification to set whether users receive email notifications about new Hybrid Calendar Service features as they are released. You can test the calendar features by simply scheduling a Cisco Webex Meeting from your calendar.

Next, we will look at how to add Hybrid Calendar Service to workspaces with Webex Room, Desk, and Board devices. This task assumes that you have already created Webex workplaces for the Webex Room, Desk, or Board devices. If you need to create the workspace, see the article "Add Shared Devices to a Workspace," available at https://help.webex.com.

Before you begin:

- Webex room devices must have email addresses that match the Google room resource format, @resource.calendar.google.com.

- If your room device email format uses a domain prefix, you must verify the domain in the prefix. For example, verify company.com for devices that have email addresses such as the following:

  company.com__3130313639353739333032@resource.calendar.google.com

- Newer resource email addresses may not include a domain prefix, as in the following example:

  c_080334862760509147 1198@resource.calendar.google.com

To add shared devices and services to a workspace:

Step 1. From the customer view in https://admin.webex.com, go to **Workspaces**, and then select the workspace that you want to update.

Step 2. Go to **Calendar** and click **Add Calendar** so that people can use OBTP from their Cisco Webex devices.

Step 3. Select **Calendar Service** from the drop-down menu.

Step 4. Enter or paste the Google resource email address from Google Workspace (**Calendar > Resources**). This is the email address that will be used to schedule meetings.

Step 5. Click **Save**.

To provide OBTP to Cisco Webex room and desk devices and Webex Boards when scheduling Webex Personal Room meetings, users must have their Personal Room associated with their Cisco Webex account. This can happen in one of the following ways:

- The Webex site is managed on Cisco Webex Control Hub.

- The users on your Webex site have been Cisco Webex linked. (For site-linking steps, see the article "Link Cisco Webex Sites to Control Hub," available at https://help. webex.com.)

- Users associate their Personal Room with Cisco Webex for themselves.

Do this task for the test user account that you will use to verify the setup, to check whether the Personal Room association needs to be added:

Step 1. Sign in to the Cisco Webex app.

Step 2. Go to **Meetings**.

Step 3.   Under My Personal Room, if the Personal Room link is missing, enter it in the format *https://company.webex.com/meet/username* or *company.webex.com/meet/username*, enter your host PIN, and click **Save**.

Step 4.   If the link was missing, have users who will schedule meetings that include room, desk devices, or boards associate their Personal Rooms with the Webex app for themselves.

Use these steps to set up a test meeting and verify the Google Calendar integration:

Step 1.   Sign in to https://calendar.google.com with one of the test Google user accounts enabled for Hybrid Calendar Service.

Step 2.   Click **Create** to start an event, and then add a space scheduling keyword (such as @webex:space or @meet) to the Where field. Fill out other meeting information, as needed, and then click **Save**.

Step 3.   Open https://web.webex.com and sign in with the test user account.

Step 4.   Verify whether a new Cisco Webex space was created and contains the calendar invite card.

Step 5.   To test out-of-office status, in https://calendar.google.com, navigate to **Settings** and turn on **Vacation Responder**. Within 20 minutes, you should see the test account's profile picture display an out-of-office overlay in the Webex app. The display picture update is triggered when others see your presence in a space. If the test user does not interact with other active users, you may need to use another account to verify the update.

Step 6.   To test One Button to Push (OBTP) with a Cisco Webex room or desk device or Webex Board:

    a.   In https://calendar.google.com, click **Create** to start an event, and then add a scheduling keyword (such as @webex) to the Location field.

    b.   Select **Rooms**, and choose the device you want to add.

    c.   Fill out other meeting information, as needed, and then click **Save**.

    d.   When the meeting is scheduled to begin, verify that the Join button appears on the device.

Another option that is outside the scope of this book is the Cisco Telepresence Management Suite (Cisco TMS) scheduling option that allows Hybrid Calendar Service to leverage your on-premises resource management and conference hosting environment for simplified meeting scheduling. This integration also extends the OBTP meeting join experience to a wide range of video devices. The integration currently works with the cloud-based Hybrid Calendar Service for Office 365 or the cloud-based Hybrid Calendar Service for Google Calendar. To deploy the integration, you first set up the cloud-based service. Then you install the Calendar Connector on your on-premises Expressway-C and configure the connector for the Cisco TMS scheduling option. However, you cannot deploy the Cisco TMS scheduling option if your Cisco Webex organization already has the Calendar Connector configured for Hybrid Calendar Service. The Cisco TMS integration must be the only Calendar Connector in the organization.

18

Office 365

When you first set up Hybrid Calendar Service, the setup asks you to have your organization's Office 365 tenant Global administrator account log in to the Office 365 portal to agree to allow Hybrid Calendar Service to access Office 365 on behalf of your users. Hybrid Calendar Service needs the permissions shown in Table 18-2 to do the corresponding actions indicated in the Usage column.

Table 18-2 Office 365 Required Permissions

Permission	Usage
Read and write calendars in all mailboxes.	■ Update the meeting text with the join details.
Sign in and read user profile.	■ Required for the other permissions listed. Hybrid Calendar Service does not use it directly.
Read and write all user mailbox settings.	■ Determine the user's language for localization purposes. ■ Read out-of-office status. ■ Set out-of-office status. (Feature is not available yet.)

When the administrator grants permission for Hybrid Calendar Service on behalf of the Office 365 tenant, Cisco Webex is notified. This permission enables Hybrid Calendar Service to get access tokens from Azure Active Directory (Azure AD) using OAuth 2.0, to authenticate and access user calendars. The Cisco Webex cloud does not see or store the administrator login credentials at any point in the process.

Hybrid Calendar Service uses the Microsoft Graph API to subscribe to changes in users' calendars, receive notifications for changes made in subscribed users' calendars, and update meeting invitations with scheduling information when the meeting location field contains keywords such as @webex or @meet, or the meeting body contains a supported video address. Hybrid Calendar Service accesses only the calendars of the users that you enable for Hybrid Calendar Service in the Cisco Webex Control Hub.

Cisco Webex follows industry-standard best practices to securely store the private key for the application. All meeting details that the service stores are encrypted using Webex end-to-end encryption. This ensures that only those who are invited to the meeting can see the details. For more information on Webex encryption, see the "Cisco Webex Meetings Security White Paper" located at cisco.com. If needed, your Exchange administrator can revoke Hybrid Calendar Service access to your Office 365 tenant user calendars from Enterprise Applications in the Azure AD management portal.

If you have already deployed the Expressway-based Calendar Connector to serve Microsoft Exchange users, Office 365 users, or a hybrid of Microsoft Exchange and Office 365 users, you can add the cloud-based Hybrid Calendar Service with Office 365, running both at the same time. Once you enable the cloud-based service, any Office 365 users who are not a part of a resource group automatically migrate from your Calendar Connector to the new cloud-based service within 24 hours. (Hybrid Calendar Service checks once a day for Office 365 users to migrate from Calendar Connectors.)

The Expressway-based Calendar Connector that you deploy with Hybrid Calendar Service for Microsoft Exchange or Office 365 has a capacity limit of 1000 Office 365 users and requires on-premises equipment. The cloud-based service allows you to scale past the capacity limit.

- Both options (Calendar Connector and cloud-based service) can be enabled at the same time.

- All Office 365 users who are *not* in a resource group migrate to the cloud-based service automatically.

- To enable some users on the cloud service first for testing, put other users who must stay homed on the on-premises Connector into a resource group before turning on the cloud-based service.

The following are the requirements for Hybrid Calendar Service with Microsoft Office 365:

- An Office 365 tenant with Exchange Online accounts for users in the organization. During setup, you must be able to sign in as a Global administrator for the tenant to grant application permissions. Note the following considerations for your Office 365 tenant:

  - Cisco currently supports only a single Office 365 tenant per Cisco Webex organization.

  - Cisco supports only the Worldwide and Germany instances of Office 365. (Other instances it does not support include USGovDoD, USGovGCCHigh, and China.)

  - Although your tenant may use Multi-Geo Capabilities in Office 365 to store data in a chosen geography, Cisco Webex stores data according to its own data residency specifications based on the country designated for the customer organization. For more information, see the article "Data Residency in Webex," available at https://help.webex.com.

- For @webex scheduling, any supported Cisco Webex Meetings release. You must enable the Personal Room feature for the Webex site and for the individual users.

- A Cisco Webex organization with a paid subscription. Currently, Cisco does not support deploying both Google Calendar and Office 365 with the cloud-based Hybrid Calendar Service in the same Cisco Webex organization.

- Users must have activated Cisco Webex accounts, with email addresses that are exact matches in Cisco Webex Meetings, Webex, and Exchange Online (the Primary Email Address). Each Webex user can have only one email address associated with only one Hybrid Calendar Service integration. In other words, Hybrid Calendar Service will only process meetings from a single address for creating spaces, decorating meetings, showing the meetings list and Join button, and sending OTBP to video devices.

18

Previously, to serve Office 365 users, you had to install the Calendar Connector on an on-premises Expressway. This on-premises deployment was required even if you did not have a hybrid Exchange environment (on-premises Microsoft Exchange and an Office 365 tenant organization). You can now choose to enable the cloud-based Hybrid Calendar Service for Office 365. With this service, hybrid Exchange environments have extra considerations:

■ You can run the Expressway-based Calendar Connector and the cloud-based Office 365 service at the same time.

■ Once you enable the cloud-based service, all Office 365 users who are not in any resource group automatically migrate to it.

■ To test the migration on a subset of users, make sure that the rest of the Office 365 users are in a resource group. Then enable the cloud-based Office 365 service.

Figure 18-3 depicts hybrid Exchange environment with Cisco Webex Hybrid Calendar Service.

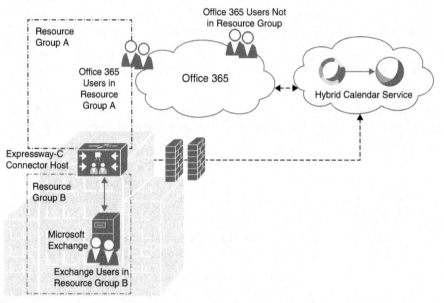

Figure 18-3   *Hybrid Exchange Environment with Cisco Webex Hybrid Calendar Service*

The Calendar Connector on the Expressway-C serves both Exchange users and Office 365 users, in Resource Group A and Resource Group B. The cloud-based service serves any Office 365 users who are not in a resource group.

Figure 18-4 illustrates the scheduling flow of cloud-based Hybrid Calendar Service with Office 365.

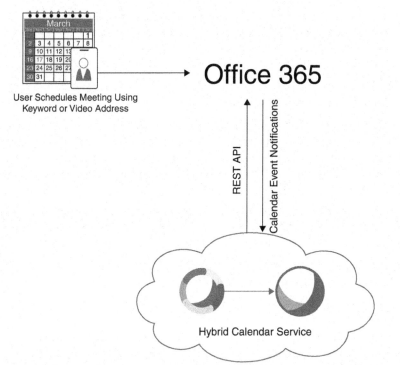

Figure 18-4 *Cloud-based Hybrid Calendar Service with Office 365 Scheduling Flow*

1. A user creates a meeting in the Office 365 calendar, putting a scheduling keyword or video address in the Location field.

2. Exchange Online sends a notification to Hybrid Calendar Service.

3. Hybrid Calendar Service requests and receives the encryption key, and then uses it to encrypt the meeting information.

4. Hybrid Calendar Service validates meeting creation and recipients, and then creates a Webex team space, if applicable.

5. Hybrid Calendar Service calls the API service and, if applicable, maps the meeting to the space.

6. Hybrid Calendar Service retrieves the meeting join information, including the Webex Personal Room if applicable.

7. Hybrid Calendar Service updates the meeting invite with the meeting join information and, if applicable, the space ID.

8. The invitees and the organizer get the updated meeting invitation.

To provide full @webex functionality, Hybrid Calendar Service needs access to user scheduling information from your Cisco Webex Meetings site. If your Webex site is managed in Cisco Webex Control Hub, you do not need do anything to make the information available. Otherwise, the preferred method for making this information available is to have an administrator link the site to Webex. If you have not yet linked the sites, your users can associate their Cisco Webex Personal Rooms with Cisco Webex themselves in the app.

Follow these steps to register your Office 365 environment to the Cisco Webex cloud, test the connection, and set the default Webex site. The setup wizard in https://admin.webex.com guides you through the process. Before you begin, you should either be the Global administrator for the Office 365 tenant or have the administrator with you when you begin the setup process.

Step 1. From https://admin.webex.com, go to **Services**.

Step 2. On the Hybrid Calendar card with the Office 365 logo, click **Set Up**.

Step 3. Follow the steps to choose an Office 365 instance (Worldwide or Germany) and authorize Cisco Webex cloud access on your Office 365 Global administrator account. The browser should redirect you to https://admin.webex.com when you have finished the authorization steps. If it does not, try these steps again.

Step 4. In Hybrid Calendar setup window, enter the email address of an account in Office 365 to test the connection, and click **Test**. Hybrid Calendar Service tests by creating an event in the user's calendar to validate access and provisioning.

Step 5. When the setup finishes, click **Done**.

Step 6. On the Hybrid Calendar card with the Office 365 logo, click **Edit Settings**.

Step 7. Choose or type the Cisco Webex Meetings site to use for @webex scheduling. Save your changes.

Step 8. If there are users with error status, click **User Status Report** to view the error details.

In Cisco Webex Control Hub, the Default Language setting controls the language of the join details that Hybrid Calendar Service adds to invitations. If you leave the setting at its default, the service uses the language in the "language":{"locale"} setting from the user's mailbox settings. To override choosing languages on a per-user basis from the "language":{"locale"}, choose a specific language to use for join details for all meetings across your organization.

Step 1. From the customer view in https://admin.webex.com, go to **Services**.

Step 2. On the Hybrid Calendar card with the Office 365 logo, click **Edit Settings**.

Step 3. Choose a language from the **Default Language** drop-down list and click **Save**. After you save the change, Hybrid Calendar Service uses the language you chose each time it adds joining details to a meeting. It does not change the language for existing join details.

By default, when users add @webex to a meeting location, Hybrid Calendar Service updates the meeting with their Cisco Webex Personal Room details. When users add @meet, by default the Calendar Service updates the meeting with Cisco Webex space details. As an administrator, you can change these default actions for either keyword. Regardless of how you set these actions, power users can add the modifier :space or :myroom to specify the action for either keyword. For example, adding @webex:space causes the service to update the meeting with Webex space details.

Step 1. From the customer view in https://admin.webex.com, go to **Services**.

Step 2. From the Hybrid Calendar card for your calendar environment, click **Edit Settings**. If you have Hybrid Calendar Service set up for multiple calendar environments, you can access the keywords settings from multiple pages in Control Hub, but the values that you set apply to all environments.

Step 3.   In the Keywords section, select the default action that you want for each keyword.

Step 4.   Click **Save**.

Use the following procedure to enable individual Cisco Webex users for Hybrid Calendar Service with Office 365. Any of the previous tasks requires that users have signed in to the Webex app to be fully activated. To enable @webex for users who have never signed in to the app, add and verify the users' domain using the Add, Verify, and Claim Domains process. (You must own a domain for it to be verifiable. You do not need to claim the domain.)

Before you begin, users must have licensed Exchange Online mailboxes and must have activated Cisco Webex accounts, with email addresses that are exact matches in Cisco Webex Meetings, Webex, and Exchange Online (the Primary Email Address).

Step 1.   From the customer view in https://admin.webex.com, go to **Users**, and then choose a specific user from the list. You can use the search function to narrow down the list of users.

Step 2.   Click the row to open an overview of the user.

Step 3.   In the Hybrid Services area, click **Calendar Service**.

Step 4.   Toggle **Calendar** on, ensure that **Microsoft Exchange/Office 365** is selected, and save your changes.

After you activate the service, the user's calendar service status changes to Pending Activation and then to Activated. The length of time for this change depends on the number of users that you are enabling for the service. Users receive an email that indicates the feature is enabled.

Hybrid Calendar Service automatically moves any Office 365 users who are not part of a resource group from your Expressway-based Calendar Connector to the cloud-based service. This process can take up to an hour because the service checks for users to move once an hour. (If you are also moving the user's mailbox from Microsoft Exchange to Office 365, it can take up to 40 minutes longer.) If you want to have users activated faster, use the following procedure to toggle Hybrid Calendar Service for users, thereby forcing the activation within minutes. Also, you must remove Office 365 users from a resource group for them to move off the Calendar Connector. This procedure also covers that process.

Step 1.   If applicable, move the user mailbox from Microsoft Exchange to Office 365.

Step 2.   From the customer view in https://admin.webex.com, go to **Users**.

Step 3.   To modify an individual user, do the following:

    a.   Search for the user in the list and click the row for that user.

    b.   In the panel that opens on the right, click **Calendar Service**.

    c.   Open the **Resource Group** drop-down list and click **None**.

18

           d.   Next to Calendar, toggle the service to **Off.**

           e.   Wait a minute, and then toggle the service back to **On.** The user should be activated within a few minutes.

Step 4.   To modify users in bulk, do the following:

           a.   Click **Manage Users,** and choose **CSV Add** or **Modify User.**

           b.   Click **Export** to download the exported_users.csv file.

           c.   Edit the exported_users.csv file. For any users that you want to move, delete the value in the Hybrid Calendar Service Resource Group column.

           d.   Save a first copy of the file in this state, for use later.

           e.   To speed the move, set Hybrid Calendar Service (Exchange) to **FALSE.**

           f.   Save a second copy of the file.

           g.   Click **Import,** select the second file copy that you saved, and click **Open.**

           h.   Choose **Add and Remove Services** and click **Submit.** If you also add new users in this process and do not suppress admin invite emails, new users receive activation emails.

           i.   Wait several minutes, and then re-import the first copy of the file. The users should be activated within a few minutes.

One Button to Push (OBTP)

Users can schedule meetings and include video devices and Webex Boards that display the Join button by using any of these methods:

- Cisco Webex Meetings

  - From a space

  - From the calendar, by entering a scheduling keyword in the meeting location field

  - From the calendar, using Cisco Webex Productivity Tools

  - From the calendar, by entering a URL in the meeting location or body

  - Using the Cisco Webex Meetings Scheduler for Google Chrome

  - Other types of meetings: From the calendar, by entering a supported video address format in the meeting location or body

To provide One Button to Push on video devices, you deploy Cisco Webex Hybrid Calendar Service. The details of the deployment depend on the type of calendar environment that you have, and on the type of device. To register devices for calendar scheduling, understand the requirements of Cisco Webex Calling and Hybrid Call Service:

- After you add a Cisco Webex Calling (formerly Spark Call) phone number to a Cisco Webex room device or board, there is a 24-hour delay before the room device caller ID is seen by others.

- Shared desk phones support all available call features except voicemail and single number reach. Room devices and Webex Boards only support basic call functions with a single line.

- For PSTN service, be aware of the following points:

  - Cloud PSTN service for room devices and boards is available in the United States and Canada.

  - You must request that your Cisco partner purchase PSTN service. If you are no longer in a trial, you must then sign the PSTN contract by DocuSign that is emailed to you.

  - Your partner must add new or port over PSTN numbers.

- To use Cisco Unified Communications Manager call control for devices in a place, you must first configure Hybrid Call Service Connect for your organization. For more information, see the *Deployment Guide for Hybrid Calling for Cisco Webex Devices (Device Connector)*.

First, create a workspace and then add shared devices and services:

Step 1. From the customer view in https://admin.webex.com, go to **Workspaces**, and then click **Add Workspace**.

Step 2. Enter a name for the workspace (such as the name of the physical room), select a room type, and add capacity. Then click **Next**.

Step 3. Choose **Cisco Webex Room Device**, and then click **Next**.

You can have only one type of device in a single space. For example, you can add up to ten desk phones to a lobby or a single Cisco Webex Room Device or a Webex Board, but not a combination of the two. The exception is Companion Mode, where you can have one Webex Board and one Room Series device in a workspace.

Step 4. Choose a call service to assign to devices in the workspace and click **Next**:

- **Free Calling (default):** For Cisco Webex app and SIP address calling.

- **Webex Calling:** To add PSTN service through a cloud preferred media provider for Webex Calling (formerly Spark Call). Assign a phone number and extension to the device, and then click **Next**.

- **Hybrid Calling:** To use call service (PSTN access or internal extension access) through your on-premises call control. UCM provides the phone number or extension for the devices in the workspace. Enter the UCM mail ID for the account that you created earlier. Then download the Device Connector to synchronize the UCM configurations to the cloud. Then click **Next**.

18

The service discovers where the email address is located on a UCM cluster. Once discovered, the service creates the Cisco Spark-RD and identifies the directory number and SIP URI associated with the account.

Step 5. (Optional) Toggle on the calendar service so that people can use OBTP on this device, and then click **Next**. Then select **Calendar Service** from the drop-down menu to add an email address and select a Resource Group. Enter or paste the email address of the room device. This is the email address that will be used to schedule meetings:

- For devices that will be scheduled in Google Calendar, enter the Google resource email address from Google Workspace (**Calendar > Resources**).

- For devices that will be scheduled in Microsoft Exchange or Office 365, enter the email address of the room mailbox. This option requires Webex Hybrid Calendar Service. To configure the service, see the *Deployment Guide for Cisco Webex Hybrid Calendar Service* at https://www.cisco.com.

Step 6. Click **Next**, and then activate the device with the code provided. Workspaces to which you added Hybrid Call Service may take approximately 5 to 10 minutes to activate while the email address, directory URI, and directory number are discovered on a Cisco Unified Communications Manager cluster. After activation, the phone number is displayed on Cisco Webex devices in the hybrid-enabled Workspace.

To provide OBTP to Cisco Webex room and desk devices and Webex Boards when scheduling Webex Personal Room meetings, users must have their Personal Room associated with their Cisco Webex account. This can happen in one of the following ways:

- The Webex site is managed on Cisco Webex Control Hub.

- The users on your Webex site have been Cisco Webex linked. (For site-linking steps, see "Link Cisco Webex Sites to Control Hub" at https://help.webex.com.)

- Users associate their Personal Room with Cisco Webex for themselves.

Do the following task for the test user account that you will use to verify the setup, to check whether the Personal Room association needs to be added:

Step 1. Sign in to the Cisco Webex app.

Step 2. Go to **Meetings**.

Step 3. Under My Personal Room, if the Personal Room link is missing, enter it in the format *https://company.webex.com/meet/username or company.webex.com/meet/username*, enter your host PIN, and click **Save**.

Step 4. If the link was missing, have users who will schedule meetings that include Webex Room, Desk devices, or Boards associate their Personal Rooms with the Webex app for themselves.

To test OBTP, use these steps to set up a test meeting and verify OBTP on registered Webex Room, Desk Devices, or Boards:

Step 1. To test a Webex team meeting in Exchange or Office 365:

    a. In Outlook, Outlook Web Access, or https://mail.office365.com, create a new meeting, and then add a keyword such as @webex:space or @meet to the Location field.

    b. Go to the Scheduling Assistant, then click **Add Room** and choose the device you want to add.

    c. Fill out other meeting information as needed and send the invitation.

    d. When the meeting is scheduled to begin, verify that the Join button appears on the device.

Step 2. To test a Personal Room meeting in Exchange or Office 365:

    a. In Outlook, Outlook Web Access, or https://mail.office365.com, create a new meeting, and then add **@webex** (or the scheduler's Personal Room URL) to the Location field.

    b. Go to the Scheduling Assistant and click **Add Room** and choose the device you want to add.

    c. Fill out other meeting information as needed and send the invitation.

    d. When the meeting is scheduled to begin, verify that the Join button appears on the device.

If there is no selectable Join button, a possible cause In hybrid Exchange environments, disabling TNEF for remote domains causes Exchange Online to strip the TMS:ExternalConferenceData and UCCapabilities user attributes for the meeting. This breaks OBTP for UCM–registered endpoints. Without these attributes, Cisco TMSXE cannot update the meeting in Cisco TMS, and Cisco TMS cannot set the OBTP dial string for the meeting.

18

Exam Preparation Tasks

As mentioned in the section "How to Use This Book" in the Introduction, you have a couple of choices for exam preparation: the exercises here, Chapter 22, "Final Preparation," and the exam simulation questions in the Pearson Test Prep practice test software.

Review All Key Topics

Review the most important topics in this chapter, noted with the Key Topics icon in the outer margin of the page. Table 18-3 lists a reference of these key topics and the page numbers on which each is found.

Table 18-3   Key Topics for Chapter 18

Key Topic Element	Description	Page Number
Paragraph	Calendar Connector overview	346
Paragraph	Impersonation account	347
Steps	Hybrid Calendar Service with Google Calendar	363
Steps	Hybrid Calendar Service with Office 365	371

Complete Tables and Lists from Memory

Print a copy of Appendix C, "Memory Tables" (found on the companion website), or at least the section for this chapter, and complete the tables and lists from memory. Appendix D, "Memory Tables Answer Key," also on the companion website, includes completed tables and lists to check your work.

Define Key Terms

Define the following key terms from this chapter and check your answers in the glossary:

application programming interface (API), certificate authority (CA), Cisco Webex cloud, Cisco Webex Control Hub, Cisco Webex Hybrid Calendar Service, Google Calendar, Hypertext Transfer Protocol Secure (HTTPS), Microsoft Exchange, Office 365, One Button to Push (OBTP), Telepresence Management Suite (TMS), Transport Layer Security (TLS)

Q&A

The answers to these questions appear in Appendix A. For more practice with exam format questions, use the Pearson Test Prep practice test software.

1. Describe the high-level process of the scheduling flow for the cloud-based Hybrid Calendar Service with Google Calendar.

2. Describe the high-level process of the scheduling flow for the cloud-based Hybrid Calendar Service with Office 365.

CHAPTER 19

Configure Webex Hybrid Message Service

This chapter covers the following topics:

Deployment Models: Provides an overview of the supported deployment models of Hybrid Message Service.

Deployment Requirements: Explains the deployment requirements, such as required versions, required network ports, and population of users.

Expressway Requirements: Recapitulates the requirements of the Expressway-C Connector needed for Hybrid Message Service.

Certificates: Focuses on the certificates associated with Hybrid Message Service.

Register Expressway Connector to the Cisco Webex Cloud: Explains the steps required for registration of the Expressway Connector to the Cisco Webex cloud.

IM and Presence Configuration: Concentrates on the configuration of the on-premises (or service provider hosted) IM&P Service.

Manage Hybrid Message Service: Focuses on managing Hybrid Message Service with understanding the service statuses and provide troubleshooting.

This chapter focuses on Hybrid Message Service and the configuration of the required components.

This chapter covers the following objective from the Implementing Cisco Collaboration Cloud and Edge Solutions (CLCEI) exam 300-820:

■ 4.2.b Configure Webex Hybrid Services/Connector: Message Service (Deployment requirements; Expressway requirements, certificates, CallManager prerequisites, IM&P prerequisites, deployment models)

"Do I Know This Already?" Quiz

The "Do I Know This Already?" quiz enables you to assess whether you should read this entire chapter thoroughly or jump to the "Exam Preparation Tasks" section. If you are in doubt about your answers to these questions or your own assessment of your knowledge of the topics, read the entire chapter. Table 19-1 lists the major headings in this chapter and their corresponding "Do I Know This Already?" quiz questions. You can find the answers in Appendix A, "Answers to the 'Do I Know This Already?' Quizzes and Review Questions."

Table 19-1 "Do I Know This Already?" Section-to-Question Mapping

Foundation Topics Section	Questions
Deployment Models	1
Deployment Requirements	2
Register Expressway Connector to the Cisco Webex Cloud	3
IM and Presence Configuration	4
Manage Hybrid Message Service	5

CAUTION The goal of self-assessment is to gauge your mastery of the topics in this chapter. If you do not know the answer to a question or are only partially sure of the answer, you should mark that question as wrong for purposes of the self-assessment. Giving yourself credit for an answer you correctly guess skews your self-assessment results and might provide you with a false sense of security.

1. How many IM and Presence (IM&P) Service users is the maximum support across multiple Expressway clusters?

    a. 195,000

    b. 75,000

    c. 5,000

    d. 15,000

2. Which of the following is *not* how you can manage your user population in Control Hub?

    a. Manually enter each individual user

    b. Hybrid Directory Service

    c. User migration tool

    d. By importing a list of users from a CSV file

3. If your on-premises environment utilizes a proxy server, where can you enter the details in the Expressway for Hybrid Message Service?

    a. Configuration > Hybrid Services > Connector Proxy

    b. System > Hybrid Services > Connector Proxy

    c. Applications > Cloud Services > Connector Proxy

    d. Applications > Hybrid Services > Connector Proxy

4. What access is needed for the Message Connector regarding IM&P?

    a. Main administrator account

    b. AXL API

    c. User account

    d. Diagnostic tools

5. Under the information page at Applications > Hybrid Services > Message Service > Message Service Status, which of the following is *not* an available category?

   a. Connectivity to Cisco Webex

   b. User and Usage Stats

   c. Hybrid Message Service

   d. Connections to IM and Presence Service Infrastructure

Foundation Topics

Deployment Models

The **Cisco Webex Hybrid Message Service** is ideal for organizations that have users on Cisco Webex that need to exchange messages with users on the on-premises Cisco Unified Communications Manager **IM and Presence (IM&P)** service. Hybrid Message Service enables exchange of one-to-one instant messages between a Cisco Webex app client and a **Cisco Jabber** client registered to Cisco Unified CM IM&P Service. Hybrid Message Service enables Cisco Jabber users to see the Presence status of Cisco Webex app users based on the users' client activity. For reference purposes, the messaging aspect of the Webex app was previously known as Webex Teams, but as of WebexOne in 2020, it is now simply named Webex. We will refer to Webex Teams as the messaging aspect of the Webex app.

Hybrid Message Service enables interoperability between on-premises deployment of Cisco Jabber and Cisco Webex. The components that make Hybrid Message Service possible are the Message Connector, hosted on Cisco Expressway infrastructure on your premises, and the Message Service, running in the **Cisco Webex cloud**.

Consider the following factors when choosing how you deploy Hybrid Message Service:

- **Scale:** How many IM&P Service users do you expect to serve? Will you need to add nodes/clusters to improve the capacity of the service to meet that requirement?

  - Cisco supports 195,000 users per organization across multiple Expressway clusters.

  - It also supports up to 5000 Message Service users per Small Expressway, up to 6500 users per Medium Expressway, and up to 15,000 users per Large Expressway. This gives a maximum number of 75,000 users on a cluster of six Expressways, because the capacity of one node is reserved for redundancy. See https://help.webex.com for an explanation of the Message Service capacity.

- **Availability:** How important is service availability to you? Do you need to deploy redundant nodes/clusters to ensure continuous service in the event of a failure?

- **Geography:** Global distribution of users means that you may have data centers in multiple time zones. Latency may be a factor to consider when choosing where to deploy your connector hosts.

In each deployment scenario, remember that:

- Each Expressway cluster has up to six nodes, including the primary.

- You must register the primary node of each Expressway cluster with Cisco Webex.

- To connect an Expressway cluster to an IM&P Service cluster, enter the publisher's details on the primary node of the relevant Expressway cluster. This action connects all nodes of the Expressway cluster with all nodes of the IM&P Service cluster.

- You must not connect all Expressway clusters to all IM&P Service clusters. Cisco does not support this scenario, because the potential benefit from redundancy is outweighed by the risk of overloading the solution.

- You must not associate multiple Expressway connector clusters with one IM&P Service cluster (even though your IM&P Service cluster may be able to home more message and presence users than your Expressway cluster can support). Cisco does not support this scenario.

- You may connect multiple IM&P Service clusters to each Expressway connector cluster.

- Cisco supports up to five IM&P Service clusters per Expressway connector cluster.

- You can use Resource Groups in **Cisco Webex Control Hub** to define your organization's geography, and then assign Expressway resources to different resource groups that represent locations. The set of users you assign to each resource group should correspond to the users in all IM&P Service clusters served by the Expressways in those resource groups.

Key Topic

One Expressway connector cluster to one IM&P Service cluster is the recommended deployment option. It requires an Expressway connector cluster per IM&P Service cluster. If you have more than one site, you can repeat the configuration in each data center, as depicted in Figure 19-1.

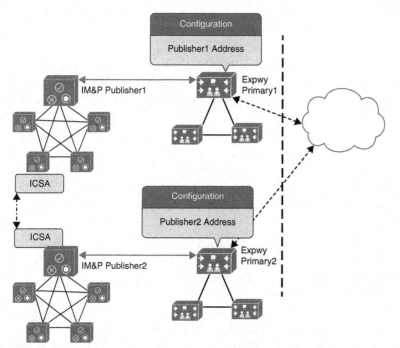

Figure 19-1 *One-to-One Expressway to IM and Presence Service Cluster*

The one Expressway connector cluster to multiple IM&P Service clusters deployment option (see Figure 19-2) requires one Expressway connector cluster across the whole IM&P Service deployment. This option is simple to configure and manage, but scalability and latency could be concerns if you have many users and/or wide geographical distribution.

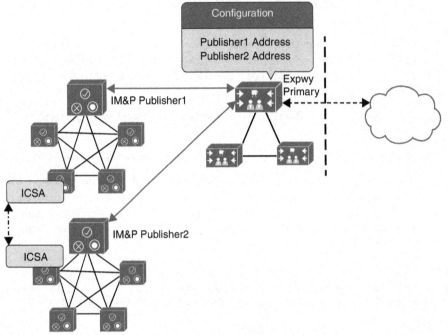

Figure 19-2   *One Expressway Connector Cluster to Multiple IM and Presence Service Clusters*

There is a performance impact for each Message Connector that connects to an IM&P Service cluster. For that reason, Cisco does not support multiple Expressway clusters connecting to one IM&P Service cluster. By extension, meshing the connectors with the IM&P Service clusters is not supported.

Cisco encrypts all instant messages that it transmits across the public Internet using the Key Management Service (KMS). By default, Webex customers use the KMS in the Cisco Webex cloud, but Hybrid Message Service also supports Cisco Webex Hybrid Data Security, which provides on-premises KMS.

The following lists cover the message flows and security. First are the messages from Cisco Jabber to Webex.

1. The sender sends a message from the Jabber client. The message goes to the IM&P Service, which sends the message on to the Jabber client of the recipient. This is the normal IM&P Service flow, which you can make secure if you want to (which is beyond the scope of this chapter).

2. If the recipient is a dual user, entitled for Hybrid Message Service, then the message may also go to the Message Connector on the Expressway. It will not go to the Message Connector if the recipient has not recently been active on the Webex app; to save

processing and memory resources, Cisco assumes that the user will not answer in the Webex app if they have not been active for more than 72 hours. You can choose to secure the connections between the IM&P Service cluster and the Expressway cluster hosting the Message Connector.

3. The Message Connector interacts with the Key Management Service (via the cloud-based messaging service) to request an encryption key. The messaging service retrieves the key for an existing space, or a new key if this is the first message, for a new space (aka "conversation" or "room") and passes the key back to the Message Connector.

4. The Message Connector creates a new conversation in Cisco Webex, if necessary, and posts the encrypted message to that conversation. This encryption is not optional and requires no configuration.

5. Cisco Webex securely sends the message to the recipient's Webex client.

The Webex app connects to Cisco Webex, which provides a server certificate to authenticate itself. The app maintains this connection while the user is active. The app interacts with the Key Management Service to dynamically generate encryption keys for each user and each space (aka "conversation" or "room"). The following list describes the messages from Webex to Cisco Jabber:

1. The sender uses Webex app to message the recipient. The Webex app encrypts the message and sends it to Cisco Webex. Cisco Webex makes the encrypted message available to the recipient's Webex client.

2. The Cisco Webex cloud checks its messaging service database to see if the sender and recipient are entitled to use Hybrid Message Service, and where to route the message towards the recipient.

3. The Cisco Webex cloud sends the encrypted message to the Message Connector.

4. The Message Connector interacts with the Key Management Service (via the cloud-based messaging service) to request the decryption key for the Webex space.

5. The Message Connector decrypts the message and sends it to the IM&P Service.

6. The IM&P Service tries to route the message onward to the Jabber client of the recipient.

7. When the message is read, the connector detects the read receipt and sends it back to Cisco Webex, so that the users' unread messages are consistent across their messaging clients.

Deployment Requirements

To enable Hybrid Message Service, you must use the supported Cisco software identified in the following list. Cisco Business Edition has Cisco Unified Communications Manager and IM&P Service as part of all its packages, so make sure you have the right version. Table 19-2 follows with the Message Service ports and protocols required for the network.

■ Cisco Unified Communications Manager and IM&P Service 11.5(1)SU3 or later (on-premises or service provider hosted)

- All publisher nodes must be running the **Administrative XML Web Service (AXL)** service. Cisco also recommends, for HA deployments, that you run the AXL service on all nodes in the IM&P Service cluster.

- If you have multiple IM&P Service clusters, you must have the Intercluster Sync Agent (ICSA) working across them.

- If any of your IM&P Service clusters have been upgraded from a version earlier than 10.5(2), you must apply a Cisco Options Package (COP file) to those clusters, to prepare them for Hybrid Message Service. (You can get the file ciscocm. cup-CSCvi79393-v1.cop.sgn, and instructions for applying it, from Cisco Software Central: https://software.cisco.com.)

- Your IM&P Service clusters must have Multiple Device Messaging (MDM) enabled (this feature is enabled by default).

- Cisco Jabber (any client platform) at least 11.9 or later

- Cisco Webex

  - You must be licensed to use Cisco Webex, so you can create your organization using Cisco Webex Control Hub.

Table 19-2 Message Service Ports

Purpose	Source IP	Source Ports	Protocol	Dest. IP	Dest. Ports
Basic messaging	Webex app clients	Ephemeral	TCP	Cisco Webex hosts	443
Persistent HTTPS registration	Connector host Expressway	30000–35999	TLS	Cisco Webex hosts	443
XMPP (IM&P)	Connector host Expressway	30000–35999	TCP	Unified CM IM&P publisher	7400
AXL queries (Administrative XML Layer)	Connector host Expressway	30000–35999	TCP	Unified CM IM&P publisher	8443
Messaging and Presence	Cisco Jabber clients	Ephemeral	TCP	Unified CM IM&P publisher	5222

The components that make Hybrid Message Service possible are the Message Connector, hosted on Cisco Expressway infrastructure on your premises, and the Message Service, running in the Cisco Webex cloud. Check the following list for licensing and entitlement factors affecting interoperability:

- Cisco assumes that all users are previously licensed for Cisco Jabber, with Jabber registered to Cisco Unified Communications Manager IM&P.

- You need any paid-for Cisco Webex offer for your organization. You can order this through Cisco Commerce Workspace.

■ You also need to have access to Cisco Webex Control Hub, with administrator privileges for your organization (you get these as part of the ordering process).

■ You should import all Jabber users into Control Hub and grant them all the "Message Free" entitlement. This entitles all the Jabber users to the basic Webex messaging functionality.

■ There are no additional paid license requirements for this basic messaging. Having this entitlement for all users improves interoperability between those who are enabled for Hybrid Message Service and those who are only licensed for Jabber.

■ Hybrid Message Service can only work between users who are in the same organization in Control Hub. The service does not enable Webex users to communicate with Jabber users outside of their organization.

■ Users who are enabled for Hybrid Message Service can use Jabber or Webex messaging to chat with all other users in the organization, irrespective of whether the recipient is using the Webex app or Jabber.

■ Users who are not enabled for Webex Hybrid Message Service can use Jabber to chat with all other users in the organization. They can use the Webex app to chat with users who are enabled for Hybrid Message Service, but the messages are not copied to the recipients' Jabber clients.

Before you connect your Jabber deployment to Cisco Webex, your Jabber users may exist in the following places:

■ Cisco Unified CM Administration

   ■ This requirement is already fulfilled by having an on-premises deployment of Jabber. The Jabber users are unable to message each other if they do not exist in Unified CM.

   ■ Users can be created manually or synchronized with your LDAP directory.

■ [Preferred] LDAP directory

   ■ If you manage your users with an LDAP directory, Cisco recommends that you synchronize users to Unified CM Administration. The alternative is that you have two places to manage users, with manual synchronization.

As part of deploying Hybrid Message Service, you must have a user population in your organization in Cisco Webex. If you have deployed other Hybrid Services, or Cisco Webex, you should already have an organization and users in Cisco Webex. Cisco recommends that you import all your Jabber users to Cisco Webex, to maximize interoperability. These users do not need paid subscriptions, but they do need to have the Message Free entitlement for Webex. There are two ways to grant this entitlement, depending on whether you have paid subscriptions:

■ If you have paid subscriptions available, enable the Automatic License Assignment Template, and Message Free entitlements will be assigned automatically by default.

19

■ If you do not have paid subscriptions, add the users manually using **Comma-Separated Values (CSV)** file import or directory synchronization, and Message Free entitlements will be assigned automatically by default.

Cisco recommends that you enable single sign-on (SSO) for your organization in Control Hub before you import Jabber users (see the article "Single Sign-On Integration in Cisco Webex Control Hub" at https://help.webex.com). With an SSO-enabled organization, you have the option to suppress email invitations to imported Jabber users, if you do not intend to give those users access to Webex (see "Suppress Automated Emails" at https://help.webex.com).

You can manage your user population the following ways:

■ Manually, by entering users individually in Control Hub.

■ By importing a list of users from a CSV file (based on a Cisco-supplied template) using Control Hub.

   ■ You can also use Control Hub to do an export-edit-import round trip with CSV files, and thus to bulk modify the users' service entitlements.

■ [Preferred] By synchronizing your organization in Cisco Webex with your on-premises directory. This option is called Hybrid Directory Service.

See "Ways to Add Users to your Control Hub Organization" at https://help.webex.com for more information.

To summarize, your user details may exist in several places, but they must at least be in Cisco Webex and in Unified CM Administration. The attribute that uniquely identifies the users in all places is their email address. Irrespective of how you create the user populations on premises and in the cloud, the users' email addresses must match in all places.

Administrators have the functionality in Control Hub to make changes to a user's email address as follows:

Step 1.   Sign in to https://admin.webex.com.

Step 2.   Click **Users** and then click a username to open that user's configuration.

Step 3.   Update the user's email address. Ensure you update the user's mail ID in Cisco Unified CM to match the new email address in Control Hub. It can take up to 10 minutes for the Message Connector to pick up the user mail ID change in Unified CM.

Step 4.   Click **Reactivate User**. Activation can take up to 10 minutes.

Expressway Requirements

Use these steps to prepare an Expressway-C for Cisco Webex Hybrid Services before you register it to the Cisco Webex cloud to host the hybrid services connector software. Note that these are the same steps detailed in Chapter 18 for the prerequisites needed for the Expressway-C Connector Host for Cisco Webex Hybrid Services, but added for convenience if not previously performed. You would not need to repeat the following if the Expressway requirements have already been met.

Cisco recommends that the Expressway-C be dedicated to hosting connectors for Cisco Webex Hybrid Services. You can use the Expressway-C connector host for other purposes, but that can change the supported number of users.

As an administrator of hybrid services, you retain control over the software running on your on-premises equipment. You are responsible for all necessary security measures to protect your servers from physical and electronic attacks.

Step 1. Obtain full organization administrator rights before you register any Expressways and use these credentials when you access the customer view in Cisco Webex Control Hub (admin.webex.com).

Step 2. Deploy the Expressway-C connector host in a cluster to account for redundancy. Follow the supported Expressway scalability recommendations:

- For Hybrid Message Service on a dedicated Expressway-C:

    - Message Connector can be hosted on multiple Expressway-C clusters of up to six nodes each.

    - Message Connector can be used with multiple Cisco Unified CM IM&P Service clusters.

Step 3. Follow these requirements for the Expressway-C connector host.

- Install the minimum supported Expressway software version. See the "Supported Versions of Expressway for Webex Hybrid Services Connectors" at https://help.webex.com for more information.

- Install the virtual Expressway OVA file according to the *Cisco Expressway on Virtual Machine Installation Guide*, after which you can access the user interface by browsing to its IP address. You can find the document in the list of Cisco Expressway Install and Upgrade Guides on Cisco.com.

    The serial number of a virtual Expressway is based on the virtual machine's MAC address. The serial number is used to validate Expressway licenses and to identify Expressways that are registered to the Cisco Webex cloud. Do not change the MAC address of the Expressway virtual machine when using VMware tools, or you risk losing service.

- You do not require a release key, or an Expressway series key, to use the virtual Expressway-C for Cisco Webex Hybrid Services. You may see an alarm about the release key. You can acknowledge it to remove it from the interface.

- Use the Expressway web interface in a supported browser. (See the *Cisco Expressway Administrator Guide* on Cisco.com.) The interface may or may not work in unsupported browsers. You must enable JavaScript and cookies to use the Expressway web interface.

Step 4. If this is your first time running the Expressway, you get a first-time setup wizard to help you configure it for Cisco Webex Hybrid Services. Select **Cisco Webex Hybrid Services**. This ensures that you will not require a release key.

19

Step 5.   Check that the following requirements are met for the Expressway-C connector host. You would normally do this during installation. See the *Cisco Expressway Basic Configuration Deployment Guide* on Cisco.com for details.

- Basic IP configuration (**System > Network Interfaces > IP**)

- System name (**System > Administration Settings**)

- DNS settings (**System > DNS**)

- NTP settings (**System > Time**)

- New password for admin account (**Users > Administrator Accounts**, click **Admin User**, then click the **Change Password** link)

- New password for root account (log on to CLI as root and run the **passwd** command)

Expressway-C connector hosts do not support dual NIC deployments.

Step 6.   Configure the Expressway-C as a "cluster of one":

- Cisco recommends that you configure the Expressway as a primary peer before you register it, even if you do not currently intend to install an extra peer.

  - When you change clustering settings on X8.11 and later, be aware that removing all peer addresses from the System > Clustering page signals to the Expressway that you want to remove it from the cluster. This causes the Expressway to factory reset itself on its next restart. If you want to remove all peers but keep configuration on the remaining Expressway, leave its address on the Clustering page and make it the primary in a "cluster of one."

  - Here are the minimum clustering settings required, but the *Cisco Expressway Cluster Creation and Maintenance Deployment Guide* at Cisco.com has more detail:

    - Enable H.323 protocol. Go to **Configuration > Protocols > H.323** page and set **H.323 Mode** to **On**. H.323 mode is required for clustering, even if the Expressway does not process H.323 calls. You may not see the H.323 menu item if you used the Service Select wizard to configure the Expressway for Hybrid Services. You can work around this problem by signing in to the Expressway console and issuing the command **xconfig H323 Mode: "On"**.

    - **System > Clustering > Cluster Name** should be an FQDN. Typically this FQDN is mapped by an SRV record in DNS that resolves to A/AAAA records for the cluster peers.

    - **System > Clustering > Configuration Primary** should be **1**.

    - **System > Clustering > TLS Verification Mode** should be **Permissive**, at least until you add a second peer. Select **Enforce** if you want cluster peers to validate each other's certificates before allowing intercluster communications.

- **System > Clustering > Cluster IP Version** should match the type of IP address of this Expressway-C.

- **System > Clustering > Peer 1 Address** should be the IP address or FQDN of this Expressway. Each peer FQDN must match that Expressway's certificate if you are enforcing **Transport Layer Security (TLS)** verification.

- To ensure a successful registration to the cloud, use only lowercase characters in the hostname that you set for the Expressway-C. Capitalization is not supported at this time.

Step 7.   If you have not already done so, open required ports on your firewall.

- All traffic between Expressway-C and the Cisco Webex cloud is **Secure Hypertext Transfer Protocol (HTTPS)** or secure web sockets.

- TCP port 443 must be open outbound from the Expressway-C. See the article "Network Requirements for Webex Services" located at help.webex.com for more details of the cloud domains that are requested by the Expressway-C.

Step 8.   Get the details of your HTTP proxy (address, port) if your organization uses one to access the Internet. You will also need a username and password for the proxy if it requires basic authentication. The Expressway cannot use other methods to authenticate with the proxy.

- Cisco has tested and verified Squid 3.1.19 on Ubuntu 12.04.5.

- Cisco has not tested auth-based proxies.

- If your organization uses a TLS proxy, the Expressway-C must trust the TLS proxy. The proxy's **certificate authority (CA)** root certificate must be in the trust store of the Expressway. You can check if you need to add it at **Maintenance > Security > Trusted CA Certificate**.

- The details of the proxy, as configured on the primary Expressway in the connector host cluster, are shared throughout the Expressway cluster. You cannot configure different proxies for different nodes in the cluster.

Step 9.   Review these points about certificate trust. You can choose the type of secure connection when you begin the main setup steps.

- Cisco Webex Hybrid Services requires a secure connection between the Expressway-C and Cisco Webex.

- You can let Cisco Webex manage the root CA certificates for you. However, if you choose to manage them yourself, be aware of certificate authorities and trust chains; you must also be authorized to make changes to the Expressway-C trust list.

19

Certificates

Table 19-3 lists the certificate authorities that your on-premises or existing environment must trust when using Cisco Webex Hybrid Services.

If you opted to have Cisco Webex manage the required certificates, then you do not need to manually append CA certificates to the Expressway-C trust list. The issuers used to sign the Cisco Webex host certificates may change in the future, and Table 19-3 may then be inaccurate. If you are manually managing the CA certificates, you must append the CA certificates of the issuing authorities that signed the currently valid certificates for the hosts listed in Table 19-3 (and remove expired/revoked CA certificates).

Table 19-3 Certificate Authorities for Hybrid Services

Cloud Hosts Signed by This CA	Issuing CA	Must Be Trusted By	For This Purpose
CDN	O=Baltimore, OU=CyberTrust, CN=Baltimore CyberTrust Root	Expressway-C	To ensure Expressway downloads connectors from a trusted host
Common identity service	O=VeriSign, Inc., OU=Class 3 Public Primary Certification Authority	Windows Server 2003 or Windows Server 2008 hosting the Cisco Directory Connector	
Expressway-C	To synchronize users from your Active Directory with Cisco Webex and to authenticate Cisco Webex Hybrid Services users		
Cisco Webex	O=The Go Daddy Group, Inc., OU=Go Daddy Class 2 Certification Authority	Expressway-C	

Register Expressway Connector to the Cisco Webex Cloud

Cisco Webex Hybrid Services use software connectors hosted on Expressway-C to securely connect Cisco Webex to your organization's environment. After completion of the Expressway-C registration of resources to the cloud, the connector software is automatically deployed on your on-premises Expressway-C.

Before you begin, make sure your Expressway-C is running on a version that is supported for hybrid services. See the "Supported Versions of Expressway for Cisco Webex Hybrid Services Connectors" documentation at https://help.webex.com for more information about which versions are supported for new and existing registrations to the cloud. Ensure you sign out of any open connections to the Expressway-C interface that are open in other browser tabs. Also, if your on-premises environment proxies the outbound traffic, you must first enter the details of the proxy server at **Applications > Hybrid Services > Connector Proxy** before you complete this procedure. Doing so is necessary for successful registration.

Step 1.   From the customer view in https://admin.webex.com, go to **Services** and then choose one of the following options:

■ If this is the first connector host that you are registering, click **Set Up** on the card for the hybrid service you are deploying, and then click **Next**.

■ If you have already registered one or more connector hosts, click **View All** on the card for the hybrid service you are deploying, and then click **Add Resource.**

The Cisco Webex cloud rejects any attempt at registration from the Expressway web interface. You must first register your Expressway through Cisco Webex Control Hub because the Control Hub needs to hand out a token to the Expressway to establish trust between premises and cloud to complete the secure registration.

Step 2.   Choose a method to register the Expressway-C:

■ New Expressways: Choose **Register a New Expressway with Its Fully Qualified Domain Name (FQDN)**, enter your Expressway-C IP address or FQDN so that Cisco Webex creates a record of that Expressway-C and establishes trust, and then click **Next**. You can also enter a display name to identify the resource in Cisco Webex Control Hub. To ensure a successful registration to the cloud, use only lowercase characters in the host name that you set for the Expressway-C. Capitalization is not supported at this time.

■ Existing Expressways: Choose **Select an Existing Expressway Cluster to Add Resources to This Service,** and then choose from the drop-down list the node or cluster that you previously registered. You can use it to run more than one hybrid service.

If you are registering a cluster, register the primary peer. You do not need to register any other peers, because they register automatically when the primary registers. If you start with one node set up as a primary, subsequent additions do not require a system reboot.

Step 3.   Click **Next**, and for new registrations, click the link to open your Expressway-C. You can then sign in to load the Connector Management window.

Step 4.   Decide how you want to update the Expressway-C trust list. A check box on the welcome page determines whether you will manually append the required CA certificates to the Expressway-C trust list or you will allow Cisco Webex to add those certificates for you. Choose one of the following options:

■ Check the box if you want Cisco Webex to add the required CA certificates to the Expressway-C trust list. When you register, the root certificates for the authorities that signed the Cisco Webex cloud certificates are installed automatically on the Expressway-C. This means that the Expressway-C should automatically trust the certificates and be able to set up the secure connection. If you change your mind, you can use the Connector Management window to remove the Cisco Webex cloud CA root certificates and manually install root certificates.

19

■ Uncheck the box if you want to manually update the Expressway-C trust list. See the Expressway-C online help at Cisco.com for the procedure.

When you register, you will get certificate trust errors if the trust list does not currently have the correct CA certificates. See "Supported Certificate Authorities for Cisco Webex Hybrid Services" at https://help.webex.com for more detail.

Step 5.   Click **Register**. After you are redirected to Cisco Webex Control Hub, read the on-screen text to confirm that Cisco Webex identified the correct Expressway-C.

Step 6.   After you verify the information, click **Allow** to register the Expressway-C for Cisco Webex Hybrid Services.

■ Registration can take up to 5 minutes depending on the configuration of the Expressway and whether it is a first-time registration.

■ After the Expressway-C registers successfully, the Cisco Webex Hybrid Services window on the Expressway-C shows the connectors downloading and installing. The Management Connector automatically upgrades itself if there is a newer version available, and then installs any other connectors that you selected for the Expressway-C connector host.

■ Each connector installs the interface pages that you need to configure and activate that connector.

This process can take a few minutes. When the connectors are installed, you can see new menu items on the **Applications > Hybrid Services** menu on your Expressway-C connector host. If registration fails and your on-premises environment proxies the outbound traffic, review this procedure and ensure correct configurations. If the registration process times out or fails (for example, you must fix certificate errors or enter proxy details), you can restart registration in Cisco Webex Control Hub.

IM and Presence Configuration

Configure an account for the Message Connector to access the AXL **application programming interface (API)** of the Cisco Unified Communications Manager IM&P Service. You must use an independent administrator account, not the main administrator account. Remember the details of this account so you can enter them in the Message Connector configuration later.

Step 1.   From Cisco Unified CM Administration, go to **User Management > Application User**, and then choose one of the following options:

■ Click **Find** and, from the list, choose the administrator account that the connector will use to communicate with Cisco Unified Communications Manager IM&P Service.

■ Click **Add New** to create a new application user account.

Step 2.   Configure the account with the **Standard AXL API Access** role.

Step 3.   Click **Save**.

To enable Hybrid Message Service, you must link the Message Connector to your IM&P Service cluster by entering server information for the publisher node. This step builds a bridge between IM&P Service and the Cisco Webex cloud, with the connector acting as a broker between the two. The connector on Expressway maintains a resilient connection between your Hybrid Message Service cluster and the cloud. You only need to add the publisher to the Expressway-C connector configuration. If a specific node goes down in the cluster, the connector will move to another server.

On each Expressway cluster that you are using for Hybrid Message Service, sign in to the primary node and complete the following configuration:

Step 1.   Go to **Applications > Hybrid Services > Message Service > Message Service Configuration**.

Step 2.   Click **New**.

Step 3.   Enter the host name or IP address of the IM&P Service publisher node that has Cisco AXL enabled. The connector uses AXL to query the publisher and discover the other nodes in the cluster.

Step 4.   Enter the credentials of the Message Connector AXL account you created on the IM&P Service publisher. This must not be the main administrator account. You must create an account explicitly for the Message Connector.

Step 5.   (Optional) Change Certificate Validation to **Disabled** if you want the Expressway to waive the check on the server certificate from the publisher node. If Certificate Validation is Enabled (which is the default), then the Tomcat certificate from the IM&P Service node must be valid and signed by a CA that the Expressway trusts. If you are using a self-signed certificate, copy it into the Expressway's Trusted CA certificate list.

Step 6.   Click **Add** to store the connector configuration on the Expressway-C.

Step 7.   Repeat this task if you need to connect this Expressway cluster to any other IM&P Service clusters.

Manually enable the Message Connector after you configured the connector with the IM&P publisher and the AXL account.

Step 1.   From Expressway-C, go to **Applications > Hybrid Services > Connector Management**, and then click **Message Connector**.

Step 2.   Choose **Enabled** from the **Active** drop-down list.

Step 3.   Click **Save**.

The connector starts and the status changes to Running on the Connector Management window. Verify that the Message Connector is running before you enable users for Hybrid Message Service. From Expressway-C, go to **Applications > Hybrid Services > Message Service > Message Service Status** and verify the configuration items in the Status column.

19

When you use bulk import or directory synchronization to import users, users must have email addresses in the source system. Those must be the addresses they use for Cisco Webex because you map them to the Cisco Webex user ID. If a user does not have an email address in IM&P Service, the Message Connector cannot discover the user. Hybrid Message Service does not work for that user. Using Cisco Directory Connector, you can map a chosen attribute (e.g., the **mail** attribute or the **userPrincipalName** attribute) to the Cisco Webex UID, but the value of the attribute must be the user's email address. See "Ways to Add Users to your Control Hub Organization" at https://help.cisco.com for other methods, such as using a bulk CSV template or Active Directory synchronization through Cisco Directory Connector.

Use this procedure to enable Cisco Webex users one at a time for Hybrid Message Service:

Step 1.   From the customer view in https://admin.webex.com, go to **Users**, choose a specific user from the list, or use the search to narrow the list, and then click the row to open an overview of the user.

Step 2.   Click **Edit**, and then ensure that the user is assigned at least one paid service under Licensed Collaboration Services. Make necessary changes, and then click **Save.**

Step 3.   Click **Message Service**, toggle the setting to turn it on, and then save your changes.

The user experiences a delay of up to one hour before reliably being able to send messages from the Webex app to Cisco Jabber.

To test Hybrid Message Service, you need at least two users who are enabled for Hybrid Message Service. They should both have Cisco Jabber and Cisco Webex enabled installed.

1. One user opens the Webex app client. Let's call this user Alice for the sake of this procedure.
2. The other user opens Cisco Jabber client. Let's call this user Bob for the sake of this procedure.
3. Send a message from Alice's Webex client to Bob's Jabber client.
4. Check that the message arrives in Bob's Jabber client and that Alice's status shows as Available.
5. Reply from Bob's Jabber client to Alice's Webex client.
6. Check in Alice's Webex client that Bob appears to be typing.
7. Repeat the test, starting from Alice's Jabber client and Bob's Webex client.

Manage Hybrid Message Service

Each Expressway connector host enables part of your Hybrid Message Service deployment and shows status information about that part only. This is useful if you already know that a specific Expressway is affected by, or responsible for, an issue. If you are looking for a more general overview of your service status, open your Hybrid Message Service deployment in Control Hub.

The status information page is at **Applications > Hybrid Services > Message Service > Message Service Status.** The information shown there falls into the following categories:

- Connectivity to Cisco Webex

- User and usage stats

- Connections to IM&P Service infrastructure

The status page and this reference topic are ordered by the level of impact that the status item will have on your service.

- Connectivity to Cisco Webex: If this status is anything other than Operational, then there is a problem between this Expressway and Cisco Webex. It could be a problem with the Expressway (check **Status > Alarms**), the service (check status.webex.com), or the network between them (check the proxy if you have one, check that firewalls allow outbound HTTPS connections, and use network diagnostic tools to establish if routes exist).

- Message Service User Totals (This Expressway): This part of the status page is about the total user populations known to this Expressway cluster. The numbers are common across this connector host cluster, because all nodes in the cluster share Hybrid Message Service configuration (where you entered the publisher address and account details).

  - Users from Connected IM&P Clusters: The count of users that the connector gathers from the directly connected IM&P Service infrastructure. These users are "homed" on (or "local" to) the IM&P clusters whose publishers' details you entered on this Expressway cluster's primary node. We need to distinguish this number because, when the connector makes AXL queries to those publishers, the publishers return all the users they know about. This includes "intercluster" users, which the queried publishers know about because ICSA (Intercluster Sync Agent) is working across multiple IM&P clusters. This number is the theoretical maximum of users that you could have using the service through this connector host cluster. In practice, you would probably enable a smaller subset of these, as part of a migration plan.

  - Users from All IM&P Clusters (ICSA): The count of users known to all IM&P clusters that are synchronized (by ICSA) with the publishers you added to the connector configuration. The number includes the count of local users (the previous number in this section). So, when you read the two numbers, you can think of them as (for example) 300 of 1000, if 300 users are homed on the directly connected IM&P clusters and 1000 are synchronized between multiple IM&P clusters. You can use the relationship between these numbers to help validate or troubleshoot your Message Service deployment. For example, if you know you should have 1000 synchronized users but the total is less, you may have an intercluster sync agent problem. If you only have one cluster, or if all the IM&P publishers are configured on this connector, then the two numbers should be the same. If both numbers are 0, it could indicate an AXL query problem or a Message Connector configuration problem.

19

■ **Users Enabled for Hybrid Message Service:** The number of Hybrid Message Service–enabled users that Cisco Webex has assigned to this Expressway cluster. It is typically smaller than the Users from Connected IM&P Clusters count. When you grant the Message Service to your users in Control Hub, the cloud communicates with the connector hosts to determine which connectors know about those users. The cloud then assigns those users to those connectors in a balanced way.

■ **Active Message Service Users:** The count of enabled users that are currently using Hybrid Message Service. Users are considered Active if, within the 72 hours leading up to now, they have used Cisco Webex messaging to read or write messages to or from Cisco Jabber. It is also shown as a percentage of Users Enabled for Hybrid Message Service.

■ **Users Not Active for 72 Hours or More:** The count of enabled users that are not currently using Hybrid Message Service. Within the rolling 72-hour period up to now, these users did not use Cisco Webex messaging to read or write messages to or from Jabber. The connector uses this characteristic to improve performance, by deleting any sessions that are held by inactive users. In typical usage across your deployment, you can expect there to be some inactive users (holidays, sick leave, etc.), but the number should typically be lower than the Active users. It is also shown as a percentage of Users Enabled for Hybrid Message Service.

■ **Message Service Status (IM&P Nodes):** This section of the status page is about the connector's relationships with directly connected IM&P nodes. For each IM&P publisher (the address you entered during configuration) there is at least one discovered node (itself) and there may be up to six in total. The following status information is shown for each node in each IM&P Service cluster:

■ **Node Version:** The IM&P Service software version, as reported by the specific node.

■ **Node Status:** Should be Operational. The Outage status indicates a problem with that IM&P Service node, or the connection to it.

■ **Certificate Validation:** Set to either On or Off, depending on the choice you made when you connected to this node's publisher. If it's On (default), then the Expressway must be able to validate the certificate presented by this node, or Hybrid Message Service will not work.

■ **Message Service Users from This Node:** The count of Hybrid Message Service–enabled users who are assigned to this connector and are homed on this IM&P Service node. Each IM&P Service node that is listed on this status page contributes a portion to the total count of Users Enabled for Message Service, shown near the top of the page.

■ **Active Message Service Users:** The count of enabled users that are currently using Hybrid Message Service and are homed on this IM&P Service node. Each IM&P Service node that is listed on this status page contributes a portion to the total count of Active Message Service Users, shown near the top of the page.

■ Users Not Active for 72 Hours or More: The count of enabled users that are not currently using Hybrid Message Service and are homed on this IM&P Service node. Each IM&P Service node that is listed on this status page contributes a portion to the total count of Users not Active for 72 Hours or more, shown near the top of the page.

The Message Connector uses AXL calls to the IM&P publisher to discover the nodes in that cluster. This is a static arrangement, and the Message Connector does not dynamically adapt when you change the IM&P cluster. For example, when you add or remove nodes. The Message Connector cannot discover IM&P nodes when the AXL service is not running on the nodes. So, if there has been some kind of failure in your deployment, the nodes may not be backed up before the Message Connector starts, or the AXL service may not have restarted. When the Message Connector has not discovered some of the IM&P nodes, you can restart the Message Connector to force a rediscovery.

Step 1.   Sign in to the primary peer of the Message Connector Expressway cluster and go to **Applications > Hybrid Services > Connector Management.**

Step 2.   Click **Message Connector.**

Step 3.   Choose **Disabled** from the **Active** drop-down list.

Step 4.   Click **Save.** You should see the connector stops.

Step 5.   Choose **Enabled** from the **Active** drop-down list.

Step 6.   Click **Save.** The connector starts and the status changes to Running.

Next, we will examine troubleshooting Hybrid Message Service. If all users are affected, the first thing you should check is whether Hybrid Message Service is operational:

Step 1.   Browse to https://status.webex.com.

Step 2.   Expand **Webex Hybrid Services > Message Service** to read the status. If the Hybrid Message Service status is not Operational, it needs to be fixed.

Check Control Hub for user activation problems:

Step 1.   Sign in to https://admin.webex.com.

Step 2.   Click **Users** and find the users you are interested in. You can sort the list by **Status.**

Step 3.   Click a username to open that user's configuration. If there is no Message Service link, you need to onboard the user for Hybrid Message Service.

Step 4.   Click **Message Service.** The slider should be on (to the right position). If it is not, slide it to on and click **Save:** the user status goes Pending for a few seconds and then Active.

Step 5.   If the user status is Error, review the message. Also, click **See History** to get more information about what is preventing this user's activation.

Step 6.   Correct the problem preventing activation, then come back to the user and click **Reactivate User.**

If the user status is still not Active, you should raise a TAC case.

19

If Hybrid Message Service is not working for all users, or a large subset, you should check the Message Connector status on Expressway:

Step 1. Sign in to the primary peer of the cluster you registered and configured for Hybrid Message Service.

Step 2. Go to **Applications > Hybrid Services > Connector Management.**

■ Is Management Connector running?

■ Is Message Connector running?

Step 3. Go to **Applications > Hybrid Services > Message Service > Message Service Status.**

Step 4. Review the page for any errors between the Expressway and the configured IM&P Service nodes. Status should be Operational. There should be users assigned on premises and subscribed to the cloud. If people are using Hybrid Message Service, then there should be some percentage of users with active sessions.

Check the IM&P Service node configuration on the Expressway:

Step 1. On the Expressway, go to **Applications > Hybrid Services > Message Service > Message Service Configuration.**

Step 2. Check the listed nodes. Are any of the status entries not Active?

There is a known issue where the software version of the IM&P node is not correctly synchronized on the Expressway after the IM&P node is upgraded. This is a purely cosmetic issue as the Message Connector does not use the version information for any purpose. You can synchronize the IM&P version by restarting the Message Connector. Cisco intends to resolve this issue in a future Message Connector release.

Step 3. Delete any affected nodes.

Step 4. Re-create the nodes you deleted. Each time, make sure to correctly enter the address, username, and password, and then save the configuration.

If the status does not improve, perhaps there is a configuration or connectivity issue on the IM&P Service nodes.

The following are some IM&P Service checks:

■ Are the users you are investigating homed on the same IM&P Service cluster that is being used with Hybrid Message Service?

■ Does the Message Connector account have the AXL role? Are the username and password of that account the same as what you entered on the Message Connector?

■ Are users in Error state in Control Hub, with "duplicate Mail ID" errors? If so, these users are probably homed on more than one IM&P cluster. This situation could be a result of the way you import users to IM&P from Active Directory. Users should not be homed on multiple IM&P clusters. Run the IM and Presence troubleshooter to check for and correct any duplicate user accounts.

■ Are the IM&P Service nodes running the Cisco AXL? Go to Cisco Unified IM&P **Serviceability > Tools > Service Activation** to check.

If one or two users are affected, try the following checks:

■ Is the user entitled for Hybrid Message Service?

■ Did the user activation fail the first time? Open the user in Control Hub, open Hybrid Message Service, and click Reactivate User.

■ Does the user have an email address (mailid) in IM&P administration?

■ Does the user's email address in IM&P match what is in Cisco Webex Control Hub?

■ Is there a new "duplicate" Webex user named after the user's Jabber ID (JID)? This could result from searching for a JID in the Webex app. When you search for a JID, Webex may create a new space based on the JID, even though there is already an account based on the same user's email address.

■ Did you use Directory Connector to import/synchronize users? Check that the LDAP attribute that you mapped to cloud UID contains the user's email address. For example, if you choose to map UserPrincipalName to cloud UID, then in Active Directory the UserPrincipalName attribute must contain the user's email address.

■ Are the users correctly entitled in Cisco Webex? The "Jabber only" users in your organization must be entitled to use the Message Free service with Webex, even though they are not using Webex, to ensure that they get messages sent via Webex by Message Service users.

   ■ To avoid getting into this situation, Cisco recommends that you assign the Message Free entitlement to all users. You can do this by configuring an Automatic License Assignment Template in Control Hub before you import users.

   ■ If you already have many users in Control Hub who do not have the correct entitlement, you can resolve the situation by exporting all users to a CSV file, and then reimporting all the users from the CSV file. This works because importing users by CSV automatically applies the Message Free entitlement. Importing users with Hybrid Directory Service does not automatically apply this entitlement unless you use an automatic license assignment template.

   ■ For a small number of affected users, you may prefer to manually apply their entitlement, especially if you have a diverse set of entitlements in your user population.

■ Are Message Service users losing messages in Jabber? When a Message Service user hides their status in the Webex app (the Show Status setting is unchecked), then that user's presence is reflected as "Away" in Jabber. However, the Message Service continues working for that user, and processes their messages from IM&P up to Webex. If the user is only using Jabber but is not actually using the client while the messages are

19

coming in, the message may not ever appear in Jabber as it does not persist messages. This could be mitigated by enabling offline storage in IM&P, but Cisco recommends that users affected like this should check the Show Status setting in the Webex app. They could also use Webex messaging, which persists the messages.

Exam Preparation Tasks

As mentioned in the section "How to Use This Book" in the Introduction, you have a couple of choices for exam preparation: the exercises here, Chapter 22, "Final Preparation," and the exam simulation questions in the Pearson Test Prep practice test software.

Review All Key Topics

Review the most important topics in this chapter, noted with the Key Topics icon in the outer margin of the page. Table 19-4 lists a reference of these key topics and the page numbers on which each is found.

Key Topic

Table 19-4   Key Topics for Chapter 19

Key Topic Element	Description	Page Number
Paragraph	Recommended deployment models	383
Paragraph	Register Expressway Connector to the Webex cloud	392

Complete Tables and Lists from Memory

There are no memory lists or tables in this chapter.

Define Key Terms

Define the following key terms from this chapter and check your answers in the glossary:

application programming interface (API), Administrative XML Web Service (AXL), certificate authority (CA), Cisco Jabber, Cisco Webex cloud, Cisco Webex Control Hub, Cisco Webex Hybrid Message Service, Comma-Separated Values (CSV), Hypertext Transfer Protocol Secure (HTTPS), IM and Presence (IM&P), Transport Layer Security (TLS)

Q&A

The answer to this question appears in Appendix A. For more practice with exam format questions, use the Pearson Test Prep practice test software.

1. What is the maximum number of IM&P Service users for Hybrid Message Service?

CHAPTER 20

Webex Edge Solutions

This chapter covers the following topics:

Webex Edge for Devices: Explains how Cisco Webex Edge for Devices allows Cisco devices on a Unified CM and VCS/Expressway to link with the Webex cloud.

Webex Edge for Calling: Describes how Webex Edge for Calling enables a unified calling architecture that connects Cisco UCM, Cisco UCM Cloud, HCS, and/or third-party PBXs.

Webex Edge Audio: Encompasses the Webex Edge Audio service and provides an overview of the solution.

Webex Edge Connect: Describes the Webex Edge Connect solution and how it peers your Webex Meetings traffic to improve the in-meeting user experience.

Webex Video Mesh: Encompasses the signaling and media flows, deployment requirements, deployment models, ports and protocols, and clustering used in a Cisco Webex Video Mesh deployment.

This chapter focuses on the Cisco Webex Edge and its extensions that are a set of services that allows you to realize savings on PSTN and bandwidth costs while providing even better meeting experiences through improved audio, video, and content quality while leveraging existing on-premises and cloud resources.

This chapter covers the following objectives from the Implementing Cisco Collaboration Cloud and Edge Solutions (CLCEI) exam 300-820:

- 4.1 Describe the signaling and media flows used in a Cisco Webex Video Mesh deployment

- 4.2.d Configure Webex Hybrid Services/Connector: Video Mesh (Deployment requirements including bandwidth, clustering, endpoint support, video call capacity, ports and protocols, deployment models)

"Do I Know This Already?" Quiz

The "Do I Know This Already?" quiz enables you to assess whether you should read this entire chapter thoroughly or jump to the "Exam Preparation Tasks" section. If you are in doubt about your answers to these questions or your own assessment of your knowledge of the topics, read the entire chapter. Table 20-1 lists the major headings in this chapter and their corresponding "Do I Know This Already?" quiz questions. You can find the answers in Appendix A, "Answers to the 'Do I Know This Already?' Quizzes and Review Questions."

Table 20-1 "Do I Know This Already?" Section-to-Question Mapping

Foundation Topics Section	Questions
Webex Edge for Devices	1
Webex Edge for Calling	2
Webex Edge Audio	3
Webex Edge Connect	4
Webex Video Mesh	5–6

CAUTION The goal of self-assessment is to gauge your mastery of the topics in this chapter. If you do not know the answer to a question or are only partially sure of the answer, you should mark that question as wrong for purposes of the self-assessment. Giving yourself credit for an answer you correctly guess skews your self-assessment results and might provide you with a false sense of security.

1. Which of the following is a supported operating system for software installation of the Cisco Webex Device Connector?

   a. Microsoft Windows 10

   b. Microsoft Server 2019

   c. Red Hat Enterprise Linux 8

   d. Windows Server 2016

2. Webex Edge for Calling architecture supports your cloud migration with services at three levels, except which of the following?

   a. Network Services

   b. User Services

   c. Enterprise Services

   d. Endpoint Services

3. What component does Cisco Webex Edge Audio use to route audio calls intelligently and automatically over VoIP or existing PSTN services?

   a. Cisco Expressway E

   b. Cisco Unity Connection

   c. Cisco Unified Communications Manager

   d. Cisco Expressway C

4. When provisioning Webex Edge Connect, which layers of connectivity are required with which entity? (Choose three.)

   a. Layer 1: Physical connectivity through Equinix

   b. Layer 3: Network connectivity with Cisco Webex

    c. Layer 2: Data-link connectivity through Equinix

    d. Layer 2: Data-link connectivity through Cisco Webex

    e. Layer 3: Network connectivity through Equinix

5. Cisco Webex Video Mesh supports which of the following call controls? (Choose two.)

    a. Cisco Unified Communications Manager 11.5(1) SU3

    b. Cisco Expressway X8.6.1

    c. Cisco Unified Communications Manager 10.5(3) SU1

    d. Cisco Expressway X8.11.4

6. Which of the following is a supported proxy and authentication type combination for Webex Video Mesh?

    a. Digest authentication with HTTP only

    b. NTLM authentication with HTTPS only

    c. Basic authentication with HTTP and HTTPS

    d. None of the above, because Webex Video Mesh does not support proxy services

Foundation Topics

Webex Edge for Devices

Hosting Webex in the cloud enables Cisco to rapidly develop and deploy services and features on its powerful cloud platform using new and innovative technologies. These new features and services can now be extended to customers with on-premises Cisco products. Video devices registered to the **Cisco Unified Communications Manager (Unified CM)** or **Video Communications Server (VCS)**/Expressway can now also be linked to the Webex cloud and benefit from features that can only be cloud delivered. With Webex Edge for Devices, customers with a mixture of on-premises and cloud video devices can monitor and manage these devices from a single administrative platform, Webex Control Hub. On-premises video devices maintain their registration to the Unified CM or VCS/Expressway and the media path for calls between these devices remains the same, but they also have an additional link to the Webex cloud for management, analytics, and more.

Currently, Webex Edge for Devices has the following features and functionality for on-premises devices:

- Online/offline connection status in Control Hub

- Device diagnostics with the ability to set admin alerts

- Device historical analytics available directly in Control Hub

- Cloud xAPI Access

- Read and write access to device configurations from Control Hub for devices running Collaboration Endpoint (CE) software version 9.13 or later

- Proxy support

- Migration to full cloud through API

- Real time media metrics when joining Webex calls for devices running CE9.13 or later

- Manage logs from Control Hub for devices running CE9.14.3 or later

- Support for Microsoft Teams WebRTC and Cisco Webex Video Integration for Microsoft Teams for devices running CE9.14.3 or later

- Workspace metrics

  - Occupancy detection

  - Call detection

  - Sound levels and ambient noise (dBa)

You can also enable the following:

- Cloud-managed software upgrade for devices running CE9.14 or later

- Native Webex Meeting experience for devices running CE9.14 or later

- Hybrid Calendar through Webex Control Hub

- Webex Assistant

- Organization-wide branding from Control Hub for devices running CE9.13 or later

The following are prerequisites needed for Webex Edge for Devices:

- Software version CE9.12 or later. For customers that have already linked devices running CE9.10, Webex Edge for Devices will continue working.

- Encrypted version of CE software.

- Unified CM or Expressway registration.

- Unified CM version 11.5(1) SU3 or 12.5(1) and later. 12.0(1) is not supported.

- For Expressway, you need HTTPS connectivity on your devices for the Device Connector tool.

- Control Hub admin access.

- Cisco Collaboration Flex Plan.

- Cisco Webex Device Connector.

The following operating systems are supported for software installation:

- Microsoft Windows 10

- macOS High Sierra (10.13) or later

20

The following are current limitations for Webex Edge for Devices:

- Enabling Hybrid Calendar disables **Telepresence Management Suite (TMS)** calendar. Only one calendaring source is supported at a time.

- Webex Edge for Devices registers devices as shared-mode devices on Control Hub.

The Cisco Webex Device Connector is a lightweight piece of software that you can use in your Control Hub–managed organization to automate your device-related tasks. It enables the onboarding of Webex devices to the cloud and provides cloud features to on-premises registered devices in your Control Hub–managed organization. The software provides a link from premises to cloud or from cloud to premises, depending on your device requirements and the features that you want to use. You get the software from Control Hub and install it on a Windows or Mac device or even a virtual machine in your network that can access your premises environment and the devices themselves.

After you sign in, the splash screen on the Cisco Webex Device Connector gives you the following device management options:

- **I want to register multiple devices to the cloud:** Use a simple CSV file to bulk register Webex devices to the cloud in one step.

- **I want cloud features for my on-premises registered device:** With Webex Edge for Devices, get access to Webex cloud capabilities, while keeping your calling and media on premises.

- **I want to add on-premises calling to my cloud registered devices:** This service provides Unified CM on-premises calling capabilities to Webex cloud-registered devices.

The Cisco Webex Device Connector also provides the following general features:

- **Upgrades notices within software interface:** When a new version of the software is available, you are notified within the interface and can manually upgrade right away. Always stay on the latest version.

- **Proxy support:** You can connect to a basic auth proxy directly by entering the required information in the Cisco Webex Device Connector.

- **FedRAMP (Webex for Government) support:** From the Settings menu, you can configure the Device Connector to point to the FedRAMP Webex cloud instead of the standard Webex cloud.

- **Report an issue:** Use the software to submit feedback and automatically upload logs to the cloud.

You sign into the software by using your Webex full administrator or device administrator credentials that you use to manage your organization in Control Hub. If you want to use the tool to bulk onboard devices to the cloud, you must run the tool on a machine that can reach the device directly over HTTP. For Hybrid Calling, the system where the software is installed requires network access to the Unified CM that contains configuration that you want to synchronize to Webex cloud-registered devices in Workspaces. Get the details of your HTTP basic proxy (address, port) if your organization uses one to access the Internet. You will also need a username and password for the proxy if it requires basic authentication. The Cisco Webex Device Connector cannot use other methods to authenticate with the proxy. Cisco has tested and verified Squid 3.1.19 on Ubuntu 12.04.5.

To install the Cisco Webex Device Connector:

Step 1.   From the customer view in https://admin.webex.com, go to **Management > Devices**, and then click **Resources**.

Step 2.   Scroll to Tools, click **Download**, and then choose **Download for Mac** or **Download for Windows**, depending on your platform.

Step 3.   Open the installer file and then follow the procedure that applies to your platform:

- For Windows:

    a. Click **Next**, check the box to accept the terms in the License Agreement, and then click **Next**.

    b. Optionally, change the destination folder or leave the default, and then click **Next**.

    c. Click **Install**, and then the setup wizard installs the software.

- For Mac:

    a. Read the introduction and then click **Continue**.

    b. Click **Continue** and then click **Agree** to accept the software license.

    c. Choose the disk where you want the software to be installed, and then click **Continue**.

    d. Optionally, click **Change Install Location** if you want to install the software somewhere else; otherwise, click **Install**.

    e. After the screen appears that says the software installed successfully, click **Close**.

Step 4.   You're ready to sign in to the Device Connector with your full or device admin credentials and use the software to onboard and manage your devices.

Step 5.   (Only required for FedRamp customers) You can go to **Settings** and choose **Connect to FedRAMP** to connect to the FedRAMP cloud instead of the Webex cloud.

Step 6.   You are notified in the software whenever an upgrade is available. Cisco recommends that you click **Update** to remain on the latest version of the software for bug fixes and security enhancements.

20

The connector uses the AXL API to retrieve the names and MAC addresses of video devices configured in the Unified CM. For Unified CM–registered devices:

Step 1. After you have installed the Device Connector tool, select **I Want Cloud Features for My On-Premises Registered Devices** and click **Link Devices Registered with Cisco Unified Communications Manager.**

Step 2. In the Host, Username (Standard AXL API Access Username), and Password fields, enter the details for your Unified CM and click **Connect.** If you have a Unified CM with public signed certificates, make sure those are valid or click **Proceed Without Certificate Validation.** The Device Connector retrieves the name and description of the Unified CM–configured devices. The Contact Info Name becomes the name for the Workspace the device is connected to. If there is no Contact Info Name set, the System Unit Name or MAC address is used.

Step 3. If you want to change the device name, you can do it from the Unified CM.

Step 4. Click **Link All** to link all the listed devices. To link an individual device, click the **Link** button next to its name.

The Device Connector sends the device information to your Webex organization, and Webex Identity Service creates activation codes for all devices. The Unified CM applies the activation code to the devices and the devices link to your Webex organization. When the device is linked to Cisco Webex cloud services, you can click the device name to open the device page directly in Control Hub. If the device says Link Pending, it is not linked yet. The activation code is provisioned from the Unified CM. The system attempts to link to the device for 7 days until the activation code expires. If the device is available during that time, it gets linked.

The connection from the Cisco Webex Device Connector to the Unified CM uses HTTPS with TLS version 1.2. The Cisco Webex Device Connector validates the Unified CM (Tomcat) certificate before proceeding with the connection. If the received server certificate is not trusted by the Java runtime default CA trust store, you will be prompted to either provide the certificate or proceed without certificate validation. If you are using a proxy server in your enterprise network, the initial Cisco Webex Device Connector login page allows you to enter the proxy server address and port number and, if required, user credentials for proxy authentication (Basic and Digest authentication are supported). TLS intercept is currently not supported between the Device Connector tool and the Webex cloud. To connect to a Unified CM cluster, you will need to activate Cisco AXL (disabled by default) and create a user account in your cluster with the Standard AXL API Access entitlement.

As shown in Figure 20-1, when the Cisco Webex Device Connector has retrieved the names and MAC addresses of video devices configured in the Unified CM, it establishes a TLS connection to the Webex cloud and sends these details to the Webex Identity Service along with details of your Webex organization. The Webex Identity Service creates an activation code for each device and returns these to the Cisco Webex Device Connector, which in turn forwards them to the Unified CM cluster.

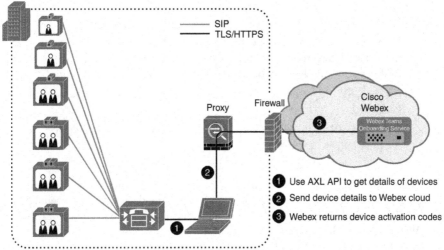

Figure 20-1   *Cisco Webex Device Connector Operation*

As shown in Figure 20-2, the Unified CM sends the activation code in a configuration file to each video device. Cisco Webex video devices running software version CE9.12.3 or above can establish a TLS connection to the Webex cloud and use the activation code received from the Unified CM to automatically onboard and link to your Webex organization. These cloud-associated on-premises devices can then be viewed and managed in Webex Control Hub.

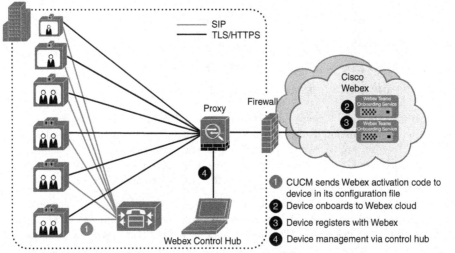

Figure 20-2   *On-Premises Devices: Cloud Onboarding and Linking*

Expressway deployments utilize a CSV file to import device details. For Expressway-registered devices:

Step 1.   After you have installed the Device Connector tool, select **I Want Cloud Features for My On-Premises Registered Devices** and click **Link Devices Using CSV or Cisco TMS Overview Export Files.**

Step 2.   Browse to the file on your computer and open the CSV or TMS Overview Export file.

Step 3.   To create the file from TMS, export a System Overview report and only select the **Network Settings > Hostname System Parameter.** Manually add columns for **Username** and **Password.**

For the CSV file, you need to create columns for **Address, Username,** and **Password.**

Step 4.   Click **Link All** to link all the listed devices. To link an individual device, click the **Link** button next to it.

The tool uses Contact Info Name for the Workspace name. If one is not available, the System Unit Name or MAC address is used. If no name is found for the device, click the Name field to enter one. The Device Connector sends the device information to your Webex organization, and Webex Identity Service creates activation codes for all devices. The activation codes are sent to the devices through the API. HTTPS must be enabled for this to work. When the device is linked to Cisco Webex cloud services, you can click the device name to open the device page directly in Control Hub.

Webex Edge for Devices allows on-premises devices to be linked over the Internet to Webex cloud services. These on-premises devices make multiple TLS/HTTPS connections to the Webex cloud for signaling, these connections are outbound only, and some connections are upgraded from HTTPS to bidirectional Secure **WebSocket** (WSS) connections. The signaling connections from on-premises devices to Webex services use TLS version 1.2 only and negotiate the following strong cipher suites with Webex services, in order of preference:

- TLS_ECDHE_RSA_WITH_AES_256_GCM_SHA384

- TLS_ECDHE_RSA_WITH_AES_128_GCM_SHA256

- TLS_ECDHE_RSA_WITH_AES_256_CBC_SHA384

- TLS_ECDHE_RSA_WITH_AES_128_CBC_SHA256

Most security-conscious customers deploy both a firewall and proxy server to control access from applications and devices in their enterprise networks to the Internet and associated cloud services, such as Webex. Specific implementations may vary, but a common deployment forces all HTTP-based traffic through a proxy server allowing only HTTP traffic originating from the proxy server to traverse the firewall and reach the Internet.

Proxies can be used to perform several security functions such as URL whitelisting and blacklisting, user authentication, IP address/domain/hostname/URI reputation lookup, and traffic decryption and inspection. HTTP proxy support has until now only been supported for full Webex deployment. The feature has been reworked for CE9.12.3 and above to support Webex Edge for Devices. When the on-premises device is linked via Webex Edge for Devices (supported from CE9.12.3 and above):

- All HTTP requests to the Webex cloud use the configured HTTP proxy.

■ Any HTTP requests targeted for provisioning (Unified CM/TMS/Expressway) or phonebook bypass the proxy settings.

Cisco Webex video devices connecting to the Webex cloud support the following proxy server features:

■ Proxy server configuration: WPAD, PAC, or Manual

■ Proxy authentication: No Auth, Basic, Digest

■ Proxy TLS inspection support: Yes

Note that the passwords used in the proxy configuration are hashed and stored locally on the on-premises registered device. The passwords used are not synchronized to the Webex cloud. To support proxy TLS inspection, the trust list downloaded into the video device during onboarding must be customized to include the enterprise CA certificate that the proxy presents to the device during TLS establishment. You can open a service request with Cisco TAC to create a custom trust list for devices in your organization.

Table 20-2 describes the URLs that are used by on-premises devices linking to Webex. If your organization uses a proxy, ensure that these URLs can be accessed.

Table 20-2   Accessible URLs for On-Premises Devices Linking to Webex

URL	Description
*.ciscospark.com	Webex services
*.wbx2.com	Webex services
*.webex.com	Authentication and Identity services
*.identrust.com	Certificate verification
*.webexcontent.com	General file storage, including ■ Device log files ■ Software updates
*.activation.webex.com *.activate.cisco.com *.webapps.cisco.com	Onboarding devices to the Webex service
speech.googleapis.com texttospeech.googleapis.com speech-services-manager-a.wbx2.com	Google speech services, used by Webex Assistant to handle speech recognition and text-to-speech; disabled by default, with opt-in via Control Hub

Enabling Webex Edge for Devices does not change the media paths that your on-premises video devices use today and no additional IP subnets for voice, video, and content sharing need to be whitelisted in your enterprise firewall.

This information is used by Webex Control Hub for monitoring and management features. CE9.13 is ready to let Cisco Webex Control Hub take care of the configuration management for devices linked via Webex Edge for Devices. Configuration Management (write) is disabled in Control Hub by default and must be enabled to take effect. If disabled, you will only be able to read the configuration from the devices. To change configurations on the device from Control Hub, you must enable it in Control Hub. Take note of that if the on-premises registered devices are registered through the Unified CM, the Configuration Control Mode setting on the device must be set to Unified CM and Endpoint for Webex Control Hub to be able to manage the on-premises device configuration.

NOTE Starting in March 2021, Cisco Webex is moving to a new certificate authority, IdenTrust Commercial Root CA 1. Due to this change, customers who are managing their device software upgrades manually must upgrade their devices to minimum CE 9.14.5 and preferably CE 9.15 at the earliest in order to be supported by Webex Edge for Devices. Failure to upgrade results in devices losing cloud connectivity and loss of all related functionality. This includes Control Hub Management, Analytics, and Hybrid calendaring, among other features. Your ability to connect and use your on-premises SIP infrastructure will not be impacted. Additionally, devices on unsupported versions lose the ability to be linked to the Webex cloud using the Webex Device Connector.

When Control Hub is set to manage configurations, the devices under such control will no longer accept most configurations from the Unified CM except configurations not exposed in Control Hub. These settings are mostly related to network services and are intended to avoid making the device unreachable from Control Hub. The device will continue to accept these settings from the Unified CM. The following list includes the most significant configurations:

- xconfig networkServices http proxy
- xconfig networkServices h323
- xconfig networkServices https
- xconfig networkServices snmp
- xconfig networkServices ssh hostkeyalgorithm
- xconfig networkServices upnp
- xconfig networkServices wifi
- xconfig conference defaultcall protocol
- xconfig conference encryption mode
- xconfig phonebook

Webex Edge for Calling

Today's large enterprises have invested in on-premises **private branch exchanges (PBXs)** and Voice over IP (VoIP) calling systems over the years and expanded through growth or acquisitions. For any given enterprise, these systems now connect multiple PBXs at different sites with multiple **public switched telephone network (PSTN)** interconnects and multinational deployments. The result is a mixed network made up of systems at various stages in their depreciation lifecycles. This disparate set of PBXs leads to inconsistent features and user experiences, high networking and telecommunication costs, along with the added complexity of multi-vendor management. This makes it difficult to drive new innovations, as enterprises simply cannot afford to replace these systems all at once.

Webex Edge for Calling is a core part of the Webex platform strategy. It provides a single calling architecture that accelerates workplace transformation and protects investments by enabling flexible, hybrid deployment paths to innovative cloud services. Offering a consistent, intelligent user experience, Webex Edge for Calling enables workplace transformation without business disruption. Webex Edge for Calling supports a hybrid architecture that connects Cisco Unified Communications Manager, Cisco UCM Cloud, Cisco **Hosted Collaboration Solution (HCS)**, and/or third-party PBXs directly into the Webex Calling cloud.

Cisco Webex Edge for Calling addresses the secure path to the challenges, which offers the following benefits:

- Enables flexible cloud migration while protecting on-premises investments by connecting all Cisco and third-party PBXs to Webex Calling to get a global dial plan and optimized call routing, add cloud innovations, and move to the cloud at a pace that makes sense for their business. This can connect Webex Calling, Cisco Unified CM, Cisco UCM Cloud, and third-party PBXs all together.

- Simplifies operations and lowers expenses through centralized application management (Webex Control Hub), databases, and enterprise services, resulting in reduced operational and capital costs by reducing network PSTN expenses.

- Creates one unified user experience, enabling users to become more productive through a consistent user experience across all collaboration workloads (calling, messaging, meetings, customer engagement) and devices. This is achieved with the modular new Webex app and Webex support for Webex Calling, Unified CM, and HCS.

- Accelerates workplace transformation by adding advanced cognitive collaboration features to in-office, mobile, remote, and contact center users, with application and device integrations that deliver a more completely connected user experience that drives productivity.

- Offers a worldwide cloud calling solution, with enterprise-grade scalability, security, features, and bundled or BYO PSTN connectivity, for instantly global calling delivery.

Through the Webex Edge for Calling architecture, Cisco can deliver a unified modular client app to serve all collaboration workloads on any desktop, laptop, mobile, or room device. Because it is modular, the app adapts according to the licensing permissions of every user. This makes it easy for users who might still be using an old Avaya phone system, for example, to use Webex for messaging, meetings, and team collaboration, while continuing to use their Avaya PBX for calling.

Webex Edge for Calling architecture supports your cloud migration with services at three levels:

- **Network Services:** Connect your sites and people to the cloud, with an option for a global enterprise dial plan for all sites, including existing PBX sites. Network Services enable you to offload on-net MPLS and off-net network traffic to the cloud.

20

- **Enterprise Services:** Centralize core enterprise routing services, like auto attendant, interactive voice response (IVR), call queues, and voicemail in the cloud. You also get centralized management of your complete collaboration suite through Webex Control Hub.

- **User Services:** Extend unified collaboration experience to all users. Even those on an Avaya PBX have access to Webex cloud collaboration services for calling, messaging, meetings, and team activities.

Webex Edge Audio

Cisco Webex Edge consists of three services (not hardware): Webex Edge Audio, Webex Edge Connect, and Webex Video Mesh. You can deploy them together for amazing and cost-effective meetings every time. Or you deploy them separately, with each service bringing its own benefit. The services reshape and re-architect the edge to maximize the power of the Webex cloud and bring that experience into the enterprise while providing even better meeting experiences through improved audio, video, and content quality.

The Cisco Webex backbone is a real-time, worldwide IP network engineered for effective meetings, enabling superior quality, reliability, and security that are nearly impossible to achieve on the public Internet or other public cloud–based services. Cisco is re-architecting the edge so that you can maximize the power of the Webex backbone directly in your own data center and improve meeting experiences. With Cisco Webex Edge, Cisco is doing this without asking users to change their behavior or requiring training on some new technology or way of meeting.

Cisco Webex Edge Audio decouples the PSTN from Cisco Webex by intelligently changing the call routing to a simple-to-deploy on-net path. It is a service that allows any company, of any size, that uses Cisco Unified Communications Manager to route audio calls intelligently and automatically over VoIP or utilize existing PSTN services.

Once Webex Edge Audio is deployed, any meeting participant automatically joins a Webex meeting through a direct VoIP route to the Webex cloud (not only from their PC but also from any Cisco-registered phone) completely transparently and with no change in behavior. This provides great cost savings because it eliminates PSTN charges created by users. At the same time, it provides those users with all the benefits of high-quality wideband codecs that Cisco Webex offers.

Webex Edge Audio also can lower PSTN costs for participants using callback from any phone, including mobile phones and home phones. When callback is requested to join a meeting from on premises, the Unified CM automatically routes the call to the desk phone. You can also choose to route callback for specific countries via their Expressways on-net and out their own PSTN gateways, providing additional costs savings over using Cisco Webex. Webex Edge Audio provides ultimate flexibility to Cisco customers in choosing the on-net path in locations/countries where they can save on PSTN and at the same time allows them to buy off-net minutes in locations/countries where they do not have an on-prem/Unified CM deployment.

In summary, for any Unified CM–registered device, Webex Edge Audio creates an end-to-end VoIP path whether users are dialing in or requesting the callback option from Webex. For all other users with a non-Unified CM–registered phone or mobile device, the company's own PSTN services can be used. Cisco has democratized audio savings while improving the audio quality for calls on Unified CM–registered devices.

Webex Edge Audio is enabled through a simple and automated provisioning process and set up with the Unified CM and Cisco Expressway. Unlike with other solutions, Cisco customers do not need to pay for edge-traversal licenses to use on third-party session border controllers. They connect to the Webex cloud through Cisco Expressway with no additional licenses.

To set up Edge Audio, you must first collect the necessary dial-in information and the Lua Normalization script from Cisco Webex Site Administration or Cisco Webex Control Hub. You will use this information to set up the dial-in numbers that users will use to dial in to their Webex services. For configurations, utilize the *Cisco Webex Edge Audio Customer Configuration Guide* available at https://help.webex.com.

Webex Edge Connect

Cisco Webex Edge Connect is a dedicated and managed, Quality-of-Service (QoS)-enabled IP link from a customer's premises to the Cisco Webex cloud through direct peering over Equinix Cloud Exchange (ECX). This dedicated peering connection insulates your meetings from the variability of the Internet, which means less congestion, packet loss, jitter, and delay. The direct connection provides enhanced meeting quality with consistent network performance and added security. Not being exposed to the public Internet also means you are better protected from potential threats and attacks.

Currently available services in Webex Edge Connect include the following:

- Webex Meetings

- Webex app, Webex Devices (Board, Room, and Desk), and Webex Video Mesh Media

- Video device-enabled Webex Meetings

- Webex Edge Audio

The following are the base requirements for establishing Edge Connect peering:

- An active connection on the Equinix Cloud Exchange that is established through Equinix; see the ECX Fabric Workflow documentation at https://docs.equinix.com/.

- A Public or Private **Border Gateway Protocol (BGP)** Autonomous System Number (ASN).

- Your IP addresses—both sides of the BGP peering connection as well as your advertised routes for performing **Network Address Translation (NAT)** from your private network to the public network:

  - Your BGP peering link address space, which is a public IP address with /30 or /31 prefix.

  - Your advertised public IP space (must be provider independent).

  - Edge Connect does not accept private prefix advertisements like RFC 1918.

- An IP space that is public and provider independent.

20

- An IT team with knowledge of BGP and peering principles.

- A network device capable of running BGP and 802.1Q tagging.

To set up Edge Connect, you first work with an Equinix representative on two tasks: establishing physical connectivity and establishing data-link connectivity. When these tasks are complete, you can continue to the third task of establishing network connectivity with Cisco Webex through the Equinix Cloud Exchange Portal. Reference the "Cisco Webex Edge Connect" article on https://help.webex.com for the most up-to-date process, IP block ranges, and BGP communities.

Webex Video Mesh

Cisco Webex Video Mesh (formerly Hybrid Media Service) dynamically finds the optimal mix of on-premises and cloud conferencing resources. On-premises conferences stay on premises when there are enough local resources. When local resources are exhausted, conferences then expand to the cloud.

Webex Video Mesh Node is software that is installed on an on-premises Cisco UCS server, registered to the cloud, and managed in Cisco Webex Control Hub. Cisco Webex meetings and events, Webex Personal Room meetings, meetings associated with a Webex space, and Webex calls (between two people) can be routed to the local, on-net Webex Video Mesh Nodes. Webex Video Mesh selects the most efficient way to use the available resources.

Webex Video Mesh provides these benefits:

Key Topic

- Improves quality and reduces latency by allowing you to keep your calls on premises.

- Extends your calls transparently to the cloud when on-premises resources have reached their limit or are unavailable.

- Manages your Webex Video Mesh clusters from the cloud with a single administrative interface: Cisco Webex Control Hub (https://admin.webex.com).

- Optimizes resources and scale capacity, as needed.

- Combines the features of cloud and on-premises conferencing in one seamless user experience.

- Reduces capacity concerns with the always-available cloud resources when additional conferencing resources are needed.

- Provides advanced analytics on capacity and usage and troubleshooting report data in https://admin.webex.com.

- Uses local media processing when users dial in to a Cisco Webex meeting from on-premises, standards-based SIP endpoints and clients:

  - SIP-based endpoints and clients (Cisco endpoints, Jabber, third-party SIP), registered to on-premises call control (Cisco Unified CM or Expressway), that call into a Cisco Webex meeting

  - Cisco Webex app (including paired with room devices) that join a Cisco Webex meeting

- Cisco Webex room and desk devices (including Cisco Webex Board) that directly join a Webex meeting

- Provides optimized audio and video interactive voice response (IVR) to on-net SIP-based endpoints and clients.

- Cisco Webex clients (internal and external) continue to join meetings from the cloud.

- H.323, IP dial-in, and Skype for Business (S4B) endpoints continue to join meetings from the cloud.

- Supports 1080p 30fps HD video as an option for meetings, if meeting participants that can support 1080p are hosted through the local on-premises Webex Video Mesh Nodes. (If a participant joins an in-progress meeting from the cloud, on-premises users continue to experience 1080p 30fps on supported endpoints.)

- Enhanced and differentiated QoS by marking separate audio (EF) and video (AF41) values.

Webex Video Mesh Nodes conform to recommended **Quality of Service (QoS)** best practices by enabling port ranges that allow you to differentiate audio and video streams in all flows to and from the Video Mesh Nodes. This change will let you create QoS policies and effectively re-mark traffic to and from the Video Mesh Nodes.

Accompanying these port changes are QoS changes. Webex Video Mesh Nodes automatically mark media traffic from SIP-registered endpoints (on-premises Unified CM or VCS Expressway registered) for both audio (EF) and video (AF41) separately with appropriate class of service and use well-known port ranges for specific media types. The source traffic from the on-premises registered endpoints is always determined by the configuration on the call control (Unified CM or VCS Expressway).

Cisco Webex apps continue to connect to Webex Video Mesh Nodes over shared port 5004. This shared port is also used by Cisco Webex apps and endpoints for Session Traversal Utilities for NAT (STUN) reachability tests to Webex Video Mesh Nodes. Webex Video Mesh Node to Webex Video Mesh Node for cascades use a destination shared port of 5004.

Call control and existing meetings infrastructure are not required to use Video Mesh, but you can integrate the two. If you are integrating Video Mesh with your call control and meeting infrastructure, make sure your environment meets the minimum criteria:

- On-premises call control

  - Cisco Unified Communications Manager, Release 11.5(1) SU3 or later (latest SU release recommended).

  - Cisco Expressway-C or E, Release X8.11.4 or later.

- Meeting infrastructure

  - Cisco Webex Meetings WBS33 or later. You can verify that your Webex site is on the correct platform if it has the Media Resource Type list available in the Cloud Collaboration Meeting Room site options.

20

- To ensure that your site is ready for Video Mesh, contact your customer success manager (CSM) or partner.

- Failover handling

  - Cisco Expressway-C or Expressway-E, Release X8.11.4 or later

- One Button to Push (OBTP)

  - Cisco TMS 15.2.1 and Cisco TMSXE5.2, WBS31 Webex Productivity Tools

- Cisco Webex app requirements:

  - Supported versions of the Cisco Webex app

  - Video Mesh supports Cisco Webex for desktop (Windows, Mac) and mobile (Android, iPhone, and iPad).

- Supported Webex-registered Room, Desk, and Board devices

  - Cisco DX70

  - Cisco Webex DX80

  - Cisco Webex Board 55

  - Cisco Webex Room Kit

  - Cisco Webex Room Kit Mini

  - Cisco Webex Room Kit Plus

  - Cisco Webex Room Kit Plus Precision 60

  - Cisco Webex Room Kit Pro

  - Cisco Telepresence SX10 Quick Set

  - Cisco Telepresence SX20 Quick Set

  - Cisco Telepresence SX80 Codec

  - Cisco Telepresence MX200 G2

  - Cisco Telepresence MX300 G2

  - Cisco Telepresence MX700

  - Cisco Telepresence MX800

In production deployments, there are two ways to deploy Webex Video Mesh Node software on a particular hardware configuration:

- You can set up each server as a single virtual machine, which is best for deployments that include many SIP endpoints.

- Using the VMNLite option, you can set up each server with multiple smaller virtual machines, which is best for deployments that mainly include Webex users and cloud-registered endpoints.

For any platform that runs Webex Video Mesh Node software, co-residency (running different Collaboration applications in dedicated VMs on the same virtualized Business Edition physical server or host) with other services is not permitted. For VMNLite deployments, co-residency of VMNLite and non-VMNLite instances has not been tested and is not supported.

Table 20-3 outlines the system and platform requirements for Webex Video Mesh Node software in a production environment:

Table 20-3 System Requirements for Cisco Webex Video Mesh Node

Hardware Configuration	Production Deployment as a Single Virtual Machine	Production Deployment with VMNLite VMs	Notes	Common Requirements
Cisco Meeting Server 1000 (CMS 1000)	■ 72vCPUs (70 for Webex Video Mesh Node, 2 for ESXi) ■ 60 GB main memory ■ 80 GB local hard disk space	Deploy as three identical virtual machine instances, each with: ■ 23 vCPUs ■ 20 GB main memory ■ 80 GB local hard disk space	Cisco recommends this platform for Webex Video Mesh Node.	■ VMware ESXi 6 or vSphere 6 or later ■ Hyperthreading enabled
Specifications-based configuration (2.6-GHz Intel Xeon E5-2600v3 or later processor required)	■ 72vCPUs (70 for Webex Video Mesh Node, 2 for ESXi) ■ 60 GB main memory ■ 80 GB local hard disk space	Deploy as three identical VM instances, each with ■ 23 vCPUs ■ 20 GB main memory ■ 80 GB local hard disk space	Use either CMS1000 or VMNLite option during configuration.	
	■ 48vCPUs (46 for Webex Video Mesh Node, 2 for ESXi) ■ 60 GB main memory ■ 80 GB local hard disk space	Deploy as two identical VM instances, each with ■ 23 vCPUs ■ 20 GB main memory ■ 80 GB local hard disk space	Use either MM410V or VMNLite option during configuration.	

20

Hardware Configuration	Production Deployment as a Single Virtual Machine	Production Deployment with VMNLite VMs	Notes	Common Requirements
Cisco Multiparty Media 410v server	■ 48vCPUs (46 for Webex Video Mesh Node, 2 for ESXi) ■ 60 GB main memory ■ 80 GB local hard disk space We do not support the first generation MM400v server.	Deploy as two identical VM instances, each with ■ 23 vCPUs ■ 20 GB main memory ■ 80 GB local hard disk space	While this platform is supported for Webex Video Mesh Node, note that it is an End of Sale/End of Life product. See the End-of-Sale and End-of-Life Announcement for the Cisco Multiparty Media 410V for more information.	

Cisco officially supports the following proxy solutions that can integrate with your Webex Video Mesh Nodes:

■ Cisco Web Security Appliance (WSA) for transparent proxy

■ Squid for explicit proxy

For an explicit proxy or transparent inspecting proxy that inspects (decrypts traffic), you must have a copy of the proxy's root certificate that you will need to upload to the Webex Video Mesh Node trust store on the web interface. Cisco supports the following explicit proxy and authentication type combinations:

■ No authentication with HTTP and HTTPS

■ Basic authentication with HTTP and HTTPS

■ Digest authentication with HTTPS only

■ NTLM authentication with HTTP only

For transparent proxies, you must use the router/switch to force HTTPS/443 traffic to go to the proxy. You can also force WebSocket/444 to go to the proxy. (WebSocket uses HTTPS.) Port 444 depends on your network setup. If port 444 is not routed through the proxy, it must be open directly from the node to the cloud.

Webex Video Mesh requires WebSocket connections to cloud services, so that the nodes function correctly. On explicit inspecting and transparent inspecting proxies, HTTP headers that are required for a proper WebSocket connection are altered and WebSocket connections fail. The symptom when this occurs on port 443 (with transparent inspecting proxy enabled) is a post-registration warning in Control Hub: "Webex Video Mesh SIP calling is not working correctly." The same alarm can occur for other reasons when proxy is not enabled. When WebSocket headers are blocked on port 443, media does not flow between apps and SIP clients. If media is not flowing, this often occurs when HTTPS traffic from the node over port 444 or port 443 is failing:

- Proxy is not inspecting, but port 444 traffic is not allowed by the proxy.

- Port 443 or port 444 traffic is allowed by the proxy, but it is an inspecting proxy and is breaking the WebSocket.

To correct these problems, you may have to "bypass" or "splice" (disable inspection) on ports 444 and 443 to *.wbx2.com and *.ciscospark.com.

Key Topic

When considering capacity, keep in mind that Webex Video Mesh is a software-based media product that works along with other Webex cloud-based services. The capacity of a Webex Video Mesh Node in a cluster can vary. Factors that influence the capacity are the type of devices and clients in a meeting, resolution, quality of network, peak load, deployment, and so on. Because of these variables, the capacity numbers that follow are a general guideline that are based on two scenarios. Cisco has used a combination of real and simulated clients for testing; these tests inherently can produce some variation. In all the scenarios, the load was placed at one call per second.

In general, adding more nodes to the cluster does not double the capacity, mainly because of overhead associated with setting up cascades. Use these numbers as general guidance. However, Cisco strongly recommends the following:

- Test out common meeting scenarios for your deployment.

- Use the analytics in Control Hub to see how your deployment is evolving and add capacity as needed.

Table 20-4 shows example scenarios under the capacity of which conferencing platform Cisco has tested. These scenarios use a controlled environment with 1:1 concurrent Webex calls at 720p or 1080p on a single server at one call per second, with static video, no sharing, and no cloud cascades:

- **Scenario 1:** Two Cisco Webex participants are in a meeting. Both the participants are within the enterprise network, using the same Webex Video Mesh Node.

- **Scenario 2:** Multiple SIP participants are in a meeting. All the participants are placed on the same Video Mesh Node.

Table 20-4 Example Scenario for Video Mesh Node Capacity

Platform	Scenario 1	Scenario 2
Cisco Meeting Server 1000 (CMS 1000) (Full Version)	100 (up to 720p) 35 (up to 1080p)	75 (up to 720p) 38 (up to 1080p)
MM410v (Full Version)	100 (up to 720p) 35 (up to 1080p)	65 (720p) 28 (1080p)

20

Cisco recommends VMNLite only for deployments that mainly include Webex and cloud-registered endpoints. In Table 20-5, the nodes utilize more switching and fewer transcoding resources than the standard configuration provides. Deploying more, smaller virtual machines on the host optimizes resources for this scenario.

Table 20-5 VMNLite Call Capacity Benchmark

Platform	Benchmark at 720p
Three VMNLite virtual machines on CMS 1000	150
Two VMNLite virtual machines on MM410v	110

Overflows on low call volume (especially SIP calls that originate on premises) are not a true reflection of scale. Video Mesh analytics (under **Control Hub > Resources > Call Activity**) indicate the call legs that originate on premises. They do not specify the call streams that came in through the cascade to the Video Mesh Node for media processing. As remote participant numbers increase in a meeting, the resulting cascade increases and consumes on-premises media resources on the Video Mesh Node.

Webex Video Mesh Nodes are deployed in clusters. A cluster defines Webex Video Mesh Nodes with similar attributes, such as network proximity. Cisco Webex participants are directed to use a particular cluster or the cloud, depending on the following conditions:

- A client on a corporate network that can reach an on-premises cluster will connect to it. This is the primary preference for clients that are on the corporate network.

- A client that cannot reach an on-premises cluster will connect to the cloud. This case is for a mobile device that is not connected to the corporate network.

- Which cluster is used also depends on latency, rather than just location. For example, a cloud cluster with lower STUN round-trip (SRT) delay than a Webex Video Mesh cluster may be a better candidate for the meeting. This logic prevents a user from landing on a geographically far cluster with a high SRT delay.

Each cluster contains logic that cascades meetings across other cloud meeting clusters, as needed. Cascading provides a data path for media between clients in their meetings. Meetings are distributed across nodes and the clients land on the most efficient node nearest to them, depending on factors such as network topology, WAN link, and resource utilization.

Reachability is determined by the client's ability to "ping" media nodes. A variety of potential connection mechanisms such as **User Datagram Protocol (UDP)** and **Transmission Control Protocol (TCP)** are used during an actual call. Before the call, the Cisco Webex device (Room, Desk, Board, and Webex app) registers with the Cisco Webex cloud, which provides a list of cluster candidates for the call.

The following guidelines apply to Webex Video Mesh cluster deployment:

- In typical enterprise deployments, Cisco recommends that customers use up to ten nodes per cluster. There are no hard limits set in the system to block a cluster size with greater than ten nodes. However, if you need to create larger clusters, Cisco strongly recommends that you review this option with Cisco engineering through your Cisco Account Team.

- Create fewer clusters when resources have similar network proximity (affinity).

- When creating clusters, only add nodes that are in the same geographical region and the same data center. Clustering across the wide-area network (WAN) is not supported.

- Typically, deploy clusters in enterprises that host frequent localized meetings. Plan where you place clusters on the bandwidth available at various WAN locations inside the enterprise. Over time, you can deploy and grow cluster-by-cluster based on observed user patterns.

- Clusters located in different time zones can effectively serve multiple geographies by taking advantage of different peak/busy hour calling patterns.

- If you have two Webex Video Mesh Nodes in two separate data centers (European Union and North America, for example), and you have endpoints join through each data center, the nodes in each data center would cascade to a single Webex Video Mesh Node in the cloud. Theses cascades would go over the Internet. If there is a cloud participant (that joins before one of the HMN participants), the nodes would be cascaded through the cloud participant's media node.

Time zone diversity can allow clusters to be shared during off-peak times. For example, a company with a Northern California cluster and a New York cluster might find that over-all network latency is not that high between the two locations that serve a geographically diverse user population. When resources are at peak usage in the Northern California cluster, the New York cluster is likely to be off peak and have additional capacity. The same applies for the Northern California cluster during peak times in the New York cluster. These are not the only mechanisms used for effective deployment of resources, but they are the two main ones.

When the capacity of all on-premises clusters is reached, an on-premises participant over-flows to the Cisco Webex cloud. This does not mean that all calls will be hosted in the cloud. Only those participants that are either remote or cannot connect to an on-premises cluster will be directed to the cloud. In a call with both on-premises and cloud participants, the on-premises cluster is bridged (cascaded) to the cloud to combine all participants into a single call.

In addition to determining reachability, the clients also perform periodic round-trip delay tests using STUN. STUN round-trip (SRT) delay is an important factor when selecting potential resources during an actual call. When multiple clusters are deployed, the primary selection criteria are based on the learned SRT delay. Reachability tests are performed in the background, initiated by several factors including network changes, and do not introduce delays that affect call setup times. Figure 20-3 depicts round-trip delay tests when the cloud device fails to reach the on-premises cluster.

20

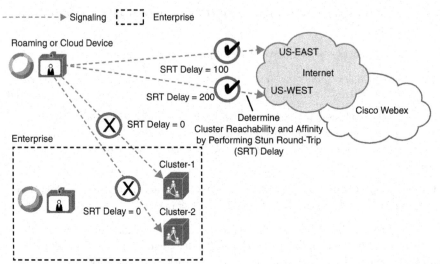

Figure 20-3 *Round-Trip Delay Tests: Cloud Device Fails to Reach On-Premises Cluster*

Figure 20-4 shows the round-trip delay tests when the cloud device successfully reaches the on-premises cluster.

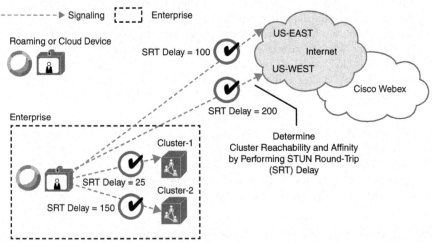

Figure 20-4 *Round-Trip Delay Tests: Cloud Device Successfully Reaches On-Premises Cluster*

Learned reachability information is provided to the Cisco Webex cloud every time a call is set up. This information allows the cloud to select the best resource (cluster or cloud), depending on the relative location of the client to available clusters and the type of call. If no resources are available in the preferred cluster, additional clusters are tested for availability based on SRT delay. A preferred cluster is chosen with the lowest SRT delay. Calls are served on premises from a secondary cluster when the primary cluster is busy. Local reachable Webex Video Mesh resources are tried first, in order of lowest SRT delay. When all local resources are exhausted, the participant connects to the cloud.

Cluster definition and location are critical for a deployment that provides the best overall experience for participants. Ideally, a deployment should provide resources where the clients are located. If not enough resources are allocated where the clients make the majority of calls, more internal network bandwidth is consumed to connect users to distant clusters.

On-premises Cisco Webex devices that have the same cluster affinity (preference, based on proximity to the cluster) connect to the same cluster for a call. On-premises Cisco Webex devices with different on-premises cluster affinities connect to different clusters and the clusters then bridge to the cloud to combine the two environments into a single call. Figure 20-5 shows an on-premises and cloud call.

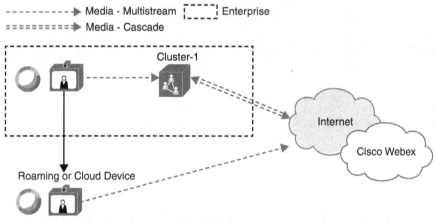

Figure 20-5   *On-Premises and Cloud Call*

The Cisco Webex device connects to either an on-premises cluster or the cloud based upon its reachability. Figure 20-6 shows the most common scenarios.

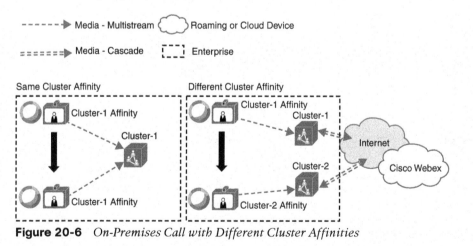

Figure 20-6   *On-Premises Call with Different Cluster Affinities*

Figure 20-7 depicts how a Cisco Webex cloud device connects to the Webex cloud.

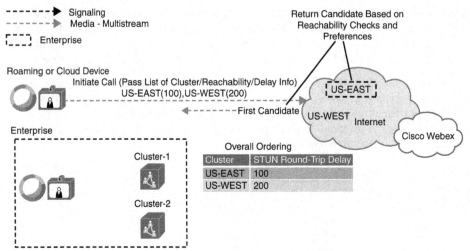

Figure 20-7   *Cisco Webex Cloud Device Connects to Cloud*

Figure 20-8 shows how a Cisco Webex on-premises device connects to an on-premises cluster.

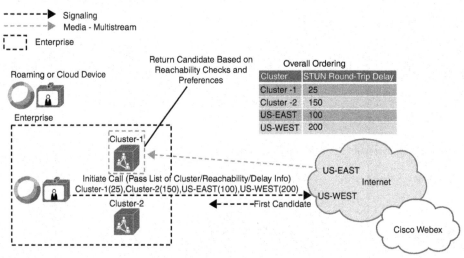

Figure 20-8   *Cisco Webex On-Premises Device Connects to On-Premises Cluster*

Figure 20-9 shows how a Cisco Webex on-premises device connects to the Webex cloud.

While the preference for node selection is your locally deployed Video Mesh Nodes, Cisco supports a scenario where, if the SRT delay to an on-premises Video Mesh cluster exceeds the tolerable round-trip delay of 250 ms (which usually happens if the on-premises cluster is configured in a different continent), then the system selects the closest cloud media node in that geography instead of a Video Mesh Node. Figure 20-10 explains the node selection, described as follows:

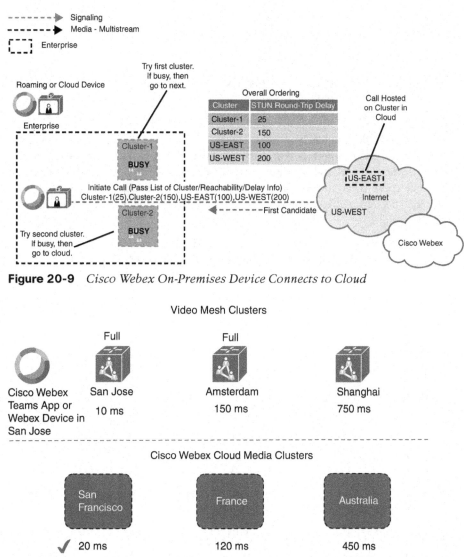

Figure 20-9 *Cisco Webex On-Premises Device Connects to Cloud*

Figure 20-10 *Cloud Cluster Selection for Overflow Based on 250-ms or Higher STUN Round-Trip Delay*

- The Cisco Webex app or device is on the enterprise network in San Jose.

- San Jose and Amsterdam clusters are at capacity or unavailable.

- SRT delay to the Shanghai cluster is greater than 250 ms and will likely introduce media quality issues.

- The San Francisco cloud cluster has an optimal SRT delay.

- The Shanghai Video Mesh cluster is excluded from consideration.

- As a result, the Cisco Webex client overflows to the San Francisco cloud cluster.

The following list describes the deployment models that are supported by Video Mesh and those that aren't:

■ Supported in a Video Mesh deployment:

  ■ You can deploy a Webex Video Mesh Node in either a data center (preferred) or demilitarized zone (DMZ). For guidance, see the section "Ports and Protocols Used by Webex Video Mesh" in the *Deployment Guide for Cisco Webex Video Mesh*.

  ■ For a DMZ deployment, you can set up the Video Mesh Nodes in a cluster with the dual network interface (NIC). This deployment lets you separate the internal enterprise network traffic (used for interbox communication, cascades between node clusters, and to access the node's management interface) from the external cloud network traffic (used for connectivity to the outside world and cascades to the cloud).

  ■ Dual NIC works on both the full version and demo version of Video Mesh Node software. You can also deploy the Video Mesh behind a 1:1 NAT setup.

  ■ You can integrate Video Mesh Nodes with your on-premises Cisco call control environment.

  ■ The following types of address translation are supported:

    ■ Dynamic NAT using an IP pool.

    ■ Dynamic Port Address Translation (PAT)

    ■ 1:1 NAT

    ■ Other forms of NAT should work if the correct ports and protocols are used, but Cisco does not officially support them because they have not been tested.

  ■ IPv4

  ■ Static IP address for the Webex Video Mesh Node

■ Not supported in a Video Mesh deployment:

  ■ IPv6

  ■ DHCP for the Webex Video Mesh Node

  ■ A cluster with a mixture of single NIC and dual NIC

  ■ Clustering Video Mesh Nodes over the WAN

  ■ Audio, video, or media that does not pass through a Webex Video Mesh Node:

    ■ Audio from phones

    ■ Peer-to-peer call between Cisco Webex app and standards-based endpoint

    ■ Audio termination on Webex Video Mesh Node

    ■ Media sent through Expressway C/E pair

    ■ Video callback

The following examples show common Webex Video Mesh deployments and help you understand where Webex Video Mesh clusters can fit into your network. Keep in mind that Webex Video Mesh deployment depends on factors in your network topology:

■ Data center locations

■ Office locations and size

■ Internet access location and capacity

In general, try to tie the Webex Video Mesh Nodes to the Unified CM or Session Management Edition (SME) clusters. As a best practice, keep the nodes as centralized as possible to the local branches. Video Mesh supports SME. Unified CM clusters can be connected through an SME deployment, and then you must create an SME trunk that connects to the Webex Video Mesh Nodes.

Figure 20-11 illustrates the hub-and-spoke architecture. This deployment model involves centralized networking and Internet access. Typically, the central location has a high employee concentration. In this case, a Webex Video Mesh cluster can be located at a central location for optimized media handling. Locating clusters in branch locations may not yield benefits in the short term and may lead to suboptimal routing. Cisco recommends that you deploy clusters in a branch only if there is frequent communication between branches.

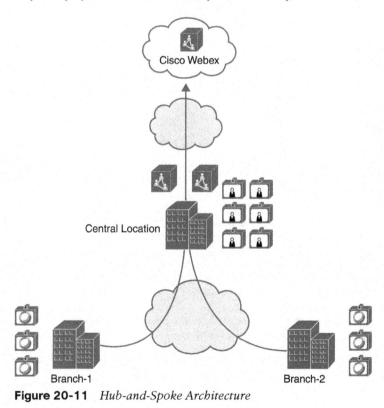

Figure 20-11 *Hub-and-Spoke Architecture*

20

The geographically distributed deployment is interconnected but can exhibit noticeable latency between regions. Lack of resources can cause suboptimal cascades to be set up in the short term when there are meetings between users in each geographical location. In this model, Cisco recommends that you allocate Webex Video Mesh Nodes near regional Internet access. Figure 20-12 depicts the geographic distribution.

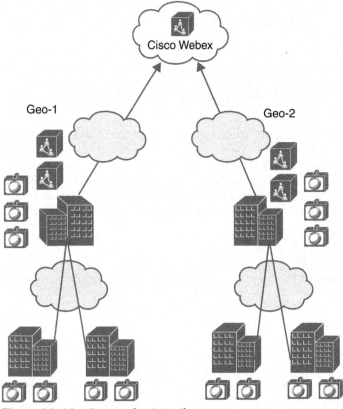

Figure 20-12   *Geographic Distribution*

The deployment model shown in Figure 20-13 contains regional Unified CM clusters. Each cluster can contain a SIP trunk to select resources in the local Webex Video Mesh cluster. A second trunk can provide a failover path to an Expressway pair if resources become limited.

To ensure a successful deployment of Video Mesh and for trouble-free operation of the Video Mesh Nodes, seek out the following documentation:

- The article "Network Requirements for Webex Services" on https://help.webex.com to understand the overall network requirements for Webex.

- The *Webex Teams Firewall Traversal* whitepaper on Cisco.com for more information about firewall and network practices for Cisco Webex services.

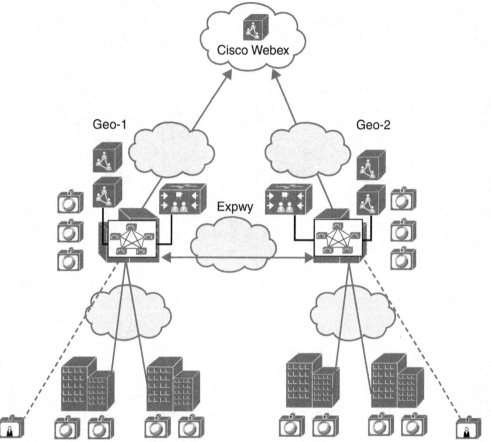

Figure 20-13   *Geographic Distribution with SIP Dialing*

- To mitigate potential **Domain Name Service (DNS)** query issues, follow the *DNS Best Practices, Network Protections, and Attack Identification* documentation on Cisco.com when you configure your enterprise firewall.

- For more design information, see the Cisco Validated Design (CVD) guide *Preferred Architecture for Cisco Webex Hybrid Services* on Cisco.com.

Table 20-6 lists the ports and protocols for management. The Webex Video Mesh Nodes in a cluster must be in the same VLAN or subnet mask. The port direction is from the management workstation to the Video Mesh Node and then the Video Mesh Node to the Cisco Webex cloud.

20

Table 20-6 Ports and Protocols for Management

Purpose	Source	Destination	Source IP	Transport Protocol	Source Port	Destination IP	Destination Port
Management	Management computer	Webex Video Mesh Node	As required	TCP, HTTPS	Any	Webex Video Mesh Node	443
SSH for access to Webex Video Mesh admin console	Management computer	Webex Video Mesh Node	As required	TCP	Any	Webex Video Mesh Node	22
Transcoding and Playback	Gateway service on Webex Video Mesh Node(s)	Webex Video Mesh Node	As required	TCP, HTTPS (WebSocket)	Any	Any	33432 or 33433
Intracluster Communication	Webex Video Mesh Node	Webex Video Mesh Node	IP address of other Webex Video Mesh Nodes in the cluster	TCP	Any	Webex Video Mesh Nodes	8443
Management	Webex Video Mesh Node	Cisco Webex cloud	As required	UDP, NTP UDP, DNS TCP, HTTPS (WebSocket)	Any	Any	123* 53*
Cascade Signaling	Webex Video Mesh Node	Cisco Webex cloud	Any	TCP	Any	Any	444 or 443
Management	Webex Video Mesh Node	Cisco Webex cloud	As required	TCP, HTTPS	Any	Any**	443
Management	Webex Video Mesh Node (1)	Webex Video Mesh Node (2)	Webex Video Mesh Node (1)	TCP, HTTPS (WebSocket)	Any	Webex Video Mesh Node (2)	5000 or 5001

* The default configuration in the OVA is configured for NTP and DNS. The OVA requires that you open those ports outbound to the Internet. If you configure a local NTP and DNS server, then ports 53 and 123 are not required to be opened through the firewall.

** Because some cloud service URLs are subject to change without warning, Any is the recommended destination for trouble-free operation of the Webex Video Mesh Nodes. If you prefer to filter traffic based on URLs, see the "Webex URLs for Hybrid Services" section of "Network Requirements for Webex Services" on https://help.cisco.com for more information.

For deployments where the Video Mesh Node sits in the enterprise side of the DMZ or inside the firewall, there is a Video Mesh Node configuration setting in Webex Control Hub that allows the administrator to optimize the port ranges used by the Video Mesh Node for QoS network marking. This Quality-of-Service setting, when enabled (enabled by default), changes the source ports that are used for audio, video, and content sharing to the values in Table 20-7. This setting allows you to configure QoS marking policies based on UDP port ranges to differentiate audio from video or content sharing and mark all audio with recommended value of EF and video and content sharing with a recommended value of AF41.

Figure 20-14 and Table 20-7 show UDP ports that are used for audio and video streams, which are the focus of QoS network configurations. While network QoS marking policies for media over UDP are the focus of Table 20-14, Webex Video Mesh Nodes also terminate TCP traffic for presentation and content sharing for Cisco Webex apps using ephemeral ports 52500–65500. If a firewall sits between the Video Mesh Nodes and the Cisco Webex apps, those TCP ports also must be allowed for proper functioning.

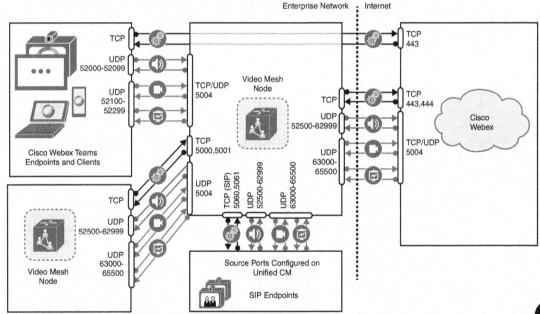

Figure 20-14 *Traffic Signatures for Video Mesh (Quality of Service Enabled)*

A Video Mesh Node marks traffic natively. This native marking is asymmetric in some flows and depends on whether the source ports are shared ports (single port like 5004 for multiple flows to various destinations and destination ports) or are not shared (where the port falls in a range but is unique to that specific bidirectional session). To understand the native marking by a Video Mesh Node, note that the Video Mesh Node marks audio EF when it is not using the 5004 port as a source port. Some bidirectional flows like Video Mesh to Video Mesh cascades or Video Mesh to Webex app will be asymmetrically marked, a reason to use the network to re-mark traffic based on the UDP port ranges provided.

Table 20-7 UDP Ports Used for Audio and Video Streams (Quality of Service Enabled)

Source IP Address	Destination IP Address	Source UDP Ports	Destination UDP Ports	Native DSCP Marking	Media Type
Video Mesh Node	Webex cloud media services	35000 to 52499	5004	AF41	Test STUN packets
Video Mesh Node	Webex cloud media services	52500 to 62999	5004	EF	Audio
Video Mesh Node	Webex cloud media services	63000 to 65500	5004	AF41	Video
Video Mesh Node	Video Mesh Node*	52500 to 62999	5004	EF/AF41*	Audio
Video Mesh Node	Video Mesh Node*	63000 to 65500	5004	AF41	Video
Video Mesh Node	Unified CM SIP endpoints	52500 to 62999	Unified CM SIP Profile	EF	Audio
Video Mesh Node	Unified CM SIP endpoints	63000 to 65500	Unified CM SIP Profile	AF41	Video
Video Mesh Node	Webex application or endpoint**	5004	52000 to 52099	AF41	Audio
Video Mesh Node	Webex application or endpoint	5004	52100 to 52299	AF41	Video

* Video Mesh to Video Mesh cascades have asymmetrically marked media for the audio. When the Video Mesh Node initiates the cascade, the source ports for audio 52500 to 62999 are used and the VMN can mark EF for that audio, but the return audio from the Video Mesh Node answering the cascade will use the shared ports (5004) and thus mark that return audio traffic AF41.

** The direction of media traffic determines the DSCP markings. If the source ports are from the Video Mesh Node (from the Video Mesh Node to Webex app), the traffic is marked as AF41 only. Media traffic that originates from the Webex app or Webex endpoints has separate DSCP markings, but the return traffic from the Video Mesh Node shared ports does not.

For deployments where the Video Mesh Node sits in the DMZ, there is a Video Mesh Node configuration setting in Webex Control Hub that allows you to optimize the port ranges used by the Video Mesh Node. This Quality-of-Service setting, when disabled (enabled by default), changes the source ports that are used for audio, video, and content sharing from the Video Mesh Node to the range 34000 to 34999. The Video Mesh Node then natively marks all audio, video, and content sharing to a single DSCP of AF41. Because the source ports are the same for all media regardless of destination, you cannot differentiate the audio from video or content sharing based on port range with this setting disabled. This configuration does let you configure firewall pin holes for media more easily than with Quality of Service enabled.

Figure 20-15 and Table 20-8 show UDP ports that are used for audio and video streams when QoS is disabled.

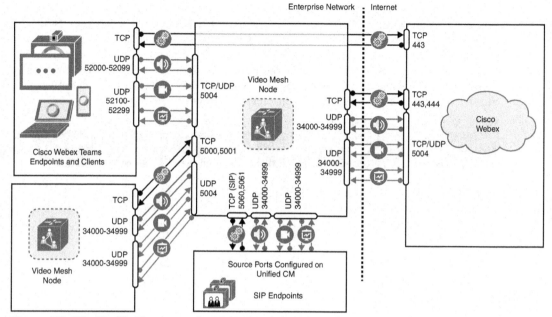

Figure 20-15 *Traffic Signatures for Video Mesh (Quality of Service Disabled)*

Table 20-8 UDP Ports Used for Audio and Video Streams (Quality of Service Disabled)

Source IP Address	Destination IP Address	Source UDP Ports	Destination UDP Ports	Native DSCP Marking	Media Type
Video Mesh Node	Webex cloud media services	34000 to 34999	5004	AF41	Audio
Video Mesh Node	Webex cloud media services	34000 to 34999	5004	AF41	Video
Video Mesh Node	Video Mesh Node	34000 to 34999	5004	AF41	Audio
Video Mesh Node	Video Mesh Node	34000 to 34999	5004	AF41	Video
Video Mesh Node	Unified CM SIP endpoints	34000 to 34999	Unified CM SIP Profile	AF41	Audio
Video Mesh Node	Unified CM SIP endpoints	34000 to 34999	Unified CM SIP Profile	AF41	Video
Video Mesh Node	Webex cloud media services	35000 to 52499	5004	AF41	Test STUN packets
Video Mesh Node	Webex application or endpoint	5004	52000 to 52099	AF41	Audio
Video Mesh Node	Webex application or endpoint	5004	52100 to 52299	AF41	Video

Table 20-9 identifies the ports and protocols for Webex Meetings traffic. The port direction would be to/from the Cisco Webex app and room or desk devices, to the Video Mesh Node, and then to/from the Cisco Webex cloud. Port 5004 is used for all cloud media and on-premises Webex Video Mesh Nodes. Cisco Webex apps continue to connect to Webex Video Mesh Nodes over shared ports (TCP/UDP) 5004. These ports are also used by Cisco Webex apps and endpoints for STUN tests to Webex Video Mesh Nodes. Webex Video Mesh Node to Webex Video Mesh Node for cascades use a destination shared port of 5004.

Table 20-9 Ports and Protocols for Cisco Webex Meetings Traffic

Purpose	Source	Destination	Source IP	Source Port	Transport Protocol	Destination IP	Destination Port
Calling to meeting	Apps (Cisco Webex desktop and mobile apps) Cisco Webex room, desk, or board device	Webex Video Mesh Node	As required	Any	UDP and TCP (Used by the Cisco Webex app) SRTP (Any)	Any****	5004
SIP device calling to meeting (SIP signaling)	Unified CM or Cisco Expressway call control	Webex Video Mesh Node	As required	Ephemeral (>=1024)	TCP or TLS	Any****	5060 or 5061
Cascade	Webex Video Mesh Node	Cisco Webex cloud	As required	34000–34999	UDP, SRTP (Any)***	Any****	5004
Cascade	Webex Video Mesh Node	Webex Video Mesh Node	As required	34000–34999	UDP, SRTP (Any)***	Any****	5004

*** TCP is also supported but not preferred because of its effect on media quality.

**** If you want to restrict by IP addresses, see the IP address ranges that are documented in "Network Requirements for Webex Services" at https://help.webex.com for the most up-to-date resource.

For the best experience using Cisco Webex in your organization, configure your firewall to allow all outbound TCP and UDP traffic that is destined toward ports 5004 as well as any inbound replies to that traffic. The port requirements that are listed above assume that Webex Video Mesh Nodes are deployed either in the LAN (preferred) or in a DMZ and that Cisco Webex apps are in the LAN.

Webex Video Mesh is adaptive depending on the available bandwidth and distributes resources accordingly. For devices in the meeting that use the Webex Video Mesh Node, the cascade link provides the benefit of reducing average bandwidth and improving the meeting experience for the user. For bandwidth provisioning and capacity planning guidelines, reference the CVD *Preferred Architecture for Cisco Webex Hybrid Services* on Cisco.com.

Based on the active speakers in the meeting, the cascade links are established. Each cascade can contain up to six streams and the cascade is limited to six participants (six in the direction of the Webex app/SIP to Webex cloud and fix in the opposite direction). Each media resource (cloud and Video Mesh) asks the remote side for the standard-definition streams that are needed to fulfill the local endpoint requirements of all remote participants across the cascade, as shown in Figure 20-16.

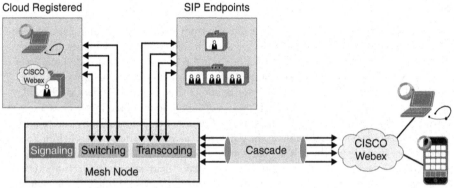

Figure 20-16 *Cascade Link*

To provide a flexible user experience, the Webex platform can do multistream video to meeting participants. This same ability applies to the cascade link between Video Mesh Nodes and the cloud. In this architecture, the bandwidth requirements vary depending on several factors, such as the endpoint layouts.

In the architecture shown in Figure 20-17, Cisco Webex–registered endpoints send signaling to the cloud and media to the switching services. On-premises SIP endpoints send signaling to the call control environment (Unified CM or Expressway), which then sends it to the Video Mesh Node. Media is sent to the transcoding service.

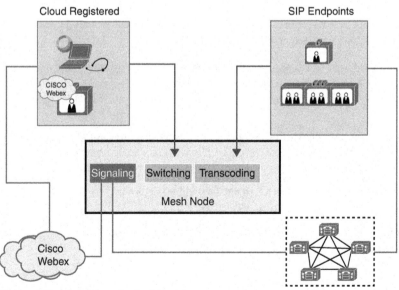

Figure 20-17 *Cascade Architecture*

20

Local on-premises participants on the Video Mesh Node request the desired streams based on their layout requirements. Those streams are forwarded from the Video Mesh Node to the endpoint for local device rendering. Each cloud and Video Mesh Node requests HD and SD resolutions from all participants that are cloud-registered devices on the Webex app. Depending on the endpoint, it will send up to four resolutions, typically 1080p, 720p, 360p, and 180p.

Most Cisco endpoints can send three or four streams from a single source in a range of resolutions (from 1080p to 180p). The layout of the endpoint dictates the requirement for the streams needed on the far end of the cascade. For active presence, the main video stream is 1080p or 720p, and the video panes (PiPS) are 180p. For equal view, the resolution is 480p or 360p for all participants in most cases. The cascade created between Video Mesh Nodes and the cloud also sends 720p, 360p, and 180p in both directions. Content is sent as a single stream, and audio is sent as multiple streams. Cascade bandwidth graphs that provide a per-cluster measurement are available in the Analytics menu in Webex Control Hub. You cannot configure cascade bandwidth per meeting in Control Hub. The maximum negotiated cascade bandwidth per meeting is 20 Mbps for main video for all sources and the multiple main video streams that they could send. This maximum value does not include the content channel or audio.

Work with your partner, Cisco Customer Success Manager (CSM), or trials representative to correctly provision the Cisco Webex site and Cisco Webex services for Video Mesh:

- You must have a Cisco Webex organization with a paid subscription to Cisco Webex services.

- To take full advantage of Webex Video Mesh, make sure your Webex site is on video platform version 2.0. (You can verify that your site is on video platform version 2.0 if it has the Media Resource Type list available in the Cloud Collaboration Meeting Room site options.)

- You must enable CMR for your Webex site under user profiles. (You can do this in a bulk update CSV with the SupportCMR attribute.)

If you have a Webex site that is managed in Site Administration, it is strongly recommended that you link it with Cisco Webex Control Hub now to have access to a wider set of features. See "Link Cisco Webex Sites to Control Hub" at https://help.webex.com for more information.

The following is the Cisco Video Mesh Deployment task flow. For further and relevant details, please reference the *Deployment Guide for Cisco Webex Video Mesh* on Cisco.com. Follow these high-level steps to deploy Webex Video Mesh Nodes:

Step 1.   Identify sites where Video Mesh clusters will be deployed.

Step 2.   Download and install the Video Mesh Node software.

Step 3.   Configure the network settings on each Video Mesh Node.

Step 4.   Register the Video Mesh Nodes to the Webex organization.

Once you have identified the sites where the Video Mesh clusters will be deployed, you can begin installation of nodes. Download the Video Mesh Node from Webex Control Hub, then perform the following steps to deploy the Video Mesh Node:

Step 1.   Deploy the Video Mesh Node OVA file.

Step 2.   Power on the Video Mesh Node and set a new password.

    a.   Power on the Video Mesh Node by right-clicking the virtual machine in the host list and choosing **Power > Power On.**

    b.   Open the **Console** to the Video Mesh Node.

    c.   Log in to the Video Mesh Node.

        ■ Username: **admin**

        ■ Password: **cisco**

    d.   On initial login, you will be prompted to change the password. For the current password, type the default password listed above and press **Enter.** Type the new password, then press **Enter** and confirm the new password.

    e.   Press **Enter** to proceed past the Unauthorized Access screen.

Step 3.   Set the network configuration on the Video Mesh Node.

    a.   From the main menu of the Video Mesh Node console, type **2** and press **Enter** to choose **Edit Configuration.**

    b.   From the screen that describes the effect of changes to the Video Mesh Node, press **Enter.**

    c.   Select **Static** for IP addressing.

    d.   On the Configure Video Mesh Node screen, configure the network details. The settings that have a * next to their name are mandatory.

        ■ Ensure that the IP address is reachable on the internal network.

        ■ Ensure that the DNS address is resolvable on the internal network.

    e.   After completing the network configurations, tab to **Save** and press **Enter.**

    f.   At the prompt to reboot, press **Enter.**

Step 4.   Register the Video Mesh Node to Webex.

    a.   Once this process has begun, it must be completed within 60 minutes. Ensure that any browser popup blockers are disabled or that an exception is applied for **admin.webex.com.**

    b.   From the browser, open **admin.webex.com** and log in with an administrator account.

    c.   Select **Services.**

    d.   From the Video Mesh card, select **Set Up.**

    e.   Select **Yes, I'm Ready to Register My Video Mesh Node** and click **Next.**

20

f.   Because this is the initial setup of Webex Video Mesh for your organization, there are no clusters configured. Create a cluster by typing a name. Cisco recommends naming clusters based on their geographical location or the name of a data center. In the second field, enter the IP address of the installed Video Mesh Node. Click **Next**.

g.   On the next screen, click **Go To Node**. A new browser opens, connecting to the Video Mesh Node. You can accept the certificate warnings.

h.   Select **Allow Access to the Video Mesh Node** and click **Continue**. The Video Mesh Node will perform several connectivity tests for Webex services.

i.   If tests are successful, go to the browser tab for **Cisco Webex Control Hub**. The Video Mesh card should show a status of Operational, indicating that node registration is now complete.

- You can add more nodes to the configured cluster by clicking **Resources** from the Video Mesh card and selecting the existing cluster in the Register Video Mesh Node window.

- You can add more clusters to the deployment by specifying a new cluster name in the Register Video Mesh Node window.

Exam Preparation Tasks

As mentioned in the section "How to Use This Book" in the Introduction, you have a couple of choices for exam preparation: the exercises here, Chapter 22, "Final Preparation," and the exam simulation questions in the Pearson Test Prep practice test software.

Review All Key Topics

Review the most important topics in this chapter, noted with the Key Topics icon in the outer margin of the page. Table 20-10 lists a reference of these key topics and the page numbers on which each is found.

Key Topic

Table 20-10   Key Topics for Chapter 20

Key Topic Element	Description	Page Number
List	Webex Video Mesh features	418
Paragraph	Webex Video Mesh capacity	423
Paragraph	Webex Video Mesh clustering	424
List	Deployment models supported by Video Mesh	430
Paragraph	Webex Video Mesh ports and protocols	432

Complete Tables and Lists from Memory

Print a copy of Appendix C, "Memory Tables" (found on the companion website), or at least the section for this chapter, and complete the tables and lists from memory. Appendix D, "Memory Tables Answer Key," also on the companion website, includes completed tables and lists to check your work.

Define Key Terms

Define the following key terms from this chapter and check your answers in the glossary:

Border Gateway Protocol (BGP), Cisco Unified Communications Manager (Unified CM), Domain Name Service (DNS), Hosted Collaboration Solution (HCS), Network Address Translation (NAT), private branch exchange (PBX), public switched telephone network (PSTN), Quality of Service (QoS), Telepresence Management Suite (TMS), Transmission Control Protocol (TCP), User Datagram Protocol (UDP), Video Communications Server (VCS), WebSocket

Q&A

The answer to this question appears in Appendix A. For more practice with exam format questions, use the Pearson Test Prep practice test software.

1. What is the Cisco Video Mesh deployment task flow for the Video Mesh Nodes?

20

CHAPTER 21

Cisco Jabber for Cloud and Hybrid Deployments with Cisco Webex Messenger

This chapter covers the following topics:

> **Deployment Requirements:** Explains the deployment models and workflows for the cloud and hybrid deployment using Webex Messenger.

> **Cisco Unified CM Requirements:** Describes how to integrate the Cisco Unified CM and UC services with a hybrid deployment using Webex Messenger.

This chapter focuses on the cloud and hybrid deployments of Cisco Jabber with Cisco Webex Messenger.

This chapter covers the following objectives from the Implementing Cisco Collaboration Cloud and Edge Solutions (CLCEI) exam 300-820:

- 4.3 Describe Cisco Jabber for Cloud and Hybrid deployments with Cisco Webex Messenger

"Do I Know This Already?" Quiz

The "Do I Know This Already?" quiz enables you to assess whether you should read this entire chapter thoroughly or jump to the "Exam Preparation Tasks" section. If you are in doubt about your answers to these questions or your own assessment of your knowledge of the topics, read the entire chapter. Table 21-1 lists the major headings in this chapter and their corresponding "Do I Know This Already?" quiz questions. You can find the answers in Appendix A, "Answers to the 'Do I Know This Already?' Quizzes and Review Questions."

Table 21-1 "Do I Know This Already?" Section-to-Question Mapping

Foundation Topics Section	Questions
Deployment Requirements	1
Cisco Unified CM Requirements	2

CAUTION The goal of self-assessment is to gauge your mastery of the topics in this chapter. If you do not know the answer to a question or are only partially sure of the answer, you should mark that question as wrong for purposes of the self-assessment. Giving yourself credit for an answer you correctly guess skews your self-assessment results and might provide you with a false sense of security.

1. Which of the following is a key service differentiator of the hybrid deployment with Webex Messenger compared to a cloud-based-only deployment?

   a. Audio

   b. Presence

   c. Contact Source

   d. Instant Messaging

2. What is the navigation path to configure the Cisco Unified Communications Manager integration under the Webex Messenger Administration Tool?

   a. Configuration > Additional Services > Messenger Administration Tool

   b. User > Additional Services > Unified Communications

   c. Configuration > Additional Services > Unified Communications

   d. Policy Editor > Additional Services > Unified Communications

Foundation Topics

Deployment Requirements

Jabber Webex Messenger IM and Jabber Team Messaging Mode were retired on March 31, 2021, and all customers will be updating to the *Cisco Webex* app. The Cisco Webex app utilizes the same Cisco Unified CM-based calling and Webex Meetings–based meeting services offered in Jabber Messenger, providing a familiar app design and user experience. This also ensures your users can transition smoothly utilizing the infrastructure, configuration, and investment you already have in place.

Cisco Webex Messenger is a cloud-delivered service that provides standards-based enterprise *Instant Messaging and Presence (IM&P)* capabilities for *Cisco Jabber* clients. Cisco Webex Messenger has been optimized for Cisco Jabber but also supports third-party desktop and mobile standards-based, *Extensible Messaging and Presence Protocol (XMPP)*-compatible presence and *Instant Messaging (IM)* clients. When deployed with these clients, Cisco Webex Messenger enables users to perform numerous functions such as instant messaging, presence, file transfer, and desktop sharing. Cisco Webex Messenger integrates with the Cisco Unified Communications Manager (Unified CM) and Cisco Webex Meeting Center to support click-to-call, phone control, voice, video, visual voicemail, and web collaboration. This highly secure, scalable, and easy-to-manage solution offers users feature-rich communication capabilities, both within and external to the organization.

Cisco Jabber streamlines communications and enhances productivity by unifying presence, instant messaging, video, voice, voice messaging, file transfer, and conferencing capabilities securely into one client. It is available for Windows, Mac, and Virtual Desktop Infrastructure (VDI) desktops and for Android and iOS mobile devices.

A cloud-based deployment utilizes Cisco Webex to host services. For cloud and hybrid deployments with Cisco Webex Messenger, you manage and monitor your cloud-based deployment using the Cisco Webex Administration Tool. You do not need to set up service profiles for your users. For cloud and hybrid deployments with Cisco Webex Platform service, you would manage and monitor your deployment using Cisco Control Hub.

For cloud-based deployment with Cisco Webex Messenger the following services are available in a cloud-based deployment using Webex Messenger:

- **Contact Source:** Cisco Webex Messenger provides contact resolution.

- **Presence:** Cisco Webex Messenger lets users show their availability and see other users' availability.

- **Instant Messaging:** Cisco Webex Messenger lets users send and receive instant messages.

- **Conferencing:** Cisco Webex Meetings Center provides hosted meeting capabilities.

Figure 21-1 shows the architecture of a cloud-based deployment.

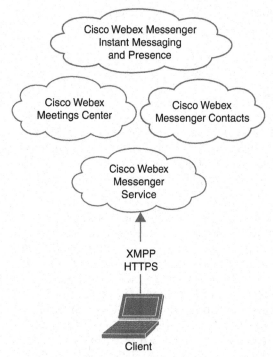

Figure 21-1 *Cloud-based Deployment Architecture*

The following is the high-level workflow analysis for a cloud deployment using Cisco Webex Messenger:

1. Configure policies.
2. Create users for cloud deployment.
3. Set up certificate validation.
4. Configure the clients.
5. (Optional) Deploy Cisco Jabber applications and Jabber Softphone for VDI.

By default, a newly provisioned Cisco Webex organization has all the capabilities granted to all the users. The policies should apply to what service or feature that would like to be disabled. The policies are created on the Policy Editor tab with a unique name and are then assigned actions to enable or disable capabilities.

Cisco Webex Administration Tool provides several ways to create users for your organization. For manual creation of users, select the User tab and then click Add. Optionally, you can select the Policy Group Assignment tab to assign a policy group to the user. You can also add other services, if enabled, to include Archive IMs, Unified Communications, assignment of users to an upgrade site or cluster, and Cisco Webex Meetings integration.

User provisioning includes specifying user-provisioning information such as registration, and fields required when creating a user's profile. The settings you make here impact when users are provisioned in your Cisco Webex Messenger organization. For example, if you set specific fields as mandatory here, the user needs to compulsorily fill in those fields when creating the user profile. Cisco Webex Messenger customers can enable self-registration when there is no SAML or Directory Integration enabled. In such a case, the organization Administrator does not need to specify the registration URL. When registration is not enabled, customers can specify a custom web page. Any user trying to register with an email address that matches the customer's domain is redirected to the custom web page. Customers can use this web page to display information about their internal processes required for creating a new Cisco Webex Messenger account.

You can easily import many users from a *Comma Separated Values (CSV)* file into your Cisco Webex Messenger organization. Similarly, you can export your users to a CSV file. Importing is a useful way of painlessly adding a bulk of users to your organization, thereby saving the effort of manually adding each user. After the import is complete, the Organization Administrator who initiated the import receives an email with the status of the import. The email states whether the import was a success, failure, or terminated. The CSV file is imported, and the users appear in the User tab.

The following services are available in a hybrid cloud-based deployment that uses Cisco Webex Messenger service:

- **Contact Source:** Cisco Webex Messenger service provides contact resolution.

- **Presence:** Cisco Webex Messenger service allows users to publish their availability and subscribe to other users' availability.

- **Instant Messaging:** Cisco Webex Messenger service allows users to send and receive instant messages.

- **Audio:** Place audio calls through desk phone devices or computers through the Unified CM.

- **Video:** Place video calls through the Unified CM.

- **Conferencing:** Cisco Webex Meetings Center provides hosted meeting capabilities.

- **Voicemail:** Send and receive voice messages through *Cisco Unity Connection (CUC)*.

Figure 21-2 shows the architecture of a hybrid cloud-based deployment.

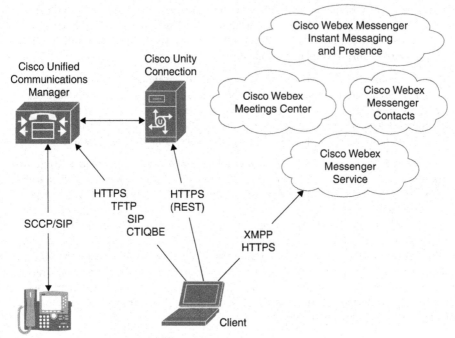

Figure 21-2   *Hybrid Cloud-based Deployment Architecture*

The following is the high-level workflow analysis for a hybrid deployment using Cisco Webex Messenger:

1. Configure policies.

2. Configure clusters.

3. Create users on the Unified Communications Manager.

4. Configure softphone.

5. Configure deskphone control.

6. Configure Extend and Connect.

7. Configure service discovery for remote access.

8. Set up certificate validation.

9. Configure the clients.

10. (Optional) Deploy Cisco Jabber applications and Jabber softphone for VDI.

11. Configure remote access.

As you can tell, the hybrid cloud-based deployment option leverages the Cisco on-premises UC infrastructure more. When deployed with the Cisco Unified Communications Manager, Cisco Jabber provides a feature-rich audio and video calling experience. In addition, the Unified CM interfaces with Cisco Webex Messenger to share the status of Cisco IP phones registered to the Unified CM. This capability helps you share your Cisco IP phone status with colleagues who are monitoring your presence state. They will see automatic updates on their Cisco Jabber or presence-enabled application, and they then can choose the best mechanism to communicate with you (for example, through an instant message, voice, or video call). Cisco Unity Connection provides access to visual voice messages. You can view, play back, or delete voice messages, including private and encrypted ones.

Creation of users and deployment of Cisco Jabber should already be performed if chosen for the primary client experience (if not, utilize the *On-Premises Deployment for Cisco Jabber* at Cisco.com). To ensure that contact data in your directory server is replicated, Cisco suggests enabling and performing a synchronization. During this process you can specify LDAP attributes for the user ID and directory URI. We will cover more of the Cisco Unified CM configuration and requirements in the next section.

For the certificate validation, Cisco Webex Messenger and Cisco Webex Meetings Center present the following certificates to the client by default:

- Central Authentication Service (CAS)

- WLAN Authentication and Privacy Infrastructure (WAPI)

Cisco Jabber validates the following XMPP certificates received from Cisco Webex Messenger. If these certificates are not included in your operating system, you must provide them.

- VeriSign Class 3 Public Primary Certification Authority – G5: This certificate is stored in the trusted root *certificate authority (CA)*

- VeriSign Class 3 Secure Server CA – G3: This certificate validates the Webex Messenger server identity and is stored in the intermediate CA.

- AddTrust External CA Root

- GoDaddy Class 2 Certification Authority Root Certificate

Service discovery enables clients to automatically detect and locate services on your enterprise network. Expressway for Mobile and Remote Access (MRA) enables you to access the services on your enterprise network. You should meet the following requirements to enable the clients to connect through Expressway for MRA and discover services:

- DNS requirements:

    - Configure a *_collab-edge* DNS SRV record on an external DNS server.

    - Configure a *_cisco-uds* DNS SRV record on the internal name server.

    - Optionally, for a hybrid cloud-based deployment with different domains for the IM and Presence server and the voice server, configure the Voice Services Domain to locate the DNS server with the *_collab-edge* record.

- Certificate requirements:

    - Before you configure remote access, download the Cisco VCS Expressway and Cisco Expressway-E Server certificate. The Server certificate is used for both HTTP and XMPP.

Finally, test external SRV *_collab-edge*:

21

Step 1. Open a command prompt.

Step 2. Enter **nslookup**. The default DNS server and address are displayed. Confirm if this is expected.

Step 3. Enter **set type=SRV**.

Step 4. Enter the name of each of your SRV records to see if they are accessible.

Cisco Unified CM Requirements

Configure *Cisco Unified Communications Manager (Unified CM)* integration:

Step 1. Select the **Configuration tab > Additional Services > Unified Communications.**

Step 2. Click the **Clusters** tab and click **Add**.

Step 3. Select **Enable Cisco UC Manager Integration with Messenger Service Client.**

Step 4. Select **Allow User to Enter Manual Settings,** users can change the Primary Server values in basic mode or the TFTP/CTI/CCMCIP server values in advanced mode. When this option is enabled, the user-entered settings will override the default or global Unified CM settings specified for the Cisco Webex organization.

Step 5. The server configuration options change based on the Cisco Unified Communications Manager Server Settings; select

- **Basic Server Settings** to enter the basic settings for the Unified CM server.

- **Advanced Server Settings** to enter detailed settings for the Unified CM server.

Step 6. Enter the following values for Basic Server Settings:

- Primary Server: Enter the IP address of the primary Unified CM server. This server is configured with Trivial File Transfer Protocol (TFTP), Computer Telephony Integration (CTI), and Cisco Unified Communications Manager IP Phone (CCMCIP) settings.

- Backup Server: Enter the IP address of the backup UC Manager server. This server is configured with TFTP, CTI, and CCMCIP settings and provides failover support in case the primary Unified CM server fails.

Step 7. If you have selected Advanced Server Settings, specify each setting for TFTP, CTI, and CCMCIP servers.

Step 8. Enter the IP address for each of the following servers. The servers listed must be in the home cluster of the users. You can specify up to two backup servers for the TFTP server and one backup server each for the CTI and CCMCIP servers. Enter the appropriate IP addresses for each backup server.

- TFTP server

- CTI server

- CCMCIP server—the address of the Cisco Unified CM (UDS) server

Step 9. In the Voicemail Pilot Number box, enter the number of the voice message service in your Unified CM server. The Organization Administrator typically provides a default voice message number for your entire Cisco Webex organization. However, you can select the **Allow User to Enter Manual Settings** check box to enable users of the cluster to override this default voice message number.

Step 10. Select **Voicemail**.

Step 11. Select **Enable Visual Voicemail** (Visual Voicemail must be configured). The Visual Voicemail settings entered here are applicable only to the users belonging to this cluster.

Step 12. In the **Clusters** tab, select **Specific Voicemail Server for This Cluster** to specify a voicemail server, which is different from the voicemail server settings provided for the entire organization.

Step 13. Select **Allow User to Enter Manual Settings** to permit users to manually enter Visual Voicemail settings for this cluster.

Step 14. Enter the following information:

- **Voicemail Server:** Enter the IP address or FQDN for the voicemail server.

- **Voicemail Protocol:** Select either **HTTP** or **HTTPS**.

- **Voicemail Port:** Enter the port number.

> **NOTE**   The Mailstore Server information is not supported, but the Cisco Webex Administration tool expects a value for this field; enter **10.0.0.0**. The mailstore Protocol, Port, and IMAP IDLE Expire Time fields are not supported; do not delete the default values from these fields.

- **Mailstore Inbox Folder Name:** Enter the name of the inbox folder configured at the mailstore server.

- **Mailstore Trash Folder Name:** Enter the name of the trash or deleted items folder configured at the mailstore server.

Step 15. Click **Save**.

For hybrid deployment, assign users to the Standard CCM End Users group.

Step 1. Open the Cisco Unified CM Administration interface.

Step 2. Select **User Management > End User**. The Find and List Users window opens.

Step 3. Find and select the user from the list. The End User Configuration window opens.

Step 4. Scroll to the Permission Information section.

Step 5. Click **Add to Access Control Group**. The Find and List Access Control Groups dialog box opens.

21

Step 6.   Select the access control groups for the user. At a minimum you should assign the user to the following access control groups:

- **Standard CCM End Users**

- **Standard CTI Enabled:** This option is used for desk phone control.

If you provision users with secure phone capabilities, do not assign the users to the Standard CTI Secure Connection group. Certain phone models require additional control groups, as follows:

- For Cisco Unified IP Phone 9900, 8900, or 8800 series or DX series, select **Standard CTI Allow Control of Phones Supporting Connected Xfer and conf.**

- For Cisco Unified IP Phone 6900 series, select **Standard CTI Allow Control of Phones Supporting Rollover Mode.**

Step 7.   Click **Add Selected.** The Find and List Access Control Groups window closes.

Step 8.   Click **Save** in the End User Configuration window.

Exam Preparation Tasks

As mentioned in the section "How to Use This Book" in the Introduction, you have a couple of choices for exam preparation: the exercises here, Chapter 22, "Final Preparation," and the exam simulation questions in the Pearson Test Prep practice test software.

Review All Key Topics

Review the most important topics in this chapter, noted with the Key Topics icon in the outer margin of the page. Table 21-2 lists a reference of these key topics and the page numbers on which each is found.

Key Topic

Table 21-2   Key Topics for Chapter 21

Key Topic Element	Description	Page Number
List	Available services in a cloud-based deployment using Webex Messenger	446
List	Available services in a hybrid cloud-based deployment using Webex Messenger	447

Complete Tables and Lists from Memory

There are no memory tables or lists in this chapter.

Define Key Terms

Define the following key terms from this chapter and check your answers in the glossary:

certificate authority (CA), Cisco Jabber, Cisco Webex, Cisco Unified Communications Manager (Unified CM), Cisco Unity Connections (CUC), Comma-Separated Values (CSV),

Extensible Messaging and Presence Protocol (XMPP), instant messaging (IM), Instant Messaging and Presence (IM&P)

Q&A

The answers to these questions appear in Appendix A. For more practice with exam format questions, use the Pearson Test Prep practice test software.

1. What is the workflow for a hybrid deployment using Cisco Webex Messenger?

2. What is the workflow for a cloud deployment using Cisco Webex Messenger?

CHAPTER 22

Final Preparation

The first 21 chapters of this book cover the technologies, protocols, design concepts, and considerations required to be prepared to pass the 300-820 Implementing Cisco Collaboration Cloud and Edge Solutions (CLCEI) exam. While these chapters supply the detailed information, most people need more preparation than simply reading the first 21 chapters of this book. This chapter details a set of tools and a study plan to help you complete your preparation for the exam.

This short chapter has two main sections. The first section lists the exam preparation tools useful at this point in the study process. The second section lists a suggested study plan now that you have completed all the previous chapters in this book.

Getting Ready

Here are some important tips to keep in mind to ensure you are ready for this rewarding exam.

- **Build and use a study tracker:** Consider taking the exam objectives shown in this book and building yourself a study tracker. This will help ensure that you have not missed anything and that you are confident for your exam. As a matter of fact, this book offers a sample Study Planner as a website supplement.

- **Think about your time budget for questions in the exam:** When you do the math, you realize that on average you have one minute per question. While this does not sound like enough time, realize that many of the questions will be very straightforward, and you will take 15 to 30 seconds on those. This builds time for other questions as you take your exam.

- **Watch the clock:** Check in on the time remaining periodically as you are taking the exam. You might even find that you can slow down pretty dramatically as you have built up a nice block of extra time.

- **Get some ear plugs:** The testing center might provide them but get some just in case and bring them along. There might be other test takers in the center with you, and you do not want to be distracted by their sighs, moans, grunts, coughing, etc.

- **Plan your travel time:** Give yourself extra time to find the center and get checked in. Be sure to arrive early.

- **Get rest:** Most students report success with getting plenty of rest the night before the exam. All-night cram sessions are not typically successful.

- **Bring in valuables but get ready to lock them up:** The testing center will take your phone, your smart watch, your wallet, and other such items. They will provide a secure place for them.

■ **Take notes:** You will be given note-taking implements, so don't hesitate to use them. If you struggle with any questions, jot them down. When you get home with a pass or fail, research those items!

Tools for Final Preparation

This section lists some information about the available tools and how to access the tools.

Pearson Test Prep Practice Test Engine and Questions on the Website

Register this book to get access to the Pearson IT Certification practice test engine (software that displays and grades a set of exam-realistic, multiple-choice questions). Using the Pearson Test Prep practice test engine, you can either study by going through the questions in study mode or take a simulated (timed) CCNP CLCEI exam.

The Pearson Test Prep practice test software comes with two full practice exams. These practice tests are available to you either online or as an offline Windows application. To access the practice exams that were developed with this book, please see the instructions in the card inserted in the sleeve in the back of the book. This card includes a unique access code that enables you to activate your exams in the Pearson Test Prep practice test software.

Accessing the Pearson Test Prep Software Online

The online version of this software can be used on any device with a browser and connectivity to the Internet including desktop machines, tablets, and smartphones. To start using your practice exams online, simply follow these steps:

Step 1. Go to **https://www.PearsonTestPrep.com**.

Step 2. Select **Pearson IT Certification** as your product group.

Step 3. Enter your email/password for your account. If you don't have an account on PearsonITCertification.com or CiscoPress.com, you will need to establish one by going to PearsonITCertification.com/join.

Step 4. In the My Products tab, click the **Activate New Product** button.

Step 5. Enter the access code printed on the insert card in the back of your book to activate your product.

Step 6. The product will now be listed in your My Products page. Click the **Exams** button to launch the exam settings screen and start your exam.

Accessing the Pearson Test Prep Software Offline

If you wish to study offline, you can download and install the Windows version of the Pearson Test Prep software. There is a download link for this software on the book's companion website, or you can just enter this link in your browser:

https://www.pearsonitcertification.com/content/downloads/pcpt/engine.zip

To access the book's companion website and the software, simply follow these steps:

Step 1. Register your book by going to **https://www.pearsonitcertification.com/register** and entering the ISBN: 9780136733720.

Step 2. Respond to the challenge questions.

Step 3.   Go to your account page and select the **Registered Products** tab.

Step 4.   Click the **Access Bonus Content** link under the product listing.

Step 5.   Click the **Install Pearson Test Prep Desktop Version** link under the Practice Exams section of the page to download the software.

Step 6.   Once the software finishes downloading, unzip all the files on your computer.

Step 7.   Double-click the application file to start the installation, and follow the onscreen instructions to complete the registration.

Step 8.   Once the installation is complete, launch the application and click the **Activate Exam** button on the My Products tab.

Step 9.   Click the **Activate a Product** button in the Activate Product Wizard.

Step 10.   Enter the unique access code found on the card in the sleeve in the back of your book and click the **Activate** button.

Step 11.   Click **Next** and then click **Finish** to download the exam data to your application.

Step 12.   You can now start using the practice exams by selecting the product and clicking the **Open Exam** button to open the exam settings screen.

Note that the offline and online versions will synch together, so saved exams and grade results recorded on one version will be available to you on the other as well.

Customizing Your Exams

Once you are in the exam settings screen, you can choose to take exams in one of three modes:

- Study Mode

- Practice Exam Mode

- Flash Card Mode

Study Mode enables you to fully customize your exams and review answers as you are taking the exam. This is typically the mode you would use first to assess your knowledge and identify information gaps. Practice Exam Mode locks certain customization options, as it is presenting a realistic exam experience. Use this mode when you are preparing to test your exam readiness. Flash Card Mode strips out the answers and presents you with only the question stem. This mode is great for late-stage preparation when you really want to challenge yourself to provide answers without the benefit of seeing multiple-choice options. This mode does not provide the detailed score reports that the other two modes do, so do not use it if you are trying to identify knowledge gaps.

In addition to these three modes, you can select the source of your questions. You can choose to take exams that cover all of the chapters or you can narrow your selection to just a single chapter or the chapters that make up specific parts in the book. All chapters are selected by default. If you want to narrow your focus to individual chapters, simply deselect all the chapters and then select only those on which you wish to focus in the Objectives area.

You can also select the exam banks on which to focus. Each exam bank comes complete with a full exam of questions that cover topics in every chapter. The two exams printed in the book are available to you as well as two additional exams of unique questions. You can have the test engine serve up exams from all four banks or just from one individual bank by selecting the desired banks in the exam bank area.

There are several other customizations you can make to your exam from the exam settings screen, such as the length of time of the exam, the number of questions served up, whether to randomize questions and answers, whether to show the number of correct answers for multiple answer questions, or whether to serve up only specific types of questions. You can also create custom test banks by selecting only questions that you have marked or questions on which you have added notes.

Updating Your Exams

If you are using the online version of the Pearson Test Prep software, you should always have access to the latest version of the software as well as the exam data. If you are using the Windows desktop version, every time you launch the software, it will check to see if there are any updates to your exam data and automatically download any changes that were made since the last time you used the software. This requires that you are connected to the Internet at the time you launch the software.

Sometimes, due to many factors, the exam data might not fully download when you activate your exam. If you find that figures or exhibits are missing, you might need to manually update your exams.

To update a particular exam you have already activated and downloaded, simply select the Tools tab and click the Update Products button. Again, this is only an issue with the desktop Windows application.

If you want to check for updates to the Pearson Test Prep exam engine software, Windows desktop version, simply select the Tools tab and click the Update Application button. This will ensure you are running the latest version of the software engine.

Premium Edition

In addition to the free practice exam provided on the website, you can purchase additional exams with expanded functionality directly from Pearson IT Certification. The Premium Edition of this title contains an additional two full practice exams and an eBook (in both PDF and ePub format). In addition, the Premium Edition title has remediation for each question to the specific part of the eBook that relates to that question.

Because you have purchased the print version of this title, you can purchase the Premium Edition at a deep discount. There is a coupon code in the book sleeve that contains a one-time-use code and instructions for where you can purchase the Premium Edition.

To view the premium edition product page, go to www.informit.com/title/9780136733799.

Chapter-Ending Review Tools

Chapters 1 through 21 each have several features in the "Exam Preparation Tasks" section at the end of the chapter. You might have already worked through these in each chapter. It can also be useful to use these tools again as you make your final preparations for the exam.

22

Suggested Plan for Final Review/Study

This section lists a suggested study plan from the point at which you finish reading through Chapter 21, until you take the 300-820 Implementing Cisco Collaboration Cloud and Edge Solutions (CLCEI) exam. Certainly, you can ignore this plan, use it as is, or just take suggestions from it.

The plan uses two steps:

Step 1.   **Review key topics and DIKTA? questions:** You can use the table that lists the key topics in each chapter, or just flip the pages looking for key topics. Also, reviewing the DIKTA? questions from the beginning of the chapter can be helpful for review.

Step 2.   **Use the Pearson Test Prep practice test engine to practice:** As previously described, you can use the Pearson Test Prep practice test engine to study using a bank of unique exam-realistic questions available only with this book.

Summary

The tools and suggestions listed in this chapter have been designed with one goal in mind: to help you develop the skills required to pass the 300-820 Implementing Cisco Collaboration Cloud and Edge Solutions (CLCEI) exam. This book has been developed from the beginning to not just tell you the facts but to also help you learn how to apply the facts. No matter what your experience level leading up to when you take the exam, it is our hope that the broad range of preparation tools, and even the structure of the book, helps you pass the exam with ease. We hope you do well on the exam!

Answers to the "Do I Know This Already?" Quizzes and Review Questions

Chapter 1

Do I Know This Already?

1. C. Although registration is allowed on both products, the Cisco VCS allows for device-based licensing, whereas the Expressway allows for user-based licensing.

2. A. The SIP URI and Expressway IP address are typically configured locally on the endpoint. These configurations can also be provisioned through Cisco Telepresence Management Suite (TMS), but TFTP is not supported as it is on the Unified CM. Once these settings have been configured, the final step in the process is for the endpoint to register to the Cisco Expressway.

3. D. The ITU defines E.164 under the international public telecommunication numbering plan as the standard with which all countries must comply that participate in audio communications across the PSTN under the H.320 umbrella. However, the ITU also defines E.64 as an alias pattern that can be used with H.323, as it is referred to in this chapter, which can include 1 to 15 digits, plus the +, *, and # symbols. Just for the record, there is also a SIP RFC for E.164 aliases (RFC 3824) that defines how E.164 aliases should be used with SIP, which is also different from the original H.320 definition.

4. A. The Cisco UWL Meetings license is the only license package Cisco offers that includes Webex licensing with it. However, Webex can be added into any CUWL Standard, UCL Enhanced, or UCL Enhanced Plus licensing plan a customer orders as an à la cart item.

5. B. FindMe, also called User Policy, is by design an advanced call forwarding mechanism. It allows calls to a specified alias to be transferred automatically if the call is busy or there is no answer within a specified time frame. Rich Media Services (RMS) licenses are used on an Expressway for special calling scenarios. Mobile and Remote Access (MRA) is a proxy registration solution. Single Number Reach is a call forwarding solution on the CUCM Express, and Extension Mobility is a call forwarding solution on the Unified CM. Neither of these is supported on the Cisco Expressway.

6. C. Once the release key and option keys have been obtained, simply use the following steps to enter them through the web interface of the Cisco Expressway. Navigate to **Maintenance > Option Keys.** If this is a new install, the Release Key section will be available as a blank field. The Release Key field for an existing Expressway installation

will not appear on this page. You can use the Upgrade window to set the release key in the event an upgrade is required.

7. D. Because the Expressway follows the user-based licensing model, you must first assess what types of devices you will register and consider how these devices will be used. Then you can apply CUWL licenses as either Room System or Desktop System licenses. Room System licenses are used for common endpoints not assigned to a specific user. This might include a Cisco Webex Room Kit Pro set up in a conference room, or a Webex Board on a cart so that it can be wheeled around to different class-rooms. These types of licenses can be applied to only one system at a time. Desktop System licenses are associated with a specific user and can be applied to only a specific type of device, such as the DX80 or the new Webex Desk Pro.

8. A. The CE1200 Appliance server and a large VM can both support up to 500 video calls and 1000 audio-only calls. The medium-density VM can support 100 video calls or 200 audio-only calls, and the small VM can support 40 MRA video or 20 non-MRA video calls and 40 audio-only calls.

Review Questions

1. The seven registration steps are as follows:

- Obtain power from the power cube.

- Load local image file.

- Obtain CDP information from the switch (optional).

- DHCP Discovery process.

- Configure SIP settings locally on the endpoint.

- Send a registration request to the Expressway.

- Wait for the 200 OK response showing registration is successful.

2. Flex licensing includes the following four subscription models:

- Cisco Collaboration Flex Plan

- Cisco Collaboration Flex Plan – Active User Meetings

- Cisco Collaboration Flex Plan – Named User

- Cisco Collaboration Flex Plan – Concurrent Agent

3. The following are the three capacity points for Expressway VM deployment:

- Small: Two vCPUs, 4 GB RAM, 132 GB disk space, two vNICs

- Medium: Two vCPUs, 6 GB RAM, 132 GB disk space, two vNICs

- Large: Eight vCPUs, 8 GB RAM, 132 GB disk space, two vNICs

Chapter 2

Do I Know This Already?

1. A. The minimum virtual hardware required to host virtual Expressway deployments is VMware ESXi 6.5.

2. A. The first time you log in to the Expressway web user interface via HTTP or HTTPS, you will automatically see the Service Setup Wizard.

3. C, E. Cisco Expressway utilizes Product Authorization Keys (PAK) as its legacy licensing, but the shift is toward the flexible and simplified Smart Licensing.

4. D. The Cisco Expressway can contain five DNS servers, although only one is needed for resolutions.

5. B, D. Expressway-C must be resolvable within the internal network and the Expressway-E must be publicly routable with the corresponding DNS server.

6. C. By default, Cisco Expressway uses the tar.gz.enc file extension to provide an encrypted backup file.

7. A, C. Cisco recommends creating regular backups, and always in the following situations:

   - Before performing an upgrade

   - Before performing a system restore

   - In demonstration and test environments, if you want to be able to restore the Expressway to a known configuration

Review Questions

1. This deployment consists of

   - DMZ subnet

     - Internal interface of Firewall A

     - LAN2 interface of the Expressway-E

   - DMZ subnet containing

     - The external interface of Firewall B

     - The LAN1 interface of the Expressway-E

   - LAN subnet containing

     - The internal interface of Firewall B

     - The LAN1 interface of the Expressway-C

     - The network interface of the Cisco TMS server

   - Firewall A is the outward-facing firewall; it is configured with a public NAT IP that is statically NATed to the LAN2 interface address of the Expressway-E.

   - Firewall B is the internally facing firewall.

Appendix A: Answers to the "Do I Know This Already?" Quizzes and Review Questions 463

A

- Expressway-E LAN1 has static NAT mode disabled.

- Expressway-E LAN2 has static NAT mode enabled with static NAT.

- Expressway-C has a traversal client zone pointing to LAN1 of the Expressway-E.

- Cisco TMS has Expressway-E added.

2. The following are the Expressway cluster restore steps:

   a. Remove the Expressway peer from the cluster so that it becomes a standalone Expressway.

   b. Restore the configuration data to the standalone Expressway.

   c. Build a new cluster using the Expressway that now has the restored data.

   d. Take each of the other peers out of their previous cluster and add them to the new cluster.

Chapter 3

Do I Know This Already?

1. B. Registration, Admission, and Status (RAS), which is used between an H.323 endpoint and a gatekeeper to provide address resolution and admission control services, falls under the H.225.0 part of the H.323 protocols.

2. A, C, F. A SIP URI address is written in *user@domain* format in a similar fashion to an email address. This enables SRV schemes to look up SIP servers associated with the DNS name. If a domain is not found (or undefined) but the name is associated with an IP address, the client directly contacts the SIP server at that IP address on port 5060, using UDP as the default protocol.

3. D. The options for the H.323 <-> SIP Interworking Mode setting are Off, Registered Only, and On.

4. B. Calls for which the Expressway acts as a SIP to H.323 gateway are Rich Media Session (RMS) calls.

5. A, D. The Expressway can act as an H.323 gatekeeper and/or SIP registrar.

6. A, C, D. When registering, the H.323 endpoint presents the Expressway with one or more of the following: one or more H.323 IDs, one or more E.164 aliases, and/or one or more URIs. When registering, the SIP endpoint presents the Expressway with its contact address (IP address) and logical address (Address of Record). The logical address is considered to be its alias and will generally be in the form of a URI.

Review Questions

1. H.323 is a system specification that describes the use of several ITU-T and IETF protocols. The protocols that comprise the core of almost any H.323 system are as follows:

   - **H.225.0:** Registration, Admission, and Status (RAS), which is used between an H.323 endpoint and a gatekeeper to provide address resolution and admission control services

- **H.225.0:** Call signaling, which is used between any two H.323 entities to establish communication based on Q.931

- **H.245:** Control protocol for multimedia communication, describes the messages and procedures used for capability exchange, opening and closing logical channels for audio, video, data, and various control and indication signals

- **RTP/RTCP:** Protocols for sending or receiving multimedia information (voice, video, or text) between any two entities

2. The options for the H.323 <> SIP Interworking Mode setting are as follows:

- **Off:** The Expressway does not act as a SIP–H.323 gateway.

- **Registered only:** The Expressway acts as a SIP–H.323 gateway but only if at least one of the endpoints is locally registered.

- **On:** The Expressway acts as a SIP–H.323 gateway regardless of whether the endpoints are locally registered.

Chapter 4

Do I Know This Already?

1. D. The Cisco Expressway uses POSIX format for regular expression syntax.

2. C. The ^ expression matches anything except the set of specified characters. This results in matching any character string as long as an @ symbol is not present.

3. B, E. The correct answers follow regex patterns. The results for the other regex patterns would not result in a match.

4. A. The correct answer follows the regex pattern. The results for the other regex patterns would not result in a match.

5. A. The correct location of the Check Pattern Tool is Maintenance > Tools > Check Pattern.

Review Questions

1. This can be answered in multiple ways (which shows the power of expressions), but opens the question of how well you would like the resulting pattern to match the desired alias. Something as simple as .* would match, but would also match nothing and everything. Matching the alias closely to a structured dial plan is recommended to avoid matches when not desired and matches when desired.

Chapter 5

Do I Know This Already?

1. D. TLS requires TCP as the reliable transport layer protocol to operate over.

2. D. A setting of auto delegates the encryption decisions to endpoints, and the Expressway does not perform any sort of RTP-to-SRTP conversion.

3. B. A certificate authority (CA) stores, issues, and signs the digital certificates.

4. A. The Trusted CA Certificate page (Maintenance > Security > Trusted CA Certificate) enables you to manage the list of certificates for the certificate authorities (CAs)

Appendix A: Answers to the "Do I Know This Already?" Quizzes and Review Questions 465

A

trusted by an Expressway. When a TLS connection to the Expressway mandates certificate verification, the certificate presented to the Expressway must be signed by a trusted CA in this list and there must be a full chain of trust (intermediate CAs) to the root CA.

5. A, B. When in secure mode, the following changes and limitations to standard Expressway functionality apply: the command line interface (CLI) and application programming interface (API) access are unavailable, and access over SSH and through the serial port is disabled and cannot be turned on (the pwrec password recovery function is also unavailable).

6. C, D. The FIPS 140 Publication Series coordinates the requirements and standards for cryptography modules that include both hardware and software components. Protection of a cryptographic module within a security system is necessary to maintain the confidentiality and integrity of the information protected by the module. This standard specifies the security requirements that will be satisfied by a cryptographic module.

Review Questions

1. The best practice is to generate a separate CSR for each server, so you have a common name for each server. If you have a cluster of Expressways, you must generate a separate signing request. Also, if you want to use a single certificate for each server in the cluster, you need to upload the private key as well.

2. There will be an alarm generated on all the nodes. The services like MRA and secured calls will be down until the certificates are renewed.

Chapter 6

Do I Know This Already?

1. C. The Call Time to Live setting determines how long the Expressway will wait to verify a call is still active. The Registration Conflict Policy setting has to do with preventing duplicate H.323 aliases from registering at the same time. Registration Time to Live is not the real name of the feature mentioned in this question. Time to Live is the timer set on H.323 devices in the registration database.

2. B. Overwrite is recommended when DHCP IP addressing is used. Reject is recommended when static IP addressing is used. Allow and Deny are Restriction Policy settings, not Conflict Policy settings.

3. D. The registration will succeed because the Deny List is enabled but there is not a rule in the Deny List to prevent registration. This is the true statement, because the Allow List and Deny List cannot be enabled at the same time. If the Deny List is enabled, then any rules in the Allow List will be ignored.

4. C. Although the two main methods the Registration Restriction Policy uses are the Allow List or Deny List, there is a third option, which is through a Policy Service that uses CPL scripts to implement the restriction policies.

5. A. SIP uses an encryption process known as Digest, and H.323 uses an encryption standard known as H.235. Both H.235 and Digest use a system called Message Digest Algorithm 5 (MD5), which is a messaging system that uses a time stamp from a time

server as part of its encryption key. Therefore, no matter if you are using H.323 or SIP with authentication, it is critical that both the Expressway and the device registering to it are pointed to the same NTP (Network Time Protocol) server or synced cluster.

6. C. You can configure the Expressway to use both the Local Database and an H.350 directory. If an H.350 directory is configured, the Expressway will always attempt to verify any Digest credentials presented to it by first checking against the Local Database before checking against the H.350 directory.

7. D. The Default Zone is the default logical connection into and out of the Local Zone. If Subzones were the interior doors of a building that separates different rooms, then Zones would be the exterior doors that allow people to enter and exit the building itself. Based on this analogy, the Default Zone would be the front door to the Expressway.

8. A. A byte is made up of 8 bits, and each bit position in a byte holds a specific numeric value. If the bit is on, then you add the value of that bit to the total for the byte. If the bit is off, then you do not add the value of that bit to the total for the byte. The bit values in an octet, from left to right, are 128, 64, 32, 16, 8, 4, 2, and 1. In this question the bits for 128 and 64 are on while all other bits are off, so the total value of 128 + 64 = 192.

Review Questions

1. Registration Restriction Policy configuration options are as follows:

   ■ Allow List

   ■ Deny List

   ■ Policy Service

2. Registration Authentication policy configuration options are as follows:

   ■ Do not check credentials

   ■ Treat as authenticated

   ■ Check credentials

3. The following are the Registration Authentication steps:

   ■ Enable authentication at the Subzone Level

   ■ Create a username and password in the Local Database

   ■ Verify NTP is enabled and synchronized

4. The default logical components of the Cisco Expressway are

   ■ Local Zone

   ■ Default Subzone

   ■ Traversal Subzone

   ■ Default Zone

   ■ Links

Chapter 7

A

Do I Know This Already?

1. **A.** This process is known as the Call Processing Order, which consists of five main components. Listed in the order each component is executed, they are Transforms, Call Policy, User Policy, Zone search, and bandwidth management. Admin Policy and Call Policy are the same thing. User Policy and FindMe are also the same thing.

2. **C.** In the regular expression ([^@]*), everything in the parentheses is a group. Working backward on the regular expression, the asterisk represents "anything." The square brackets with the caret symbol inside mean "does not include." Because the square brackets also include an @ symbol, together this means "does not include @." Couple that with the asterisk, and this expression represents anything that does not include an @.

3. **C.** A Call Policy is implemented using a programming language designed to control Internet telephony services called Call Processing Language Script, or CPL Script. CPL Script is an XML-based language for defining call handling. So, when the built-in tool is used to create rules, the Expressway is creating a CPL Script on behalf of the administrator within the database itself. Programmers who understand CPL Scripts can create even more intricate rules beyond "allow" or "reject" that change the dialed alias completely from its originally dialed form.

4. **B.** A script, like an English book, is read from the top down and from left to right. Therefore, policy matches listed first are applied and no other policy will be searched. When using the built-in tool to create Call Policy, the top of the list is highest priority and therefore searched first. Each additional Call Policy in order from top to bottom assumes its position in the search order because this is how the script will be created in the Expressway database.

5. **D.** User Policy, also known as FindMe, is an option on the Expressway that works similarly to call forward or Single Number Reach, where a call can be rerouted to other aliases based on a set of user-defined settings.

6. **C.** The user can edit their assigned user account only after it has been created. For the user to access their user account, the user must navigate to the URL of the TMSPE FindMe user portal screen. Once logged in, the user can make changes to their account, such as adding and removing devices, and create locations with different call routing behaviors.

7. **F.** To access the Locate tool, from the web interface of the Expressway, navigate to **Maintenance > Tools > Locate.**

Review Questions

1. List the five main components of the Call Processing Order.
   a. Transforms (pre-search)
   b. Call Policy or Admin Policy (pre-search)
   c. User Policy or FindMe (pre-search)
   d. Zone search (based on Search Rules)
   e. Bandwidth management

2. List the three services in the Cisco Expressway that require an authentication setting of Treat As Authenticated or Check Credentials.

   a. All Call Policy

   b. Registration Restriction Policy using Policy Service

   c. Search Rules using Policy Service

Chapter 8

Do I Know This Already?

1. D. There are two methods for implementing bandwidth restrictions on an Expressway: using Pipes or using Subzones. Using either of these methods, bandwidth restrictions can be applied to the call in two ways: on a per-call basis and on a total-bandwidth basis.

2. C. When a call is placed between two endpoints that are registered to the same Subzone but the call must be interworked using the Traversal Subzone, the in and out bandwidth restriction is used. For example, a call between a SIP endpoint and an H.323 endpoint would fall into this category. No endpoints can ever register to the Traversal Subzone, so calls between an H.323 endpoint and a SIP endpoint within the same Traversal Subzone would not even be possible.

3. C. The Default Call Bandwidth setting is not a limitation. Some endpoints allow the internal bandwidth setting to be auto-negotiated. If one of those endpoints places a call but does not specify the desired bandwidth, the Expressway implements whatever limit has been established here. The default value is 384 kbps, but this setting can be changed to whatever limit is desired. If this limit is set to a high rate, such as 2048 Mbps, and there are bandwidth restrictions set in Subzones or Pipes that would restrict the per-call rate to a lower limit, such as 768 kbps, then that restricted rate of 768 kbps will take precedence over the Default Call Bandwidth rate.

4. B. A Pipe is a bandwidth restriction that is applied to Links. Remember that Links have no bandwidth restriction capability in and of themselves. Zones do not have bandwidth restrictions either, only Subzones do.

5. A. Each pipe may be applied to multiple Links. There is no limit to the number of Links to which a Pipe can be applied.

6. C. Each link may have up to two Pipes that are associated with it.

7. D. When a call is routed between Subzones or between a Subzone and Zone, the call will always take the shortest path. If that path is blocked, then the call will not reroute across another logical path. The call will simply fail.

Review Questions

1. The three bandwidth restriction modes are No Bandwidth, Limited, and Unlimited.

2. Pipes can be applied to Links in the following three ways:

   ■ One Pipe, one Link

   ■ One Pipe, two or more Links

   ■ Two Pipes, one Link

Chapter 9

Do I Know This Already?

1. D. Zones that exist within the Cisco Expressway include the Local Zone, Default Zone, Neighbor Zones, Traversal Zones (not Transversal), and DNS and ENUM Zones.

2. A. The Calls to Unknown IP Addresses setting on the Expressway Core should be set to Indirect. This allows the Expressway Core to forward the call request across the Traversal Zone to the Expressway Edge. The Calls to Unknown IP Addresses setting on the Expressway Edge should then be set to Direct. This allows the call to traverse through the firewall in order to connect to the endpoint that exists outside the corporate network.

3. D. Zones are searched based on the priority of the Search Rules. Priority values can be set between 1 and 65,534. 1 is the highest value, so the higher the number, the lower the value.

4. B. When a non-traversal call is set up through the Cisco Expressway, the signaling for call setup must travel through the Expressway before it is sent to the destination endpoint. However, the actual UDP media and signaling for the audio and video are direct between the endpoints. With traversal calls, the media must always traverse through the Expressway. The Expressway supports four types of traversal calls: firewall traversal, SIP/H.323 interworking, IPv4/IPv6 interworking, and dual network traversal, the last of which is available only on the Expressway Edge server.

5. C. The Call Loop Detection Mode setting on the Cisco Expressway prevents search loops from occurring. Each search has a call serial number and a call tag. The serial number is unique to the search, but the call tag information is passed with a Location Request (LRQ). The Expressway uses the tag to identify a call that has already been received and hence ignored, preventing loopback errors.

6. B. The real key to this structured dial plan is the use of a site code of sorts.

7. B. Call Signaling Optimization is the setting on a Cisco Expressway that allows for optimal call routing, which is the function of limiting hops between Expressways for call setup signaling when more than two Expressways are being used in a video network.

8. C. A Neighbor Zone is essentially a trunk that can be used to connect like devices over the same network type. These zones can be used to connect two Expressway Cores on an internal network or two Expressway Edges in a DMZ or on a public network. Neighbor Zones are not used to connect an Expressway Core with an Expressway Edge. Even though the devices are essentially the same, the network parameters they operate within are not. Traversal Zones should be used in this type of scenario, which will be discussed in Chapter 10. You can also use a Neighbor Zone to connect an Expressway Core to a Unified CM, but the Unified CM uses a SIP trunk to connect to the Expressway Core.

9. B. If you change the SIP Transport setting, you need to change the port as well. TCP uses port 5060 and TLS uses port 5061.

10. A. Unfortunately, the Neighbor Zone to a Unified CM will not appear as active unless an active SIP trunk exists on the Unified CM that points to the Expressway Core.

However, a Unified CM SIP trunk to an Expressway Core will show active without a Neighbor Zone ever being created. Therefore, it is best practice to create the SIP trunk on the Unified CM first, then go back and create the Neighbor Zone on the Expressway Core.

Review Questions

1. The following three Traversal Zones can be configured on the Cisco Expressway:

   a. Traversal Client Zone

   b. Traversal Server Zone

   c. Unified Communications Traversal Zone

2. The Zone search order is

   a. Local Zone

   b. Neighbor Zones

   c. Traversal Zones

   d. DNS and ENUM Zones

3. Five advantages of a hierarchical video network with a structured dial plan are as follows:

   a. It's a more scalable solution.

   b. Full mesh is not needed (not all Expressways need to neighbor to each other).

   c. Minimized number of LRQs for each call attempt.

   d. Calls consume bandwidth only within the local Expressway locations.

   e. Some resiliency is provided when Expressways go down.

4. The following are the four basic steps to creating a SIP trunk from the Unified CM to the Expressway Core:

   a. Configure a SIP Trunk Security Profile.

   b. Configure a SIP trunk.

   c. Configure a Route Pattern.

   d. Transform the pattern once it arrives at the Cisco VCS.

Chapter 10

Do I Know This Already?

1. D. Most firewalls use ports to mark TCP outgoing traffic so that reply messages from outside the network coming in on the same ports will be allowed back into the private corporate network. This means that any two-way communication must be started by an internal system. UDP ports are unidirectional, so any UDP packets originating from outside the network will be blocked.

2. C. The ranges for private IP addresses are

   ■ Class A addresses: 10.0.0.0–10.255.255.255, with 16,777,216 available addresses

   ■ Class B addresses: 172.16.0.0–172.31.255.255, with 1,048,576 available addresses

   ■ Class C addresses: 192.168.0.0–192.168.255.255, with 65,536 available addresses

Appendix A: Answers to the "Do I Know This Already?" Quizzes and Review Questions   471

A

3. C. Session Traversal Utilities for NAT (STUN) requires that the NAT server allow all traffic that is directed to a particular port to be forwarded to the client on the inside. This means that STUN only works with less-secure NATs, so-called "full-cone" NATs, exposing the internal client to an attack from anyone who can capture the STUN traffic. STUN may be useful within asymmetric network environments but is generally not considered a viable solution for enterprise networks. In addition, STUN cannot be used with symmetric NATs. This may be a drawback in many situations because most enterprise-class firewalls are symmetric. For more information about STUN, see RFC 8489.

4. B. Traversal Using Relays around NAT (TURN) relay services are the only IETF services available on the Expressway-E. Neither ICE nor STUN can be used with the Expressways. ASSENT and H.460.18/19 are not IETF protocols. For more information about TURN, see RFC 8656.

5. A. Interactive Connectivity Establishment (ICE) is a complex solution to the problem of NAT traversal, but because it encompasses multiple solutions, it is regarded as one that will always enable the connection, regardless of the number of NATs involved. ASSENT and H.460.18/19 are not IETF protocols. For more information about ICE, see RFC 8445.

6. C. H.460.18 works just like Assent, except it requires de-multiplexed ports 36,000 to 59,999 to be opened on the firewall. H.460.19 works as a layer on H.460.18 to allow multiplexing the media ports so only two ports need to be opened for RTP and RTCP media streams, 2776 and 2777. However, this question only asked about H.460.18.

7. D. The Traversal Zone options on the Expressway Edge include the Traversal Server Zone, Traversal Client Zone, and Unified Communications Traversal Zone. A typical traversal deployment scenario uses the Traversal Server Zone on the Expressway Edge and the Traversal Client Zone on the Expressway Core. There is a scenario where you may want to configure a Traversal Client Zone on the Expressway Edge as well. The Unified Communications Traversal Zone is used for Mobile Remote Access (MRA).

8. E. Only two types of Traversal Zones are available on the Expressway Core: the Unified Communications Traversal Zone, which is used for MRA, and the Traversal Client Zone, which you will use in this type of deployment. The Expressway Core cannot ever act as a Traversal Server; therefore, the Traversal Server Zone is not available on this server.

9. C. The dual NIC DMZ deployment scenario is the method Cisco recommends using for most DMZ deployments. It is a more secure solution that prevents the internal firewall and external firewall from communicating directly with one another.

10. A. ENUM Zones on the Cisco Expressway work on the same principle as DNS Zones. ENUM stands for Enumerated dialing, or E.164 Number Mapping. It is a way of using DNS NAPTR (Name Authority PoinTeR) records to convert E164 numbers into routable URIs. ENUM is defined in RFC 6116.

Review Questions

1. The private IP address classes are as follows:

    ■ Class A addresses: 10.0.0.0–10.255.255.255

    ■ Class B addresses: 172.16.0.0–172.31.255.255

    ■ Class C addresses: 192.168.0.0–192.168.255.255

2. The Traversal Zone components are as follows:

    ■ Expressway Core

        i.   Traversal Client Zone

        ii.   Search Rule(s)

    ■ Traversal Server Zones

        i.   Authentication username and password

        ii.   Traversal Server Zone

        iii.   Search Rule(s)

3. The following are A record and SRV record formats:

    a. _service._protocol.<fqdn>. TTL Priority Weight Port Target

    b. sip._tcp.company.com 7200 20 5 5060 vcs1.company.com

    c. sips._tcp.<fully.qualified.domain>

    d. sip._tcp.<fully.qualified.domain>

    e. sip._udp.<fully.qualified.domain>

    f. h323ls._udp.<fully.qualified.domain> —for UDP RAS messaging, for example: LRQ

    g. _h323cs._tcp.<fully.qualified.domain> —for H.323 call signaling

Chapter 11

Do I Know This Already?

1. B. Clustering can increase the capacity of an Expressway deployment by a maximum factor of four, compared with a single Expressway. There is no capacity gain after four peers. So, if you deploy a maximum six-peer cluster, the fifth and sixth Expressways do not add extra call capacity to the cluster. Resilience is improved with the extra peers, but not capacity.

2. D. All peers in the cluster must operate within the same domain. No federation or dual-homed domain spaces are supported within an Expressway cluster. All peers must be running the same version of firmware, because how you configure a cluster may diverge between different versions. Therefore, if the firmware version is different, the cluster may not work. All peers within the cluster must have the same set of option keys installed. Exceptions to this rule include Rich Media Session (RMS) licenses and Room System and Desktop System registration licenses.

Appendix A: Answers to the "Do I Know This Already?" Quizzes and Review Questions   473

A

3. C. Each peer within the cluster must be able to support a round-trip-delay time of up to 80 ms. This is an improvement over previous versions of the Expressway that required a 30-ms round-trip-delay time. This means that each Expressway in the cluster must be within a 40-ms hop to any other peer within the cluster.

4. D. To use DNS with a cluster of Expressways, the cluster name must be created in DNS as a fully qualified domain name (FQDN). The DNS server configuration does not replicate, so each cluster member must also be created in DNS with both forward and reverse A records. Reverse lookups are frequently provided through Pointer (PTR) records. SRV records may also be required for the cluster. Multiple entries for each service with equal weights can be entered to cover each peer in the cluster. This configuration is advised for video interoperability and business-to-business (B2B) video calling but is not required for Mobile and Remote Access (MRA). For MRA, create a collab-edge SRV record for each peer in the Expressway Edge cluster. For B2B-only calls the expressway Edge cluster has a DNS SRV record that defines all cluster peers.

5. F. When you are configuring a zone between two clusters, it is not necessary to have the same number of peers in each cluster. For example, a cluster of three Expressway Cores can traverse to a cluster of six Expressway Edges.

Review Questions

1. The following common settings must be configured the same on each Expressway Peer within a cluster:

■ Same Configuration menu settings

■ Same domain

■ Same version of software

■ Same option keys (except RMS and Registration)

■ H.323 mode enabled on all peers

■ Firewall rules on the Expressways block connections from all IP addresses except those of its peers

2. The following are two common settings that must be configured differently on each Expressway Peer within a cluster:

■ Different system names

■ Different LAN addresses

3. List the three ways a cluster of Expressways will forward incoming call requests when using Zones:

■ To one of its locally registered endpoints, if the endpoint is registered to that Peer

■ To one of its peers, if the endpoint is registered to another Peer in that cluster

■ To one of its external Zones, if the endpoint has been located elsewhere

Chapter 12

Do I Know This Already?

1. D. The Registration Rejected – Unknown Domain error message would only pertain to SIP registration attempts. Because H.323 uses a gatekeeper, anything related to a gatekeeper would not pertain to domains. To resolve this issue, check the domain configured on both the endpoint and the Cisco Expressway to ensure they match.

2. A. Search History is a log that aids in troubleshooting call setup issues. It captures all search events of every call attempt on the Expressway as it utilizes the Call Processing Order, except for bandwidth consumption.

3. C. Typically, the Source Alias optional field is only relevant if the routing process uses Call Processing Language (CPL) that has rules dependent on the source alias. The Alias field is the only field required to use the Locate tool. This provides the destination alias to test the call attempt against. The Source field determines where the simulated search will originate from. The Authenticated field is used to select whether or not the request should be treated as authenticated.

4. B. If the supplied host is fully qualified, then DNS is queried first for *host*. If the lookup for *host* fails, then an additional query for *host.<system_domain>* is performed, where *<system_domain>* is the domain name as configured on the DNS page of the Expressway. If the supplied host is not fully qualified, then DNS is queried first for *host.<system_domain>*. If the lookup for *host.<system_domain>* fails, then an additional query for *host* is performed.

5. A, C. Cisco has provided two troubleshooting tools on the Cisco Expressway that can aid administrators in troubleshooting certificate issues: the Client Certificate Testing page and the Server Traversal Test page.

6. D. There are three ways to view alarms on the Expressway. A red triangle appears in the top-right corner when there is an alarm, with a banner identifying how many alarms exist on the system. Clicking the triangle takes you to the Alarms page. If there are no alarms, or the alarms have been dismissed, then the triangle no longer appears. Alternatively, you can navigate to **Status > Alarms** (not **System > Alarms**), which takes you to the same menu. The third option is to log in using SSH through IP or a serial connection. After successfully logging in, all open alarms are listed in text at the top of the console window.

Review Questions

1. The following registration issues are possible:

   ■ Registration Rejected – Unknown Domain

   ■ Registration Rejected – Alias Conflicts with an existing registration

   ■ Registration Rejected – Not Permitted by Policy

   ■ Registration Rejected – Received from Unauthenticated Source

2. The ten SRV queries are as follows:

   ■ _h323ls._udp.*<domain>*

   ■ _h323rs._udp.*<domain>*

Appendix A: Answers to the "Do I Know This Already?" Quizzes and Review Questions   475

A

- _h323cs._tcp.<domain>

- _sips._tcp.<domain>

- _sip._tcp.<domain>

- _sip._udp.<domain>

- _collab-edge._tls

- _cisco-uds._tcp

- _turn._udp.<domain>

- _turn._tcp.<domain>

Chapter 13

Do I Know This Already?

1. D. The Expressway Series also offers a secure VPN-less solution for unified communications, known as Mobile and Remote Access (MRA). MRA allows for endpoints outside the firewall to register to an internal Cisco Unified Communications Manager from anywhere outside the corporate network through a proxied registration rather than through a VPN. This limits the need for small and medium-sized businesses to install complex VPN routers and improves the media flow of calls between internal endpoints and external endpoints.

2. A. MRA is only supported for SIP; there is no H.323 support in the MRA solution.

3. B. Mutual TLS (MTLS) authentication, or TLS Verify, is required between the Expressway Core and Edge servers. Trust between TLS entities is established based on certificates. The final component that needs to be mentioned regarding the MRA solution is the SIP Trunk Security Profile on the Cisco Unified CM that is used in connection with the Expressway Core. MTLS is not required between these two servers. However, if MTLS is used, then a trust needs to be established between the Unified CM and Expressway Core certificates, and the subject alternative names (SANs) in the Expressway Core certificate need to be included in the SIP Trunk Security Profile.

4. B. The internal firewall must allow the following outbound connections from the Expressway-C to the Expressway-E:

    - SIP: TCP 7001

    - Traversal media: UDP 2776 to 2777 (or 36000 to 36011 for large VM/appliance)

    - XMPP: TCP 7400

    - HTTPS (tunneled over SSH between C and E): TCP 2222

5. A. Cisco AXL Web Service must be running on the publisher node. If you have Cisco Jabber clients using OAuth authentication over MRA, make sure that your Jabber users' User Profiles allow MRA. This is not required if OAuth is not being used. If you are using OAuth on the Expressway, you must also enable OAuth Refresh

Logins on Unified CM as well. Again, this is not required if OAuth is not being used. High volumes of MRA calls may trigger denial of service thresholds on Unified CM when all calls arrive at the Unified CM from the same Expressway-C (cluster). If necessary (but not required), Cisco recommends that you increase the level of the SIP Station TCP Port Throttle Threshold service parameter to 750 KB/second.

Review Questions

1. The following are the six required MRA components:

   ■ DNS

   ■ MTLS Certificate

   ■ Firewall Traversal Services

   ■ Unified Communications configuration settings

   ■ Reverse HTTPS proxy

   ■ SIP Trunk Security Profile on Cisco Unified CM

2. The approaches to domain configuration with MRA are as follows:

   ■ Single domain with split DNS

   ■ Dual domain without split DNS

   ■ Single domain without split DNS

   ■ URL for Cisco Meeting Server Web Proxy and MRA domain cannot be the same

   ■ Multiple external domains for MRA

Chapter 14

Do I Know This Already?

1. A. The external DNS server must be configured with a _collab-edge._tls.*<domain>* SRV record so that external endpoints can discover that they should use the Cisco Expressway-E for Mobile and Remote Access. Service records for secure SIP are also required, not specifically for MRA but for deploying a secure SIP service on the Internet. The _sip._tcp.*<domain>* SRV is not for secure SIP. The SRV records must point to each cluster member of the Cisco Expressway-E server.

2. D. The service discovery occurs as follows. First, a Cisco Jabber client located outside the corporate network, and without a VPN connection, sends a DNS SRV record lookup for _cisco-uds._tcp.company.com to a public DNS server. The public enterprise DNS that manages company.com should not have such an SRV record and, therefore, the lookup fails. Next, the Cisco Jabber client sends another DNS SRV record lookup for _collab-edge._tls.company.com. This time the lookup is successful, and the address of the Cisco Expressway Edge is provided to the Jabber client in the DNS response.

3. A, B. Six different certificate pairs can be configured in an MRA deployment. However, only two pairs are required to set up the solution. The other four exist in an ideal environment for absolute security pertaining to registration and calling. The first certificate required is a public or enterprise CA certificate chain used to sign the

Appendix A: Answers to the "Do I Know This Already?" Quizzes and Review Questions   477

A

Expressway-C. The second certificate required is a public or enterprise CA certificate chain used to sign the Expressway-E.

4. B. Self-signed certificates will not fulfill the TLS Verify requirements, so they cannot be used on Expressways for MRA. Wildcard certificates are not supported on Expressways at all. So the only option left is single host/domain certificates, which are the most common certificate used. Also supported are UCC/Multiple SAN/Cert, not listed in this question.

5. C, D. Two Cisco Unified Communications Manager certificates are significant for Mobile and Remote Access: the CallManager certificate and the Tomcat certificate.

6. D. Certificates can be signed in either a DER-encoded or Base64-encoded format. DER stands for Distinguished Encoding Rules, which is a binary format. Base64 is an encoding method that converts binary to plain ASCII text. Some scenarios prevent copying and transferring data in binary, so plain text is needed. Therefore, it is recommended to choose the Base 64 Encoded option before downloading the certificate.

7. B. High volumes of Mobile and Remote Access calls may trigger denial-of-service thresholds on the Cisco Unified Communications Manager. The reason is that all the calls arriving at the Unified CM are from the same Expressway-C cluster. If necessary, Cisco recommends that you increase the level of the SIP Station TCP Port Throttle Threshold to 750 kbps.

8. A. After MRA has been enabled on the Expressway-E, no more MRA-specific settings have to be configured. However, several settings need to be configured on the Expressway-C. Domain settings must be configured, Tomcat certificates might need to be uploaded, and the Unified CM must be discovered by the Expressway-C. The IM and Presence server and the Cisco Unity Connection server might need to be configured as well.

9. B. The Unified CM IM and Presence Service and Cisco Unity Connections servers can also be discovered by the Expressway-C if these servers are being used. However, be aware that the status will not show Active on these until the Traversal Zones are configured and active.

10. B. The Cisco MRA reverse proxy settings provide a mechanism to support visual voicemail access, contact photo retrieval, Cisco Jabber custom tabs, and other data applications. HTTPS reverse proxy is a function that is provided by the Cisco Expressway-E using port TCP 8443 for HTTPS traffic. Initial MRA configuration allows inbound authenticated HTTPS requests to the following destinations:

- TCP 6970 (TFTP file download) and TCP 8443 (SOAP API) to all discovered Unified CM nodes

- TCP 7400 (XCP router) and TCP 8443 (SOAP API) to all Unified CM IM and Presence nodes

11. D. Navigate to **Configuration > Zones > Zones** and add a new Traversal Server Zone. Because this zone is specifically for MRA, the zone Type setting should be set to Unified Communications Traversal.

Review Questions

1. The following are the six certificate types:

   ■ Public or enterprise CA certificate chain used to sign Expressway Core certificate

   ■ Public or enterprise CA certificate chain used to sign Expressway Edge certificate

   ■ Cisco Unified CM Tomcat certificates or CA chain

   ■ Cisco Unified CM CallManager certificates or CA chain

   ■ IM&P Tomcat certificates or CA chain

   ■ Cisco Unified CM CAPF certificates

2. The seven Cisco Unified CM steps for MRA preparation are as follows:

   ■ Make sure that the Cisco AXL Web Service is activated on the publisher node.

   ■ Optionally, configure region-specific settings for MRA endpoints.

   ■ Assign your region to the device pool that your MRA endpoints use.

   ■ Set up a phone security profile to be used by MRA endpoints.

   ■ (Cisco Jabber only) Set up an MRA Access Policy for Cisco Jabber users. Cisco Jabber users must be enabled with MRA access within their user profiles to use the MRA feature.

   ■ (Cisco Jabber only) Apply the user policy that was set up previously to the appropriate end user.

   ■ Configure and provision endpoints that will use the MRA feature.

3. The following three Expressway-C MRA settings must be configured after MRA is enabled:

   ■ Configure a SIP domain to route registrations to the Cisco Unified CM.

   ■ Install the Unified CM Tomcat certificate (if TLS Verify is being used).

   ■ Discover the Unified CM from the Expressway Core.

Chapter 15

Do I Know This Already?

1. B. You might see invalid services errors if you changed any of the following items on the Cisco Expressway. A system restart is required to be sure the configuration changes take effect.

   ■ Server or CA certificates

   ■ DNS configuration

   ■ Domain configuration

2.   E. The Collaboration Solutions Analyzer, or CSA, is a tool set provided by Cisco TAC. It can be used to help with deploying and troubleshooting MRA. The Cisco Expressway release notes provide instructions on how to access the CSA. This tool set is composed of a validator tool and a log analysis tool.

3.   A, E, F. To configure the diagnostic log level from the Expressway web interface, navigate to **Maintenance > Diagnostics > Advanced > Support Log Configuration** and select the following logs:

   ■ developer.edgeconfigprovisioning

   ■ developer.trafficserver

   ■ developer.xcp

   Click Set to Debug.

4.   A. Endpoints may not be able to register to the Unified CM if there is also a SIP trunk configured between the Unified CM and the Cisco Expressway-C. If a SIP trunk is configured, you must ensure that it uses a different listening port on the Unified CM from that used for SIP line registrations to the Unified CM.

5.   D. When Jabber doesn't register for phone services, there is a case-handling mismatch between the Cisco Expressway and the User Data Service (UDS). Another issue unique to Jabber that you might encounter with MRA is a Jabber popup window that warns about an invalid certificate when connecting from outside the network. This is a symptom of an incorrectly configured server certificate on the Cisco Expressway-E. Jabber can fail to sign in due to the SSH tunnels failing to be established. The Traversal Zone between the Cisco Expressway-C and Cisco Expressway-E will work normally in all other respects even when this issue occurs. This can occur if the Cisco Expressway-E DNS host name contains underscore characters. Jabber sign-in failures have also occurred when there is inconsistency of the DNS domain name between Cisco Expressway-E peers in a cluster.

6.   C. A 502 message on the Cisco Expressway-E indicates that the next hop failed, which is typically to the Cisco Expressway-C. If you get the error No Voicemail Service "403 Forbidden" response, then ensure that the Cisco Unity Connection (CUC) host name is included on the HTTP server allow list on the Cisco Expressway-C. A "403 Forbidden" response many also occur for any other service requests. You may see call failures due to a 407 Proxy Authentication Required error message or a 500 Internal Server Error message. Call failures can occur if the Traversal Zones on Cisco Expressway are configured with an Authentication Policy setting of Check Credentials. Ensure that the Authentication Policy setting on the Traversal Zones used for Mobile and Remote Access is set to Do Not Check Credentials. A 401 Unauthorized failure message can occur when the Cisco Expressway attempts to authenticate the credentials presented by the endpoint client. The reasons for this error may could be the client supplying an unknown username or the wrong password. It could also be that the Cisco Intercluster Lookup Service (ILS) has not been set up on all of the Unified CM clusters.

Review Questions

1. Three settings requiring a restart:

   - Server or CA certificated

   - DNS configuration

   - Domain configuration

2. The CSA tool set includes

   - CollabEdge validator tool

   - Log analysis tool

3. Five setting changes on Unified CM can cause MRA deployment failure:

   - Number of nodes within a Unified CM cluster

   - Host name or IP address of an existing node

   - Listening port numbers

   - Security parameters

   - Phone security profiles

Chapter 16

Do I Know This Already?

1. B. Cisco cloud provider partners can implement Cisco HCS for end customers as a partner-hosted or partner-managed Unified Communications-as-a-Service (UCaaS) solution.

2. D. Cisco UCM Cloud supports central (cloud) breakout, local breakout, and mixed mode for its PSTN connectivity models.

3. A. Webex provides the highest level of protection for meeting data with support for AES 256-bit GCM encryption.

4. D. Cisco Cloudlock monitors all Cisco Webex spaces that contain members internal to the organization for data loss prevention (DLP). When a violation is detected, Cloudlock can take Webex-specific actions.

5. B. Hybrid Calendar Service also enables Cisco Webex users to utilize One Button to Push (OBTP) so that when a scheduled meeting includes video devices, a green Join button appears on the devices right before the meeting begins, just as it does in the Cisco Webex app.

6. D. Cisco Hybrid Directory Service uses the Cisco Directory Connector to automatically synchronize Microsoft Active Directory and Azure Active Directory users into Webex Control Hub (creating, updating, deleting) so that user account information is always current in the cloud.

Review Questions

1. A Cisco Validated Design (CVD) is a specific bundle of Cisco products and products from our partners designed to address the business needs of customers. CVDs are

Appendix A: Answers to the "Do I Know This Already?" Quizzes and Review Questions   481

A

created based on Cisco's observation of market trends and inside knowledge of future directions of Cisco and its partners. As a complete solution, each CVD consists of both hardware and software.

2. Add @webex or their Personal Room URL to automatically share the host's Webex Personal Room and join information in the invitation. Add @meet to automatically create a Cisco Webex space and corresponding join link for the space.

Chapter 17

Do I Know This Already?

1. B, E. The core components for Cisco Webex Hybrid Directory Service include the Cisco Directory Connector and Microsoft Active Directory.

2. A. Download the Cisco Directory Connector software from https://admin.webex.com to ensure the most up-to-date version is downloaded.

3. D. There is no upper limit for how many Active Directory objects can be synchronized to the cloud. Any limits on premises directory objects are tied to the specific version of and specifications for the Active Directory environment that is being synchronized to the cloud, not the connector itself.

4. D. The attribute mapped to the uid field must be in email format.

5. A. Site administrators can only set a user's privileges if the user has Cisco Webex Enterprise Edition.

Review Questions

1. For a Cisco Directory Connector deployment, keep the following requirements and recommendations in mind if you are going to synchronize Active Directory information from multiple domains into the cloud:

    ■ A separate instance of the Cisco Directory Connector is required for each domain.

    ■ The Cisco Directory Connector software must run on a host that is on the same domain that it will synchronize.

    ■ Cisco recommends that you verify or claim your domains in Cisco Webex Control Hub.

    ■ If you want to synchronize more than 50 domains, you must open a ticket to get your organization moved to a large org list.

    ■ If desired, you can synchronize room resource information along with user accounts.

2. The following are the high-level steps required to deploy Webex Hybrid Directory Service:

    ■ Virtual Microsoft Windows Server instances are created and deployed in the enterprise data center.

    ■ After the Windows servers are deployed, the administrator logs in to the Webex Control Hub at https://admin.webex.com to enable directory synchronization and download the Cisco Directory Connector software installation package.

- Directory Connector is installed on the Windows servers.

- After Directory Connector is installed, the administrator configures the connector, and an initial synchronization occurs between Microsoft Active Directory and the Directory Connector and between the Directory Connector and Webex.

- Once the initial synchronization completes, the administrator configures the schedule for periodic incremental and full synchronizations.

- The administrator manages users and provisions them for cloud services as appropriate.

Chapter 18

Do I Know This Already?

1. C. The meetings list in Cisco Webex lets users see upcoming meetings for the next 4 weeks.

2. A. The Calendar Connector is the on-premises component of Webex Hybrid Calendar Service.

3. B. The Expressway-C Connector Hosts do not support dual NIC deployments.

4. D. Each user in your Webex organization can have only one email address associated with only one Hybrid Calendar Service integration. In other words, Hybrid Calendar Service will only process meetings from a single address for creating spaces, decorating meetings, showing the meetings list and Join button, and sending One Button to Push (OTBP) to video devices.

5. A. Webex Hybrid Calendar Service uses the Microsoft Graph API to subscribe to changes in users' calendars, receive notifications for changes made in subscribed users' calendars, and update meeting invitations with scheduling information when the meeting's location field contains keywords such as @webex or @meet, or the meeting body contains a supported video address. Hybrid Calendar Service accesses only the calendars of the users that you enable for Hybrid Calendar Service in the Cisco Webex Control Hub.

6. B. To provide One Button to Push on video devices, you deploy the Cisco Webex Hybrid Calendar Service.

Review Questions

1. The Hybrid Calendar Service with Google Calendar scheduling flow is as follows:

    - A user creates a meeting in Google Calendar, putting a scheduling keyword or video address in the location field.

    - Google sends a notification to Hybrid Calendar Service.

    - Hybrid Calendar Service requests and receives the encryption key, and then uses it to encrypt the meeting information.

    - Hybrid Calendar Service validates meeting creation and recipients, and then creates a Webex team space, if applicable.

    - Hybrid Calendar Service calls the API service and maps the meeting to the space.

Appendix A: Answers to the "Do I Know This Already?" Quizzes and Review Questions   483

A

- Hybrid Calendar Service retrieves the meeting join information, including the Personal Room if applicable.

- Hybrid Calendar Service updates the meeting invite with the meeting join information and, if applicable, the space ID.

- The updated meeting information appears in Google Calendar.

2. The cloud-based Hybrid Calendar Service with Office 365 scheduling flow is as follows:

- A user creates a meeting in the Office 365 calendar, putting a scheduling keyword or video address in the Location field.

- Exchange Online sends a notification to Hybrid Calendar Service.

- Hybrid Calendar Service requests and receives the encryption key, and then uses it to encrypt the meeting information.

- Hybrid Calendar Service validates meeting creation and recipients, and then creates a Webex team space, if applicable.

- Hybrid Calendar Service calls the API service and, if applicable, maps the meeting to the space.

- Hybrid Calendar Service retrieves the meeting join information, including the Webex Personal Room if applicable.

- Hybrid Calendar Service updates the meeting invite with the meeting join information and, if applicable, the space ID.

- The invitees and the organizer get the updated meeting invitation.

Chapter 19

Do I Know This Already?

1. A. Currently, Hybrid Message Service supports up to 195,000 users per organization across multiple Expressway clusters.

2. C. You can manage your user population in Webex Control Hub by manually adding/removing users, importing users (and selected services) through a CSV file, and by utilizing Hybrid Directory Service to synchronize users from an existing on-premises directory environment.

3. D. If your on-premises environment proxies the outbound traffic, you must first enter the details of the proxy server on the Applications > Hybrid Services > Connector Proxy page.

4. B. An account for Message Connector needs to access the Administrative XML Web Service (AXL) API of the Cisco Unified Communications Manager IM&P Service. You must use an independent administrator account, not the main administrator account.

5. C. The status information page at **Applications > Hybrid Services > Message Service > Message Service Status** shows information in the following categories: Connectivity to Cisco Webex, User and Usage Stats, and Connections to IM and Presence Service Infrastructure.

Review Questions

1. Cisco supports 195,000 users per organization across multiple Expressway clusters. Cisco also supports up to 5000 Message Service users per Small Expressway, up to 6500 users per Medium Expressway, and up to 15,000 users per Large Expressway. This gives a maximum number of 75,000 on a cluster of six Expressways, because the capacity of one node is reserved for redundancy.

Chapter 20

Do I Know This Already?

1. A. Supported operating systems for software installation of the Cisco Webex Device Connector are Microsoft Windows 10 and macOS High Sierra (10.13) or later.

2. D. Webex Edge for Calling architecture supports your cloud migration with services at three levels: Network Services, Enterprise Services, and User Services.

3. C. Cisco Webex Edge Audio decouples the PSTN from Cisco Webex by intelligently changing the call routing to a simple-to-deploy on-net path. It is a service that allows any company, of any size, that uses Cisco Unified Communications Manager (Unified CM) to route audio calls intelligently and automatically over VoIP or utilize existing PSTN services.

4. A, B, C. To set up Webex Edge Connect, you first work with an Equinix representative on two tasks: establishing physical connectivity and establishing data-link connectivity. When these tasks are complete, you can continue to the third task of establishing network connectivity with Cisco Webex through the Equinix Cloud Exchange Portal.

5. A, D. Webex Video Mesh supports Cisco Unified Communications Manager, Release 11.5(1) SU3 or later, and Cisco Expressway-C or Expressway-E, Release X8.11.4 or later.

6. C. Cisco supports the following explicit proxy and authentication type combinations:

   ■ No authentication with HTTP and HTTPS

   ■ Basic authentication with HTTP and HTTPS

   ■ Digest authentication with HTTPS only

   ■ NTLM authentication with HTTP only

Review Questions

1. The following is a high-level task flow for deployment of the Video Mesh Node:

   ■ Identify sites where Video Mesh clusters will be deployed.

   ■ Download and install the Video Mesh Node software.

   ■ Configure the network settings on each Video Mesh Node.

   ■ Register the Video Mesh Nodes to the Webex organization.

Chapter 21

Do I Know This Already?

1. A. Cloud-based deployment with Cisco Webex Messenger service includes contact source, presence, instant messaging, and conferencing (Webex Meeting provided). Hybrid cloud-based deployment with Cisco Webex Messenger service includes contact source, presence, instant messaging, conferencing, and Unified CM–provided audio, video, and voicemail (Unity Connection).

2. C. The menu to configure the Unified CM integration is accessed via **Configuration > Additional Services > Unified Communications**.

Review Questions

1. The following is the high-level workflow analysis for a hybrid deployment using Cisco Webex Messenger:

   ■ Configure policies.

   ■ Configure clusters.

   ■ Create users on the Unified Communications Manager.

   ■ Configure softphone.

   ■ Configure deskphone control.

   ■ Configure Extend and Connect.

   ■ Configure service discovery for remote access.

   ■ Set up certificate validation.

   ■ Configure the clients.

   ■ (Optional) Deploy Cisco Jabber applications and Jabber softphone for VDI.

   ■ Configure remote access.

2. The following is the high-level workflow analysis for a cloud deployment using Cisco Webex Messenger:

   ■ Configure policies.

   ■ Create users for cloud deployment.

   ■ Set up certificate validation.

   ■ Configure the clients.

   ■ (Optional) Deploy Cisco Jabber applications and Jabber Softphone for VDI.

CCNP Implementing Cisco Collaboration Cloud and Edge Solutions (CLCEI) 300-820 Exam Updates

Over time, reader feedback allows Pearson to gauge which topics give our readers the most problems when taking the exams. To assist readers with those topics, the authors create new materials clarifying and expanding on those troublesome exam topics. As mentioned in the Introduction, the additional content about the exam is contained in a PDF on this book's companion website, at https://www.ciscopress.com/title/9780136733720.

This appendix is intended to provide you with updated information if Cisco makes minor modifications to the exam upon which this book is based. When Cisco releases an entirely new exam, the changes are usually too extensive to provide in a simple update appendix. In those cases, you might need to consult the new edition of the book for the updated content. This appendix attempts to fill the void that occurs with any print book. In particular, this appendix does the following:

- Mentions technical items that might not have been mentioned elsewhere in the book

- Covers new topics if Cisco adds new content to the exam over time

- Provides a way to get up-to-the-minute current information about content for the exam

Always Get the Latest at the Book's Product Page

You are reading the version of this appendix that was available when your book was printed. However, given that the main purpose of this appendix is to be a living, changing document, it is important that you look for the latest version online at the book's companion website. To do so, follow these steps:

Step 1. Browse to https://www.ciscopress.com/title/9780136733720.

Step 2. Click the **Updates** tab.

Step 3. If there is a new Appendix B document on the page, download the latest Appendix B document.

NOTE The downloaded document has a version number. Comparing the version of the print Appendix B (Version 1.0) with the latest online version of this appendix, you should do the following:

- **Same version:** Ignore the PDF that you downloaded from the companion website.

- **Website has a later version:** Ignore this Appendix B in your book and read only the latest version that you downloaded from the companion website.

Technical Content

The current Version 1.0 of this appendix does not contain additional technical coverage.

GLOSSARY OF KEY TERMS

401 Unauthorized   Failure message that can occur when the Cisco Expressway attempts to authenticate the credentials presented by the endpoint client. The reasons for this error may be due to the client supplying an unknown username or the wrong password. It could also be that the Intercluster Lookup Service (ILS) has not been set up on all of the Cisco Unified CM clusters.

403 Forbidden   Error message that can occur for any service request. These services may fail if the Cisco Expressway-C and Cisco Expressway-E are not synchronized to a reliable NTP server. The services may also need to be added to the HTTP allow list.

404 Not Found   Type of error that occurs when client HTTPS requests are dropped by the Cisco Expressway. This can be caused by the automated intrusion protection feature on the Cisco Expressway-E if it detects repeated invalid attempts, which are 404 errors, from a client IP address to access resources through the HTTP proxy.

407 Proxy Authentication Required   Type of error that can cause call failures if the Traversal Zones on Cisco Expressway are configured with an Authentication Policy setting of Check Credentials. Ensure that the Authentication Policy setting on the Traversal Zones used for Mobile and Remote Access is set to Do Not Check Credentials. This could also be a 500 Internal Server Error message.

502 Bad Gateway   A type of message on the Cisco Expressway-E that indicates the next hop failed, which is typically to the Cisco Expressway-C.

A record   A mapping record used by DNS servers to map a URI address to an IP address. A records consist of a host name and domain name, which make up the URI, and an IP address.

Active Directory Certificate Service (ADCS)   A service that runs on a Microsoft Windows Server. This service can be used to sign private certificates for use within an enterprise.

Address of Record (AOR)   An identifier in a SIP registrar for the SIP URI and IP address.

Administrative XML Web Service (AXL)   An XML/SOAP-based interface that provides a mechanism for inserting, retrieving, updating, and removing data from the Unified Communication configuration database. Developers can use AXL and the provided WSDL to create, read, update, and delete objects such as gateways, users, devices, route patterns, and much more.

Admission Request (ARQ)   The RAS message sent from an endpoint to a gatekeeper to request permission to place a call. The gatekeeper responds with either an Admission Confirmation (ACF) or Admission Reject (ARJ).

Advanced Encryption Standard (AES)   A specification for the encryption of electronic data established by the U.S. National Institute of Standards and Technology (NIST); also known by its original name, Rijndael.

Application Layer Gateway (ALG)   This service will identify SIP and H.323 traffic as it passes through the router/firewall. It inspects and, in some cases, modifies the payload of the SIP and H.323 messages. The purpose of modifying the payload is to help the H.323 or SIP application from which the message originated to traverse NAT. ALG is so referred to as Fixup, Inspection, Application Awareness, Stateful Packet Inspection, Deep Packet Inspection, and so forth.

application programming interface (API)   A set of functions and procedures allowing the creation of applications that access the features or data of an operating system, application, or other service.

Assent   Cisco proprietary protocol used for firewall and NAT traversal of audio and video media and signaling over UDP ports for RTP and RTCP packets.

asymmetric cryptography   Same process as symmetric cryptography, except the identity of the communicating parties can be authenticated using public-key cryptography.

asymmetric network   A network that contains multiple entry and exit points for traffic to take with each new transmission.

Automatic Certificate Management Environment (ACME)   A communications protocol for automating interactions between CAs and their users' web servers, allowing the automated deployment of public key infrastructure (PKI) at low cost. It was designed by the Internet Security Research Group (ISRG) for its Let's Encrypt service.

back-to-back user agent (B2BUA)   A logical network element in SIP applications. It is a type of SIP UA that receives a SIP request, then reformulates the request and sends it out as a new request.

bandwidth   A measure of the rate at which data can be sent or received across a network.

Base64-encoded format   An encoding method for certificates that converts binary to plain ASCII text.

Border Gateway Protocol (BGP)   An interdomain routing protocol designed to provide loop-free routing between separate routing domains that contain independent routing policies (autonomous systems).

business-to-business (B2B)   Describes communications between two businesses.

business-to-customer (B2C)   Describes communications between a business and its customers.

Call Admission Control (CAC)   A mechanism on the Unified CM and the Cisco Expressway that is used to control if calls are allowed and how bandwidth is used across an enterprise network.

Call Loop Detection Mode   A setting on the Cisco Expressway that prevents search loops occurring. Each search has a serial number and tag. The serial number is unique to the search but the tag information is passed with a Location Request. The Expressway uses the tag to identify a call that has already been received and hence ignored, preventing loopback errors.

Call Policy   Also known as Administrator Policy, or Admin Policy, a list of rules that are used to control call behavior through the Expressway.

Call Processing Order   A systematic process used to gauge incoming call requests against a series of criteria that can be fashioned by an administrator.

Call Processing Language (CPL)   A machine-generated programing language that is often used in telephony to create calling behavior within a PBX or telco environment.

Call Processing Language (CPL) Script   An XML-based language for defining call handling designed to control Internet telephony services.

Call Setup Mode   An H.323 setting configured on an endpoint that can be set to either Direct or Gatekeeper. If set to Direct, the endpoint never attempts to register to a gatekeeper and is only able to dial by IP address. When Gatekeeper mode is used, the endpoint is completely subservient to a gatekeeper and will perform no function until it has registered.

Call Signaling Optimization   Setting on the Cisco Expressway that enables optimal call routing. This setting can be configured as On or Off (the default value).

certificate authority (CA)   The certificate server that issues and verifies the authenticity of certificates.

certificate revocation list (CRL)   A list of digital certificates that have been revoked by the issuing certificate authority (CA) before their scheduled expiration date and should no longer be trusted.

certificate signing request (CSR)   A template used to submit information to a CA so that a certificate can be signed.

Cisco Collaboration Flex Plan   Entitles customers to use Cisco's industry-leading collaboration tools with one simple subscription-based offer. It helps with transitions to the cloud, and investment protection, by including cloud, premises, hosted, and hybrid deployments, with the flexibility to use them all.

Cisco Directory Connector   Synchronizes Microsoft Active Directory users into Webex Control Hub (creating, updating, deleting) so that user account information is always current in the cloud.

Cisco Discovery Protocol (CDP)   A proprietary protocol used at Layer 2 of the network for device and information discovery across a network.

Cisco Hosted Collaboration Solution (HCS)   A cloud offering for Cisco Collaboration through service providers.

Cisco Jabber   A software client tool that utilizes the on-premises or hosted Cisco Unified CM and IM&P services.

Cisco Meeting Server (CMS)   An on-premises conferencing server used for rich media multipoint conferencing between three or more participants.

Cisco Unified Communications (UC)   A set of Cisco products that provides a consistent, unified user interface and experience across multiple devices and media types.

Cisco Unified Communications Manager (Unified CM)   A Cisco call control server that supports SIP devices and many different call features.

Cisco Unified Workspace Licensing (CUWL)   A Cisco licensing type that was designed for medium to large organizations that offers both voice and video capabilities plus many other product solutions, such as voicemail systems and conferencing solutions.

Cisco Unity Connections (CUC)   A unified messaging and voicemail solution within Cisco's collaboration suite of products.

Cisco User Connect Licensing (CUCL)   A Cisco licensing type that was designed for smaller voice-only networks.

Cisco Webex   A secure cloud team collaboration platform that works with devices and apps to enable better teamwork for every worker.

Cisco Webex Control Hub   A web-based, intuitive, single-pane-of-glass management portal that enables you to provision, administer, and manage Cisco Webex services and Webex Hybrid Services, such as Hybrid Call Service, Hybrid Calendar Service, Hybrid Directory Service, and Video Mesh.

Cisco Webex Hybrid Calendar Service   Supports Microsoft Exchange, Office 365, and Google Calendar and makes it easy to schedule and join meetings from any device, no matter where the user is located.

Cisco Webex Hybrid Message Service   Ideal service for organizations that have users on Cisco Webex who need to exchange messages with users on Cisco Unified Communications Manager IM and Presence (IM&P) Service.

CollabEdge validator tool   A part of the CSA tool set used to simulate a Jabber client sign-in process to validate an MRA deployment and provide feedback on the results.

Collaboration Endpoint (CE)   Software that comes preloaded onto DX, MX, SX, and Webex endpoints. This software is based on the legacy TC software.

Collaboration Solutions Analyzer (CSA)   A tool set that can be provided by Cisco TAC to help troubleshoot an MRA solution.

Comma-Separated Values (CSV)   A simple file format used to store tabular data, such as a spreadsheet or database. Files in the CSV format can be imported to and exported from programs that store data in tables, such as Microsoft Excel and OpenOffice Calc.

command line interface (CLI)   A text-based command structure that allows an administrator to interact with a system. The CLI can be used over an IP connection or through a console connection.

data loss prevention (DLP)   The practice of detecting and preventing data breaches, exfiltration, or unwanted destruction of sensitive data. Organizations use DLP to protect and secure their data and comply with regulations.

Default Call Bandwidth   A setting that enables the Expressway to apply a bandwidth value when an endpoint does not request a specific bandwidth rate for a call. This bandwidth setting is not a limitation. Some endpoints allow the internal bandwidth setting to be auto-negotiated. If one of those endpoints places a call but does not specify the desired bandwidth, the Expressway implements whatever limit has been established here. The default value is 384 kbps, but this setting can be changed to whatever limit is desired.

Default Subzone   A logical group within the Local Zone that all endpoints register to by default.

Default Zone The default logical connection into and out of the Local Zone.

demilitarized zone (DMZ) A parameter network that exists outside an organization's main corporate network and acts as a buffer for services that are public facing, such as the Expressway Edge.

Diffie-Hellman key exchange A method of securely exchanging cryptographic keys over a public channel and was one of the first public-key protocols.

Digest Authentication mechanism built into SIP.

Directory Expressway A designation given to an Expressway in a Hierarchical Video Network with a Structured Dial Plan model. The directory Expressway essentially acts as a call distribution point between other Expressways that each represent a different collection of registered endpoints within a single location.

Directory Number (DN) A numeric dialing pattern used on the Cisco Unified CM. A DN is assigned to the line on a phone and essentially becomes the phone number for that phone.

Distinguished Encoding Rules (DER)-encoded format A binary format used with certificates.

Domain Name System (DNS) A type of service that allows URL addresses to be used in place of IP addresses. DNS resolves the URLs to their IP address mapping.

Domain Validation (DV) Certificate A type of certificate for which the CA only checks the right of the applicant to use a specific domain name. No company identity information is vetted and no information is displayed other than encryption information within the Secure Site Seal.

Downspeed Mode A setting that is used to down speed calls on the Expressway. The options are Downspeed Per Call Mode and Downspeed Total Mode.

Downspeed Per Call Mode A setting that pertains to bandwidth down speeding for each individual call attempt and can be set to On or Off.

Downspeed Total Mode A setting that pertains to bandwidth down speeding for all call attempts and can be set to On or Off.

DNS Zone Trunk used for communication between the Expressway and a Domain Name System (DNS) server.

dual-tone multifrequency (DTMF) An in-band communications system that has been used for many years by telephone companies and allows the end user to communicate by pressing keys on their phone.

Dynamic Host Configuration Protocol (DHCP) An open-source protocol used by network devices to automatically discover network addressing information so that communication across the network is possible. The DHCP process is a four-step process that involves Discovery, Offer, Request, and Acknowledgment.

E.164 An ITU-T recommendation that defines a general format for international telephone numbers. Numeric-only values containing 1 to 15 digits that are assigned to an endpoint. They work in the same manner as any phone number would in a typical telephony environment.

E.164 alias   Numeric only values containing 1 to 15 digits that are assigned to an endpoint. They work in the same manner as any phone number would in a typical telephony environment.

E.164 Number Mapping (ENUM)   A way of using DNS NAPTR (Name Authority PoinTeR) records to convert E.164 numbers into routable URIs. ENUM is defined in RFC 6116, which obsoletes the original RFC 3761.

endpoint   An audio-only or audio- and video-capable device used for communication.

Extended Validation (EV) Certificate   A type of certificate for which the CA checks the right of the applicant to use a specific domain name and conducts a thorough vetting of the organization.

Extensible Messaging and Presence Protocol (XMPP)   A set of open technologies for instant messaging, presence, multiparty chat, voice and video calls, collaboration, lightweight middleware, content syndication, and generalized routing of XML data.

FindMe   Trademarked term that describes a call forwarding feature within the Cisco Expressways.

FindMe ID   Alias assigned to a user account in the Expressway that initiates the FindMe search within the Cisco Expressway. The FindMe ID must be a unique alias that is not assigned to another endpoint.

firewall   Controls IP traffic entering your network. Firewalls generally block unsolicited incoming requests, meaning that any communication originating from outside your network will be prevented. However, firewalls can be configured to allow outgoing requests to certain trusted destinations, and to allow responses from those destinations. Allowing traffic in both directions prevents the firewall from doing its job. Therefore, a firewall exists to protect the inside of a corporate network from outside attack.

fully qualified domain name (FQDN)   A domain name that specifies its exact location in the tree hierarchy of DNS. It specifies all domain levels, including the top-level domain and the root zone.

gatekeeper   A call control device used with H.323. Gatekeepers provide registration, security, and call control into an otherwise unsecure and uncontrolled environment.

Gatekeeper Request (GRQ)   A RAS broadcast message initiated by an endpoint and used to locate a gatekeeper within the broadcast domain. The gatekeeper that responds sends a Gatekeeper Confirmation (GCF).

Google Calendar   Time-management and scheduling calendar service developed by Google.

H.225   The ITU substandard for call setup under the H.323 umbrella standard. H.225 consists of RAS and Q.931 messaging.

H.235   Authentication mechanism built into the H.323 standard.

H.245   A process used in H.323 for capability set exchange, conflict control, and opening logical channels, or ports. H.245 is also responsible for closing logical channels at the end of the call.

H.320   An ITU umbrella standard for circuit-switched communication.

H.323   An ITU umbrella standard for packet-switched communication.

H.323 ID   A string-based alias assigned to the endpoint that can use any combination of numbers, letters, and special characters except spaces. Because of this capability, an H.323 ID can be in the form of a URI. However, an H.323 ID is not a URI, because it is not dependent on the domain being an FQDN.

H.350   Communications standard used for LDAP messaging between a client and an LDAP server.

H.460.18 and H.460.19   ITU-T standard used for firewall traversal communication between a traversal client and traversal server. H.460.18/19 can only support the H.323 communication standard.

hair pinning   Also known as toll fraud, a fraudulent action where someone enters your network via IP and then hijacks your PSTN to make toll calls at your company's expense.

Hosted Collaboration Solution (HCS)   A cloud offering for Cisco collaboration through service providers.

HTTPS reverse proxy   A function that is provided by the Cisco Expressway-E using port TCP 8443 for HTTPS traffic. The Cisco MRA Reverse Proxy settings provide a mechanism to support visual voicemail access, contact photo retrieval, Cisco Jabber custom tabs, and other data applications.

Hypertext Transfer Protocol (HTTP)   An application layer protocol for distributed, collaborative, hypermedia information systems and is the foundation of data communication for the Internet.

Hypertext Transfer Protocol Secure (HTTPS)   Used for secure communication over computer networks and is widely used on the Internet. The communication protocol is encrypted using Transport Layer Security (TLS) or, formerly, Secure Sockets Layer (SSL).

IM and Presence (IM&P)   The Cisco Unified Communications Manager service that provides native standards-based, dual-protocol, enterprise instant messaging (IM) and network-based presence as part of Cisco Unified Communications.

instant messaging (IM)   A text-based communications tool that allows real-time text messages to be sent over the Internet.

Instant Messaging and Presence (IMP)   The Cisco Unified Communications Manager IM and Presence Service that provides native standards-based, dual-protocol, enterprise instant messaging (IM) and network-based presence as part of Cisco Unified Communications.

Integrated Services Digital Network (ISDN)   Similar to plain old telephone service (POTS), but the original analog signal is converted to digital format before it is sent across a wire. That digital signal must be converted back to analog at the receiving phone.

Interactive Connectivity Establishment (ICE)   A framework capable of assessing the networked environment a request comes from, and can then act as either a STUN or TURN server on behalf of the client's needs. ICE is not a NAT traversal protocol in and of itself.

International Telecommunications Union (ITU)   A specialized agency of the United Nations that is responsible for standardizing communications technologies.

Internet Engineering Task force (IETF)   An open standards organization that develops Internet standards.

Internet Protocol version 4 (IPv4)   An addressing system used to send communication packets across a packet-switched network. IPv4 addresses use a 32-bit binary numbering system divided into four octets made up of 8 bits, or 1 byte each.

Internet Protocol version 6 (IPv6)   An addressing system originally designed to replace the IPv4 addressing system. IPv6 addresses use a 128-bit hexadecimal numbering system that is capable of producing 340 undecillion addresses.

interworking   A gateway function of the Expressway used to bridge communication when two dissimilar protocols are trying to communicate.

Lightweight Directory Access Protocol (LDAP)   A search protocol used most commonly for extracting user information from a corporate directory.

Link   A logical connection between two Subzones or between a Subzone and a Zone.

local-area network (LAN)   A network within a single confined area.

Local Zone   A logical representation of the Cisco Expressway itself, and all other logical components are defined by how they relate back to the Local Zone.

Locate   Tool on the Cisco Expressway that operates just like the Search History log, except it only simulates a call.

Location Confirm (LCF)   The response sent in reply to the LRQ message confirming the location of the requested node.

Location Request (LRQ)   An H.323-based communication protocol used to request the location information of a node that is registered to a different server. Although LRQs are based on the H.323 standard, they are used by SIP communication as well.

log analysis tool   A part of the CSA tool set used to analyze logs that were collected on a Cisco Expressway to help identify issues with an MRA setup.

Loopback   A call routing error that can occur when a call request that has been sent out is somehow sent back to the requesting server.

Membership Rules   Rules created on the Expressway that determine to what Subzone an endpoint will register based on either the Subnet mask or an alias pattern match.

Message Digest Algorithm 5 (MD5)   A messaging system that uses a time stamp from a time server as part of its encryption key.

Microsoft Active Directory (AD)   A Microsoft-branded LDAP directory service that runs on a Microsoft Windows Server platform.

Microsoft Active Directory Lightweight Directory Services (AD LDS)   An independent mode of Active Directory that provides dedicated directory services for applications.

Microsoft Exchange   Software installed on Microsoft Exchange Server that provides the back end to an integrated system for email, calendaring, messaging, and tasks.

Mobile and Remote Access (MRA)   A Cisco feature that uses the Expressway Series devices to proxy registrations to the Cisco Unified CM from endpoints outside the corporate network without the use of a VPN. MRA also provides call capabilities into and out from the internal network through the firewall traversal components.

Multiprotocol Label Switching (MPLS)   A transport protocol that uses labels rather than network addresses to route traffic. Packets are forwarded based on the content of the label, so deciphering between voice, video, and data is simple. It is protocol agnostic, so it will function in circuit-switched or packet-switched networks.

Name Authority Pointer (NAPTR) record   A record in a DNS server that can be used to convert E.164 aliases into routable URIs.

Neighbor Zone   A trunk on the Cisco Expressway that is used to communicate with other communication servers within the same LAN or WAN.

Network Address Translation (NAT)   An IETF protocol designed to masquerade private IP addresses with public IP addresses so that communications can be sent across the public Internet space from a private network.

network interface card (NIC)   A computer card on a computing device that allows that device to access a network over Ethernet.

Network Time Protocol (NTP)   A protocol for synchronizing computer system clocks over IP networks. NTP has a hierarchical organization that is based on clock strata. Stratum 0 is an extremely precise clock source, such as an atomic clock or radio clock. A stratum 1 server is directly connected to a stratum 0 clock and can provide time information to other (stratum 2) devices, which in turn serves stratum 3 devices.

NT LAN Manager (NTLM)   A suite of Microsoft security protocols intended to provide authentication, integrity, and confidentiality to users. NTLM is the successor to the authentication protocol in Microsoft LAN Manager, an older Microsoft product.

Office 365   Line of subscription services offered by Microsoft as part of the Microsoft Office product line.

One Button to Push (OBTP)   A Cisco videoconferencing feature that enables users to easily join a scheduled meeting. This feature can be utilized with Hybrid Calendar Service or Cisco TMS.

Online Certificate Status Protocol (OCSP)   An Internet protocol used for obtaining the revocation status of an X.509 digital certificate. It is as an alternative to certificate revocation lists (CRL), specifically addressing certain problems associated with using CRLs in a public key infrastructure (PKI).

OpenLDAP   Open-source LDAP platform that was originally created by Oracle, which made the source code publicly available for businesses to use freely.

optimal call routing   A function on Cisco Expressways that limits the number of hops that occur for passing call setup signaling. This in turn also reduces the number of call licenses needed to host calls within an Expressway environment. The configuration setting for optimal call routing is named Call Signaling Optimization.

Organization Validation (OV) Certificate   A type of certificate for which the CA checks the right of the applicant to use a specific domain name and conducts some vetting of the organization. Additional vetted company information is displayed to customers when clicking the Secure Site Seal, giving enhanced visibility into who is behind the site and associated enhanced trust.

Pipe   A bandwidth limitation between two Subzones or between a Subzone and a Zone that is applied to Links.

Port Address Translation (PAT)   Works similar to NAT but uses ports to map communication between a private IP address and a public IP address.

Portable Operating System Interface (POSIX)   A family of standards specified by the IEEE Computer Society for maintaining compatibility between operating systems.

private branch exchange (PBX)   Operates similarly to the Automatic Telephone Exchange but its only purpose is to route calls within a business exclusively. A PBX can also connect to the outside world over the public telephone network, but it operates on the same circuit-switched network using POTS or ISDN.

product authorization key (PAK)   A product key (i.e., not a license key) that enables a customer to register a product they purchased to Cisco, so that they can generate the license keys for their product.

public key infrastructure (PKI)   An encryption solution that works by using two different cryptographic keys: a public key and a private key. Whether these keys are public or private, they encrypt and decrypt secure data to allow for secure communication between two devices.

Public Switched Telephone Network (PSTN)   A circuit-switched telephony network that encompasses the globe. The PSTN provides infrastructure and services for public telecommunications.

Q.931   Contains the source and destination IP address, in hexadecimal format, and any crypto-hash token if the call is to be encrypted. Q.931 is also responsible for the Alerting and Connect messages sent from the destination endpoint.

Quality of Service (QoS)   Any technology that manages data traffic to reduce packet loss, latency, and jitter on a network. QoS controls and manages network resources by setting priorities for specific types of data on the network.

Real-time Transport Control Protocol (RTCP)   A protocol that is used over UDP to carry real-time signaling traffic.

Real-time Transport Protocol (RTP)   A protocol that is used over UDP to carry real-time media traffic.

Registration, Admission, and Status (RAS)   An ITU communication protocol that identifies all messaging schemes between any device and a gatekeeper using H.323.

Registration Authentication An authentication service used on the Expressway to control endpoint registration based on registration credentials presented by an endpoint and challenged against an authoritative database.

Registration Confirm (RCF) An H.323 message sent from a gatekeeper to a device confirming the registration was successful.

Registration Conflict Policy Security policy automatically enabled on the Expressway that prevents duplicate H.323 aliases from registering at the same time. Can be configured as Reject, which is the default value, or Overwrite.

Registration Reject (RRJ) An H.323 message sent from a gatekeeper to a device denying registration.

Registration Request (RRQ) An H.323 RAS message initiated by an endpoint to request to registration to a gatekeeper. The gatekeeper responds with either a Registration Confirm (RFC) or a Registration Reject (RRJ).

Registration Restriction Policy Security policy that can be used on the Expressway to control both H.323 and SIP endpoint registrations using either an Allow List or a Deny List.

regular expression (regex) A sequence of characters that defines a search pattern. Usually, such patterns are used by string-searching algorithms for "find" or "find and replace" operations on strings, or for input validation.

Request for Comments (RFC) A type of publication from the technology community that describes methods, behaviors, research, or innovations applicable to the working of the Internet and Internet-connected systems.

Request in Progress (RIP) An H.323 RAS message sent from a gatekeeper to a device that is used to inform the device that the request was received and is being processed.

rich media session (RMS) A type of license that can be installed on the Expressway Core and Expressway Edge servers. These licenses allow for B2B calling and SIP to Microsoft interworking capabilities.

Rivest-Shamir-Adleman (RSA) A public-key cryptographic system used for secure data transmission.

root CA The certificate server that generates, signs, and authenticates certificates used for authentication. This is the authority for all certificates signed by it.

root CA certificate Establishes a trusted chain that begins at the root CA, through the root CA certificate, and ending at the certificate that was signed.

Routing Prefix Type of prefix that is configured on a gateway or bridge and registers to an H.323 gatekeeper. It is used to route all calls to that server regardless of the following digits.

Search History Log on the Cisco Expressway that allows administrators to view and troubleshoot call attempts by examining how the Expressway invoked the Call Processing Order.

Search Rule A dialing rule created on the Cisco VCS and Cisco Expressway servers that determines what Zones can be searched during a call setup and the order in which Zones are searched. Search Rules match destination aliases based on pattern matches, and can also be configured to transform a destination alias for one specific search.

Secure Real-time Transport Protocol (SRTP)   A secure protocol over TLS used over UDP to carry real-time media traffic.

Secure Sockets Layer (SSL)   A legacy cryptographic protocol that provides communications security over a computer network for TCP and UDP traffic. SSL has been replaced by the more secure TLS.

Server Name Indication (SNI)   An extension to the TLS computer networking protocol by which a client indicates which hostname it is attempting to connect to at the start of the handshaking process.

Service (SRV) record   A location service within DNS that can be used to identify protocols, port numbers, and hostnames of servers for particular services.

Session Description Protocol (SDP)   A protocol that is used during SIP call setup to exchange capabilities and identify UDP ports to be used.

Session Initiation Protocol (SIP)   An IETF signaling protocol used for real-time sessions, such as voice, video, and instant messaging.

Session Traversal Utilities for NAT (STUN)   An IETF NAT traversal solution designed for an asymmetric network. STUN servers are used to assign a port to a client but are not involved with the sending and receiving of packets.

SIP Proxy   Function of the SIP server used to connect devices in voice or video calls.

SIP registrar   A function of the SIP server used to map SIP URI addresses to IP addresses for SIP endpoints when they register.

SIP server   The call control device for SIP voice and video systems.

Smart Account   A central repository where you can view, store, and manage licenses across an entire organization. Comprehensively, you can get access to your software licenses, hardware licenses, and subscriptions through your Smart Account. Smart Accounts are required to access and manage Smart License–enabled products.

Smart Licensing   A new type of license Cisco created that enables customers to more easily purchase, deploy, and manage licenses through a cloud-based license management system. Smart licenses are tied to the user's Smart Account rather than to a specific system.

Subnet mask   A networking parameter that defines a range of IP addresses.

Subzone   Logical groupings of registered devices, such as endpoints, conference bridges, gateways, and so on, for the purposes of bandwidth management and access control.

symmetric cryptography   Process of negotiating between a server and client the details as to which encryption algorithm and cryptographic keys to use before the first byte of data is transmitted. Identification is usually in the form of digital "certificates" that contain the server name, the trusted CA, and the server's public encryption key.

symmetric network   A restricted network with a single entry or exit point. All traffic must use this single point of access to enter or leave the network with every transmission.

Telepresence Management Suite (TMS)   A management software solution for Telepresence endpoints and infrastructure. It can only be installed in a Microsoft Windows Server, and can be used to schedule conference calls, create and manage phonebooks, and perform many other duties.

Telepresence Management Suite – Provisioning Extension (TMSPE)   An applet that can be added to the TMS software to allow TMS to perform many provisioning functions, such as provisioning FindMe for users.

Time to Live   Setting within the Cisco Expressway that determines how long an H.323 registration remains in the database before the device needs to renew the registration. The default value is 1800 seconds.

TLS Verify   Also known as Mutual TLS, this is a form of TLS that requires certificate authentication from both the client and the server before communication can be established.

Transform   A rule that, when applied, changes an alias based on the criteria it has been configured to change. Transforms can be applied pre-search or during a Search Rule.

Transmission Control Protocol (TCP)   A routing protocol that ensures communication by use of acknowledgments. If an acknowledgment is not received, the packet will be retransmitted.

Transport Layer Security (TLS)   A cryptographic protocol that provides communication security over a computer network for TCP and UDP traffic.

traversal   Term use to describe movement from one side to another. Firewall traversal describes moving data from one side of a firewall to another. NAT traversal describes moving data from one side of a NAT server to another.

Traversal Chaining   A more secure means of traversing firewalls when one Expressway is placed within a DMZ. As well as acting as a traversal server, an Expressway-E can act as a traversal client to another Expressway-E. If you chain two Expressway-Es, the first Expressway-E is a traversal server for the Expressway-C. That first Expressway-E is also a traversal client of the second Expressway-E. The second Expressway-E is a traversal server for the first Expressway-E.

Traversal Client Zone   Zone type created on the Expressway Core that is used to initiate a traversal communication for media traversal through the firewall during voice and video calls. Traversal Client Zones can sometimes be created on the Expressway Edge Server.

Traversal Server Zone   Zone type created on the Expressway Edge that is used to receive a traversal communication for media traversal through the firewall during voice and video calls. Traversal Client Zones can only be configured on the Expressway Edge.

Traversal Subzone   A Subzone that is different from all other Subzones because it is only used to manage and throttle bandwidth for any traversal calls through the Expressway. Devices registering to the Expressway will never register to the Traversal Subzone.

Traversal Using Relays around NAT (TURN)   An IETF NAT traversal solution designed for a symmetric network. TURN servers are used to assign a port to a client and handle the relay of all packets sent and received.

Traversal Zone   Used for communication through a firewall. An Expressway Core and an Expressway Edge are required to set up a traversal communication through a firewall. The Expressway Core needs to be located inside the firewall, while the Expressway Edge needs to be located outside the firewall or in a DMZ.

Unified Communications Traversal Zone   A special type of traversal zone on Expressway servers that are used for MRA deployments. This type of traversal zone requires TLS Verify be used for the highest security in communications.

Uniform Resource Indicator (URI)   A string of characters that identifies a particular resource. URIs typically take the form of User@FQDN.

Uniform Resource Locator (URL)   A reference to a web resource that specifies its location on a computer network and a mechanism for retrieving it. URLs typically take the form of *User.FQDN*.

Universal Measurement and Calibration Protocol (XCP)   A network protocol from the Association for Standardization of Automation and Measuring Systems (ASAM) for connecting calibration systems to electronic control units (ECUs). It enables read and write access to variables and memory contents of microcontroller systems at runtime.

User Data Service (UDS)   A REST-based set of operations that provides authenticated access to user resources and entities such as users' devices, subscribed services, speed dials, and much more from the Unified Communications configuration database.

User Datagram Protocol (UDP)   A fast routing protocol that does not use acknowledgments to confirm packet delivery.

User Policy   Also known as FindMe, a call forward tool similar to Single Number Reach. When one alias is dialed, the call is sent to other aliases based on how each user account is configured.

Video Communications Server (VCS)   A call control server originally created by Tandberg, which was acquired by Cisco. This product is the model from which the Expressway Core and Edge servers were built for its ability to support firewall and NAT traversal.

virtual local-area network (VLAN)   A virtual partition at Layer 2 of the network used to decouple traffic and logically group data packets being sent across the network. VLANs can be used for QoS.

Virtual Private Network (VPN)   A protocol used to connect two autonomous networks across a WAN.

Voice over IP (VoIP)   Audio technology that allows voice communication to be broken down into packets and sent across an IP network.

Webex Zone   Zone introduced in version X8.11.4 that not only automates and simplifies Hybrid Call Service configuration, but is also a single zone entry that ensures that all calling and meetings solutions under the Webex banner precisely route to the correct cloud microservices and are handled accordingly.

WebSocket A computer communications protocol providing full-duplex communication channels over a single TCP connection. The WebSocket protocol was standardized by the IETF as RFC 6455 in 2011, and the WebSocket API in Web IDL is being standardized by the W3C.

wide-area network (WAN) A network topology that covers a wider geographical area than a local-area network (LAN). WANs are typically regionally located, but are not restricted to this parameter.

Index

Symbols

A

B

J

O

S

V

REGISTER YOUR PRODUCT at CiscoPress.com/register
Access Additional Benefits and SAVE 35% on Your Next Purchase

- Download available product updates.
- Access bonus material when applicable.
- Receive exclusive offers on new editions and related products.
  (Just check the box to hear from us when setting up your account.)
- Get a coupon for 35% for your next purchase, valid for 30 days.
  Your code will be available in your Cisco Press cart. (You will also find
  it in the Manage Codes section of your account page.)

Registration benefits vary by product. Benefits will be listed on your account page under Registered Products.

CiscoPress.com – Learning Solutions for Self-Paced Study, Enterprise, and the Classroom
Cisco Press is the Cisco Systems authorized book publisher of Cisco networking technology, Cisco certification self-study, and Cisco Networking Academy Program materials.

At **CiscoPress.com** you can
- Shop our books, eBooks, software, and video training.
- Take advantage of our special offers and promotions (ciscopress.com/promotions).
- Sign up for special offers and content newsletters (ciscopress.com/newsletters).
- Read free articles, exam profiles, and blogs by information technology experts.
- Access thousands of free chapters and video lessons.

Connect with Cisco Press – Visit CiscoPress.com/community
Learn about Cisco Press community events and programs.

Cisco Press